Y0-BCS-385

SEXUAL BEHAVIOR IN MODERN CHINA

Dalin Liu, Man Lun Ng, Li Ping Zhou,
and Erwin J. Haeberle

Sexual Behavior in Modern China

中国当代性文化

Report on the Nationwide Survey of 20,000 Men and Women

English-Language Edition by
Man Lun Ng and Erwin J. Haeberle

Continuum • New York

1997

The Continuum Publishing Company
370 Lexington Avenue
New York, NY 10017

Printed in the United States of America

Library of Congress Cataloging-in-Publication Data

Chung-kuo tang tai hsing wen hua. English
Sexual behavior in modern China : report on the nationwide survey of 20,000 men and women / Dalin Liu, Man lun Ng, Li ping Zhou, and Erwin J. Haeberle ; English-language edition by Man lun Ng and Erwin J. Haeberle.
p. cm.
Includes bibliographical references.
ISBN 0-8264-0886-9 (Hardcover : alk. paper)
1. Chinese—Sexual behavior. 2. Sexual ethics—China. 3. Sexual behavior surveys—China. I. Liu, Ta-lin.
HQ18.C6C53813 1997
306.7'0951—dc20 96-1072
CIP

Contents

Foreword

It is both a great honor and a great pleasure for me to contribute a few welcoming words to this first major survey of sexual behavior in China.

Such systematic surveys already have a respectable tradition in many countries, from Magnus Hirschfeld's pioneering efforts in Germany in 1903 and 1904 to Alfred C. Kinsey's famous American "reports" of 1948 and 1953. Unfortunately, these and other pioneering sexological studies were neither fully appreciated nor universally acclaimed when they were first published. On the contrary, Hirschfeld's work was terminated by court order, and Kinsey's private financial support was withdrawn as a result of political pressure. It was only much later, after the the outbreak of AIDS, that the same governments that before had strangled sex research realized their mistake and very belatedly began clamoring for data. After decades of neglect, ridicule, interference, and outright suppression, sexologists were suddenly asked by the health authorities to tell them immediately and exactly how much pre- and extramarital intercourse, how much homosexual and bisexual behavior, and how much prostitution existed in each country, city, or rural district, as well as the prevalence of various sexual techniques in different populations in order to get a picture of possible chains of infection.

The embittered researchers pointed out that the answers to such questions cannot be found overnight; that they themselves had, for a long time and in vain, asked for funding; that sex research needs steady support and a great deal of time to obtain meaningful results; that a single study is never sufficient, but must be repeated several times in order to yield sufficient insight; that sex research is extremely difficult under any circumstances and requires special training; and, finally, that such training is possible only within special sexological institutes which should have been set up years ago.

In other words, in most countries around the world sex research has never received the recognition it deserves and, as a result, the actual sexual behavior in these countries is unknown.

In their desperation, and since nothing else was available, epidemiologists turned to older surveys, mainly to Kinsey's "reports" and tried to extrapolate the data not only to the present and future, but also to countries other than the United States. This way they hoped to arrive at some predictions as to the course the AIDS pandemic might take. However, it soon became clear that this simplistic approach could not result in accurate forecasts.

In the meantime, researchers in the United States as well as in Great Britain, France, Finland, and some other countries have conducted new, representative or near-representative national surveys of sexual behavior. However, helpful as these efforts have been, they have not produced certainty. Greeted with relief by many health officials because of the "conservative" picture they painted, they have been questioned and doubted by sexologists who know the pitfalls and shortcomings of all existing research methods.

Sexologists also know something else: Each country, indeed, each social class, ethnic group, and generation within the same country has a different "sexual culture," and they all need to be investigated. Most countries also have a number of sexual "subcultures" in which members of otherwise very different social groups may interact, thereby creating specific erotic milieux and "lifestyles." Examples are prison populations, youth gangs, homosexual communities, "swingers" clubs, sadomasochistic circles, and the various types of prostitution, from street prostitution to brothels and "call girl rings." Such subcultures by no means exist in all countries, and they may show an enormous variability from one country to another. They do become important, however, as "target groups" for AIDS prevention campaigns, since they themselves are the best experts on their own sexual behavior. Therefore they can be very helpful in designing appropriate prevention campaigns and materials. They also know how to distribute such materials in the most effective manner, and they command the necessary trust.

In short, where such sexual subcultures exist, they can be the most valuable allies of health workers in preventing the spread of sexually transmitted deseases including AIDS. Conversely, those health officials who try to coerce or suppress such potential allies will fail in protecting not only the members of these subcultures, but also the general population. It is therefore necessary for sex researchers to find the various sexual groups that might exist in a particular society, to befriend them, to support them, and to learn from them. In this respect Hirschfeld and Kinsey were also role models for their successors.

The sexological pioneers also showed us that sex research is socially beneficial quite apart from the issue of disease prevention. They documented an enormous variety of sexual behaviors and thus enabled legislators to obtain a more realistic view of human nature. This, in turn, led to the reform of many unnecessary, counterproductive or downright destructive sex laws in Europe and the United States. As a result, the amount of sexual misery and hypocrisy in these countries was greatly reduced, the police had more time to fight serious crime, and the social peace in general was strengthened.

Another area where sex research has proved immensely valuable is in the treatment of sexual dysfunctions. Especially noteworthy is the work of Masters and Johnson in the 1960s and 1970s, which led to a new and much better understanding of the physiological processes underlying human sexual expression. This, in turn, made it possible to develop new therapeutic techniques that benefited dysfunctional couples. Today, "sex therapy" has become a recognized academic and professional enterprise in many countries, and many couples and individuals who were formerly beyond help have regained their sexual capacities.

However, quite apart from all of these utilitarian arguments it must clearly be stated that sex research is meaningful in itself as a part of humankind's overall effort to understand itself and the world. It should therefore be obvious that, above all, basic sex research needs support regardless of any immediate practical application. Only on this neutral, disinterested basis will researchers be able to maintain an open mind and will the deeper truths of sex reveal themselves. Such basic research can and must involve many academic disciplines, from biology and medicine to history, economics, and sociology. The proper way to conduct sex research is therefore to set up interdisciplinary teams. Again, Hirschfeld and Kinsey recognized this and acted accordingly.

Magnus Hirschfeld, who had edited the world's first *Journal for Sexology* in 1908 and was a co-founder of the first *Society for Sexology* 1913, established the first *Institute for Sexology* in 1919 in Berlin. (Two years later, he also convened the first international sexological congress in Berlin.) His institute, from the very beginning, combined biological, medical, historical, sociological and anthropological approaches. This was also reflected in its publications and, above all, in its unique collection and library. It attracted visitors from all over the world, including André Gide, Margaret Sanger, and Jawaharlal Nehru, who later acted as Hirschfeld's host in Allahabad, when he visited India on his world journey.

During this journey, which took almost two years (1930–32), Hirschfeld traveled from Berlin to New York, Chicago, Los Angeles, and San Francisco, from there to Japan, China, the Philippines, Indonesia, India, Egypt, Palestine, Greece, Austria, and Switzerland, lecturing everywhere about the new science of sexology and various sexological topics. In the summer of 1931 Hirschfeld lectured at all Chinese national universities. Especially in Beijing and Nanjing the audiences were very large, and at Sun Yat Sen University in Guangzhou over one thousand students appeared for a lecture. Of course, he also visited Shanghai. (There still exists a photo showing Hirschfeld with members of the Chinese Women's Club.)

In view of this historical connection between Chinese and German sexology, I was especially gratified to hear about Professor Liu's plans for a first great sex survey in 1988. We began corresponding, and, in the spring of 1989, I finally had the privilege of meeting him and his collaborators in Shanghai. In a series of fascinating and personally rewarding meetings, I had the opportunity to contribute to the research design, to discuss details of the questionnaire and interviewing techniques, to make various methodical and technical suggestions and to offer my encouragement. As the president of the German Society for Social-Scientific Sex Research (DGSS) I also asked Prof. Liu to join our scientific advisory board, and he invited me, in turn, to become an advisor to the Shanghai Sex Sociology Research Center. After that we continued our collaboration by correspondence and also met several more times for working sessions—for example in Hong Kong at the First Conference on Sexuality in Asia and in Berlin at the national conferences of our own society in 1990 and 1992. We met again in Shanghai in 1992 for the first international sexological Conference in China. On that occasion, we presented the original Chinese edition of our book to participants from many Asian countries.

Finally, in Berlin in 1994, our society was pleased to award Professor Liu the Magnus Hirschfeld Medal for outstanding contributions to sex research. In short, our collaboration has intensified, and we are now looking forward to strengthening our ties even further. For example, in the summer of 1995 we were able to present an exhibition in Berlin of his extraordinary personal collection of art and artifacts under the title "Five Thousand Years of Sexual Culture in China." This exhibition at the State Library proved an enormous success with extensive coverage in all national media—the press, radio, and television. As a result, the German general public for the first time learned something about a hitherto hidden aspect of Chinese culture.

Professor Liu stands in the tradition of the great sexological pioneers Hirschfeld and Kinsey, making a total commitment to his science along with great personal sacrifices for the sake of his research. As these great men did, he also seeks and finds allies and collaborators from various academic disciplines, and from official agencies as well as industry and large and small organizations. This careful building of local, national, and international alliances is the best proof of the seriousness of his intentions and it also offers the best guarantee that his research will continue.

Obviously, the first large Chinese sex survey whose results are published here, can only be a beginning. Like all good research, it raises more questions than it answers. In many respects, the findings are almost predictable, since they are similar to those in most other countries. For example, the fact that an overwhelming majority of college students find sex education too conservative mirrors very similar sentiments almost everywhere in our fast-changing world. The fact that a considerable number of people have sexual intercourse before marriage also reflects a nearly universal finding.

Considering the earlier physical maturation of boys and girls today and the rising age at which young men and women get married, this can hardly be a surprise to anyone. On the contrary, future, more specialized research will probably confirm this trend and raise the present percentages. Certain other numbers in the present report, on the other hand, seem low compared to findings in other countries. For example, to experienced sex researchers it is quite surprising that less than half of the male college students masturbate. According to our reasoned expectations, this figure should be much higher.

Perhaps, in this first survey, the respondents were still too shy and did not tell the truth, or some other factor falsified the answer. It seems reasonable to assume that the number will be higher in future surveys. It is also intriguing to find that well over 7 percent of college students reported homosexual experiences. A surprise is also the figure of just over 10 percent who had heterosexual intercourse. In fact, the last two findings should prove very interesting to all sex researchers who learn about them. A variety of interpretions are possible. It seems safe to assume, however, that in future surveys both figures will turn out to be different, and that especially the percentage of those with heterosexual experiences will grow dramatically. The percentage of those with homosexual experiences may eventually also be found to be at least somewhat larger.

On the other hand, the recent nationwide surveys in the United States, Great Britain, and France report much smaller figures with regard to homosexual behavior than had been anticipated on the basis of the earlier reports by Kinsey and his collaborators. However, while his figures, for certain technical reasons, were probably too high, the new numbers may well be too low for entirely different reasons. The debate among sex researchers about the best survey techniques is by no means over.

It would certainly be interesting to keep an eye on the percentage of those with both homosexual and heterosexual experiences. In any case, sex research in other countries—no matter where it is being conducted—has shown time and again that there is no clear demarcation line between those with heterosexual and homosexual interests. Of course, the vast majority of men and women do not maintain homosexual behavior for long (if at all), but some of them show some homosexual behavior after puberty for at least a few years, and in perhaps half of these cases it will probably remain significant throughout life. This has always been, and will remain true all over the world. After all, as the zoologist Kinsey pointed out, a certain amount of homosexual behavior in a minority of the population is simply "part of our mammalian heritage." There is no biological reason why the Chinese should be an exception.

This is not to say, however, that cultural factors do not play a very subtantial role in shaping all sexual (including homosexual) behavior. Especially the interpretation of such behavior varies greatly from one culture and historical period to another. I understand that Professor Liu is planning to give special attention to this whole issue in his next study. I am certain that this also will be a very illuminating, pioneering work.

Another fascinating discovery of the present survey is the fact that over sixteen percent of the married report masturbation. This certainly has a ring of truth. Finally, the finding that over half of the couples practice sexual intercourse in various ways sounds both true and reassuring about Chinese sexual culture. On the whole, the present survey reveals a picture of "average" and in part even robust sexual health in China with a few fuzzy spots that need to be cleared up.

Needless to say, Professor Liu will have to prepare for a great deal of criticism from a number of quarters. Sex researchers are always criticized. And it is true that no sex survey can be perfect or cover everything that readers would like to know about. Professional colleagues will undoubtely point out various shortcomings in the research design or in its execution. This criticism is also unavoidable and must be borne with equanimity. Actually, as everybody is going to discover, serious professional criticism is the most valuable response any researcher can hope for. More than anything else it promotes interest in more and better research. Thus, no matter how this survey itself is eventually judged, Professor Liu will have every reason to be pleased, since he has provided the first and greatest impetus to the growth of sexology in China. It remains the enviable position of pioneers like Professor Liu to promote their field no matter how their work is received. Even the strongest attack will have the effect of pointing to the importance of what he is saying. Agree or disagree, his main objective will be achieved: Everyone will see that a survey such as this had to be conducted and will have to be repeated.

To foreigners like myself, the Chinese often appear both fascinating and "inscrutable." It is Professor Liu's unique contribution that he has begun to show us that, in matters of sex, his compatriots are very much like most other people, that they are—not surprisingly—part of the same human race with the same personal satisfications and problems. Most importantly, however, by enabling the Chinese to learn something about themselves which they might not have realized, he has opened the way to a multifaceted, inner-Chinese dialogue, in which the people themselves examine their values, hopes, and aspirations for happiness.

I for one hope that this dialogue will also result in establishing sexology as a scientific enterprise in its own right in China. Few things could be more welcome to us European and American sexologists than to see the growth of the Chinese institutes of sex research, especially those with a sociological orientation. After all, sex research in China, expanded and maintained over years and decades, could significantly increase our understanding not only of China, but of "the human condition."

Hirschfeld's own research, his collection and library, indeed his whole institute, fell victim to Hitler and the Nazis in 1933. To this day, this pioneering institute has not been rebuilt in Berlin, because the city's three universities have taken no note of international developments and consequently have never understood their responsibilities and opportunities in this area. Finally, in 1994, seventy-five years after the opening of Hirschfeld's institute, the Robert Koch Institute, a German federal health research institution, took the initiative to open an Archive of Sexology in Berlin. It could become the nucleus of an urgently needed German research center.

In any case, I was very pleased to be able to reestablish the interrupted Chinese–German sexological connections, to travel repeatedly to

China and to welcome Professor Liu even more often in Germany. I wish this book the grateful reception it deserves, and I am looking forward to helping the further development of Chinese sexology in any way I can.

The present English-language edition of the book was prepared jointly by two of the original four co-authors: Dr. M. L. Ng of Hong Kong and myself.

We have endeavored to remain very faithful to the Chinese edition in order to give the Western reader an accurate impression of the work and its context. For example, we left all of the scanty original reference notes without making additions. Thus, the Western reader will clearly see how limited the access to current American and European sexological literature remains even in present China.

Moreover, we have retained the style and structure of the original, with a rather rigid (if not pedantic) narrative in order to convey an impression of the dispassionate "seriousness" which allowed the work to be published in the first place. Even so, as in the original, some of the paragraphs contain surprising anecdotes and asides, and some of the tables are startling. Therefore we hope that the work as a whole will be well received even by impatient Western readers. After all, few of us have the opportunity to get a good look at the "hidden" side of a culture of which we are only now beginning to become aware.

Professor Erwin J. Haeberle, Ph.D., Ed.D.
Robert Koch Institute
Archive for Sexology
Berlin

Introduction

This is a report on the nationwide survey of sexual behavior conducted in China in the period ranging from February 1989 to April 1990.

In our survey, we included data on adolescent sexual physiological development, the extent and source of sexual knowledge, sexual attitudes and their changes, marital relationships, family planning, and sexual offenses. We considered all of this to be part of our sexual and social culture. The findings touch on the most personal experiences of the individual and have important implications for family life and society as a whole.

In the China of the late eighties, people looked, above all, for social stability and therefore paid a great deal of attention to their marital and familial systems. However, in doing so, they overlooked some important things. As Kinsey wrote:

> Sociologists and anthropologists generally consider that the family is the basis of human society, and at least some students believe that the sexual attraction between the anthropoid male and female has been fundamental in the development of the human and infra-human family. . . . But whatever the phylogenetic history of the human family, the evidence is clear that the sexual factor contributes materially to its maintenance today. . . . Success or failure of a marriage usually depends upon a multiplicity of factors, of which the sexual are only a part. Nevertheless . . . where the sexual adjustments are poor, marriages are maintained with difficulty.[1]

Of course, the purpose of studying sexual matters is not only the strengthening of marriage or family. It will also benefit adolescent education, and ultimately it will contribute to the stabilization and solidarity of society.

This report can only give an introductory analysis of the data obtained in the survey. It is introductory because the wealth of the data is too great for an in-depth analysis within a short time. More detailed studies on the results may take another eight to ten years. In this report and introductory analysis, we hope to make a modest contribution in several areas:

1. Information

This is basic to any survey. We are aware of the limitations of any single survey. However, we make certain comparisons with other, smaller Chinese sex surveys of the last ten years and also with surveys in neighboring countries such as Japan.

2. Theory

By analyzing the large amount of data obtained, we aim to define and clarify a number of issues concerning the sexuality of the modern Chinese:

[a] The relationship between sexual attitude and behavior on the one hand and sociocultural factors on the other: As social and cultural factors keep changing, parallel changes are expected in sexual attitudes and behavior. It is the task of this survey to identify these changes and their relationships to find out the direction of the work needed in sex education and sexual policies.

[b] The commonalities and differences in Chinese sexuality: The Chinese are an ethnically heterogenous people. Their sexual attitudes and habits are also heterogenous. The current process of modernization forces the Chinese to accept many great changes, including those in their sexual attitudes and behavior. It will be helpful to see how modernization influences sexuality in general and what the Chinese could or should do on their road to further development.

[c] The quality of marriage in China: Poverty and backwardness often go hand in hand with unhappy marriages. It would be good to know how much and what kind of marital counseling is needed, and to whom and how much adult sex education should be provided.

[d] Adolescent sexual problems: Adolescents are our future leaders. Their need for sexual knowledge and sexual ethics has to be recognized, characterized, and measured for the planning of adolescent sex education.

[e] Women's problems: Sexual oppression especially victimizes women. Any sexual liberation should therefore begin with women. This survey aims to study the sexuality of Chinese women, how oppressed they are in their sex lives and how repressed in their sexual attitudes. On the other hand, are the rates of female sex offenses indicative of degrees of sexual liberation?

[f] Sexual control: In all societies, sexuality is regulated in many ways. This survey aims to discover how these control mechanisms work in modern China. Are they effective? Are they humane? Can or should they be changed? Should they be stricter or more lenient?

3. Instruction

Information leads to theoretical formulation. We hope to be able to arrive at some guidelines for teachers, health professionals, and policy makers in China.

However, in our present society where multiple ethical rules coexist, it is very difficult for any suggestions to be absolutely neutral. Biases may be due to problems in information collection, e.g., in the selection of study areas, the way questions are framed, and the method of conducting the study. All we can do is try hard, looking at the facts from a distance, then make an preliminary analysis. Most importantly: We should not draw any rash conclusions.

In our simple survey there are many inadequacies of which we are well aware. It is practically impossible to estimate the number of subjects required for a representative sample for the whole population of 1.16 billion Chinese, not only because the population is vast but because of the multiple racial and social characteristics in the many different regions of China. A large proportion of Chinese are farmers. Our sample on the other hand had only 20 percent who were farmers. This was much lower than we originally planned, because of the difficulty in doing field studies in some of the areas where many of the villagers were also illiterate.

Another problem is that because of the national attitudes toward sex, we either could not ask certain questions or could not find out significant details. For example, in the case of married couples, we could only ask about changes in sexual positions, but dared not ask about the frequency of each type of position. Considering the general degree of sexual knowlege, we also only asked about the feeling of sexual pleasure and not about orgasm. These modifications made our studies less precise.

Also, we only asked those groups of subjects that were of special concern to us, i.e., high school and college students, married couples, and sex offenders. We did not survey the physically disabled, minority groups, the army, old people, or self-defined homosexuals. All of these are, without question, very important for a truly comprehensive survey. Such groups need to be surveyed in the future.

However, we did make some effort to ensure a certain degree of representativeness of our information. In our survey design, we aimed at surveying two large groups of subjects: a large group presumed to consist of social conformists, and a smaller group of nonconformists, in this case: sex offenders. In the conformist group, subdivisions were made into married and unmarried (students). The unmarried were further divided into those who were below or above age eighteen (high school and college students). By this way of linking and grouping, we try to trace the information following the paths of physiological, psychological, and social development. Thus, we tried to make sure that the information can be crossvalidated. We hope that, by tracing the main line of development, we can obtain some reliable information about the sexual behavior of "mainstream" modern China.

All scientific research has its subjectivity and its limitations, and our survey is no exception. We see this survey as a first step on a long road to truly meaningful sexological research. It was a difficult, yet rewarding step. We dedicate this survey to all those interested in sexological studies. It has to be emphasized that this survey represents the work of forty researchers and five hundred additional field workers. The present book was written by the few of us who synthesized, analyzed, and reported the results.

Notes

1. A. C. Kinsey, W. B. Pomeroy, and C. E. Martin, *Sexual Behavior in the Human Male* (Philadelphia: W. B. Saunders Co., 1948), 563.

1

HOW THE SURVEY WAS CONDUCTED

This survey was organized by the Shanghai Sex Sociology Research Center. We wanted to obtain data on the physiological development in both sexes, sexual knowledge, sources of sexual knowledge, the sexual attitudes of young people, the marital and sexual relationships of married couples, and their family planning practices. We also wanted some information about sex offenders. Thus, the subjects of our survey were high school students, college students, married couples in cities and rural areas, and sex offenders. A total of 21,500 questionnaires were distributed, 20,712 were returned. This means a return rate of 96.3 percent. Of the returns, 19,559 were usable, meaning an effective return rate of 94.4 percent. Of the usable questionnaires, 6092 (31.1 percent) were from high school students, 3360 (17.2 percent) were from college students, 7971 (40.8 percent) were from married couples and 2136 (10.9 percent) were from sex offenders.

The regions covered in this survey were Heilong Jiang, Liaoning, Beijing, Tianjin, Shandong, Shanxi, Jiangsu, Shanghai, Zhejiang, Fujian, Guangdong, Henan, Sichuan, Xinjiang, and Ningxia. All in all, there were twenty-eight regions located in fifteen provinces of China. Five hundred and thirty field workers participated in the research. The field work began in February 1989 and ended in April 1990.

1. Social Background

The fact that this survey could be conducted at all was mainly due to the changing social and political climate in the China of the late 1980s.

Beginning in the early 1980s, China took rather bold steps to implement a new "open policy." With an increasing exchange between the Chinese and Western societies, a market economy developed and greatly elevated the average Chinese living standard. As a result, new and varied social contacts became possible, with an increase in basic needs. More and more people escaped from the prison of traditional thinking and came face to face with reality. Seeking love, affection, and marital happiness, they felt entitled to a healthy and harmonious life. These aspirations gradually led the Chinese of all ages to investigate the hitherto secret world of sex for themselves and talk more openly about it.

Another reason for this new preoccupation with sex was an increase in sexual problems manifesting themselves in the wake of the "open policy." Generally speaking, the speed of reform greatly exceeded the psychological ability to follow. Most people were unable to anticipate and study, much less modify the negative influences of Western civilization and of the new market economy suddenly growing in China.[1] Sexual problems became more prevalent, and sex education was unable to keep up.[2] Problems became visible in the following major areas:

1. An increasing rate of early love relationships between young people: According to the yearly Shanghai 1985–88 survey, of the senior high school students, about 60 percent had love affairs. There also was significant percentage among junior high school students.

2. A great increase in premarital sex: According to the statistics of a few major hospitals, in 1986 there was an 16 percent overall increase of premarital pregnancies and requests for induced abortions in one year.

3. A great increase in extramarital sex: According to a few surveys from 1988, the number of divorces due to adultery increased to the point of accounting for 25–40 percent of all divorces.[3]

4. An increase in the reported cases of sexual disharmony in married couples: In 1984, in Shanghai, 23 percent of divorces were due to sexual disharmony. Two years later, in 1986, nearly twice as many couples, namely 45 percent reported sexual disharmony.[4]

5. An increase in sex offenses: According to Shanghai statistics, from 1979 to 1983, the number of rapes increased more than 3½ times, and the age of rapists became lower. There were more

group rapes, and these were not only more violent, but they also turned out to have been premeditated.[5]

6. An increase in prostitution: In the last ten years, prostitution has spread from coastal cities to medium-sized cities in the country's interior and from there even to the villages. In 1987 the number of prostitutes arrested in China was 240 times of that in 1979.

7. Spread of sexually transmitted diseases: In recent years, the rate of sexually transmitted diseases has been increasing by 300 percent a year in China. AIDS has reached China as well.[6]

8. An increase in pornographic publications: The government reported an increasing number of campaigns to eradicate pornography, indicating a spread of these materials in China.

9. Confusion in sexual attitudes: In China, feudalistic sexual attitudes still retain some influence. Add to these Western capitalist ideas which seeped into China over the last one hundred years, mixed with communist teachings in the new China, modified again by the latest American and European fads and fashions, and the predictable result is a great deal of confusion among Chinese young people. China is still searching for a new, healthy, and rational attitude toward sexuality.[7]

10. Family planning is facing great difficulties: China aims to control population, trying to keep it under 1.2 billion, but in view of the difficulties in teaching and implementing family planning in distant regions, there is a high probability that the goal cannot be reached. This is another reason why the government and the people both realize the importance of sex education.

All of the above are real problems, but most of them are difficult to admit—especially prostitution and sexually transmitted diseases. Some people think that to admit these problems is to shame the country and the communist doctrine. Yet, with the progress of modernization and the open door policy, facts cannot be hidden for long, and it is therefore a historical necessity to face and solve these problems.

2. Basic Support for This Survey

After the establishment of the new China, sexological studies began in the early eighties. The pioneers were physicians in the country's north:

for example the Director of the Beijing Academy of Medical Science, Dr. J.P. Wu and the assistant professor at Beijing Medical University, Professor F. F. Ruan. Similar to the development of Western sexology, sex research in the new China began with sexual physiology. In 1982, Wu translated and edited *Human Sexual Reponse* by Masters and Johnson. In 1985, Ruan edited *A Manual of Sexual Knowledge*. The two books attracted a wide readership and much public attention.

Despite these initial efforts, no organized effort on behalf of sexology developed in China. Nothing effective was done to promote an academic or social atmosphere favorable to sex research. The first organized effort began in the early eighties in Shanghai.

In March 1985, the editorial board of the journal *Sociology* edited by the Faculty of Arts of Shanghai University organized a series of public seminars on "Sexual Problems in Today's Society." This series consisted of ten sessions, with one hundred thousand participants. Reactions were enthusiastic. Some sexological workers and sex educators scattered in various parts of Shanghai had their first chance to meet each other. They decided to join forces and begin some organized scientific work on sexuality.

They also felt that they should spread their influence over the country. Hence, from July to August 1985, the editorial board of the journal *Sociology*, the Shanghai College of Traditional Chinese Medicine, and the Shanghai Family Planning Promotion and Education Center organized another series of sex education courses for eighty participants from eighteen different regions of China. Many of the teachers and participants of this series also decided to continue their work on human sexuality, and, as a group, they became the backbone of Chinese sexology in the years that followed. In August 1985, they formed the organizing committee of The Society of Chinese Sex Education. Unfortunately, however, the society was refused registration, and the committee gave up any further efforts.

At the same time, there were other advocates of change in Shanghai. They were the Youth Study Center of the Shanghai, the Academy of Social Sciences, the Office of Shanghai Health Education, and some workers of the Shanghai Education Bureau. Beginning in 1985, they conducted sex education trials in one hundred high schools throughout Shanghai. The results were good and received recognition by various national bodies. As a result, such trials were repeated in other parts of China.

In 1985, the many sex education forces coalesced into one. In June 1986, the first sexological organization in China was established—the Shanghai Sex Education Research Society. In December 1988, the

Shanghai Sex Sociology Research Center was also established. Both of these initiatives led to the infusion of new blood into the sexology movement, with many new talents being trained and spread out over the whole country.

Sexology in Shanghai was only one step ahead of the developments in other parts of China. From 1986 to 1989, many sexological organizations were established in different regions, such as the Heilongjiang Sexological Society, the Shenzhen Sex Education Research Society and others.

With this foundation having been laid, Chinese sexology made rapid advances. Many more sexological books of a greater variety were published. Some were translated foreign works, and some were original works reflecting Chinese culture and Chinese concerns. The first book in Shanghai of this latter kind was the *Adolescent Education of High School Students* and *A Reader for Adolescent Knowledge* by P. K. Yao. Then came *Sex Sociology* and *A Critique of Sexual Liberation* by D. L. Liu as well as *Sex Education* by J. H. Hong and his colleagues. In 1988, Shanghai published the first series of *The Journal of Sex Education* with an international circulation. At the same time, Dr. Pan of the China People's University translated the "Kinsey Reports" and wrote the *Mystical Holy Fire*, a history of sexology. In Beijing University, Li and his associates translated the *Fundamentals of Sexology*, Wang wrote *A Sex Psychology* and Guo *Sex and Life*, all of which had an extensive influence on the country. In 1989, the Guangdong Family Planning Commission published *The Beginning of Man*, the first popular sex education magazine for open circulation. This marked the end of the first stage of the movement towards a complete sex education system in China.

It was with the help of this system and its resulting network that the present survey could be planned. The many small-scale surveys conducted in the course of the development of this system gave us ideas with a theoretical background for the planning of this survey. The experiences of the various pilot workers also informed our survey methods.

3. The Tortuous Path

A few years ago, although worried about its feasibility, we had thought of doing a large-scale national sex survey. Obviously, we would need enormous resources as well as government and public support.

By the autumn of 1988, however, there were some hopeful signs. A letter from Jiang of Xiamen University invited us to help organize a sex survey. We explored the possibilities, and, to our surprise, there were more people throughout the country willing to help than we had expected. Not a single request we mailed out received a negative reply.

Hence, the initiation of this survey was not the result of some capricious impulse on the part of a few workers, but the answer to a true social need. There were, of course, warnings that we should be cautious. A colleague in Beijing wrote to us that such a survey should be planned very carefully, that it should take national sentiments into account, and that 80-90 percent of the attempts at this type of survey were known to fail anyway. In response to such warnings, we decided to undertake some pilot studies in what were possibly the most difficult regions.

Thus, we decided on a pilot survey in the villages. Farmers constitute 80 percent of the population of the whole country. Yet they are the least educated and usually the most conservative group. If the villagers would receive our project well, there would be even fewer problems in the cities.

The village pilot survey was made possible with the help of Huang, vice principal of Shanghai Women Officials Training College, who was also a member of Shanghai Sex Sociology Research Center. Through the Women's Unions of four *xians* (towns), Jinshan, Jiading, Qinpu, and Songjiang, four hundred men and women in the villages were surveyed. We learned from the experience and modified the questionnaire in order to make it more acceptable. We also reinforced the efforts to prepare the respondents by giving detailed instructions and explanations and by assuring them of the strictest confidentiality.

The last step before starting this large survey was to secure adequate financial resources. China had very limited funds for any kind of scientific research. The Shanghai Sex Sociology Research Center, being just a public academic body, in order to run a survey of this caliber, had to look beyond its own resources. At the beginning, some business companies within and outside of China promised support, and therefore we started the survey. The well-known events in June 1989, however, caused some unexpected difficulty; foreign financial restrictions imposed on China and the recession which followed caused many of the original resources we had relied on to disappear. But since we had started, we decided not to give up. We solicited new financial assistance from different sources in the following one and a half years, ultimately obtaining sufficient funds from:

1. Mr. Ding Ke, Director of *The Journal of Democracy and the Law* (RMB 25,000)
2. Shanghai Planned Parenthood Committee Research Fund (RMB 3000)

3. Shanghai University, Faculty of Arts research fund (RMB 1700)
4. Joint contribution from twenty-one enterprise companies (RMB 22,500)
5. Prof. Dalin Liu, Shanghai Sex Sociology Research Center (RMB 29,000)

The first national coordinating meeting of the Sex Civilization Survey was held in Shanghai in May 1989. Thirty representatives from thirteen participating regions in China were in attendance. The sexologist Erwin J. Haeberle of the German Federal Health Office also came from Berlin to give us valuable advice on various aspects of planning.

Soon after the beginning of the actual survey, however, we were unfortunate enough to confront a number of social campaigns which caused us serious difficulties. There was a campaign against permitting capitalism, followed closely by a national campaign against obscenity. To our way of thinking, however, the best way of eradicating obscenity was the dissemination of scientific information about sex and the promotion of healthy and rational ideas. But it seemed that the general public was not yet ready for our approach. Anything relating to sex was considered obscene and was therefore faced with the threat of eradication. Some people aked our field workers: "Is this really the right time to ask people about sex?"

Hence, many of our field workers could not successfully interview the selected subjects as planned. One of the regional team leaders, Yao of Shanghai, started with an agreement from ten universities to participate in the survey with their students, but when she approached the universities after the social campaigns mentioned above, all ten universities refused to honor that agreement. So did the high schools which earlier had made the same promises to Liu of Beijing. At the universities in Xinjiang, after half of the students were surveyed, cooperation was suspended by higher officials, and other universities had to be found as substitutes in order to complete the survey. One field worker was criticized and disciplined by her superiors for having participated in the survey.

These were not the only difficulties. Many villagers were illiterate so that the field worker had to read the questions to them one by one and then fill in the answers. Interviewing prison inmates, the field workers had to endure poor and hot environments and deal with the resentment of people to whom the survey made no sense at all. A great deal of effort was required to help inmates understand the questions in order to obtain their cooperation.

There were some advantages, as well. A closely linked structure is a characteristic of Chinese society. Our survey made full use of this and thus was channeled through all regional bureaus concerned, such as Planned Parenthood committees, the Women's Federation, the Workers' Union, schools, police departments, correctional facilities, social science institutes, publication networks, and others. The implementation moved all they way down from provincial bodies to cities, to towns and villages, step by step. Hence the process of work distribution and duty allocation was quite simple.

Because our survey was implemented through official organizations, our surveys on students and sex offenders were conducted in groups. Group questionnaire completion is a better method in this kind of situation because: [1] When conducted in groups and administered by a trusted official, the subjects are more likely to cooperate, as they find it easier to believe in the worth and seriousness of the survey. [2] When so many others are filling in the questionnaires at the same time, some of the individual fears of "sticking out" or being identified diminish. [3] Individual interviews, especially on sexual matters, tend to provoke anxiety in the individual.

All questionnaires were collected by October 1989. Data entry was made in the following few months, with the first analysis meeting held in the spring of 1990. In May of 1990, the preliminary results were released to the news agencies and reported at the First Asian Congress of Sexology held in Hong Kong. There, another analysis meeting was held with our overseas consultants M. L. Ng and E. J. Haeberle, with whom we had remained in close contact by correspondence. In July 1990, some preliminary results were reported at the Third International Berlin Conference of Sexology held at Humboldt University and the Reichstag. On that occasion, a third meeting with our co-author E. J. Haeberle took place. In August 1990, Mr. Yamamoto and his Japanese Sexuality and Life Society visited China and were introduced to the survey. In September 1990, at the Adolescent Sexuality Conference organized by the East–West Center in Honolulu, Hawaii, still another preliminary report of the survey results was presented.

4. Sampling and Statistics

The ideal sampling procedure for this type of survey is random sampling, but under the current conditions in China, on a topic which most people were yet unable to fully understand, it is a sampling method that could not be used. Since the survey was neither funded nor officially supported by the government, we did not have access to the central governmental population statistics and their breakdowns according to age, occupation, marital status, level of education, and other demographic characteristics. This made the process of random sampling or stratified random sampling in the cities and villages impossible. The lack of uniform cooperation in a district area also made the selection of representative samples using random or semirandom procedures impossible.

Thus, although we realized the value of using random sampling as much as possible, we could only use nonrandom procedures. Our procedures can be divided into two stages. In the first stage, we selected survey points. Based on our knowledge of the size of the cities and their locations, we chose about the same number of cities and villages in the interior, coastal, northern, and southern regions of the country. However, admittedly, our choice was also influenced by "convenience" in the sense that we picked places where cooperation was likely to be obtained.

In the second stage, we specified the sample characteristics and calculated the sample size needed for getting representative data at the survey spot. The team leader for that region then was free to decide how he would go about obtaining the sample by random or intentional sampling, as long as the subjects met the required characteristics and number. Hence, in this second stage, various types of sampling procedures were used by different regions: intentional, random, convenience, or others.

By these standards, the survey should be seen as a nonrandom sampling survey. Since it is impossible to eliminate sampling errors under these conditions, the data obtained from the sample cannot be generalized to the whole population. We believe however, because of our interest in and our acquaintance with the population in question, that our intentional choice of the subjects represent those that are of interest to us, as well as to sex educators and policy makers in China, and that they have a certain degree of representativeness for all Chinese.

Using the SPSS package, the frequencies and percentage of single variables and the correlation of selected paired variables were worked out. Where appropriate, one variable (e.g., sex) was controlled to study the correlation of two other associated variables. We used the Gamma index as the correlation measure since it is a sensitive index for interval data (most of our data were interval data or could be interpreted as such). For some correlations which involved both categorical and interval data, we still used Gamma for convenience, in order to indicate the trend of change which in most cases can be interpreted even from percentage tables.

Gamma values can be positive or negative, indicating the direction of correlation. This directional sign however, will be omitted in our presentation since the direction of correlation is always obvious in the descriptive text.

For paired data of a categorical nature, chi-square was used with its associated p values. Since the sampling in this survey was mainly non-random, all correlations must be interpreted with caution, applicable only to the subjects surveyed. This is to give an outline impression to readers, preventing generalization outside surveyed samples.

In interpreting the results, some other defects of this survey must be acknowledged and taken into account. The questionnaire design left much to be desired in terms of the method of measurement, sequencing, and categorization. Occasionally, the vocabulary and usage of terms might not have been clear enough to prevent misinterpretation. Some answers were missing for various reasons, and the sample distribution could still be biased despite a deliberate attempt to survey representative regions and groups.

We believe, however, that our experience with this survey—including shortcomings and mistakes—could serve as a basis for better studies of a similar nature in the future. During our survey period for example, Keng successfully finished a sexuality survey on two thousand and fifty city couples and two thousand and eighty university students using more representative samples. We are glad to know that her findings closely match ours in many of the sexual behaviors surveyed, e.g., on physiological sexual development, masturbation frequency, the ways couples get married, the rate of premarital sex, sexual satisfaction, and so on.

Notes

1. Dalin Liu, *Sex Sociology* (Jinan: Shandong People's Publications, 1986).
2. Ibid.
3. Ibid.
4. Ibid.
5. Ibid.
6. Bai Mu, Ba Di, "Chase away the Darkness under the Sun," *Sociology* 1 (1990): 24.
7. Fan Min-Sheng, "Analysis of the Cause for the Resurgence of Sexually Transmitted Diseases," *Sociology* 12 (1990): 27.

2
High School Students

1. General Background

In China, high school students (i.e., those students in the three years of junior high and the three years of senior high school) constitute a large group of people. According to national statistics, in 1989, the population of China was 1111.91 million, of which 45.54 million (4.1 percent) were high school students. Of these, 26.227 million were male, 18.873 female. Outside this group, there were also 21.77 million vocational high school students, of which 11.89 million were male and 0.988 million were female. The two groups together made a total of 4.3 percent of the whole population.

This part of the sexual behavior survey on high school students was performed in twenty-eight high schools in Beijing, Shanghai, Qingdao, Guangzhou, Xiamen, Chengdu, Jinzhou, Ningxia, Nanjing and Wuxi. In all, 6900 questionnaires were distributed; 6092 were returned, of which 3065 (50.3 percent) were from male students and 3023 (49.6 percent) from female students. In only four of the returned questionnaires could the sex of the respondents not be determined. Since the male and female percentages of the high school students in China were 58 percent and 42 percent respectively, the sex ratio of our subjects came close to the national ratio.

The detailed distribution of the subjects was as in table 2–1: The selection principle for this survey was to include a proportionate balance of students from both major and ordinary schools and to focus on the second and third years of junior high and the first and second years of senior high (avoiding the youngest and oldest classes). The classes were meant to be representative in character and scholastic performance.

DISTRIBUTION OF HIGH SCHOOL STUDENTS SURVEYED		
CITY	NUMBER OF SUBJECTS	PERCENTAGE
Beijing	1166	19.1
Shanghai	2237	36.7
Qindao	578	9.5
Guangzhou	373	6.1
Xiamen	80	1.3
Chengdu	496	8.1
Jinzhou	195	3.2
Ningxia	298	4.9
Nanjing	292	4.8
Wuxi	377	6.2
TOTAL	6092	100.0

Table 2–1

Once a class was selected, the head teacher assembled the students in the classroom and asked them to fill out the questionnaires. Before doing this, however, they were instructed about the objective and meaning of the survey. Its importance was explained and confidentiality assured. Little resistance to participation was encountered from the students.

However, some high school principals were unable to appreciate the importance of this study and were reluctant to allow their students to participate. They were worried that this type of survey could cause sexual misconduct among students. In every case of such a refusal, another school was selected.

An advantage of doing a sex survey of high school students was that, in the past, some similar, fairly large-scale surveys had been performed in China. In 1988, the National Education Committee pioneered and supported an "Adolescent Education Research Work Group" (Yao 1990) to study the living environment, as well as the physiological and psychosexual development and development of sexual awareness of three thousand high school students in five major provinces. This pilot study helped us to avoid a great many unnecessary difficulties and obstacles. Its results provided a good basis for comparison with our own survey.

Another good source of comparison comes from Japan. In the last twenty years, Japan has performed adolescent sexuality studies on a national scale three times (JASE 1974, 1981, 1987). Its third survey had a sample size similar to ours.

In 1986, China announced and put into effect the National Free Education Law. Because of this, in 1990, 97.8 percent of school age children in the whole country were able to enter primary schools, and 74.6 percent of primary school graduates entered secondary schools (*Liberation Daily,* 1991). Since the law requires a set age for entering schools, secondary school students generally are between twelve to eighteen years old. This is also the range of our high school students in this part of the survey, with a mode between fourteen to seventeen. The mean age was 15.53 years, with standard deviation at 1.78. There was no significant difference between the male and female students (table 2–2).

AGE DISTRIBUTION OF THE HIGH SCHOOL STUDENTS					
TOTAL	<=13	14-15	16-17	>=18	MISSING
6092	599 (9.8%)	2330 (38.2%)	2344 (38.5%)	617 (10.1%)	202 (3.3%)

Table 2–2

AGE DISTRIBUTION OF MALE AND FEMALE HIGH SCHOOL STUDENTS					
	TOTAL	<=13	14-15	16-17	>=18
Male	2948	277 (9.4%)	1099 (37.3%)	1242 (42.1%)	330 (11.2%)
Female	2938	322 (11.0%)	1230 (41.9)	1100 (37.4)	286 (9.7)

P=0.001

Table 2–3

As to the scholastic performance of the subjects, most of them were good (33.0 percent) and average (47.4 percent). 6.0 percent were excellent, 11.0 percent were poor and 0.9 percent were very poor. This shows that most of the students paid attention to their studies and achieved results within or above the expected standard (table 2–4). The male–female breakdown of the distribution follows in table 2–5.

DISTRIBUTION OF SCHOLASTIC PERFORMANCE						
TOTAL	EXCELLENT	GOOD	AVERAGE	POOR	VERY POOR	MISSING
6092	366 (6.0%)	2010 (33.0%)	2890 (47.4%)	672 (11.0%)	57 (0.9%)	97 (1.6%)

Table 2–4

DISTRIBUTION OF SCHOLASTIC PERFORMANCE OF MALE AND FEMALE SUBJECTS						
	TOTAL	EXCELLENT	GOOD	AVERAGE	POOR	VERY POOR
Male	3 034	192 (6.3%)	954 (31.4%)	1417 (46.7%)	427 (14.1%)	44 (1.5%)
Female	2957	174 (5.9%)	1056 (35.7%)	1471 (49.7%)	243 (8.2%)	13 0.4%)

P=0.001

Table 2–5

The distribution of students in different grades is shown in table 2–6. Although we surveyed students of all six grades, we focused on the middle four grades because the students in these grades, being of age between thirteen to sixteen, should be in the period of greatest psycho-sexual change and deserve the most intensive study.

DISTRIBUTION ACCORDING TO GRADE LEVELS							
TOTAL	J1	J2	J3	S1	S2	S3	MISSING
6092	531 (8.7%)	1115 (18.3%)	1326 (21.8%)	1387 (22.8%)	1072 (17.6%)	621 (10.2%)	40 (0.6%)

Table 2–6

SEX DISTRIBUTION ACCORDING TO GRADE LEVELS							
	TOTAL	J1	J2	J3	S1	S2	S3
Male	3039	275 (9.0%)	530 (17.4%)	644 (21.2%)	762 (25.1%	529 (17.4%)	299 (9.8%)
Female	3009	256 (8.5%)	584 (19.4%)	682 (22.7%)	624 (20.7%)	541 (18.0)	322 (10.7%)

Table 2–7

The parents of the subjects came from all occupations (table 2–8). Most of the parents were laborers. Officials came next. The relatively small number of peasants is disproportionate to the percentage in the national population. This is because the schools surveyed were all located in cities. The result is a certain bias in our results which should be rectified in future studies.

Occupation of Parents					
	TOTAL	WORKMAN	PEASANT	COMMERCE	SERVICE
Father	6092	1931 (31.7%)	322 (5.3%)	126 (2.1%)	123 (2.0%)
Mother	6092	2305 (37.8%)	537 (8.8%)	323 (5.3%)	413 (6.8%)
	OFFICIAL	HIGH OFFICIAL	SPECIALIST	OTHER	UNKNOWN
Father	1218 (20.0%)	866 (14.2%)	860 (14.1%)	569 (9.3%)	77 (1.3%)
Mother	949 (15.6%)	198 (3.3%	629 (10.3%)	640 (10.5%)	98 (1.6%)

Table 2–8

The educational levels of the parents are shown in table 2–9. Compared with tables 4–2 and 4–3, which show the general educational level of urban married couples, this distribution is typical of urban parents.

Parental Educational Level				
PARENT	TOTAL	ILLITERATE	PRIMARY	JUNIOR HIGH
Father	6092	47 (0.8%)	594 (9.8%)	1515 (24.9%)
Mother	6092	154 (2.5%)	998 (16.4%)	1985 (32.6%)
	HIGH SCHOOL	COLLEGE	POST-GRAD	MISSING
Father	1512 (24.8%)	748 (12.43%)	1622 (26.6%)	54 (0.9%)
Mother	1649 (27.1%)	466 (7.6%)	777 (12.8%)	63 (1.0%)

Table 2–9

As to the relationship of the parents, according to the respondents, 83.7 percent of the parents had a very good or good relationship; 12.0 percent had a fair relationship. This shows that most of the subjects were living in relatively stable and happy families. This family atmosphere provides a favorable background for the psychosexual development of the subjects.

PARENTAL RELATIONSHIP

TOTAL	EXCELLENT	GOOD	FAIR	FIGHT OFTEN	VIOLENT
6092	2450 (40.2%)	2622 (43.0%)	730 (12.0%)	119 (2.0%)	5 (0.1%)

SEPARATED	DIVORCED	NOT CLEAR	MISSING
16	80	37	33

Table 2–10

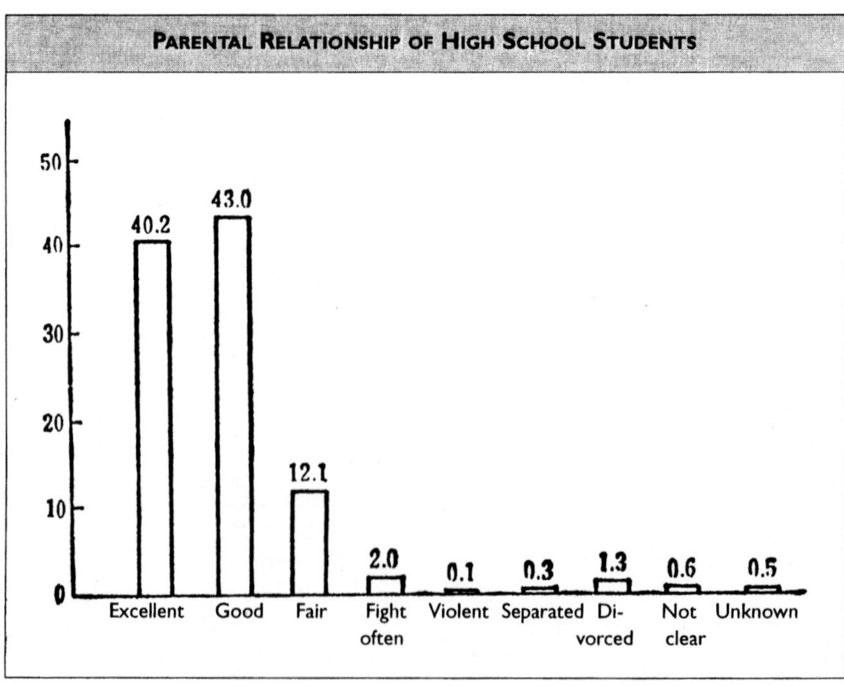

Figure 2–1

This result is similar to that of the National Adolescent Education Survey of 1988. In that survey, 82.2 percent of the parents had good or very good relationships; 11.8 percent were fair; 3.15 percent were poor; and 0.7 percent were very poor. Moreover, the survey revealed that more than 82 percent of the parents had a good relationship with the students; 5 percent had a poor relationship; and 1 percent had a very poor relationship.

In our survey, 22.9 percent of the subjects were the only child. A large majority of the rest had only one sibling. (table 2–11 and 2–12).

SUBJECTS WITH SIBLINGS			
TOTAL	NO SIBLING	WITH SIBLING	UNKNOWN
6092	1361	4574	157

Table 2–11

NUMBER OF SIBLINGS						
TYPE	TOTAL	1	2	3	4	>=5
OlderBrother	1657	1419 (85.6%)	195 (11.8%)	28 (1.7%)	10 (0.6%)	5 (0.3%)
Younger Brother	1056	1021 (96.7%)	 (3.2%)	34 (0.1%)	— —	1 —
Older Sister	1797	1369 (76.2%)	311 (17.3%)	95 (5.3%)	18 (1.0%)	4 (0.3%)
Younger Sister	1041	949 (91.2%)	65 (6.2%)	26 (2.5%)	1 (0.1%)	— —

Table 2–12

2. Physiological Sexual Development

Adolescence is a period in life when physiological and psychological changes are very obvious and rapid. Sexual changes are the most characteristic because they mark the onset of puberty and also the end of childhood.

Usually, the beginning of puberty is marked in girls by the first menstruation (menarche) and in boys by the first ejaculation. At the same time, the secondary sexual characteristics appear. The usual sequence of changes is:

A. Girls: breast enlargement, pubic hair, growth spurt, menarche, and axillary hair.

B. Boys: growth of testicles, pubic hair, change of voice, ejaculation, growth spurt, axillary hair, and beard.

1. Sexual Physiological Development of Female High School Students

Of the 3023 high school students, 2843 (94.0 percent) reported to have had their first mentruation, 166 (5.5 percent) had no menstruation yet, the rest gave no or unclear answers. The earliest age of menarche in our subjects was nine years, the latest eighteen years. The mean age of menarche was 13.04 years (S.D.=1.16). Menarche occurred most often in the summer season (table 2–14).

AGE AT MENARCHE					
TOTAL	<=10	11-12	13-14	>=15	UNKNOWN
2843	28 (1.0%)	865 (30.4%)	1649 (58.0%)	264 (9.3%)	37 (1.3%)

Table 2–13

SEASON OF MENARCHE					
TOTAL	JAN–MAR	APR–JUN	JUL–SEP	OCT–DEC	UNKNOWN
2843	551 (19.4%)	555 (19.5%)	1005 (35.3%)	470 (16.5%)	262 (9.2%)

Table 2–14

The age of first menstruation varies from one nation and region to another (table 2–15). A survey in Beijing 1963–1964 (Yap 1964) on high school students showed that the mean age of first menstruation at that time was 14.5 years (figure 2–3), 1.9 years earlier than the age of first ejaculation of the male students. Yet in 1988, the National Adolescence Education Survey (Yao 1988) showed that the mean age of first menstruation was 13.4 years. This comes closer to our present finding and shows that with the progress of social development and improvement in living conditions, the age of first menstruation has been lowered by about one year over a period of twenty years. This finding is in agreement with that of other countries. According to statistics in some countries, the age of first menstruation tends to lower by three months for every ten years; others reported a lowering of one year in fifty years (figure 2–4).

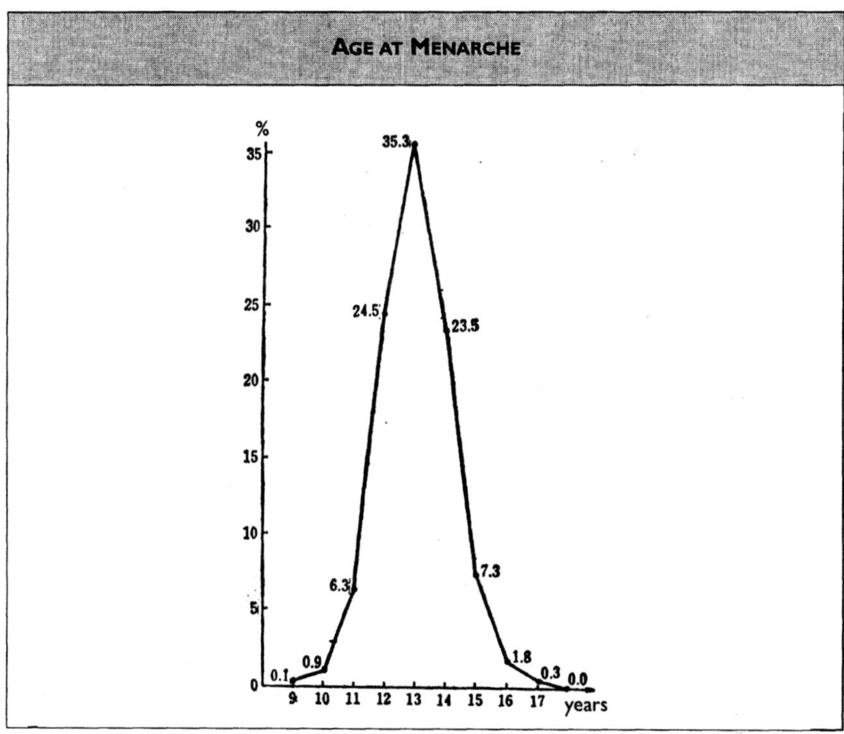

Fig 2–2

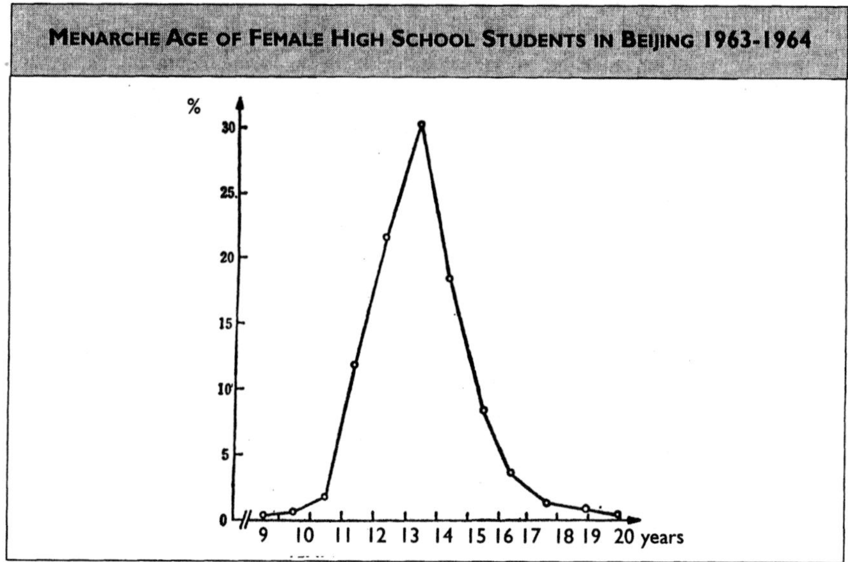

Figure 2–3

YEAR OF MENARCHE AGE IN DIFFERENT COUNTRIES[1]		
COUNTRY/REGION	YEAR	MEAN AGE
Sweden	1968	12.9+_0.05
Netherlands	1965	13.4
Great Britain	1966	13.0+_0.02
France	1967	13.2+_0.06
Poland	1967	14.0+_0.02
Yugoslavia	1963	14.3+_0.06
Rumania	1963	13.5+_0.06
Russia(Moscow)	1970	13.0+_0.08
India	1971	13.3
Hong Kong	1962	12.8+_0.20
New Guinea	1967	18.0+_0.19
Australia	1970	13.0
U.S.A.	1968	12.72
Guatemala	1963	15.1+_0.25
Egypt	1966	15.2+_0.30
South Africa	1958	15.0+_0.03

Table 2–15

VARIATION OF AGE OF MENARCHE IN DIFFERENT COUNTRIES FROM 1830–1960[2]

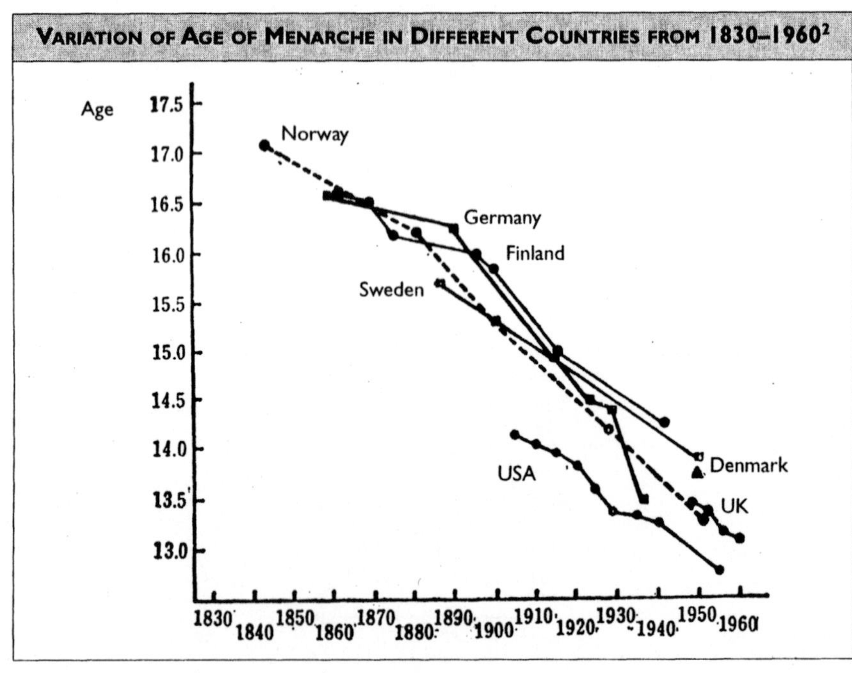

Figure 2–4

Associated with the first menstruation is the development of the secondary sexual characteristics: i.e., enlargement of the breasts, the growth of pubic and axillary hair. Acne is infrequent. Only 8.2 percent had acne; 50.3 percent did not have any (table 2–16).

SECONDARY SEXUAL CHARACTERISTICS OF FEMALE HIGH SCHOOL STUDENTS				
TYPE	TOTAL	NOT YET	OBSERVABLE	OBVIOUS
Breast	2926	39 (1.3%)	1458 (49.8%)	1429 (48.8%)
Pubic Hair	2849	144 (5.0%)	1361 (47.8%)	1344 (47.2%)
Axillary Hair	2804	471 (16.8%)	1703 (60.7%)	630 (22.5%)
Acne	2513	1264	1042	207

Table 2–16

2. *Sexual Physiological Development of Male High School Students*

Of the 3065 students surveyed, 2031 (66.3 percent) reported to have had ejaculated; 867 (28.3) reported no ejaculation; the rest did not answer the question. The age of first ejaculation was lower than the age of first menstruation (table 2–17).

EJACULATION EXPERIENCE OF MALE HIGH SCHOOL STUDENTS			
TOTAL	YES	NO	MISSING
3065	2031 (66.3%)	867 (28.3%)	167 (5.4%)

Table 2–17

Because of the difficulty in remembering the time of first ejaculation accurately, only 1671 subjects responded to the question properly. The mean age of first ejaculation of these respondents was 14.4 years, S.D. 2.01. It is in agreement with Yao's (1988) figure of 14.4, but earlier than the Beijing figure of 1963–1964 (Yap 1980) which was 16.6 year, thus, within one generation, the male sexual physiological development has advanced by about 2 years. The detailed distribution of the age of first ejaculation is shown in table 2–18.

DISTRIBUTION OF AGE OF FIRST EJACULATION IN MALE HIGH SCHOOL STUDENTS				
TOTAL	<=12	13-14	15-16	>=17
1671	122 (7.3%)	777 (46.5%)	715 (42.8%)	57 (3.4%)

Table 2–18

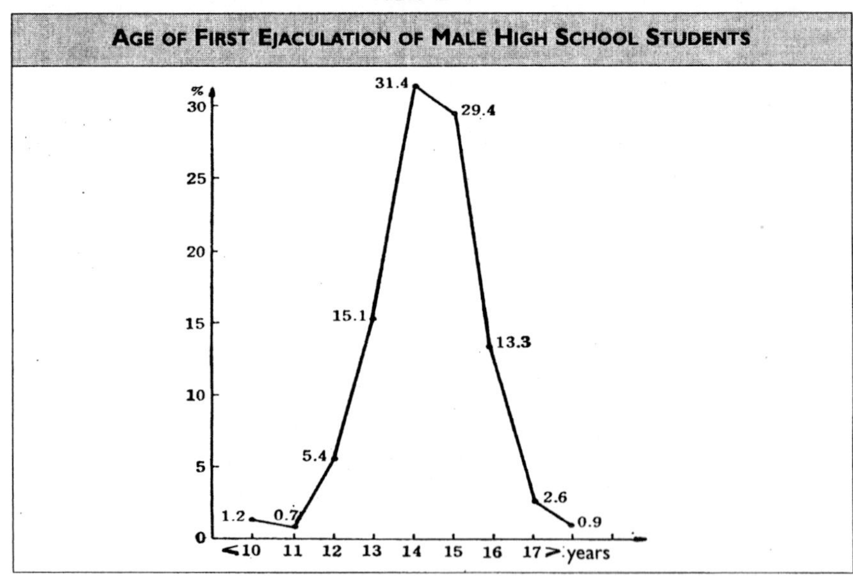

Figure 2–5

Most of the male subjects (79.5 percent) had their first ejaculation in the form of nocturnal emission; 11.0 percent had it in a semiconsciousness state; 4.5 percent by masturbation and 5.1 percent in other circumstances which were not specified (table 2–19).

CIRCUMSTANCES DURING FIRST EJACULATION				
TOTAL	SLEEP	SEMICONSCIOUS	MASTURBATION	OTHER
2016	1602 (79.5%)	222 (11.0%)	90 (4.5%)	102 (5.1%)

Table 2–19

SECONDARY SEXUAL CHARACTERISTICS OF MALE HIGH SCHOOL STUDENTS

TYPE	TOTAL	NOT YET	OBSERVABLE	OBVIOUS
Adam's Apple	2922	357 (12.2%)	1672 (57.2%)	893 (30.6%)
Beard	2898	690 (23.8%)	1681 (58.0%)	527 (18.2%)
Axillary Hair	2875	734 (25.5%)	1290 (44.9%)	851 (29.6%)
Pubic Hair	2883	251 (8.7%)	979 (34.0%)	1653 (57.3%)
Acne	2648	1050 (39.6%)	1166 (44.0%)	432 (16.3%)

Table 2–20

Most male students had an observable or obvious development of the Adam's apple, beard, axillary hair, and pubic hair, but few (16.31 percent) had obvious acne and 39.65 percent had no acne. Yet the number of male students who had acne was double that of the females; those who had observable acne (44.0 percent) were about the same as the females (41.5 percent).

AGE COMPARISON OF MENARCHE IN JAPANESE AND CHINESE STUDENTS

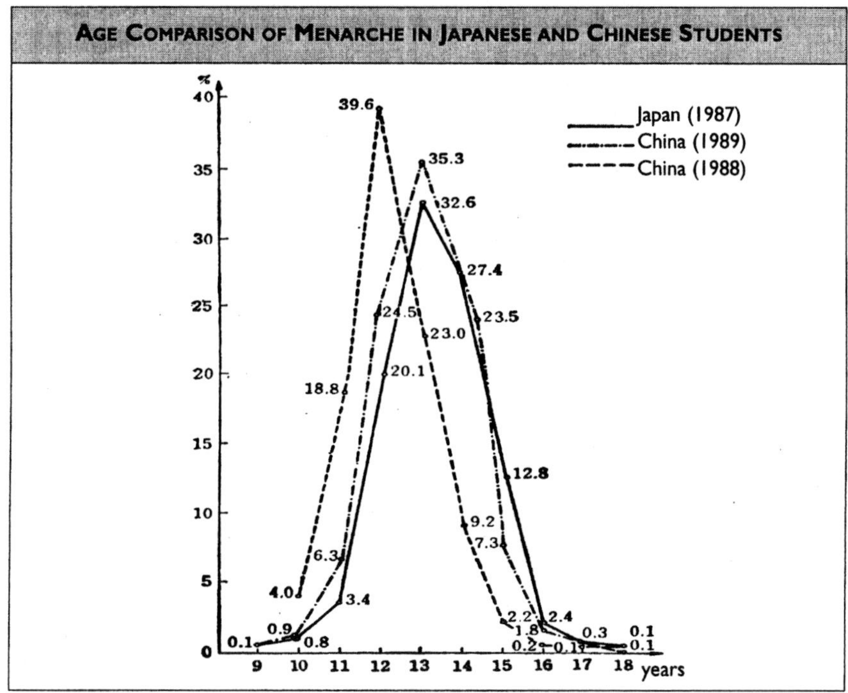

Figure 2–6

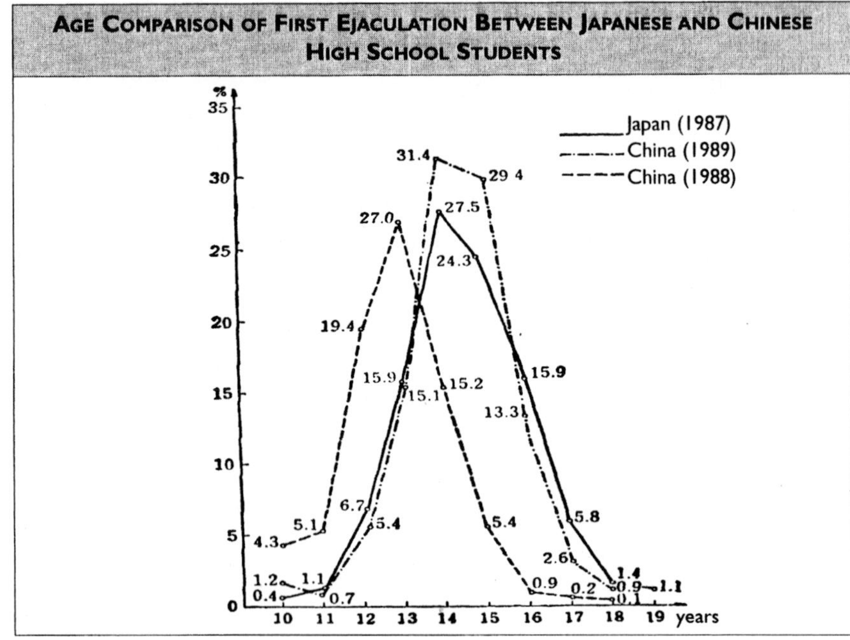

AGE COMPARISON OF FIRST EJACULATION BETWEEN JAPANESE AND CHINESE HIGH SCHOOL STUDENTS

Figure 2–7

Compared with the 1988 and 1989 surveys of China (Yap 1980) and the 1987 survey of Japan (JASE 1987), the Japanese youths have the earliest age of first ejaculation and menarche, the Chinese youths of 1989 come next, and of 1988 last (figures 2–6 and 2–7)

3. Development of Sexual Awareness

With body changes and the development of secondary sexual characteristics, the sexual awareness of youths heightens as well. This period marks the end of childhood and the beginning of adolescence, with a new awareness concerning how individuals view members of the opposite sex, feelings of sexual attraction, and the formation of views about love, relationships, and so forth.

1. Interest in Sexual Matters

Interest in sexual matters is usually the beginning of sexual awareness. It is accompanied by the realization of sexual and sex role differences.

According to the 1988 Adolescence Education Survey (Yao 1988), 36.37 percent reported interest in sexual matters. The youngest age for this was ten years, the oldest nineteen years, and the mean 14.64 years.

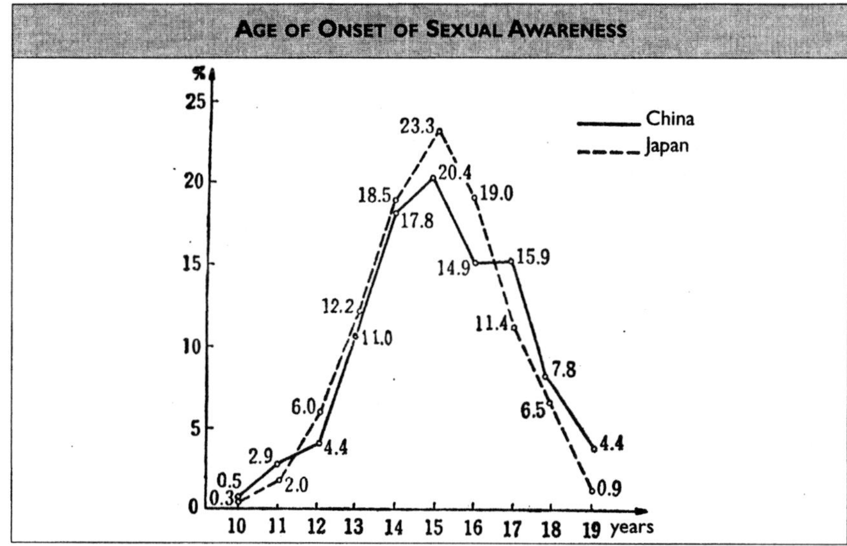

Figure 2–8

Of the 1092 female students, 32.23 percent reported interest in sexual matters. The youngest age was ten years,the eldest nineteen, and the mean was 14.71 years, showing that the onset of sexual awareness was in general later than the onset of first ejaculation and menarche (figure 2–8).

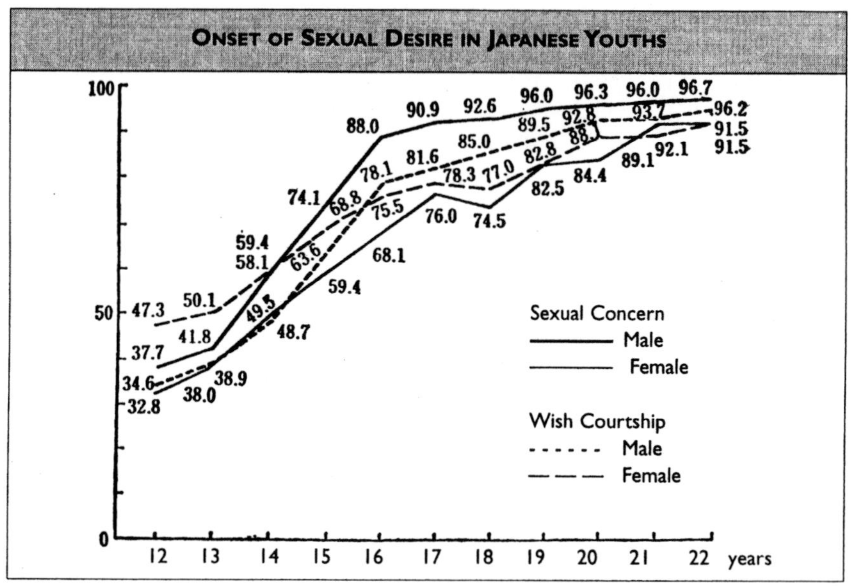

Figure 2–9

The 1987 Third National Youth Sexuality Survey of Japan (JASE 1987) showed that 79.5 percent of the male high school students and 70.6 percent of the females reported sexual desire. As can be seen from figure 2–9, at age fourteen, 59.4 percent Japanese male students and 49.5 percent females already reported sexual desire. At sixteen, 88.0 percent male and 68.1 percent female students experienced sexual desire. From figure 2–10, it can be seen that for males, the earliest age of onset of sexual desire was ten and the highest age seventeen, while the most common age of onset was from twelve to thirteen. For the females, the earliest age was ten, the latest twenty, and the most common age was also between twelve and thirteen years.

In comparing the Chinese and the Japanese students, we found that Japanese students had an earlier onset of sexual desire. This is probably an indication that the Japanese society is sexually more liberal, so that young people have earlier and freer access to sexual information and stimulation.

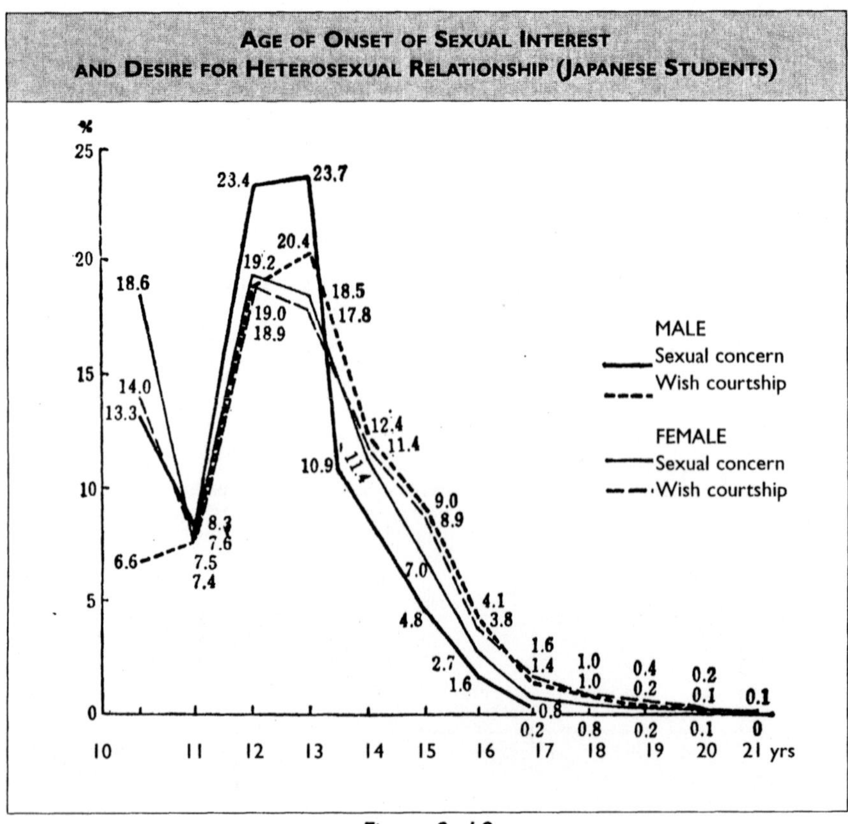

Figure 2–10

2. Desire for a Heterosexual Relationship

With psychosexual development, young people often feel the force of sexual attraction, progressing to a need for affection and relationships with the other sex. In our survey, 3503 subjects (57.5 percent) reported heterosexual relationships, 2485 (40.8 percent) did not, and 104 (1.7 percent) gave no answers.

Table 2–21 shows that 1934 (64.4 percent) of male students and 1569 (52.6 percent) of the female felt sexual desire. These proportions are higher than those reported in the 1988 Adolescent Education survey which showed only 47.1 percent of males and 47.4 percent of females giving positive answers. It suggests that young people tend to wish for a heterosexual relationship at an earlier age.

DESIRE FOR HETEROSEXUAL RELATIONSHIPS			
GENDER	TOTAL	YES	NO
Male	3004	1934 (64.4%)	1070 (35.6%)
Female	2984	1569 (52.6%)	1415 (47.4%)

Table 2–21

GRADE LEVEL AND DESIRE FOR HETEROSEXUAL RELATIONSHIPS							
DESIRE	TOTAL	JUNIOR GRADES			SENIOR GRADES		
		1	2	3	1	2	3
No	2466	377 (72.1%	727 (66.3%)	608 (46.5%)	415 (30.4%)	20 (21.0%)	119 (19.4%)
Yes	3483	146 (27.9%)	69 (33.7%)	699 (23.5%)	948 (69.6%)	828 (79.0%))	93 (80.6%)

Table 2–22

With respect to grade levels, the higher grade students show a higher percentage for the desire (table 2–22), with G at 0.51.

The average age of initial desire for a heterosexual relationship was 13.89 years, SD 2.11. The mode was from thirteen to sixteen years, the peak age was from thirteen to fourteen years (42.2 percent), and the next peak age was at fifteen to sixteen years (33.7 percent) (table 2–23).

The cross tabulation of current age with age of onset for heterosexual desire shows that onset of the desire has a significant tendency to become lower with the younger students (G=0.57) (table 2–24).

Age of Onset for Heterosexual Desire					
TOTAL	<=10	11-12	13-14	15-16	>=17
2686	157 (5.8%)	344 (12.8%)	1134 (42.2%)	906 (33.7%)	145 (5.4%)

Table 2–23

Current Age and Age of Onset for Heterosexual Desire						
CURRENT AGE	TOTAL	<=10	11-12	13-14	15-16	>=17
<=13	124	25 (20.2%)	39 (31.4%)	60 (48.4%)	0 (0%)	0 (0%)
14-15	870	65 (7.5%)	159 (18.3%)	520 (59.8%)	126 (14.5%)	0 (0%)
16-17	1244	50 (4.0%)	117 (9.4%)	453 (36.4%)	588 (47.3%)	36 (2.9%)
>=18	363	13 (3.6%)	19 (5.2%)	71 (19.6%)	164 (45.3%)	95 (26.2%)

Table 2–24

Age of Onset of Heterosexual Desire in High School Students

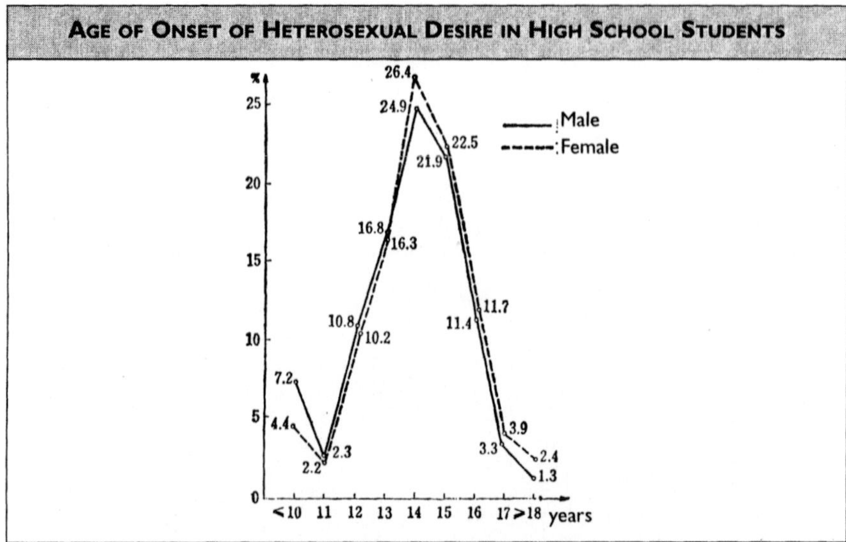

Figure 2–11

The 1988 Adolescent Education Survey[3] showed that in male students, the earliest age for heterosexual desire was eight, the latest nineteen; for females, the earliest was ten and the latest also nineteen. The peak age for both males and females was between fourteen and fifteen. The mean age for males was 14.2 and females 14.5 years.

The Japanese 1987[4] survey showed that a greater proportion of Japanese high school students had a desire for heterosexual relationships. The figures were 68.5 percent for males and 70.0 percent for females.

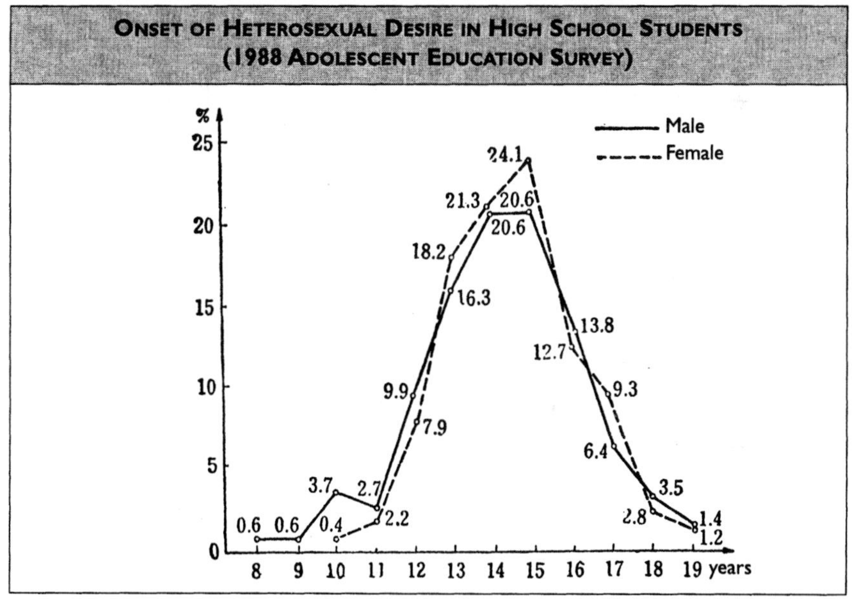

Figure 2–12

Their onset for the desire was also earlier. In table 2–10, it can be seen that at age ten, already 18.6 percent of the males and 14.0 percent of the females had the desire. The peak age was twelve to thirteen, earlier than in the Chinese students by one to two years.

Male and female students had different reasons for desiring heterosexual relationships. For the males, the reasons were, in descending order of frequency: physical attraction, tenderness, social need, pleasure, support, and security. For the females, the order was support, social need, pleasure, physical attraction, tenderness (table 2–25).

Of the reasons for not desiring heterosexual relations, the main ones were "not feeling the need," "not liking it," "being busy with studying,"

REASONS FOR PHYSICAL ATTRACTION TO THE OTHER SEX			
REASON	TOTAL	MALE	FEMALE
Appearance	863 (23.3%)	772 (38.8%)	91 (5.3%)
Tenderness	511 (13.8%)	389 (19.6%)	122 (7.1%)
Attractiveness	243 (6.6%)	6 (0.3%)	237 (13.8%)
Pleasing	503 (13.6%)	229 (11.5%)	274 (16.0%)
Support	671 (18.1%)	205 (10.3%)	466 (27.2%)
Emotional security	121 (3.3%)	12 (0.6%)	109 (6.4%)
Social need	587 (15.8%)	281 (14.1%)	306 (17.8%)
Others	205 (5.5%)	95 (4.8%)	110 (6.4%)
Total	3704	1989	1715

Table 2–25

REASONS FOR ATTRACTION TO MEMBERS OF THE OTHER SEX IN HIGH SCHOOL STUDENTS (1988 ADOLESCENCE EDUCATION SURVEY)

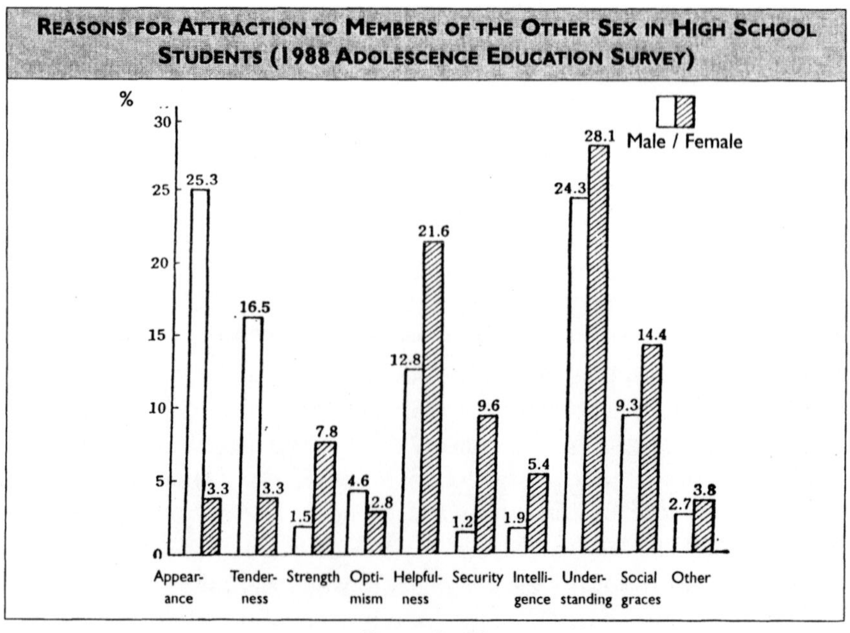

Figure 2–13

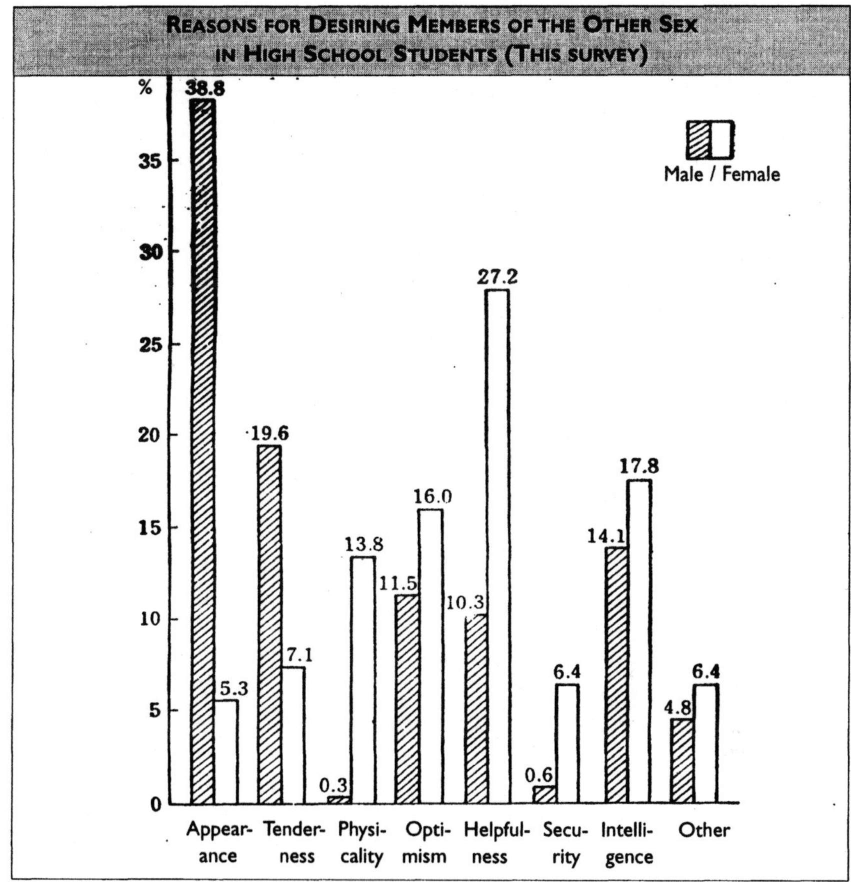

Figure 2–14

and "shyness." This shows that how much the high school students were controlled by their school work and social restraints (table 2–26).

In the 1988 survey, the reasons males gave were physical attraction, mutual understanding, tenderness, support; the reasons female students provided were mutual understanding, support, social need, security, and stability. Compared with this survey, a greater proportion of male students in the 1988 survey (38.8 percent) were attracted to the other sex physically, more female students (27.2 percent) looked for emotional support and both male and female students placed more emphasis on social need (figures 2–13 and 2–14).

3. Wish for Physical Contact with the Other Sex

In all, 5666 subjects answered the question on this subject (table 2–27):1,213 (21.4 percent) of them had the wish; 4453 (78.6 percent)

Reasons for No Physical Attraction to the Other sex		
REASON	TOTAL	PERCENT
Not liking it	416	(14.3%)
Shyness	39	(13.5%)
No need	1131	(38.8%)
Fear of gossip	229	(7.9%)
Busy	403	(13.8%)
Others	340	(11.7%)
Total	12,911	(100.0%)

Table 2–26

did not. Among the males, 35.7 percent had the wish; among the females,7.4 percent The gender differences were obvious.

In the 1988 Adolescent Education Survey, in a total of 1033 male students, 289 (27.98 percent) had the wish for heterosexual physical contact—ages ranging from ten to nineteen years, with the mean age being 14.83 years. In 1045 female students, 88 (8.42 percent) had the

Wish for Heterosexual Physical Contact in High School Students			
GENDER	TOTAL	NO	YES
Male	2807	1806 (64.3%)	1001 (35.7%)
Female	2859	2647 (92.6%)	212 (7.4%)

Table 2–27

desire, with ages ranging from ten to eighteen with a mean of 14.94 years (figure 2–17). The figures suggested that the proportion of male students desiring heterosexual contact had risen between the years 1988 and 1989, but had decreased in the females. Both surveys showed a significant difference between male and female students.

Japanese high school students showed higher figures in this respect. The 1987 Adolescent Sexuality Survey had 66.9 percent male students and 20.6 percent female showing a desire for physical contact with the other sex. Although desire differences also occurred between the male and female Japanese students, the Japanese males showed an overall greater desire than the Chinese. From figure 2–15, it can be seen that at age fourteen, already 43.1 percent Japanese male students and 35.2 percent female wished for heterosexual physical contact. At age sixteen, the male figure rose to 79.6 percent, the female to 76.8 percent. Most likely, the liberal sexual culture in Japanese society greatly influences the sexual awareness of its young people. This comparison between Chinese and Japanese adolescents suggests the effect of different cultures on the development of sexual desires.

Our survey data provides a G index of 0.44 for the relationship between grade level and the desire for heterosexual physical contact, with a greater desire being found in higher grades (table 2–28). For the age of onset of the desire, ages thirteen and fourteen and ages fifteen and sixteen are the peak ages (35.3 percent and 43.8 percent respectively).

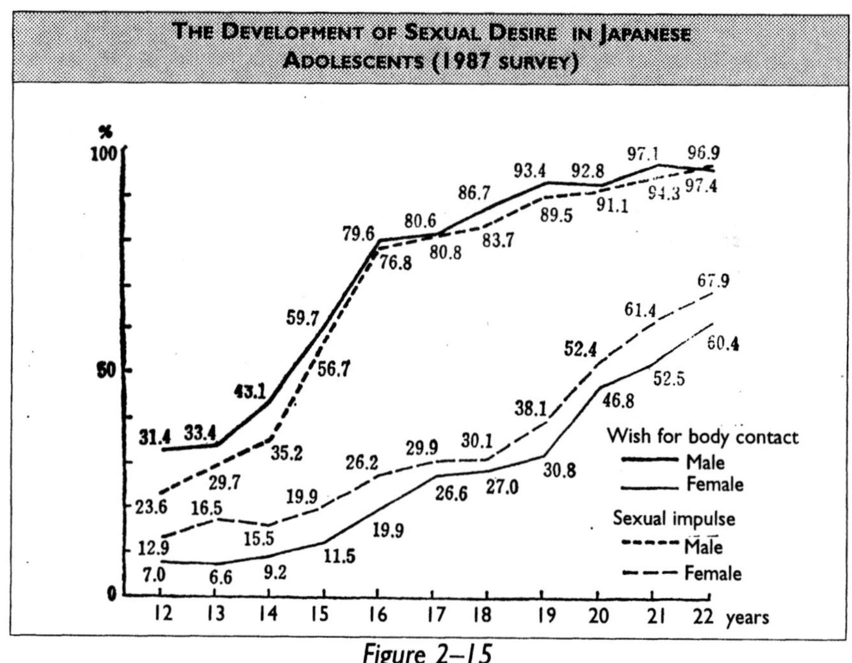

Figure 2–15

The mean age was 14.48 years with a SD of 2.47 (table 2–29 and figure 2–16). There was a significantly positive association between the students' current age and their onset of the desire (G=0.64). This suggests that there is a trend for this desire to start at progressively lower ages (table 2–30).

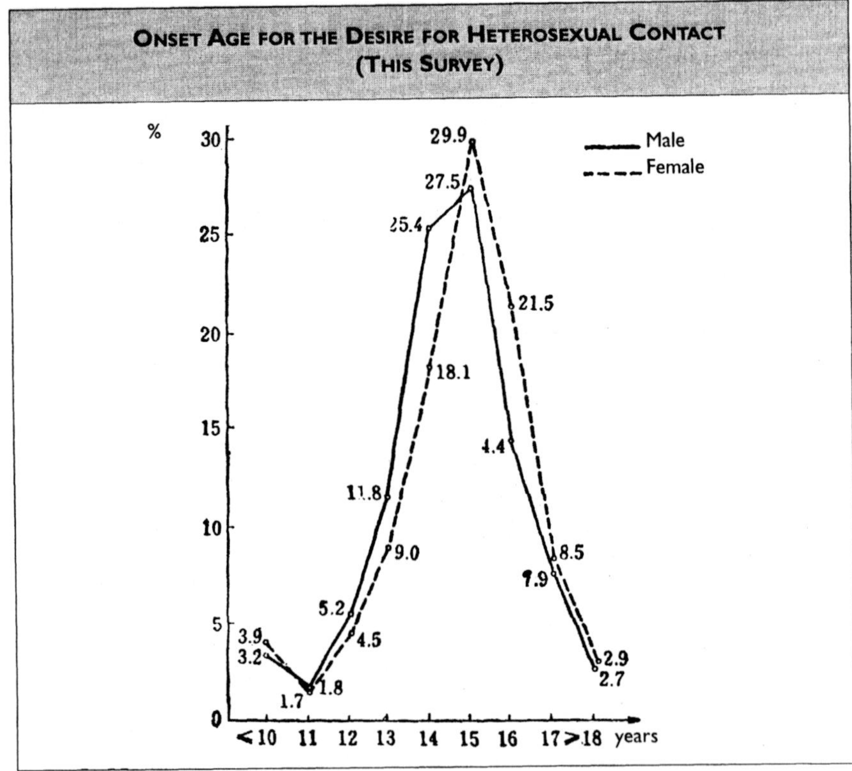

Figure 2–16

GRADE LEVEL AND DESIRE FOR HETEROSEXUAL PHYSICAL CONTACT							
DESIRE	TOTAL	J1	J2	J3	S1	S2	S3
No	4424	464 (94.1%)	97 (92.4%)	1053 (84.1%)	907 (71.6%)	663 (66.1%)	360 (63.3%)
Yes	1208	9 (5.9%)	80 (7.6%)	199 (15.9%)	359 (28.4%)	32 (33.4%)	209 (36.7%)

Table 2–28

AGE OF ONSET OF THE DESIRE FOR HETEROSEXUAL CONTACT OF THE HIGH SCHOOL STUDENTS					
TOTAL	<=10	11-12	13-14	15-16	>=17
912	31 (3.4%)	62 (6.8%)	322 (35.3%)	399 (43.8%)	98 (10.7%)

Table 2–29

Current Age and the Onset of Desire for Heterosexual Physical Contact						
CURRENT AGE	TOTAL	<=10	11-12	13-14	15-16	>=17
<=13	22 (4.5%)	1 (45.4%)	10 (50.0%)	11 (0%)	0 (0%)	0
14-15	244 4.9%)	12 (9.4%)	23 (62.7%)	153 23.0%)	56 (0%)	0
16-17	476	14 (2.9%)	25 (5.3%)	128 (26.9%)	277 (58.2%)	32 (6.7%)
>=18	137	4 (2.9%)	3 (2.2%)	18 (13.1%)	50 (36.5%)	62 (45.3%)

Table 2–30

In the 1988 Adolescent Education Survey, among the male high school students, the earliest onset age of the desire for heterosexual physical contact was ten, the latest was nineteen. The mean age was 14.83. For the females, the earliest age was ten, the latest eighteen with a mean of 14.94. The peak age for male students was fourteen to fifteen and seventeen while the peak for females was fourteen and sixteen. They showed differences in peak ages but both have a trough in the developmental curve of this desire (figure 2–17).

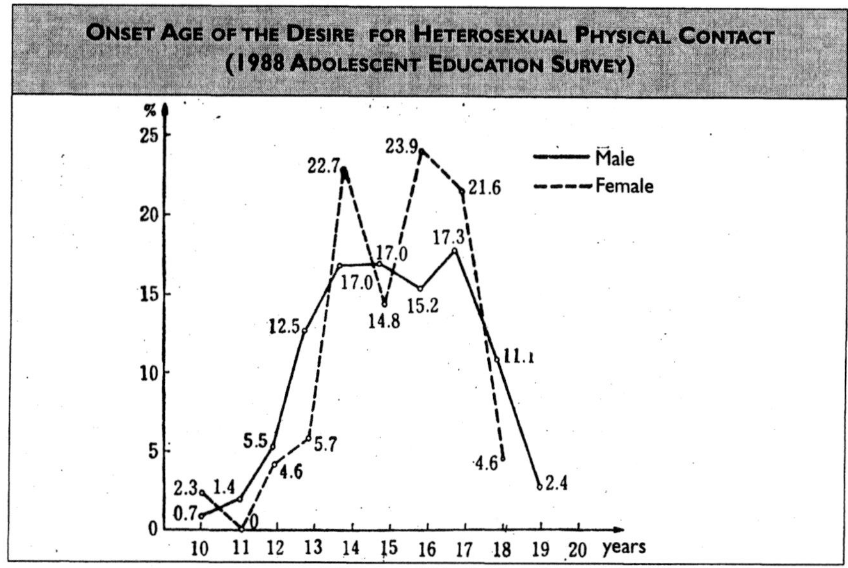

Figure 2–17

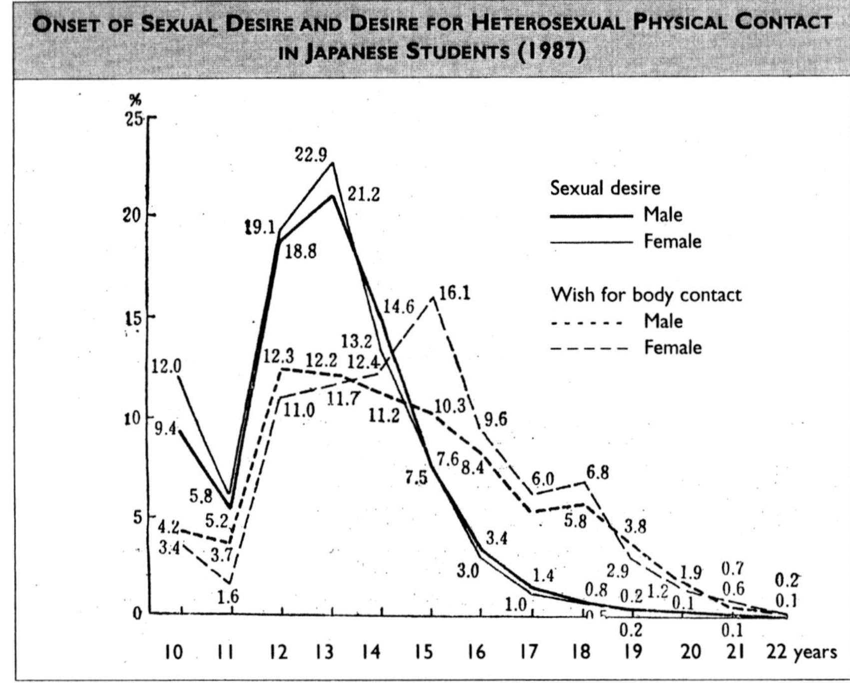

Figure 2–18

The Japanese data showed that the earliest age of onset for heterosexual physical contact was ten, the latest at twenty, with a peak at age thirteen (22.9 percent). For females, the earliest was ten, latest twenty-two, and the peak fifteen (16.1 percent). The female onset was about one to two years later than the male (figure 2–18).

4. Sexual Impulse

In all, 5669 subjects answered this question. 1552 (27.4 percent) reported experience of sexual impulse; 4117 (72.6 percent) did not report any. Those who reported the experience constituted 42.9 percent of all the males and 12.1 percent of all the females; 57.1 percent of the males and 87.9 percent of the females did not report any (table 2–31). The gender differences in sexual impulse is obvious. Table 2–32 also showed that experience of sexual impulse increases with grade level (G=0.47).

Compared with the 1988 survey, the the figures were slightly higher. In the older survey, 35.7 percent of the 1185 male subjects and 11.93 percent of the 1266 female subjects reported experience of a sex

Experience of Sexual Impulse			
GENDER	TOTAL	NO	YES
Male	2818	1610 (57.1%)	1208 (42.9%)
Female	2851	2507 (87.9%)	344 (12.1%)

p=0.001

Table 2–31

Grade Level and Experience of Sexual Impulse							
EXPERIENCE	TOTAL	J.1	J.2	J.3	S.1	S.2	S.3
No	4089	455 (92.7%)	943 (90.2%)	998 (79.6%)	820 (63.9%)	553 (56.0%)	320 (55.8%)
Yes	1544	36 (7.3%)	103 (9.8%)	255 (20.4%)	463 (36.1%)	434 (44.0%)	253 (44.2%)

p=0.001

Table 2–32

impulse. In the Japanese 1987 survey, 68.8 percent of the male and 34.6 percent of the females had the experience, showing a higher percentage than the Chinese. In the Japanese male students, 56.7 percent of those at age fifteen and 76.8 percent of those at the age of sixteen had the experience; in the Japanese female students, the corresponding percentages were 19.9 percent and 26.2 percent (figure 2–15). The females developed more slowly than the males in this respect. Up to age nineteen, only 38.1 percent of them had the experience of a sexual impulse compared with 89.5 percent of the males.

The peak age for the onset of sexual impulse was from thirteen to sixteen, with the mean age being 14.63, and the SD 1.86 (table 2–33 and figure 2–19). In the 1988 Adolescent Education Survey, the earliest onset age for male students was eight, and the latest was eighteen, with the mean being at 14.5. For the females, the earliest age was eight, the latest nineteen, and the mean was 15.2 (figure 2–20). The percentages in males were higher than in females.

Japanese students had an earlier onset of sexual impulses than the Chinese. Their peak age of onset was twelve to thirteen (figure 2–18). At twelve, there was 18.8 percent male and 12.3 percent female students who had their first experience of a sexual impulse. At thirteen, there was 21.2 percent males and 12.2 percent females.

AGE AND ONSET OF SEXUAL RESPONSE					
TOTAL	<=10	11-12	13-14	15-16	>=17
1174	18 (1.5%)	74 (6.3%)	421 (35.9%)	543 (46.3%)	118 (10.1%)

Table 2–33

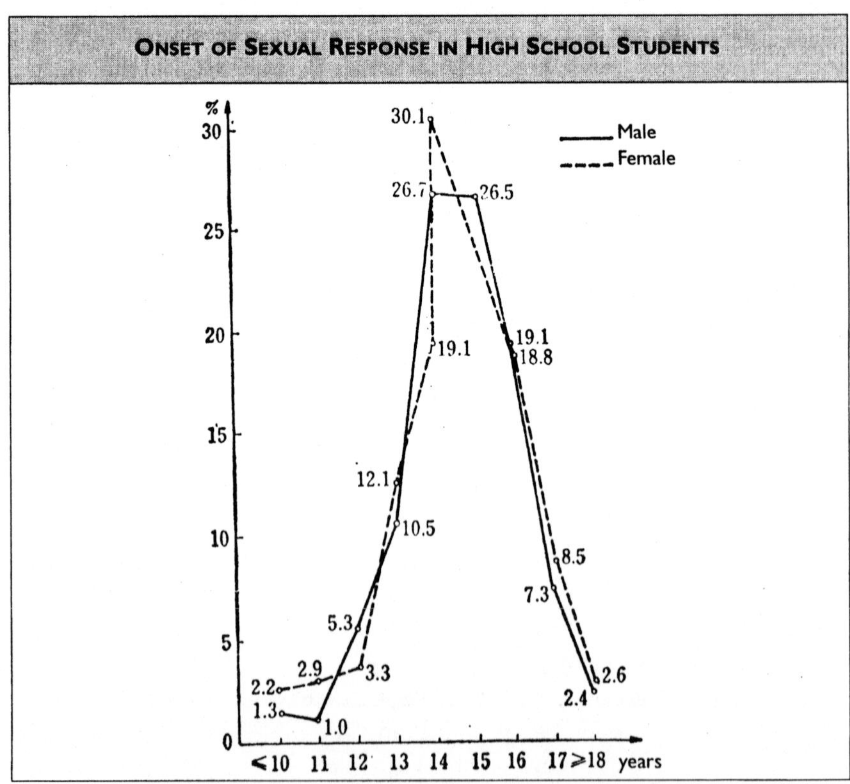

Figure 2–19

Although physiological changes are the most important factor for the onset of sexual impulses, the role of external stimulation cannot be neglected, and these in turn depend highly on the gender of the subject, as well as on cultural and individual factors.

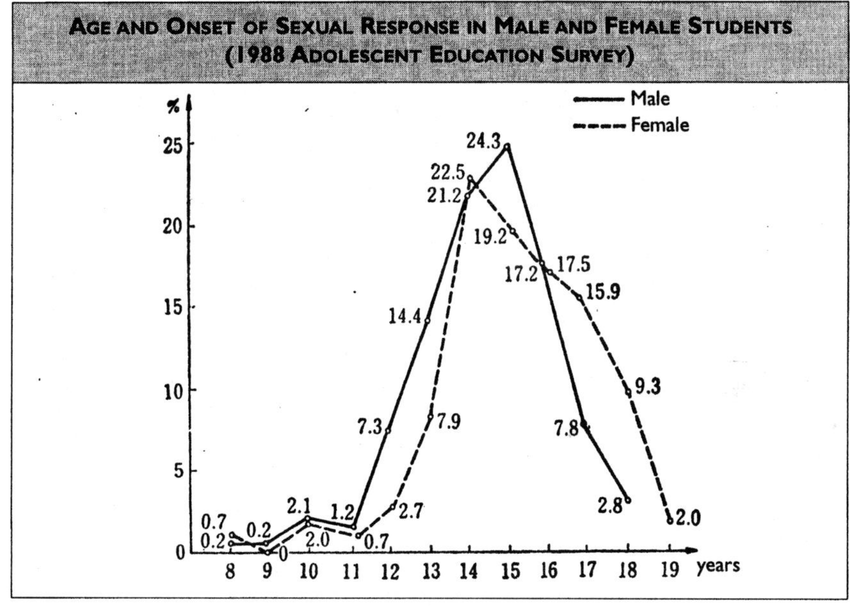

AGE AND ONSET OF SEXUAL RESPONSE IN MALE AND FEMALE STUDENTS (1988 ADOLESCENT EDUCATION SURVEY)

Figure 2–20

In our survey, the male students reported that they could be stimulated sexually by a large variety of means, in the following descending order of frequency: erotic pictures, sexual depictions in movies, occasional physical contact with the other sex, and observing the nude body of the other sex. For the females, the order was: sexual depictions in movies, erotic pictures, occasional physical contact, and occasional talks about sex (table 2–34). It can be seen that the males were more frequently aroused (14.9 percent) than females (7.8 percent) by witnessing the nude body of the other sex. This suggests that males are more easily aroused by visual stimuli.

Comparing the data with the Japanese (figure 2–21), the order of the stimulants in the three Japanese surveys was quite similar to ours. But more Japanese males were stimulated by erotic movies and more Chinese students were stimulated by body contact. This could be related to the traditional Chinese taboo of heterosexual body contact, even in social circumstances, as reflected by the ancient saying "Do not touch the other person even when handing over an object!" Given the rarity of physical contact with the other sex, occasional contact becomes an impressive, sexually arousing experience.

STIMULANTS FOR SEXUAL RESPONSES			
STIMULANT	TOTAL	MALE	FEMALE
Erotic pictures	1842 (22.3%)	1093 (23.2%)	749 (21.1%)
Erotic movies	1844 (22.3%)	1015 (21.5%)	829 (23.3%)
Body contact	1253 (15.2%)	702 (14.9%)	551 (15.5%)
Live visual stimulation	980 (11.9%)	702 (14.9%)	278 (7.8%)
Talking about sex	851 (10.3%)	506 (10.7%)	345 (9.7%)
Dating	601 (7.3%)	272 (5.8%)	329 (9.3%)
Leisure	431 (5.2%)	227 (4.8%)	204 (5.7%)
Dancing	241 (2.9%)	95 (2.0%)	146 (4.1%)
Others	224 (2.7%)	104 (2.2%)	120 (3.4%)
Total	8267 (100.0%)	4716 (100.0%)	3551 (100.0%)

Table 2–34

From the data given on the facing page, it can be seen that:

1. There is a certain sequence in the psychological development of youths. Associated with physiological development, there is first the development of sexual interest, followed by a desire for a heterosexual relationship, the desire for heterosexual physical contact, and then a sexual impulse in a specific sense. From figure 2–22, it can be seen that the onset of sexual awareness follows a sequence too. When a youth is around the age of ten or below, the various forms of sexual awareness are in this sequence: desire for heterosexual relations, desire for heterosexual physical contact, and sexual impulse, with the peak ages of each also following the same sequence. From figures 2–9, 2–10, 2–15, and 2–18, it can be seen that Japanese adolescents followed the same sequence too. Furthermore, some relationship can be observed between any sequential pair of growing sexual awareness. As shown in figure 2–22, the value of desire for physical contact is close to that of the sexual impulse. The shape of their curves are also quite similar. The same pattern was found in the 1988 Adolescent Education Survey.

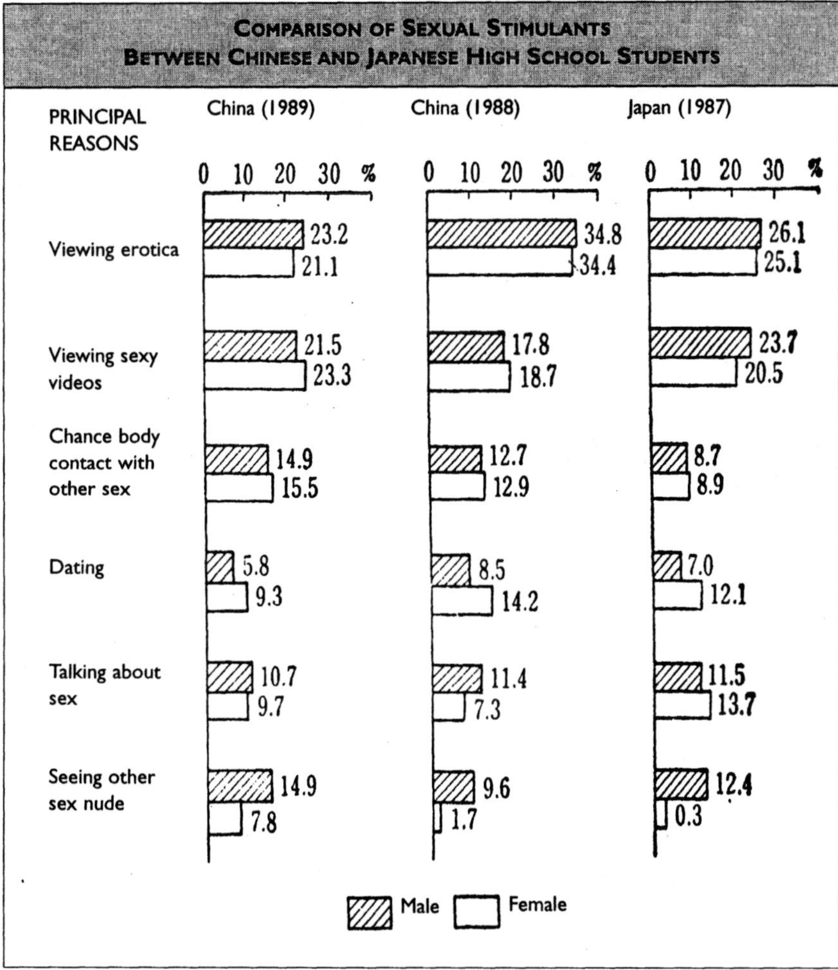

Figure 2–21

2. There are differences betweens the two genders. The females usually show a weaker awareness as measured in the percentages of their positive replies and their age of onset of the various types of awareness.

3. There is possibly a cultural influence on the development of sexual awareness. In figure 2–23, it can be seen that for every item, the Japanese values are invariably higher than the Chinese values. It is likely that in societies which are sexually more open, the development of sexual awareness tends to start earlier and reach a higher level. If this hypothesis is true, the importance of sex education for young people becomes apparent.

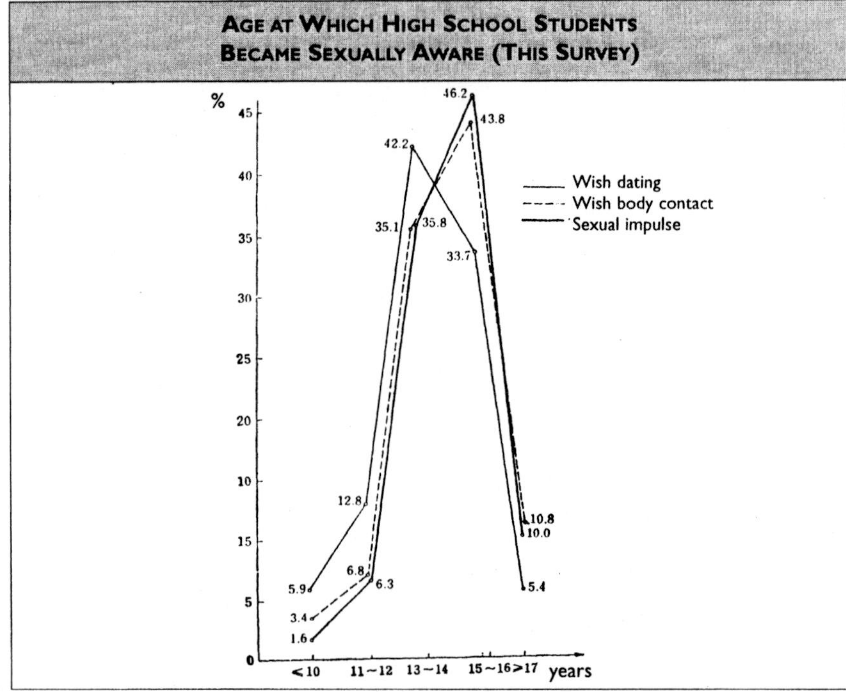

Figure 2–22

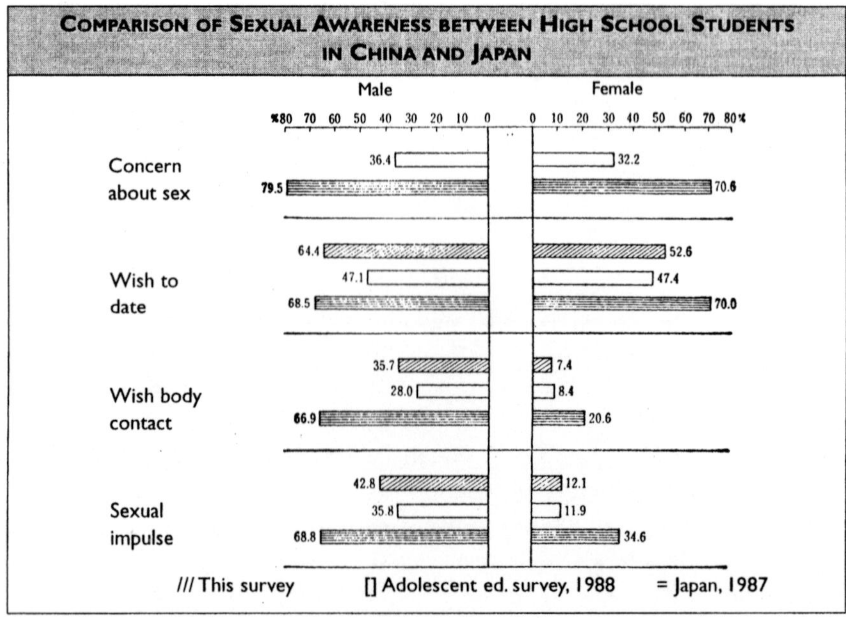

Figure 2–23

4. Heterosexual Relations and Early Love

The sexual awareness of youths can be divided into three developmental stages: sexual feelings, sexual desire and sexual love. The stage of sexual feeling begins at the time of menarche or the first ejaculation. At this stage, the sexual attention of youths is focused on the body. Yet, the interest is not limited to one's own body. The awareness of bodily functions has a deeper meaning only when there is a social relationship allowing realistic comparisons. Without external influence, one's sexual impulse is only a subconsciously driven behavior, and one's sexual awareness is also only a vague condition lacking a social dimension. Generally speaking, when one's sexual feeling is awakened by a specific person, there develops an emotional attachment, a feeling that the object is pleasing. This, in turn, leads to sexual desire. Then, following the process of further socialization and intensification, with the development of a personal relationship, the infatuation turns into love.

This division of developmental stages is theoretical. It is the task of sex educators to check the validity of this hypothesis, to comprehend the mechanism of the psychosexual development of youths and to assist young people in their proper socialization.

1. Heterosexual Relationships

From a developmental point of view, young people have a need for friendship. From the psychological point of view, peers are a major factor in identity formation, especially for those looking for self-realization, exploring the question "Who am I?" The 1988 Adolescence Education

INDIVIDUALS' RELATIONSHIP WITH THEIR BEST FRIENDS (1988 ADOLESCENT EDUCATION SURVEY)		
	MALE (%)	FEMALE (%)
HAVE AS BEST FRIENDS		
Parents	8.1	9.6
Sister	1.8	8.2
Brothers	3.6	0.5
Schoolmates	16.8	20.8
Friend	23.3	29.5
Others	0.3	0.4
NO BEST FRIENDS	46.1	31.1

Table 2-35

Survey showed that in high school students, 16.8 percent of the males found their same-sex friends among their classmates, 23.3 percent among those outside the school. For females, the figures were 20.8 percent and 29.5 percent respectively (table 2–35).

More than half of the students had best friends who were of the same sex (53.9 percent for males, 68.9 percent for females, table 2–35). Yet, quite a sizable proportion of the students had close friends of the other sex. The 1988 survey shows that 22.2 percent males and 18.3 percent females reported that they had close friends of the other sex. In the males, the earliest age for this was eight, the eldest nineteen, with a mean age of 14.3. For the females, the earliest was eight and the eldest eighteen, with a mean of fourteen (figure 2–24).

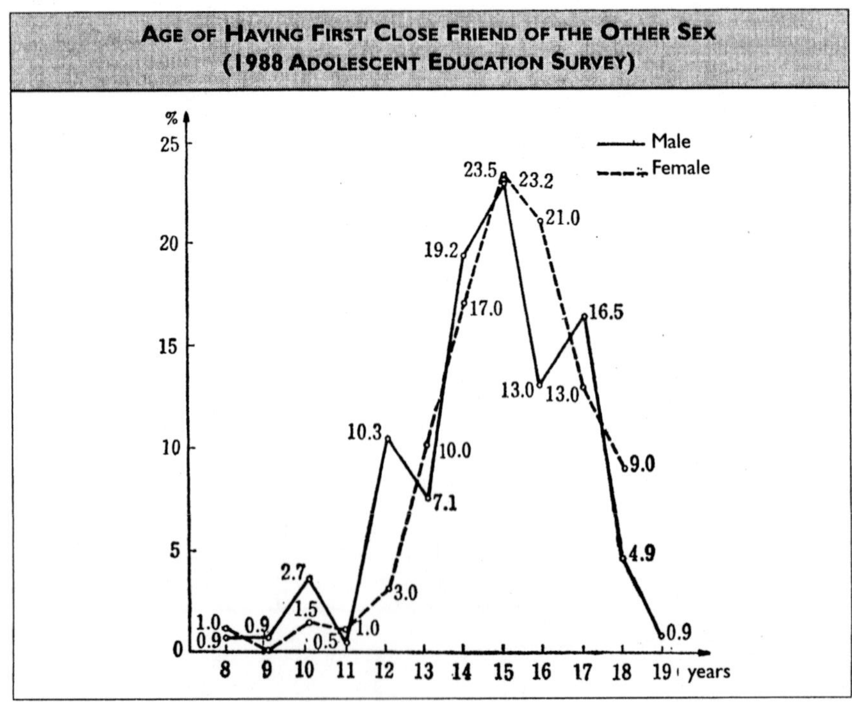

Figure 2–24

In our survey, 5339 subjects answered the question about friends of the other sex: 2074 (38.8 percent) reported having friends of the other sex; 3265 (61.2 percent) reported not having such friends. Answering yes were 41.6 percent of the males and 36.1 percent of the females (table 2–36).

STUDENTS HAVING FRIENDS OF THE OTHER SEX			
GENDER	TOTAL	YES	NO
Male	2666	1108 (41.6%)	1558 (58.4%)
Female	2673	966	1707

P=0.001

Table 2–36

ONSET OF FRIENDSHIPS WITH THE OTHER SEX IN HIGH SCHOOL STUDENTS					
TOTAL	<=10	11–12	13–14	15–16	>=17
1582	127 (8.0%)	165 (10.4%)	558 (35.3%)	583 (36.9%)	149 (9.4%)

Table 2–37

GRADE LEVEL AND FRIENDS OF THE OTHER SEX							
FRIEND	TOTAL	J1	J2	J3	S1	S2	S3
No	3245	362 (76.2%)	683 (72.0%)	800 (67.4%)	660 (54.8%)	494 (52.6%)	246 (44.7%)
Yes	2059	113 (23.8%)	265 (28.0%)	87 (32.6%)	545 (45.2%)	445 (47.4%)	304 (55.3%)

Table 2–38

In the high school students, the peak age of starting to have friends of the other sex was thirteen to fifteen years (table 2–37, figure 2–25). The mean age was 14.98, SD=2.61. Students in the last year of junior high and the first two years of high school had more friends of the other sex. The association between grade levels and having friends of the other sex had a G index of 0.28, with higher grade students having a higher proportion (table 2–38).

Comparing this table with table 2–36, it can be seen that the age of having friends of the other sex came later than the wish for such friends (table 2–39). It shows a natural sequence.

Table 2–40 examines the relationship between the current age of the subjects and the onset of heterosexual realtionships among them, with an

THE WISH FOR FRIENDS OF THE OTHER SEX AND ITS FULFILLMENT						
AGE SEX-WISH BEGINS	TOTAL	<=10	11–12	13–14	15–16	>=17
<=10	77 (50.6%)	39 (16.9%)	13 (22.1%)	17 (6.5%)	5 (3.9%)	3
11–12	171 (5.8%)	10 (39.8%)	68 (38.6%)	66 (14.0%)	24 (1.8%)	3
13–14	499 (2.2%)	11 (4.6%)	23 (64.1%)	320 (25.3%)	126 (3.8%)	19
15–16	409 (2.0%)	8 (1.2%)	5 (8.8%)	36 (78.2%)	320 (9.8%)	40
>=17	61 –	– –	1 (1.6%)	3 (4.9%)	7 (11.5%)	50 (82.0%)

Table 2–39

CURRENT AGE AND ONSET AGE OF HETEROSEXUAL FRIENDSHIP						
CURRENT AGE	TOTAL	ONSET AGE OF HETEROSEXUAL FRIENDSHIP				
		<=10	11–12	13–14	15–16	>=17
<=13	79	23 (29.1%)	27 (34.2%)	29 (36.7%)	0 0	0 0
14–15	481	63 (13.1%)	73 (15.2%)	254 (52.8%)	91 (18.9%)	0 0
16–17	737	34 (4.6%)	50 (6.8%)	235 (31.9%)	370 (50.2%)	48 (6.5%)
>=18	230	5 (2.2%)	13 (5.7%)	30 (13.0%)	94 (40.9%)	88 (38.3%)

Table 2–40

association index G of 0.63. This suggests that there is a significant trend toward engaging in such behavior at younger and younger ages.

The Japanese Third Adolescent Sexuality Survey shows that Japanese youths had more friends of the same sex than of the other sex, with the females more so. For friends of the opposite sex, the male and female distributions are about the same. For example, at age fourteen, 31.7 percent males and 30.2 percent females had friends of the other sex. At age

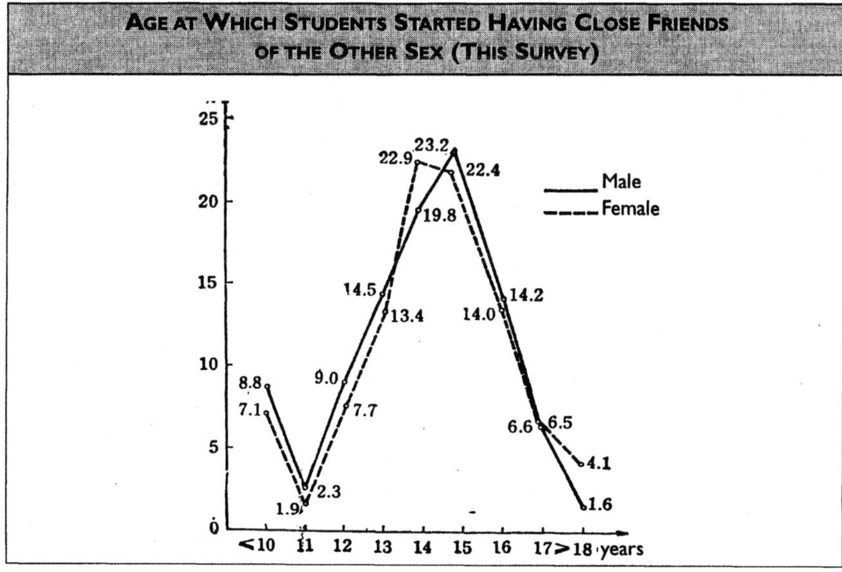

Figure 2–25

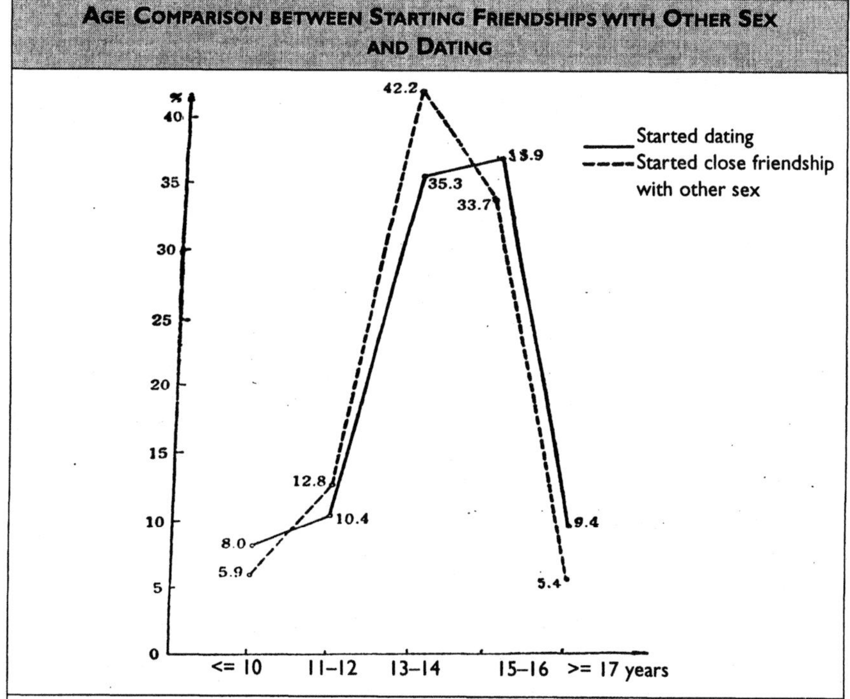

Figure 2–26

nineteen, 44.2 percent male and 45.6 percent female had them (figure 2–27). This condition might have something to do with the sexual openness of Japanese society. At a certain age, males begin to have female friends and females begin to have male friends. They do not show any great difference in this respect.

FAVORED ATTITUDE OF RELATING TO THE OTHER SEX IN HIGH SCHOOL STUDENTS (1988 ADOLESCENT EDUCATION SURVEY)				
ATTITUDE	MALE		FEMALE	
	No.	Percent	No	Percent
Mutual respect	1037	(80.6%)	1141	(85%)
Just fun	216	(16.8%)	186	(13.9%)
Mutual pleasure	34	(2.6%)	15	(1.1%)
Total	1287		1342	

Table 2–41

FAVORED WAY OF RELATING TO THE OTHER SEX (1988 ADOLESCENT EDUCATION SURVEY)				
WAY	MALE		FEMALE	
	No.	Percent	No.	Percent
No contact	50	(3.9%)	38	(2.8%)
In groups	1187	(91.7%)	1283	(95.5%)
In pairs	58	(4.5%)	23	(1.7%)
Total	1295		1344	

Table 2–42

The 1988 Adolescent Education Survey also looked into the attitude of the students towards other–sex friendships. Most students (80.57 percent males and 85.02 percent females) believed such friendships should be characterized by mutual respect and chastity. Only a minority believed mutual pleasure and physical gratification to be important (table 2–41). Moreover, most subjects (91.7 percent males and 95.5 percent female) thought that in the high school period, other-sex friendships should be made and maintained openly in groups.

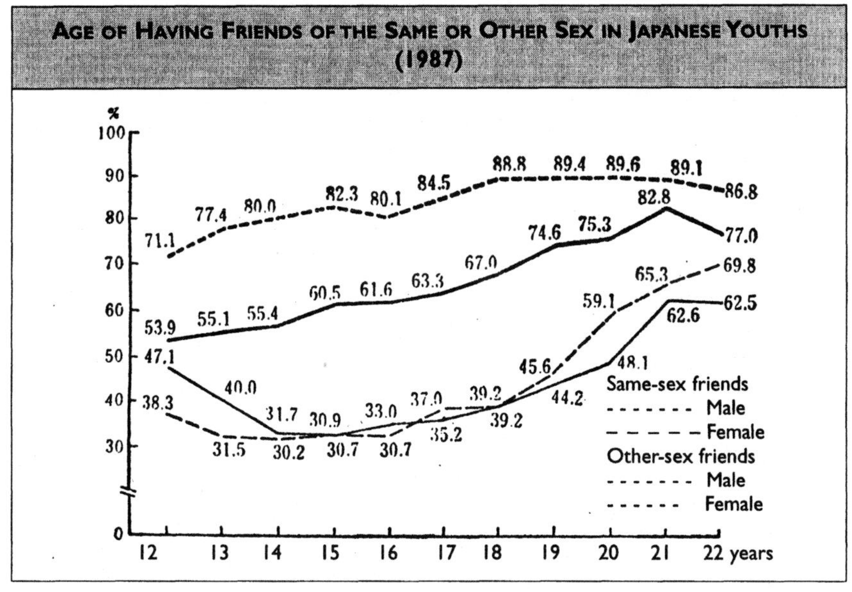

Age of Having Friends of the Same or Other Sex in Japanese Youths (1987)

Figure 2–27

Only a minority (4.5 percent male and 1.7 percent female) were in favor of intimate relations between individual couples (table 2–42). It can be inferred that in high school students, their attitude regarding heterosexual contacts follows that of traditional teachings or that it is still vague and naive, ignoring possible physical aspects.

2. Early Love

The 1988 Adolescent Education Survey showed that in 1053 male high school students, 7.9 percent (83) already had girlfriends and in 1070 females, 5.7 percent (61) had boyfriends. Our survey of one year later shows similar results. Out of 4978 who responded to this question, 4603 (92.5 percent) reported no lovers, 375 (7.5 percent) reported having boyfriends or girlfriends, with 7.6 percent males and 6.0 percent females.

The peak age of starting to have such relationships was thirteen to sixteen (table 2–43, figure 2–28), the mean age being 14.2 with a SD of 2.63. Of those who had lovers, students of junior high third year made up 22.7 percent and those at senior high first year made up 20.3 percent. The association index between grade and percentage of students having such relationships had a G index of 0.18, showing some relationship between grade and proportion of having boyfriends or girlfriends.

ONSET AGE OF STUDENTS HAVING A DATING PARTNER					
TOTAL	<=10	11–12	13–14	15–16	>=17
375	21 (5.6%)	36 (9.6%)	125 (33.3%)	149 (39.7%)	44 (11.7%)

Table 2–43

GRADE LEVELS OF STUDENTS HAVING DATING PARTNERS							
BOYFRIEND GIRLFRIEND	TOTAL	J1	J2	J3	S1	S2	S3
No	4608	431 (94.3%)	879 (95.6%)	1050 (93.2%)	1042 (93.8%)	803 (92.6%)	403 (86.7%)
Yes	335	26 (5.7%)	40 (4.4%)	76 (6.7%)	68 (6.1%)	63 (7.3%)	62 (13.3%)

Table 2–44

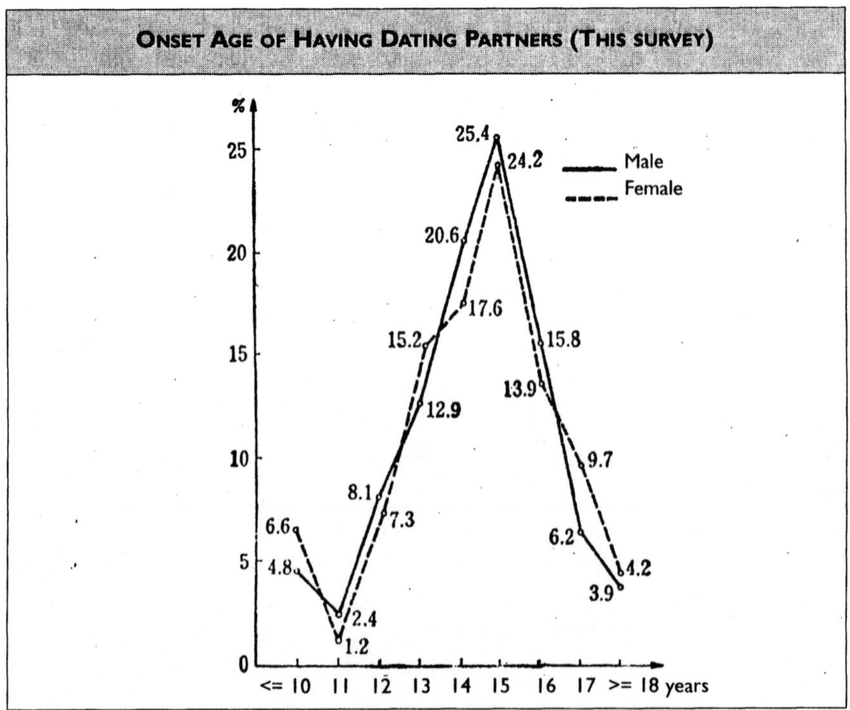

Figure 2–28

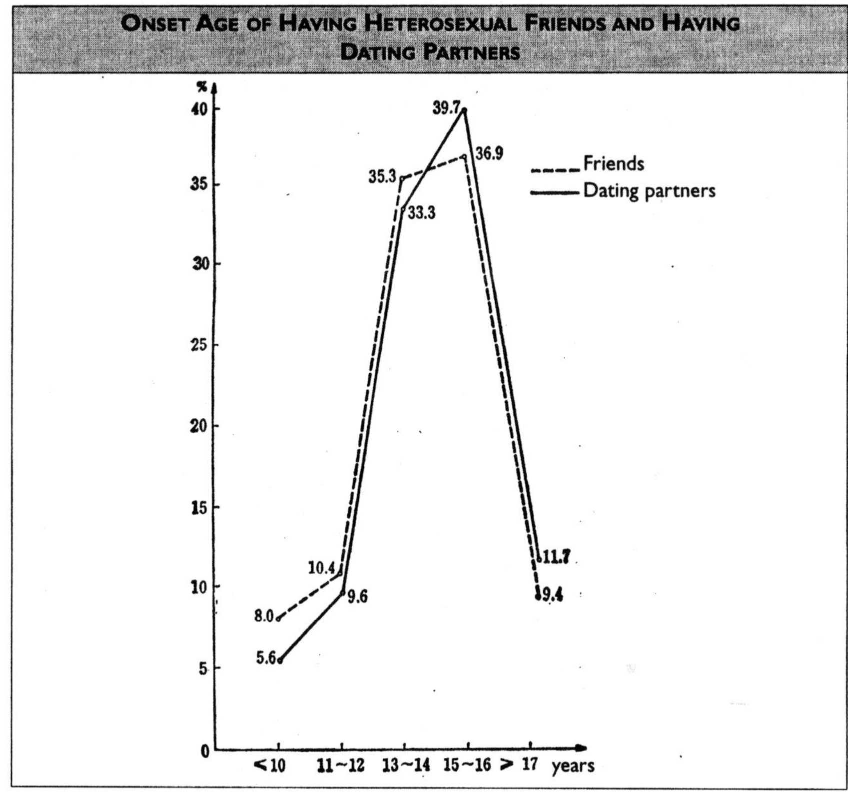

Figure 2–29

In the 1988 Adolescent Education Survey, the earliest age for the males to have dating partners of the other sex was ten, the latest nineteen, the mean being 15.16; for females, the youngest was twelve, the eldest nineteen, mean 15.3 (figure 2–30). But from figure 2–30, it can be seen that the peak onset age of having dating partners was higher in the females. In the 1987 Japan third Adolescent Sexuality Survey, in the younger age section, a greater proportion of the males had dating partners of the opposite sex, but in the elder age section, (after age fifteen), the females were more (figure 2–31). For example, at twelve years, 9.4 percent males and 5.5 percent females had dating partners of the other sex; at age sixteen, the proportions changed to 14 percent males and 18.4 percent females; at age nineteen, the males were 22.7 percent, the females were 29.0 percent. This trend might be associated with the fact that females usually marry earlier than males.

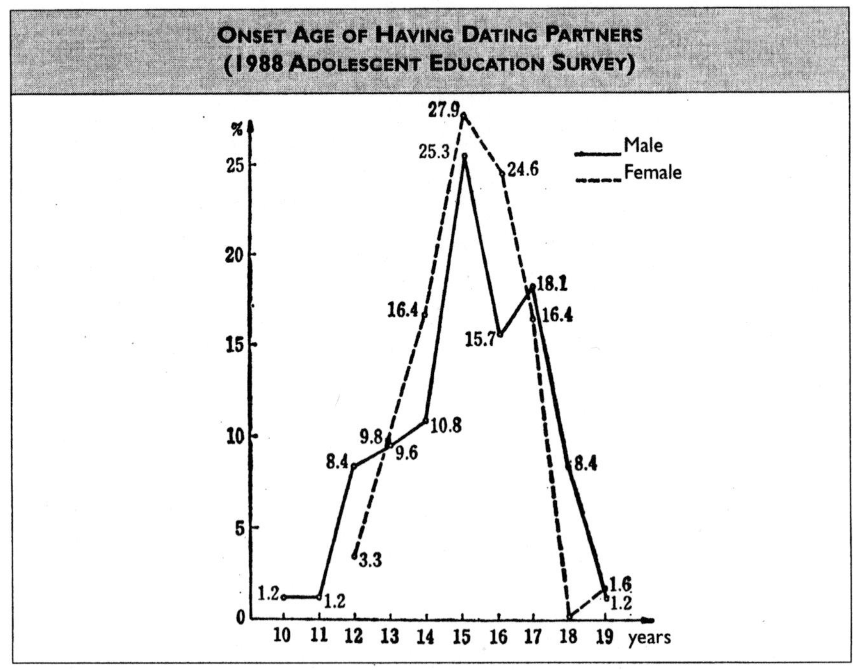

Figure 2–30

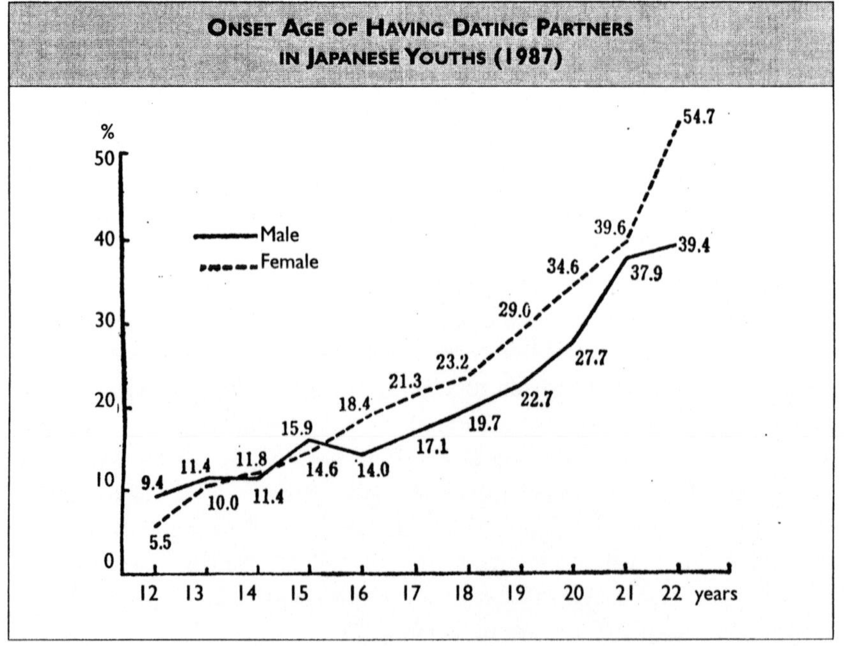

Figure 2–31

Generally, the age where individuals first have friends of the other sex is lower than the age for having dating partners (figure 2–29), but the two ages come rather close. For example, at ages eleven and twelve, 48.1 percent of those who began to have friends of other sex also had dating partners; at ages thirteen and fourteen, the proportion became 66.6 percent (table 2–45). This condition shows that for a proportion of the high school students, their sexual awareness led quite readily to target objects.

ONSET OF HETEROSEXUAL FRIENDSHIP AND ONSET OF DATING						
ONSET OF FRIENDSHIPS	TOTAL	ONSET OF DATING				
		<=10	11–12	13–14	15–16	>=17
<=10	18 (33.3%)	6 (27.8%)	5 (27.8%)	5 (11.1%)	2	0
11–12	27	0	13 (48.1%)	10 (37%)	4 (14.8%)	0
13–14	102	0	0	68 (66.6%)	30 29.4%)	4 (3.9%)
15–16	112	0	0	13 (11.6%)	89 (79.5%)	10 (8.9%)
>=17	24	0	0	0	4	20

Table 2–45

Our survey found an association between having boyfriends or girlfriends and parental relationships. Compared with those whose parents had a good relationship, a significantly higher proportion of those whose parents had poor or average relationships had dating partners (G=0.21, table 2–46).

Of course, adolescent love is a complicated issue. Family and parental relationships can be one factor. Other factors could be physiological and the various sociocultural conditions which were not specifically studied in this project.

At present, adolescent love is an issue of wide concern. Generally speaking, what is early love should not be defined simply by age. A young person's ability to be independent should be taken into consideration. If one is socially and financially self-sufficient, it cannot be said that it is too early to fall in love. But if another person of the same age is not self-sufficient, then their love might be considered by society as premature. Another criterion might be a legal one. According to Chinese law, the

PARENTAL RELATIONSHIP IN RELATION TO HAVING DATING PARTNERS			
RELATIONSHIP	TOTAL	NO LOVER	HAS LOVER
Excellent	2004 (40.5%)	1891 (94.4%)	113 (5.6%)
Good	2161 (43.7%)	2031 (94.0%)	130 (6.0%)
Fair	579 (11.7%)	507 (87.6%)	72 (12.4%)
Quarrelsome	91 (1.8%)	82 (90.1%)	9 (9.9%)
Fights	2 (0%)	2 (100.0%)	0 (0%)
Separated	15 (0.3%)	13 (86.7%)	2 (13.3%)
Divorced	66 (1.4%)	61 (92.4%)	5 (7.6%)
Unknown	31 (0.6%)	27 (87.1%)	4 (12.9%)
Total	4949 (100.0%)	4614 (93.2%)	335 (6.8%)

Table 2–46

lowest age for marriage is twenty-two for males and twenty for females. Falling in love after these legal ages can never be considered too early.

Table 2–47 showed that in this survey many high school students cannot say clearly what is meant by early love (33.6 percent males and 42.1 percent females). Some students thought that love during the high school period was already early love (28.5 percent males and 30.2 percent females). table 2–48 shows that the higher the grade, the more

HOW DO YOU DEFINE EARLY DATING?					
GENDER	TOTAL	BEFORE AGE 15	IN HIGH SCHOOL	BEFORE MARITAL AGE	UNCLEAR
Male	2813	377 (13.4%)	803 (28.5%)	687 24.4%)	946 (33.6%)
Female	2818	320	851 (11.4%)	461 (30.2%)(16.4%)	1186 (42.1%)

Table 2–47

students found it difficult to define early love. This could be because the junior high students had a simplistic view of things, while the higher grade students could understand the complexity of this issue.

GRADE LEVEL AND DEFINITION OF EARLY DATING							
DEFINITION	TOTAL	J1	J2	J3	S1	S2	S3
Dating before 15	695	52 (7.5%)	154 (15.7%	172 (13.8%)	147 (11.2%)	88 (8.4%)	82 (13.7%)
Dating in high school	647	101 (24.3%)	230 (23.5%)	396 (31.7%)	436 (33.2%)	321 (30.7%)	163 (27.2%)
Dating before marital age	1133	154 (37.0%)	272 (27.8%)	287 (23.0%)	236 (17.9%)	133 (12.7%)	51 (8.5%)
Unclear	2127	10 26.2%)	22 (32.9%	93 (31.5%)	496 (37.7%)	504 (48.2%)	303 (50.6%)
Total	5602 (100%)	416 (100%)	978 (100%)	1248 (100%)	1315 (100%)	1046 (100%)	599 (100%)

Table 2–48

GRADE AND ATTITUDE TOWARD EARLY DATING							
ATTITUDE	TOTAL	J1	J2	J3	S1	S2	S3
Normal	1369	32 (7.2%)	107 10.6%)	23 (18.9%)	35 (28.1%)	367 (37.1%)	270 (48.0%)
Not good	1449	193 (43.3%)	356 (35.3%)	397 (31.7%)	275 (26.6%)	131 (13.2%)	97 (17.3%)
Will improve scholastic performance	153	4 (0.9%)	16 1.6%)	35 (2.8%)	50 (3.9%)	33 (3.3%)	15 (2.7%)
Could affect studies badly	2238	20 (46.0%)	505 (50.1%)	539 (43.1%)	496 (39.0%)	373 (37.7%)	120 (21.4%)
No better chance in future	33	5 (1.1%)	4 (0.4%)	7 (0.6%)	8 (0.6%)	4 (0.4%)	5 (0.9%)
Others	286	7	20	37	86	81	55

p=0.001

Table 2–49

Of the 5562 students who responded, most students (40.5 percent) thought early love could have an adverse effect on scholastic performance; 24.7 percent thought it was normal, 26.2 percent thought it was no good, and 2.8 percent thought it could improve scholastic performance.

Generally, less females had a positive view about early love. More of them thought negatively (figure 2–32). These views could of course be the students' "intellectual views."

Table 2–49 shows that the higher grade students had more positive views regarding early love.

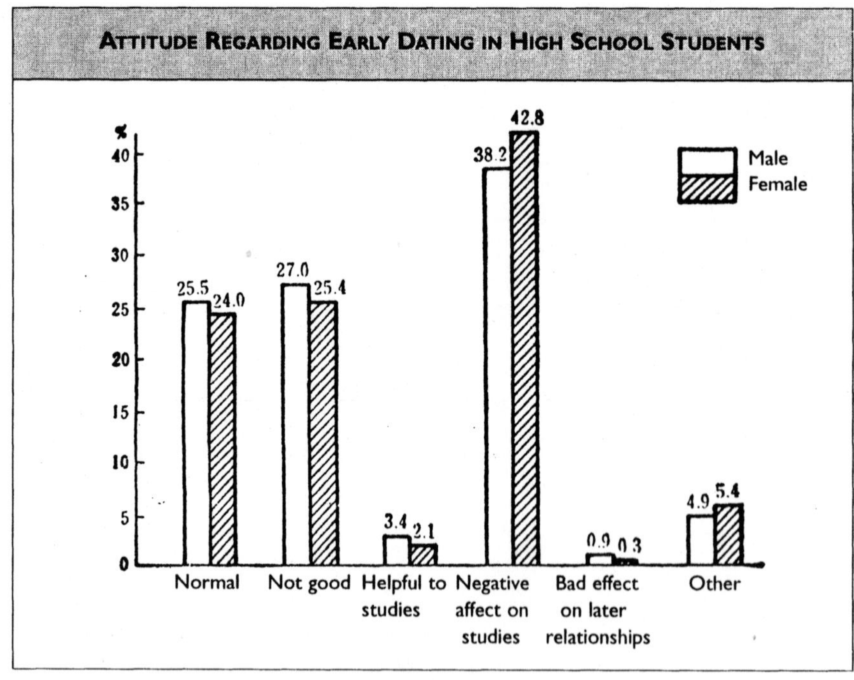

Figure 2–32

In the 1988 survey, of 1273 male students, 12.7 percent (162) reported having the experience of dating. The earliest age of dating was eleven, the latest nineteen, with a mean of 15.3. In 1283 females, 11.1 percent (142) reported having a dating experience, with the earliest age being eleven, the latest nineteen, with a mean of 15.2 (figure 2–33). The peak age of starting dating was earlier in the females. The proportion of students with dating experience is earlier than those with dating partners of the same age, which indicates that dating, as defined for youths falls somewhere between friendship and a love relationship—not the same as courtship with adults.

The Japan 1987 survey showed that the Japanese students started dating at about the same age, with a similar relationship pattern i.e., the desire for the opposite sex and early love (figure 2–34).

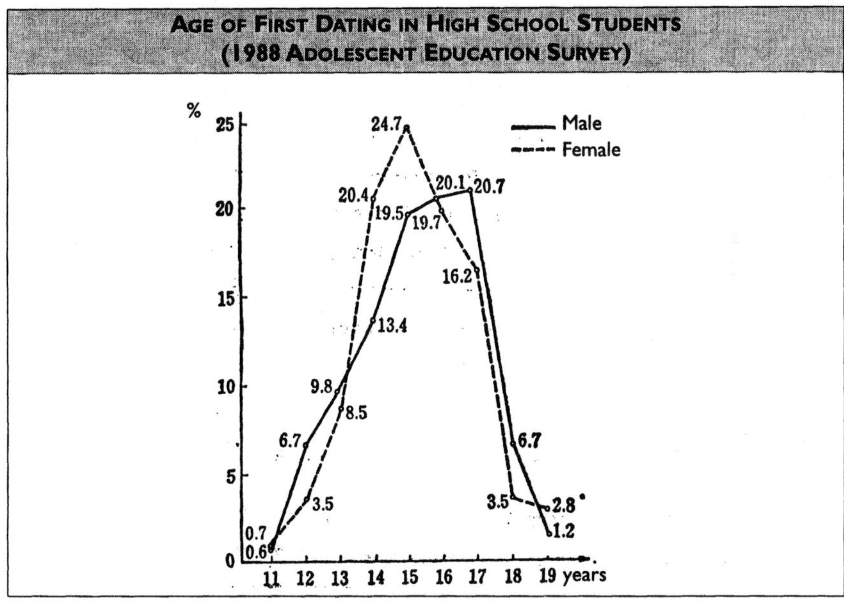

Figure 2–33

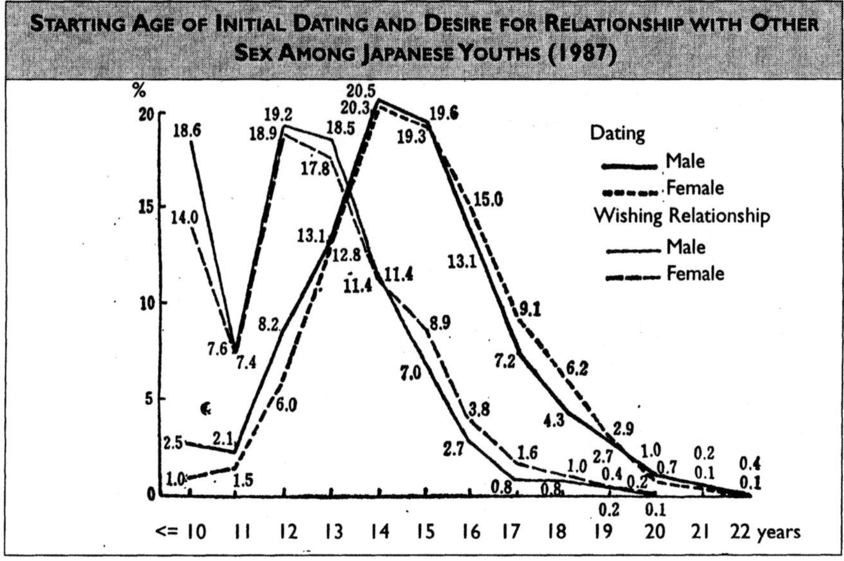

Figure 2–34

5. Early Sexual Activities

1. Masturbation

The Kinsey Reports showed masturbation in American youths is quite common: 92 percent (97 percent of the males, 55–68 percent of the females had the experience. Available data in China, however, suggest a lower rate. In our survey, 5636 subjects answered the question. 488 (8.7 percent) reported having masturbated; 3566 (63.3 percent) gave a negative answer; 1582 (28.1 percent) answered "don't know." Separating the sexes, 359 (12.5 percent) males and 129 (4.7 percent) females reported having had the experience (table 2–50).

MASTURBATION AMONG HIGH SCHOOL STUDENTS				
GENDER	TOTAL	YES	NO	DON'T KNOW
Male	2861	359 (12.5%)	1806 (63.1%)	696 (24.3%)
Female	2771	129 (4.7%)	1757 (63.4%)	885 (31.9%)

Table 2–50

MASTURBATION AMONG JAPANESE YOUTHS (1987)							
EDUCATION LEVEL	SEX	YES	NO	UNKNOWN	MISSING	TOTAL	
						%	No.
JUNIOR HIGH	M	30.0	38.6	23.5	7.9	100	1800
	F	6.9	63.3	25.7	4.1	100	1799
HIGH SCHOOL	M	81.2	7.0	5.6	6.2	100	1621
	F	10.7	73.9	8.1	7.3	100	1649
COLLEGE	M	92.2	2.1	2.5	3.2	100	896
	F	21.1	65.7	5.6	7.6	100	916
TOTAL (%)		36.6	43.6	13.6	6.2	100	8681

Table 2–51

In the 1988 Adolescent Education Survey, 18.43 percent males and 5.29 percent females reported masturbation. In the 1987 Japanese Third

National Sexuality Survey, 30.0 percent junior middle male and 6.9 percent junior high school female students had the experience, and 81.2 percent high school males and 10.7 percent high school females had the experience. In college students, 92.2 percent males and 21.1 percent females had the experience (table 2–51). The low rate of masturbation found among the Chinese could be due to sociocultural reasons causing some students to deny what had, in fact, occurred. Another reason could be that some students did not know what "masturbation" meant. It cannot be excluded, however, that the results reflect a true difference in the Chinese after all.

The rate of masturbation increased with the grade level of the students. The number of students giving a "don't know" answer decreased with the grade level. In those students who had masturbated, 53.3 percent reported that they were still masturbating recently within the previous month (table 2–53).This rate is also lower than that of the Japanese students. In the 1987 Japanese survey, the corresponding percentage in the junior high students was 64.0 percent for females and 78.9 percent

Grade Level and Masturbation

	TOTAL	J1	J2	J3	S1	S2	S3
Don't know	1568	165 (33.8%)	339 (2.8%)	373 (31.2%)	302 (23.4%)	223 (22.2%)	166 (28.3%)
No	3546	306 (62.7%)	631 (61.1%)	691 (57.8%)	886 (68.6%)	680 (67.6%)	352 (60.0%)
Yes	486	17 (3.5%)	63 (6.1%)	131 (11.0%)	103 (8.0%)	103 (10.2%)	69 (11.7%)
Total	5600 (100%)	488 (100%)	1033 (100%)	1195 (100%)	1291 (100.%)	1006 (100%)	587 (100%)

Table 2–52

Recent Masturbation in Students with Masturbation Experience

	NUMBER	%
Recent masturbation	260	53.3
Not recently	228	46.7
Total	488	100

Table 2–53

JAPANESE STUDENTS WHO HAD RECENTLY MASTURBATED						
EDUCATION LEVEL	GENDER	YES	NO	MISSING	TOTAL	
					%	No.
Jr. High	M	78.9	15.7	5.4	100	540
	F	64.0	28.0	8.0	100	125
High School	M	88.4	8.0	3.6	100	1317
	F	59.9	33.3	6.8	100	177
College	M	89.0	8.1	2.9	100	826
	F	56.5	35.8	7.8	100	193

Table 2–54

AGE OF FIRST MASTURBATION IN HIGH SCHOOL STUDENTS

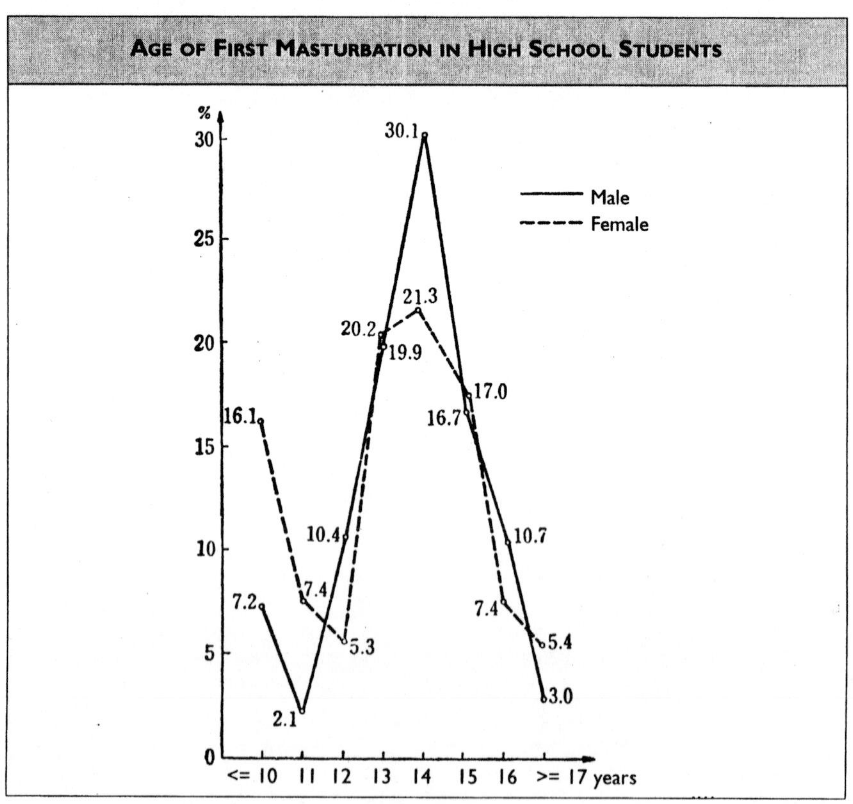

Figure 2–35

P=0.001

for males. In the high school students, the percentages were 59.9 percent and 88.4 percent respectively.

First Masturbation in High School Students						
AGE	MALE	%	FEMALE	%	TOTAL	%
<=10	24	7.2	15	16.0	139	9.1
11	7	2.1	7	7.4	14	3.3
12	35	10.4	5	5.3	40	9.3
13	67	19.9	19	20.2	86	20.0
14	101	30.1	20	21.3	121	28.1
15	56	16.7	16	17.0	72	16.7
16	36	10.0	7	77.0	443	10.0
>=17	10	3.0	5	5.0	415	3.4

Table 2–55

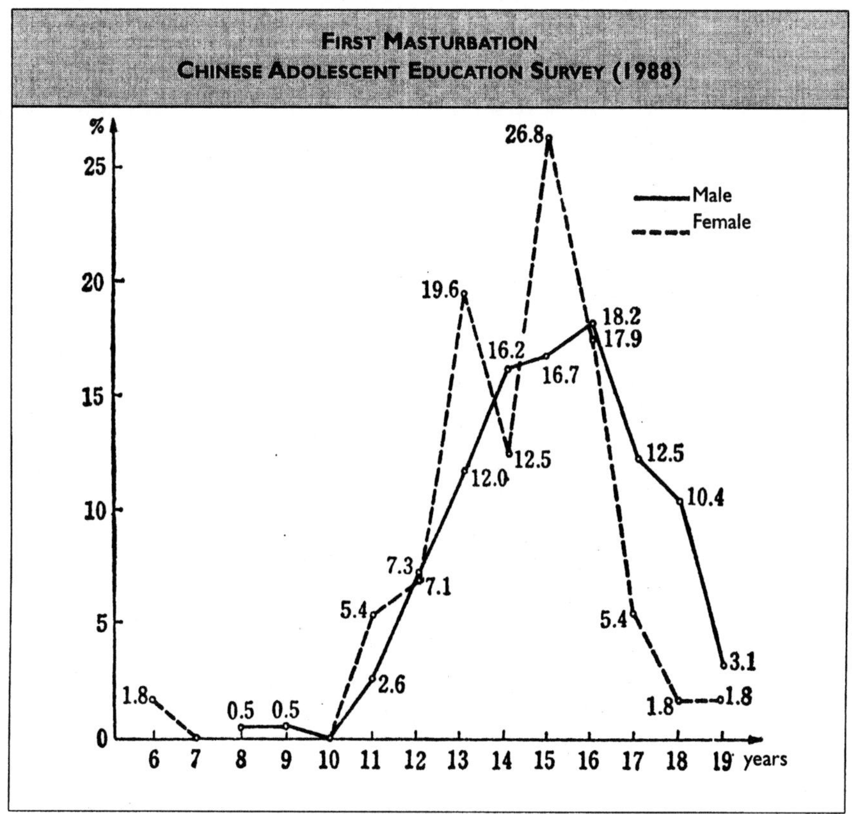

Figure 2–36

The mean age of the students starting to masturbate was 13.46, SD 2.71, with peak ages at thirteen through sixteen (table 2–55, figure 2–35).

In the 1988 Adolescent Education Survey, male and female students showed some difference in the age of first masturbation. The peak age for males was from ages fourteen to sixteen, with that of the females being at thirteen and fifteen (figure 2–36).

The onset age of masturbation in Japanese students is obviously higher than the Chinese (figure 2–37). The male Japanese students had their peak age of starting masturbation at thirteen to fourteen, about one year earlier than the Chinese. The peak age for the female Japanese students was also one year earlier than their Chinese peers. They also showed two peak ages, one at twelve and the other at fourteen (figure 2–38).

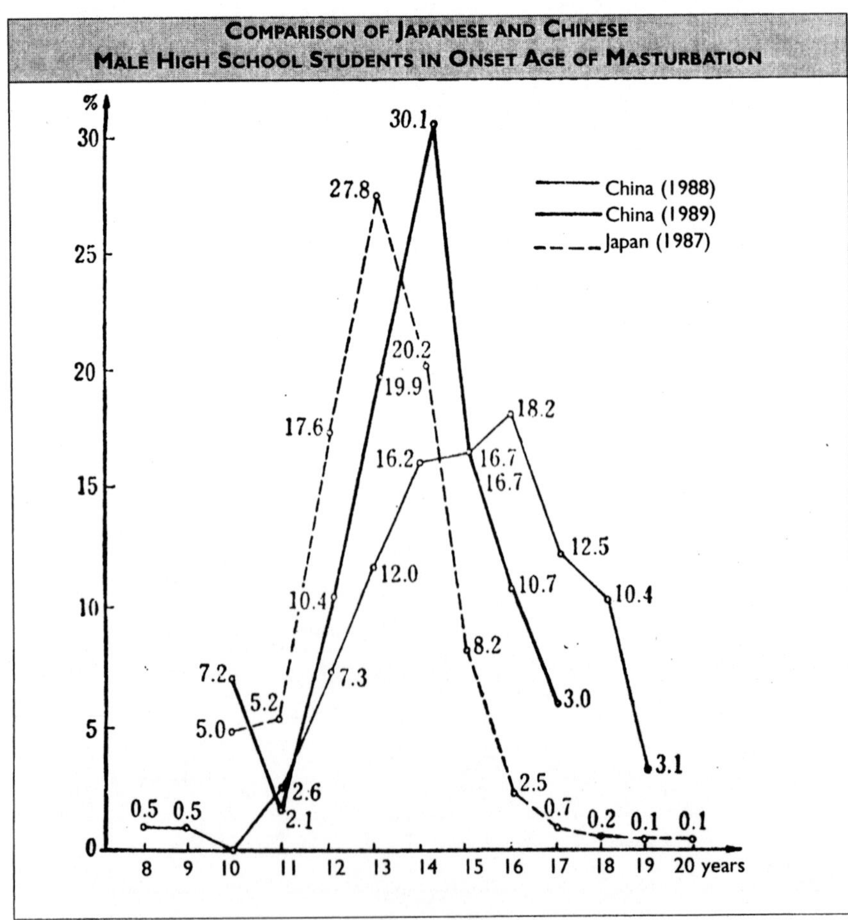

Figure 2–37

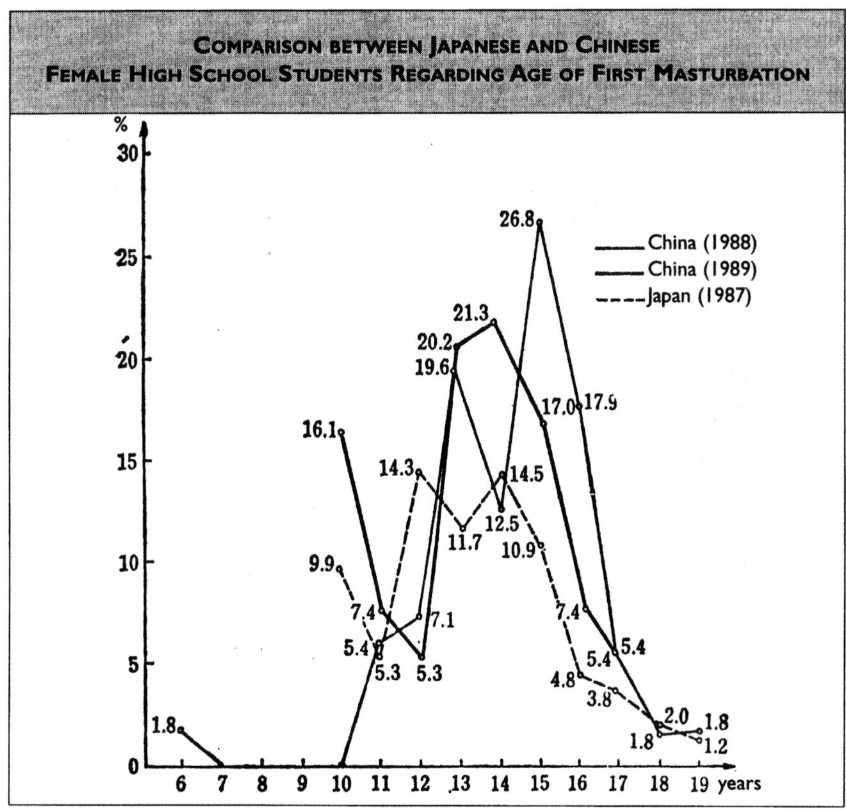

Figure 2–38

FREQUENCY OF MASTURBATION IN HIGH SCHOOL STUDENTS

TIMES PER WEEK	MALE		FEMALE		TOTAL	
	No.	%	No	%	No.	%
0	58	18.3	29	22.5	87	19.5
1	53	16.7	11	8.5	64	14.3
2	37	11.7	5	3.9	42	9.4
3	36	11.4	7	5.4	43	9.6
Missing	133	42.0	77	59.7	210	47.1
Total	317	100	129	100	446	100

Table 2–56

The frequency of masturbation of Japanese students was much higher than the Chinese (table 2–57).

FREQUENCY OF MASTURBATION IN JAPANESE STUDENTS									
# WEEKLY	<1	1	2	3	4	>5	MISSING	TOTAL	
								%	No.
Junior High									
Male	9.9	12.2	21.4	22.1	8.0	21.4	5.2	100	426
Female	25.0	15.0	23.8	20.0	3.8	10.0	2.5	100	80
High School									
Male	9.6	14.2	25.3	24.4	7.6	14.3	4.6	100	1164
Female	37.7	12.3	21.7	15.1	4.7	5.7	2.8	100	106

Table 2–57

The difference between the Japanese and Chinese students in their masturbatory practice may be due to a cultural difference. For a long time in China, there has been a lack of sexual education and dissemination of scientific sexual knowledge. The ignorance has led most people to think that masturbation is harmful. Ancient theories in China encourage people "to guard the ejaculatory gate, to have coitus but no ejaculation." The "Precious Recipe" of the Tang dynasty theories that "scanty semen could lead to sickness and exhaustion of semen could lead to death. One should be very cautious and thoughtful about ejaculation. If one ejaculates only once in several acts of coitus, vitality will be increased." The understanding is therefore that masturbation will "drain the bone marrow" and "damage seriously the vital essence." The classics of Western medicine from the eighteenth century to the early twentieth century hold similar views, postulating a causal relationship between masturbation and mental illness. The Swiss physician Tissot in 1767 wrote "A Treatise on the Various Diseases Caused by Masturbation" which had a great influence up to end of the nineteenth century, making it a widely held belief in Western medicine of that time that mental illness was caused by masturbation. In the 1950s, medical books on psychiatry in China still wrote about masturbation as an early symptom of neuroticism and many mental illnesses. In 1981, at the fifth World Congress of Sexology, two Indian doctors reported that in India, 90 percent of doctors there still maintained that masturbation was harmful and 98 percent of college students also thought so.

It is exactly because of this superstition concerning masturbation that our subjects in this survey were affected. Although in the West this fear of masturbation has begun to be eradicated in the last thirty to forty years, our results show that the effect in China has remained significant (table 2–58 and 2–59). Of those surveyed, 50.3 percent of the students (55.8 percent male and 44.3 percent female) thought it a misbehavior. Only 10.8 percent (14.0 percent male and 7.4 percent female) thought it was normal; 4.4 percent (4.5 percent male and 4.3 percent female) thought it a tolerable behavior. A large proportion of the 30.1 percent (21.2 percent male and 39.9 percent female) did not know what masturbation was. Such answers show that current students in China have only a rather vague idea about masturbation. Compared with Japanese studies, more Japanese students (27.7 percent male and 9.3 percent female) thought masturbation was normal, and fewer of them (3.4 percent male and 4.7 percent female) thought it was misbehavior.

Views on Masturbation						
Gender	Total	Normal	Misbehavior	Tolerance	Don't Know	Other
Male	2754	395 (14.0%)	1538 (55.8%)	123 (4.5%)	583 (21.2%)	125 (4.5%)
Female	2525	187 (7.4%)	1118 (44.3%)	107 (4.2%)	1007 (39.9%)	106 (4.2%)

Table 2–58

Grade Level and Views on Masturbation						
Grade	Total	Normal	Misbehavior	Tolerable	Don't know	Others
J1	404	17 (4.2%)	192 (47.5%)	6 (1.5%)	160 (39.6%)	29 (7.2%)
J2	933	63 (6.7%)	422 (45.2%)	25 (2.7%)	385 (41.3%)	38 (4.1%)
J3	1111	103 (9.3%)	562 (50.6%)	56 (5.0%)	341 (30.7%)	49 (4.4%)
S1	1236	161 (13.0%)	646 (52.3%)	52 (4.2%)	338 (27.3%)	39 (3.2%)
S2	993	135 (13.6%)	522 (52.6%)	65 (6.5%)	224 (22.6%)	47 (4.7%)
S3	569	92	297	26	128	26

Table 2–59

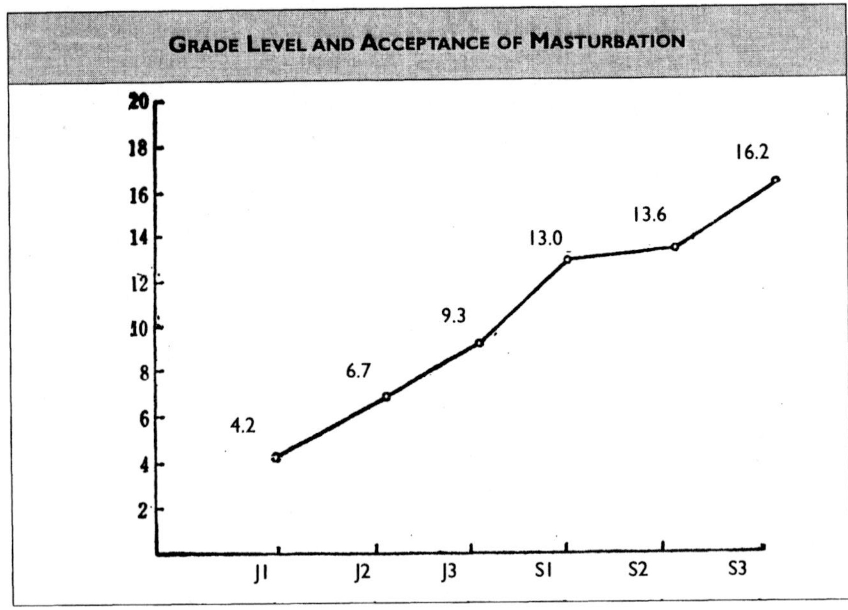

Figure 2–39

Compared with the 1988 survey in China however, our findings show more students accepting masturbation as normal (figure 2–40). This suggests an improvement in the sexual knowledge of our students, probably due to the widely applied efforts of adolescent sex education in various regions in China in recent years (figure 2–40).

Different grade levels of high school students show differences in their beliefs concerning masturbation. Table 2–59 shows that higher grades are associated with a greater acceptance of masturbation, excluding those who thought of it as misbehavior. It appears that higher general education does not necessarily lead to greater acceptance in this area.

In regard to the effect of sex education on this belief, table 2–60 shows that 12.4 percent of those who had sex education believed that masturbation was normal, while only 6.6 percent of those who had no sex education held such a belief. As to those who did not know what masturbation was, 25.8 percent had received sex education while 40.8 percent had received none. The number of those who believed masturbation to be misbehavior (medically, ethically, psychologically, or socially), was slightly greater among those who had received sex education. This complex result shows that sex education helps only partially in removing masturbation anxiety.

Sex Education and Beliefs Concerning Masturbation						
EDUC.	TOTAL	NORMAL	MISBEHAVIOR	TOLERABLE	UNSURE	OTHER
No	1479	97 (6.6%)	650 (43.9%)	51 (3.4%)	604 (40.8%)	77 (5.2%)
Yes	3639	453 (12.4%)	1920 (52.8%)	176 (4.8%)	939 (25.8%)	151 (4.1%)

Table 2–60

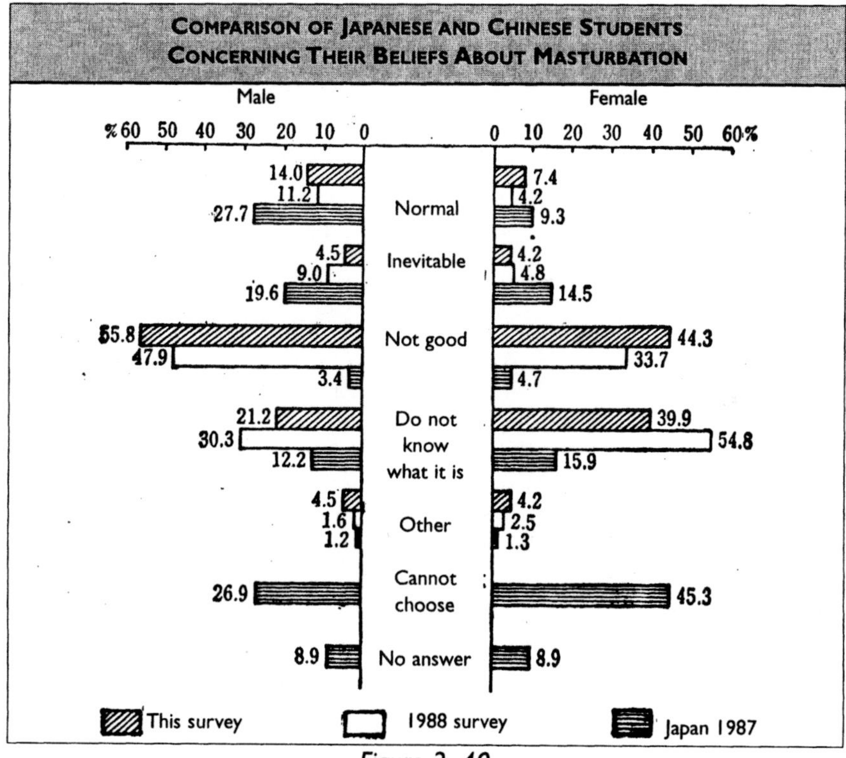

Figure 2–40

2. Other Early Sexual Activities

Although Chinese law does not allow high school students to have sexual intercourse, a small proportion of the students tried kissing, embracing, petting, and even sexual intercourse. Worldwide, sexual activities in the young seem to occur at an ever earlier age. In Sweden, in the 1920s, the median age of first sexual intercourse was twenty, but in the 1960s, it had decreased to 18.5 years. In the 1980s, it further decreased to 16.5. In the 1920s and 1960s, the age of first sexual intercourse in Swedish males was lower than the females by one year. In the 1980s, the situation reversed, with the females having their first intercourse one year earlier. Table 2–61 shows the age of first sexual intercourse in Swedish high school students in 1980. From the table, it can be seen that at age thirteen, 14 percent of the students had coital experience. At age fourteen, 22.5 percent and at fifteen, 37 percent had the experience. Many Western countries are following this trend.

Occurrence Rate of Sexual Experience in Swedish High School Students (1980)			
AGE	MALE	FEMALE	TOTAL
13	18%	10%	14%
14	22%	23%	22.5%
15	33%	41%	37%

Table 2–61

In China, due to legal restrictions and social mores, the rate of sexual experience in the young is much lower. Even if they have such experiences, it is difficult for them to admit it. Hence, the results obtained in our survey may not reflect the actual, greater extent of the behavior.

In our survey, 461 subjects admitted to physical contact with the opposite sex in the form of kissing, embracing, petting, and sexual intercourse. Table 2–62 shows the percentages of each type of physical intimacy. Including those who did not answer in the total percentage, of 602 students surveyed, 2.9 percent (174) had engaged in kissing, 1.2 percent (76) in embracing, 2.5 percent (154) in petting, and 0.9 percent (57) in sexual intercourse. The general results are much lower than in the West. Students of southern China had higher rates than those of northern regions (table 2–62).

In table 2–63, which shows the male and female percentages of sexual experience, the female percentage is 20.5—much higher than the male, which is only 8.4 percent. This reflects a problem worth noticing, because it suggests that female adolescents are being sexually exploited.

In the 1987 Japanese Youth Sexuality Survey, 5.6 percent junior high school male students and 6.6 percent of the female had a kissing experience. In the senior high school students, 23.1 percent of the males and

STUDENTS WHO HAD PHYSICAL CONTACT WITH THE OTHER SEX					
REGION	KISSING	EMBRACE	PETTING	COITUS	TOTAL
Shanghai	56 (32.9%)	26 (15.3%)	62 (36.5%)	26 (15.3%)	170 (100%)
Beijing	39 (41.5%)	24 (25.5%)	24 (25.5%)	7 (7.4%)	94 (100%)
Qindao	25 (44.6%)	5 (8.9%)	20 (35.7%)	6 (10.7%)	56 (100%)
Guangzhou Xiamen	9 (30.0%)	8 (26.7%)	7 (23.3%)	6 (20.0%)	30 (100%)
Chengdu	27 (50.9%)	5 (9.4%)	20 (37.7%)	1 (1.9%)	53 (100%)
Jinzhou	0 0 1 0 (0.00%)	1 (0.00%)	(1000%)	(0.00%)	(100%)
Ningxia	3 (25.0%)	1 (8.3%)	6 (50.0%)	2 (16.7%)	12 (100%)
Nanjing Wuxi	15 (33.3%)	7 (15.6%)	14 (31.1%)	9 (20.0%)	45 (100%)

Table 2–62

GENDER AND EXPERIENCE OF PHYSICAL CONTACT WITH THE OTHER SEX			
ACTIVITY	TOTAL	MALE	FEMALE
Kissing	174	114 (36.8%)	60 (39.7%)
Embracing	76	57 19 (18.4%)	(12.6%)
Petting	154	113 (36.4%)	41 (27.2%)
Intercourse	57	26 (8.4%)	31 (20.5%)
Total	461	310	151

P=0.001

Table 2–63

percent of the females had kissed; 2.2 percent of the junior high males and 1.8 percent of the females had had sexual intercourse; 11.5 percent of the high school males and 8.7 percent of the high school females had had sexual intercourse (tables 2–64, 2–65, 2–66).

Japanese Students Who Desire Kissing (1987)

GRADE	YES	NO	MISSING	TOTAL (% No.)	
Junior high male	31.8	62.9	5.3	100	1800
Junior high female	29.4	65.8	4.8	100	1799
High school male	64.6	31.8	3.6	100	1621
High school female	41.3	51.7	7.0	100	1649
College male	85.6	12.8	1.6	100	896
College female	54.8	40.2	5.0	100	916

Table 2–64

Japanese Youths Who Have Experienced Kissing (1987)

GRADE	YES	NO	MISSING	TOTAL (% No.)	
Junior high male	5.6	90.3	4.1	100	1800
Junior high female	6.6	89.9	3.5	100	1799
High school male	23.1	74.6	2.3	100	1621
High school female	25.5	70.9	3.6	100	1649
College male	59.4	38.7	1.9	100	896
College female	49.7	48.0	2.3	100	916
Total (%)	23.1	73.8	3.1	100	8681

Table 2–65

Japanese Youths Who Have Experienced Coitus (1987)

GRADE	YES	NO	MISSING	OTHER	TOTAL (% No.)	
Junior high male	2.2	87.3	6.6	3.9	100	1800
Junior high female	1.8	91.6	3.1	3.5	100	1799
High school male	11.5	81.4	4.6	2.5	100	1621
High school female	8.7	86.4	1.9	3.0	100	1649
College male	46.5	48.4	2.3	2.7	100	896
College female	26.1	68.8	1.0	4.1	100	916
Total (%)	12.2	80.9	3.6	3.3	100	8681

Table 2–66

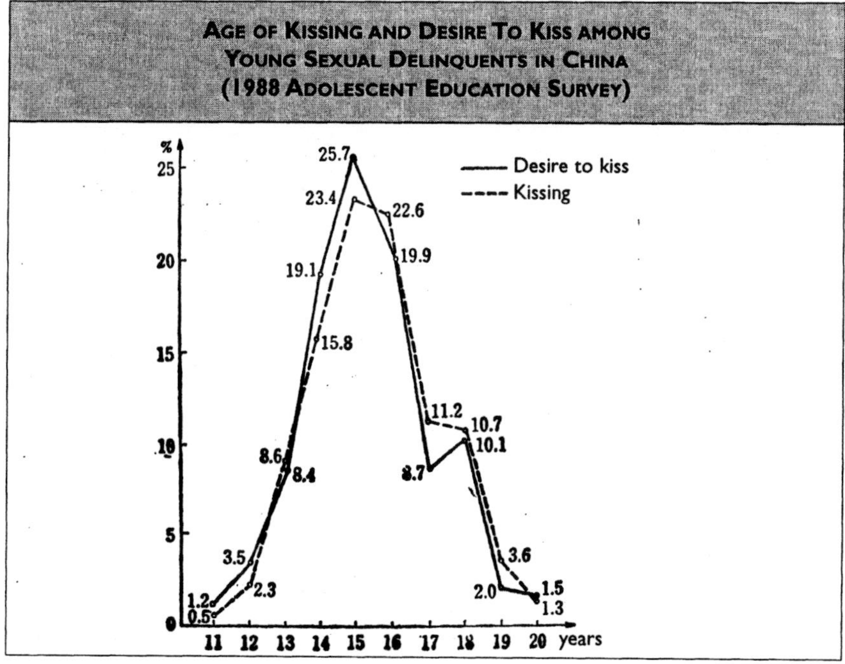

Figure 2–41

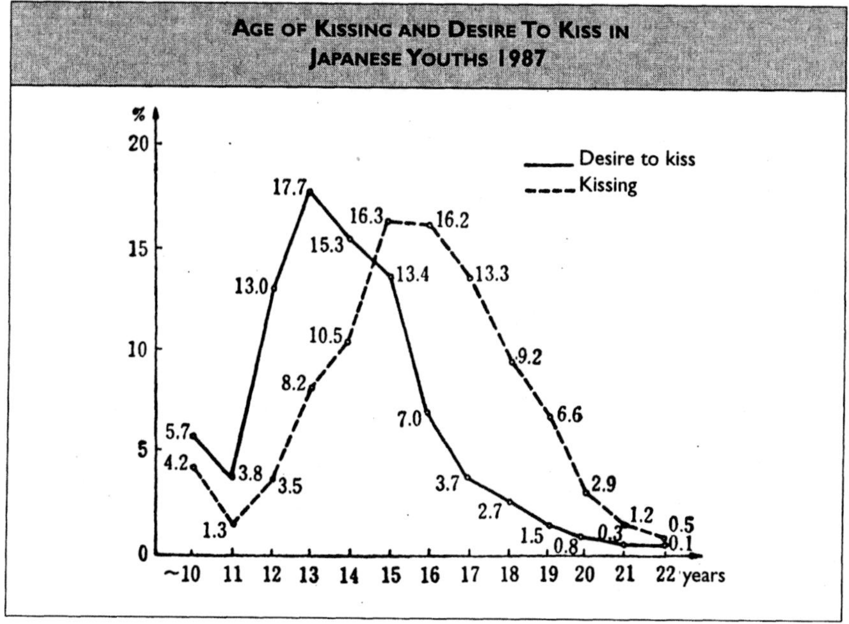

Figure 2–42

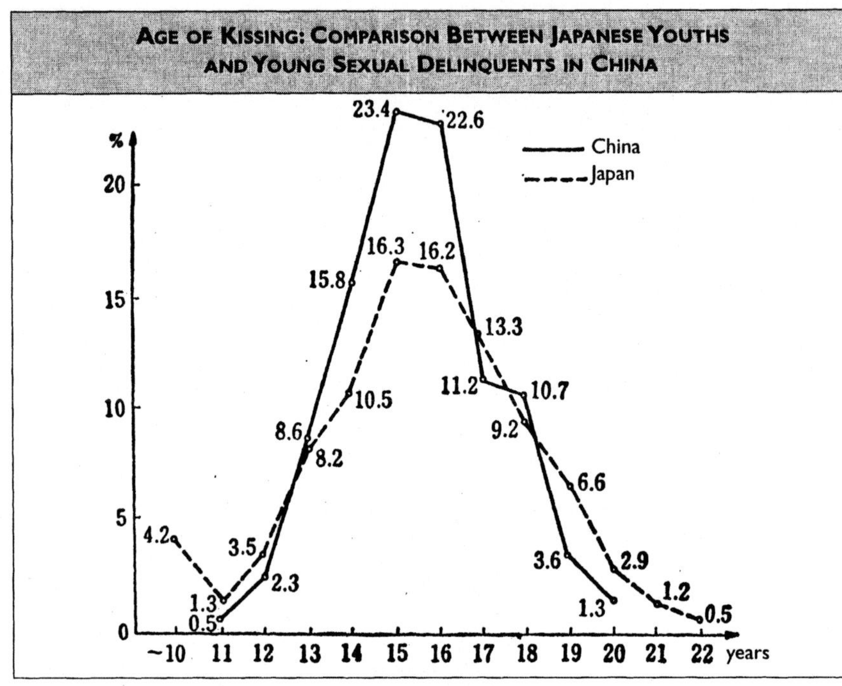

Age of Kissing: Comparison Between Japanese Youths and Young Sexual Delinquents in China

Figure 2–43

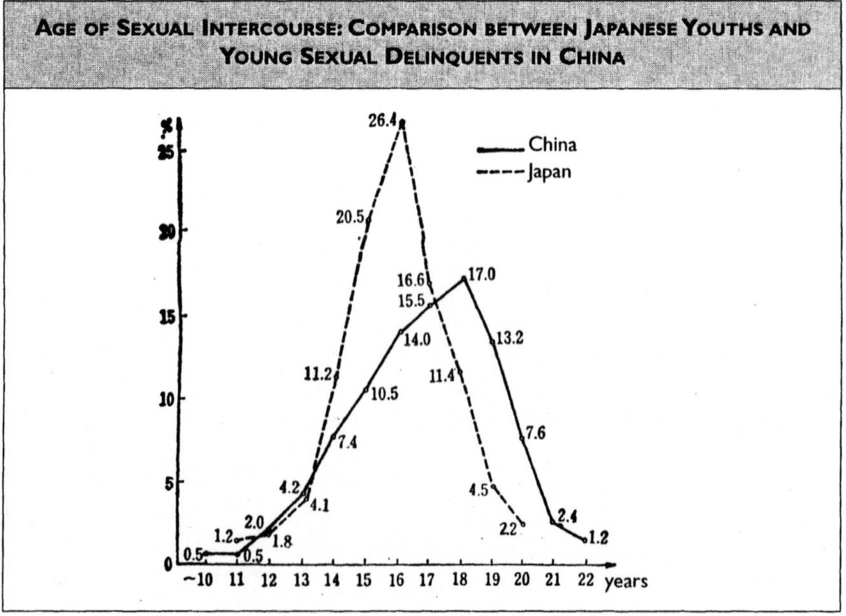

Age of Sexual Intercourse: Comparison between Japanese Youths and Young Sexual Delinquents in China

Figure 2–44

6. Sociocultural Conditions and Sexual Problems of Students

1. Source of Sexual Knowledge:

The 1988 Adolescent Education Survey showed that the public media were an important source of sexual information for 74.6 percent of the male students and 70.1 percent of the female. Among the various types of media, medical books ranked first, followed by magazines and newspapers. Important people as source of information were classmates and friends (for 11.3 percent males and 10.0 percent females). Parents and siblings were of little importance, as were schools, which appeared as a source of sexual knowledge for less than 4 percent of the students (table 2–67).

The 1987 Japanese survey showed a similar picture. The mass media ranked first in importance and among direct contacts, friends ranked the highest while the parents and teachers ranked low (table 2–68).

Source of Sexual Knowledge (1988 Adolescent Education Survey)

SOURCE	MALE		FEMALE	
	No.	%	No.	%
Parents	36	2.9	81	6.3
Teacher	68	5.6	50	3.9
Classmates / Friends	138	11.3	128	10.0
Siblings	6	0.5	16	1.3
Medical books	359	29.3	295	23.1
Magazines and newspapers	267	21.8	271	21.2
Television	85	6.9	118	9.2
Radio	42	3.4	83	6.5
Fiction	172	14.1	154	12.1
School	33	2.7	48	3.8
Others	18	1.5	34	2.7
Total	1224	100	1278	100

Table 2–67

Table 2–69 shows that in our survey, classroom education was the main source of the subjects' sexual knowledge (34.4 percent of the males and 39.6 percent of the females). This a result different from that of the 1988 survey, suggesting that high school adolescent education has begun

SOURCE OF SEXUAL KNOWLEDGE AT DIFFERENT GRADE LEVELS (1987 JAPANESE THIRD ADOLESCENT SEXUALITY SURVEY)							
SOURCE	JUNIOR HIGH		HIGH SCHOOL		COLLEGE		TOTAL
	M	F	M	F	M	F	
Parents	1.0	2.5	0.8	1.4	1.6	4.6	1.8
Friends	32.3	29.9	40.5	34.9	42.6	44.2	36.2
Teacher	1.7	1.7	1.1	0.8	1.0	0.5	1.2
School	3.6	5.1	1.5	3.7	0.8	3.7	3.3
Magazines Newspapers	12.3	14.8	17.1	20.9	19.6	16.5	16.6
TV/Radio	12.6	15.2	13.3	13.4	12.3	10.3	13.1
Books	9.7	6.3	13.8	8.1	14.0	7.8	9.6
Other	4.1	2.1	2.3	1.8	2.8	2.6	2.6
Missing	22.7	22.4	9.7	14.9	5.4	9.8	15.6
Total	1800	1799	1621	1649	896	916	8681

Table 2–68

SOURCE OF SEXUAL KNOWLEDGE AMONG STUDENTS			
SOURCE	TOTAL	MALE	FEMALE
Magazine / Newspaper	1308 (23.2%)	679 (23.7%)	629 (22.7%)
Television Movies (Local)	69 (1.2%)	36 (1.3%)	33 (1.2%)
Television Movies (Foreign)	256 (4.5%)	118 (4.1%)	138 (5.0%)
Local Fiction	106 (1.9%)	62 (2.2%)	44 (1.6%)
Foreign fiction	118 (2.1%)	60 (2.1%)	58 (2.1%)
Medical books	1254 (22.3%)	675 (23.6%)	579 (20.9%)
Social chats	124 (2.2%)	72 (2.5%)	52 (1.9%)
Erotic publications	196 (3.5%)	113 (4.0%)	83 (3.0%)
Classroom	2082 (37.0%)	985 (34.4%)	1097 (39.6%)
Other	120 (2.1%)	60 (2.1%)	60 (2.2%)
Total	5633	2860	2773

Table 2–69

to take its effect. Magazines and newspapers ranked second in our survey (237 percent of the males and 22.7 percent of the females), followed by medical books (23.6 percent of the males and 20.9 percent of the females).

The sources for the males and females were quite similar in importance, but more males received sexual knowledge from local fiction, social chats, and erotic publications.

GRADE LEVEL AND SOURCE OF SEXUAL KNOWLEDGE							
SOURCE	TOTAL	J1	J2	J3	S1	S2	S3
Magazine	1301	63 (15.0%)	180 (18.2%)	243 (19.9%)	306 (23.3%)	309 (29.6%)	200 (32.8)
Local TV & Movies	69	8 (1.9%)	10 (1.0%)	19 (1.6%)	16 (1.2%)	9 (0.9%)	7 (1.1%)
Foreign TV & Movies	256	27 (6.4%)	69 (7.0%)	46 (3.8%)	54 (4.1%)	34 (3.3%)	26 (4.3%)
Local fiction	104	5 (1.2%)	6 (0.6%)	14 (1.1%)	29 (2.2%)	20 (1.9%)	30 (4.9%)
Foreign fiction	116	1 (0.2%)	16 (1.6%)	11 (0.9%)	27 (2.1%)	29 (2.8%)	32 (5.3%)
Medical books	1247	64 (15.2%)	169 (17.1%)	245 (20.1%)	327 (24.8%)	289 (27.7%)	153 (25.1%)
Social chats	122	5 (1.2%)	28 (2.8%)	30 (2.5%)	25 (1.9%)	22 (2.1%)	12 (2.0%)
Erotic publ.	196	7 (1.7%)	36 (3.6%)	35 (2.9%)	57 (4.3%)	43 (4.1%)	18 (3.0%)
Classroom	2073	225 (53.4%)	446 (45.0%)	539 (44.2%)	464 (35.3%)	280 (26.8%)	119 (19.5%)
Other	118	16 (3.8%)	31 (3.1%)	38 (3.1%)	11 (0.8%)	10 (1.0%)	12 (2.0%)
Total	5602	421	991	1220	1316	1045	609

Table 2–70

2. The Influence of Other People

Of the high school students, 40.3 percent thought that the sexual knowledge provided by teachers was the most rich and useful; 24.4 percent thought that classmates and friends were the most informative;

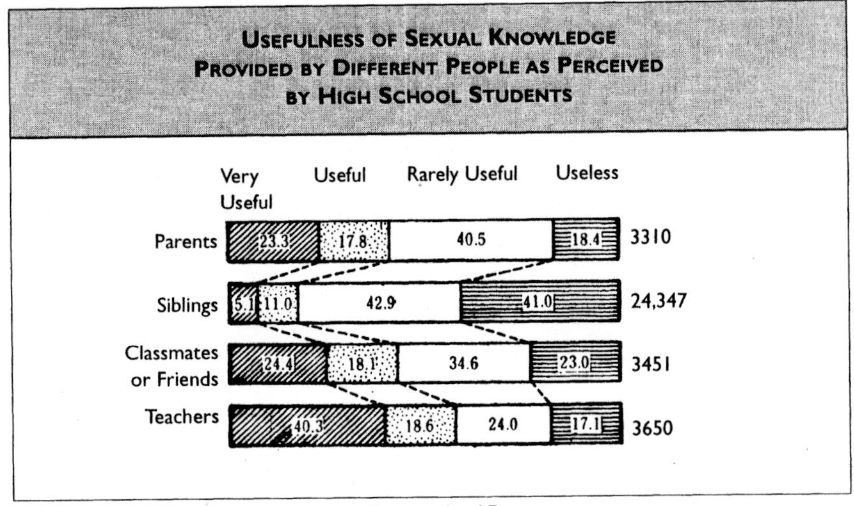

Figure 2–45

23.3 percent thought that parents were. On the other hand, 41 percent of the students thought that the sexual knowledge given by siblings was useless, followed by that of classmates and friends (23.0 percent), parents (18.4 percent), and teachers (17.1 percent) (figure 2–45).

Our survey also found that most students (86.7 percent of the males and 50.9 percent of the females) talked about sexual matters more with people other than their parents, siblings, or friends. For people of the same gender, only 7.5 percent of the male students talked

People of the Same Gender to Whom One Talked Most about Sexual Matters

GENDER	TOTAL	FATHER	MOTHER	TEACHER	SIBLINGS	OTHERS
Male	1219	91 (7.5%)	—	11 (0.9%)	60 (4.9%)	1007 (86.7%)
Female	1010	—	340 (33.7%)	14 (1.4%)	142 (14%)	514 (50.9%)

Table 2–71

most with the fathers, but 33.7 percent of the female students talked most with their mothers. This suggests that mothers are usually more concerned with the sexual lives of their daughters than the fathers are with those of their sons.

PEOPLE OF THE OPPOSITE SEX TO WHOM ONE TALKED MOST ABOUT SEXUAL MATTERS						
GENDER	TOTAL	FATHER	MOTHER	TEACHER	SIBLING	OTHER
Male	389	—	37 (9.5%)	18 (4.6%)	9 (2.3%)	325 (83.5%)
Female	194	39 (20.1%)	—	11 (5.7%)	8 (4.1%)	136 (70.1%)

Table 2–72

For people of the opposite sex, "others" still were considered the most important source of sexual information (83.5 percent of the males and 70.1 percent of the females, table 2–72). "Others" usually means classmates and friends. This proves the importance of peer influence in the formation of the adolescent personality.[5] Hence, in sex education for young people, the effective mobilization of peer influence in group activities and discussions appears to be essential.

3. Responses to Erotic Depictions

The responses included "hot" feelings, palpitation and shortness of breath (33.4 percent of the males and 31.7 percent of the females), tension (19.0 percent of the males and 15.8 percent of the females), disgust (13.5 percent of the males and 24.4 percent of the females), pleasure (7.6 percent of the males and 1.9 percent of the females) and no response (26.4 percent of the males and 26.3 percent of the females) (table 2–73). Generally, males showed a more intense response than the females, but more females found the depictions disgusting. This could be because

RESPONSES TO EROTIC READING MATERIAL						
GENDER	TOTAL	HOT	PLEASURE	TENSION	DISGUST	NOTHING
Male	2751	920 (33.4%)	210 (7.6%)	523 (19.0%)	371 (13.5%)	727 (26.4%)
Female	2791	885 (31.7%)	53 (1.9%)	440 (15.8%)	680 (24.4%)	733 (26.3%)

Table 2–73

Grade Levels and Responses to Erotic Depictions							
	TOTAL	J1	J2	J3	S1	S2	S3
Hot	1797	95 (20.1%)	262 (25.9%)	374 (30.8%)	463 (37.1%)	388 (39.5%)	215 (36.9%)
Pleasure	261	120 (4.2%)	14 (1.4%)	44 (3.6%)	74 (5.9%)	54 (5.5%)	55 (9.5%)
Tension	959	64 (13.6%)	133 (13.2%)	229 (18.8%)	227 (18.2%)	205 (20.9%)	101 (17.4%)
Disgust	1042	159 (33.7%)	296 (29.3%)	258 (21.2%)	165 (13.2%)	103 (10.5%)	61 (10.5%)
Nothing	1453	134 (28.4%)	306 (30.3%)	311 (25.6%)	320 (25.6%)	232 (23.6%)	150 (25.8%)
Total	5512	472	1011	1216	1249	982	582

Table 2–74

females are usually more sexually inhibited in Chinese society. From table 2–74, it can be seen that we found more intense or pleasurable responses and less disgust with the increasing age of the respondents.

The students did not have any agreed-upon views concerning sexual depictions in print or television or movies. Of the students surveyed, 30.9 percent felt these would be all right for them, 32.6 percent felt that they should be permitted to watch them under the guidance of adults, while 36.5 percent (more females than males) felt they should not see them (table 2–75).

Students at higher grade levels felt the depictions should be permitted. As for watching under guidance, the students in the middle grades favored it the most (correlation coefficient gamma=0.16, table 2–76).

Views on High School Students Reading Erotic Materials				
GENDER	TOTAL	PERMITTED	UNDER ADULT GUIDANCE	PROHIBITED
Male	2867 (36.6%)	1049 (29.2%)	837 (34.2%)	981
Female	2896 (25.2%)	729 (36.0%)	1044 (38.8%)	1123

Table 2–75

GRADE LEVELS AND VIEWS ON HIGH SCHOOL STUDENTS READING EROTIC MATERIALS							
VIEWS	TOTAL	J1	J2	J3	S1	S2	S3
Permitted	1771	54 (10.7%)	174 (16.2%)	303 (23.9%)	454 (35.4%)	455 (45.1%)	331 (56.0%)
Under adult guidance	1872	136 (26.9%)	323 (30.1%)	448 (35.3%)	469 (36.6%)	336 (33.3%)	160 (27.1%)
Prohibited	2087	315 (62.4%)	577 (53.7%)	518 (40.8%)	360 (28.0%)	217 (21.5%)	100 (16.9%)

p=0.001

Table 2–76

This shows a probable relationship with the subject's general knowledge in sex. Hence, in sex education with the junior high students, some training in the critical evaluation of erotic publications might help in promoting their understanding of pornographic materials.

7: Sex Education

In China, sex education is a difficult task. After the establishment of new China, some people made a relentless effort to promote this kind of work, especially after the nation's decision to open up and modernize. Under the government's lead, from the beginning of the 1980s, Shanghai began its trial of sex education with a sample of high school students, and then later spread the effort to other regions in China. This is an important landmark of education in the 1980s in China.

Now, although many educators are aware of the importance of sex education in secondary schools with many schools actually trying it, the actual outcomes are quite different from one place to another. Our survey shows that in many aspects, the outcomes are still far from satisfactory and there is still much hard work ahead.

1. The Advance of Sex Education

Of the 6092 high school students surveyed, 4088 (67.1 percent) reported having received sex education; 1737 (28.5 percent) had not received it; and 267 (4.4 percent) did not answer. With respect to gender, 70.1 percent of the male and 70.2 percent of the female students had received

STUDENTS HAVING RECEIVED SEX EDUCATION			
GENDER	TOTAL	NO	YES
Male	2925	874 (29.9%)	2051 (70.1%)
Female	2897	863 (29.8%)	2034 (70.2%)

Table 2–77

SEX EDUCATION AND GRADE LEVEL					
GRADE	TOTAL	NO		YES	
		No.	%	No.	%
J1	489	219	44.8	270	55.2
J2	1051	412	39.2	639	60.8
J3	1291	430	33.3	861	66.7
S1	1327	317	23.9	1010	76.1
S2	1034	196	18.9	838	81.1
S3	594	146	24.6	448	75.4

Table 2–78

sex education; 29.9 percent of the males and 29.8 percent of the females had not (table 2–77).

This result shows that the percentage of students who had received sex education was higher than that of 1988 survey. In the 1988 survey, 1169 (55.9 percent) of the males and 1149 (57.4 percent) of the females had received sex education. The rise was probably a consequence of a "Notice to develop adolescent education in secondary schools" issued by the National Education and Family Planning Professional Committee in 1988.

The percentage of students having received sex education increased with grade levels, from 55.2 percent in J1 to 81.1 percent in S2 and 75.4 percent in S3.

Different regions showed large differences in the rate of students having received sex education. The Shanghai students had the highest rate (78.9 percent), followed by Chengdu (73.0 percent). Nanjing, Wuxi, Guangzhou, Xiamen, Beijing, Qindao all had around 60 percent to 70 percent; Jinzhou was lower at 49.2 percent; Yinchuan lowest at 33.6 percent. This shows the uneven distribution of sex education in China, with a lower rate in distant rural areas.

STUDENTS HAVING RECEIVED SEX EDUCATION				
REGION	TOTAL	NO	YES	UNKNOWN
Shanghai	2237	369 (16.5%)	1764 (78.9%)	104 (4.6%)
Beijing	1166	369 (31.6%)	772 (66.2%)	25 (2.1%)
Qindao	578	182 (31.5%)	358 (61.9%)	38 (6.6%)
Guangzhou & Xiamen	453	175 (38.6%)	253 (55.8%)	25 (5.5%)
Chengdu	496	112 (22.6%)	362 (73.0%)	22 (4.4%)
Jinzhou	195 87	96 (44.6%)	12 (49.2%)	(6.2%)
Yinchuan	298	182 (61.1%)	100 (33.6%)	16 (5.4%)
Nanjing Wuxi	668	261 (39.1%)	383 (57.3%)	24 (3.6%)

Table 2–79

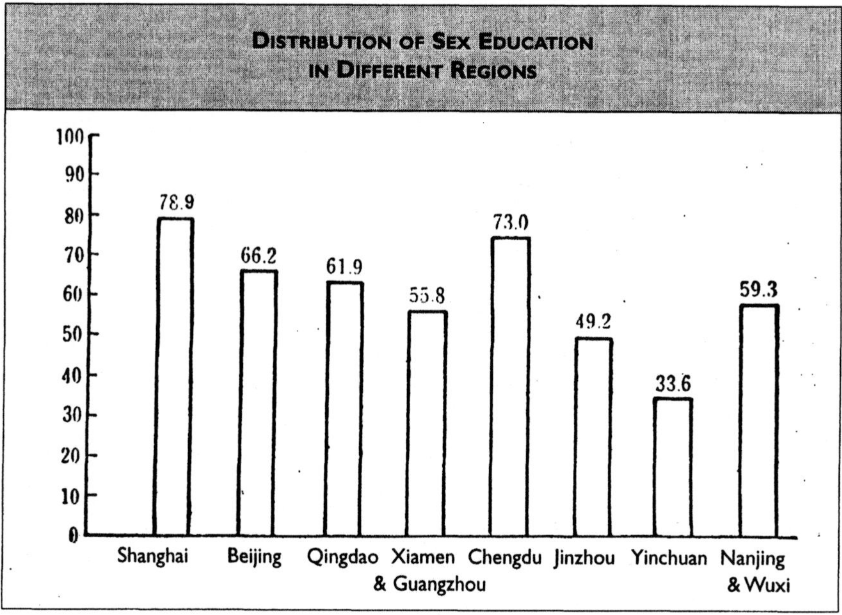

Figure 2–46

SEX EDUCATION CONTENTS RECEIVED BY JAPANESE HIGH SCHOOL AND COLLEGE STUDENTS (1987)							
	JUNIOR HIGH		HIGH SCHOOL		COLLEGE		MEAN %
	M	F	M	F	M	F	
Genital anatomy	58.3	48.4	81.8	77.7	80.4	74.8	69.1
Menarche	61.1	95.1	77.0	96.7	73.8	98.7	85.3
Nocturnal emission	69.2	48.0	81.9	68.2	78.3	60.8	66.6
Secondary sex characteristics	75.3	75.9	81.8	82.1	82.3	84.4	80.0
Pregnancy & delivery	41.8	42.5	74.6	81.2	71.3	84.9	65.2
Sexual determination	16.5	8.9	50.8	45.1	52.9	58.3	36.5
Psychobehavioral differences	19.7	20.4	23.5	26.4	20.2	23.9	22.6
Sex role	13.3	10.9	24.8	19.0	24.9	24.7	18.8
Courtship	14.6	13.1	25.5	23.0	22.4	24.6	20.2
Adolescent psychology	31.3	35.5	47.6	40.4	44.5	41.0	39.8
Love	8.1	7.0	19.6	14.4	21.2	20.0	14.2
Marriage	4.7	2.2	24.7	26.9	15.7	22.3	16.1
Family planning	4.5	6.0	38.7	45.8	38.8	52.1	29.8
STD & sex crimes	5.6	5.0	39.9	37.8	51.1	45.7	28.6
Sex culture and tradition	4.7	3.0	19.6	9.7	18.0	14.7	10.8
Sexual ethics	6.2	4.3	14.9	8.3	20.9	17.8	10.8
Others	2.1	0.2	1.8	0.5	1.3	0.8	1.0
Total	1042	1476	1278	1523	683	865	6867

Table 2–80

From the percentage of students who had received each type of sex education content, the most often taught content was adolescent psychology, followed by sexual physiology, pregnancy and childbirth. Contents relating to sexual ethics were low (figure 2–47). Hence the emphasis, like that for the Japanese students, has been mostly on sexual psychology (table 2–80).

Although sexual psychology was the top content taught, high school students were most eager to know about adolescent psychology (males 26.2 percent, females 39.7 percent), followed by "courtship" (males 25.5

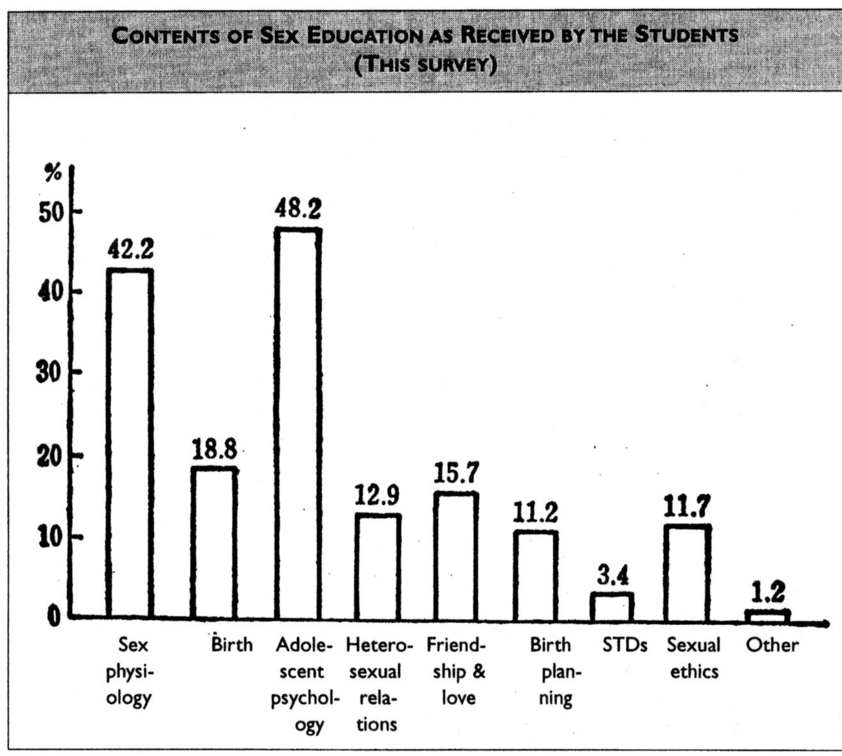

Figure 2–47

percent, females 25.8 percent), and sexual physiological development was low at 13.9 percent. For sexual intercourse, more males desired to know about it than females (table 2–81). Students' desire to know about contraception was also low (0.9 percent).

The interest in the topic adolescent psychology decreased at higher grade levels, while the wish for other types of sexual knowledge increased, except for that relating to sexual variations (as shown in table 2–82).

Our survey also showed that those who had received sex education had a greater wish to learn about courtship. This reflects the inadequacy of their sex education on this topic and the probable sequence of needs of the youngsters on sexual knowledge (table 2–83). Hence, in planning a sex education curriculum, the selection of topics and their sequences should take the age and background of the students into consideration.

SEXUAL CONTENTS WHICH THE STUDENTS WISHED TO LEARN						
	TOTAL	SEX PHYSIOLOGY	ADOLESCENT PSYCHOLOGY	COURT-SHIP	LOVE	SEXUAL DESIRE
Male	2620	405 (15.5%)	687 (26.2%)	669 (25.5%)	239 (9.1%)	235 (9.0%)
Female	2660	330 (12.4%)	1057 (39.7%)	686 (25.8%)	256 (9.6%)	107 (4.0%)
	COITUS	CONTRA-CEPTION	STDs	SEXUAL VARIATIONS		OTHER
Male	132 (5.0%)	28 (1.1%)	77 (2.9%)	100 (3.8%)		48 (1.8%)
Female	66 (2.5%)	19 (0.7%)	31 (1.2%)	79 (3.0%)		29 (1.1%)

p=0.001

Table 2–81

GRADE LEVEL AND THE TYPE OF SEX EDUCATION TOPIC DESIRED							
	TOTAL	J1	J2	J3	S1	S2	S3
Physiology	728	74 (18.9%)	168 (18.8%)	211 (17.6%)	145 (11.8%)	91 (9.3%)	39 (6.9%)
Adol. psych.	1736	189 (48.3%)	402 (44.9%)	497 (41.4%)	326 (26.5%)	217 (22.2%)	105 (18.0%)
Courtship	1348	28 (7.2%)	128 (14.3%)	224 (18.7%)	390 (31.7%)	374 (38.3%)	204 (36.2%)
Love	495	29 44 (7.4%)	91 (4.9%)	130 (7.6%)	105 (10.6%)	96 (10.8%)	(17.1%)
Sexual desire	342	18 (4.6%)	84 (5.4%)	65 (5.4%)	87 (7.1%)	73 (7.5%)	51 (9.1%)
Coitus	197	9 31 (2.3%)	36 (3.5%)	46 (3.0%)	50 (3.7%)	25 (5.1%)	(4.4%)
Contra-ception	47	4 3 (1.0%)	10 (0.3%)	13 (0.8%)	7 (1.1%)	10 (0.7%)	(1.8%)
STDs	107	12 (3.1%)	17 (1.9%)	16 (1.3%)	30 (2.4%)	21 (2.2%)	11 (2.0%)
Sexual variations	179	13 (3.3%)	30 (3.3%)	33 (2.8%)	54 (4.4%)	31 (3.2%)	18 (3.2%)
Others	77	15 (3.8%)	25 (2.8%)	17 (1.4%)	9 (0.7%)	7 (0.7%)	4 (0.7%)
Total	5256	391	86	1200	1230	976	563

Table 2–82

SEX EDUCATION EXPERIENCE AND ADDITIONAL TOPICS DESIRED					
SEX EDUC. RCVD	TOTAL	PHYSI-OLOGY	ADOLESCENT PSYCHOLOGY	COURTSHIP	LOVE
No	1399	268 (19.2%)	516 (36.9%)	244 (17.4%	128 (9.1%)
Yes	3706	444 (12.0%)	1160 (31.3%)	1078 (29.1%)	356 (9.6%)
SEXUAL DESIRE	COITUS	CONTRA-CEPTION	STDs	SEXUAL VARIATIONS	OTHER
No 33 (2.4%)	74 (5.3%)	52 (3.7%)	8 (0.6%)	35 (2.5%)	41 (2.9%)

Table 2–83

2. *Effects of Sex Education on Students*

Sex education increases the factual sexual knowledge of students. In tables 2–84 and 2–85, more of those who had received sex education could give correct answers to the question "How is a baby born?" Yet, the results are not totally satisfactory: 23.2 percent of those who had received sex education could not give a correct answer to this question, and 7.4 percent of them did not know that the fetus grows in the uterus. The good news is that much more of those educated knew the correct cause of the transmission of STDs.

Sex education also improves the students' understanding of their own sexual development (table 2–87): 83.6 percent of those who had received sexual education, compared with 66.1 percent for those who had not, thought that ejaculation was a healthy, normal bodily function. Yet, a fairly similar proportion of those sexually uneducated (1.1 percent) and educated (0.8 percent) felt ejaculation was obscene and ugly as well as those who felt it to be harmful to health (2.3 percent of uneducated and 2.4 percent of the educated). This shows that sex education as it was given had some flaws in need of correction.

WHERE DOES THE FETUS GROW?						
SEXUALLY EDUCATED	TOTAL	VAS DEFERENS	SPERM	URETHRA	UTERUS	PENIS
No	944	2 (0.2%)	3 (0.3%)	3 (0.3%)	831 (88.0%)	2 (0.2%)
Yes	3159	9 (0.3%)	4 (0.1%)	10 (0.3%)	2924 (92.6%)	0 (0.0%)
	ABDOMEN	FALLOPIAN TUBE	OVARY	VAGINA		
No	45 (4.8%)	6 (0.6%)	43 (4.6%)	9 (1.0%)		
Yes	49 13	138 12				

Table 2–84

FROM WHERE IS A BABY BORN?						
SEXUALLY EDUCATED	TOTAL	OVARY	BELLY BUTTON	VAS DEFERENS	PENIS	SPERM
No	593	24 (4.0%)	82 (13.8%)	5 (0.8%)	15 (2.5%)	1 (0.2%)
Yes	2397	109 (4.5%)	235 11 (9.8%)	51 4 (0.5%)	(2.1%)	(0.2%)
SEXUALLY EDUCATED	VAGINA	TESTES	FALLOPIAN TUBE	URETHRA		
No	427 (72.0%)	0 (0.0%)	17 (2.9%)	22 (3.7%)		
Yes	1840 (76.8%)	3 (0.1%)	68 (2.8%)	76 (3.2%)		

Table 2–85

As for initial ejaculation and menstruation, table 2–88 and 2–89 show that the sexually educated were more psychologically prepared, but psychological preparation did not make them less apprehensive. There was also a sizable portion who were educated and yet felt psychologically unprepared and frightened. It shows the need to strengthen the psychological concern or counseling element in our sex education efforts.

CAUSE FOR STD					
SEXUALLY EDUCATED	TOTAL	PROMIS-CUITY	AUTO-IMMUNE PROBLEM	HETERO-SEXUAL INTER-COURSE	UNKNOWN
No	1638	664 (40.5%)	27 (1.6%)	79 (4.8%)	868 (53.0%)
Yes	3937	2689 (68.3%)	72 (1.8%)	125 (3.2%)	1051 (26.7%)

Table 2–86

SEXUAL EDUCATION AND VIEWS ON EJACULATION AMONG MALE STUDENTS						
EDUCATED	TOTAL	HARMFUL	NORMAL	UNCLEAR	OBSCENE	OTHER
No	732	17 (2.3%)	484 (66.1%)	192 (26.2%)	8 (1.1%)	31 (4.2%)
Yes	1949	46 (2.4%)	1629 (83.6%)	232 (11.9%)	15 27 (0.8%)	(1.4%)

Table 2–87

SEX EDUCATION AND FEELING IN MALE STUDENTS CONCERNING FIRST EJACULATION						
EDUCATED	TOTAL	PREPARED &		UNPREPARED &		OTHER
		Afraid	Not afraid	Afraid	Not afraid	
No	436	36 (8.3%)	94 (21.6%)	81 (18.6%)	205 (47.0%)	20 (4.6%)
Yes	1525	152 (10.0%)	460 (30.2%)	200 (13.1%)	679 (44.5%)	34 (2.2%)

Table 2–88

Of the sexually educated 12.4 percent thought that masturbation was normal, compared with 6.6 percent of the uneducated; 25.8 percent of the educated replied "don't know," while 40.8 percent of the uneducated gave that reply (table 2–60).

SEX EDUCATION AND FEELING IN FEMALE STUDENTS CONCERNING FIRST MENSTRUATION						
EDUCATED	TOTAL	PREPARED &		UNPREPARED &		OTHER
		Afraid	Not afraid	Afraid	Not afraid	
No	780	121 (15.5%)	143 (18.3%)	258 (33.1%)	206 (26.4%)	52 (6.7%)
Yes	326	524 (16.9%)	476 (27.1%)	530 (24.6%)	76 (27.4%)	(4.0%)

Table 2–89

To further explore the sexual attitude of the students, a hypothetical question was asked: "What would you think if a fellow female classmate became pregnant?" Of the 5329 students who answered this question, 2295 (43.1 percent) said they would persuade her to get an abortion (36.1 percent of the males and 49.9 percent of the females). 13.0 percent of the students (17.9 percent of the males and 8.2 percent of the females) said it was normal and acceptable. Only 6.8 percent (8.8 percent of the males and 4.7 percent of the females) thought the girl should be punished by the school and only 11.0 percent (11.2 percent of the males and 10.7 percent of the females) took a scornful and rejecting attitude (table 2–90 and 2–91). This attitude is much more accepting than it was a few years ago, when pregnant students received absolutely no respect in school, were afraid of seeing their classmates, and even committed suicide. This change in attitude illustrates the importance of sex education and the teaching of sexual ethics. Students should know how to avoid sexual intercourse at an early age in order to prevent unwanted pregnancies.

WHAT WOULD YOUR ATTITUDE BE CONCERNING A PREGNANT STUDENT IN YOUR CLASS?						
GENDER	TOTAL	SCORN & REJECT	PERSUADE ABORTION	SCHOOL PUNISHMENT	NORMAL	OTHER
Male	2631	295 (11.2%)	950 (36.1%)	233 (8.8%)	472 (17.9%)	681 (25.9%)
Female	2698	290 (10.7%)	1345 (49.9%)	128 (4.7%)	222 (8.2%)	713 (26.4%)

Table 2–90

Grade Level and Attitude Regarding Pregnant Classmate							
	TOTAL	J1	J2	J3	S1	S2	S3
Scorn & rejection	579	56 (9.7%)	124 (21.4%)	161 (27.8%)	112 (19.3%)	87 (15.0%)	39 (6.7%)
Suggest abortion	2283	229 (10.00%)	423 (18.5%)	483 (21.2%)	508 (22.3%)	397 (17.4%)	243 (10.6%)
School punishment	359	45 (12.5%)	99 (27.6%)	80 (22.3%)	73 (20.3%)	38 (10.6%)	24 (6.7%)
Normal	691	49	75	116	190	146	115
Other	1389	84 (6.0%)	218 (15.7%)	342 (24.6%)	335 (24.1%)	279 (20.1%)	131 (9.4%)

Table 2–91

Conclusion

1. The high school students of China are progressively reaching puberty at an earlier age. They develop an earlier sexual awareness, including the desire for physical contact with the other sex. Some students put their desire into action, in the form of early love, masturbation, petting and other forms of sexual activity. Their sexual awareness is closely related to their social environment, especially peer influence. All of these indicate that their sexual attitudes and intentions are at a crossroads.

2. In order to deal with this problem, sex education has to be strengthened. It should include the teaching of sexual ethics. Further essential topics are relationships, emotions and biological, medical, psychological, and sociological facts. As the the study by Yao (1988) demonstrated, sex education for high school students produces positive results (table 2–92).

3. The results of sex education are still tentative. Our survey found that the sex education materials in China were not well balanced. They contain too much sexual physiology and hygiene, with little attention paid to sexual ethics. Sex education is also not well developed in the more outlying districts and rural regions.

4. Our survey did not include the views of the teachers. In the 1988 survey by Yao, the teachers found some inadequacies in sex education (table 2–93).

POSITIVE EFFECT OF SEX EDUCATION	
EFFECT	% INCREASE
Psychosexual development of the self	10.59
Social relationships between female and male students	12.14
Proper management of heterosexual friendship or love	11.37
Self-control and regulation of sexual desire	18.35
Concentration on studies	30.75
Improved relation with teachers and classmates	11.37
Improved relationship with parents	1.29
Less sexual misconduct	0.78
More interest in sex	2.07
More heterosexual relationships	0.26
Others	1.03
(Total number of students surveyed 387)	

Table 2–92

INADEQUACIES OF SEX EDUCATION IN CHINA AS ASSESSED BY TEACHERS						
Teacher + Resouce -	Teachers + Resource -	Resource + Teacher -	Teachers ignorant	Course absent	No leader support	Other
20.8%	33.10%	1.89%	8.27%	33.57%	0.95%	1.42%

Table 2–93

They also had some misunderstanding and disagreement on the planning and purpose of sex education (table 2–94).

Adolescent sex education still has no fixed place in the Chinese school curriculum. Although many schools have set up a course, teaching hours are not fixed or secure enough to be effective (table 2–95).

There is still no national policy, curriculum, or teaching aid for sex education in China: 33.1 percent of the schools had difficulties with offering sex education because of a lack of support and materials. The "Government Committee" instruction was that "the National Teachers Committee should set up a standard teaching guide and curriculum of adolescent sex education as soon as possible," and "a good set of teaching materials should be made available soon."

There is a need for more sex education courses for teachers: 64.06 percent of teachers had difficulty in teaching sex because of their own

TEACHERS VIEWS ON THE PLANNING AND PURPOSE OF SEX EDUCATION	
VIEWS	%
Should be compulsory for students and adults	28.39
Necessary for students' adolescent development	38.63
Necessary for students' personal growth	7.89
Can reduce students' sexual misconduct	0.59
Can reduce students' early love affairs	2.36
Can improve discipline in class	9.19
Too indecent to be taught in class	1.06
Children automatically know when they grow up	3.65
Seductive to children when they know too much	4.95
Others	3.30

Table 2–94

PLACE OF SEX EDUCATION IN HIGH SCHOOL CURRICULUM	
	% SCHOOLS
An important part of the curriculum	19.87
Part of health education	22.89
Part of moral education	25.80
Duty of the teacher	10.82
Part of physical education	0.75
Part of extracurricular activity	2.26
No place	15.97
Others	1.76

Table 2–95

inadequate sexual knowledge. Currently, except for a few experienced pioneers in adolescent sex education, most teachers still lack the basic knowledge and training for the job. In some pilot schools, the job is mostly taken on by teachers of biology, physiology, political education, or the school clinic doctor. There are no teachers specifically trained for sex education. China currently has about 15,000 high schools with about 45,000,000 students overall. In order to provide sex education for all of them, the need for a qualified teaching staff must be met.

There is still not enough support from the students' families and society in general. In our survey, the students' parents were not helpful in giving sex education (table 2–96).

PARENTS' RESPONSES TO SEX QUESTIONS ASKED BY THEIR CHILDREN						
	GOOD ANSWER	AVOID REPLY	SCOLD	OCC. ANSWER	%	No.
Father M	17.5	26.86	16.66	34.31	9.61	1020
F	7.93	30.38	6.28	29.21	24.70	907
Mother M	11.32	28.95	13.89	32.06	12.75	1051
F	30.37	9.57	3.69	53.03	3.34	1139

Table 2–96

Notes

1. Yap Gong-Shao, *Children and Adolescent Health* (Beijing: People's Health Publications).
2. Ibid.
3. Yao Pei-Kuan, *Report of the Adolescent Education Survey* (Shanghai: Xuelin Publication, 1990).
4. JASE (Japanese Association for Sex Education), *Sexuality of the Youths, Third Survey* (Tokyo: JAS, August, 1988). See also "Sexuality of the Youths–a Comparison of Japanese and Chinese Reports," (Tokyo: JASE, May, 1990). Sample distribution of students in the Japan 1987 third National Adolescent Sexual Behavior Survey:

	JUNIOR	SENIOR	MATRICULATION	COLLEGE	TOTAL
Male (%)	1800 50.0	1621 49.6		896 67.7	4317 49.7
Female (%)	1799 50.0	1649 50.4	489 1000	427 32.3	4364 50.3
Total	3599	3270	489	1323	8681

5. Zhu Pei-Li, *Adolescent Psychology* (Shanghai: People's Publications, 1986).

3

College Students

1. Overview

College students represent a highly educated part of the younger population. After graduation, they begin all sorts of careers and become the backbone of many enterprises. Therefore, although they constitute only a small proportion of the entire population,[1] they can be presumed to influence the direction of social development, and their thinking and behavior may very well be a character model for many other people.

Because college students are generally more open in their thinking, and because they usually live together on campus, it was relatively easy for us to survey them. (This is also true for most researchers in Western countries, where many sex surveys have been conducted using student populations.) However, a conservative attitude still prevails among university administrators. Thus, we were unwelcome in many of the colleges we approached. Finally, we succeeded in obtaining the cooperation of twenty-four colleges and universities in nine regions of China: Shanghai, Beijing, Xiamen, Chengdu, Nanjing, Qindao, Hangzhou, Xinjiang Shihezi, and Yinchuan. The colleges were: Tungji University, Shanghai University, Fudan University, Shanghai College of Chinese Medicine, Zhejiang University, Nanjing University, Xiamen University, Shiheji Medical College, Beijing Teachers' Training College, Beijing Architectural College, Huasi Medical College, Qinda University, Qindao Marine University, Qindao Teachers' Training College, Nanjing Teachers' Training College, Nanjing Arts College, Hehai University, Dongnan University, Jiangsu Police Training College, Jiangsu Mechanical College, Jiangsu Youth Management Professionals College, Military Engineering College, and Ningxia Education College. Eventually, a total of 3360 answered questionnaires were usable.

DISTRIBUTION OF COLLEGE STUDENTS SURVEYED		
CITY	NO. OF SUBJECTS	PERCENTAGE
Shanghai	994	29.6
Beijing	283	8.4
Xiamen	724	21.5
Chengdu	421	12.5
Nanjing	148	4.4
Qindao	224	6.7
Hangzhou	322	9.6
Shihezi	198	5.9
Tinchuen	46	1.4
Total	3360	100.0

Table 3–1

Our choice of cities aimed for equal proportions of colleges in big cities, middle-sized cities, southern and northern cities, as well as coastal and inland cities. Since the small cities and villages in China do not have colleges, no surveys of college students could be done there. There was no deliberate preselection as to age groups, majors, or minors, but a special effort was made to include all classes and fields of study.

Our sampling in this part of the survey was therefore stratified and well focused. The principals of the colleges and the headmasters of the classes chosen were asked for their consent. The headmaster then assembled the class for a questionnaire session. The aim and meaning of the survey were explained to the students, confidentiality and anonymity were guaranteed, and instruction and counseling were given to individual students upon request. Unfortunately, we were unable to do any pilot study, and there were some restrictions in the explicitness and clarity of the questionnaires used. Nevertheless, since the college students were more knowledgeable

GENDER DISTRIBUTION OF THE COLLEGE STUDENTS		
GENDER	NO. OF SUBJECTS	PERCENTAGE
Male	1907	56.8
Female	1291	38.4
Unknown	162	4.8
Total	3360	100.0

Table 3–2

AGE DISTRIBUTION OF THE COLLEGE STUDENTS		
AGE	NO. OF SUBJECTS	PERCENTAGE
<=19	1010	30.1
20	843	25.1
21	625	18.6
22	311	9.3
>=23	210	6.3
	361	10.7
Total	3360	100.0

Table 3–3

and open-minded than their elders, and since they trusted the teachers who administered the questionnaires, we believe that the answers obtained have a satisfactory degree of validity.

The gender distribution of subjects is shown in table 3–2.

The age distribution of the students is shown in table 3–3 and 3–4. More than half of the students were under age twenty. Most of them were in years two to four (sophomore to senior year). Their mean age was 20.28, SD 3.13, median and mode at age twenty.

Class Distribution of the College Students

YEAR	NO. OF SUBJECTS	PERCENTAGE
1	501	14.9
2	1086	32.3
3	842	25.1
4	724	21.5
5	86	2.6
Postgrad	53	1.6
Unknown	68	2.0

Table 3–4

Profession Distribution of the College Students

	NO. OF STUDENTS	PERCENTAGE
Arts	1141	34.0
Science	548	16.3
Engineering	745	22.2
Agriculture	41	1.2
Medicine	740	21.1
Unknown	175	5.2
Total	3360	100.0

Table 3–5

Parental Occupation of College Students

OCCUPATION	FATHER		MOTHER	
	NO.	%	NO.	%
Factory worker	451	13.4	563	16.8
Farmer	518	15.4	725	21.6
Commercial	61	1.8	127	3.8
Service	46	1.4	159	4.7
Official	675	20.1	613	18.2
High official	690	20.5	181	5.4
Professional	564	16.8	486	14.5
Other	185	5.5	338	10.1
Unknown	170	5.1	168	5.0
Total	3360	100.0	3360	100.0

Table 3–6

EDUCATIONAL LEVEL OF THE PARENTS				
LEVEL OF EDUCATION	FATHER		MOTHER	
	NO.	%	NO.	%
Illiterate	122	3.6	384	11.4
Primary	510	15.2	650	19.3
Junior high	550	16.4	615	18.3
Senior high	600	17.9	617	18.4
College	543	16.2	452	13.5
Postgrad	858	25.5	501	14.9
Unknown	177	5.3	141	4.2
Total	3660	100.0	3360	100.0

Table 3–7

The students majored in the following subjects: arts, science, engineering, agriculture, and medicine—with most coming from the arts, engineering, and medicine. We expected certain differences in the sexual attitudes and behaviors among different study areas, because they might represent different social subcultures.

For the students' family background, the parents' occupations and educational levels were surveyed. In table 3–6, it can be seen that the majority of the fathers (57.4 percent) were officials in government units or private enterprises or professionals. The others were factory workers or farmers.

Furthermore, 41.7 percent of the fathers and 28.4 percent of the mothers had a college or even graduate school education. Thus, the subjects' parental education was higher than ordinary.

We found that the college students' sexuality differed very little by region, but more by age, gender, and profession.

2. Physiological Sexual Development

The college students had been secondary school students only a few years before. Their sexual physiological development can therefore serve a good comparison with our findings on the current high school students.

1. Age of Pubertal Changes

The male subjects' mean age of first ejaculation was 14.14, SD 1.63; the female subjects' mean onset of breast development was 14.56 with SD at 2.78. The mean age of onset of pubic hair and axillary hair growth was 14.47, SD 2.02.

AGE OF SEXUAL DEVELOPMENT													
SIGNS	TOTAL	<=10		11–12			13–14			15–16		>=17	
		NO.	%	NO.	%	NO.	%	NO.	%	NO.	%	NO.	%
First ejac./mens.	3360	11	0.3	428	12.7	1336	39.8	891	26.5	199	5.9	495	14.7
Breast/ beard	3360	112	3.3	422	12.6	747	22.2	821	24.4	502	14.9	756	22.5
Pubic/ axillary hair	3360	47	1.4	286	8.5	900	26.8	990	29.5	263	7.8	874	26.0

Table 3–8

Generally, the females experienced the onset of pubertal changes earlier than the males. As can be seen in table 3–9, at ages eleven and twelve, the rate of menarche was 24.4 percent while the rate of males having the first ejaculation was 7.6 percent. At ages thirteen and fourteen, the corresponding rates were 56.0 percent and 39.5 percent. The mean age of first ejaculation of the males was 14.59 with SD at 1.63. That of the menarche was 13.43 with SD at 1.37. Pubertal development, therefore, occurred earlier in males than females. At age fifteen and sixteen, the rate of males' first ejaculation was higher at 41.2 percent and menarche was 17.9 percent. It was the age when females had already passed the developmental milestone. In table 3–11, it can be seen that the males were also later in developing the other secondary sexual characteristics. For the onset of pubic and axillary hair growth, the mean age for the male was 14.79, SD 1.57 while for the female was 13.77 with SD at 1.73. So was the age of males' onset of beard growth and females' onset of breast development. The male onset of beard growth was 15.37 with SD at 1.75. The female onset of breast development was 13.77 with SD at 1.73.

GENDER AND AGE OF FIRST EJACULATION OR MENARCHE												
GENDER	TOTAL NO.	<=10		11–12		13–14		15–16		>=17	
		NO.	%	NO.	%	NO.	%	NO.	%	NO.	%
Ejaculation	1532	9	0.6	117	7.6	605	39.5	631	41.2	170	11.1
Menarche	1203	2	0.2	293	24.4	674	56.0	215	17.9	19	1.6

Table 3–9

GENDER AND ONSET OF BEARD OR BREAST DEVELOPMENT											
GENDER	TOTAL NO.	<=10		11–12		13–14		15–16		>=17	
		NO.	%	NO.	%	NO.	%	NO.	%	NO.	%
Male	1518	10	0.7	70	4.6	377	24.8	614	40.4	447	29.4
Female	965	98	10.2	334	34.6	337	34.9	171	17.7	25	2.6

Table 3–10

GENDER AND ONSET OF PUBIC AND AXILLARY HAIR GROWTH											
GENDER	TOTAL NO.	<=10		11–12		13–14		15–16		>=17	
		NO.	%	NO.	%	NO.	%	NO.	%	NO.	%
Male	1521	13	0.9	84	5.5	527	34.6	706	46.4	191	12.6
Female	851	33	3.9	185	21.7	335	39.4	240	28.2	58	6.8

Table 3–11

Generally, the females in our survey experienced breast development before their menarche, but in our college sample, the breast development came slightly later. The reason could be that the students had some difficulty in noticing breast development.

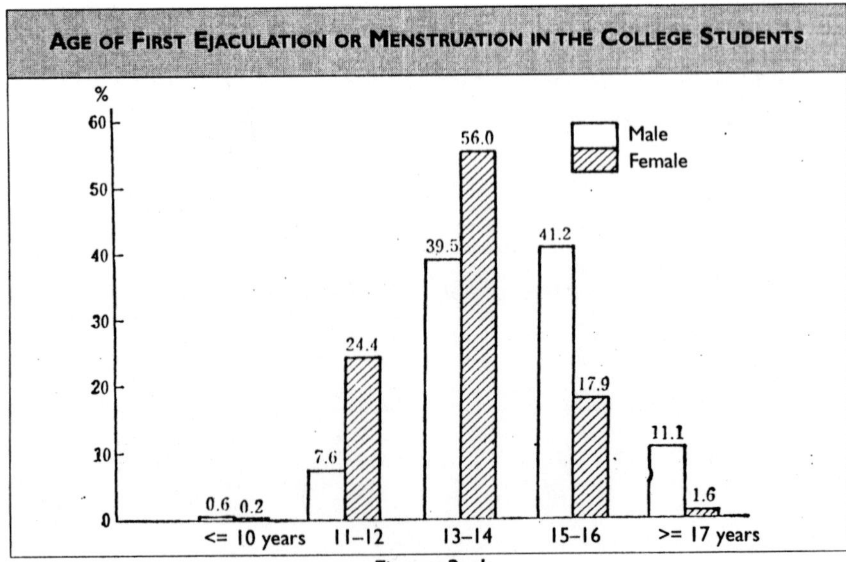

Figure 3–1

Missing answers were quite high in table 3–8, probably due to the difficulty in recalling pubertal changes that, for the subjects, were "events of a distant past." This can be observed more clearly in figures 3–1, 3–2, and 3–3.

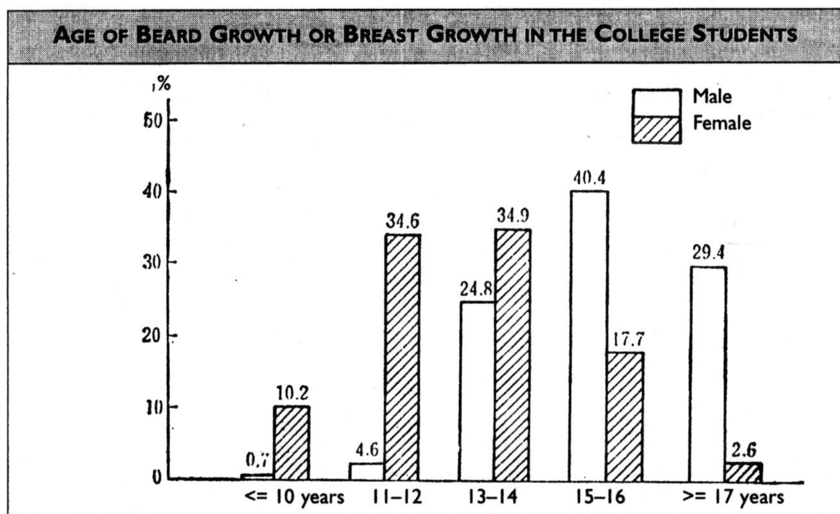

Figure 3–2

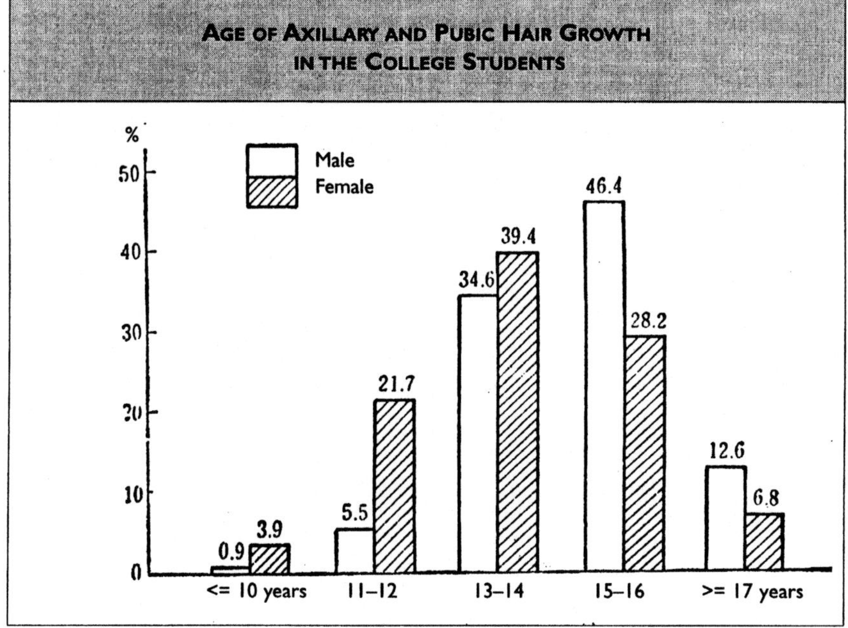

Figure 3–3

Currently, college students fall mostly within the age range between eighteen and twenty-three. Correlating the subjects' age with their age of menarche or first ejaculation, age of beard or breast growth, or age of pubic

Current Age and Onset Age of Menstruation or Ejaculation

CURRENT AGE	TOTAL NO.	<=10		11–12		13–14		15–16		>=17	
		NO.	%	NO.	%	NO.	%	NO.	%	NO.	%
<=19	879	2	0.2	157	17.9	435	49.5	249	28.3	36	4.1
20	735	2	0.3	106	14.4	347	47.2	227	30.9	53	7.2
21	539	6	1.1	78	14.5	257	47.7	158	29.3	40	7.4
22	273	0	0	39	14.3	126	46.2	83	30.4	25	9.2
>=23	179	0	0	12	6.7	64	35.8	77	43.0	26	14.5

P=0.001

Table 3–12

Current Age and Onset Age of Beard or Breast Development

CURRENT AGE	TOTAL NO.	<=10		11–12		13–14		15–16		>=17	
		NO.	%	NO.	%	NO.	%	NO.	%	NO.	%
<=19	795	41	5.2	147	18.5	243	30.6	252	31.7	112	14.1
20	662	33	5.0	128	19.3	178	26.9	193	29.2	130	19.6
21	485	23	4.7	67	13.8	141	29.1	171	35.3	83	17.1
22	257	6	2.3	37	14.4	70	27.2	75	29.2	69	26.8
>=23	173	2	1.2	13	7.5	38	22.0	64	37.0	56	32.4

P=0.001

Table 3–13

Current Age and Onset Age of Axillary and Pubic Hair Growth

CURRENT AGE	TOTAL NO.	<=10		11–12		13–14		15–16		>=17	
		NO.	%	NO.	%	NO.	%	NO.	%	NO.	%
<=19	753	10	1.3	89	11.8	300	39.8	313	41.6	41	5.4
20	628	24	3.8	81	12.9	219	34.9	230	36.6	74	11.8
21	466	8	1.7	52	11.2	173	37.1	191	41.0	42	9.0
22	251	2	0.8	27	10.8	84	33.5	98	39.0	40	15.9
>=23	160	0	0	8	5.0	51	31.9	68	42.5	33	20.6

P=0.001

Table 3–14

or axillary hair growth, the G indices were found to be 0.13, 0.14, and 0.11 respectively. It shows that for the older subjects, the onset of physiological sexual development came later. This could be due to the rapid changes in China within the last ten years, including social openness, westernization, change of sexual attitudes, and improving health conditions.

2. Sexual Concerns or Worries

The questionnaire explored the subjects' concerns and worries about their sexual attractiveness; 1260 (37.5 percent) had concerns and 2404 (71.5 percent) had worries. (tables 3–15 and 3–16).

Our findings show that a large percentage of the students had sexual concerns or worries. For the male students, worry over a small penis ranked highest, much higher than worry over a large penis. This could

CONCERNS OVER SEXUAL CHARACTERISTICS													
	TOTAL NO.												
		NO.	%	NO.	%	NO.	%	NO.	%	NO.	%	NO.	%
Male	650	83	12.8	69	10.6	294	45.2	6	0.9	17	2.6	181	27.8
Female	548	30	5.5	0	0	0	0	131	23.9	298	54.4	89	16.2

P=0.001

Table 3–15

WORRIES OVER PHYSICAL APPEARANCE									
GENDER	TOTAL NO.	SHORT		ACNE		OVER–WEIGHT		THIN	
		NO.	%	NO.	%	NO.	%	NO.	%
Male	1318	646	49.0	279	21.2	73	5.5	55	4.2
Female	980	247	25.2	222	22.6	10	1.0	2	0.2

GENDER	OBESE		BALD		WHITE HAIR		HAIRY	
	NO.	%	NO.	%	NO.	%	NO.	%
Male	88	6.7	27	2.0	101	7.7	49	3.7
Female	369	37.7	5	0.5	30	3.1	95	9.7

P=0.001

Table 3–16

be due to the popular belief that a large penis is needed for sexual satisfaction or impregnation. For the females, the top worry was over small breasts, much more than over large breasts. Again, this could be due to the popular fashion of large breasts. Large breasts had not been a fashion in Chinese tradition. In ancient China, females took slimness as beauty, including inconspicuous breasts. Women tied their breasts tightly during their growth period, much to the detriment of their health. Nowadays, the opposite is encouraged as a sign of health. Small breasts became a source of worry, leading to an increase in the popularity of breast pumps in China at this time.

From table 3–17, it can be seen that 80 percent of female students wore bras for the proper development of breasts. Only 4.9 percent used bras to try to limit the size of their breasts.

Obviously, a strong healthy body does not mean a fat body; 37.7 percent of the female students worried about being too fat. For the males, worry over being fat was less. Their top worry was being too short (49.0 percent).This is also related to the aesthetic fashion of our time. Young girls nowadays generally like boys of an athletic build. Some girls even specify that their partners should be at least 1.75 meters high and consider those shorter than 1.70 meters as being stunted or disabled. These views might have added stress to the male concern over body build. Table

INITIAL BRA USAGE						
TOTAL NO.	ONSET OF BREAST DEVELOPMENT		AFTER FULL BREAST DEVELOPMENT		NEVER	
	NO.	%	NO.	%	NO.	%
1318	392	29.3	844	63.0	103	7.7

Table 3–17

REASON FOR WEARING BRAS						
TOTAL NO.	FOR PROPER BREAST DEVELOPMENT		FOR BETTER BREAST SHAPE		TO LIMIT BREAST SIZE	
	NO.	%	NO.	%	NO.	%
1264	1011	80.0	191	15.1	62	4.9

Table 3–18

4–15 shows that even 25.2 percent of the females worried that they might be too short.

The worry over sexual characteristics and the individual body image are related to the extent of sexual knowledge, and also to social background.[2] Table 3–19, however, shows that the worries are unrelated to the number of years spent in college (gamma all < 0.1). The lack of a clear correlation is apparent in figure 3–4.

YEAR AND WORRY OVER PHYSICAL APPEARANCE

APPEARANCE	YR. 1		YR.2		YR.3		YR.4		YR.5		POSTGD.	
	NO.	%	NO.	%	NO.	%	NO.	%	NO.	%	NO.	%
Height	154	43.0	324	39.0	219	37.1	183	36.7	21	38.9	17	56.7
Acne	68	19.0	191	23.0	120	20.3	115	23.0	12	22.2	8	26.7
Beard	17	4.7	29	3.5	17	2.9	21	4.2	2	3.7	1	3.3
No beard	8	2.2	19	2.3	17	2.9	15	3.0	4	7.4	0	0
Obese	74	20.7	164	19.7	133	22.5	89	17.8	4	7.4	1	3.3
Bald	2	0.6	9	1.1	11	1.9	7	1.4	2	3.7	1	3.3
White hair	14	3.9	42	5.1	37	6.3	35	7.0	6	11.1	2	6.7
Hairy	21	5.9	53	6.4	37	6.3	34	6.8	3	5.6	0	0
Total	358	100.0	831	100.0	591	100.0	499	100.0	54	100.0	30	100.0

P=0.001

Table 3–19

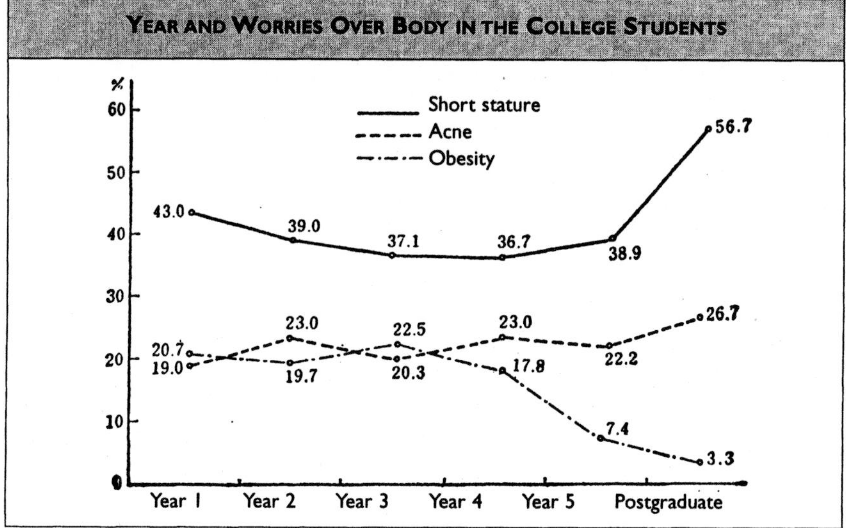

Figure 3–4

3. Worry over Sexual Functioning

As table 3–20 shows, 30.7 percent of male students and 13.3 percent of the females worried about their sexual functioning. The percentages were quite similar between the students of the arts, science, and medicine, but the engineering students had significantly higher rates (table 3–21).

GENDER AND WORRY OVER SEXUAL FUNCTION

	TOTAL NO.	YES		NO		NOT THOUGHT ABOUT	
		NO.	%	NO.	%	NO.	%
Male	1870	574	30.7	823	44.0	473	25.3
Female	1253	167	13.3	339	27.1	747	59.6

P=0.001

Table 3–20

PROFESSION AND WORRY OVER SEXUAL FUNCTION

WORRY	TOTAL	ARTS		SCIENCE		ENGIN.		AGRICUL.		MEDICINE	
		NO.	%	NO.	%	NO.	%	NO.	%	NO.	%
Yes	744	261	23.7	120	22.4	223	30.3	6	14.6	134	19.2
No	1153	409	37.1	202	37.8	272	27.0	19	46.3	251	36.0
No such thought	1214	432	39.2	213	39.8	241	32.7	16	39.0	312	44.8
Total	3111	1102	100.0	535	100.0	736	100.0	41	100.0	697	100.0

Table 3–21

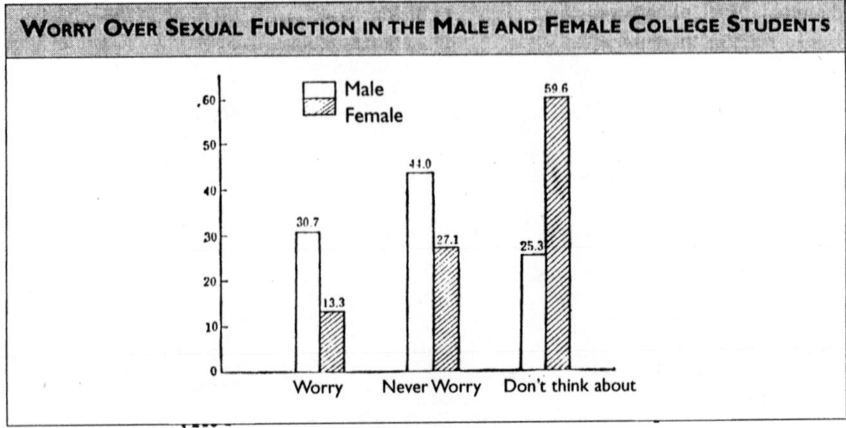

Figure 3–5

There is no evidence that the worries of the students were justified. They were probably due only to a lack of sexual knowledge, even among the well-educated college students.

3. Sexual Psychology

1. Gender Acceptance

An overall of 69.2 percent of the students liked being of their own gender, 7.9 percent disliked it, and 21.5 percent remained neutral, and 1.5 percent did not answer. Of the male students, 2.6 percent disliked their gender, and of the female, the figure was 15.6 percent, six times that of the male. From table 3–23 and figure 3–7, age has no significant association with gender acceptance, except that those below nineteen had a lower percentage of subjects accepting their gender.

GENDER AND GENDER ACCEPTANCE

	TOTAL	ACCEPT		NOT ACCEPT		NEUTRAL	
		NO.	%	NO.	%	NO.	%
Male	1879	1516	80.7	49	2.6	314	16.7
Female	1272	700	55.0	198	15.6	374	29.4

P=0.001

Table 3–22

AGE AND GENDER ACCEPTANCE

AGE	TOTAL	ACCEPT		NOT ACCEPT		NEUTRAL	
		NO.	%	NO.	%	NO.	%
<=19	994	660	66.4	93	9.4	241	24.2
20	832	591	71.0	51	6.1	190	22.8
21	620	442	71.3	49	7.9	129	20.8
22	304	216	71.1	26	8.6	62	20.4
>=23	205	158	77.1	18	8.8	29	14.1

P=0.001

Table 3–23

Of the overall subjects, 55.7 percent wished to be male, 15.6 percent wished to be female, 26.5 percent made no special choice and 2.2 percent did not answer; 8.3 percent of the males and 42.8 percent of the females were willing to choose the other gender. The number of females wishing to be male was five times higher than that of the males wishing to be female. Table 3–7 shows no change of the wish in association with age.

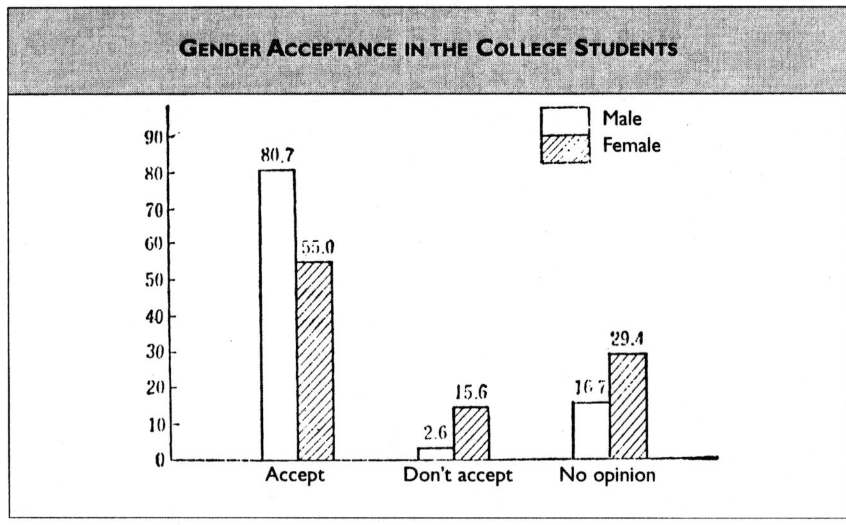

Figure 3–6

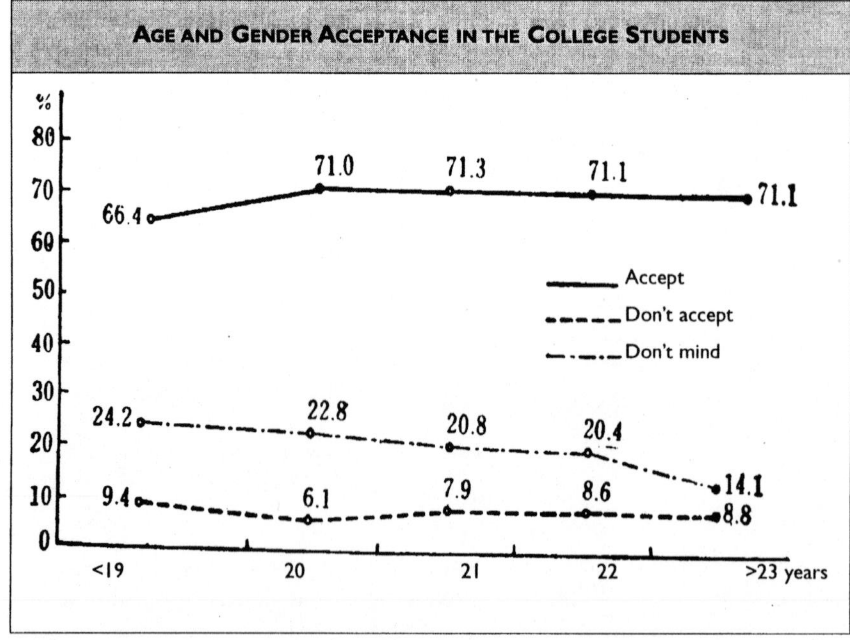

Figure 3–7

GENDER AND GENDER CHOICE							
	TOTAL	FOR MALE		FOR FEMALE		NEUTRAL	
		NO.	%	NO.	%	NO.	%
Male	1869	1235	66.1	155	8.3	479	25.6
Female	1258	539	42.8	350	27.8	369	29.3

P=0.001

Table 3–24

AGE AND GENDER CHOICE							
AGE	TOTAL	FOR MALE		FOR FEMALE		NEUTRAL	
		NO.	%	NO.	%	NO.	%
<=19	989	563	56.9	166	16.8	260	26.3
20	820	441	53.8	151	18.4	228	27.8
21	614	350	57.0	89	14.5	175	28.5
22	306	177	57.8	47	15.4	82	26.8
>=23	204	129	63.2	30	14.7	45	22.1

P=0.001

Table 3–25

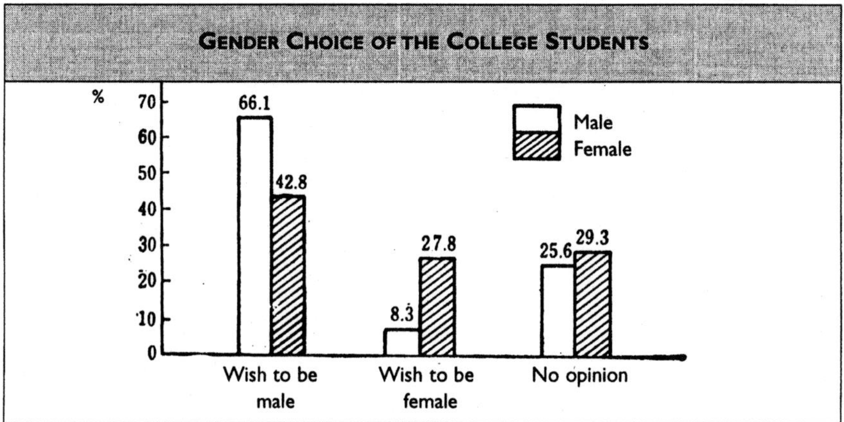

Figure 3–8

The phenomenon of females preferring to be males appears to have become noticeable since the privatization of property and the establishment of patriarchy. Among the ancient Greeks, it was said that nearly all females wished to be males but no males to be females. The sexological pioneer Havelock Ellis estimated that in his time one in one hundred

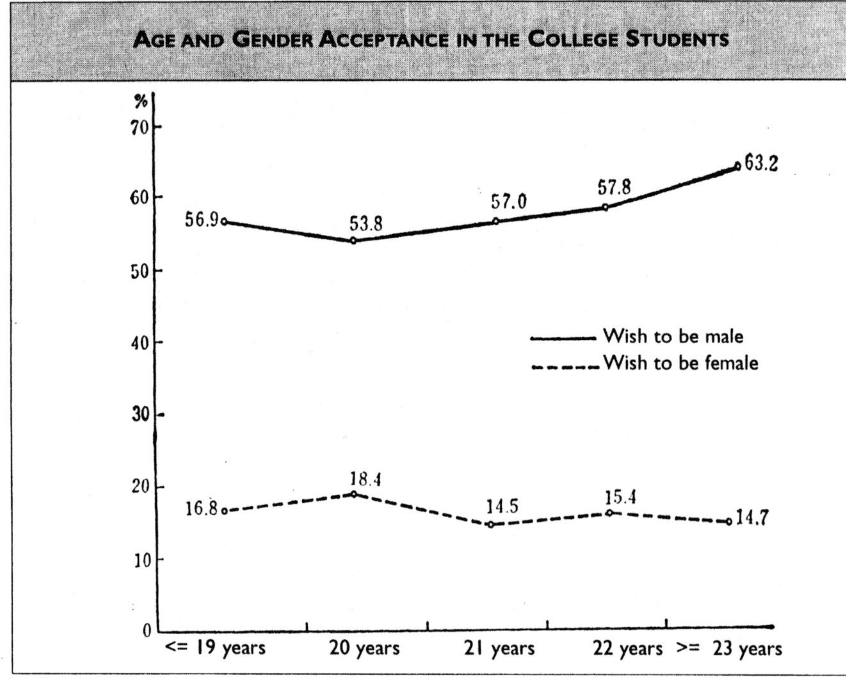

Figure 3–9

males wished to be female but 75 percent of all females wished to be male. This type of mentality is bred in certain cultures where children are taught at an early age that females are likely to experience greater difficulties in life. In China, the situation is especially serious because of traditional beliefs and the modern one-child policy, which forces parents to choose whether to have a boy or a girl. Very often, they prefer a boy. This is already resulting in a worrysome scarcity of females in certain regions of the country. Only in some short periods in Chinese history were females deemed more precious, because the emperor might select them for his household and favor them.

It must be emphasized, however, that our survey questions here dealt only with the "superficial" wish to change one's gender, because of perceived material or social advantages. None of the preceding remarks are meant to illuminate the more specific problem of genuine gender dysphoria (transsexualism) or to give even a hint of an explanation about transvestism. These complicated issues were not addressed by us and, in any case, cannot be explored by means of a simple questionnaire.

2. Desire for Heterosexual Relations

There is a Chinese saying that "All boys like to fall in love, all girls love romances."[3] In our subjects, 70.1 percent reported a strong desire to have heterosexual relations, 24.5 percent denied this, and 5.4 percent did not answer. Of the males, 81.8 percent had a strong desire; for the females the figure was 63.4 percent. The males had a higher percentage probably because of social expectations that they should be the ones to initiate sex.

GENDER AND DESIRE FOR HETEROSEXUAL RELATIONS

	TOTAL	YES		NO	
		NO.	%	NO.	%
Male	1815	1484	81.8	331	18.2
Female	1219	773	63.4	446	36.6

P=0.001

Table 3–26

AGE AND DESIRE FOR HETEROSEXUAL RELATIONS

AGE	TOTAL	YES		NO	
		NO.	%	NO.	%
<=19	955	654	68.5	301	31.5
20	810	596	73.6	214	26.4
21	598	464	77.6	134	22.4
22	299	249	83.3	50	16.7
>=23	199	165	82.9	34	17.1

P=0.001

Table 3–27

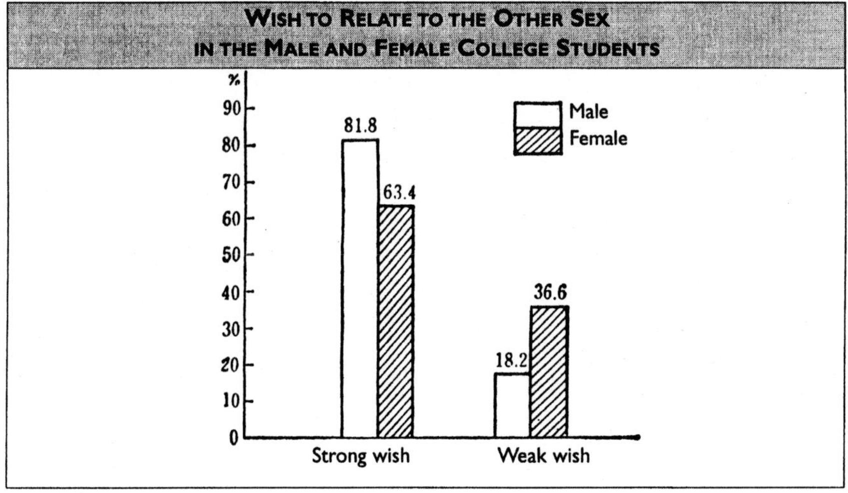

Figure 3–10

GRADE AND DESIRE FOR HETEROSEXUAL RELATIONS					
YEAR	TOTAL	YES		NO	
		NO.	%	NO.	%
1	463	302	65.2	161	34.8
2	1038	755	72.7	283	27.3
3	799	604	75.6	195	24.4
4	690	543	78.7	147	21.3
5	80	63	78.7	17	21.3
Postgd.	53	46	86.8	7	13.2

P=0.001

Table 3–28

Figures 3–11 and 3–12 show that age and grade levels had a positive correlation with desire for heterosexual relations (G=0.20 and 0.17 respectively).

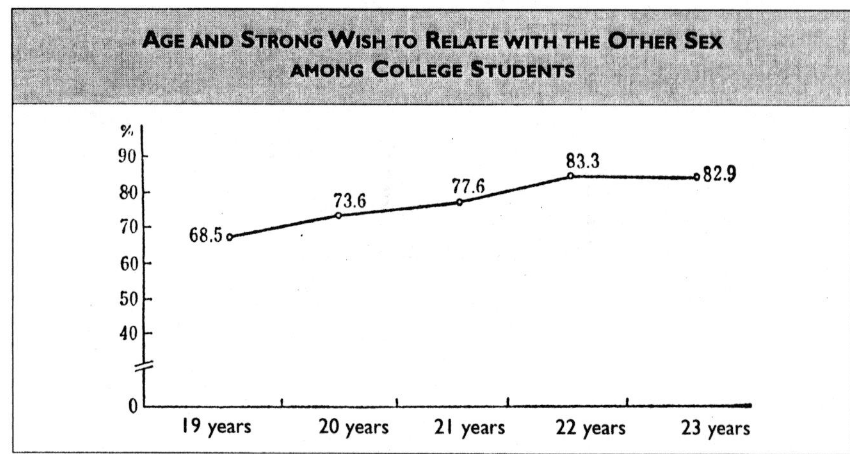

Figure 3–11

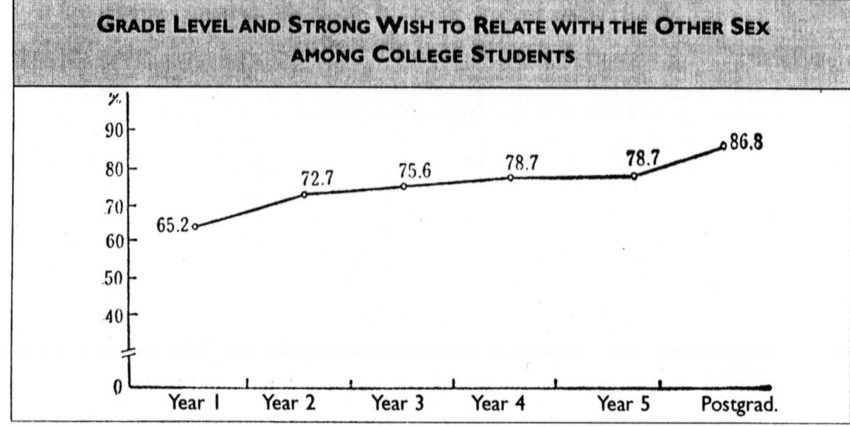

Figure 3–12

3. Sexual Fantasies

Sexual fantasies cannot wholly gratify sexual wishes, but can offer a temporary escape from sexual frustrations. Of our subjects, 5 percent reported sexual fantasies nearly every day within the past month, 64.1 percent reported occasional fantasies, and 26.7 percent did not report any; 3.5 percent of the subjects did not answer the question.

Table 3–29 and figure 3–13 show that more male students had frequent sexual fantasies. This is in contrast with Ellis's survey[4] on 352 subjects which listed 47 percent of the females and 17 percent of the males as having sexual fantasies. This may be due to a more traditional orientation of the Chinese females or because in Ellis's survey, the fantasy was specified to be in form of long stories which were more suited to female inclinations.

Frequencies of sexual fantasy were found to have a positive correlation with year and grades (tables 3–30 and 3–31).

GENDER AND SEXUAL FANTASIES IN THE PAST ONE MONTH

	TOTAL	DAILY		OCCASIONALLY		NEVER	
		NO.	%	NO.	%	NO.	%
Male	1868	156	8.3	1451	77.7	261	14.0
Female	1228	26	2.1	604	49.2	598	48.7

P=0.001

Table 3–29

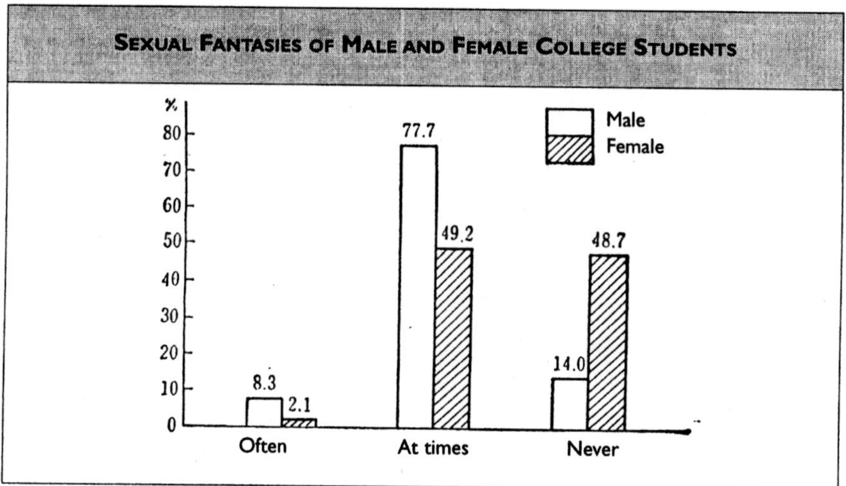

Figure 3–13

AGE AND SEXUAL FANTASY							
AGE	TOTAL	DAILY		OCCASIONALLY		NEVER	
		NO.	%	NO.	%	NO.	%
<=19	978	44	4.5	629	64.3	305	31.2
20	820	54	6.6	530	64.6	236	28.8
21	609	40	6.6	418	68.6	151	24.8
22	305	20	6.6	206	67.5	79	25.9
>=23	204	21	10.3	146	71.6	37	18.1

P=0.001

Table 3–30

YEAR AND SEXUAL FANTASY							
YEAR	TOTAL	DAILY		OCCASIONALLY		NEVER	
		NO.	%	NO.	%	NO.	%
1	480	14	2.9	314	65.4	152	31.7
2	1057	65	6.1	706	66.8	286	27.1
3	815	59	7.2	523	64.2	233	28.6
4	704	37	5.3	481	68.3	186	26.4
5	84	4	4.8	57	67.8	23	27.4
Postgd.	51	6	11.8	39	76.5	6	11.7
Total	3191	185	5.8	2120	66.4	886	27.8

Table 3–31

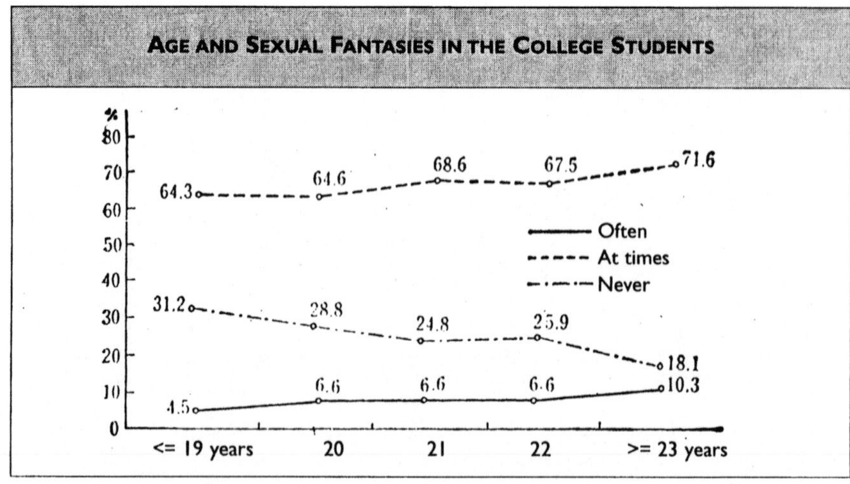

Figure 3–14

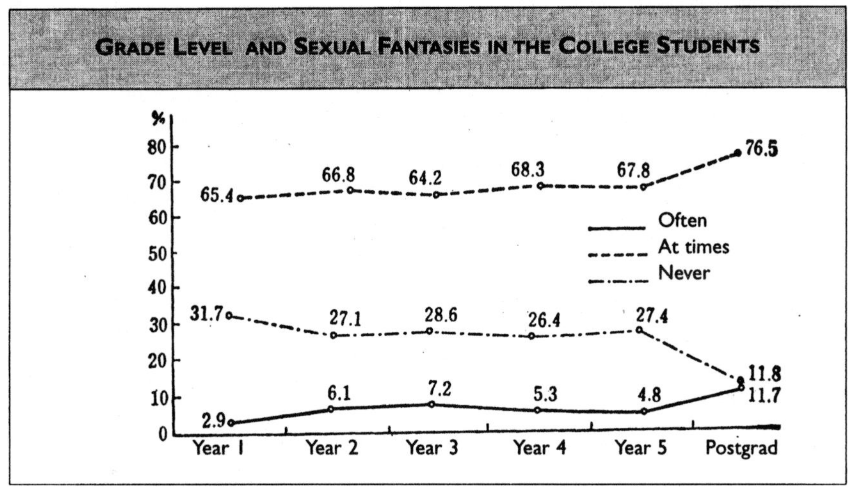

Figure 3–15

Table 3–32 shows that the rate of sexual fantasies did not change for students of different professions.

PROFESSION AND SEXUAL FANTASIES

RATE OF FANTASY	TOTAL	ARTS		SCIENCE		ENGINE		AGRICUL.		MEDICINE	
		NO.	%	NO.	%	NO.	%	NO.	%	NO.	%
Often	182	77	7.0	35	6.6	48	6.5	0	0	22	3.2
Occass.	2046	741	67.7	357	67.4	516	70.4	27	69.2	405	58.9
Never	857	277	25.3	138	26.0	169	23.1	12	30.8	261	37.9
Total	3085	1095	100.0	530	100.0	733	100.0	39	100.0	688	100.0

Table 3–32

4. Sexual Dreams

When asked "Do you have sexual contact with members of the other sex in your dreams?", 12.8 percent of the students answered "frequently," 57.5 percent answered "rarely," 26.2 percent answered "never," and 3.5 percent did not answer. The frequency of sex dreams in the students was therefore no less than that of sexual fantasies. Comparing table 3–33 and table 3–29, a close similarity can be found. In the male students, the rate of sexual dreams was even double that of sexual fantasies. It might be that, in dreams, people tend to be less inhibited, or the respondents were for some reason more willing to admit to sexual dreams than to fantasies.

Gender and Sex Dreams							
	TOTAL	OFTEN		RARE		NEVER	
		NO.	%	NO.	%	NO.	%
Male	1857	361	19.4	1246	67.1	250	13.5
Female	1237	43	3.5	610	49.3	584	47.2

P=0.001

Table 3–33

Percentage of Male and Female College Students Who had Sexual Dreams

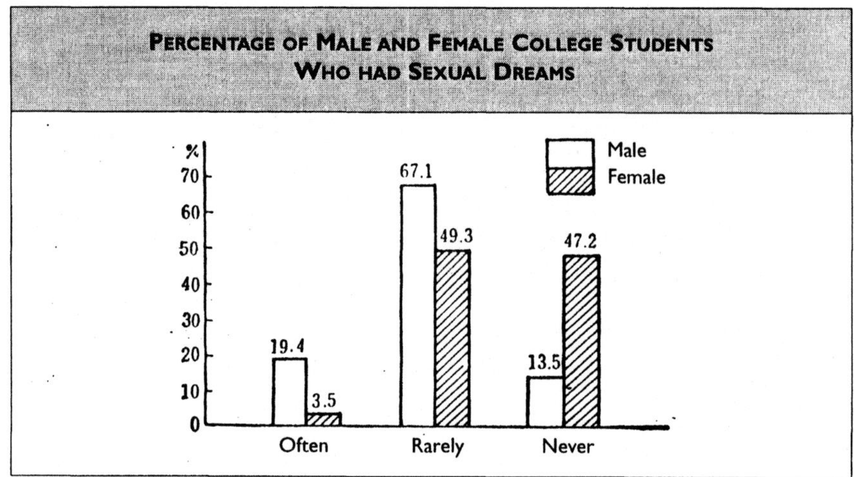

Figure 3–16

Two thousand two hundred and seventy-eight subjects disclosed the details of their sex dreams. 30.9 percent contained kissing, 28.5 percent contained petting, 20.9 percent contained coitus, and 19.6 percent contained other types of behavior. Table 3–33 shows that female students had more dreams about petting than the males, while the males had many more dreams about coitus. This may be due to the higher sexual

Gender and Content of Sex Dreams									
	TOTAL	KISSING		PETTING		COITUS		OTHERS	
		NO.	%	NO.	%	NO.	%	NO.	%
Male	1553	465	29.9	406	26.1	411	26.5	271	17.5
Female	631	208	33.0	224	35.5	42	6.7	157	24.9

P=0.001

Table 3–34

need and aggressiveness of the males. In fact, some modern Chinese women restrict their sexual wishes to tenderness, kissing, and petting rather than pursuing actual sexual intercourse.

The degree of sexual intimacy in dreams increased with the grade level and age of the students (tables 3–35 and 3–36), with G indices at 0.21 and 0.16 respectively.

GENDER AND CONTENT OF SEX DREAMS

	TOTAL	KISSING		PETTING		COITUS		OTHERS	
		NO.	%	NO.	%	NO.	%	NO.	%
Male	1553	465	29.9	406	26.1	411	26.5	271	17.5
Female	631	208	33.0	224	35.5	42	6.7	157	24.9

P=0.001

Table 3–34

AGE AND SEX DREAMS

AGE	TOTAL	OFTEN		RARE		NEVER	
		NO.	%	NO.	%	NO.	%
<=19	970	89	9.2	551	56.8	330	34.0
20	820	112	13.7	477	58.2	231	28.2
21	607	90	14.8	382	62.9	135	22.2
22	307	52	16.9	206	67.1	49	16.0
>=23	204	41	20.1	127	62.3	36	17.61

P=0.001

Table 3–35

YEAR AND SEX DREAMS

YEAR	TOTAL	OFTEN		RARE		NEVER	
		NO.	%	NO.	%	NO.	%
1	481	39	8.1	259	53.8	183	38.0
2	1046	143	13.7	616	58.9	287	27.4
3	818	106	13.0	497	60.8	215	26.3
4	705	99	14.0	458	65.0	148	21.0
5	83	15	18.1	49	59.0	19	22.9
Postgd.	53	20	37.7	23	43.4	10	18.9

Table 3–36

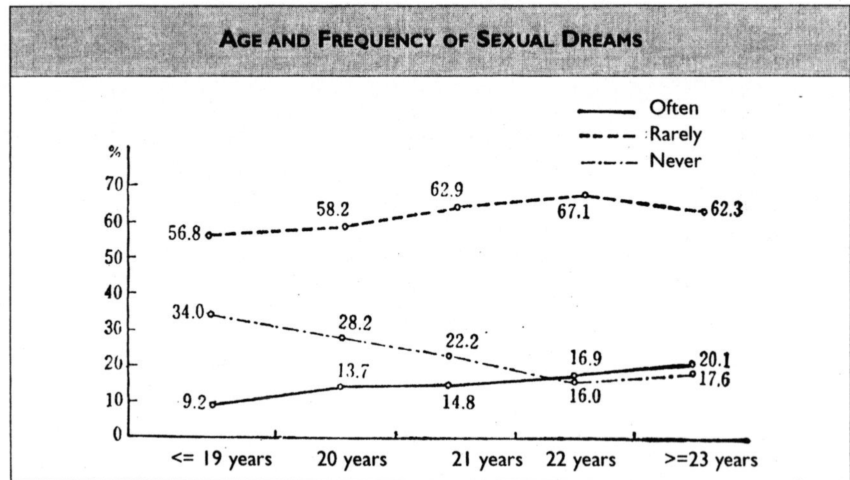

Figure 3–17

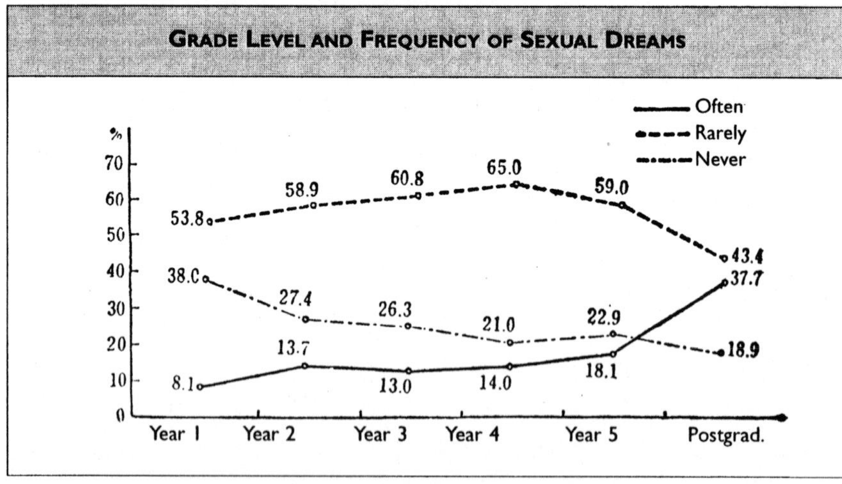

Figure 3–18

Of the women surveyed in the second Kinsey Report, about 65 percent had explicit sexual dreams, and at least 20 percent of them experienced orgasm in the course of that dream, but 45 percent never had an orgasm.[5] Kinsey's 65 percent is close to our figure of 52.8 percent in the female students.

There was no obvious correlation between the frequency of sexual dreams and the profession of the students (table 3–37).

PROFESSION AND FREQUENCY OF SEX DREAMS											
FREQUENCY	TOTAL	ARTS		SCIENCE		ENGIN.		AGRICUL.		MEDICINE	
		NO.	%	NO.	%	NO.	%	NO.	%	NO.	%
Often	409	175	15.9	61	11.5	108	15.0	3	7.7	62	9.0
Rare	1833	633	57.7	331	62.3	437	60.5	25	64.1	407	58.9
Never	839	290	26.4	139	26.2	177	24.5	11	28.2	222	32.1
Total	3081	1098	100.0	531	100.0	722	100.0	39	100.0	691	100.0

Table 3–37

PROFESSION AND CONTENT OF SEX DREAMS											
CONTENT	TOTAL	ARTS		SCIENCE		ENGIN.		AGRICUL.		MEDICINE	
		NO.	%	NO.	%	NO.	%	NO.	%	NO.	%
Kissing	665	259	32.9	122	33.1	171	32.2	13	46.4	100	22.4
Petting	621	215	27.3	112	30.4	146	27.5	12	42.9	136	30.4
Coitus	452	174	22.1	59	16.0	115	21.7	0	0	104	23.3
Other	425	140	17.8	76	20.6	99	18.6	3	10.7	107	23.9
Total	2163	788	100.0	369	100.0	531	100.0	28	100.0	447	100.0

Table 3–38

5. Sex and Sexual Arousal

1. AROUSAL BY SEXUAL DEPICTIONS

As a reaction to sexual representations in books or pictures, 75.6 percent of the students reported excitement as evidenced by blushing, palpitations, arousal, and the temptation to engage in some sexual activity; 3.4 percent reported feelings of disgust; 14.5 percent felt nothing; and 6.5 percent did not answer. Some 87.6 percent of the male students and 71.2 percent of the females reported excited reactions. There was a higher proportion of males than females who reported a temptation to try sexual

GENDER AND REPORTED REACTION TO SEXUAL DEPICTIONS											
	TOTAL	BLUSH		PLEASURE		TEMPTED		DISGUST		NONE	
		NO.	%	NO.	%	NO.	%	NO.	%	NO.	%
Male	1805	689	38.2	468	25.9	424	23.5	19	1.1	205	11.4
Female	1208	729	60.3	64	5.3	67	5.5	86	7.1	262	21.7

P=0.001

Table 3–39

activities. Only 1.1 percent of males and 7.1 percent of females reported feelings of disgust (table 3–39).

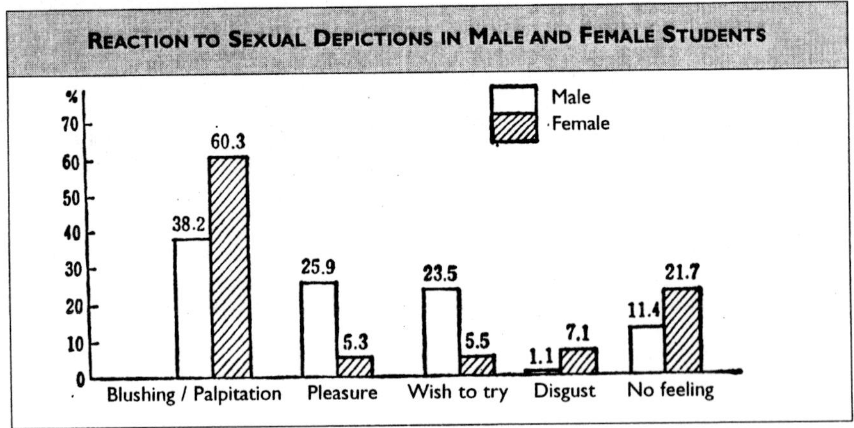

Figure 3–19

AGE AND REACTION TO SEXUAL DEPICTIONS

AGE	TOTAL	BLUSH		PLEASURE		TEMPTED		DISGUST		NONE	
		NO.	%	NO.	%	NO.	%	NO.	%	NO.	%
<=19	954	509	53.4	121	12.7	132	13.8	57	6.0	135	14.2
20	815	396	48.6	128	15.7	135	16.6	19	2.3	137	16.8
21	598	264	44.1	124	20.7	105	17.6	13	2.2	92	15.4
22	301	122	40.5	72	23.9	57	18.9	9	3.0	41	13.6
>=23	198	68	34.3	53	26.8	47	23.7	2	1.0	28	14.1

P=0.001

Table 3–40

PROFESSION AND REACTION TO SEXUAL DEPICTIONS

REACTION	TOTAL	ARTS		SCIENCE		ENGINE		AGRICUL.		MEDICINE	
		NO.	%	NO.	%	NO.	%	NO.	%	NO.	%
Blush	1423	511	46.8	245	46.8	327	45.4	27	67.5	313	46.8
Pleasure	529	201	18.4	92	17.6	139	19.3	8	20.0	89	13.3
Tempted	509	196	17.9	81	15.5	139	19.3	1	2.5	92	13.8
Disgust	113	39	3.6	16	3.1	26	3.6	2	5.0	30	4.5
None	471	145	13.3	90	17.2	89	12.4	2	5.0	145	21.7
Total	3045	1092	100.0	524	100.0	720	100.0	40	100.0	669	100.0

Table 3–41

The older students reported less excitement or disgust in response to sexual depictions. Obviously, this is due to a higher degree of desensitization to the materials as one gets older. The more mature and open attitude to sex that develops with the advancing years may also make the subjects feel less disgusted by the materials. Yet, it is also with age that there is an increase in arousal and a temptation to engage in sexual activities.

There was no correlation between profession and the various reactions.

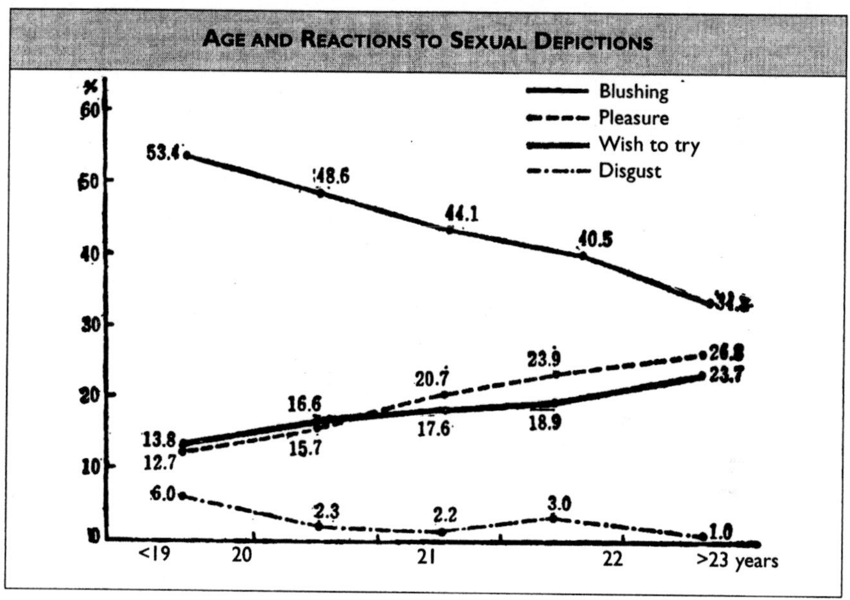

Figure 3–20

2. REACTION TO NUDITY

Students were asked about reactions to viewing nude bodies of the members of the other sex in pictures or in real life, excluding those of parents or dead bodies. Only 62.8 percent of the subjects had such experiences, 34.4 percent never had them, and 2.8 percent did not answer.

Table 3–42 shows that more male students had seen the other gender nude. Of all the subjects, 54.0 percent reported seeing this in magazines, 8.9 percent in public movies or on television, 7.9 percent on videotapes, 5.9 percent in photographs, and 17.9 percent in real life. The finding that most of the subjects had seen nudity in magazines is probably due to the fact that in the 1980s, some material of this kind was allowed to be published. Although very few had viewed live nude subjects, more females had this experience than males.

GENDER AND EXPERIENCE OF VIEWING OTHER-SEX NUDITY					
	TOTAL	YES		NO	
		NO.	%	NO.	%
Male	1864	1319	70.8	545	29.2
Female	1252	695	55.5	557	44.5

P=0.001

Table 3–42

GENDER AND SOURCE OF VIEWING OTHER-SEX NUDITY											
	TOTAL	MAGAZINE		MOVIE/TV		VIDEO		PHOTOS		LIVE	
		NO.	%	NO.	%	NO.	%	NO.	%	NO.	%
Male	1313	648	49.4	189	14.4	148	11.3	109	8.3	219	16.7
Female	677	423	62.5	96	14.2	7	1.0	7	1.0	144	21.3

P=0.001

Table 3–43

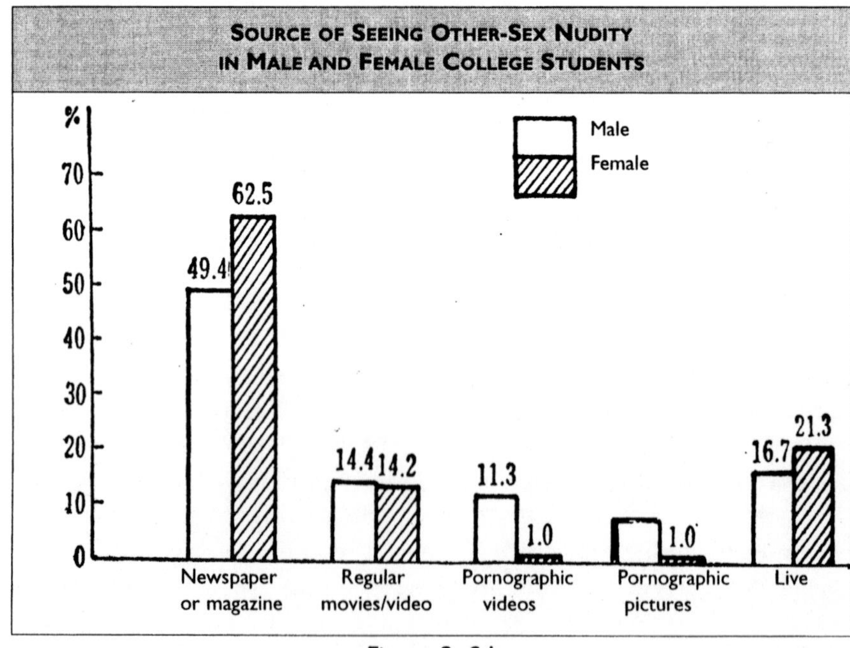

Figure 2–21

Table 3–44 and 3–45 show that the experience increased with age and grade level. Table 3–45 shows no obvious difference between regions.

YEAR AND EXPERIENCE OF SEEING OTHER-SEX NUDITY					
YEAR	TOTAL	YES		NO	
		NO.	%	NO.	%
1	484	256	52.9	228	47.1
2	1055	648	61.4	407	38.6
3	822	560	68.1	262	31.9
4	709	517	72.9	192	27.1
5	84	51	60.7	33	29.3
Postgd.	52	40	76.9	12	23.1

P=0.001

Table 3–45

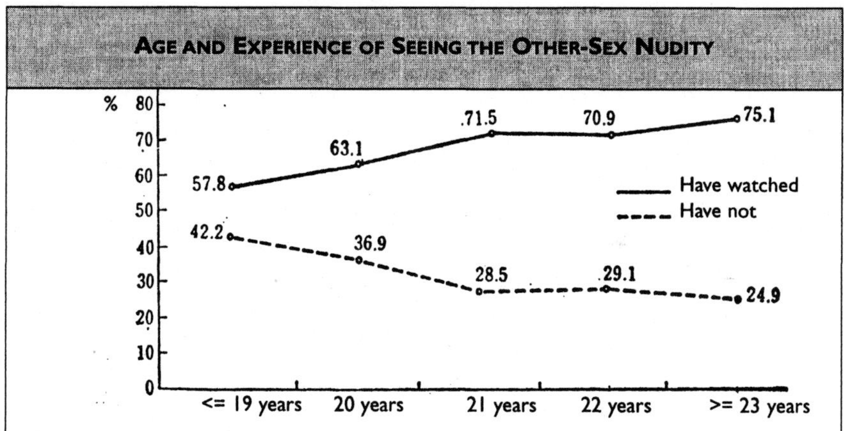

Figure 3–22

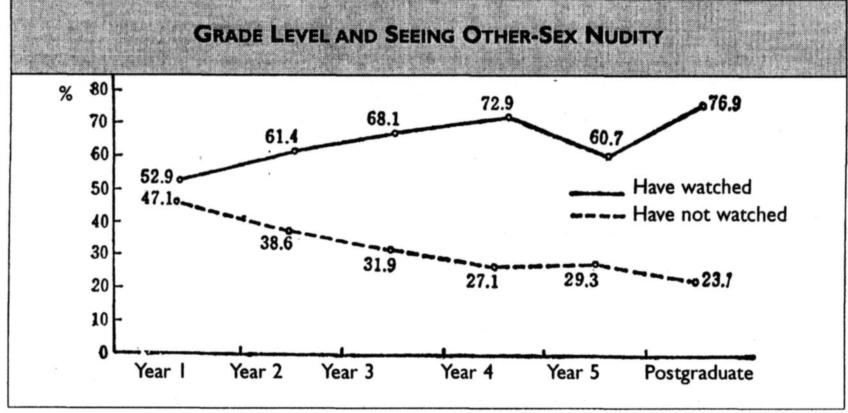

Figure 3–23

REGION AND FREQUENCY OF HAVING SEEN OTHER-SEX NUDITY											
REGION	TOTAL	<=19		20		21		22		>=23	
		NO.	%	NO.	%	NO.	%	NO.	%	NO.	%
Chengdu	410	81	60.0	75	72.1	61	75.3	13	61.9	8	66.7
Xiamen	689	169	59.7	92	68.1	64	79.0	37	86.0	29	82.9
Shanghi Fudan U	302	36	48.6	32	42.1	41	63.1	23	69.7	22	81.5

Table 3–46

3. Sexual Arousal

In this section, we asked the subjects to choose from ten proposed situations those which would arouse them sexually. Three thousand seven hundred and seven subjects made such choices. The most frequently chosen situation was viewing a nude body of the other sex live or in photos (table 3–47). The male and female frequencies were quite similar.

The next question asked concerned the subjects' feeling when seeing the nude body of the same gender in public baths or changing rooms: 4.8 percent responded that they liked it, 5.0 percent felt disgusted, 87.3 percent did not feel anything, and 2.9 percent did not give any clear answer. The males had a higher proportion of pleasurable feelings (table 3–48) This may be taken as an indication of homosexual inclinations, since it was not possible for us to ask more direct questions without risking the prohibition of the whole survey.

SITUATIONS CAUSING SEXUAL AROUSAL									
BODILY CONTACT IN CROWDS		VIEWING STATUES		VIEWING LIVE NUDITY		CROSS DRESSING		BODILY CONTACT WITH CHILDREN	
FREQ.	%	FREQ.	%	FREQ.	%	FREQ.	%	FREQ.	%
945	25.5	471	12.7	1720	46.4	103	2.8	54	1.5

PHYSICAL PAIN		TORTURING OTHERS		SELF EXPOSURE		CONTACT ANIMALS		SEXUAL COERCION		TOTAL	
FREQ.	%	FREQ.	%	FREQ.	%	FREQ.	%	FREQ.	%	FREQ.	%
49	1.3	41	1.1	206	5.6	26	0.7	92	2.5	3707	100.0

Table 3–47

GENDER AND SITUATIONS CAUSING SEXUAL AROUSAL

GENDER	BODILY CONTACT IN CROWDS		VIEWING STATUES		VIEWING LIVE NUDITY		CROSS DRESSING		BODILY CONT. W. CHILDREN	
	FREQ.	%	FREQ.	%	FREQ.	%	FREQ.	%	FREQ.	%
Male	762	25.9	375	12.8	1380	47.0	78	2.7	27	0.9
Female	150	24.2	74	11.9	275	44.4	20	3.2	23	3.7

PHYSICAL PAIN		TORTURING OTHERS		SELF EXPOSURE		CONTACT ANIMALS		SEXUAL COERCION		GENDER
FREQ.	%	FREQ.	%	FREQ.	%	FREQ.	%	FREQ.	%	
32	1.1	27	0.9	164	5.6	21	0.7	73	2.5	Male
13	2.1	12	1.9	36	5.8	3	0.5	14	2.3	Female

Table 3–48

GENDER AND FEELING WHEN SEEING THE NUDE BODY OF THE SAME SEX

	TOTAL	PLEASURE		DISGUST		NOT NOTICE	
		NO.	%	NO.	%	NO.	%
Male	1873	101	5.4	89	4.8	1683	89.9
Female	1255	49	3.9	72	5.7	1144	90.4

P=0.05

Table 3–49

4. Sexual Behavior

Sexual behavior is more than sexual intercourse. For Chinese college students, any form of sexual contact is considered antisocial and punishable, and even lesser degrees of sexual intimacy such as embracing, kissing, and petting were only allowed gradually after 1986. Hence, in college students, sexually open attitudes are still in sharp contrast with their cautious and secretive sexual behavior.

1. Masturbation

A. NUMBER

Of the whole student sample, 39.0 percent had masturbated, 51.5 percent had not, and 9.5 percent did not answer. Many more males had masturbated than had females (table 3–50 and figure 3–24).

GENDER AND MASTURBATORY EXPERIENCE					
GENDER	TOTAL	YES		NEVER	
		NO.	%	NO.	%
Male	1794	1059	59.0	735	41.0
Female	1111	183	16.5	928	83.5

P=0.001

Table 3–50

AGE AND MASTURBATORY EXPERIENCE					
AGE	TOTAL	YES		NEVER	
		NO.	%	NO.	%
<=19	916	352	38.5	354	61.5
20	767	307	40.0	460	60.0
21	577	278	48.2	299	51.8
22	291	141	48.5	150	51.5
>=23	191	110	57.6	81	42.4

Table 3–51

Table 3–51 shows that masturbatory experience increased with age (G index=0.16). This could be because college students are usually not yet able to marry and, as a result, masturbation becomes the only readily available sexual activity.

Comparing the professions of the students, the engineering students

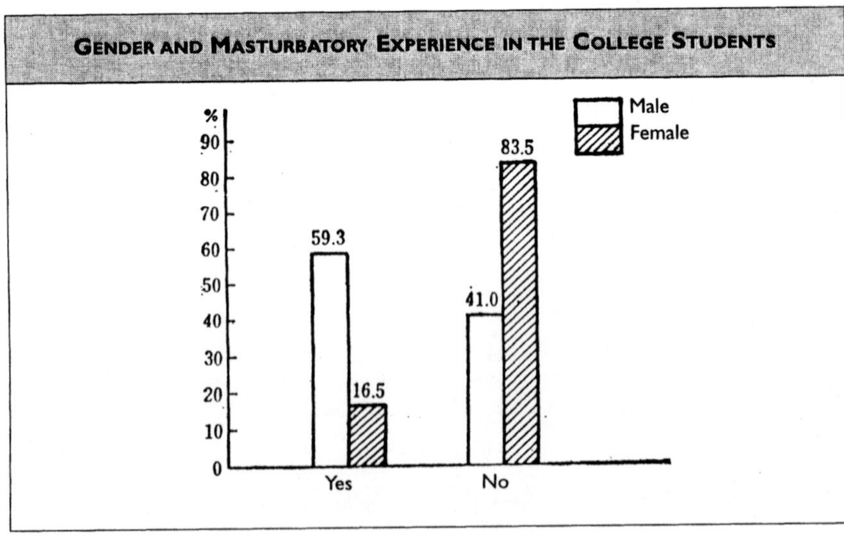

Figure 3–24

showed a higher frequency of masturbation. Table 3–21 also shows that engineering students worried more about their sexual functioning. This is an interesting correlation for which we cannot yet find any explanation.

Data on masturbation have always been controversial in sex research. Kinsey found that, in the United States, 92 percent of subjects had achieved orgasm by self-stimulation and the percentage varied little with level of education. Other surveys show similar or much lower rates. Kinsey believed that those low rate reports could be due to underreporting,[6] since masturbation is often considered a disgraceful behavior.

Our own data are also controversial, even within China. In 1989, Lee surveyed 679 college students and found that 93.1 percent of them had masturbatory experience.[7] How then can we explain the lower rates in our sample? Can our findings be considered reliable? We believe that they can. After all, our survey profited from a higher degree of cooperation than Lee's in general, and if the students were frank and provided plausible data on behaviors such as oral and anal sex, why should they be unreliable on masturbation?

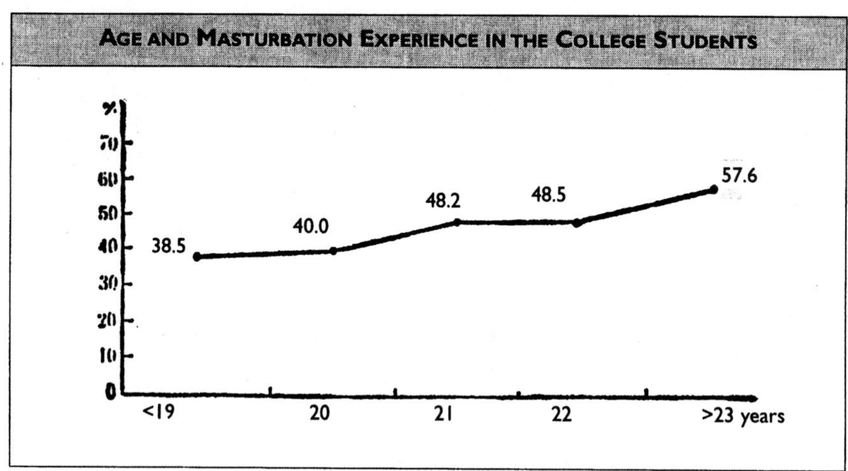

Figure 3–25

PROFESSION AND MASTURBATORY EXPERIENCE

	TOTAL	ARTS		SCIENCE		ENGIN.		AGRICUL.		MEDICINE	
		NO.	%	NO.	%	NO.	%	NO.	%	NO.	%
Yes	1242	453	44.3	210	42.2	336	48.5	13	35.1	230	35.9
No	1648	569	55.7	288	57.8	357	51.5	24	64.9	410	64.1
Total	2890	1022	100.0	498	100.0	693	100.0	37	100.0	640	100.0

Table 3–52

B. Frequency of Masturbation

According to the responses given from the report of 892 subjects who masturbated during the teenage period, 44.2 percent said they masturbated about once per week during that period , 24.2 percent twice per week, 14.6 percent thrice per week, and 17.0 percent four times or more per week. The mean frequency was 2.34 times per week with a SD of 1.82. Table 3–53 and 3–54 showed that the males and females had similar frequencies. Lower masturbation rates were found in subjects who were below age nineteen and or age twenty-three at the time of survey.

For current masturbatory frequency of the subjects (in the last three months), 492 of those who masturbated answered the question. 63.6 percent masturbated once per week, 23.2 percent twice, 5.3 percent three times, and 7.9 percent four times or more. The mean frequency was 1.72 per week with SD at 1.42. The frequency was obviously lower than that during the teenage period.

An interesting finding is that from the teenage period to the current period, there was a rise in the percentage of female students who masturbated at five times per week, from 14.9 percent to 15.7 percent. Table 3–50 and figure 3–26 show that the rate of masturbation in the females was lower than in the males in general, but in the range of high activity

Gender and Mean Masturbation Rate per Week During the Teenage Period

GENDER	TOTAL	<=2		3–4		5–6		>=7	
		NO.	%	NO.	%	NO.	%	NO.	%
Male	737	505	68.5	151	20.5	35	4.7	46	6.2
Female	107	69	64.5	22	20.6	10	9.3	6	5.6

P=0.20

Table 3–53

Age and Mean Masturbation Rate per Week During the Teenage Period

AGE	TOTAL	<=2		3–4		5–6		>=7	
		NO.	%	NO.	%	NO.	%	NO.	%
<=19	240	167	69.6	52	21.7	14	5.8	7	2.9
20	224	150	67.0	43	19.2	15	6.7	16	7.1
21	177	117	66.1	36	20.3	9	5.1	15	8.5
22	94	57	60.6	18	19.1	7	7.4	12	12.8
>=23	82	58	70.7	18	22.0	1	1.2	5	6.1

P=0.20

Table 3–54

GENDER AND CURRENT MEAN MASTURBATION RATE PER WEEK									
GENDER	TOTAL	<=2		3–4		5–6		>=7	
		NO.	%	NO.	%	NO.	%	NO.	%
Male	416	366	88.0	32	7.7	9	2.2	9	2.2
Female	51	39	76.5	4	7.8	3	5.9	5	9.8

P=0.20

Table 3–55

there were many more females than males. One explanation could be that for the females, it is generally more difficult to overcome traditional sexual taboos, but that those who do overcome them are much less inhibited as a result. Another explanation might be the small sample of females with masturbatory experience, causing statistical biases.

C. AGE OF FIRST MASTURBATION

According to the 954 subjects who reported, 7.3 percent began masturbation at age ten or below, 7.3 percent at age eleven and twelve, 23.5 percent at age thirteen and fourteen, 36.3 percent between fifteen and sixteen, and 25.6 percent at age seventeen or above. The mean age was at 14.88, SD 2.74.

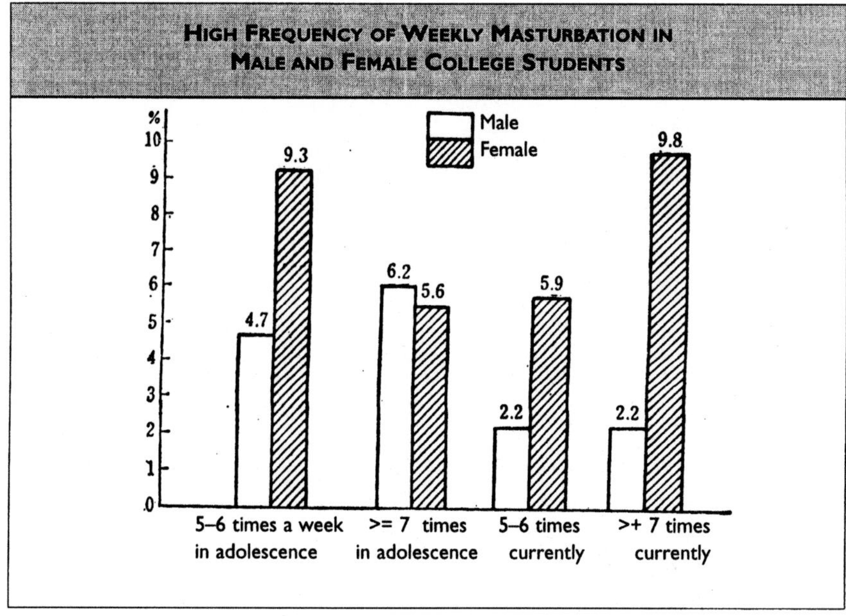

Figure 3–26

Table 3–56 shows that for the males, most of them began masturbation between the ages of thirteen and sixteen, and 10.7 percent began at age twelve or below. For the females, a much higher proportion of 34.6 percent began masturbation at age twelve or below, indicating earlier sexual development for the females.

D. Views on Masturbation

The Chinese traditional view on masturbation is that it is harmful to one's health. For thousands of years, it has been propagated that "one drop of semen is worth ten drops of blood," thus wasting this "basic yang" in the body shortens one's life. This threatening view of masturbation has imposed a heavy psychological burden on Chinese youths, adversely affecting their learning and working efficiency. In the 1980s, however, the advancement of sexual knowledge in China has gradually changed this traditional view, and thus we tried to pinpoint the attitudinal changes that might have occurred.

Gender and Age of First Masturbation

GENDER	TOTAL	<=10		11–12		13–14		15–16		>=17	
		NO.	%	NO.	%	NO.	%	NO.	%	NO.	%
Male	769	37	4.8	45	5.9	173	22.5	305	39.7	209	27.2
Female	133	27	20.3	19	14.3	37	27.8	27	20.3	23	17.3

P=0.001

Table 3–56

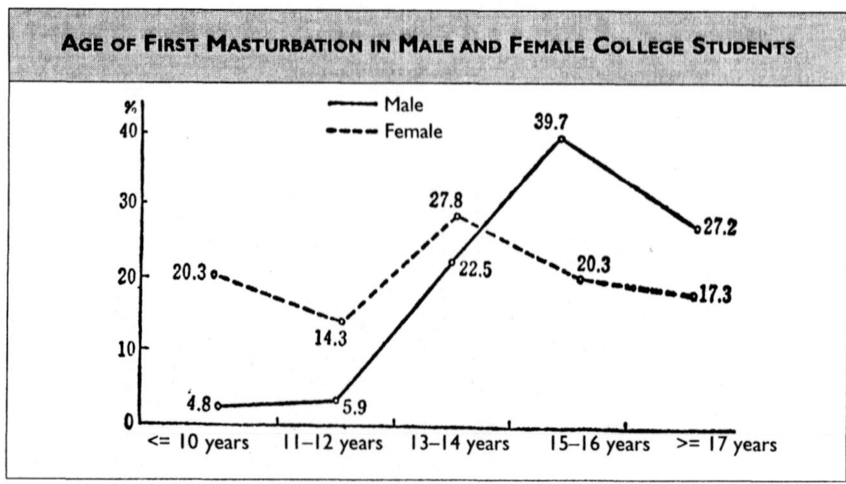

Figure 3–27

NUMBER OF COLLEGE STUDENTS CURRENTLY MASTURBATING					
GENDER	TOTAL	HAS MASTURBATION HISTORY	ENDED MASTURBATION	CURRENTLY MASTURBATING	
				NO.	%
Male	1907	1059	305	754	39.5
Female	1291	183	77	106	8.2

Table 3–57

GENDER AND TRADITIONAL VIEWS ON THE EFFECTS OF MASTURBATION							
	TOTAL	AGREE		PARTLY AGREE		DISAGREE	
		NO.	%	NO.	%	NO.	%
Male	1858	75	4.0	781	42.0	1002	53.9
Female	959	21	2.2	461	48.1	477	49.7

P=0.01

Table 3–58

PROFESSION AND TRADITIONAL VIEWS ON MASTURBATION											
VIEW	TOTAL	ARTS		SCIENCE		ENGIN.		AGRICUL.		MEDICINE	
		NO.	%	NO.	%	NO.	%	NO.	%	NO.	%
Agree	100	36	3.7	17	3.6	22	3.3	1	2.9	24	3.7
Partly agree	1236	414	42.2	222	46.9	287	42.7	15	42.9	298	46.1
Disagree	1470	530	54.1	234	49.5	363	54.0	19	54.3	324	50.2
Total	2806	980	100.0	473	100.0	672	100.0	35	100.0	646	100.0

Table 3–59

GENDER AND MORAL VIEWS ON MASTURBATION							
	TOTAL	NORMAL		UNETHICAL		CRIMINAL	
		NO.	%	NO.	%	NO.	%
Male	1823	1522	83.5	231	12.7	70	3.8
Female	1077	591	54.9	348	32.3	138	12.8

P=0.001

Table 3–60

Only 3.7 percent of the 2956 students who responded to this question strongly agreed with the view that "One drop of semen is as precious

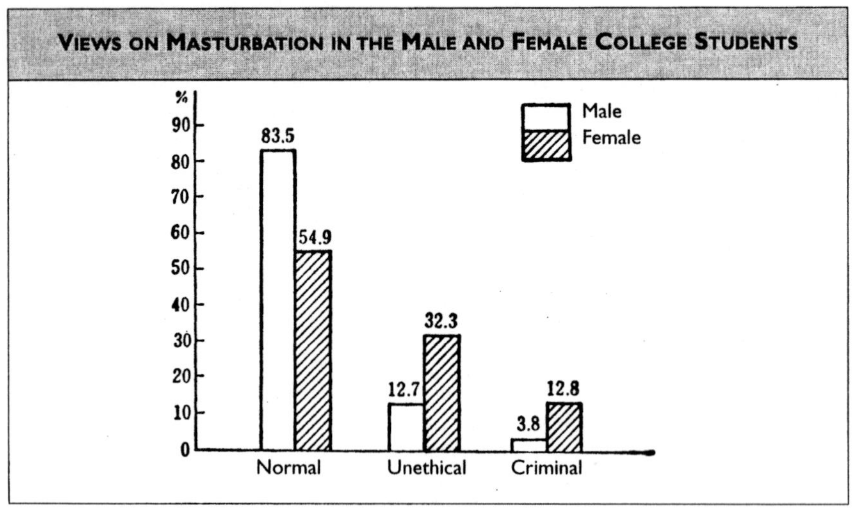

Figure 3–28

REGIONAL DISTRIBUTION BY AGE OF SUBJECTS WHO FELT MASTURBATION WAS NORMAL

REGION	TOTAL	<=19		20		21		22		>=23	
		NO.	%	NO.	%	NO.	%	NO.	%	NO.	%
Chengu	228	85	67.5	65	70.7	54	76.1	14	70.0	10	90.9
Xiamen	401	167	67.9	114	87.0	59	79.7	32	86.5	29	82.9
Shanghi Fudan U	186	37	54.4	47	64.4	52	86.7	28	87.5	22	95.7

Table 3–61

as ten drops of blood," 44.0 percent agreed somewhat, and 52.3 percent disagreed. This shows that many college students have abandoned the traditional view, but nearly half of them are still influenced by it. More males than females disagreed with the traditional view (table 3–58).

The division of views was found in all regions and professions. Slightly more of the arts or medical students disagreed with the traditional view, most likely because they were more sexually open or knowledgeable.

Another type of view on masturbation is a moralistic one. 65.0 percent of all those surveyed thought masturbation was normal, 18.2 percent thought it was unethical, 6.4 percent thought it criminal, and 9.6 percent did not answer. Fewer males than females thought that masturbation was unethical or criminal, showing that females were much more influenced by tradition.

AGE AND VIEW ON MASTURBATION

AGE	TOTAL	NORMAL		UNETHICAL		CRIMINAL	
		NO.	%	NO.	%	NO.	%
<=19	903	580	64.2	240	26.6	83	9.2
20	771	569	73.8	149	19.3	53	6.9
21	571	443	77.6	95	16.6	33	5.8
22	290	236	81.4	36	12.4	18	6.2
>=23	195	162	83.1	24	12.3	9	4.6

Table 3–62

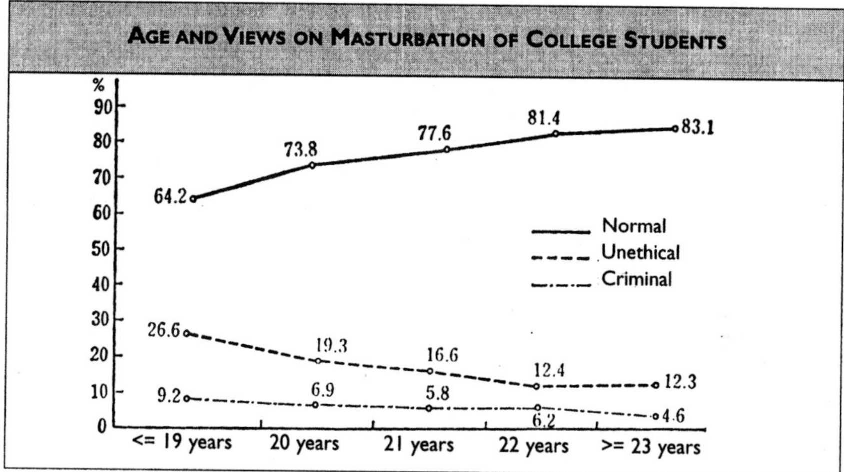

Figure 3–29

The older a subject was, the more he/she felt that masturbation was normal (G=0.23). This was irrespective of regional differences (tables 3–61 and 3–62).

PROFESSION AND VIEW ON MASTURBATION

VIEW	TOTAL	ARTS		SCIENCE		ENGIN.		AGRICUL.		MEDICINE	
		NO.	%	NO.	%	NO.	%	NO.	%	NO.	%
Normal	2101	771	74.9	351	71.3	511	75.0	24	60.0	444	69.5
Unethical	572	183	17.8	110	22.4	131	19.2	10	25.0	138	21.6
Criminal	209	76	7.4	31	6.3	39	5.7	6	15.0	57	8.9
Total	2882	1030	100.0	492	100.0	681	100.0	40	100.0	639	100.0

Table 3–63

Gender and View on Effect of Masturbation

GENDER	TOTAL	GOOD IF PROPERLY		NOT GOOD OR HARMFUL		SMALL HARM		GREAT HARM	
		NO.	%	NO.	%	NO.	%	NO.	%
Male	1844	748	40.6	380	20.6	454	24.6	262	14.2
Female	1080	220	20.4	194	18.0	262	24.3	404	37.4

P=0.001

Table 3–64

Age and View on the Effect of Masturbation

AGE	TOTAL	GOOD IF PROPERLY		NOT GOOD OR HARMFUL		SMALL HARM		GREAT HARM	
		NO.	%	NO.	%	NO.	%	NO.	%
<=19	896	249	27.8	173	19.3	226	25.2	248	27.7
20	779	260	33.4	153	19.6	187	24.0	179	23.0
21	582	209	35.9	111	19.1	143	24.6	119	20.4
22	297	120	40.4	58	19.5	67	22.6	52	17.5
>=23	198	80	40.4	38	19.2	51	25.8	29	14.6

P=0.001

Table 3–65

Of those who thought masturbation was normal, art students represented the greatest number. It appeared that on many sexual matters, art students were more open. This tendency becomes more obvious in the following sections.

We also asked the subjects about their overall attitude toward masturbation. In all the subjects surveyed, 30.1 percent thought masturbation was proper and beneficial, 17.9 percent thought it was neither harmful nor

View on the Consequences of Masturbation in the Male and Female College Students

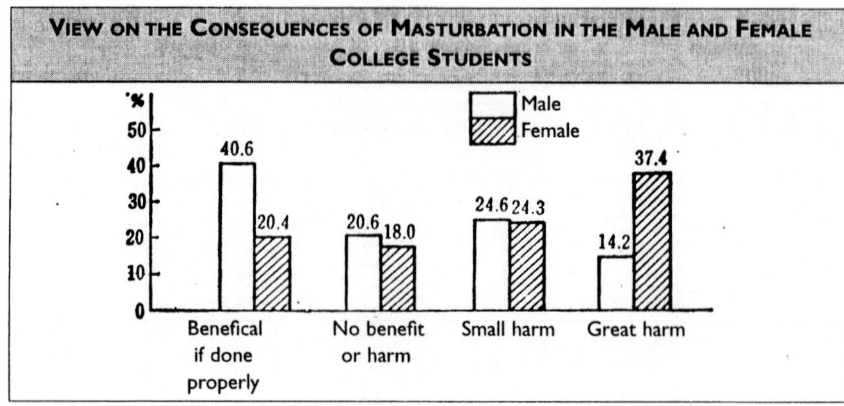

Figure 3–30

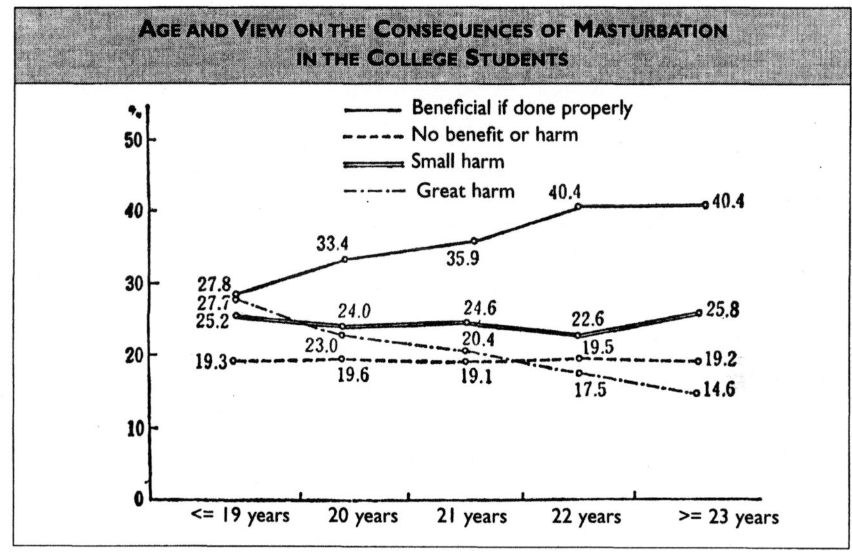

Figure 3–31

GENDER AND EXPERIENCE OF MASTURBATING WITH SAME SEX

	TOTAL	YES		NO	
		NO.	%	NO.	%
Male	1778	153	8.6	1625	91.4
Female	1108	35	3.2	1073	96.8

P=0.001

Table 3–66

beneficial, 22.3 percent thought it was mildly harmful, 20.8 percent thought it very harmful, and 8.9 percent did not answer.

In table 3–64, grouping the students according to their view, it was shown that in males the ratio between "is harmless" and "is harmful" was about six to four; in the females, the ratio was about four to six. The older the students, the higher the percentage of them held a positive attitude toward masturbation (G=0.12).

GENDER AND NUMBER OF SEXUAL PARTNERS

GENDER	TOTAL	NO		YES		1		2–5		>=6	
		NO.	%	NO.	%	NO.	%	NO.	%	NO.	%
Male	454	216	47.6	238	52.4	144	60.5	84	35.3	10	4.2
Female	168	87	51.8	81	48.2	63	77.8	15	18.5	3	3.7

Table 3–67

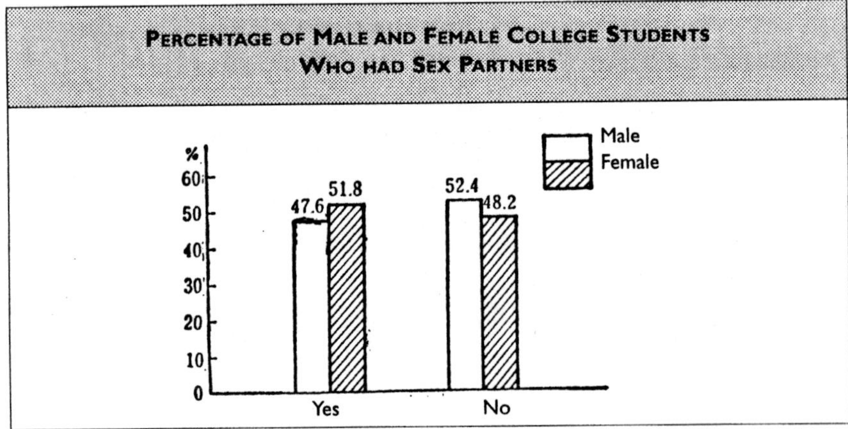

Figure 3–32

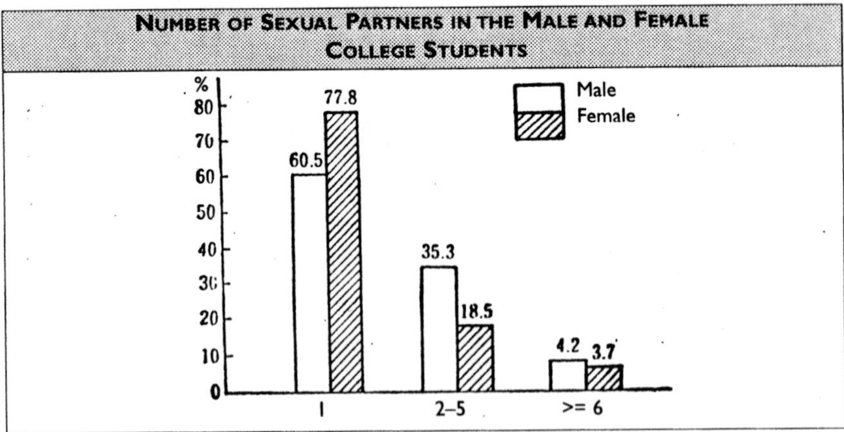

Figure 3–33

As for same-sex mutual masturbation, 5.8 percent of the respondents reported having had the experience, 8.4 percent answered no, and 10.2 percent did not answer. There were more males than females reporting such experiences. It is difficult to say whether the experiences were simply due to curiosity or reflected genuine homosexual interests.

Kinsey reported that 90 percent of the whole population had a history of masturbation. Our findings also show a high proportion of such.

2. Sexual Partners

By sexual partner, we mean a partner with whom one engages in coitus. Of the 640 subjects who answered this question, 312 (48.8 percent) reported

PROFESSION AND NUMBER OF SEX PARTNERS											
NUMBER	TOTAL	ARTS		SCIENCE		ENGIN.		AGRICUL.		MEDICINE	
		NO.	%	NO.	%	NO.	%	NO.	%	NO.	%
0	298	62	33.2	37	42.0	122	61.3	4	50.0	73	57.9
1	201	73	39.0	34	38.4	56	28.1	2	25.0	36	28.6
2–5	96	46	24.6	13	14.8	20	10.1	2	25.0	15	11.9
6–10	5	2	1.1	2	2.3	0	0	0	0	1	0.8
>10	8	4	2.1	2	2.3	1	0.5	0	0	1	0.8
Total	608	187	100.0	88	100.0	199	100.0	8	100.0	126	100.0

Table 3–68

AGE AND NUMBER OF SEX PARTNERS									
AGE	TOTAL	UNKNOWN		1		2–5		>=6	
		NO.	%	NO.	%	NO.	%	NO.	%
<=19	1010	962	95.2	34	3.4	13	1.3	1	0.1
20	843	786	93.2	37	4.4	17	2.0	3	0.4
21	625	546	87.4	48	7.7	26	4.2	5	0.8
22	311	245	78.8	46	14.8	18	5.8	2	0.6
>=23	210	156	74.3	30	14.3	23	11.0	1	0.5

Table 3–69

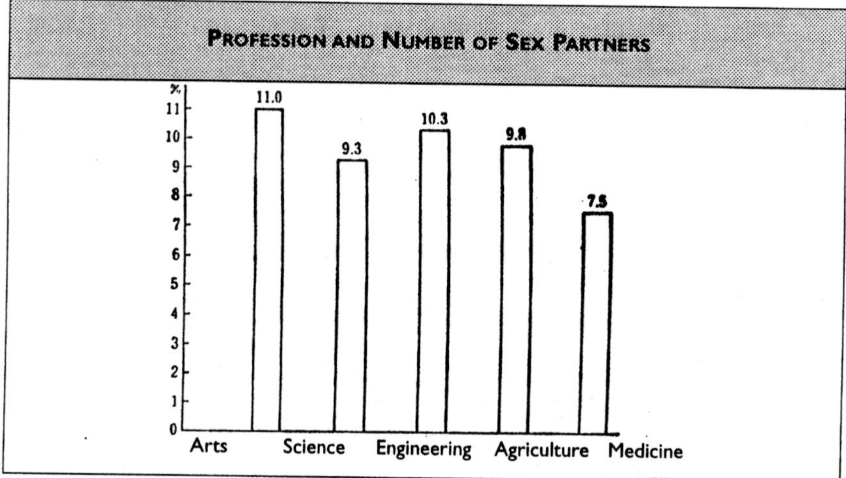

Figure 3–34

none; 213 (33.3 percent) reported having one such partner; 101 (15.8 percent) reported having had two to five; 6 (0.9 percent) reported having

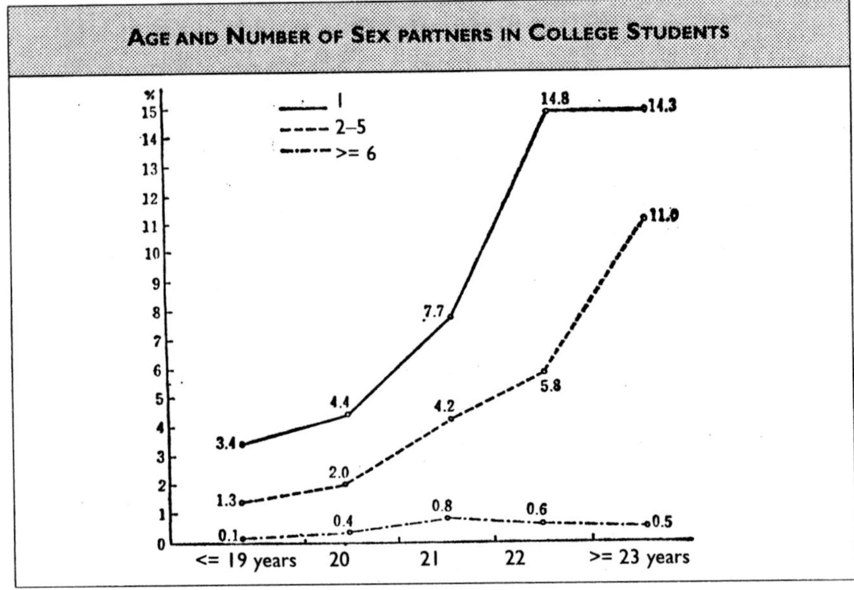

Figure 3–35

had six to ten and 8 (1.3 percent) reported having ten or more partners. Hence, a total of 328 subjects (9.8 percent) of the college students had had sexual partners (gender distribution: table 3–67).

Of the male students, 12.5 percent had sexual partners; of the females, 6.3 percent had such partners. A greater proportion of the males had multiple sexual partners (table 3–67, figures 3–32 and 3–33). Based on the desired professions of the students, those with partners were: arts 11.0 percent, science 9.3 percent, engineering 10.3 percent, agriculture 9.8 percent, and medicine 7.5 percent. The detailed number of partners are listed in table 3–68.

The older the subjects were, the higher the percentage became of those who had sex partners (G=0.45) (table 3–69, figure 3–35).

Of those who had sex partners, 328 used contraception. Of these, fifty-eight (17.7 percent) took pills, twenty-five (7.6 percent) used spermicide, sixty (18.3 percent) used condoms, fifteen (4.6 percent) used a diaphragm, forty-two (12.8 percent) practiced coitus interruptus, ninety-nine (30.2 percent) used the rhythm method, twenty-seven (8.2 percent) used miscellaneous methods, and two (0.6 percent) did not specify any method. This shows that among college students, there was sufficient knowledge of contraception, but the fact that 30.2 percent of them used the rhythm period indicates that they either could not afford the cost of other, more effective contraceptive methods or were ignorant of its poore effectiveness.

3. Heterosexual Activity

A. TYPES OF HETEROSEXUAL ACTIVITY

We divided sexual contact into coital and noncoital activities.

Of the surveyed population,1004 subjects (29.9 percent) reported having experienced erotic hugging of the opposte sex; 902 (26.8 percent) reported kissing, 362 (10.8 percent) gential touching, and 215 (6.4

GENDER AND EXPERIENCE OF EROTIC HUGGING OF THE OTHER SEX

	FREQUENCY					MANNER							FEELING						
	Often		Occ.		T	Active		Passive		Forced		T	Good		Bad		None		T
	NO.	%	NO.	%		NO.	%	NO.	%	NO.	%		NO.	%	NO.	%	NO.	%	
Male	187	33.8	366	66.2	553	491	91.1	45	8.3	3	0.6	539	466	87.3	5	0.9	63	11.8	534
Female	124	29.2	301	70.8	425	134	32.4	270	65.4	9	2.2	413	324	77.9	25	6.0	67	16.1	416

Table 3–70

GENDER AND EXPEREIENCE WITH OTHER SEX ON KISSING

	FREQUENCY					MANNER							FEELING						
	Often		Occ.		T	Active		Passive		Forced		T	Good		Bad		None		T
	NO.	%	NO.	%		NO.	%	NO.	%	NO.	%		NO.	%	NO.	%	NO.	%	
Male	177	35.8	318	64.2	495	441	91.7	34	7.1	6	1.2	481	428	88.8	12	2.5	42	8.7	482
Female	112	29.1	273	70.9	385	115	31.5	234	64.1	16	4.4	365	271	74.0	28	7.7	67	18.3	366

Table 3–71

GENDER AND EXPERIENCE OF TOUCHING GENITALS WITH OTHER SEX

	FREQUENCY					MANNER							FEELING						
	Often		Occ.		T	Active		Passive		Forced		T	Good		Bad		None		T
	NO.	%	NO.	%		NO.	%	NO.	%	NO.	%		NO.	%	NO.	%	NO.	%	
Male	64	25.3	187	74.7	253	215	89.2	22	9.1	4	1.7	241	197	82.1	11	4.6	32	13.3	240
Female	14	14.1	85	85.9	99	25	25.8	61	62.9	11	11.3	97	55	57.3	21	21.9	20	20.8	96

Table 3–72

Gender and Experience of Coitus with the Other Sex																			
	FREQUENCY					MANNER							FEELING						
	Often		Occ.		T	Active		Passive		Forced		T	Good		Bad		None		T
	NO.	%	NO.	%		NO.	%	NO.	%	NO.	%		NO.	%	NO.	%	NO.	%	
Male	39	25.2	116	74.8	155	146	94.8	4	2.6	4	2.6	154	139	89.7	5	3.2	11	7.1	155
Female	8	14.5	47	85.5	55	18	34.0	32	60.4	3	5.7	53	39	75.0	6	11.5	7	13.5	52

Table 3–73

percent) had coitus. There could, of course, be a great deal of overlapping among these behaviors, but if sensual hugging is used as an indicator of subjects engaging in intimate relationships, then 30.0 percent of the college students could be said to have arrived at or passed this stage. The percentage of male students in this category was 29.0 percent, with females at 32.9 percent.

In 1989, Ming-xiao Zhou of Shanghai did a survey on the love life of 150 female college students. She found that thirty-two (21.3 percent) of them had suitors whom they rejected; twenty-one (14 percent) of them had "fancied" somebody but did not put the feeling into action; thirty-one (20.6 percent) of them were in love; and sixty-three (42.0 percent) of them decided not to have any heterosexual friendship while in college. These figures are lower than ours, but not to any significant degree.

Tables 3–70, 3–71, 3–72, and 3–73 show the frequency of sexual intercourse, as well as attitudes and feelings about the experience.

From these tables, it can be seen that most of the students had only occasional sexual intercourse, probably because of the surrounding moral attitudes which forced them into secrecy. In these experiences, it was the males who most often took the initiative, with most of them enjoying the experience.

Age of First Coitus											
GENDER	TOTAL	<=13		14–16		17–19		20–22		>=23	
		NO.	%	NO.	%	NO.	%	NO.	%	NO.	%
Male	269	32	11.9	34	12.6	79	29.4	91	33.8	33	12.3
Female	89	3	3.4	9	10.1	32	36.0	36	40.4	9	10.1

Table 3–74

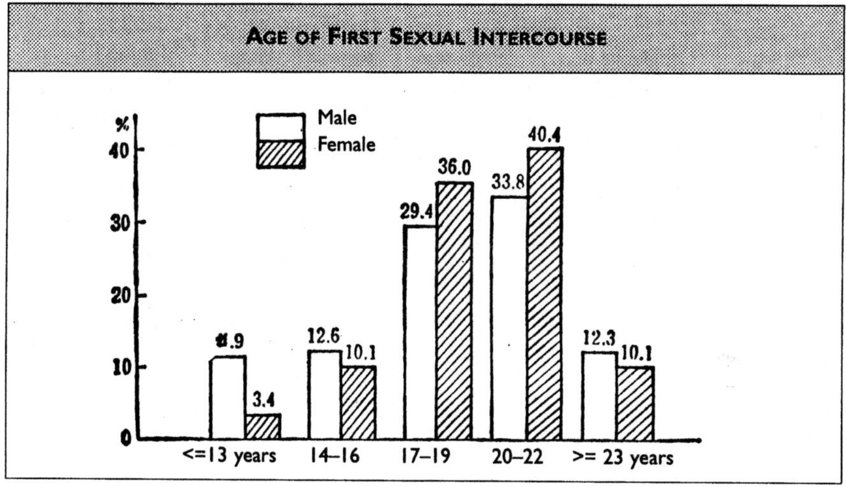

Figure 3–36

B. AGE OF FIRST SEXUAL INTERCOURSE

In the self-report of 372 students, 40 (10.8 percent) started having sexual intercourse before age thirteen, 43 (11.6 percent) between fourteen and sixteen, 114 (30.6 percent) between seventeen and nineteen, 130 (34.9 percent) between twenty-one and twenty-two, and 45 (12.1 percent) above age twenty-three. The mean age starting for sexual intercourse was 18.78 years, the standard deviation being 3.44.

From the facing table and figure above, it can be seen that most of the students had first engaged in sexual intercourse between the ages of seventeen and twenty-two; 63.2 percent of the male students and 76.4 percent of the females who had sexual intercourse started the activity in this age range. In those who started before age sixteen, there were many more males (24.5 percent) than females (13.5 percent). This shows that the males in China are today relatively free and easy in respect to sex, even in comparison with many Western counties.

The mean age in college students of starting to embrace a friend of the other sex was 18.74 (SD=4.52), to kiss 19.06 (SD=4.02), to begin

GENDER AND AGE STARTED EROTIC HUGGING OF THE OTHER SEX

GENDER	TOTAL	<=13		14–16		17–19		20–22		>=23	
		NO.	%	NO.	%	NO.	%	NO.	%	NO.	%
Male	452	22	4.9	44	9.7	199	44.0	161	35.6	26	5.8
Female	382	7	1.8	31	8.1	177	46.3	158	41.4	9	2.4

Table 3–75

GENDER AND AGE STARTING KISSING WITH THE OTHER SEX											
GENDER	TOTAL	<=13		14–16		17–19		20–22		>=23	
		NO.	%	NO.	%	NO.	%	NO.	%	NO.	%
Male	400	11	2.8	33	8.3	181	45.3	149	37.3	26	6.5
Female	336	4	1.2	14	4.2	159	47.3	152	45.2	7	2.1

Table 3–76

GENDER AND AGE OF STARTING TOUCHING GENITALIA WITH THE OTHER SEX											
GENDER	TOTAL	<=13		14–16		17–19		20–22		>=23	
		NO.	%	NO.	%	NO.	%	NO.	%	NO.	%
Male	199	25	12.6	24	12.1	68	34.2	64	32.2	18	9.0
Female	85	1	1.2	8	9.4	25	29.4	46	54.1	5	5.9

Table 3–77

GENDER AND AGE STARTING COITUS WITH THE OTHER SEX											
GENDER	TOTAL	<=13		14–16		17–19		20–22		>=23	
		NO.	%	NO.	%	NO.	%	NO.	%	NO.	%
Male	121	12	9.9	17	14.0	32	26.4	44	36.4	16	13.2
Female	50	6	12.0	5	10.0	13	26.0	23	46.0	3	6.0

Table 3–78

AGE AND PERCENTAGE OF MALE AND FEMALE COLLEGE STUDENTS WHO HAD SEXUAL EMBRACE WITH THE OTHER SEX

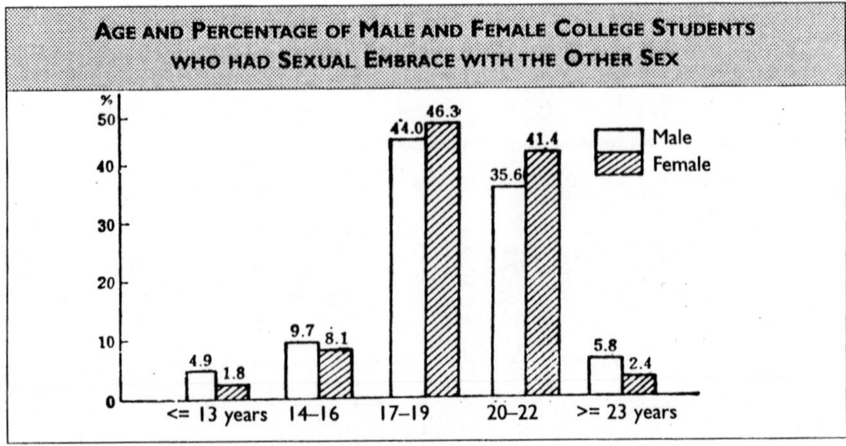

Figure 3–37

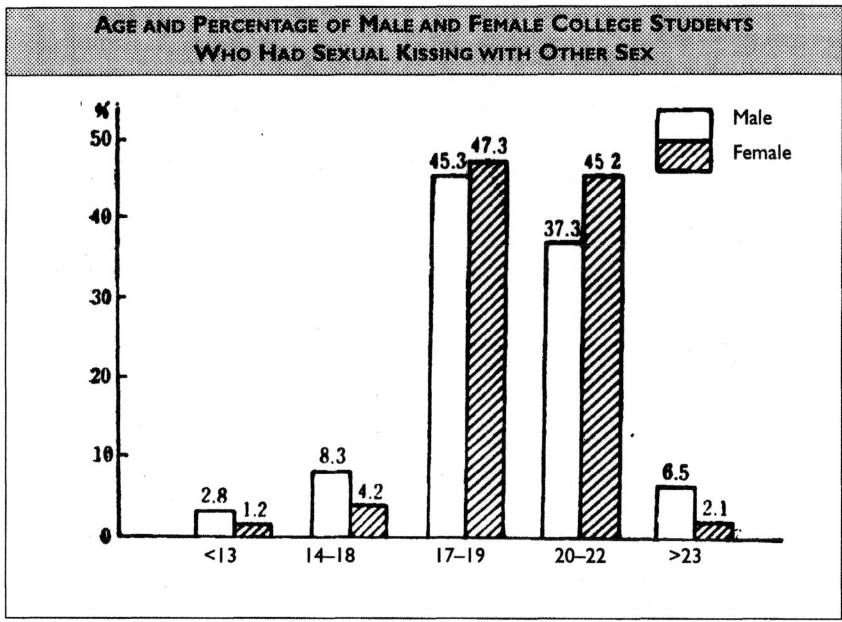

Age and Percentage of Male and Female College Students Who Had Sexual Kissing with Other Sex

Figure 3–38

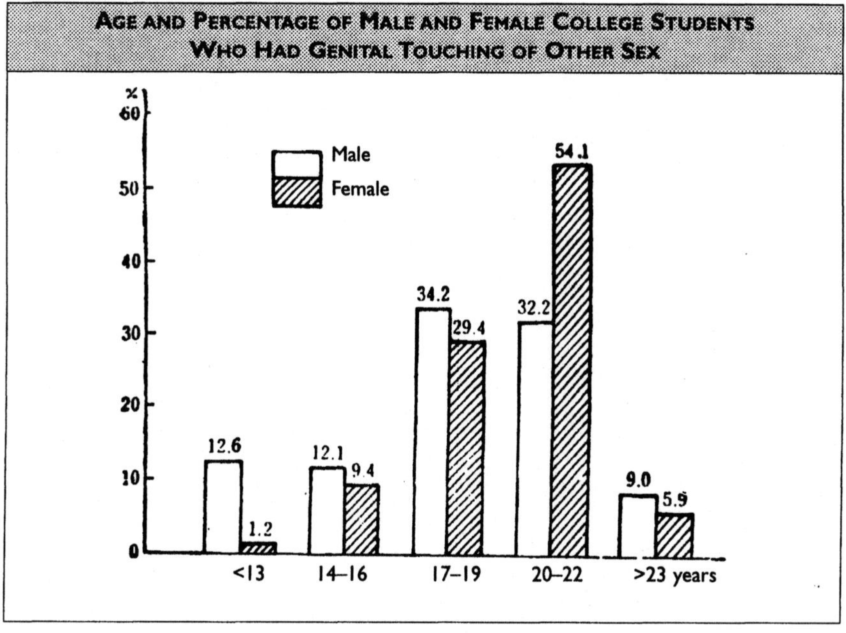

Age and Percentage of Male and Female College Students Who Had Genital Touching of Other Sex

Figure 3–39

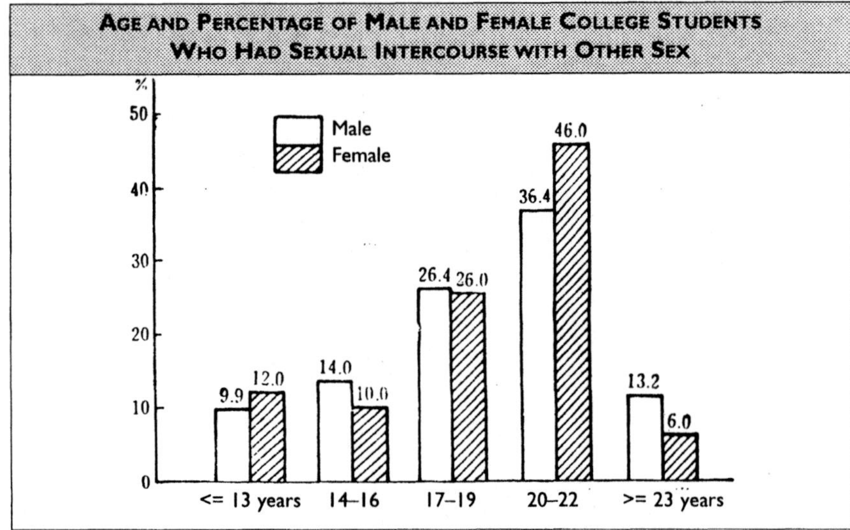

Figure 3–40

genital fondling 18.35 (SD=4.03), and to start sexual genital intercourse 18.41 (SD=4.13), to start anal intercourse 17.41 (SD=5.16), and to start oral sex 17.10 (SD=6.69).

The ages for male and female students starting to engage in various sexual activities are shown in tables 3–75, 3–76, 3–77, 3–78.

The tables show that the majority of college students who engaged in various sexual activities fell within the same age range as those students who first had sexual intercourse, between seventeen and twenty-two. The preceding tables show that the majority of college students who engaged in various sexual activities fell within the same age range as those students who first had sexual intercourse, between seventeen and twenty-two.

4. Homosexual Activity

It was very difficult to elicit much truly meaningful information concerning homosexual interests by means of our relatively simple questionnaire. We could only rely on specific behavior as a more objective and concrete indicator. Even so, it was still difficult to ensure that the respondents really understood the question. They had to realize that we were asking about behaviors that express genuine homosexual desires. For example, hugging a person of the same sex, in our sense, was not supposed to mean ordinary hugging between son and father or between social friends for nonerotic reasons. We were talking about hugging that

Gender and Experience of Erotic Hugging of Same Sex																					
	FREQUENCY					MANNER							FEELING								
	Often		Occ.		T	Active		Passive		Forced		T	Good		Bad		None		T
	NO.	%	NO.	%		NO.	%	NO.	%	NO.	%		NO.	%	NO.	%	NO.	%	
Male	28	20.4	106	77.4	137	92	73.0	25	19.8	9	7.1	126	68	49.6	11	8.0	58	42.3	137
Female	35	30.7	74	64.9	114	78	75.0	20	19.2	6	5.8	104	73	64.0	6	5.8	35	30.7	114

Table 3–79

Gender and Experience Kissing Same Sex																					
	FREQUENCY							MANNER							FEELING						
	Often		Occ.		Miss'g.		T	Active		Passive		Forced		T	Good		Bad		None		T
	NO.	%	NO.	%		NO.	%	NO.	%	NO.	%	NO.	%		NO.	%	NO.	%	NO.	%	
M	18	30.5	34	47.6	7	11.9	59	39	72.2	11	20.4	4	7.4	54	35	59.3	10	16.9	14	23.7	59
F	9	32.1	19	67.9	0	0	28	17	77.3	4	18.2	1	4.5	2	19	67.9	0	0	9	32.1	28

Table 3–80

Gender and Experience Touching Genitalia with Same Sex																					
	FREQUENCY							MANNER							FEELING						
	Often		Occ.		Miss'g.		T	Active		Passive		Forced		T	Good		Bad		None		T
	NO.	%	NO.	%		NO.	%	NO.	%	NO	%	NO.	%		NO.	%	NO.	%	NO.	%	
M	18	28.6	40	63.5	5	7.9	63	38	62.3	18	29.5	5	8.2	61	41	65.1	10	15.9	12	19.0	63
F	1	11.1	8	88.9	0	0	9	2	33.3	3	50.0	1	16.7	6	3	37.5	3	37.5	2	25.0	8

Table 3–81

Gender and Experience of Sexual Intercourse with the Same Sex																					
	FREQUENCY							MANNER							FEELING						
	Often		Occ.		Miss'g.		T	Active		Passive		Forced		T	Good		Bad		None		T
	NO.	%	NO.	%		NO.	%	NO.	%	NO.	%	NO.	%		NO.	%	NO.	%	NO.	%	
M	6	14	23	53.5	14	32.5	43	13	35.1	17	45.9	7	18.9	37	16	37.2	17	39.5	10	23.3	43
F	0	0	4	66.6	2	33.3	6	1	20.0	2	40.0	2	40.0	5	3	50.0	0	0	3	50.0	6

Table 3–82

involved at least a certain erotic interest of some sort on the part of at least one of the participants. Unfortunately, it is very difficult to draw a clear line here, since different degrees of intimacy or arousal on one side or the other can and do creep into the picture.

Of all the respondents, 251 (7.5 percent) reported an experience of same-sex erotic hugging, eighty-two (2.4 percent) reported kissing, sixty-eight (0.2 percent) reported genital fondling, twenty (0.6 percent) reported anal sex, and thirteen (0.4 percent) reported oral sex. If same-sex erotic hugging is taken as an indicator of homosexual interest, then 7.5 percent of the college students had homosexual interests (i.e., 7.0 percent of the males and 8.4 percent of the females).

Tables 3–79, 3–80, 3–81, and 3–82 show that most of the students' homosexual activities were performed occasionally, not frequently or

GENDER AND AGE OF BEGINNING EROTIC HUGGING WITH SAME SEX											
GENDER	TOTAL	<=13		14–16		17–19		20–22		>=23	
		NO.	%	NO.	%	NO.	%	NO.	%	NO.	%
Male	105	24	22.9	28	26.7	40	38.1	12	11.4	1	1.0
Female	78	19	24.4	30	38.5	21	26.9	7	9.0	1	1.3

Table 3–83

GENDER AND AGE BEGINNING KISSING SAME SEX											
GENDER	TOTAL	<=13		14–16		17–19		20–22		>=23	
		NO.	%	NO.	%	NO.	%	NO.	%	NO.	%
Male	50	8	16.0	13	26.0	20	40.0	7	14.0	2	4.0
Female	20	4	20.0	7	35.0	5	25.0	4	20.0	0	0

Table 3–84

GENDER AND AGE BEGINNING TOUCHING GENITALIA OF SAME SEX											
GENDER	TOTAL	<=13		14–16		17–19		20–22		>=23	
		NO.	%	NO.	%	NO.	%	NO.	%	NO.	%
Male	51	14	27.5	18	35.3	15	29.4	2	3.9	2	3.9
Female	8	3	37.5	2	25.0	2	25.0	1	12.5	0	0

Table 3–85

GENDER AND AGE BEGINNING SEXUAL CONTACT WITH SAME SEX												
GENDER	TOTAL	<=13		14–16		17–19		20–22		>=23	
		NO.	%	NO.	%	NO.	%	NO.	%	NO.	%
Male	32	8	25.0	6	18.7	11	34.4	4	12.5	3	9.4
Female	5	0	0	3	60.0	1	20.0	1	20.0	0	0

Table 3–86

AGE AND PERCENTAGE OF MALE AND FEMALE COLLEGE STUDENTS WHO EXPERIENCED EROTIC HUGGING OF SAME SEX

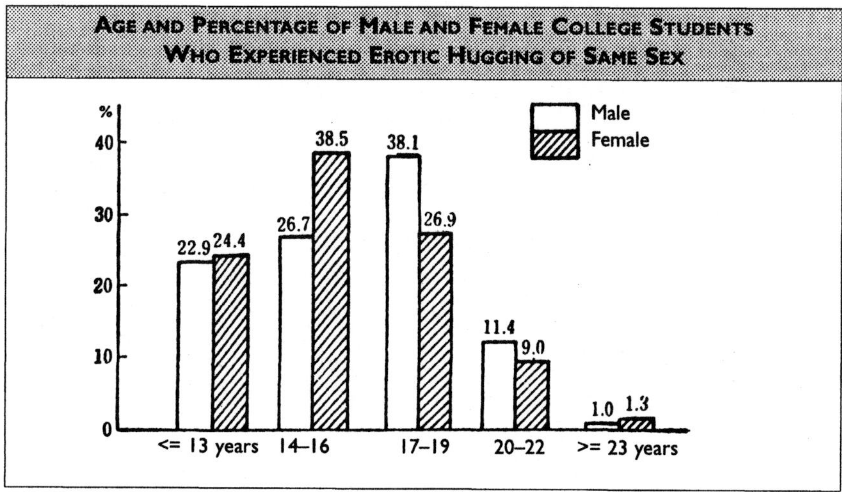

Figure 3–41

AGE AND PERCENTAGE OF MALE AND FEMALE COLLEGE STUDENTS WHO KISSED SOMEONE OF THE SAME SEX

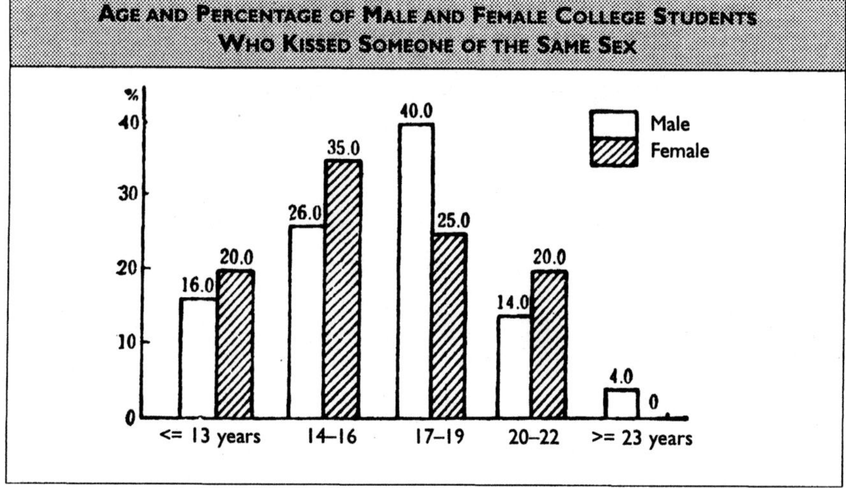

Figure 3–42

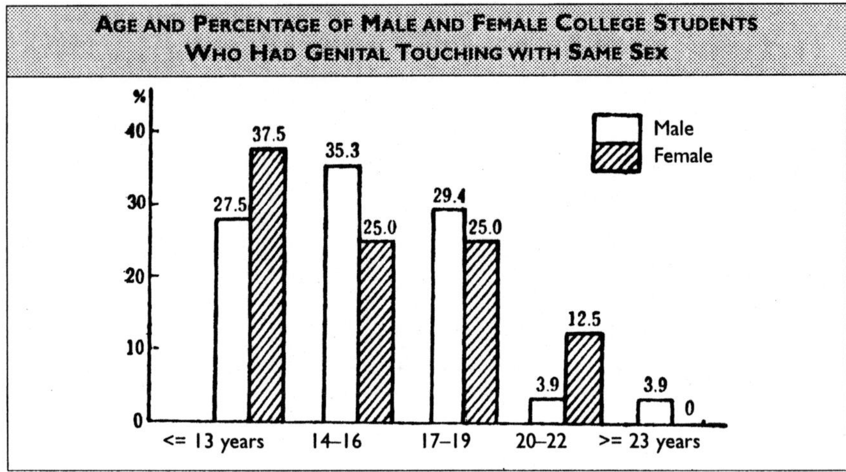

Figure 3–43

regularly. This, of course, may also be due to the living conditions on campus. They took the initiatives in embracing, and kissing, but were more passive in genital fondling and oral or anal sex. Compared with heterosexual activities, more homosexual activities were forced upon the subjects against their will.

It was found that 50-60 percent of the college students who had engaged in homosexual activities had begun this behavior before the age of sixteen. Quite a number of them had started before the age of thirteen. In view of the vagueness of the questionnaire and the likelihood of misunderstandings on the part of the subjects, we cannot be sure whether or not everyone had really understood the questions or had perhaps included playful behaviors of a nonsexual nature. The possibility of misunderstanding is even higher as we come to our findings in the preceding tables, which show that sexual activities such as anal and oral intercourse happened to a considerable number of subjects before the age of thirteen. Could the figures really be true, indicating that our children are becoming progressively precocious, or are we dealing here with simple exploratory childhood games due to sexual ignorance and attempts at satisfying a "normal" curiosity?

Kinsey faced similar problems of definition in his reports. He spoke generally of "homosexual experiences,"[8] but also more specifically of "physical intimacy leading to orgasm."[9] He counted purely psychological reactions as well as overt acts and combined both in his famous "Kinsey scale" ranging from zero (exclusively heterosexual behavior) to six (exclusively homosexual behavior). In any case, the social and financial constraints of our survey precluded us from going into the same detail as Kinsey. Thus, it also became impossible to gather enough data for distribution along a Kinsey-type scale. Thus, unfortunately, our results in this area are more than unsatisfactory. Again, we can only point to the very real difficulties of obtaining any data at all. Inadequate as they are, they do, however, show that homosexual interests and indeed acts are to be found in modern China.

Great discrepancies exist among different surveys on the rate of homosexuality. In 1936, Ellis estimated the rate in the United Kingdom to be 2-5 percent. Hirschfeld, before World War I, estimated a similar rate in Germany. In 1947, Singer found the rate to be 27 percent among college students in the United States, and in Kinsey's survey, practically one half (50 percent) of the male subjects had at least one homosexual experience to the point of orgasm after reaching puberty.[10] This, of course, did not mean that all these men were "homosexuals," a term Kinsey declined to use for the characterization of persons. He spoke only of homosexual behavior. Because of our inadequate research instrument, our results help little to clarify the existing confusion.

Gender and Anticipatory Knowledge about Ejaculation and Menstruation

GENDER	TOTAL	YES		NO	
		NO.	%	NO.	%
Male	1863	1289	69.2	574	30.8
Female	1275	918	72.0	357	28.0

P=0.05

Table 3–87

Gender & Psychological Reaction to First Ejaculation or Menstruation

GENDER	TOTAL	PREPARED, NOT AFRAID		PREPARED, BUT AFRAID		UNPREPARED, AFRAID		UNPREPARED, NOT AFRAID	
		NO.	%	NO.	%	NO.	%	NO.	%
Male	1845	354	19.2	133	7.2	197	10.7	1161	62.9
Female	1271	253	19.9	277	21.8	326	25.6	415	32.7

P=0.001

Table 3–88

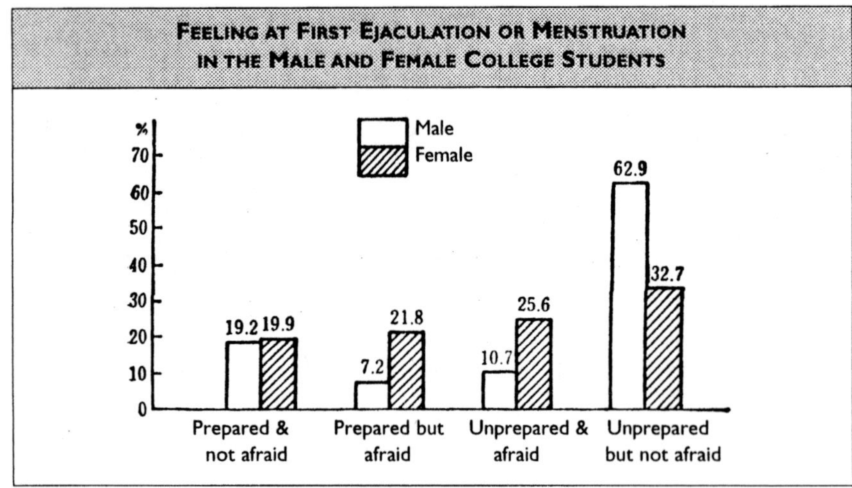

Figure 3–44

5. Sexual Knowledge and Education

A. FUNDAMENTAL KNOWLEDGE

We found that 68.6 percent of the students anticipated emissions during sleep or menstruation before puberty, 29.2 percent did not, 2.2 percent did not answer. Males and females were about the same, showing that the preparation for the sexual development during puberty was generally inadequate (table 3–87).

Of all college students, 18.8 percent had some psychological preparation and no fearful reaction to the first physiological sign of puberty, 12.6 percent had fearful reactions despite some psychological preparation, 16.4 percent had no preparation and were fearful, 49.3 percent were not prepared but were also not fearful, and 2.7 percent did not answer the question. Overall, 73.6 percent of the males and 58.3 percent of the females were poorly prepared, indicating a lack of correct sexual knowledge (table 3–88 and figure 3–44).

Our data suggests many similarities between the Chinese and Westerners, as well as between the past and the present. For example, in 1896 Havelock Ellis surveyed 125 female students in America, thirty-six (28.8 percent) of which reported a total ignorance concerning menstruation at the time of menarche. It seems that our situation in China is not much better than the situation in America, dating back about one hundred years ago.

Of those who knew about and expected menstruation or nocturnal emissions, 56.8 percent obtained the information in biology or health

GENDER AND SOURCE OF KNOWLEDGE AFTER EJACULATION OR MENSTRUATION														
	TOTAL NO.	HYGIENE LESSONS		OUTSIDE READING		PARENTS		SIBLINGS		CLASS-MATES		OTHERS	
		NO.	%	NO.	%	NO.	%	NO.	%	NO.	%	NO.	%
Male	1313	873	66.5	354	27.0	11	0.8	5	0.4	48	3.7	22	1.7
Female	911	385	42.3	89	9.8	165	18.1	46	5.0	191	21.0	35	3.8

P=0.001

Table 3–89

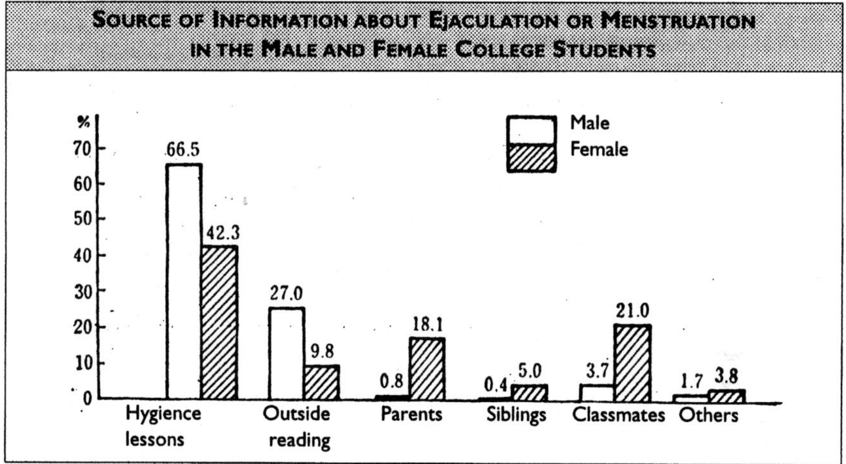

Figure 3–45

classes, 19.7 percent obtained it through extracurricular reading, 7.7 percent were taught by their parents, 2.3 percent by their siblings, 11.0 percent by their senior classmates, and 2.5 percent were informed by miscellaneous sources.

From table 3–89, many more male college students than females received the information in biology or health classes. More females were informed by relatives or classmates. This illustrates that our society pays more attention to developmental changes among females.

The same differences occurred when young people had to seek answers concerning pubertal changes. On menstruation or nocturnal emissions, 1.1 percent of the subjects asked their fathers, 28.7 percent asked the mothers, 3.4 percent their friends or classmates, 0.4 percent their teachers, 2.65 their senior classmate, 60.3 percent asked no one, and 3.3 percent did not give any clear answer.

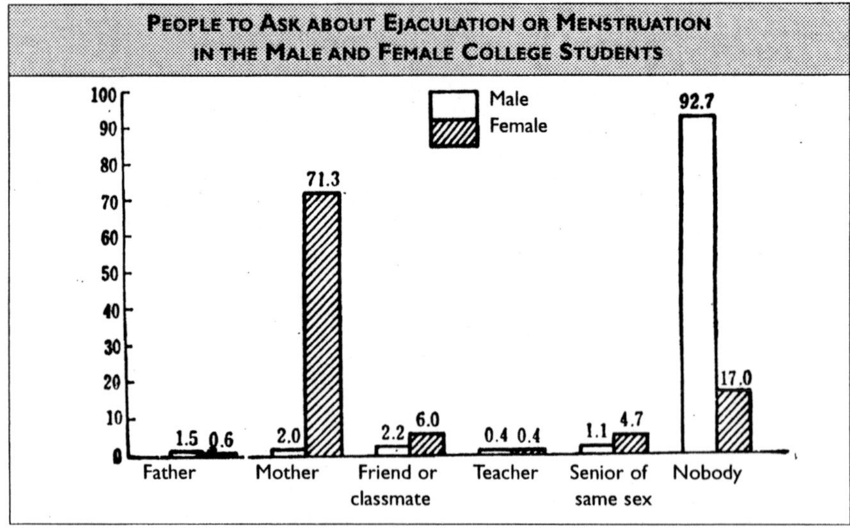

Figure 3–46

Table 3–90 and figure 3–46 showed that a large majority of the male students did not ask anyone. Most of the females however, asked their mothers, showing that in China, the communication distance between mother and daughter is the shortest among the family members. There

GENDER AND PERSON TO ASK ON FIRST EJACULATION OR MENSTRUATION

	TOTAL NO.	HYGIENE LESSONS		OUTSIDE READING		PARENTS		SIBLINGS		CLASS-MATES		OTHERS	
		NO.	%	NO.	%	NO.	%	NO.	%	NO.	%	NO.	%
Male	1838	27	1.5	37	2.0	41	2.2	8	0.4	21	1.1	1704	92.7
Female	1261	7	0.6	899	71.3	76	6.0	5	0.4	59	4.7	215	17.0

P=0.001

Table 3–90

GENDER AND EARLIEST SOURCE OF SEXUAL KNOWLEDGE

	TOTAL	FATHER		MOTHER		SIBLING		TEACHER		CLASSMATE		FRIEND		BOOK		OTHER SENIOR	
		NO.	%	NO.	%	NO.	%	NO.	%	NO.	%	NO.	%	NO.	%	NO.	%
Male	1810	30	1.7	18	1.0	16	0.9	79	4.4	371	20.5	149	8.2	1120	61.9	27	1.5
Female	1240	21	1.7	184	14.8	22	1.8	69	5.6	109	8.8	64	5.2	765	61.7	6	0.5

P=0.001

Table 3–91

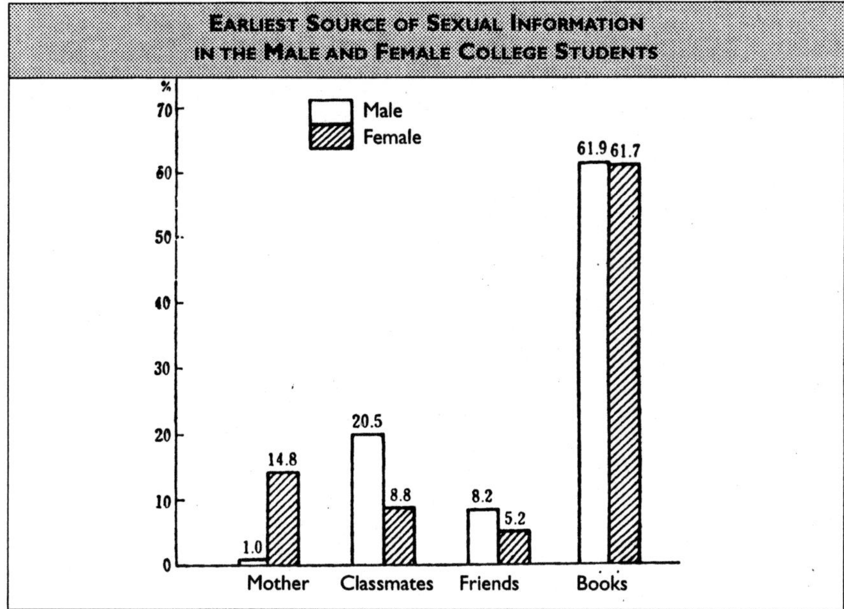

Figure 3–47

was a tradition in ancient China for the mother to give sexual instructions to her daughter just before her wedding day. This form of traditional sex education might be a reason that mothers are still the best sex educators for their daughters in modern China.

With regard to sex education on matters other than pubertal milestones, parents again emerged as a rather unimportant source. Of all subjects, 8.1 percent said they received information from the parents, 1.3 percent from their siblings, 4.8 percent from their teachers, 21.8 percent from friends or classmates, 58.5 percent from books, 1.0 percent from

AGE AND EARLIEST SOURCE OF SEXUAL KNOWLEDGE

AGE	TOTAL	FATHER		MOTHER		SIBLING		TEACHER		CLASSMATE		FRIEND		BOOK		OTHER SENIOR	
		NO.	%	NO.	%	NO.	%	NO.	%	NO.	%	NO.	%	NO.	%	NO.	%
<=19	961	13	1.4	92	9.6	13	1.4	44	4.6	141	14.7	48	5.0	603	62.7	7	0.7
20	810	16	2.0	43	5.3	11	1.4	44	5.4	136	16.8	57	7.0	493	60.9	10	1.2
21	595	11	1.8	38	6.4	9	1.5	26	44.4	96	16.1	56	9.4	349	58.7	10	1.7
22	301	3	1.0	15	5.0	4	1.3	20	6.6	49	16.3	23	7.6	183	60.8	4	1.3
<=23	194	6	3.1	7	3.6	1	0.5	6	3.1	32	16.5	15	7.7	126	64.9	1	0.5

P=0.001

Table 3–92

other adults, and 4.6 percent did not answer clearly. Hence, about 80 percent of the students received their earliest sexual knowledge from books, classmates, or friends. It indicates how unsuccessful schools and families are in providing sex education for children.

Gender & People One Can Talk with About Personal Matters					
	TOTAL	NO		YES	
		NO.	%	NO.	%
Male	1861	463	24.9	1398	78.1
Female	1277	193	15.1	1084	84.9

P=0.001

Table 3–93

Table 3–91 shows that the girls obtained sexual knowledge from their mothers, much more than boys. Hence, next to books, for the boys, the sources of sexual knowledge are classmates and friends, while the girls are instructed by their mothers.

The sources of sexual knowledge remain about the same, even if we divided the subjects by age (correlation alpha=0).

B. Bosom Friends

By bosom friend, we mean one's close friend or trusted relative to whom one can talk about intimate matters, including personal sexual matters.

Of all subjects, 77.4 percent said they had bosom friends, 20.7 percent said they had none, and 1.9 percent did not answer (table 3–93). In table 3–93, it can be seen that fewer of the male students had bosom friends.

Of the bosom friends, 9.1 percent were the subjects' parents, 5.8 percent were their sisters, 3.0 percent were brothers, 58.5 percent were friends of the same sex, 22.2 percent were friends of the other sex, 0.6 percent were teachers, and 0.9 percent were other people (table 3–94)

For the males, brothers and friends of the same sex ranked highest in importance. For the females, parents and sisters were at the top.

It is important to note that parents and teachers ranked very low in the minds of students as bosom friends. The parents constitute 10 percent

Type of People One Can Talk with About Personal Matters																
	TOTAL	PARENTS		SISTER		BROTHER		SAME SEX FRIEND		OTHER SEX FRIEND		TEACHER		OTHER SENIORS	
		NO.	%	NO.	%	NO.	%	NO.	%	NO.	%	NO.	%	NO.	%
Male	1413	103	7.3	35	2.5	59	4.2	876	62.0	320	22.6	6	0.4	14	1.0
Female	1098	125	11.4	109	9.9	15	1.4	597	54.4	236	21.5	7	0.6	9	0.8

P=0.001

Table 3–94

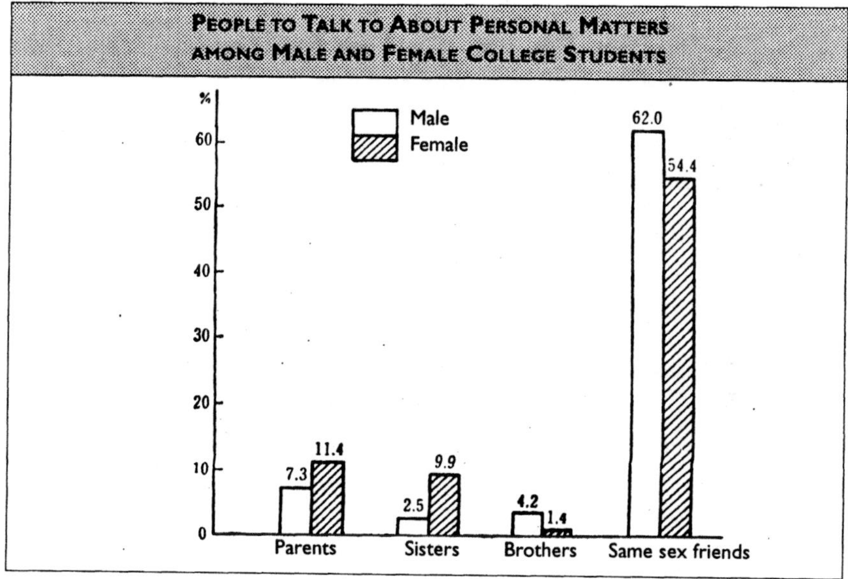

Figure 3–48

while the teachers constituted less than 1 percent. It could be a sign of crisis in our educational system and family relationships. In a more optimistic interpretation, however, it is a sign of maturity and independence for college students to turn to their peers for bosom friends.

C. Sexual Knowledge

In our questionnaire, we tried to get an impression of the students' sexual knowledge by asking them to indicate their understanding of the following terms: fertilization, pregnancy, menstruation, love, kissing, parturition, nocturnal emission, masturbation, penis, vagina, uterus, ovulation, orgasm, contraception, testosterone, ejaculation, sexual intercourse, homosexuality, prostitution, rape, sexually transmitted diseases, testes, and ovaries. All the terms except orgasm were understood by more than 75 percent of the students. It could be that they were really very knowledgeable about the meaning of basic sexual terms, or that they made correct assumptions. In 1988, Zhou surveyed 150 female students and asked them about their understanding of the physiology of menstruation. Twelve thought that menstruation came from the unfertilized ovum, 137 thought it was shredded from the uterine mucosa, and one student did not know what it was.[11] The results showed that the students were quite knowledgeable concerning basic sexual physiology.

The main sources of sexual knowledge for college students are medical books, newspapers, magazines, and works of fiction. The detailed percentages of the various sources for all the subjects were: newspaper and magazines 28.6 percent, Chinese movies and videos 0.5 percent, foreign movies and videos 2.7 percent, literature 10.3 percent, medical books 50.6 percent, pornography 4.4 percent, others 1.1 percent, unknown 1.8 percent. In table 3–95, it can be seen that more male students than females obtained sexual knowledge from medical books and pornography, and more female students than males received it from

Gender and Source of Sexual Knowledge

	TOTAL	NEWSPAPER MAGAZINE		LOCAL VIDEO/ MOVIES		FOREIGN		LITERATURE		MEDICAL BOOKS		EROTIC BOOKS		OTHERS	
		NO.	%	NO.	%	NO.	%	NO.	%	NO.	%	NO.	%	NO.	%
Male	1880	521	27.7	6	0.3	35	1.9	179	9.5	996	53.0	119	6.3	24	1.3
Female	1246	401	31.7	7	0.6	46	3.6	149	11.8	629	49.8	20	1.6	12	0.9

P=0.001

Table 3–95

Principle Source of Sexual Information in Male and Female College Students

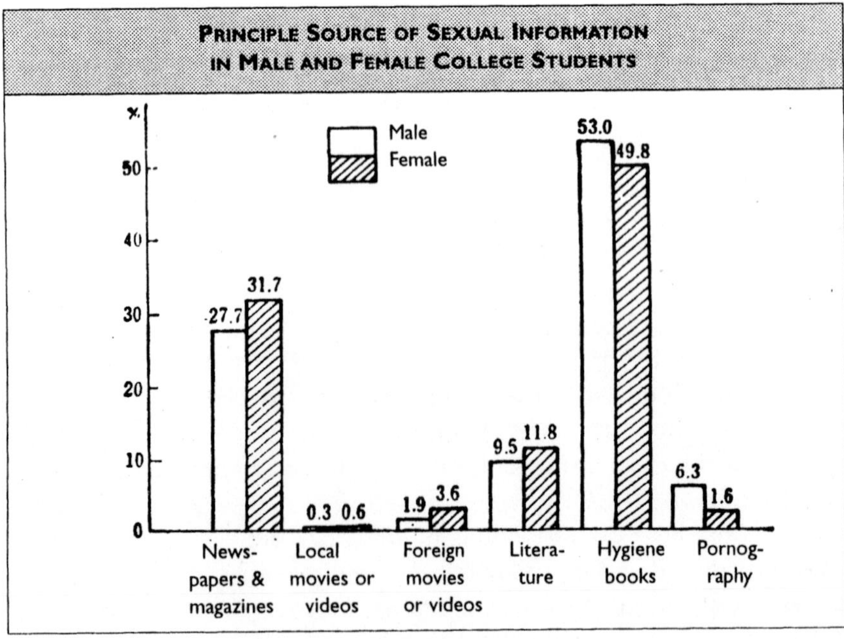

Figure 3–49

Age and Principal Source of Sexual Knowledge																
AGE	TOTAL	NEWSPAPER MAGAZINE		LOCAL VIDEO/ MOVIES		FOREIGN		LITERATURE		MEDICAL BOOKS		EROTIC BOOKS		OTHERS	
		NO.	%	NO.	%	NO.	%	NO.	%	NO.	%	NO.	%	NO.	%
<=19	990	308	31.1	4	0.4	33	3.3	106	10.7	492	49.7	29	2.9	18	1.8
20	832	247	29.7	4	0.5	22	2.6	90	10.8	423	50.8	37	4.4	9	1.1
21	616	155	25.2	2	0.3	13	2.1	76	12.3	337	54.7	30	4.9	3	0.5
22	309	83	26.9	3	1.0	9	2.9	23	7.4	174	56.3	17	5.5	0	0
>=23	208	56	26.9	0	0	2	1.0	14	6.7	116	55.8	17	8.2	3	1.4

P=0.01

Table 3–96

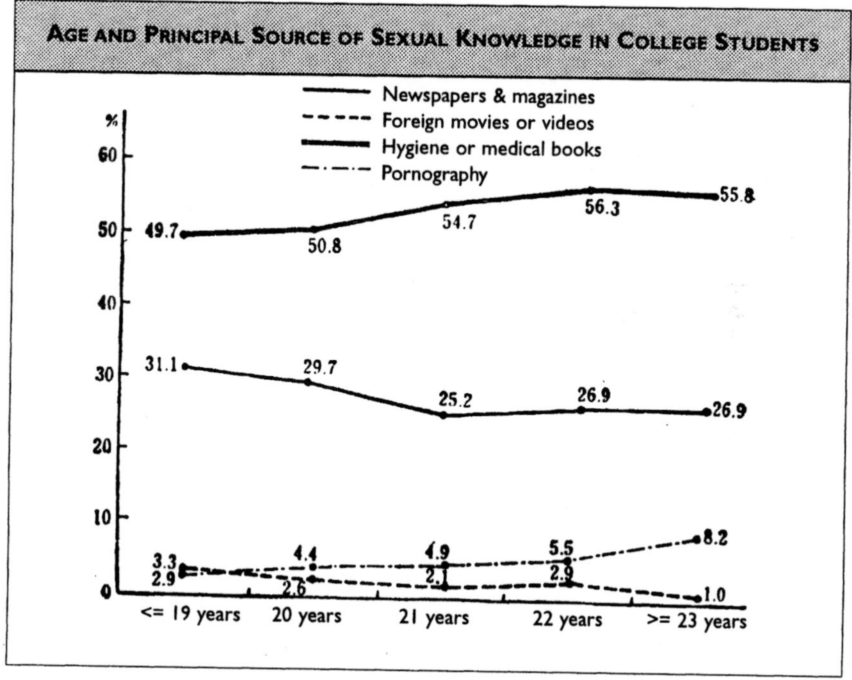

Figure 3–50

newspapers, magazines, and other literature. Table 3–96 shows that magazines and newspapers were the main source for students below the age of twenty-one, while for those twenty-one and above, medical books were the main source. Pornography as a source became more important as the subjects grew older.

Should Students Read Erotic Materials?

GENDER	TOTAL	YES		SHOULD BE ALLOWED		ALLOWED SELECTIVELY		SHOULD FORBID	
		NO.	%	NO.	%	NO.	%	NO.	%
Male	1856	588	31.7	213	11.5	982	52.9	73	3.9
Female	1251	223	17.8	37	3.0	929	74.2	62	5.0

P=0.01

Table 3–97

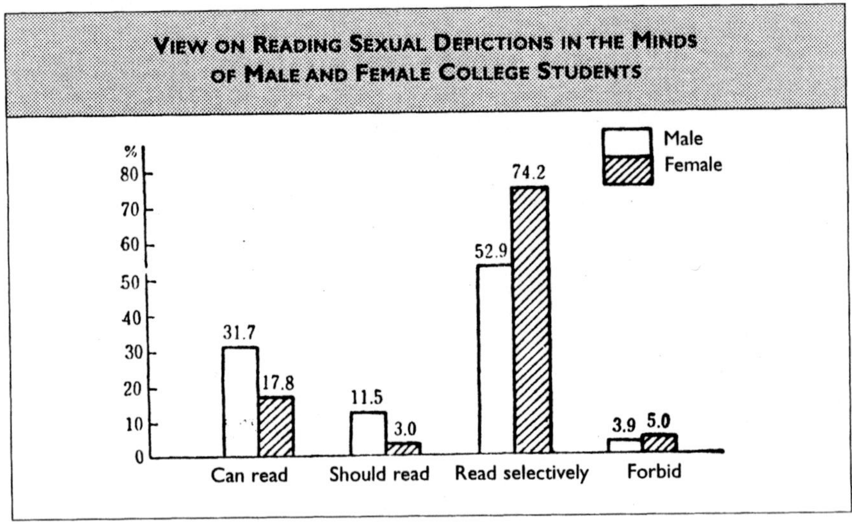

Figure 3–51

In our questionnaires, we also asked the students' opinions on reading materials containing sexual depictions. Of all the subjects, 25.2 percent replied that they should be allowed to read such material, 8.1 percent replied that they should have to read it, 59.0 percent replied that they should read it selectively, 4.3 percent replied that they should be forbidden to do so, and 3.4 percent did not give a clear answer. More male students than females replied that they should be allowed to read sexually explicit books, but more female students replied that these should be read selectively.

D. Evaluation of Contemporary Sex Education in China

Currently, sex education courses in colleges are very rare. They only exist at Tongji University (Shanghai), Zhejiang University, and a few others.

The situation is much worse than that in the high schools. This could be because the chancellor and the teachers of colleges think that their students should no longer be concerned with sexual matters. They may also think that since the college students read more anyway, it is not necessary to teach them about sex. Most of the college students (85.1 percent) believed that the sex education currently available for them was "too

Evaluation of Sex Education in China							
GENDER	TOTAL	APPROPRIATE		CONSERVATIVE		LIBERAL	
		NO.	%	NO.	%	NO.	%
Male	1830	124	6.8	1675	91.5	31	1.7
Female	1218	117	9.6	1078	88.5	23	1.9

P=0.02

Table 3–98

Age and Evaluation of Sex Education in China							
AGE	TOTAL	APPROPRIATE		CONSERVATIVE		LIBERAL	
		NO.	%	NO.	%	NO.	%
<=19	957	90	9.4	851	88.9	16	1.7
20	822	53	6.4	757	92.1	12	1.5
21	603	52	8.6	544	90.2	7	1.2
22	298	25	8.4	268	89.9	5	1.7
>=23	201	14	7.0	181	90.0	6	3.0

P=0.50

Table 3–99

Year and Evaluation of Sex Education in China							
YEAR	TOTAL	APPROPRIATE		CONSERVATIVE		LIBERAL	
		NO.	%	NO.	%	NO.	%
1	467	64	13.7	395	84.6	8	1.7
2	1044	76	7.3	946	90.6	22	2.1
3	813	50	6.1	746	91.8	17	2.1
4	692	57	8.2	626	90.5	9	1.3
5	84	11	13.1	73	86.9	0	0
Postgd.	51	2	3.9	48	94.1	1	2.0

P=0.50

Table 3–100

conservative." Of the students, 7.9 percent thought it was appropriate, 1.7 percent thought it too open, and 5.3 percent of them did not give a clear answer. More male than female students thought the sex education was too conservative. Fewer of them thought it was appropriate (table 3–98). Age or grade did not appear to correlate with any difference in the views (table 3–99, 3–100).

We conclude, therefore, that sex education for college students in China is very inadequate. It may be too late to teach anyone at that age. Efforts should concentrate more on the younger high school students. As Bertrand Russell suggested, "Tell them everything about sex."[12]

6. Sexual Attitudes

The core content of sexual attitudes is one's ethical evaluation of sexual issues. There are three levels of sexual ethics: The level of penal law, the level of social mores, and the level of personal convictions and choices. Of all segments of the population, college students represent most those that are young, knowledgeable, and sexually open-minded. Their sexual attitudes are likely to influence individuals of the immediate future in China.

1. Views on Dating in College Students

Of all the students surveyed, 0.9 percent replied that dating among college students should be forbidden, 1.8 percent thought that it should be

VIEW ON COLLEGE STUDENTS DATING										
GENDER	TOTAL	TO FORBID		TO RESTRICT		TO GUIDE		TO BE FREE		
		NO.	%	NO.	%	NO.	%	NO.	%	
Male	1885	17	0.9	31	1.6	1233	65.4	604	32.0	
Female	1252	7	0.6	22	1.7	905	72.3	318	25.4	

P=0.001

Table 3–101

controlled, 66.4 percent thought it should be put under guidance, 28.8 percent thought it should be freely allowed, and 2.1 percent did not answer clearly.

Of those who replied that it should be put under guidance, males were significantly less than females. For those who thought it should be freely allowed, males were significantly higher than the females.

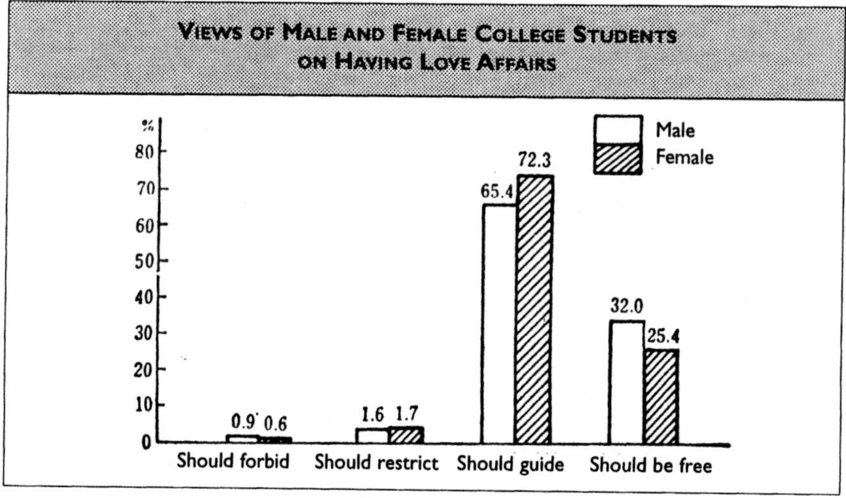

Figure 3–52

YEAR AND VIEW ON COLLEGE STUDENTS DATING

VIEW	YR. 1		YR.2		YR.3		YR.4		YR.5		POSTGD.	
	NO.	%	NO.	%	NO.	%	NO.	%	NO.	%	NO.	%
Forbid	10	2.0	8	0.8	6	0.7	5	0.7	2	2.4	0	0
Restrict	16	3.3	15	1.4	14	1.7	12	1.7	2	2.4	1	1.9
Guide	353	72.3	749	70.3	539	65.4	456	63.9	59	70.2	33	63.5
Free	109	22.3	293	27.5	265	32.2	241	33.8	21	25.0	18	34.6
Total	488	100.0	1065	100.0	824	100.0	714	100.0	84	100.0	52	100.0

Table 3–102

PROFESSION AND VIEW ON COLLEGE STUDENT DATING

VIEW	TOTAL	ARTS		SCIENCE		ENGIN.		AGRICUL.		MEDICINE	
		NO.	%	NO.	%	NO.	%	NO.	%	NO.	%
Forbid	28	7	0.6	10	1.9	10	1.4	0	0	1	0.1
Restrict	58	17	1.5	18	3.4	11	1.5	1	2.4	11	1.6
Guide	2117	728	65.1	346	64.8	518	71.3	37	90.2	488	69.2
Free	923	367	32.8	160	30.0	188	26.9	3	7.3	205	29.1
Total	3126	1119	100.0	534	100.0	727	100.0	41	100.0	705	100.0

Table 3–103

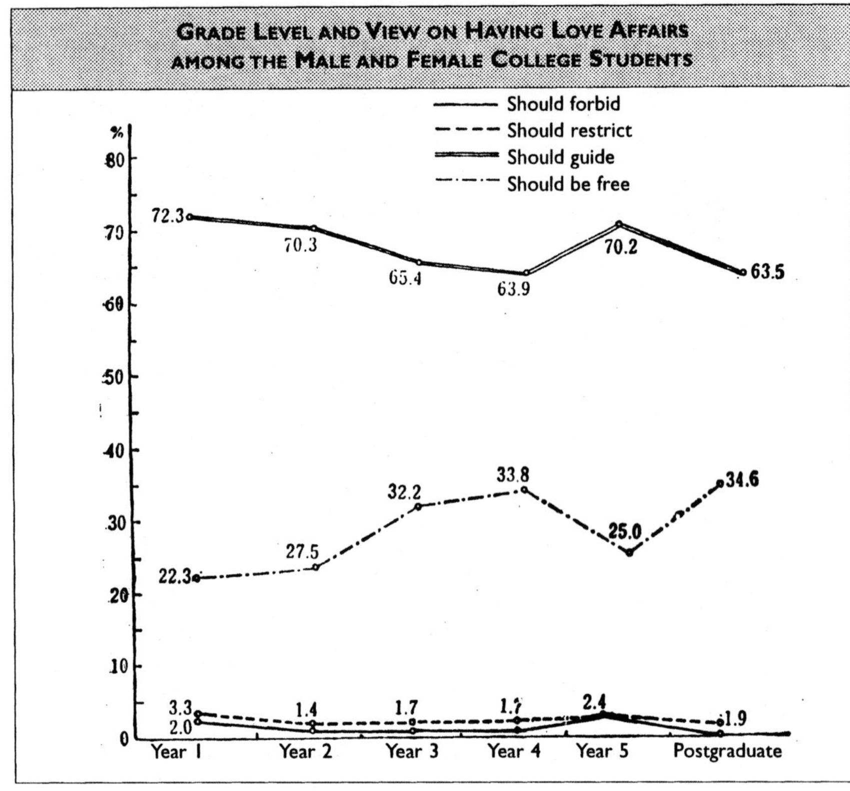

Figure 3–53

Table 3–103 and figure 3–53 show that views change with the grade levels of the students. The higher the grade level, the more students think that dating should be freely allowed. The reverse is true for those who thought it should be guided (G=0.12 in both occasions). This shows that the senior students were more confident of their ability to take care of their own affairs, and did not wish to have their dating behavior interfered with by others.

Of the various professions, the highest percentage of arts students thought that their dating behavior should be allowed to develop freely.

Before 1985, dating among college students was considered misconduct. The students involved were criticized, re-educated, and even punished. But this policy proved to be impractical. It only drove the students to secret or underground dating and to outright lying. It also put them under tremendous pressure. After 1985, friendships among male and female college students were allowed to be more open. The school authorities in general did not interfere with dating, although they hardly encouraged it. But this policy still did not face reality. The result was that dating affairs could not receive any proper guidance, something very much needed as shown by the responses of the students in this survey. We agree with Russell[13] who suggested that college students should be allowed to get married, or should be allowed to love and date freely, but in current China, this still cannot be done.

2. Aim of Sexual Intercourse

To know the students' view on sexual intercourse, we could not ask questions like "Do you think college students should have sexual intercourse?" because this is strictly forbidden in colleges. Hence, we decided to ask a more theoretical and vague question. We asked them to rank the various aims of sexual intercourse by importance, for physical pleasure, development of love, raising a family, companionship, or for satisfying the other individual.

Results show that love, physical pleasure, and raising a family were among the top three. Love was the most frequent one in the top rank. From rank two to four, family raising appeared most frequently. If we added the rank scores of each choice, the items in descending order were family raising, love, physical pleasure, satisfying the other individual, companionship, and reproduction. It is important to note that in college

RANKING OF AIM OF SEXUAL INTERCOURSE

AIM	FIRST		SECOND		THIRD		FOURTH		FIFTH		SIXTH	
	NO.	%	NO.	%	NO.	%	NO.	%	NO.	%	NO.	%
Pleasure	717	21.3	640	19.0	425	12.6	407	12.1	379	11.3	436	13.0
Love	1838	54.7	630	18.8	332	9.9	167	5.0	44	1.3	49	1.5
Family	220	6.5	927	27.6	737	21.9	631	18.8	552	16.4	162	4.8
Reproduction	97	2.9	233	6.9	667	19.9	604	18.0	534	15.9	601	17.9
Companion	131	3.9	306	9.1	374	11.1	538	16.0	710	21.1	908	27.0
Satisfy partner	51	1.5	295	8.8	470	14.0	628	18.7	735	21.9	789	23.5
Unknown	306	9.1	329	9.8	355	10.5	385	11.4	406	12.0	415	12.4
Total	3360	100.0	3360	100.0	3360	100.0	3360	100.0	3360	100.0	3360	100.0

Table 3–104

students, reproduction is already last in the number of reasons for sexual intercourse (table 3–104). This is the logical outcome of a social policy restricting each couple to one child. The political ideal of a one-child family automatically severs the ancient connection between reproduction

GENDER AND FIRST AIM OF SEXUAL INTERCOURSE							
	TOTAL	PLEASURE		LOVE		FAMILY	
		NO.	%	NO.	%	NO.	%
Male	1790	546	30.5	947	52.9	133	7.4
Female	1135	148	13.0	822	72.4	74	6.5

P=0.001

Table 3–105

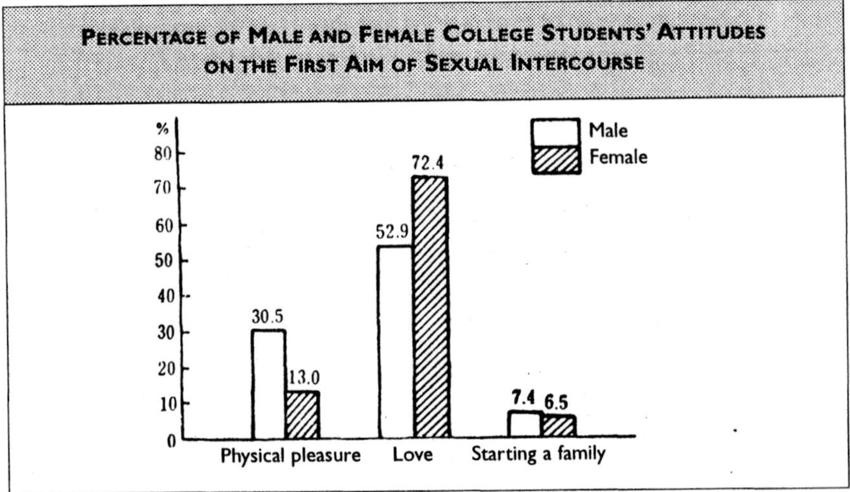

Figure 3–54

PROFESSION AND FIRST AIM OF SEXUAL INTERCOURSE												
AIM	TOTAL	ARTS		SCIENCE		ENGIN.		AGRICUL.		MEDICINE		
		NO.	%	NO.	%	NO.	%	NO.	%	NO.	%	
Pleasure	1687	283	27.1	128	26.1	157	22.6	5	12.8	114	17.7	
Love	752	610	58.4	280	57.1	425	61.2	25	64.1	412	64.0	
Family	212	74	7.1	34	6.9	50	7.2	5	12.8	49	7.6	
Reproduction	91	19	1.8	18	3.7	22	3.2	3	7.7	29	4.5	
Companion	122	43	4.1	23	4.7	32	4.6	0	0	24	3.7	
Satisfy partner	49	16	1.5	7	1.4	9	1.3	1	2.6	16	2.5	
Total	2913	1045	100.0	490	100.0	695	100.0	39	100.0	644	100.0	

Table 3–106

and sex, giving the latter a much greater importance as a goal in itself, as a means of binding couples together.

In table 3–105 we see that there is a higher percentage of males than females who think physical pleasure is an important aim, with the reverse being true for love as an aim.

Table 3–106 shows that among those who took physical pleasure as an aim, the arts students were most prominent.

AGE AND FIRST AIM OF SEXUAL INTERCOURSE							
AGE	TOTAL	PLEASURE		LOVE		FAMILY	
		NO.	%	NO.	%	NO.	%
<=19	902	175	19.4	575	63.7	67	7.4
20	782	184	23.5	482	61.6	50	6.4
21	590	134	22.7	356	60.3	42	7.1
22	298	83	27.8	168	56.4	20	6.7
>=23	193	75	38.9	87	45.1	19	9.8

P=0.001

Table 3–107

GENDER AND SECOND AIM OF SEXUAL INTERCOURSE							
	TOTAL	PLEASURE		LOVE		FAMILY	
		NO.	%	NO.	%	NO.	%
Male	1782	382	21.4	433	24.3	457	25.6
Female	1122	220	19.6	169	15.1	443	39.5

P=0.001

Table 3–108

AGE AND SECOND AIM OF SEXUAL INTERCOURSE							
AGE	TOTAL	PLEASURE		LOVE		FAMILY	
		NO.	%	NO.	%	NO.	%
<=19	895	171	19.1	169	18.9	282	31.5
20	775	168	21.7	159	20.5	244	31.5
21	585	139	23.8	115	19.7	174	29.7
22	298	58	19.5	67	22.5	91	30.5
>=23	193	39	20.2	61	31.6	51	26.4

P=0.001

Table 3–109

Table 3–107 shows that the older the students were, the more he/she took physical pleasure as an important aim. This may be related to the maturity of their sexual physiology or psychology.

The high frequency of family rasing as the second choice, especially in the females (table 3–108) and the older ages (table 3–109), shows that although love or sexual pleasure were of importance in the students' minds, they also realized the importance of raising a family as a social need, as well as a stabilizing force for love or sexual pleasure.

3. Female Sex Life

A. Views on Coitus During Menstruation

Of all the subjects, 5.7 percent thought it was normal, 3.5 percent thought it impossible, 84.8 percent saw it as unhygienic, 1.8 percent as unethical, and 4.1 percent did not answer. From table 3–110, it can be seen that 92.2 percent of the males and 96.8 percent of the females held negative attitudes toward the behavior. Most of those who held negative views gave hygiene as a reason.

Students of different faculties did not show any significant differences in their views concerning this item. From table 3–112 however, it is

View on Sex During Menstruation

GENDER	TOTAL	NORMAL		INCONCEIVABLE		UNHYGIENIC		UNETHICAL	
		NO.	%	NO.	%	NO.	%	NO.	%
Male	1833	143	7.8	51	2.8	1599	87.2	40	2.2
Female	1245	40	3.2	62	5.0	1127	90.5	16	1.3

P=0.001

Table 3–110

Profession and View on College Student Dating

VIEW	TOTAL	ARTS		SCIENCE		ENGIN.		AGRICUL.		MEDICINE	
		NO.	%	NO.	%	NO.	%	NO.	%	NO.	%
Normal	182	68	6.2	31	6.0	42	5.9	1	2.5	40	5.7
Inconc'ble	111	39	3.5	25	4.8	24	3.4	0	0	23	3.3
Unhygienic	2717	981	89.1	446	86.3	628	87.9	39	97.5	623	89.5
Unethical	58	13	1.2	15	2.9	20	2.8	0	0	10	1.4
Total	3068	1101	100.0	517	100.0	714	100.0	40	100.0	696	100.0

Table 3–111

YEAR AND VIEW ON SEX DURING MENSTRUATION										
YEAR	TOTAL	NORMAL		INCONCEIVABLE		UNHYGIENIC		UNETHICAL	
		NO.	%	NO.	%	NO.	%	NO.	%
1	465	34	7.3	28	6.0	398	85.6	5	1.1
2	1042	56	5.4	39	3.7	927	89.0	20	1.9
3	818	43	5.3	27	3.3	726	88.7	22	2.7
4	706	43	6.1	22	3.1	630	89.2	11	1.6
5	84	7	8.3	2	2.4	73	86.9	2	2.4
Postgd.	49	6	12.3	0	0	43	87.7	0	0

Table 3–112

shown that the older the students were, the more of them thought the behavior normal. It could be because the senior students knew more and changed their views.

B. SHOULD WIVES TAKE THE INITIATIVE IN SEXUAL INTERCOURSE?

The traditional Chinese view is that women should always be passive in sex. Even if they want sex, they should only show a halfhearted willingness.

VIEW ON WOMEN TAKING INITIATIVE IN SEX									
GENDER	TOTAL	NORMAL		INCONCEIVABLE		UNHYGIENIC		UNETHICAL	
		NO.	%	NO.	%	NO.	%	NO.	%
Male	1877	1770	94.3	83	4.4	10	0.5	14	0.7
Female	1249	1080	86.5	148	11.8	12	1.0	9	0.7

P=0.001

Table 3–113

YEAR AND VIEW ON WOMEN TAKING INITIATIVE IN SEX									
YEAR	TOTAL	NORMAL		INCONCEIVABLE		UNHYGIENIC		UNETHICAL	
		NO.	%	NO.	%	NO.	%	NO.	%
1	486	441	90.7	30	6.2	9	1.9	6	1.2
2	1061	958	90.3	94	8.9	4	0.4	5	0.5
3	828	758	91.5	56	6.8	7	0.8	7	0.8
4	709	654	92.2	48	6.8	3	0.4	4	0.6
5	83	77	92.8	5	6.0	0	0	1	1.2
Postgd.	52	50	96.2	2	3.8	0	0	0	0

Table 3–114

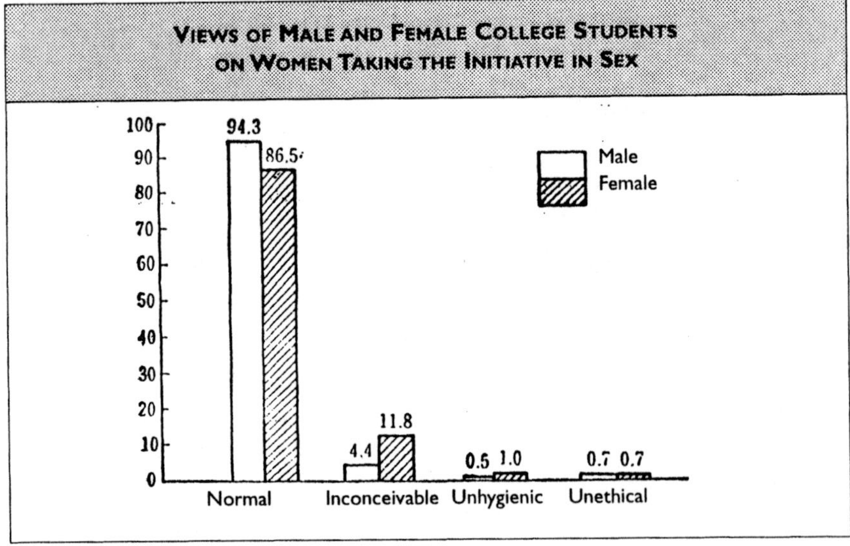

Figure 3–55

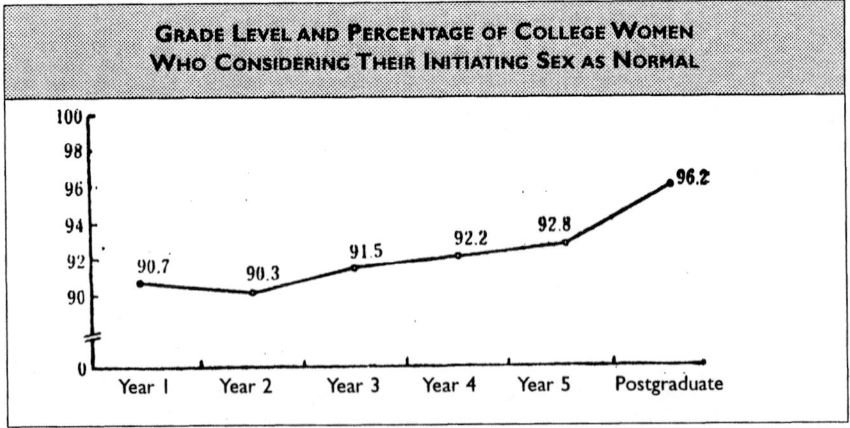

Figure 3–56

Otherwise, they would be considered licentious or troublesome. However, this survey shows that most of the students had discarded this traditional view; 94.8 percent of them thought it normal for women to take the initiative, 2.6 percent thought it impossible, 0.8 percent thought it unhygienic, 0.7 percent unethical, and 1.1 percent did not answer clearly. The older the students were, the more of them thought it normal.

PROFESSION AND VIEW ON WOMEN TAKING INITIATIVE IN SEX												
VIEW	TOTAL	ARTS		SCIENCE		ENGIN.		AGRICUL.		MEDICINE		
		NO.	%	NO.	%	NO.	%	NO.	%	NO.	%
Normal	2840	1020	91.2	473	88.9	672	92.6	37	72.5	638	91.0
Inconc'ble	231	80	7.2	47	8.8	47	6.5	3	7.5	54	7.7
Unhygienic	23	12	1.1	7	1.3	3	0.4	0	0	1	0.1
Unethical	23	6	0.5	5	0.9	4	0.6	0	0	8	1.1
Total	3117	1118	100.0	532	100.0	726	100.0	40	100.0	701	100.0

Table 3–115

But, as shown in table 3–113, more female students than males thought it impossible.

Table 3–115 shows no differences on this view among the different professions for which the students were training.

4. Views on Variant Sex Styles:

A. ON PREMARITAL SEX

Of all the respondents, most were positive about premarital sex. 40.2 percent considered it was all right if it was based on love; 34.7 percent thought it all right if it was by mutual consent; 19.6 percent thought it was unethical; 0.4 percent thought it should be punishable by the administration; 0.8 percent thought it should be punishable by law; 4.3 percent did not give a clear answer. More females than males took sex based on love as a positive reason, but more males than females emphasized mutual consent. More females also thought the behavior was unethical or punishable.

VIEW ON PREMARITAL SEX											
GENDER	TOTAL	YES IF LOVE		YES IF CONSENT		UNETHICAL		ADMINST. PENALTY		LEGAL PENALTY	
		NO.	%	NO.	%	NO.	%	NO.	%	NO.	%
Male	1860	753	40.5	855	46.0	238	12.8	6	0.3	8	0.4
Female	1212	548	45.2	254	21.0	390	32.2	5	0.4	15	1.2

Table 3–116

In 1987, Ling and Liu surveyed 352 students of Zhongshan University, Shenzhen University, China West Medical University, and East–West Technical College. In this survey, 48.2 percent of the fourth

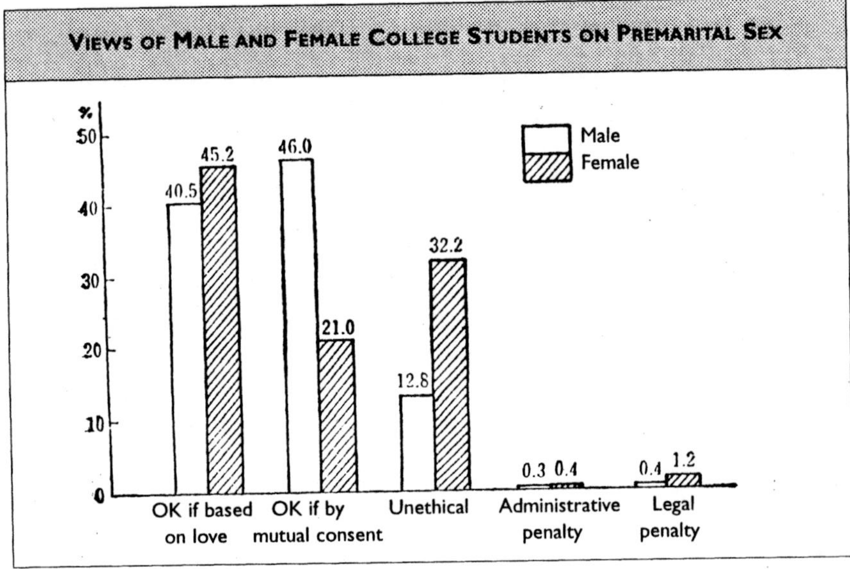

Figure 3–57

year male students, 28.3 percent of the female fourth year, 51.7 percent of the male first year, and 11.6 percent of the female first year thought that premarital sex was acceptable if the individuals were in a deep affectionate relationship and preparing for marriage. For those who thought that sex was all right as long as a loving relationship was established, the respective percentages were 25.9 percent, 5.4 percent, 13.5, percent and 3.5 percent.[14] These figures show the relative permissiveness of the college students regarding premarital sex, with the females being of a lesser

PROFESSION AND VIEW ON PREMARITAL SEX

VIEW	TOTAL	ARTS		SCIENCE		ENGIN.		AGRICUL.		MEDICINE	
		NO.	%	NO.	%	NO.	%	NO.	%	NO.	%
Yes if love	1306	467	42.3	220	41.3	311	42.5	17	43.6	291	43.3
Yes if consent	1107	410	37.1	191	35.8	296	40.5	7	17.9	203	30.2
Unethical	627	222	20.1	113	21.2	112	15.3	12	30.8	168	25.0
Ad. penalty	12	1	0.1	2	0.4	3	0.4	2	5.1	4	0.6
Legal penalty	27	4	0.4	7	1.3	9	1.2	1	2.6	6	0.9
Total	3079	1104	100.0	533	100.0	731	100.0	39	100.0	672	100.0

Table 3–117

degree. A permissive attitude, of course, does not necessarily mean permissive behavior.

Medical students were found to be the less permissive in this respect. Could this be due to their higher medical knowledge about the risk of unwanted pregnancy?

The results show that it might not be reasonable or sufficient to forbid sex between college students. By the end of the last decade, in a Shanghai college, two students entered a sexual relationship and the female became pregnant. A great deal of pressure was put on both of them by their relatives and by the school authorities. Finally, they killed themselves in a suicide pact. Their funeral was extraordinary and attended by many of their classmates who dressed the dead couple in beautiful clothing and covered them with flowers. It is interesting to contemplate what the students were trying to express.

B. Attitude toward Extramarital Sex

For extramarital sex involving two consenting adults, 3.9 percent of the students thought it should be punishable by law, 34.5 percent thought it

Gender and View on Extramarital Sex

	TOTAL	YES IF LOVE		YES IF CONSENT		UNETHICAL		ADMINST. PENALTY		LEGAL PENALTY	
		NO.	%	NO.	%	NO.	%	NO.	%	NO.	%
Male	1848	71	3.8	626	33.9	11	0.6	609	33.0	531	28.7
Female	1203	50	4.2	484	40.2	15	1.2	339	28.2	315	26.2

Table 3–118

Profession and View on Extramarital Sex

VIEW	TOTAL	ARTS		SCIENCE		ENGIN.		AGRICUL.		MEDICINE	
		NO.	%	NO.	%	NO.	%	NO.	%	NO.	%
Legal penalty	127	43	3.9	31	5.9	24	3.4	4	10.5	25	3.7
Unethical	1112	383	34.7	193	36.6	263	37.0	20	52.6	253	37.6
Ad. penalty	27	9	0.8	2	0.4	9	1.3	2	5.3	5	0.7
Yes if love	940	362	32.8	148	28.1	211	29.6	8	21.1	211	31.4
Yes if consent	846	307	27.8	153	29.0	204	28.7	4	10.5	178	26.5
Total	3052	1104	100.0	527	100.0	711	100.0	38	100.0	672	100.0

Table 3–119

was unethical, 0.8 percent thought it should be punishable by the administration, 29.5 percent replied that it should be acceptable if the affair was based on love, 26.0 percent replied that if the spouse tolerated it, no one else should interfere, and 5.3 percent did not give any clear answer.

In those who thought extramarital sex should be tolerated, male students were more numerous than the females.

The attitudes did not show obvious variation. The arts students had the highest percentage of those who showed a positive attitude toward extramarital sex and the medical students were the lowest at 53.2 percent.

C. Attitude toward Chastity

The question asked here is "If you found out your fiancé or fiancée had sex with somebody else before you, what would be your attitude toward him/her?"

Most of the replies were tolerant and positive. Only 17.0 percent replied that they would terminate their relationship; 14.0 percent said that they would marry with reluctance, yet feel irreparable damage at heart; 57.0 percent thought their relationship would not be affected; and 11.5 percent did not give any clear answer.

Attitude If Future Spouse Has Previously Had Sex with Others

	TOTAL	SEPARATE		MARRY BUT HURT		NO PROBLEM	
		NO.	%	NO.	%	NO.	%
Male	1736	343	19.8	315	18.1	1078	62.1
Female	1120	193	17.2	163	14.6	764	68.2

P=0.05

Table 3–120

Profession and View on Future Spouse Had Sex with Others

VIEW	TOTAL	ARTS		SCIENCE		ENGIN.		AGRICUL.		MEDICINE	
		NO.	%	NO.	%	NO.	%	NO.	%	NO.	%
Separate	541	199	19.3	86	17.5	129	19.1	10	30.3	117	18.7
Marry but hurt	472	178	17.3	91	18.5	104	15.4	4	12.1	95	15.2
No problem	1843	654	63.4	314	64.0	442	65.5	19	57.6	414	66.1
Total	2856	1031	100.0	491	100.0	675	100.0	33	100.0	626	100.0

Table 3–121

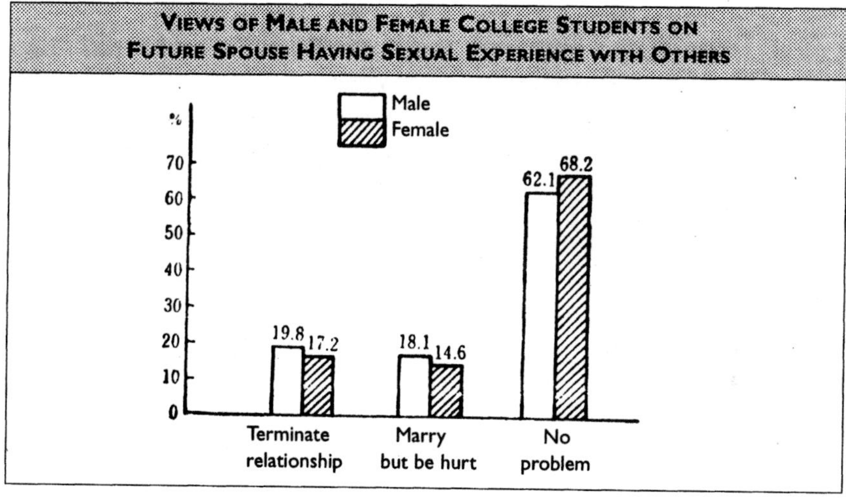

Figure 3–58

From table 3–120, it can be seen that more females than males felt that their relationship would not be affected and more males felt there would be irreparable damage. Hence, the traditional attitude on female chastity is still quite influential. In traditional China, chastity was very important for females, but not for males.

There were no significant differences between different professions concerning the attitudes toward chastity (table 3–121).

One has to realize, of course, that attitudes may not carry over to behavior. There are people who just cannot accept a lack of chastity if they are personally involved. A college student once said, "I know she should not be blamed. I know it should not affect our future. But as long I remember what has happened, I feel disgusted."

D. Attitude toward Sex in the Elderly and the Disabled

Of the students, 90.3 percent thought that it was normal for the elderly to have a sex life; 6.0 percent thought it was not possible, 2.0 percent thought it unhealthy; 0.6 percent thought it unethical, and 1.2 percent did not give any clear answer. The respective figures for the physically disabled were 94.8 percent, 2.6 percent, 0.8 percent, 0.7 percent and, 1.1 percent.

Table 3–122 and 3–123 show that more males than females thought it normal for the elderly to have sex. For the physically disabled, approximately the same proportion of males and females thought it to be normal. For those who thought old people could not possibly have any sex life, females were higher than the males. This shows that in China, the females, including female college students, are generally more traditional and inhibited than the males.

In the 1960s, a survey in America showed that in 646 college students surveyed, about 1/4 thought their parents should have stopped any sexual

VIEW ON THE DISABLED HAVING SEX										
GENDER	TOTAL	NORMAL		INCONCEIVABLE		UNHYGIENIC		UNETHICAL	
		NO.	%	NO.	%	NO.	%	NO.	%
Male	1888	1815	96.1	50	2.6	13	0.7	10	0.5
Female	1281	1228	95.9	30	2.3	13	1.0	10	0.8

P=0.001

Table 3–122

VIEW ON THE ELDERLY HAVING SEX									
GENDER	TOTAL	NORMAL		INCONCEIVABLE		UNHYGIENIC		UNETHICAL	
		NO.	%	NO.	%	NO.	%	NO.	%
Male	1890	1769	93.6	79	4.2	34	1.8	8	0.4
Female	1267	1128	88.3	110	8.6	29	2.3	10	0.8

P=0.70

Table 3–123

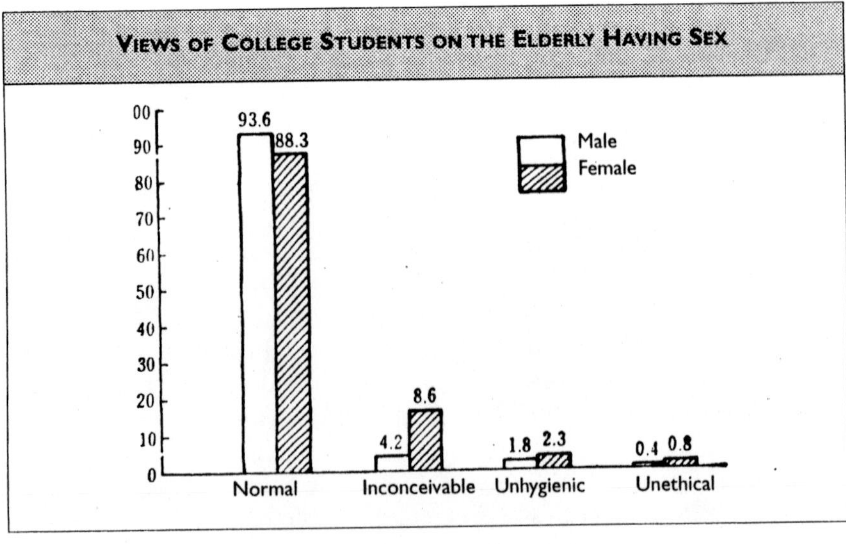

Figure 3–59

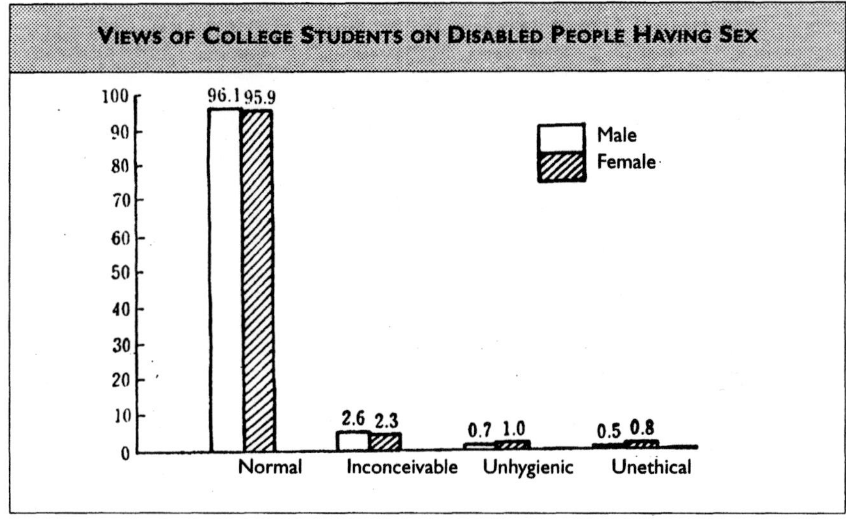

Figure 3–60

activities, but in fact, their parents were only between forty and fifty years old. More than half of the students thought that their parents might have sex about once per week or even less.[15] This low estimation about their parental sexual activities reflect the degree of sexual conservatism. It could be that the Chinese college students of the 1980s are a little more enlightened than those in the America of the 1960s.

E. Attitude toward Homosexual Behavior

The dominant attitude in China toward homosexuality is that it is a sexually deviant behavior. The same is reflected in this college student survey. Of all the respondents, 9.6 percent thought it was the normal behavior of a minority, 79.0 percent considered it a form of sexual deviancy, 4.3 percent thought it unethical, 3.1 percent thought it to be a crime, and 3.8 percent did not give any clear answer.

More male students took a positive attitude toward the homosexual behavior, and more females thought it to be deviant and expressed negative attitudes.

When asked about their attitudes in the event that they found out one of their classmates was a homosexual, 11.2 percent of the total respondents said they would end their relationship with him/her, 15.1 percent said they would be sympathetic but keep the classmate at a distance, 67.5 percent would persuade the classmate to see a doctor, 1.2 percent would join into the homosexual activity, and 4.9 percent did not

VIEWS ON HOMOSEXUALITY										
GENDER	TOTAL	NORMAL		DEVIANT		UNETHICAL		CRIMINAL	
		NO.	%	NO.	%	NO.	%	NO.	%
Male	1861	222	11.9	1526	82.0	60	3.2	53	2.8
Female	1239	79	6.4	1047	84.5	73	5.9	40	3.2

P=0.001

Table 3–124

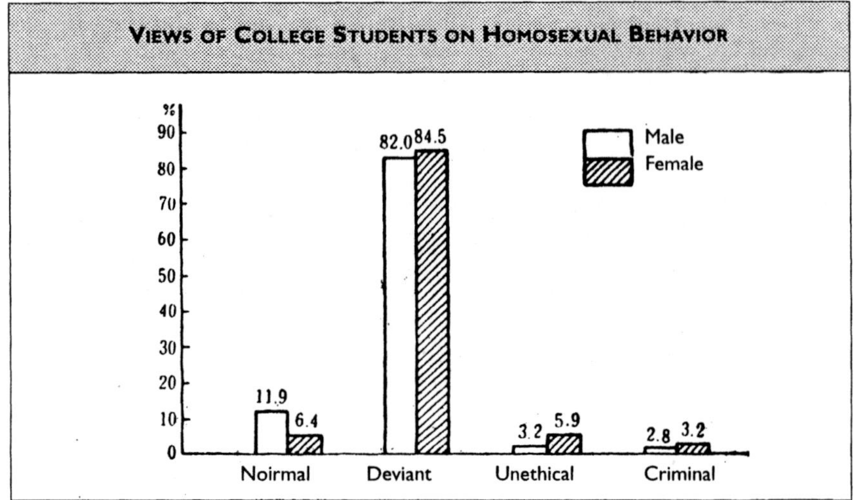

Figure 3–61

give any clear answer. The males and females did not show any significant differences in their attitudes concerning this event (table 3–125).

This shows that many Chinese consider homosexuality a medical problem that doctors might solve or alleviate. This belief was, at one time, probably imported from Western countries which, ironically, no longer share it today.

When asked the question of what their feelings would be if they found out that a member of their family was a homosexual, 30.4 percent answered that they would feel embarrassed, 38.6 percent said they would feel just like the member had a serious illness, 24.4 percent would feel neutral, and 6.6 percent did not give any definite answer. This confirms that most of the respondents still thought the condition was an illness. There was no significant difference between the two sexes in response to the question. (table 3–126).

ATTITUDE TOWARD A FRIEND BEING A HOMOSEXUAL									
GENDER	TOTAL	SEPARATE		DISTANT		ADVISE DOCTOR		JOIN IN	
		NO.	%	NO.	%	NO.	%	NO.	%
Male	1838	208	11.3	296	16.1	1306	71.1	28	1.5
Female	1228	151	12.3	187	15.2	881	71.7	9	0.7

P=0.10

Table 3–125

When asked if a great man they admired was a homosexual, 23.0 percent replied that they would give the same respect, 57.6 percent said they would consider it a pity, 15.0 percent said the man would lose all of their respect, and 4.4 percent did not give any clear answer. More males than females felt no difference in their respect. More females felt a loss of respect (table 3–127).

Another question asked was the respondents' opinion if Tchaikovsky had been executed for his homosexuality. Of those who answered, 51.5

VIEW OF A RELATIVE BEING HOMOSEXUAL							
	TOTAL	SHAME		HE/SHE IS SICK		NO PROBLEM	
		NO.	%	NO.	%	NO.	%
Male	1014	581	32.0	753	41.5	480	26.5
Female	1195	398	33.3	497	41.6	300	25.1

P=0.05

Table 3–126

percent thought such a punishment too severe, 37.4 percent felt it was totally wrong, 7.4 percent said Tchaikovsky would have deserved it, and 3.8 percent did not give any clear answer. Many more males thought the punishment totally wrong. More females thought the punishment would have been too severe and undeserved (table 3–128). Generally speaking, therefore, male students were more accepting of homosexuality.

As for differences between different professions, table 3–130 shows no significant differences with respect to feeling toward a friend being a homosexual. Table 3–129 shows more arts students took homosexuality to be the normal tendency of a minority; table 3–131 shows that more arts students felt neutral if one of their family members were a homosexual; table 3–132 shows that more arts students did not lose respect for their idols even if they were found to be a homosexual; table 3–133

View toward an Idol Being Homosexual							
GENDER	TOTAL	SAME RESPECT		A PITY		LOSE RESPECT	
		NO.	%	NO.	%	NO.	%
Male	1849	538	29.1	1081	58.5	230	12.4
Female	1234	200	16.2	790	64.0	244	19.8

P=0.001

Table 3–127

View if Tschaikovsky Had Been Executed for Being a Homosexual							
GENDER	TOTAL	DESERVE IT		TOO MUCH		WRONG	
		NO.	%	NO.	%	NO.	%
Male	1856	132	7.1	878	47.3	846	45.6
Female	1245	103	8.3	781	62.7	361	29.0

P=0.001

Table 3–128

Profession and View toward Homosexuality											
VIEW	TOTAL	ARTS		SCIENCE		ENGIN.		AGRICUL.		MEDICINE	
		NO.	%	NO.	%	NO.	%	NO.	%	NO.	%
Normal	306	142	12.7	64	12.0	60	8.3	0	0	40	5.8
Deviant	2561	887	79.4	426	79.9	608	84.1	38	92.7	602	87.5
Unethical	138	48	4.3	27	5.1	35	4.8	0	0	28	4.1
Criminal	97	40	3.6	16	3.0	20	2.8	3	7.3	18	2.6
Total	3102	1117	100.0	533	100.0	723	100.0	41	100.0	688	100.0

Table 3–129

Profession and View of Friend Being Homosexual											
VIEW	TOTAL	ARTS		SCIENCE		ENGIN.		AGRICUL.		MEDICINE	
		NO.	%	NO.	%	NO.	%	NO.	%	NO.	%
Separate	355	121	11.0	64	12.2	97	13.5	5	12.8	68	10.0
Distant	489	198	18.0	98	18.7	114	15.9	2	5.1	77	11.3
Adv. doctor	2176	760	69.3	349	66.5	501	69.7	32	82.1	534	78.4
Join it	41	18	1.6	14	2.7	7	1.0	0	0	2	0.3
Total	3061	1097	100.0	525	100.0	719	100.0	39	100.0	681	100.0

Table 3–130

PROFESSION AND VIEW OF RELATIVE BEING A HOMOSEXUAL											
VIEW	TOTAL	ARTS		SCIENCE		ENGIN.		AGRICUL.		MEDICINE	
		NO.	%	NO.	%	NO.	%	NO.	%	NO.	%
Shame	981	370	34.2	164	31.9	237	33.5	9	23.7	201	29.7
He/she sick	1255	425	39.2	223	43.4	276	39.0	22	57.9	309	45.7
No problem	782	287	36.6	127	24.7	195	27.5	7	18.4	166	24.6
Total	3018	1082	100.0	514	100.0	708	100.0	38	100.0	676	100.0

Table 3–131

PROFESSION AND VIEW OF IDOL BEING HOMOSEXUAL											
VIEW	TOTAL	ARTS		SCIENCE		ENGIN.		AGRICUL.		MEDICINE	
		NO.	%	NO.	%	NO.	%	NO.	%	NO.	%
No problem	748	315	28.5	111	21.1	171	23.7	5	12.8	146	21.1
Pity	1858	632	57.1	322	61.3	448	62.0	29	74.4	427	61.8
Lost respect	477	159	14.4	92	17.5	103	14.3	5	12.8	118	17.1
Total	3083	1106	100.0	525	100.0	722	100.0	39	100.0	691	100.0

Table 3–132

PROFESSION AND VIEW IF TCHAIKOVSKY EXECUTED FOR BEING HOMOSEXUAL											
VIEW	TOTAL	ARTS		SCIENCE		ENGIN.		AGRICUL.		MEDICINE	
		NO.	%	NO.	%	NO.	%	NO.	%	NO.	%
Deserve it	230	71	6.4	45	8.5	55	7.6	3	7.3	56	8.1
Too much	1668	575	51.6	276	51.9	377	52.1	28	68.3	412	59.4
Wrong	1206	468	42.0	211	39.7	291	40.2	10	24.4	226	32.6
Total	3104	1114	100.0	532	100.0	723	100.0	41	100.0	694	100.0

Table 3–133

shows more arts students also thought that the death penalty for Tchaikovsky would have been totally wrong.

The results above show that students of different academic fields did not show any significant differences in sexual attitudes, except that arts students appeared to be more enlightened and permissive and in some other aspects, even progressive. This may be because their studies dealt more with human nature, thoughts, and feelings.

Conclusion

1. College students still have inadequate sexual knowledge. Their sexual attitudes are rather conventional and, in part, immature.
2. Only 0.1 percent of the students considered their teachers to be persons to whom they could talk about intimate personal matters.
3. Sex education in the colleges, necessary as it is, might come too late for most young people. This insight should guide our strategy in sex education.
4. Probably due to the mixed messages received from Chinese and Western sources, college students in China show both traditional and unconventional sexual attitudes. How to help them integrate their knowledge and feelings, and how to get the best information from both sides, should be a major concern of college sex education.
5. The necessary process of integration has to take the need for family and social harmony as well as the needs of the country into account.
6. Love relationships among students are quite common. This reflects their psychological and physical need. This need has to be faced honestly by administrators. It cannot be dealt with by mere authoritarian suppression and punishment. A proper channeling of this need should be permitted together with education on healthy sexual attitudes, practices, and responsibilities.

Notes

1. The National Statistics Bureau of 1990 census showed that in 1989, there were a total of 82,000 tertiary students, making a rate of 1422 per one hundred thousand population.
2. It is known that the size of the flaccid penis has little to do with satisfaction during intercourse, since the size of the erect penis can be quite different. Also, the elasticity of the vagina can easily compensate for different-sized penises.
3. Bai Ju-Yi (Tang Dynasty), *Song of Eternal Remorse.*
4. Havelock Ellis, *Psychology of Sex* (London: Heinemann, 1933). Chinese translation, G. D. Pan (Beijing: Joint Publishing, 1987), 72, 130
5. A. C. Kinsey, W. B. Pomeroy, C. E. Martin, and P. H. Gebherd. *Sexual Behavior in the Human Female* (Philadelphia: W. B. Saunders Co., 1943). (Chinese translation, Pan Sui-Ming (Beigjing: People's Publications, 1990).

6. Ibid.
7. Lee Guang-Hui, unpublished data, 1989, Shanghai, Long March Hospital.
8. A. C. Kinsey, W. B. Pomeroy, and C. E. Martin. *Sexual Behavior in the Human Male* (Philadelphia: W. B. Saunders Co., 1948). Chinese tranlation, Pan Sui-Ming (Beijing: People's Publications, 1990).
9. Ibid.
10. Ibid.
11. Zhou Ming-Xiao, "Solutions to the Unspeakable Questions of Female Univesity Students," *Sex Education* 1 (1988):28.
12. Bertrand Russell, *Marriage and Morals* (London: Allen & Unwin, 1976). Chinese translation, anon. (Shanghai: Eastern Publications, 1990), 78.
13. Ibid., 71–72.
14. Unpublished data.
15. Dalin Liu, *Sex Sociology*, 141

4
Married Couples

1. Overview

The survey of married couples was carried out in fifteen cities (Qingdao, Kaifeng, Chengdu, Wuxi, Shanghai, Nanjing, Tianjin, Jinzhou, Guangzhou, Juhai, Shenzhen, Shaoxing, Shaoguan, Shantou, and Foshan) and in three villages (Yuci, Suzhou, and Qixian). The total number of couples was 7602, of which 6210 (81.7 percent) were from the cities and 1392 (18.3 percent) from the villages. Since the majority of the Chinese population are farmers, a much greater number of villagers would have been desirable in this survey, but because of the enormous obstacles to conducting sex research in rural areas, the sample we obtained was small.

We started by looking for married, healthy husbands or wives with a high school education, since some minimum educational standard was necessary to answer the questions adequately.

Our survey and questionnaire focused on the wives, because traditionally Chinese women—more than men—are held responsible for the consequences of sexual activity. Chinese women are also known to be more submissive, oppressed, and restricted in their sexual lives. They have the greatest share of our social–sexual problems. We therefore felt that, in order to understand the sexual problems of married couples, the wives' problems should be considered first.

The questionnaires were given to the subjects with the instruction to fill them out and return them anonymously. Whenever there were difficulties in answering due to a lack of education (mostly in rural areas), the couples were interviewed and helped in answering the questions. Since most of the interviewers were women from women's organizations, they were able to obtain reliable answers, at least from the wives.

The detailed sample disribution is shown on table 4–1. Of the 6210 subjects surveyed in the cities, 1806 (29.1 percent) were husbands, 4231 (68.1 percent) were wives, 173 (2.8 percent) could not be identified. Of the 1392 subjects from the villages, 301 (21.6 percent) were males, 1088 (78.2 percent) were females, and 3 (0.2 percent) could not be identified. Of all the subjects surveyed, there were 2107 males (27.7 percent), 5319 females (70.0 percent) and 176 (2.3 percent) were unidentified.

Most of the subjects had a secondary education. Generally, the city dwellers were better educated than the villagers. In the cities, the husbands were better educated than the wives, but in the villages, the husbands and wives were of a comparable educational level (tables 4–2 and 4–3). Because of the character of our survey, our sample was, on the average, better educated than the general population in China.

Since illiterate subjects and those with post-secondary education represented less than 5 percent of our total, we combined, for the sake of analysis, illiterates and the primary school educated into one single group, and similarly, we combined those with a high school and post-secondary education into another single group.

Sample Distribution of the Couple Survey		
DISTRICT		NO. SURVEYED
Cities	Qingdao	139
	Chengdu	906
	Wuxi	483
	Shanghai	2573
	Nanjing	179
	Tianjin	1010
	Jinzhou	395
	Guangzhou, Xiamen	525
	(Subtotal)	*6210*
Villages	Suzhou	494
	Yuci, Qi Xian	898
	Shanghai	369
	(Subtotal)	*1961*
Total		7971

Table 4–1

Educational Level of Wives													
REGION NO.	TOTAL	ILLITERATE		PRIMARY		J. HIGH		S. HIGH		COLLEGE OR ABOVE		UNKNOWN	
		NO.	%	NO.	%	NO.	%	NO.	%	NO.	%	NO.	%
City	4231	19	0.4	155	3.7	1416	31.1	1870	44.2	790	18.7	81	1.9
Village	1088	35	3.2	245	22.5	502	46.1	294	27.0	12	1.1	0	0

Table 4–2

EDUCATIONAL LEVEL OF HUSBANDS														
REGION	TOTAL NO.	ILLITERATE		PRIMARY		J. HIGH		S. HIGH		UNIVERSITY OR ABOVE		UNKNOWN	
		NO.	%	NO.	%	NO.	%	NO.	%	NO.	%	NO.	%
City	1806	13	0.7	36	2.0	350	19.4	642	35.5	706	39.1	59	3.3
Village	301	13	4.3	61	20.3	125	41.5	87	28.9	12	4.0	3	1.0

Table 4–3

Most of the subjects were between the ages of twenty-six and forty-five. The mean age of city subjects was 37.42 (SD=9.30). The mean age of village subjects was 34.85 (SD=8.80). The overall mean age was 36.94 (SD=9.26) (tables 4–4, 4–5).

AGE OF WIFE														
	TOTAL NO.	<=25		26–35		36–45		46–55		>=56		UNKNOWN	
		NO.	%	NO.	%	NO.	%	NO.	%	NO.	%	NO.	%
City	4231	242	5.7	1650	39.0	1547	36.6	618	14.6	124	2.9	50	1.2
Village	1088	110	10.1	546	50.2	338	31.1	80	7.4	14	1.3	0	0

Table 4–4

AGE OF HUSBAND														
	TOTAL NO.	<=25		26–35		36–45		46–55		>=56		UNKNOWN	
		NO.	%	NO.	%	NO.	%	NO.	%	NO.	%	NO.	%
City	1806	76	4.2	681	37.7	578	32.0	307	17.0	130	7.2	34	1.9
Village	301	21	7.0	106	35.2	105	34.9	48	15.9	21	7.0	0	0

Table 4–5

Of the city wives, the three most common occupations were technicians, workers, and executives. Of the city husbands, the three most common were technicians, executives, and administrators. Of the village subjects, the occupation of the couples were farming and fishing (tables 4–6, 4–7).

Nearly all of the subjects, i.e., 95.8 percent of the city husbands, 93.1 percent of the city wives, 97.3 percent of the village husbands, and 97.4 percent of the village wives claimed to be healthy (tables 4–8, 4–9).

OCCUPATION OF HUSBAND	TOTAL	FACTORY		AGRICUL.		SERVICE		COMMERCE		OFFICAL	
		NO.	%	NO.	%	NO.	%	NO.	%	NO.	%
City	1806	306	16.9	30	1.7	63	3.5	165	9.1	342	18.9
Village	301	21	7.1	167	56.4	227	9.1	8	2.7	15	5.1

	SENIOR OFFICIAL		PROFESSIONAL		SOLDIER		OTHER		UNKNOWN	
	NO.	%	NO.	%	NO.	%	NO.	%	NO.	%
City	317	17.6	440	24.4	32	1.8	42	2.3	69	3.8
Village	26	8.8	13	4.4	3	1.0	16	5.4	5	1.7

Table 4–6

OCCUPATION OF WIFE	TOTAL	FACTORY		AGRICUL.		SERVICE		COMMERCE		OFFICAL	
		NO.	%	NO.	%	NO.	%	NO.	%	NO.	%
City	4231	860	20.3	93	2.2	266	6.3	461	10.9	773	18.3
Village	1088	218	20.0	581	53.4	91	8.4	25	2.7	25	2.3

	SENIOR OFFICIAL		PROFESSIONAL		SOLDIER		OTHER		UNKNOWN	
	NO.	%	NO.	%	NO.	%	NO.	%	NO.	%
City	477	11.3	1044	24.7	10	0.3	139	3.3	108	2.6
Village	41	3.8	44	4.0	0	0	59	5.4	0	0

Table 4–7

HEALTH OF WIFE	TOTAL	HEALTHY		ORDINARY		SICK		UNKNOWN	
		NO.	%	NO.	%	NO.	%	NO.	%
City	4231	1817	42.9	1919	45.4	279	6.6	216	5.1
Village	1088	723	66.5	332	30.5	28	2.6	5	0.5

Table 4–8

HEALTH OF HUSBAND									
	TOTAL	HEALTHY		ORDINARY		SICK		UNKNOWN	
		NO.	%	NO.	%	NO.	%	NO.	%
City	1806	991	54.9	565	31.3	68	3.8	182	10.1
Village	301	239	79.4	49	16.3	8	2.7	5	1.7

Table 4–9

AGE OF FIRST MARRIAGE (WIFE)											
	TOTAL	<=20		21–25		26–30		>=31			
		NO.	%	NO.	%	NO.	%	NO.	%	NO.	%
City	4231	184	4.3	2189	51.7	1651	39.0	162	3.8	45	1.1
Village	1088	183	16.8	787	72.3	106	9.7	12	1.1	0	0

Table 4–10

AGE OF FIRST MARRIAGE (HUSBAND)											
	TOTAL	<=20		21–25		26–30		>=31			
		NO.	%	NO.	%	NO.	%	NO.	%	NO.	%
City	1806	37	3.7	559	31.0	994	55.0	153	8.5	33	1.8
Village	301	27	9.0	198	65.8	72	23.9	4	1.3	0	0

Table 4–11

Most of the subjects married between the ages of twenty-one to thirty-nine (tables 4–10, 4–11). In the city husbands, the mean age of marriage was 25.98 (SD=3.39); that of the city wives was 24.64 (SD=3.2). For the village husbands and wives the mean ages were 23.38 (SD=2.96) and 22.26 (SD=2.77) respectively. The age difference in

DURATION OF MARRIAGE IN YEARS															
	TOTAL	<=2		3–5		6–10		11–15		16–20		>=21		UNKNOWN	
		NO.	%	NO.	%	NO.	%	NO.	%	NO.	%	NO.	%	NO.	%
City	6210	801	12.9	827	13.3	1518	24.4	887	14.3	685	11.0	1189	19.1	303	4.9
Village	1392	147	10.6	224	16.1	323	23.2	247	17.7	208	14.9	240	17.2	3	0.2

Table 4–12

marriage between the husbands and wives were 1.34 in the cities and 1.12 in the villages.

The duration of marriage in the subjects was quite variable between two to twenty years. Most had been married between six to ten years (table 4–12). The mean duration of marriage in the city subjects was 11.05 (SD=7.41) and in the village subjects was 11.14 (SD=7.19).

2. Marriage and Love

1. The Paths to Marriage

How the spouses become acquainted and how they get married, to a certain extent, influences the mutual perception of the marriage. It can be an important factor in the subsequent development of their feelings for each other. For the Chinese, there are many different ways of finding a spouse. These ways could be divided into two groups: free and arranged marriages. The free marriages result from chance acquaintances or from informal introductions by various intermediaries. The arranged marriages are usually set up by parents, sometimes for economic reasons, and there are also cases of forced marriage.

As shown in table 4–13, 2.0 percent of city couples and 4.3 percent of village couples were married through arranged marriages. For free marriages, the percentages were 97.0 percent and 95.2 percent respectively. More city couples than villagers got acquaintd by themselves.

Our results are quite similar to those of previous studies. By the 1987 survey of Social Science Research Unit of the China National Social Science Institute, in fourteen villages scattered over the country, 74.3 percent of the couples were married by free choice, 18.4 percent were brought together by matchmakers, and 7.1 percent by parental arrangement.[1]

Terms of Marriage

	TOTAL	ARRANGED		PARENTS INTRODUCED		FRIENDS INTRODUCED		SELF ACQUAINTED		UNKOWN	
		NO.	%	NO.	%	NO.	%	NO.	%	NO.	%
City	6210	126	2.0	907	14.6	2899	46.7	2215	35.7	63	1.0
Village	1392	60	4.3	244	17.5	734	52.7	348	25.0	6	0.4

Table 4–13

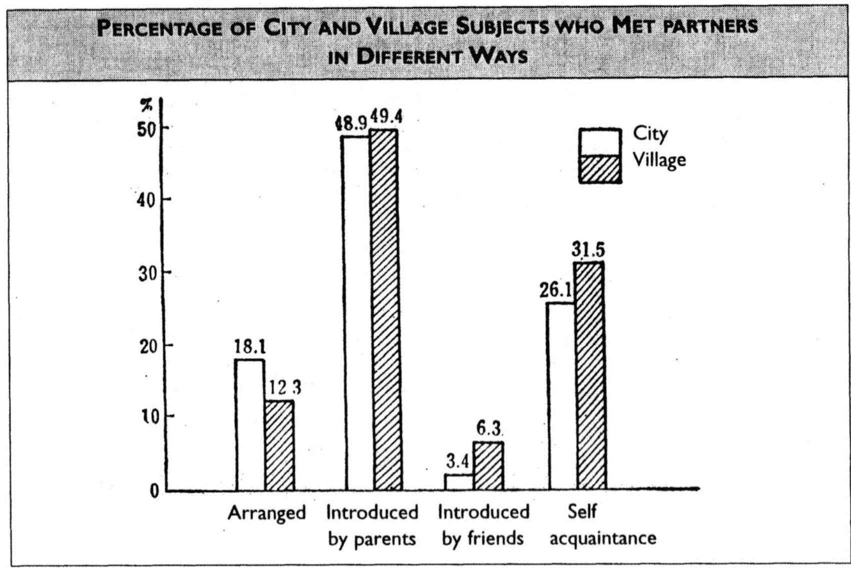

Figure 4–1

The results show that arranged marriages are few, both in the cities or villages. This form of marriage is disappearing in China. Historically, the decline began in the late 1940s, with the rate of arranged marriages decreasing from 47.37 percent in 1945 to 35.56 percent in 1949. In 1950, China announced its first marriage law. The arranged marriage rate decreased further to 28.99 percent in 1952. In 1982, it reached a low level of 1.69 percent, and free marriages rose to 25 percent. But in 1982, because the family enterprise began to replace the hitherto more typical larger enterprises, young people in the villages had fewer chances to socialize. As a result, there was a slight decline in free marriages to 24.29 percent.[2]

Our data show that most couples had met as a result of some introduction by others. In a survey of 1984 in Shanghai, Beijing, and Guangzhou, 65.1 percent, 68.3 percent and 60.8 percent of couples were married as a result of introduction.[3] A survey in Helungjiang in 1986 showed also that in the period from 1982 to 1986, 67.23 percent of newly married couples reported that they had met as a result of introduction.[4] This dominant form of getting acquainted was found not only in the less-educated, but also in the well-educated. In a survey in Tianjin in 1983, 71 percent of the college graduates had found their spouses through introduction.[5] This shows that the social circle of many Chinese is probably rather small.

Factors found to be associated with the types of marriage were:

1. REGION

Table 4–13 already shows that in the villages, there are more arranged marriages, about twice as many as in the cities. These findings are quite similar everywhere, even if we compare cities and villages individually (table 4–14). The only exception is the region around Shanghai, where quite a large number of the village couples there had originally become acquainted on their own. This may be because Shanghai is an especially large city with extensive links to the countryside. As a result, life in the entire region is less restricted.

TERMS OF MARRIAGE IN DIFFERENT REGIONS

		TOTAL	ARRANGED		PARENTS INTRODUCED		FRIENDS INTRODUCED		SELF ACQUAINTED	
			NO.	%	NO.	%	NO.	%	NO.	%
City	Shanghai	2544	34	1.3	330	13.0	1172	46.1	1008	39.6
	Tienjin	1002	30	3.0	176	17.6	553	55.2	243	24.2
	Chengdu	897	14	1.6	122	13.6	425	47.4	336	37.4
	Guangzhou	523	14	2.7	62	11.8	196	37.5	251	48.0
Village	Suzhou	494	20	4.0	115	23.3	236	47.8	123	24.9
	Yuci	892	40	4.5	129	14.5	498	55.8	225	25.2
	Shanghai	367	18	4.9	78	21.3	159	43.3	112	30.5

Table 4–14

2. GENDER

Table 4–15 shows that gender has no significant bearing on the type of marriages the subjects had (alpha=0.01) although more male subjects found their spouses on their own.

GENDER AND TERMS OF MARRIAGE

GENDER	TOTAL	ARRANGED		PARENTS INTRODUCED		FRIENDS INTRODUCED		SELF ACQUAINTED	
		NO.	%	NO.	%	NO.	%	NO.	%
Male	2064	85	4.1	305	14.8	916	44.4	758	36.7
Female	5260	96	1.8	799	15.2	2619	49.8	1746	33.2

Table 4–15

3. AGE

Age has a greater bearing on the type of marriage. The G index for city husband, village husband, and village wives were 0.15, 0.43, and 0.12 respectively. Only the city wives had low G index. The age of the subjects in fact reflects the era in which the subjects got married. Older subjects were still under the influence of traditional practices and hence had more arranged marriages. (tables 4–16, 4–17, 4–18, 4–19)

AGE AND TERMS OF MARRIAGE (CITY HUSBANDS)

	<=25		26–35		36–45		46–55		>=56	
	NO.	%	NO.	%	NO.	%	NO.	%	NO.	%
Arranged	2	2.7	15	2.2	8	1.4	8	2.6	26	20.3
Parent introduced	10	13.3	78	11.6	89	15.5	64	21.0	21	16.4
Friend introduced	21	28.0	319	47.4	252	43.9	121	39.8	49	38.3
Self acquainted	42	56.0	261	38.8	225	39.2	111	36.5	32	25.0
Total	75	100.0	673	100.0	574	100.0	304	100.0	128	100.0

P=0.001

Table 4–16

AGE AND TERMS OF MARRIAGE (CITY WIVES)

	<=25		26–35		36–45		46–55		>=56	
	NO.	%	NO.	%	NO.	%	NO.	%	NO.	%
Arranged	0	0	10	0.6	19	1.2	17	2.8	13	10.5
Parents introduced	28	11.7	221	13.5	248	16.2	81	13.3	23	18.5
Friend introduced	100	41.7	832	50.8	759	49.6	279	45.7	48	38.7
Self acquainted	112	46.7	574	35.1	504	32.9	234	38.3	40	32.3
Total	240	100.0	1637	100.0	1530	100.0	611	100.0	124	100.0

P=0.001

Table 4–17

AGE AND TERMS OF MARRIAGE (VILLAGE HUSBANDS)

	<=25		26–35		36–45		46–55		>=56	
	NO.	%	NO.	%	NO.	%	NO.	%	NO.	%
Arranged	0	0	5	4.7	6	5.9	5	10.4	8	38.1
Parents introduced	2	9.5	13	12.3	14	13.7	13	27.1	6	28.6
Friend introduced	5	23.8	48	45.3	65	63.7	20	41.7	6	28.6
Self acquainted	14	66.7	40	37.7	17	16.7	10	20.8	1	4.8
Total	21	100.0	106	100.0	102	100.0	48	100.0	21	100.0

P=0.001

Table 4–18

AGE AND TERMS OF MARRIAGE (VILLAGE WIVES)										
	<=25		26–35		36–45		46–55		>=56	
	NO.	%	NO.	%	NO.	%	NO.	%	NO.	%
Arranged	1	0.9	8	1.5	10	3.0	8	10.1	8	57.1
Parents introduced	16	14.5	94	17.3	64	18.9	19	24.1	2	14.3
Friend introduced	62	56.4	315	57.9	178	52.7	33	41.8	2	14.3
Self acquainted	31	28.2	127	23.3	86	25.4	19	24.1	2	14.3
Total	110	100.0	544	100.0	338	100.0	79	100.0	14	100.0

P=0.001

Table 4–19

4. EDUCATIONAL LEVEL

There was high correlation between educational level and type of marriage. Table 4–17 and 4–18 show that, in general, the better educated the subjects, the fewer arranged marriages. The G indices for city husbands, city wives, village husbands, and village wives are 0.11, 0.15, 0.44, and 0.16 respectively.

EDUCATIONAL LEVEL AND TERMS OF MARRIAGE (CITY HUSBANDS)										
	ILLITERATE		PRIMARY		J. HIGH		S. HIGH		C. OR ABOVE	
	NO.	%	NO.	%	NO.	%	NO.	%	NO.	%
Arranged	4	30.8	2	5.7	11	3.2	20	3.1	24	3.4
Parents introduced	3	23.1	8	22.9	61	17.6	96	15.1	87	12.4
Friend introduced	2	15.4	15	42.9	154	44.5	289	45.4	294	42.3
Self acquainted	4	30.8	10	1.5	120	34.7	231	36.3	293	41.8
Total	13	100.0	35	100.0	346	100.0	636	100.0	700	100.0

Table 4–20

EDUCATIONAL LEVEL AND TERMS OF MARRIAGE (CITY WIVES)										
	ILLITERATE		PRIMARY		J. HIGH		S. HIGH		C. OR ABOVE	
	NO.	%	NO.	%	NO.	%	NO.	%	NO.	%
Arranged	4	21.1	13	8.4	20	1.5	18	1.0	5	0.6
Parents introduced	4	21.1	37	24.0	197	15.1	259	14.0	100	12.8
Friend introduced	9	47.4	74	48.1	651	50.0	925	49.8	336	42.9
Self acquainted	2	10.5	30	19.5	435	33.4	654	35.2	342	43.7
Total	19	100.0	154	100.0	1303	100.0	1856	100.0	783	100.0

Table 4–21

EDUCATIONAL LEVEL AND TERMS OF MARRIAGE (VILLAGE HUSBANDS)

	ILLITERATE		PRIMARY		J. HIGH		S. HIGH		C. OR ABOVE	
	NO.	%	NO.	%	NO.	%	NO.	%	NO.	%
Arranged	9	69.2	9	15.0	2	1.6	4	4.6	0	0
Parents introduced	2	15.4	13	21.7	22	17.9	8	9.2	2	16.7
Friend introduced	2	15.4	30	50.0	68	55.3	39	44.8	4	33.3
Self acquainted	0	0	8	13.3	31	25.2	36	41.4	6	50.0
Total	13	100.0	60	100.0	123	100.0	87	100.0	12	100.0

Table 4–22

EDUCATIONAL LEVEL AND TERMS OF MARRIAGE (VILLAGE WIVES)

	ILLITERATE		PRIMARY		J. HIGH		S. HIGH		C. OR ABOVE	
	NO.	%	NO.	%	NO.	%	NO.	%	NO.	%
Arranged	11	31.4	11	4.5	7	1.4	4	1.4	2	16.7
Parents introduced	10	28.6	54	22.1	79	15.8	52	17.7	0	0
Friend introduced	9	25.7	135	55.3	276	55.1	163	55.6	7	58.3
Self acquainted	5	14.3	44	18.0	139	27.7	74	25.3	3	25.0
Total	35	100.0	244	100.0	501	100.0	293	100.0	12	100.0

Table 4–23

LEVEL OF EDUCATION AND PERCENTAGE OF CITY AND VILLAGE SUBJECTS WHOSE MARRIAGE WAS ARRANGED

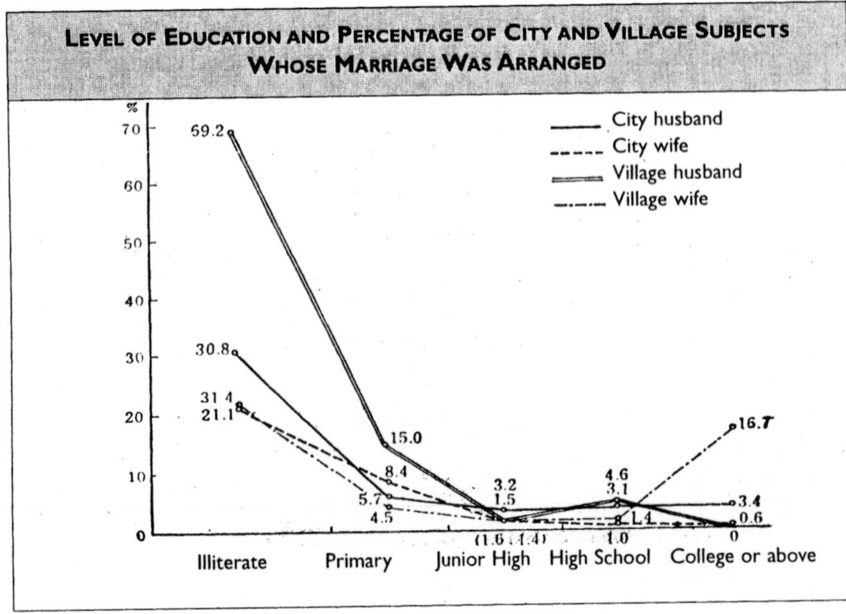

Figure 4–2

The overall finding relating to the type of marriage is that the proportion of arranged marriages in modern China is low—at around 2.4 percent of all marriages. Yet, if the large Chinese population in China is considered, this percentage represents a total of about five million couples in arranged marriages. This is about the total number of couples in a medium-sized country. Furthermore, arranged marriages are still found in some subjects under the age of thirty-five. This shows that freedom of marital choice has not yet been achieved everywhere in China.

In 1978 in Helungjiang, of the toal 13,427 newly married couples, 867 were found to be in arranged marriages. In 1985, in twenty-three villages around Yulin Xian (city), 2559 couples were in arranged marriages, representing 30 percent of the total marriages in that region. From 1980 to 1986, in Gaozhou Xian of Guangdong province, of eighty-three newlyweds, forty were in arranged marriages.[6] In Anhui province, in the Xu'an district court of Lu'an Xian, of the 366 divorce cases handled in 1985, 141 dealt with arranged marriages.[7] In some villages, the parents still say, "We are not used to seeing free relationships and free marriages. Any boys and girls who find their own partners are bound to be criticized."

Arranged marriages in China are not due only to low educational levels; economic need is also a cause. Under the pressure of poverty, women are still considered family property to be "given in marriage" for profit. There are many ways in which one can dispose of this property. A direct way is to actually sell women in the market, as still practiced in the northeastern villages. In the 1950s and 1960s, the price was two hundred yuen for single-eyelid women, four hundred yuen for double eyelids. The price is known to have increased considerably in the 1980s. More commonly, however, parents gave a girl away in return for a "wedding gift" (often a certain sum of cash) from the bridegroom. According to the study of the National Marriage and Family Research Society, in 1980, about 0.5 percent of villages asked for wedding gifts at a price of over three thousand yuen. In 1986, the percentage rose to 10.5 percent, and in certain provinces, the percentage was up to 47 percent. This over tenfold increase is disproportional to the average income of the inhabitant which barely doubled during the same period.

There is another way to sell a bride directly. For example, in Helungjiang, a father had twice forced his daughter to get married in order to pay debts, first for one thousand yuan and later for three thousand yuan. In Shaanxi province, a villager sold his three daughters to three mental patients for 13,300 yuan.[8] Many female suicides were found to be related to this kind of forced marriage.

In short, forced or arranged marriages for women still exist in China in many forms. Although the government is trying hard to discourage it, economic hardship still keeps the practice alive in various parts of China. This is another social problem waiting to be solved.

3. Love

Modern views of marriage hold that it should be based on love. The traditional Chinese view, however, emphasizes not love, but the different roles and identities of husband and wife and their duties to each other.

1. Definitions of Love

Historically, writers have offered many different definitions of love.[9] Ellis thought that love, in the sense of being the spiritual side of a sexual relationship, was the same as life.[10] He also thought of love as the sum of all impulses, including the sexual impulse.[11] Warseleff thought that although love is based on sex, it exists on a much higher level of affection, stimulating higher psychological functions and creating happiness.[12] In China, however, theoreticians understand love as an afffection based on a particular social relationship and a shared aspiration. It is not solely physical or psychological.

2. Must Marriages Be Based on Love?

Asking our subjects for a definition of love would have been too difficult and abstract. Hence, we asked a more concrete question: "Must marriages be based on love?" A majority answered in the affirmative, with more city dwellers doing so than villagers (table 4–24).

Table 4–25 shows that fewer males gave an affirmative answer regarding this question.

For all the subjects except the village wives, the higher the educational level was, the greater the importance of love in marriage became (G>0.1). This may be a result of the fact that the better educated tend

Region and Attitude toward the Need for Love in Marriage

	TOTAL	HEALTHY		ORDINARY		SICK		UNKNOWN	
		NO.	%	NO.	%	NO.	%	NO.	%
City	6210	5488	88.4	131	2.1	519	8.4	72	1.2
Village	1392	1165	83.7	44	3.2	179	12.9	4	0.3

Table 4–24

GENDER AND ATTITUDE TOWARD THE NEED FOR LOVE IN MARRIAGE							
	TOTAL	YES		NO		MAYBE	
		NO.	%	NO.	%	NO.	%
Male	2063	1786	86.5	48	2.3	229	11.1
Female	5255	4692	89.2	117	2.2	446	8.5

P=0.001

Table 4–25

PERCENTAGE OF VILLAGE AND CITY SUBJECTS ON DIFFERENT VIEWS ON LOVE IN MARRIAGE

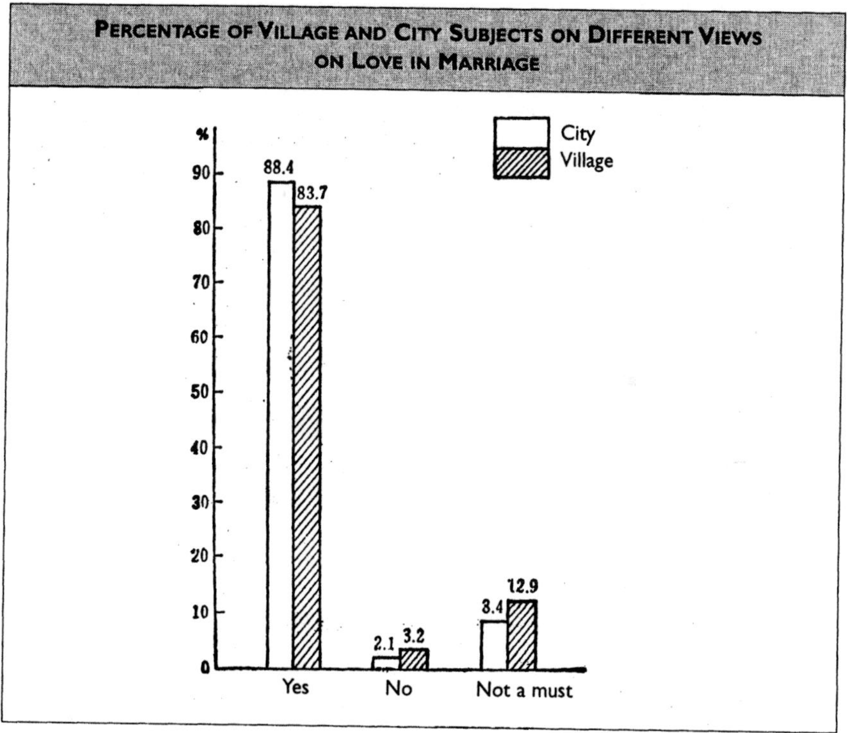

Figure 4–3

EDUCATION AND ATTITUDE ON THE NEED FOR LOVE IN MARRIAGE (CITY HUSBAND)										
	ILLITERATE		PRIMARY		J. HIGH		S. HIGH		C. OR ABOVE	
	NO.	%	NO.	%	NO.	%	NO.	%	NO.	%
Yes	9	75.0	26	72.2	299	86.9	548	86.3	626	89.3
No	0	0	1	2.8	9	2.6	15	2.4	11	1.6
Maybe	3	25.0	9	25.0	36	10.5	72	11.3	64	9.1
Total	12	100.0	36	100.0	344	100.0	635	100.0	701	100.0

Table 4–26

to look for more emotional and spiritual satisfaction. (tables 4–26 to 4–29, figure 4–4)

In 1986, a similar survey on this aspect was conducted among Helungjiang villagers.[13] The question asked was: "What do you think is the most important factor in making a marriage last?" Of the subjects surveyed, 930 (64.5 percent) answered that love was the most important. Other factors mentioned were mutual understanding (17.42 percent), personal compatibility (7.77 percent), common interests

Education and Attitude on the Need for Love in Marriage (City Wives)

	ILLITERATE		PRIMARY		J. HIGH		S. HIGH		C. & ABOVE	
	NO.	%	NO.	%	NO.	%	NO.	%	NO.	%
Yes	13	68.4	128	84.8	1155	89.1	1687	90.9	731	92.9
No	2	10.5	5	3.3	30	2.3	36	1.9	13	1.7
Maybe	4	21.1	18	11.9	112	8.6	132	7.1	43	5.5
Total	19	100.0	151	100.0	1297	100.0	1855	100.0	787	100.0

Table 4–27

Education and Attitude on the Need for Love in Marriage (Villge Husband)

	ILLITERATE		PRIMARY		J. HIGH		S. HIGH		C. & ABOVE	
	NO.	%	NO.	%	NO.	%	NO.	%	NO.	%
Yes	10	76.9	46	76.7	102	81.6	77	89.5	11	91.7
No	1	7.7	1	1.7	7	5.6	4	4.7	0	0
Maybe	2	15.4	13	21.7	16	12.8	5	5.8	1	8.3
Total	13	100.0	60	100.0	125	100.0	86	100.0	12	100.0

Table 4–28

Education and Attitude on the Need for Love in Marriage (Village Wives)

	ILLITERATE		PRIMARY		J. HIGH		S. HIGH		C. & ABOVE	
	NO.	%	NO.	%	NO.	%	NO.	%	NO.	%
Yes	27	77.1	202	82.8	426	84.9	250	85.0	10	90.9
No	1	2.9	8	3.3	12	2.4	7	2.4	1	9.1
Maybe	7	10.0	34	13.9	64	12.7	37	12.6	0	0
Total	35	100.0	244	100.0	502	100.0	294	100.0	11	100.0

Table 4–29

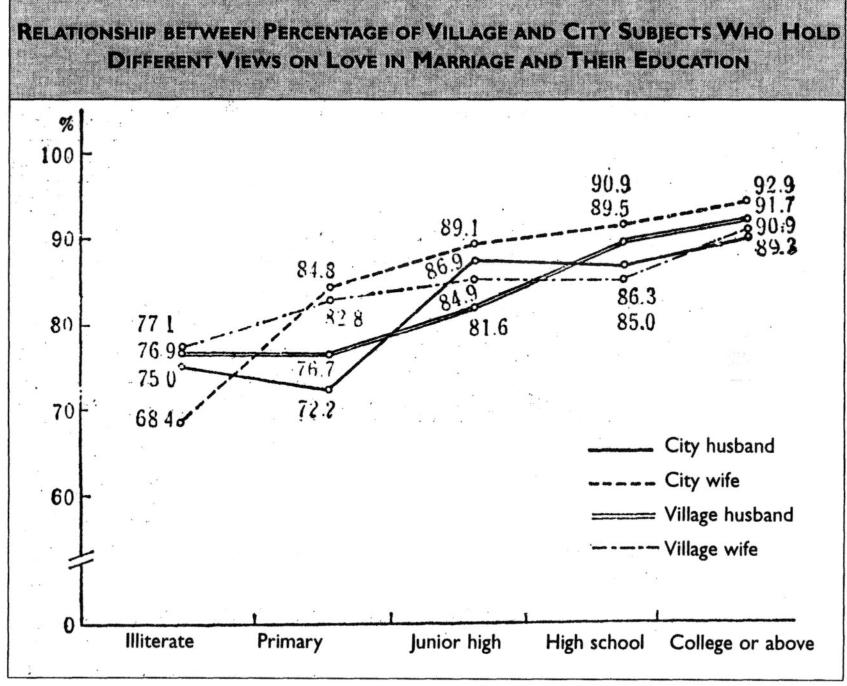

Figure 4–4

(2.49 percent), material benefits (2.22 percent), social approval (1.46 percent), cultural aspiration (0.21 percent), and others (0.14 percent). The percentage of subjects seeing love as the most important factor was smaller than ours, but since the older survey allowed answers to overlap with other emotional factors, the difference might be less than it appears.

In a survey in Russia, Jachoubin (1987) did a more detailed study on the types of emotional relationships accepted by married couples. Of the seven hundred subjects surveyed, twenty could not accept unrequited love between married couples. Of the females in the remaining 680 subjects, 70 percent would rather have been loved by a spouse whom they themselves did not love, and 30 percent would rather have loved someone who did not love them. This Russian survey showed how love relationships among marital couples can vary. As Engels said, "Love that is free from monetary considerations can appear only in societies that are highly developed in spiritual and material wealth."[14]

3. Nothing but Love?

A commonly held view is that love is more important than anything else: "Everything can be given up for the sake of love!" For young people, this view translates into the following conviction: "As long as a pair of lovers are in love, they can have sex, even if they are not married to each other." With this view, as table 4–30 shows, 34.3 percent of the males and 16.0 percent of the females agreed. And this agreement did not vary with the educational level of the subjects (tables 4–31, 4–32, 4–33, and 4–34).

ATTITUDE TOWARD SEX WITH LOVE BUT WITHOUT MARRIAGE							
	TOTAL	AGREE		DISAGREE		NOT MIND	
		NO.	%	NO.	%	NO.	%
Male	2053	339	16.5	1348	65.7	366	17.8
Female	5263	397	7.5	4422	84.1	444	8.4

P=0.001

Table 4–30

EDUCATION AND ATTITUDE ON SEX WITH LOVE BUT WITHOUT MARRIAGE (CITY HUSBAND)										
	ILLITERATE		PRIMARY		J. HIGH		S. HIGH		C. OR ABOVE	
	NO.	%	NO.	%	NO.	%	NO.	%	NO.	%
Agree	3	23.1	6	16.7	54	15.8	103	16.2	125	18.1
Disagree	7	53.8	27	75.0	224	65.5	416	65.3	433	62.6
Not mind	3	23.1	3	8.3	64	18.7	118	18.5	134	19.4
Total	13	100.0	36	100.0	342	100.0	637	100.0	692	100.0

Table 4–31

EDUCATION AND ATTITUDE ON SEX WITH LOVE BUT WITHOUT MARRIAGE (CITY WIVES)										
	ILLITERATE		PRIMARY		J. HIGH		S. HIGH		C. OR ABOVE	
	NO.	%	NO.	%	NO.	%	NO.	%	NO.	%
Agree	2	10.5	11	7.2	98	7.5	140	7.5	61	7.8
Disagree	16	84.2	131	86.2	1094	83.8	1571	84.7	634	81.0
Not mind	1	5.3	10	6.6	114	8.7	144	7.8	88	11.2
Total	19	100.0	152	100.0	1306	100.0	1855	100.0	783	100.0

Table 4–32

Education and Attitude on Sex with Love but without Marriage (Village Husband)										
	ILLITERATE		PRIMARY		J. HIGH		S. HIGH		C. & ABOVE	
	NO.	%	NO.	%	NO.	%	NO.	%	NO.	%
Agree	2	15.4	10	16.9	11	8.8	3	3.4	1	8.3
Disagree	8	61.5	40	67.8	100	80.0	76	87.4	11	91.7
Not mind	3	23.1	9	15.3	14	11.2	8	9.2	0	0
Total	13	100.0	59	100.0	125	100.0	87	100.0	12	100.0

Table 4–33

Education and Attitude on Sex with Love but without Marriage (Village Wives)										
	ILLITERATE		PRIMARY		J. HIGH		S. HIGH		C. & ABOVE	
	NO.	%	NO.	%	NO.	%	NO.	%	NO.	%
Agree	4	11.8	20	8.2	36	7.2	30	10.3	0	0
Disagree	27	79.4	205	83.7	424	84.6	237	81.4	11	91.7
Not mind	3	8.8	20	8.2	41	5.2	24	8.2	1	8.3
Total	34	100.0	245	100.0	501	100.0	291	100.0	12	100.0

Table 4–34

Type of First Sex Partner and Attitude toward Sex with Love but without Marriage (City Subjects)						
TYPE OF FIRST SEX PARTNER	AGREE		DISAGREE		NOT MIND	
	NO.	%	NO.	%	NO.	%
Spouse	504	89.5	3945	97.8	574	92.9
Non-spouse	59	10.5	89	2.2	44	7.1
Total	563	100.0	4034	100.0	618	100.0

Table 4–35

Type of First Sex Partner and Attitude toward Sex with Love but without Marriage (Village Subjects)						
TYPE OF FIRST SEX PARTNER	AGREE		DISAGREE		NOT MIND	
	NO.	%	NO.	%	NO.	%
Spouse	105	92.9	1061	96.8	115	98.3
Non-spouse	8	7.1	35	3.2	2	1.7
Total	113	100.0	1096	100.0	117	100.0

Table 4–36

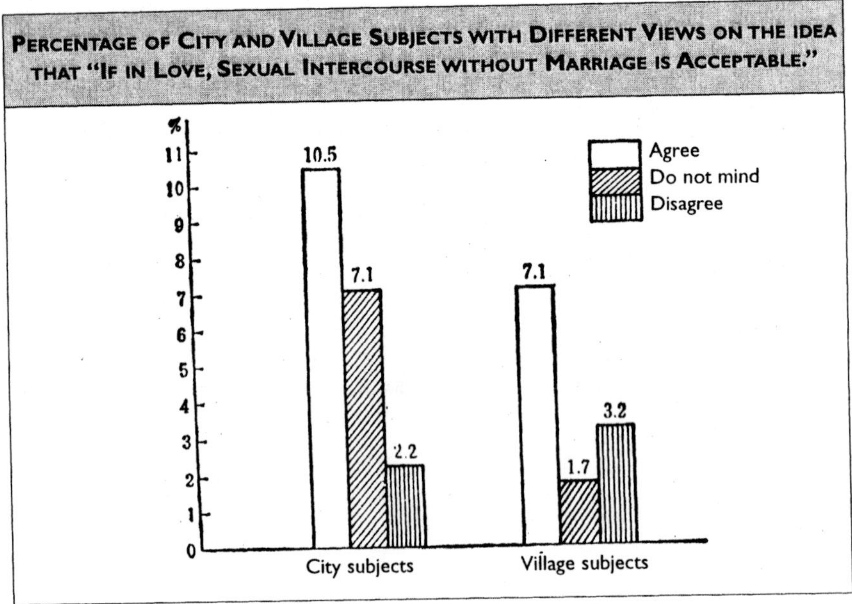

Figure 4–5

The agreement, however, had a significant relationship with the subjects' sexual histories. Most of these subjects had not had their first sexual experience with their spouse or future marital partner. This shows how much sexual attitudes influence sexual behavior.

Most scholars do not agree that love should be put above all other concerns. After all, love must be considered within the context of other good things in life which it enhances and which, in turn, color its character. If the importance of love is exaggerated to such a degree that it renders everything else insignificant, it loses its original meaning and purpose. As a Chinese scholar Fu Lei said, "In my whole life, I have never taken love as being above everything."[15]

4. Views on the Portrayal of Love in the Mass Media

Views on the portrayal of love in the mass media can be an indirect reflection of the subjects' attitude toward love. Tables 4–37 and 4–38 and figure 4–6 show the subjects views on the portrayal of kissing and hugging in the mass media.

In table 4–37 and 4–38, more males liked to watch kissing and hugging on television than females. More subjects in the villages considered these depictions revolting. But on the whole, the majority of the subjects felt neutral about this.

Attitude toward Kissing and Embracing Scenes in Movies and Videos							
	TOTAL	AGREE		DISAGREE		NOT MIND	
		NO.	%	NO.	%	NO.	%
Male	2070	393	19.0	317	15.3	1360	65.7
Female	5260	663	12.6	1092	20.7	3505	66.5

P=0.001

Table 4–37

Region and Attitude toward Kissing and Embracing in Movies and Videos									
	TOTAL	LIKE IT		OFFENDED		NOT MIND		UNKNOWN	
		NO.	%	NO.	%	NO.	%	NO.	%
City	6210	922	14.8	1027	16.5	4196	67.6	65	1.0
Village	1392	167	12.0	419	30.1	803	57.7	3	0.2

Table 4–38

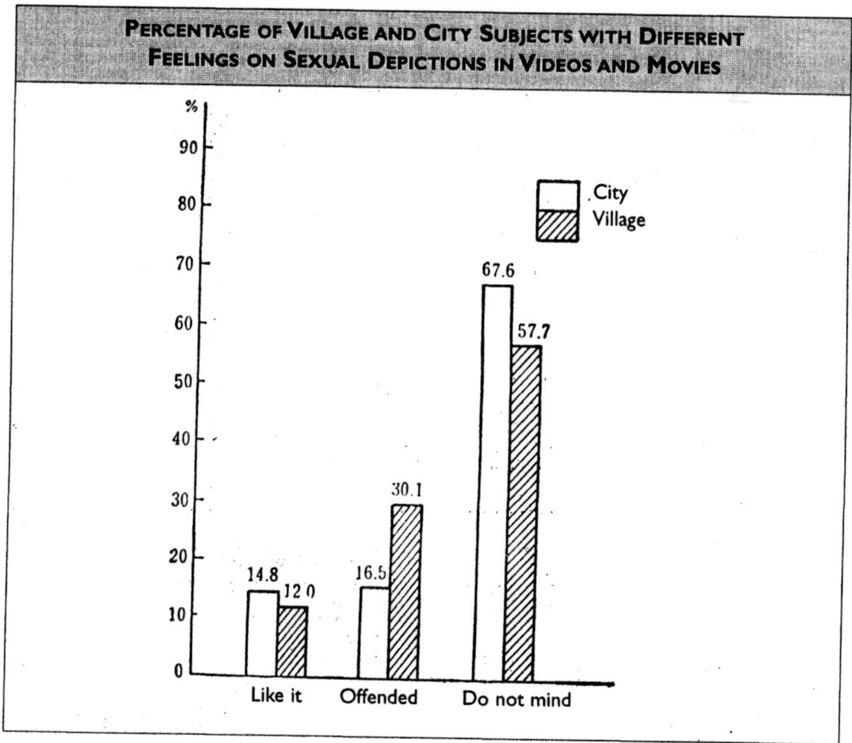

Figure 4–6

Except for village husbands, the higher the subjects' educational level, the more they liked to watch sexual scenes on television (tables 4–39, 4–40, 4–41, 4–42). Among the better educated, a much smaller percentage felt any revulsion over such scenes.

Table 4–38 shows one more finding. The subjects here were not very interested in watching depictions of love. Only 14.8 percent of the city

EDUCATION AND ATTITUDE TOWARD KISSING AND EMBRACING IN MOVIES AND VIDEOS (CITY HUSBANDS)

	ILLITERATE		PRIMARY		J. HIGH		S. HIGH		C. OR ABOVE	
	NO.	%	NO.	%	NO.	%	NO.	%	NO.	%
Like it	2	15.4	4	11.1	83	23.9	112	17.6	138	19.7
Offended	3	23.1	12	33.3	56	16.1	77	12.1	70	10.0
Not mind	8	61.5	30	55.6	208	59.9	447	70.3	493	70.3
Total	13	100.0	36	100.0	347	100.0	636	100.0	701	100.0

Table 4–39

EDUCATION AND ATTITUDE TOWARD KISSING AND EMBRACING IN MOVIES AND VIDEOS (CITY WIVES)

	ILLITERATE		PRIMARY		J. HIGH		S. HIGH		C. OR ABOVE	
	NO.	%	NO.	%	NO.	%	NO.	%	NO.	%
Like it	0	0	12	7.8	176	13.6	253	13.6	95	12.1
Offended	5	26.3	48	31.2	270	20.8	309	16.7	122	15.5
Not mind	4	73.7	94	61.0	852	65.6	1293	69.7	569	74.4
Total	19	100.0	154	100.0	1298	100.0	1855	100.0	786	100.0

Table 4–40

EDUCATION AND ATTITUDE TOWARD KISSING AND EMBRACING IN MOVIES AND VIDEOS (VILLAGE HUSBANDS)

	ILLITERATE		PRIMARY		J. HIGH		S. HIGH		C. OR ABOVE	
	NO.	%	NO.	%	NO.	%	NO.	%	NO.	%
Like it	2	15.4	11	18.3	19	15.2	8	9.2	2	16.7
Offended	4	30.8	20	33.3	30	24.0	24	27.6	2	16.7
Not mind	7	53.8	29	48.3	76	60.8	55	63.2	8	66.7
Total	13	100.0	60	100.0	125	100.0	87	100.0	12	100.0

Table 4–41

EDUCATION AND ATTITUDE TOWARD KISSING AND EMBRACING IN MOVIES AND VIDEOS (VILLAGE WIVES)										
	ILLITERATE		PRIMARY		J. HIGH		S. HIGH		C. OR ABOVE	
	NO.	%	NO.	%	NO.	%	NO.	%	NO.	%
Like it	5	14.3	23	9.4	53	10.6	41	14.0	2	16.7
Offended	12	34.3	82	33.5	150	29.9	91	31.1	2	16.7
Not mind	18	51.4	140	57.1	298	59.5	161	54.9	8	66.7
Total	35	100.0	245	100.0	501	100.0	263	100.0	12	100.0

Table 4–42

couples and 12.0 percent of the village couples enjoyed watching these depictions. Most of the rest felt indifferent, especially the middle-age couples. They said, "We are old couples already. What has love got to do with us anymore?" This attitude is quite different from that of Russell, who taught the special value of long-term sexual relationship.[16]

5. Marital Satisfaction

The wedding is often just the beginning of a sexual relationship. It is no guarantee of happiness. Some scholars are even pessimistic about the value of marriage for achieving happiness: "In real life, marriage is more often a painful hell for modern people."[17] In our survey, we included questions that explore the marital satisfaction of the Chinese couples interviewed.

1. Subjective Satisfaction

Table 4–43 shows that 59.1 percent of the city couples felt good about heir marriage, and 32.1 percent felt all right about it. Of the village couples, 64.8 percent felt good, and 26.5 percent felt all right. The differences between city and village couples are not great.

SEX AND MARITAL SATISFACTION											
REGION	TOTAL	SATISFIED		ORDINARY		NOT SATISFIED		CANNOT TELL		UNKNOWN	
		NO.	%	NO.	%	NO.	%	NO.	%	NO.	%
City	6210	3670	59.1	1996	32.1	255	4.1	263	4.2	26	0.4
Village	1392	902	64.8	369	26.5	40	2.9	80	5.7	1	0.1

Table 4–43

City Subjects and Marital Satisfaction									
REGION	TOTAL	SATISFIED		NOT SATISFIED		CANNOT TELL		UNKNOWN	
		NO.	%	NO.	%	NO.	%	NO.	%
Male	1796	1097	61.1	564	31.4	67	3.7	68	3.8
Female	4215	2485	59.0	1364	32.4	177	4.2	189	4.5

P=0.5

Table 4–44

Village Subjects and Marital Satisfaction									
REGION	TOTAL	SATISFIED		NOT SATISFIED		CANNOT TELL		UNKNOWN	
		NO.	%	NO.	%	NO.	%	NO.	%
Male	301	192	63.8	83	27.6	7	2.3	19	6.3
Female	1087	709	65.2	285	26.2	32	2.9	61	5.6

P=0.9

Table 4–45

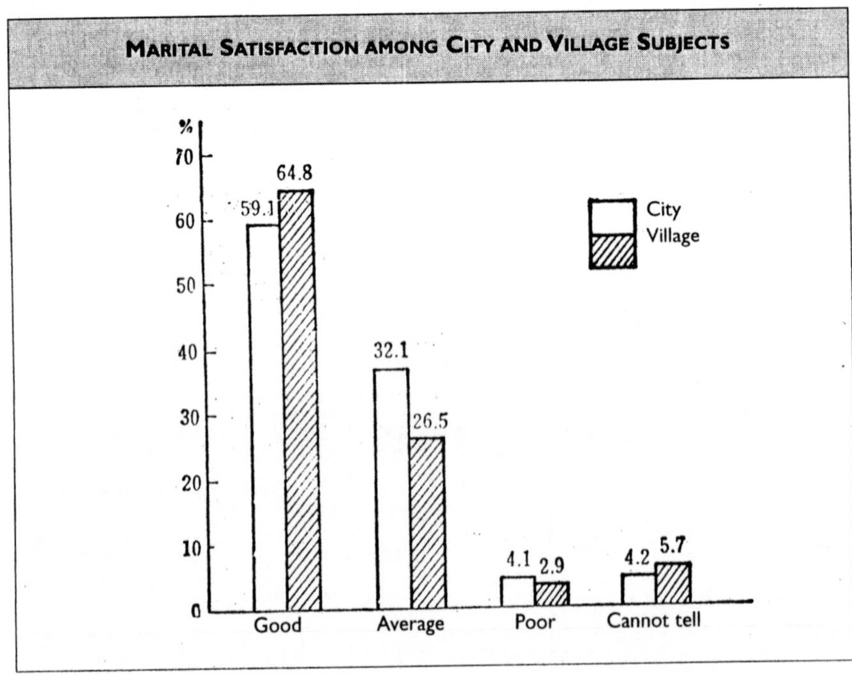

Figure 4–7

Tables 4–44 and 4–45 show that in the cities, the marital satisfaction of the wives was lower than that of the husbands. Yet, the reverse was true in the villages. This may mean that city women have higher expectations of their marriages or that city wives encounter more serious problems.

The low percentage of dissatified couples shows that Chinese couples score higher in satisfacton than westerners. In the United States, a magazine did a survey on the readers' estimation of happily married wives in America. The results showed that 27 percent of the readers thought there were about 25 percent happy wives, 15 percent of the readers gave 26 to 49 percent, 20 percent of the readers gave 50 percent, and 3 percent gave 100 percent. The estimate therefore expressed the view that less than half of American wives were satisfied with their marriage.

Our results agree well with other Chinese surveys on marital satisfaction,[18] but our survey went further, asking for more details. To the question about the subjects' feeling when they had to separate temporarily from their spouses, 22.7 percent of city subjects and 34.7 percent of village subjects answered that they had no special feelings. In regard to the question of whether they would feel more relaxed in case of a temporary separation, 39.1 percent of the city subjects and 40.5 percent of the village subjects answered no. To the question of whether they had ever thought that they would be happier with another spouse, 34.7

Do You Miss Your Spouse When You Are Not Together?									
	TOTAL	YES		NO		NO FEELING		UNKNOWN	
		NO.	%	NO.	%	NO.	%	NO.	%
City	6210	4708	75.8	283	4.6	1123	18.1	96	1.5
Village	1392	908	65.2	80	5.7	403	29.0	1	0.1

Table 4–46

Do You Feel More Relaxed When Not with Your Spouse?									
	TOTAL	YES		NO		NO FEELING		UNKNOWN	
		NO.	%	NO.	%	NO.	%	NO.	%
City	6210	899	14.5	3629	58.4	1530	24.6	152	2.4
Village	1392	115	8.3	827	59.4	448	32.2	2	0.1

Table 4–47

HAVE YOU THOUGHT THAT YOU MIGHT BE HAPPIER IF YOU HAD MARRIED SOMEBODY ELSE?										
	TOTAL	OFTEN		SOMETIMES		NO		UNKNOWN		
		NO.	%	NO.	%	NO.	%	NO.	%	
City	3210	217	3.5	1940	31.2	3897	62.8	156	2.5	
Village	1392	59	4.2	371	26.7	956	68.7	6	0.4	

Table 4–48

percent of the city subjects and 30.9 percent of village subjects said that they often had such thoughts. These three items were related to marital satisfaction with high G indices of 0.58, 0.49, and 0.69 respectively. Although one can attribute different meanings to these answers, and although they may not necessarily indicate marital satisfaction or dissatisfaction, overall, it is quite plausible that the subjects' satisfaction in their marriages was real. This means that only about one third of the couples were not satisfied or felt indifferent about their marriages.

2. Other Factors Associated with the Marital Relationship

Most Chinese scholars agree that people of different age, social background, and sex have different expectations and criteria on marital satisfaction.[19] Our survey confirms this view.

A. AGE

Tables 4–43, 4–44, and 4–45 already show the regional differences in marital satisfaction. Tables 4–49, 4–50, 4–51, and 4–52 show that age is not associated with variations in marital satisfaction (G less than 0.1), although there is a relative trend that subjects at the age of twenty-five

AGE AND MARITAL SATISFACTION (CITY HUSBANDS)										
	<=25		26–35		36–45		46–55		>=56	
	NO.	%	NO.	%	NO.	%	NO.	%	NO.	%
Satisfied	48	64.0	412	60.8	342	59.4	201	65.7	76	58.9
Ordinary	19	25.3	212	31.3	192	33.3	92	30.1	42	32.6
Not satisfied	4	5.3	22	3.2	24	4.2	8	2.6	5	3.9
Cannot tell	4	5.3	32	4.7	18	3.1	5	1.6	6	4.7
Total	75	100.0	678	100.0	576	100.0	306	100.0	129	100.0

P=0.001

Table 4–49

Age and Marital Satisfaction (City Wives)										
	<=25		26–35		36–45		46–55		>=56	
	NO.	%	NO.	%	NO.	%	NO.	%	NO.	%
Satisfied	160	66.7	972	59.1	880	57.1	371	60.1	71	57.7
Ordinary	52	21.7	515	31.3	543	35.3	202	32.7	38	30.9
Not satisfied	11	4.6	75	4.6	60	3.9	18	2.9	10	8.1
Cannot tell	17	7.1	83	5.0	57	3.7	26	4.2	4	3.3
Total	240	100.0	1645	100.0	1540	100.0	617	100.0	123	100.0

P=0.5

Table 4–50

Age and Marital Satisfaction (Village Husbands)										
	<=25		26–35		36–45		46–55		>=56	
	NO.	%	NO.	%	NO.	%	NO.	%	NO.	%
Satisfied	15	71.4	67	63.2	68	64.8	30	62.5	12	57.1
Ordinary	3	14.3	32	30.2	27	25.7	13	27.1	8	38.1
Not satisfied	1	4.8	2	1.9	3	2.9	1	2.1	0	0
Cannot tell	2	9.5	5	4.7	7	6.7	4	8.3	1	4.8
Total	21	100.0	106	100.0	105	100.0	48	100.0	21	100.0

P=0.95

Table 4–51

Age and Marital Satisfaction (Village Wives)										
	<=25		26–35		36–45		46–55		>=56	
	NO.	%	NO.	%	NO.	%	NO.	%	NO.	%
Satisfied	80	72.7	357	65.5	216	63.9	48	60.0	8	57.1
Ordinary	21	19.1	138	25.3	97	28.7	25	31.3	4	28.6
Not satisfied	4	3.6	18	3.3	8	2.4	1	1.3	1	7.1
Cannot tell	5	4.5	32	5.9	17	5.0	6	7.5	1	7.1
Total	110	100.0	545	100.0	338	100.0	80	100.0	14	100.0

P=0.90

Table 4–52

and below have the highest percentage of satisfaction. From age twenty-six to forty-five, the percentage of satisfied subjects declines steadily. Another period of decline is after the age of fifty-six. It is possible that the young and the middle-aged experience fewer challenges. For example,young people might still be free from the burden of a child. The elderly, one the other hand, might have difficulties in adapting to the physiological and psychological changes of old age.

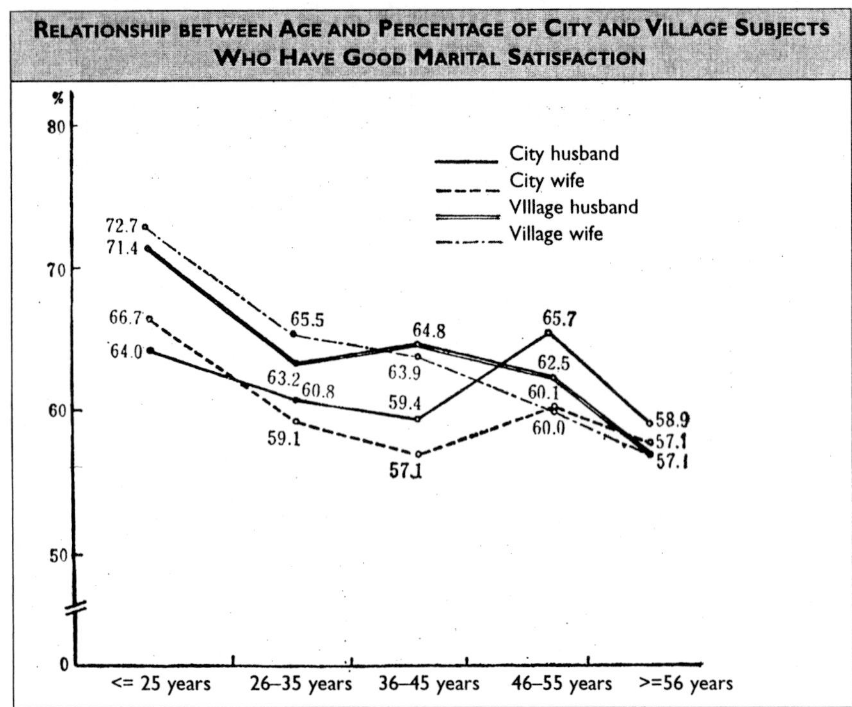

Figure 4–8

EDUCATIONAL LEVEL AND MARITAL SATISFACTION (CITY HUSBANDS)

	ILLITERATE		PRIMARY		J. HIGH		S. HIGH		C. OR ABOVE	
	NO.	%	NO.	%	NO.	%	NO.	%	NO.	%
Satisfied	4	30.8	16	44.4	215	61.6	375	58.7	458	65.4
Ordinary	5	38.5	13	36.1	110	31.5	221	34.6	193	27.6
Not satisfied	1	7.7	3	8.3	11	3.2	19	3.0	29	4.1
Cannot tell	3	23.1	4	11.1	13	3.7	24	3.8	20	2.9
Total	13	100.0	36	100.0	349	100.0	639	100.0	700	100.0

Table 4–53

B. EDUCATION

The marital satisfaction and the educational level of the city and village husbands have a relationship G index of 0.10 and 0.14 respectively. The wives show an even weaker asociation. The trend, however, is still recognizable: The higher the level of education, the greater the satisfaction in marriage. It may be that the better educated have more resources available to them to tackle their problems or know better how to tolerate or adapt to their partners.

EDUCATIONAL LEVEL AND MARITAL SATISFACTION (CITY WIVES)

	ILLITERATE		PRIMARY		J. HIGH		S. HIGH		C. OR ABOVE	
	NO.	%	NO.	%	NO.	%	NO.	%	NO.	%
Satisfied	3	15.8	85	55.6	757	57.8	1107	59.4	479	60.8
Ordinary	11	57.9	49	32.0	412	31.5	621	33.3	251	31.9
Not satisfied	0	0	10	6.5	78	6.0	59	3.2	26	3.3
Cannot tell	5	26.3	9	5.9	63	4.8	77	4.1	32	4.1
Total	19	100.0	153	100.0	1310	100.0	1864	100.0	788	100.0

Table 4–54

EDUCATIONAL LEVEL AND MARITAL SATISFACTION (VILLAGE HUSBANDS)

	ILLITERATE		PRIMARY		J. HIGH		S. HIGH		C. OR ABOVE	
	NO.	%	NO.	%	NO.	%	NO.	%	NO.	%
Satisfied	8	61.5	36	59.0	75	60.0	62	71.3	9	75.0
Ordinary	4	30.8	19	31.1	40	32.0	17	19.5	2	16.7
Not satisfied	1	7.7	1	1.6	3	2.4	2	2.3	0	0
Cannot tell	0	0	5	8.2	7	5.6	6	6.9	1	8.3
Total	13	100.0	61	100.0	125	100.0	87	100.0	12	100.0

Table 4–55

EDUCATIONAL LEVEL AND MARITAL SATISFACTION (VILLAGE WIVES)

	ILLITERATE		PRIMARY		J. HIGH		S. HIGH		C. OR ABOVE	
	NO.	%	NO.	%	NO.	%	NO.	%	NO.	%
Satisfied	21	60.0	160	65.3	324	64.7	194	66.0	10	83.3
Ordinary	13	37.1	64	26.1	136	27.1	71	24.1	1	8.3
Not satisfied	0	0	11	4.5	10	2.0	11	3.7	0	0
Cannot tell	1	2.9	10	4.1	31	6.2	18	6.1	1	8.3
Total	35	100.0	245	100.0	501	100.0	294	100.0	12	100.0

Table 4–56

C. TYPE OF MARRIAGE

Those who married by parental arrangement were obviously less satisfied than those in a freely sought marriage (G=0.13 for city subjects and 0.08 for village subjects) (tables 4–57, 4–58, and figure 4–9). In figure 4–9, it can be seen that the discrepancy in satisfaction was much smallers in the village couples than in the city couples. It shows that in the villages, probably due to a strict, traditional, conservative, and closed environment, the couples there were more used to arranged marriages anyway.

TERMS OF MARRIAGE AND MARITAL SATISFACTION (CITY)

	ARRANGED		PARENT INTRODUCED		FRIEND INTRODUCED		SELF ACQUAINTED	
	NO.	%	NO.	%	NO.	%	NO.	%
Satisfied	46	36.5	504	55.9	1676	58.0	1409	63.9
Ordinary	40	31.7	320	35.5	983	34.0	632	28.7
Not satisfied	21	16.7	37	4.1	124	4.3	72	3.3
Cannot tell	19	15.1	41	4.5	106	3.7	92	4.2
Total	126	100.0	902	100.0	2889	100.0	2205	100.0

Table 4–57

TERMS OF MARRIAGE AND MARITAL SATISFACTION (VILLAGE)

	ARRANGED		PARENT INTRODUCED		FRIEND INTRODUCED		SELF ACQUAINTED	
	NO.	%	NO.	%	NO.	%	NO.	%
Satisfied	35	58.3	154	63.1	468	63.8	241	69.3
Ordinary	17	28.3	70	28.7	203	27.7	78	22.4
Not satisfied	4	6.7	7	2.9	19	2.6	10	2.9
Cannot tell	4	6.7	13	5.3	43	5.9	19	5.5
Total	60	100.0	244	100.0	733	100.0	348	100.0

Table 4–58

RELATIONSHIP BETWEEN ARRANGED MARRIAGE AND PERCENTAGE OF CITY AND VILLAGE SUBJECTS WHO HAVE MARITAL SATISFACTION.

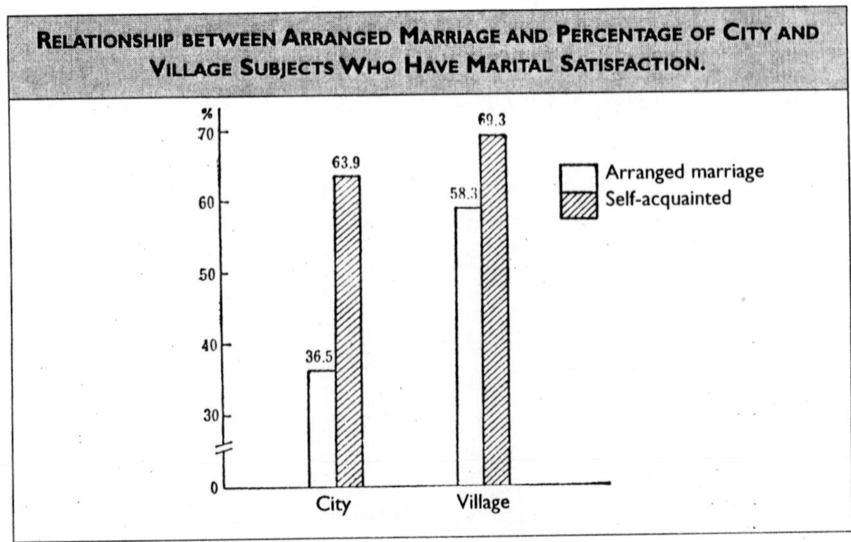

Figure 4–9

Occupation and Marital Satisfaction (City Husbands)

	FACTORY		AGRICULTURE		SERVICE		COMMERCE	
	NO.	%	NO.	%	NO.	%	NO.	%
Satisfied	178	58.7	20	66.7	45	71.4	97	58.8
Ordinary	93	30.7	8	26.7	16	25.4	59	35.8
Not satisfied	13	4.3	0	0	2	3.2	2	1.2
Cannot tell	19	6.3	2	6.7	0	0	7	4.2
Total	303	100.0	30	100.0	63	100.0	165	100.0

	OFFICIALS		S. OFFICIAL		PROFESSIONAL		SOLDIERS		OTHERS	
	NO.	%	NO.	%	NO.	%	NO.	%	NO.	%
Satisfied	195	57.4	208	66.2	276	62.9	20	64.5	23	54.8
Ordinary	123	36.2	86	27.4	133	30.3	7	22.6	12	28.6
Not satisfied	11	3.2	11	3.5	19	4.3	3	9.7	2	4.8
Cannot tell	11	3.2	9	2.9	11	2.5	1	3.2	5	11.9
Total	340	100.0	314	100.0	439	100.0	31	100.0	42	100.0

Table 4–59

Occupation and Marital Satisfaction (City Wives)

	FACTORY		AGRICULTURE		SERVICE		COMMERCE	
	NO.	%	NO.	%	NO.	%	NO.	%
Satisfied	504	58.9	51	54.8	137	51.7	261	56.7
Ordinary	257	30.0	31	33.3	90	34.0	160	34.8
Not satisfied	53	6.2	1	1.1	16	6.0	21	4.6
Cannot tell	42	4.9	10	10.8	22	8.3	18	3.9
Total	856	100.0	93	100.0	265	100.0	460	100.0

	OFFICIALS		S. OFFICIAL		PROFESSIONAL		SOLDIERS		OTHERS	
	NO.	%	NO.	%	NO.	%	NO.	%	NO.	%
Satisfied	458	59.6	314	66.0	608	58.4	8	80.0	69	50.0
Ordinary	256	33.3	138	29.0	363	34.9	2	20.0	41	29.7
Not satisfied	25	3.3	11	2.3	31	3.0	0	0	16	11.6
Cannot tell	30	3.9	13	2.7	39	3.7	0	0	12	8.7
Total	769	100.0	476	100.0	1041	100.0	10	100.0	138	100.0

Table 4–60

Occupation and Marital Satisfaction (Village Husbands)

	FACTORY		AGRICULTURE		SERVICE		COMMERCE	
	NO.	%	NO.	%	NO.	%	NO.	%
Satisfied	14	66.7	101	60.5	18	66.7	4	50.0
Ordinary	4	19.0	54	32.3	7	25.9	1	12.5
Not satisfied	1	4.8	4	2.4	0	0	0	0
Cannot tell	2	9.5	8	4.8	2	7.4	3	37.5
Total	21	100.0	167	100.0	27	100.0	8	100.0

	OFFICIALS		S. OFFICIAL		PROFESSIONAL		SOLDIERS		OTHERS	
	NO.	%	NO.	%	NO.	%	NO.	%	NO.	%
Satisfied	8	53.3	23	88.5	9	69.2	2	66.7	9	56.3
Ordinary	6	40.0	1	3.8	3	23.1	1	33.3	5	31.3
Not satisfied	0	0	1	3.8	1	7.7	0	0	0	0
Cannot tell	1	6.7	1	3.8	0	0	0	0	2	12.5
Total	15	100.0	26	100.0	13	100.0	3	100.0	16	100.0

Table 4–61

Occupation and Marital Satisfaction (Village Wives)

	FACTORY		AGRICULTURE		SERVICE		COMMERCE	
	NO.	%	NO.	%	NO.	%	NO.	%
Satisfied	145	66.8	391	67.3	39	42.9	20	80.0
Ordinary	48	22.1	145	25.0	44	48.4	3	12.0
Not satisfied	11	5.1	14	2.4	4	4.4	0	0
Cannot tell	13	6.0	31	5.3	4	4.4	2	8.0
Total	217	100.0	581	100.0	91	100.0	25	100.0

	OFFICALS		S. OFFICIAL		PROFESSIONAL		SOLDIERS		OTHERS	
	NO.	%	NO.	%	NO.	%	NO.	%	NO.	%
Satisfied	13	52.0	28	68.3	34	77.3	0	0	36	61.0
Ordinary	9	36.0	9	22.0	8	18.2	0	0	19	32.2
Not satisfied	1	4.0	1	2.4	0	0	0	0	1	1.7
Cannot tell	2	8.0	3	7.3	2	4.5	0	0	3	5.1
Total	25	100.0	41	100.0	44	100.0	0	0	59	100.0

Table 4–62

D. Occupation

The relationship between occupation and marital satisfaction was weak. Administrators, professionals, and technicians were generally more satisfied (tables 4–59, 4–60, 4–61, and 4–62). It could be that they are more resourceful in coping with marital stress. Another point worth noting is that, in both cities and villages, among service workers, many more husbands were satisfied with their marriages than were the wives.

It has to be realized that marital dissatifaction is not necessarily a negative thing. It can motivate a couple to work harder on improving the relationship.[20]

3. Sexual Behavior

"Sexual behavior" is a broader concept than "sexual intercourse." It includes any activity that involves sexual pleasure. One can distinguish between target sexual behavior, process sexual behavior, and marginal sexual behavior.[21] In more detail, Kinsey identified six sexual "outlets" leading to orgasm: sexual dreams, self-stimulation, heterosexual petting, heterosexual intercourse, homosexual activity, and sexual contact with animals.[22] Harmonious sexual activity in married couples is a source of marital satisfaction, but it depends, among other things, on their sexual attitudes and beliefs.[23] This section tries to elicit information about the subjects' sexual attitudes.

1. Marital Sex

Like many surveys abroad,[24] our own asked the subjects why they thought sex was important in marriage. Table 4–63 shows that more city than village couples thought it fulfilled both an emotional and a physical need. When asked whether they felt embarrassed by their sexual activities, more city couples answered that they were not embarrassed (table 4–64).

View on Marital Sex																
	TOTAL	WIFE'S DUTY		MUTUAL DUTY		MUTUAL PHYSICAL NEED		MUTUAL PSYCHO-PHYSICAL NEED		REPRO-DUCTION		ROUTINE		UNKNOWN	
		NO.	%	NO.	%	NO.	%	NO.	%	NO.	%	NO.	%	NO.	%
City	6210	170	2.7	265	4.3	646	10.4	4652	74.9	74	1.2	302	4.9	101	1.6
Village	1392	19	1.4	41	2.9	231	16.6	849	61.0	67	4.8	178	12.8	7	0.5

Table 4-63

DO YOU FEEL THAT SEX BETWEEN COUPLES IS EMBARRASSING?										
	TOTAL	YES		NO		CANNOT TELL		UNKNOWN		
		NO.	%	NO.	%	NO.	%	NO.	%
City	6210	378	3.4	4767	76.8	937	15.1	128	2.1
Village	1392	109	7.8	837	60.1	443	31.8	3	0.2

Table 4–64

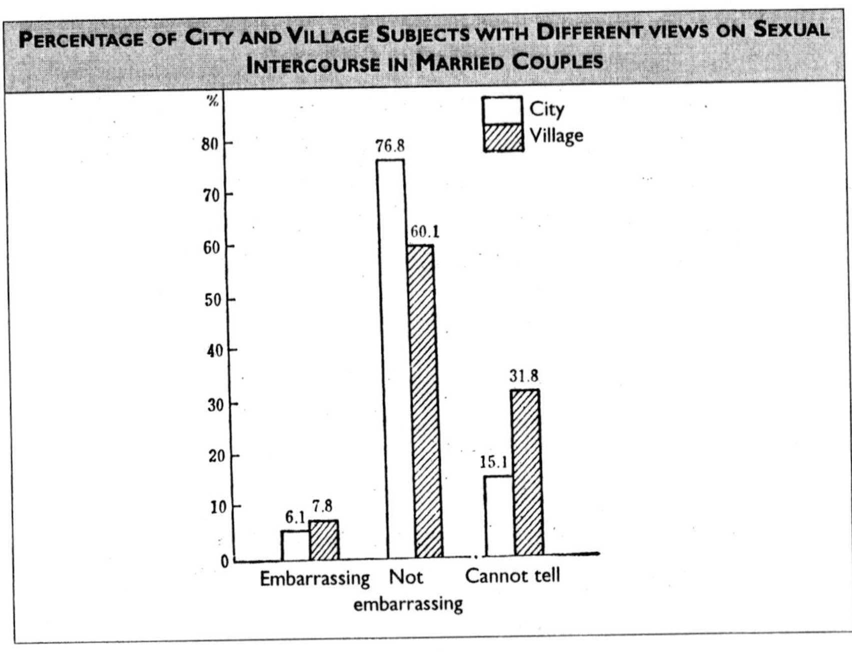

Figure 4–10

Four times more village couples than city couples viewed the need for reproduction as an important function of sex in marriage.

In 1986, the Helungjiang Women's Federation conducted a survey on 1441 families. In that survey, 1402 subjects answered the question "Do you think marriage is for the purpose of legalizing sexual intercourse?" Of those who responded, 904 answered positively, 102 answered that it was mainly for this purpose; another 102 answered that it was partly so; 103 answered that it was only one small reason among many; 191 answered in the negative. That is, about 79.0 percent of the subjects agreed, at least partially, to this purpose of marriage. To another question asking whether they thought marriage was for reproduction, of the 1405 subjects who answered, 837 (59.6 percent) answered positively; 137 (9.7 percent) said it was mainly so; 132 (9.4 percent) said it was partly so; 121 (8.6 percent) said it was a small purpose; 178 (12.7 percent) answered negatively.[25] This data could serve as reference, but could not be strictly compared with ours since the questions were different.

GENDER AND VIEW ON MARITAL SEX														
	TOTAL NO.	WIFE'S DUTY		MUTUAL DUTY		MUTUAL PHYSICAL NEED		MUTUAL PSYCHO-PHYSICAL NEED		REPRO-DUCTION		ROUTINE	
		NO.	%	NO.	%	NO.	%	NO.	%	NO.	%	NO.	%
Male	2056	40	1.9	98	4.8	278	13.5	1496	72.8	38	1.8	106	5.2
Female	5235	144	2.8	200	3.8	574	11.0	3852	73.6	101	1.9	364	7.0

Table 4–65

GENDER AND FEELING OF EMBARRASSMENT CONCERNING SEX BETWEEN COUPLES							
	TOTAL	YES		NO		NOT MIND	
		NO.	%	NO.	%	NO.	%
Male	2058	78	3.8	1640	79.6	340	16.5
Female	5211	392	7.5	3816	73.2	1003	19.2

P=0.001

Table 4–66

EDUCATIONAL LEVEL AND VIEW ON MARITAL SEX (CITY HUSBANDS)										
	ILLITERATE		PRIMARY		J. HIGH		S.HIGH		C.AND ABOVE	
	NO.	%	NO.	%	NO.	%	NO.	%	NO.	%
Wife's duty	2	15.4	5	14.3	11	3.2	11	1.7	5	0.7
Mutual duty	0	0	2	5.7	28	8.2	23	3.6	32	4.6
Mutal physical need	3	23.1	7	20.0	49	14.3	72	11.4	70	10.1
Mutual psycho-physical need	5	38.5	18	51.4	222	64.7	491	77.7	566	81.4
Reproduction	1	7.7	0	0	10	2.9	6	0.9	5	0.7
Routine	2	15.4	3	8.6	23	6.7	29	4.6	17	2.4
Total	13	100.0	35	100.0	343	100.0	632	100.0	695	100.0

Table 4–67

Table 4–65 shows that husbands and wives did not differ significantly in their feelings about sex in marriage. Twice as many wives felt that sex was embarrassing, showing that women are still more affected by traditional, conservative sexual attitudes.

EDUCATIONAL LEVEL AND VIEW ON MARITAL SEX (CITY WIVES)										
	ILLITERATE		PRIMARY		J. HIGH		S.HIGH		C.AND ABOVE	
	NO.	%	NO.	%	NO.	%	NO.	%	NO.	%
Wife's duty	3	16.7	10	6.7	32	4.0	45	2.4	19	2.4
Mutual duty	0	0	7	4.7	62	4.8	71	3.8	22	2.8
Mutal physical need	4	22.2	20	13.3	162	12.5	164	8.9	49	6.3
Mutual psycho-physical need	5	27.8	76	50.7	910	70.2	1479	80.1	669	85.7
Reproduction	0	0	7	4.7	22	1.7	19	1.0	2	0.3
Routine	6	33.3	30	20.0	88	6.8	68	3.7	20	2.6
Total	18	100.0	150	100.0	1296	100.0	1846	100.0	781	100.0

Table 4–68

EDUCATIONAL LEVEL AND VIEW ON MARITAL SEX (VILLAGE HUSBANDS)										
	ILLITERATE		PRIMARY		J. HIGH		S.HIGH		C.AND ABOVE	
	NO.	%	NO.	%	NO.	%	NO.	%	NO.	%
Wife's duty	0	0	3	4.9	2	1.6	1	1.1	0	0
Mutual duty	0	0	1	1.6	3	2.4	2	2.3	0	0
Mutal physical need	2	15.4	10	16.4	24	19.2	16	18.4	1	8.3
Mutual psycho-physical need	8	61.5	44	72.1	80	64.0	55	63.2	11	91.7
Reproduction	2	15.4	0	0	4	3.2	3	3.4	0	0
Routine	1	7.7	3	4.9	12	9.6	10	11.5	0	0
Total	13	100.0	61	100.0	125	100.0	87	100.0	12	100.0

Table 4–69

The degree of sexual enlightenment showed a slightly positive relationship with the level of education in the city subjects. The relationship was not obvious, however, in the village subjects (tables 4–67, 4–68, 4–69, 4–70).

Tables 4–71 to 4–74 show that the educational level of the city husbands had an inverse relationship with the feeling of embarrassment

EDUCATIONAL LEVEL AND VIEW ON MARITAL SEX (VILLAGE WIVES)	ILLITERATE		PRIMARY		J. HIGH		S.HIGH		C.AND ABOVE	
	NO.	%	NO.	%	NO.	%	NO.	%	NO.	%
Wife's duty	1	2.9	2	0.8	6	1.2	4	1.4	0	0
Mutual duty	0	0	7	2.9	17	3.4	11	3.8	0	0
Mutal physical need	4	11.4	45	18.6	80	16.0	43	14.7	5	41.7
Mutual psycho-physical need	27	77.1	144	59.5	295	59.1	177	60.4	5	41.7
Reproduction	1	2.9	14	5.8	26	5.2	16	5.5	1	8.3
Routine	2	5.7	30	12.4	75	15.0	42	14.3	1	8.3
Total	35	100.0	242	100.0	499	100.0	273	100.0	12	100.0

Table 4–70

PERCENTAGE OF CITY SUBJECTS WHO TOOK SEX AS A MUTUAL PSYCHOPHYSICAL NEED AND THEIR EDUCATIONAL LEVEL

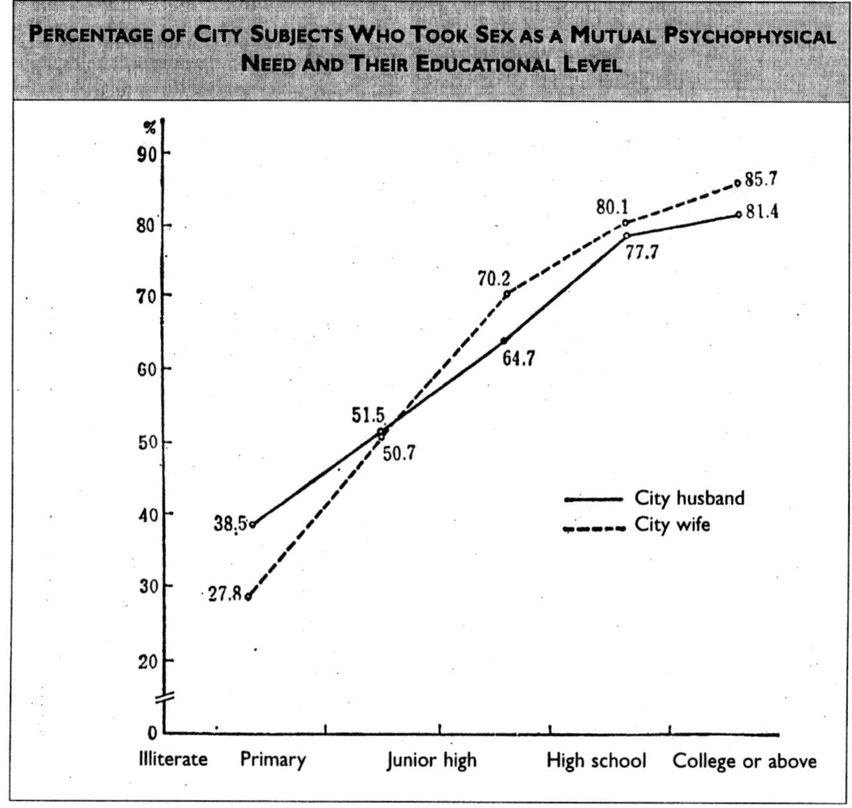

Figure 4–11

Education Level and Feeling of Embarrassment in Marital Sex (City Husbands)										
	ILLITERATE		PRIMARY		J. HIGH		S.HIGH		C.AND ABOVE	
	NO.	%	NO.	%	NO.	%	NO.	%	NO.	%
Yes	2	15.4	2	5.7	15	4.4	19	3.0	17	2.4
No	7	53.8	18	51.4	260	26.2	533	84.2	625	89.0
Do not mind	4	30.8	15	42.9	66	19.4	81	12.8	60	8.5
Total	13	100.0	35	100.0	341	100.0	633	100.0	702	100.0

Table 4–71

Education Level and Feeling of Embarrassment in Marital Sex (City Wives)										
	ILLITERATE		PRIMARY		J. HIGH		S.HIGH		C.AND ABOVE	
	NO.	%	NO.	%	NO.	%	NO.	%	NO.	%
Yes	6	35.3	30	20.4	103	8.0	123	6.7	43	5.5
No	4	23.5	81	55.1	921	71.6	1455	79.0	637	81.9
Do not mind	7	41.2	36	24.5	262	20.4	263	14.3	98	12.6
Total	17	100.0	17	100.0	1286	100.0	1841	100.0	778	100.0

Table 4–72

Education Level and Feeling of Embarrassment in Marital Sex (Village Husbands)										
	ILLITERATE		PRIMARY		J. HIGH		S.HIGH		C.AND ABOVE	
	NO.	%	NO.	%	NO.	%	NO.	%	NO.	%
Yes	1	7.7	6	9.8	10	8.0	6	6.9	0	0
No	8	61.5	29	47.5	79	63.2	55	63.2	10	83.3
Do not mind	4	30.8	26	42.6	36	28.8	26	29.9	2	16.7
Total	13	100.0	61	100.0	125	100.0	87	100.0	12	100.0

Table 4–73

Education Level and Feeling of Embarassment in Marital Sex (Village Wives)										
	ILLITERATE		PRIMARY		J. HIGH		S. HIGH		C.AND ABOVE	
	NO.	%	NO.	%	NO.	%	NO.	%	NO.	%
Yes	2	5.9	16	6.5	47	9.4	20	6.8	1	8.3
No	19	55.9	149	60.8	311	62.1	163	55.6	10	83.3
Do not mind	13	38.2	80	32.7	143	28.5	110	37.5	1	8.3
Total	34	100.0	245	100.0	501	100.0	293	100.0	12	100.0

Table 4–74

PERCENTAGE OF CITY AND VILLAGE SUBJECTS WHO DO NOT FEEL SEXUAL INTERCOURSE IS EMBARRASSING AND THEIR EDUCATIONAL LEVEL

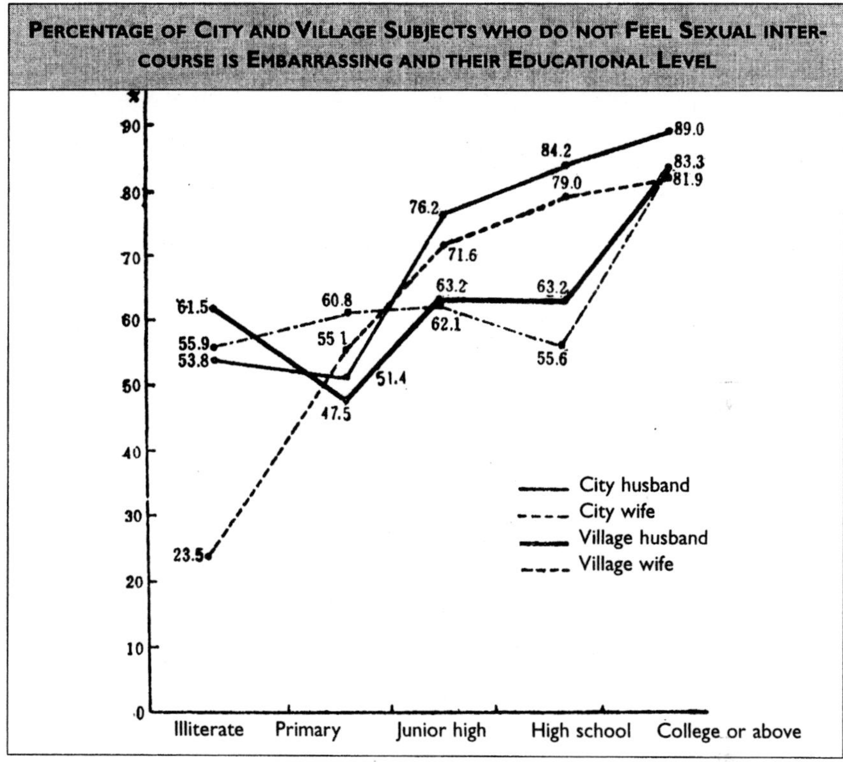

Figure 4–12

about marital sex (G=0.22). For the city wives and the village couples, although the relationship indices were small, figure 4–12 shows that the trends were similar.

The data show that the modern Chinese are developing a more enlightened sexual attitude. However, this does not necessarily mean that sexual practices have become more spontaneous and uninhibited.[26] Hence, the survey went on to ask more practical questions. To the

WHAT WOULD YOU DO IF YOUR SEX LIFE WAS NOT HARMONIOUS?

	TOTAL	CONSULT DOCTOR		CONSULT FRIEND		TALK WITH SPOUSE		LET IT BE		UNKNOWN	
		NO.	%	NO.	%	NO.	%	NO.	%	NO.	%
City	6210	834	13.4	444	7.1	2739	44.1	1496	24.1	698	11.2
Village	1392	323	23.2	141	10.1	610	43.8	292	21.0	26	1.9

Table 4–75

Percentage of City and Village Subjects with Different Responses to Sexual Disharmony in Their Marriage

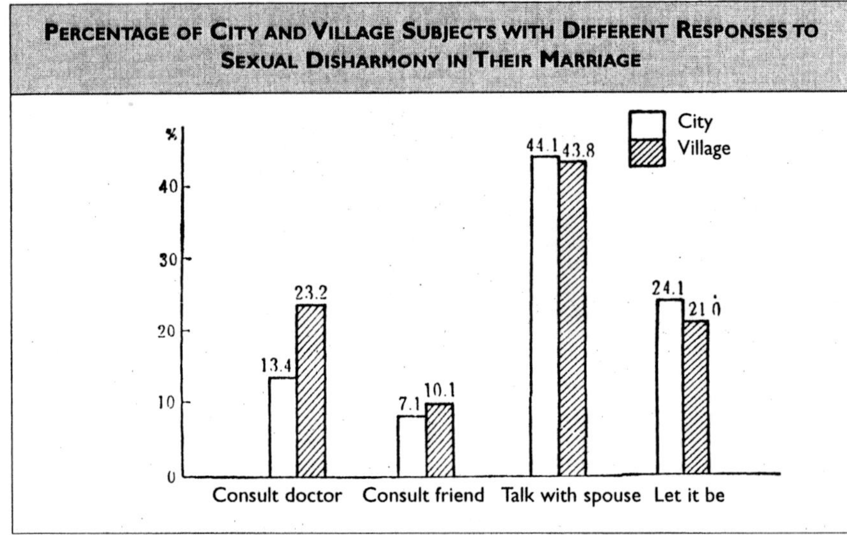

Figure 4–13

question "If your sex life was unhappy with your spouse, how would you deal with it?" about one quarter of both city and village couples replied that they would leave it as it is. Hence, in practice, the prevalence of conservative and complacent attitudes is still significant (table 4–75).

2. First Sexual Intercourse

A. Age of First Sexual Intercourse

The mean age was 25.45 (SD=3.53) for the city couples, and 22.88 (SD=2.42) for the village couples. The mode was between twenty-one and thirty. Intercourse age before twenty-one (i.e., below the nation's legal age of marriage), was reported by 5.7 percent of city couples and 17.6 percent

Age of First Sexual Intercourse

	TOTAL NO.	<=25		21-25		26-30		31-35		>=36		UNKNOWN	
		NO.	%	NO.	%	NO.	%	NO.	%	NO.	%	NO.	%
City	6210	356	5.7	2741	44.1	2491	40.1	251	4.0	39	0.6	332	5.3
Village	1392	245	17.6	971	69.8	168	12.1	3	0.2	1	0.1	4	0.3

Table 4–76

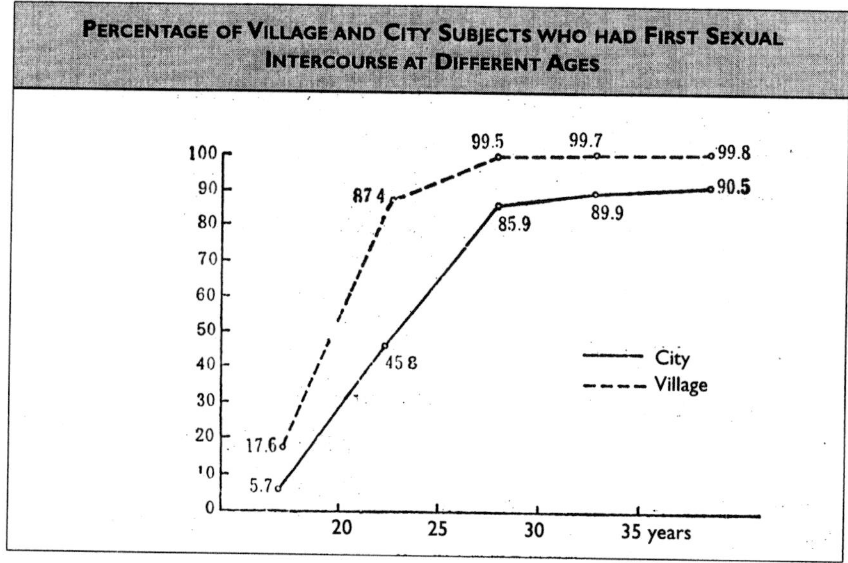

Figure 4–14

of village couples. Obviously then, to a certain extent, early (illegal) marriage or premarital sex is being practiced, more so in the villages.

B. PARTNER OF FIRST SEXUAL INTERCOURSE

Of all the subjects, 81.9 percent of the city subjects and 92.5 percent of the village subjects had their first sexual intercourse with the individual who would later be their spouse; 3.1 percent of city subjects and 3.2 percent of the village subjects were with non-spouses (table 4–77, figure 4–15).

TYPE OF FIRST SEX PARTNER

	TOTAL	SPOUSE		NON-SPOUSE		UNKNOWN	
		NO.	%	NO.	%	NO.	%
City	6210	5084	81.9	195	3.1	931	15.0
Village	1392	1288	92.5	45	3.2	59	4.2

Table 4–77

Table 4–78 and figures 4–15 and 4–16 show that more females had their first sexual intercourse with their eventual spouses, indicating that probably the females were more cautious with their first sexual partners and took the whole encounter more seriously. Of all the cities,

Guangzhou and Xiamen had the greatest number of subjects who had sex with non-spouses (figures 4–17 and 4–18), probably indicating the degree of sexual permissiveness in these cities.

GENDER AND TYPE OF FIRST SEX PARTNER

		MALE		FEMALE		
		NO.	%	NO.	%	
City	Spouse	1469	93.6	3499	97.4	
	Non-spouse	100	6.4	92	2.6	
	Total	1569	100.0	3591	100.0	P=0.001
Village	Spouse	274	95.8	1011	96.8	
	Non-spouse	12	4.2	33	3.2	
	Total	286	100.0	1044	100.0	P=0.50

Table 4–78

PERCENTAGE OF CITY AND VILLAGE SUBJECTS WITH DIFFERENT TYPES OF FIRST SEXUAL PARTNERS

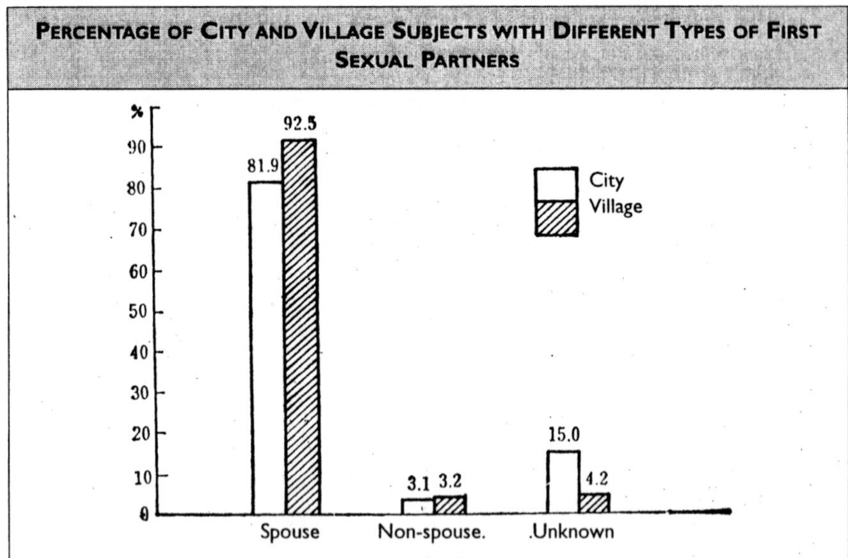

Figure 4–15

Tables 4–79 to 4–82 show that in the city subjects, the younger the subjects, the more they had their first sexual intercourse with non-spouses (G=0.14 for husbands and 0.13 for wives). It could be that the city subjects, especially the younger ones, were more liberal in their sexual attitudes. They were also less likely to get married due to financial constraints, high mobility, and a time-consuming education.

For the village subjects, however, there was no significant relationship with age. For the village wives, those who had first sex with non-spouse were subjects of ages forty-six to fifty-five, or below age twenty-six.

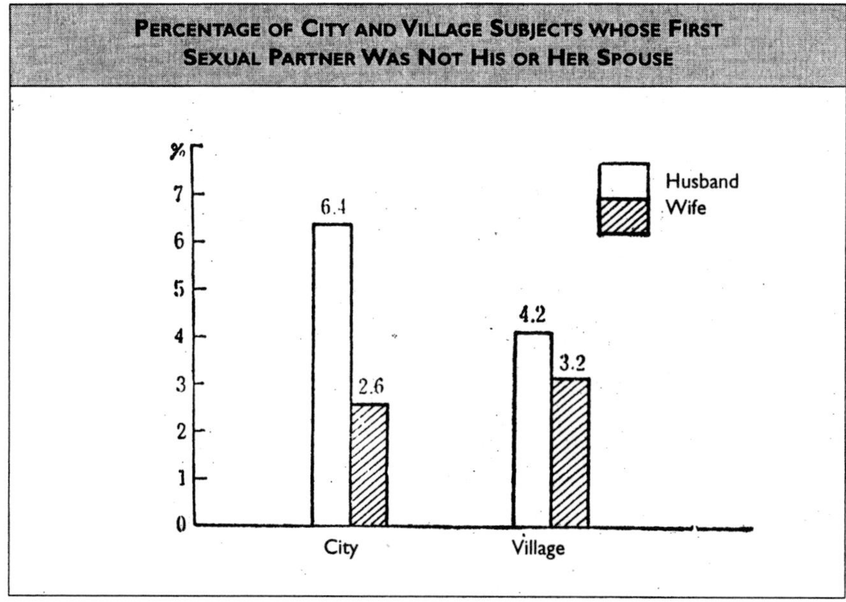

Figure 4–16

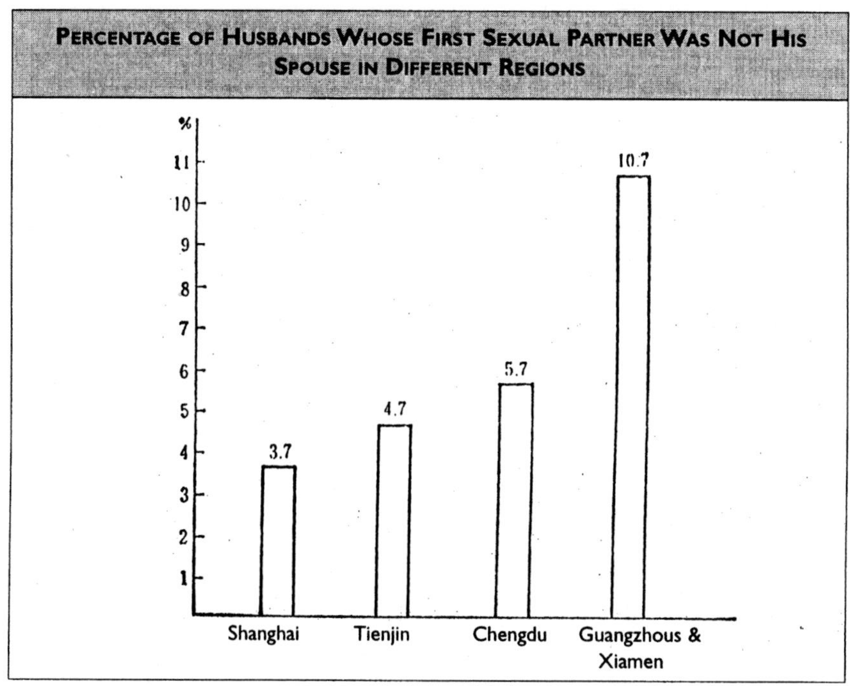

Figure 4–17

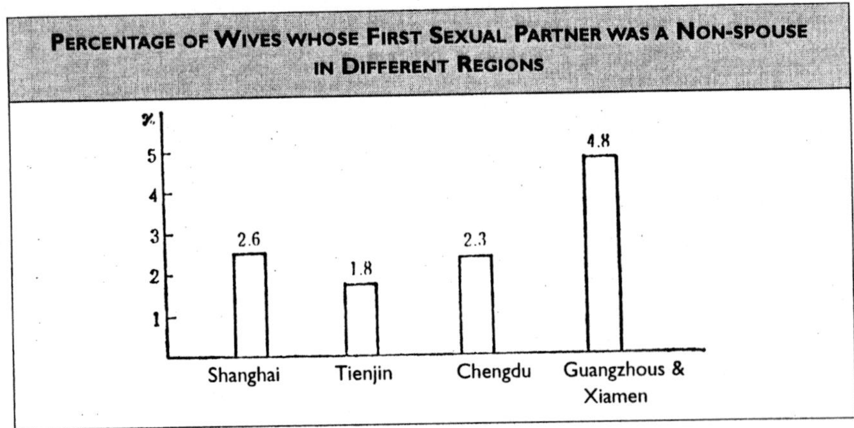

Figure 4–18

The village husbands showed even a reverse relationship; that is, the older the subjects were, the more they had had their first sexual encounter with non-spouses (G=0.22) (tables 4–79 to 4–82).

In the city subjects, the educational level had little to do with the type of partner for first sexual intercourse (G=0.09), but more of the less

AGE AND TYPE OF FIRST SEX PARTNER (CITY HUSBANDS)

	<=25		26-35		36-45		46-55		>=56	
	NO.	%	NO.	%	NO.	%	NO.	%	NO.	%
Spouse	64	91.4	554	92.5	481	94.3	247	93.9	102	96.2
Non-spouse	6	8.6	45	7.5	29	5.7	16	6.1	4	3.8
Total	70	100.0	599	100.0	510	100.0	263	100.0	106	100.0

P=0.001

Table 4–79

AGE AND TYPE OF FIRST SEX PARTNER (CITY WIVES)

	<=25		26-35		36-45		46-55		>=56	
	NO.	%	NO.	%	NO.	%	NO.	%	NO.	%
Spouse	195	94.7	1408	97.4	1273	97.8	502	97.9	86	95.6
Non-spouse	11	5.3	37	2.6	28	2.2	11	2.1	4	4.4
Total	206	100.0	1445	100.0	1301	100.0	513	100.0	90	100.0

P=0.05

Table 4–80

AGE AND TYPE OF FIRST SEX PARTNER (VILLAGE HUSBANDS)										
	<=25		26-35		36-45		46-55		>=56	
	NO.	%	NO.	%	NO.	%	NO.	%	NO.	%
Spouse	20	100.0	98	96.1	94	95.9	43	93.5	19	95.0
Non-spouse	0	0	4	3.9	4	4.1	3	6.5	1	5.0
Total	20	100.0	102	100.0	98	100.0	46	100.0	20	100.0

P=0.90

Table 4–81

AGE AND TYPE OF FIRST SEX PARTNER (VILLAGE WIVES)										
	<=25		26-35		36-45		46-55		>=56	
	NO.	%	NO.	%	NO.	%	NO.	%	NO.	%
Spouse	105	96.3	513	97.2	308	96.6	71	95.9	14	100.0
Non-spouse	4	3.7	15	2.8	11	3.4	3	4.1	0	0
Total	109	100.0	528	100.0	319	100.0	74	100.0	14	100.0

P=0.90

Table 4–82

EDUCATIONAL LEVEL AND TYPE OF FIRST SEX PARTNER (CITY HUSBANDS)										
	ILLITERATE		PRIMARY		J. HIGH		S.HIGH		C.AND ABOVE	
	NO.	%	NO.	%	NO.	%	NO.	%	NO.	%
Spouse	7	87.5	23	82.1	286	94.4	522	93.7	589	94.2
Non-spouse	1	12.5	5	17.9	17	5.6	35	6.3	36	5.8
Total	8	100.0	28	100.0	303	100.0	557	100.0	625	100.0

Table 4–83

EDUCATIONAL LEVEL AND TYPE OF FIRST SEX PARTNER (CITY WIVES)										
	ILLITERATE		PRIMARY		J. HIGH		S.HIGH		C.AND ABOVE	
	NO.	%	NO.	%	NO.	%	NO.	%	NO.	%
Spouse	12	92.3	109	94.8	1066	97.6	1554	97.4	704	97.9
Non-spouse	1	7.7	86	5.2	26	2.4	42	2.6	15	2.1
Total	13	100.0	115	100.0	1092	100.0	1596	100.0	719	100.0

Table 4–84

EDUCATIONAL LEVEL AND TYPE OF FIRST SEX PARTNER (VILLAGE HUSBANDS)										
	ILLITERATE		PRIMARY		J. HIGH		S.HIGH		C.AND ABOVE	
	NO.	%	NO.	%	NO.	%	NO.	%	NO.	%
Spouse	13	100.0	53	93.0	111	94.1	82	98.8	12	100.0
Non-spouse	0	0	4	7.0	7	5.9	1	1.2	0	0
Total	13	100.0	57	100.0	118	100.0	83	100.0	12	100.0

Table 4–85

EDUCATIONAL LEVEL AND TYPE OF FIRST SEX PARTNER (VILLAGE WIVES)										
	ILLITERATE		PRIMARY		J. HIGH		S.HIGH		C.AND ABOVE	
	NO.	%	NO.	%	NO.	%	NO.	%	NO.	%
Spouse	34	100.0	222	95.7	464	96.7	279	97.6	12	100.0
Non-spouse	0	0	10	4.3	16	3.3	7	2.4	0	0
Total	34	100.0	232	100.0	480	100.0	286	100.0	12	100.0

Table 4–86

educated had their first sexual encounter with non-spouses. For the villagers, there was significant relationship with education (G=0.37 for husbands and 0.13 for wives). (tables 4–83 to 4–86)

Ocupation had very little to do with the type of partner one had first sexual intercourse with(tables 4–87 to 4–90).

OCCUPATION AND TYPE OF FIRST SEX PARTNER (CITY HUSBANDS)								
	FACTORY		AGRICULTURE		SERVICE		COMMERCE	
	NO.	%	NO.	%	NO.	%	NO.	%
Spouse	241	91.6	27	96.4	52	98.1	134	94.4
Non-spouse	22	8.4	1	3.6	1	1.9	8	5.6
Total	263	100.0	28	100.0	53	100.0	142	100.0

	OFFICAL		S. OFFICIAL		PROFESSIONAL		SOLDIER		OTHERS	
	NO.	%	NO.	%	NO.	%	NO.	%	NO.	%
Spouse	271	93.8	248	94.3	377	93.8	29	96.7	37	92.5
Non-spouse	18	6.2	15	5.7	25	6.2	1	3.3	3	7.5
Total	289	100.0	263	100.0	402	100.0	30	100.0	40	100.0

Table 4–87

OCCUPATION AND TYPE OF FIRST SEX PARTNER (CITY WIVES)

	FACTORY		AGRICULTURE		SERVICE		COMMERCE	
	NO.	%	NO.	%	NO.	%	NO.	%
Spouse	700	97.5	76	96.2	213	95.5	396	97.3
Non-spouse	18	2.5	3	3.8	10	4.5	11	2.7
Total	718	100.0	79	100.0	223	100.0	407	100.0

	OFFICIAL		S. OFFICIAL		PROFESSIONAL		SOLDIER		OTHERS	
	NO.	%	NO.	%	NO.	%	NO.	%	NO.	%
Spouse	640	98.3	383	97.0	907	97.6	9	100.0	108	97.3
Non-spouse	11	1.7	12	3.0	22	2.4	0	0	3	2.7
Total	651	100.0	395	100.0	929	100.0	9	100.0	111	100.0

Table 4–88

OCCUPATION AND TYPE OF FIRST SEX PARTNER (VILLAGE HUSBANDS)

	FACTORY		AGRICULTURE		SERVICE		COMMERCE	
	NO.	%	NO.	%	NO.	%	NO.	%
Spouse	21	100.0	142	93.4	26	96.3	8	100.0
Non-spouse	0	0	10	6.6	1	3.7	0	0
Total	21	100.0	152	100.0	27	100.0	8	100.0

	OFFICIAL		S. OFFICIAL		PROFESSIONAL		SOLDIER		OTHERS	
	NO.	%	NO.	%	NO.	%	NO.	%	NO.	%
Spouse	15	100.0	26	100.0	12	92.3	3	100.0	16	100.0
Non-spouse	0	0	0	0	3	7.7	0	0	0	0
Total	15	100.0	26	100.0	15	100.0	3	100.0	16	100.0

Table 4–89

C. PREMARITAL SEX

Of those surveyed, 62.4 percent of the city husbands, 70.8 percent of the city wives, 69.3 percent of the village husbands, and 62.3 percent of the village wives had their first sexual intercourse on their wedding day (tables 4–91 and 4–92).

The younger the couples were, the more they had had premarital sex (tables 4–93 to 4–96, figure 4–22). The G index for city husbands was 0.21, city wives 0.12, village husbands insignificant, and village wives 0.16.

Occupation and Type of First Sex Partner (Village Wives)

	FACTORY		AGRICULTURE		SERVICE		COMMERCE	
	NO.	%	NO.	%	NO.	%	NO.	%
Spouse	208	97.2	531	96.0	88	97.8	23	100.0
Non-spouse	6	2.8	22	4.0	2	2.2	0	0
Total	214	100.0	553	100.0	90	100.0	23	100.0

	OFFICIAL		S. OFFICIAL		PROFESSIONAL		SOLDIER		OTHERS	
	NO.	%	NO.	%	NO.	%	NO.	%	NO.	%
Spouse	23	95.8	40	100.0	40	95.2	0	0	56	100.0
Non-spouse	1	4.2	0	0	2	4.8	0	0	0	0
Total	24	100.0	40	100.0	42	100.0	0	0	56	100.0

Table 4–90

The educational level had little to do with premarital sex, except for villages wives (G=0.21). In general, the trend indicates that the more highly educated had premarital sex (tables 4–97 to 4–100).

Occupation also had little to do with premarital sex. (Alpha less than 0.1) (tables 4–101 to 4–104).

Our findings were different from those of Kinsey who found that the better educated had less premarital sex. In Kinsey's view, it was because the well-educated had more self-control.[27]

In the past, the Chinese believed premarital sex to be a corruptive

Gender and Time of First Sexual Intercourse (City)

	MALE		FEMALE	
	NO.	%	NO.	%
Premarital	441	24.9	645	15.7
Wedding night	1103	62.4	2911	70.8
After marriage	224	12.7	554	13.5
Total	1768	100.0	4110	100.0

P=0.001

Table 4–91

Sex and Time of First Sexual Intercourse (City)

	MALE		FEMALE	
	NO.	%	NO.	%
Premarital	22	7.3	188	17.3
Wedding night	208	69.3	677	62.3
After marriage	70	23.3	221	20.3
Total	300	100.0	1086	100.0

P=0.001

Table 4–92

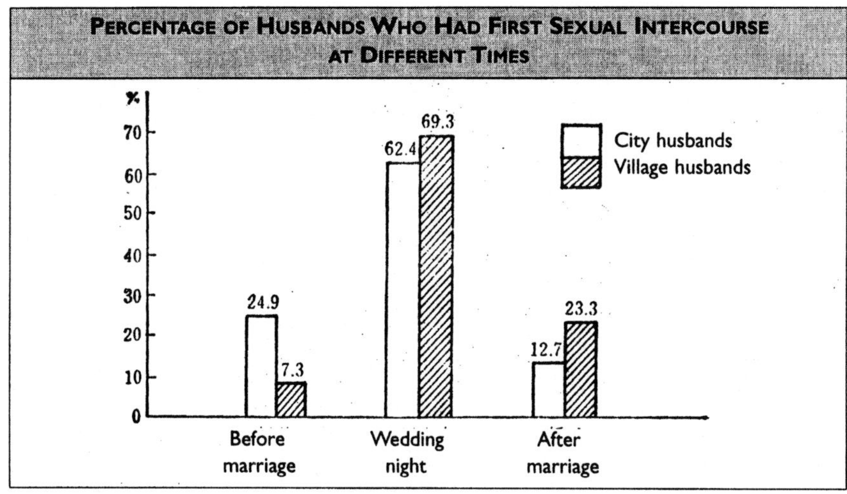

Figure 4–19

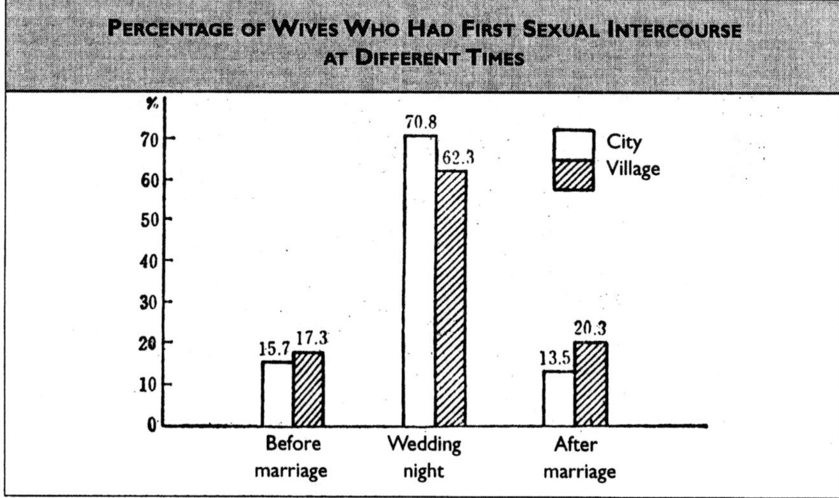

Figure 4–20

influence from the West. But in the 1980s, premarital sex gradually spread in China, almost becoming a common practice. The figures of premarital pregnancies can give an idea of the increase. In 1982 in Shanghai, the figure of premarital abortions was 39,000. In 1983, it had grown to 50,000. In 1984, it was 65,000.[28] In Wuxi, in 1986, the figure was 5112 and 16 percent of the subjects were above age twenty.[29] In Jinhua Xian of Zhejiang in 1988, there were 1704 cases of induced

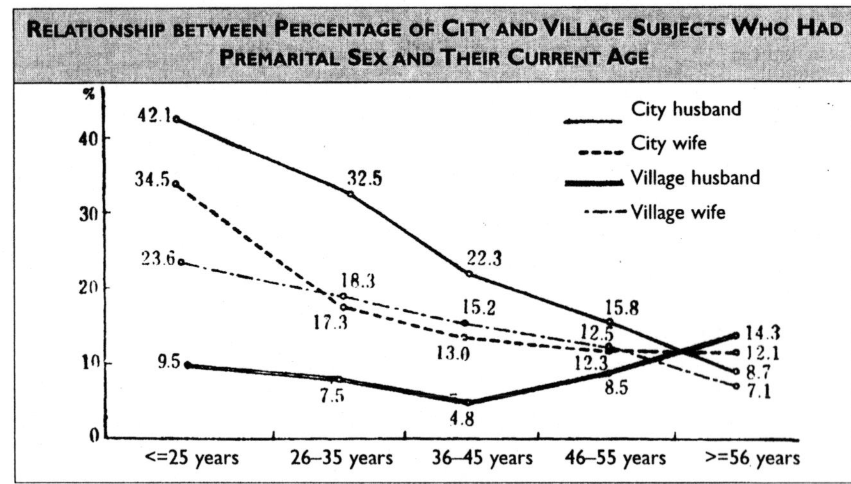

Figure 4–21

AGE AND TIME OF FIRST SEXUAL INTERCOURSE (CITY HUSBANDS)

	<=25		26-35		36-45		46-55		>=56	
	NO.	%	NO.	%	NO.	%	NO.	%	NO.	%
Premarital	32	42.1	216	32.5	126	22.3	48	15.8	11	8.7
Wedding night	39	51.3	357	53.7	371	65.5	220	72.6	97	76.4
After marriage	5	6.6	92	13.8	69	12.2	35	11.6	19	15.0
Total	76	100.0	665	100.0	566	100.0	303	100.0	127	100.0

P=0.001

Table 4–93

AGE AND TIME OF FIRST SEXUAL INTERCOURSE (CITY WIVES)

	<=25		26-35		36-45		46-55		>=56	
	NO.	%	NO.	%	NO.	%	NO.	%	NO.	%
Premarital	80	34.5	279	17.3	197	13.0	73	12.3	13	12.1
Wedding night	122	52.6	1121	69.5	1118	73.6	438	73.9	78	72.9
After marriage	30	12.9	214	13.3	203	13.4	82	13.8	16	15.0
Total	232	100.0	1614	100.0	1518	100.0	593	100.0	107	100.0

P=0.001

Table 4–94

abortion for first pregnancies and 90 percent of these were premarital. Some of the subjects had induced abortions up to ten times.[30]

AGE AND TIME OF FIRST SEXUAL INTERCOURSE (VILLAGE HUSBANDS)	<=25		26-35		36-45		46-55		>=56	
	NO.	%	NO.	%	NO.	%	NO.	%	NO.	%
Premarital	2	9.5	8	7.5	5	4.8	4	8.5	3	14.3
Wedding night	15	71.4	72	67.9	74	70.5	32	68.1	15	71.4
After marriage	4	19.0	26	24.5	26	24.8	11	23.4	3	14.3
Total	21	100.0	106	100.0	105	100.0	47	100.0	21	100.0

P=0.90

Table 4–95

AGE AND TIME OF FIRST SEXUAL INTERCOURSE (VILLAGE WIVES)	<=25		26-35		36-45		46-55		>=56	
	NO.	%	NO.	%	NO.	%	NO.	%	NO.	%
Premarital	26	23.6	100	18.3	51	15.2	10	12.5	1	7.1
Wedding night	72	65.5	346	63.4	194	57.7	55	68.8	10	71.4
After marriage	12	10.9	100	18.3	91	27.1	15	18.8	3	21.4
Total	110	100.0	546	100.0	336	100.0	80	100.0	14	100.0

P=0.01

Table 4–96

EDUCATIONAL LEVEL AND TIME OF FIRST SEXUAL INTERCOURSE (CITY HUSBANDS)	ILLITERATE		PRIMARY		J. HIGH		S.HIGH		C.AND ABOVE	
	NO.	%	NO.	%	NO.	%	NO.	%	NO.	%
Premarital	4	36.4	10	27.8	80	23.7	154	24.4	172	24.7
Wedding night	5	45.5	21	58.3	212	62.9	392	62.1	439	63.2
After marriage	2	18.2	5	13.9	45	13.4	85	13.5	84	12.1
Total	11	100.0	36	100.0	337	100.0	631	100.0	695	100.0

Table 4–97

EDUCATIONAL LEVEL AND TIME OF FIRST SEXUAL INTERCOURSE (CITY WIVES)	ILLITERATE		PRIMARY		J. HIGH		S.HIGH		C.AND ABOVE	
	NO.	%	NO.	%	NO.	%	NO.	%	NO.	%
Premarital	3	17.6	21	14.5	190	14.9	290	16.0	126	16.2
Wedding night	13	76.5	101	69.7	930	72.7	1273	70.3	544	69.7
After marriage	1	5.9	23	15.9	150	12.4	249	13.7	110	14.1
Total	17	100.0	145	100.0	1279	100.0	1812	100.0	780	100.0

Table 4–98

EDUCATIONAL LEVEL AND TIME OF FIRST SEXUAL INTERCOURSE (VILLAGE HUSBANDS)										
	ILLITERATE		PRIMARY		J. HIGH		S.HIGH		C.AND ABOVE	
	NO.	%	NO.	%	NO.	%	NO.	%	NO.	%
Premarital	1	7.7	8	13.1	5	4.0	8	9.3	0	0
Wedding night	8	61.5	41	67.2	90	72.0	56	65.1	12	100.0
After marriage	4	30.8	12	19.7	30	24.0	22	25.6	0	0
Total	13	100.0	61	100.0	125	100.0	86	100.0	12	100.0

Table 4–99

EDUCATIONAL LEVEL AND TIME OF FIRST SEXUAL INTERCOURSE (VILLAGE WIVES)										
	ILLITERATE		PRIMARY		J. HIGH		S.HIGH		C.AND ABOVE	
	NO.	%	NO.	%	NO.	%	NO.	%	NO.	%
Premarital	1	2.9	29	11.8	83	16.6	71	24.1	4	33.3
Wedding night	23	65.7	155	63.3	318	63.6	176	59.9	5	41.7
After marriage	11	31.4	61	24.9	99	19.8	47	16.0	3	25.0
Total	35	100.0	245	100.0	500	100.0	294	100.0	12	100.0

Table 4–100

OCCUPATION AND TIME OF FIRST SEXUAL INTERCOURSE (CITY HUSBANDS)								
	FACTORY		AGRICULTURE		SERVICE		COMMERCE	
	NO.	%	NO.	%	NO.	%	NO.	%
Premarital	76	26.1	11	36.7	11	17.7	41	24.8
Wedding night	178	61.2	17	56.7	42	67.7	101	61.2
After marriage	37	12.7	2	6.7	9	14.5	23	13.9
Total	291	100.0	30	100.0	62	100.0	165	100.0

	OFFICIAL		S. OFFICIAL		PROFESSIONAL		SOLDIER		OTHERS	
	NO.	%	NO.	%	NO.	%	NO.	%	NO.	%
Premarital	75	22.6	68	22.0	119	27.2	5	15.6	12	29.3
Wedding night	215	64.8	206	66.7	263	60.0	20	62.5	22	53.7
After marriage	42	12.6	35	11.3	56	12.8	7	21.9	7	17.1
Total	332	100.0	309	100.0	438	100.0	32	100.0	41	100.0

Table 4–101

OCCUPATION AND TIME OF FIRST SEXUAL INTERCOURSE (CITY WIVES)	FACTORY		AGRICULTURE		SERVICE		COMMERCE	
	NO.	%	NO.	%	NO.	%	NO.	%
Premarital	125	15.2	15	16.7	55	21.1	78	17.1
Wedding night	602	73.2	61	67.8	176	67.4	317	69.7
After marriage	95	11.6	14	15.6	30	11.5	60	13.2
Total	822	100.0	90	100.0	261	100.0	455	100.0

	OFFICIAL		S. OFFICIAL		PROFESSIONAL		SOLDIER		OTHERS	
	NO.	%	NO.	%	NO.	%	NO.	%	NO.	%
Premarital	119	15.8	70	15.1	139	13.6	2	20.0	28	20.9
Wedding night	529	70.4	332	71.7	730	71.3	5	50.0	91	67.9
After marriage	103	13.7	61	13.2	155	15.1	3	30.0	15	11.2
Total	751	100.0	463	100.0	1024	100.0	10	100.0	134	100.0

Table 4–102

OCCUPATION AND TIME OF FIRST SEXUAL INTERCOURSE (VILLAGE HUSBANDS)	FACTORY		AGRICULTURE		SERVICE		COMMERCE	
	NO.	%	NO.	%	NO.	%	NO.	%
Premarital	2	9.5	13	7.8	1	3.7	0	0
Wedding night	13	61.9	110	65.9	20	74.1	5	62.5
After marriage	6	28.6	44	26.3	6	22.2	3	37.5
Total	21	100.0	167	100.0	27	100.0	8	100.0

	OFFICIAL		S. OFFICIAL		PROFESSIONAL		SOLDIER		OTHERS	
	NO.	%	NO.	%	NO.	%	NO.	%	NO.	%
Premarital	1	6.7	4	16.0	1	7.7	0	0	0	0
Wedding night	12	80.0	17	68.0	10	76.9	2	66.7	15	93.8
After marriage	2	13.3	4	16.0	2	15.4	1	33.3	1	6.2
Total	15	100.0	25	100.0	13	100.0	3	100.0	16	100.0

Table 4–103

This survey has not questioned the total rate of premarital sex directly, but it could be calculated from the available figures. Of the city husbands, 22.0 percent had their first sexual intercourse before their marriage. The percentages for city wives was 15.7 percent, for village

OCCUPATION AND TIME OF FIRST SEXUAL INTERCOURSE (VILLAGE WIVES)

	FACTORY		AGRICULTURE		SERVICE		COMMERCE	
	NO.	%	NO.	%	NO.	%	NO.	%
Premarital	52	23.9	87	15.0	13	14.3	3	12.0
Wedding night	123	56.4	370	63.9	56	61.5	19	76.0
After marriage	43	19.7	122	21.1	22	24.2	3	12.0
Total	218	100.0	579	100.0	91	100.0	25	100.0

	OFFICIAL		S. OFFICIAL		PROFESSIONAL		SOLDIER		OTHERS	
	NO.	%	NO.	%	NO.	%	NO.	%	NO.	%
Premarital	6	24.0	6	14.6	8	18.2	0	0	13	22.0
Wedding night	14	56.0	32	78.0	25	56.8	0	0	36	61.0
After marriage	5	20.0	3	7.3	11	25.0	0	0	10	16.9
Total	25	100.0	41	100.0	44	100.0	0	0	59	100.0

Table 4–104

husbands 34.6 percent and for village wives 14.8 percent. The overall figure for premarital sex was therefore 17.9 percent.

Another way of calculating the same figure is found in table 4–77. 3.2 percent of the subjects had non-spouses as their first sexual partners. Since tables 4–91 and 4–92 show that a total of 1296 subjects (i.e., 17.84 percent of 7264) had premarital sex, the approximate total percentage of subjects who had premarital sex should be:

$$3.2\% + 83.6\% \times 17.84\% = 18.1\%$$

The two calculations come close to matching. The rate of premarital sex was about 18 percent. This figure is also similar to some national statistics. This phenomenon may indicate that, as time passes, people are becoming more accepting of premarital sex, irrespective of their educational level. In spite of his findings, Kinsey already thought that most males could accept and actually want premarital sex. He believed that it was a natural result of normal sexual development.[31] The Russian sociologists Hazev and Walord surveyed 3620 college students and technicians and found 91 percent of the males accepted premarital sex with their girl friends; 60 percent thought that it could happen even on the first date. Of the girls, 14 percent also thought that it was all right to have sex whether or not the partners were their spouses.[32]

It is difficult to decide whether this change in attitude is good or bad. Perhaps, as Kinsey believed, there is no harm as long as the partners involved truly accept premarital sex without guilt.[33]

3. Frequency of Sexual Intercourse

Table 4–105 shows the mean monthly frequency of sexual intercourse in the past year as claimed by the subjects. The mean frequency for city subjects was 4.66 (SD=3.72) and for village subjects 5.43 (SD=3.79). The overall frequency was 4.8 (SD=3.75). Hence, village subjects had a generally higher frequency of sexual intercourse (table 4–105, figure 4–23).

In China, there have been few surveys on the frequency of sexual intercourse. In 1986, the Women's Federation of Helungjiang surveyed 1104 subjects of a wide age range and found 534 (48.4 percent) of them had sexual intercourse once a week, 409 (37.0 percent) had it once to

MONTHLY RATE OF SEXUAL INTERCOURSE

	TOTAL	<=1		2–3		4–5		6–7		8–15					
		NO.	%	NO.	%	NO.	%	NO.	%	NO.	%	NO.	%	NO.	%
City	6210	730	11.8	1891	30.5	1529	24.6	1168	18.8	499	8.0	115	1.9	778	12.5
Village	1392	109	7.8	294	21.1	415	29.8	362	26.9	159	11.4	30	2.2	23	1.7

Table 4–105

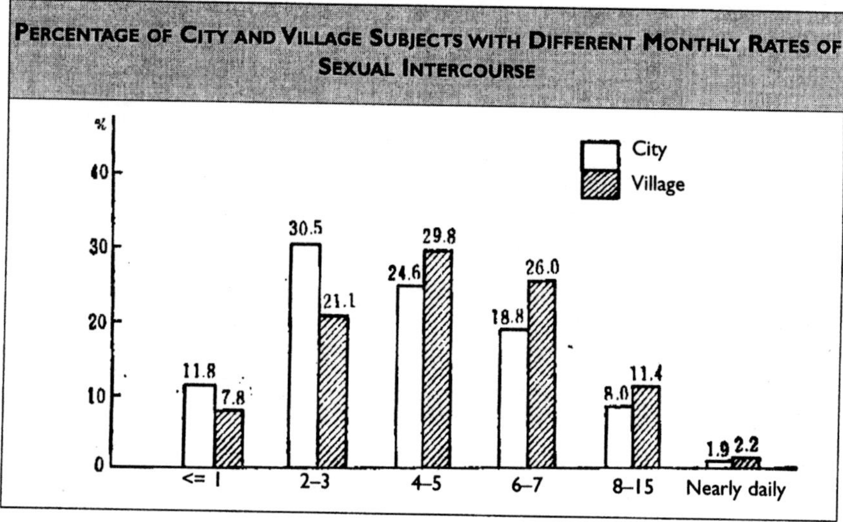

Figure 4–22

twice a week, and 136 (12.3 percent) had it more than twice a week.[34] These results are similar to ours.

The findings in table 4–105 seem to agree well with traditional beliefs in the proper frequency of sexual intercourse. The physician Sun Si-Miao of the Tang dynasty, in his "Essentials of Precious Prescriptions," proposed that the frequency of sexual intercourse should be adjusted according to age. At age twenty, it could be once every four days. At age thirty, it should be once every eight days. At forty, once every sixteen days, and at fifty once every twenty days. A colloquial verse of the Ching dynasty proposes: "In adolescence, do it daily; at twenty-four or twenty-five, do not do it daily; above thirty, do it as if spending money; around forty, do it like a church ceremony; after fifty, as if in a temple; approaching sixty, like paying the rent; around seventy, retire peacefully."[35]

There are many surveys of intercourse frequency in various parts of the world.[36] There is a great deal of variation in these data. Most likely, it is something that varies from person to person and does not necessarily depend on age alone.

Some variation in frequency is also found according to region. In coastal regions, the frequencies are higher. In the villages or less developed areas, the frequencies are also high, showing only a little drop in the middle age range. For example, in Guangzhou and Xiamen, 15.5 percent of subjects had sexual intercourse about eight to fifteen times per month, and 2.1 percent had it once daily. In Shaanxi Yuci and Xin xian, 11.8 percent had sex eight to fifteen times per month; 3.1 percent had it daily. These two regions had high frequencies of sexual intercourse, but they are quite different in location and many other aspects. Hence, there are probably many factors affecting the frequency of sexual intercourse.

REGION AND MONTHLY RATE OF SEXUAL INTERCOURSE

		TOTAL	<=1		2–3		4–5		6–7		8–15		DAILY	
			NO.	%	NO.	%	NO.	%	NO.	%	NO.	%	NO.	%
City	Shanghai	2482	337	13.6	840	33.8	682	27.5	456	18.4	141	5.7	26	1.0
	Tienjin	995	156	15.7	329	33.1	246	24.7	157	15.8	88	8.8	19	1.9
	Chengdu	875	74	8.4	253	28.9	208	23.8	223	25.5	92	10.5	25	2.9
	Guangzhou	515	38	7.4	125	24.3	138	26.8	123	23.9	80	15.5	11	2.1
Village	Suzhou	493	36	7.3	127	25.8	157	31.8	114	23.1	56	11.3	3	0.6
	Yuci	876	73	8.3	167	19.1	258	29.4	248	28.3	103	11.8	27	3.1
	Shanghai	354	28	7.9	81	22.9	113	31.9	77	21.7	49	13.8	6	1.7

Table 4–106

AGE AND MONTHLY RATE OF SEXUAL INTERCOURSE (CITY HUSBANDS)

	<=25		26–35		36–45		46–55		>=56	
	NO.	%	NO.	%	NO.	%	NO.	%	NO.	%
<=1	2	2.7	31	4.7	47	8.4	49	16.3	43	35.5
2–3	15	20.5	148	22.4	182	32.4	125	41.7	47	38.8
4–5	16	21.9	165	25.0	168	29.9	68	22.7	20	16.5
6–7	21	28.8	186	28.1	112	19.9	43	14.3	10	8.3
8–15	13	17.8	110	16.6	44	7.8	12	4.0	0	0
Daily	6	8.2	21	3.2	9	1.6	3	1.0	1	0.8
Total	73	100.0	661	100.0	562	100.0	300	100.0	121	100.0

P=0.001

Table 4–107

AGE AND MONTHLY RATE OF SEXUAL INTERCOURSE (CITY WIVES)

	<=25		26–35		36–45		46–55		>=56	
	NO.	%	NO.	%	NO.	%	NO.	%	NO.	%
<=1	9	3.9	123	7.8	192	12.8	165	28.6	39	37.1
2–3	60	26.0	472	29.8	529	35.4	204	35.4	29	27.6
4–5	48	20.8	438	27.7	418	28.0	115	19.9	17	16.2
6–7	55	23.8	361	22.8	258	17.3	68	11.8	13	12.4
8–15	42	18.2	154	4.7	85	5.7	23	4.0	4	3.8
Daily	17	7.4	35	2.2	13	0.9	2	0.3	3	2.9
Total	231	100.0	1583	100.0	1495	100.0	577	100.0	105	100.0

P=0.001

Table 4–108

AGE AND MONTHLY RATE OF SEXUAL INTERCOURSE (VILLAGE HUSBANDS)

	<=25		26–35		36–45		46–55		>=56	
	NO.	%	NO.	%	NO.	%	NO.	%	NO.	%
<=1	0	0	7	6.7	9	8.8	2	4.3	0	0
2–3	3	14.3	22	21.2	19	18.6	6	12.8	1	5.0
4–5	4	19.0	34	32.7	32	31.4	22	46.8	8	40.0
6–7	11	52.4	32	30.8	29	28.4	10	21.3	8	40.0
8–15	2	9.5	7	6.7	10	9.8	4	8.5	2	10.0
Daily	1	4.8	2	1.9	3	2.9	3	6.4	1	5.0
Total	21	100.0	104	100.0	102	100.0	47	100.0	20	100.0

P=0.50

Table 4–109

AGE AND MONTHLY RATE OF SEXUAL INTERCOURSE (VILLAGE WIVES)										
	<=25		26–35		36–45		46–55		>=56	
	NO.	%	NO.	%	NO.	%	NO.	%	NO.	%
<=1	8	7.3	44	8.2	23	6.9	11	13.9	4	28.6
2–3	19	17.3	111	20.7	85	25.5	25	31.6	3	21.4
4–5	36	32.7	144	26.9	108	32.4	21	26.6	5	35.7
6–7	32	29.1	154	28.7	72	21.6	11	13.9	2	14.3
8–15	12	10.9	74	13.8	37	11.1	11	13.9	0	0
Daily	3	2.7	9	1.7	8	24	0	0	0	0
Total	110	100.0	536	100.0	333	100.0	79	100.0	14	100.0

P=0.02

Table 4–110

RELATIONSHIP BETWEEN PERCENTAGE OF CITY HUSBANDS WITH DIFFERENT RATES OF SEXUAL INTERCOURSE AND THEIR AGE

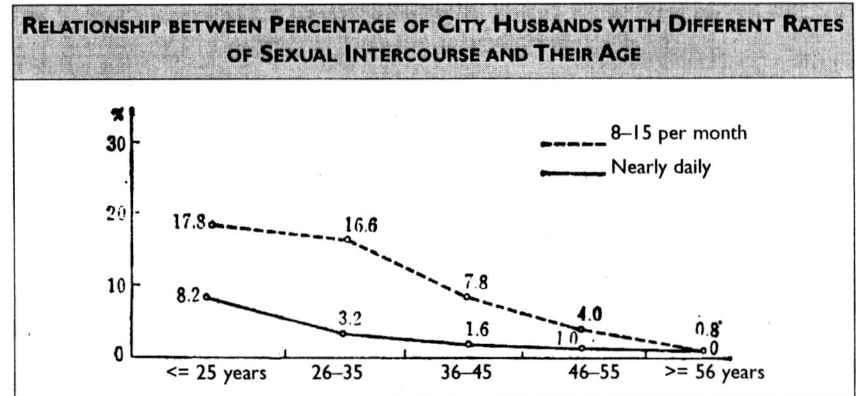

Figure 4–23

In our subjects, sexual frequency decreases with advancing age (G=0.39 for city husband, 0.29 for city wives, 0.12 for village wives, but insignificant for village husbands) (tables 4–107 to 4–110, figures 4–24 and 4–25). The relationship is weaker for the village subjects.

The frequency of sexual intercourse bears no relation to the educational level of the subjects. No obvious pattern of variation can be seen in tables 4–111 to 4–114.

The relationship of sexual intercourse frequency with occupation is also weak. The administrators and professionals have less sexual intercourse than the other occupations, but the difference is not significant (tables 4–115 to 4–118).

Generally, the frequency of sexual intercourse also decreases with the duration of marriage. The G index was 0.31 for city husbands, 0.24

EDUCATIONAL LEVEL AND MONTHLY RATE OF SEXUAL INTERCOURSE (CITY HUSBANDS)										
	ILLITERATE		PRIMARY		J. HIGH		S. HIGH		C. OR ABOVE	
	NO.	%	NO.	%	NO.	%	NO.	%	NO.	%
<=1	2	20.0	6	17.1	37	11.1	58	9.3	65	9.4
2–3	2	20.0	7	20.0	96	28.9	199	31.8	204	29.6
4–5	1	10.0	10	28.6	96	28.9	163	26.0	165	23.9
6–7	4	40.0	8	22.9	65	19.6	148	23.6	143	20.8
8–15	1	10.0	2	5.7	26	7.8	49	7.8	95	13.8
Daily	0	0	2	5.7	12	3.6	9	1.4	17	2.5
Total	10	100.0	35	100.0	332	100.0	626	100.0	689	100.0

Table 4–111

EDUCATIONAL LEVEL AND MONTHLY RATE OF SEXUAL INTERCOURSE (CITY WIVES)										
	ILLITERATE		PRIMARY		J. HIGH		S. HIGH		C. OR ABOVE	
	NO.	%	NO.	%	NO.	%	NO.	%	NO.	%
<=1	0	0	31	21.8	164	13.1	230	12.8	99	13.1
2–3	8	47.1	45	31.7	455	36.5	563	31.4	217	28.6
4–5	2	11.8	34	23.9	323	25.9	485	27.0	189	24.9
6–7	5	29.4	22	15.5	224	17.9	340	18.9	153	20.2
8–15	1	5.9	6	4.2	63	5.0	151	8.4	82	10.8
Daily	1	5.9	4	2.8	19	1.5	26	1.5	18	2.4
Total	17	100.0	142	100.0	1248	100.0	1795	100.0	758	100.0

Table 4–112

EDUCATIONAL LEVEL AND MONTHLY RATE OF SEXUAL INTERCOURSE (VILLAGE HUSBANDS)										
	ILLITERATE		PRIMARY		J. HIGH		S. HIGH		C. OR ABOVE	
	NO.	%	NO.	%	NO.	%	NO.	%	NO.	%
<=1	0	0	6	10.5	7	5.7	5	5.7	0	0
2–3	2	15.4	6	10.5	22	18.0	18	20.7	1	8.3
4–5	5	35.5	16	28.1	46	37.7	28	32.2	5	41.7
6–7	6	46.2	19	33.3	33	27.0	26	29.9	5	41.7
8–15	0	0	8	14.0	9	7.4	7	8.0	1	8.3
Daily	0	0	2	3.5	5	4.1	3	3.4	0	0
Total	13	100.0	57	100.0	122	100.0	87	100.0	12	100.0

Table 4–113

EDUCATIONAL LEVEL AND MONTHLY RATE OF SEXUAL INTERCOURSE (VILLAGE WIVES)										
	ILLITERATE		PRIMARY		J. HIGH		S. HIGH		C. OR ABOVE	
	NO.	%	NO.	%	NO.	%	NO.	%	NO.	%
<=1	4	11.4	18	7.5	42	8.5	24	8.3	2	16.7
2–3	9	25.7	61	25.4	119	24.0	50	17.3	4	33.3
4–5	11	31.4	71	29.6	153	30.8	79	17.3	0	0
6–7	9	25.7	56	23.3	122	24.6	81	28.0	3	25.0
8–15	2	5.7	26	10.8	51	10.3	52	18.0	3	25.0
Daily	0	0	8	3.3	9	1.8	3	1.0	0	0
Total	35	100.0	240	100.0	496	100.0	289	100.0	12	100.0

Table 4–114

OCCUPATION AND MONTHLY RATE OF SEXUAL INTERCOURSE (CITY HUSBANDS)								
	FACTORY		AGRICULTURE		SERVICE		COMMERCE	
	NO.	%	NO.	%	NO.	%	NO.	%
<=1	23	7.9	0	0	3	4.8	19	11.9
2–3	75	25.8	7	25.0	13	21.0	45	28.1
4–5	73	25.1	7	25.0	19	30.6	47	29.4
6–7	86	29.6	8	28.6	20	32.3	33	20.6
8–15	24	8.2	3	10.7	5	8.1	15	9.4
Daily	10	3.4	3	10.7	2	3.2	1	0.6
Total	291	100.0	28	100.0	62	100.0	160	100.0

	OFFICIAL		S. OFFICIAL		PROFESSIONAL		SOLDIER		OTHERS	
	NO.	%	NO.	%	NO.	%	NO.	%	NO.	%
<=1	36	10.7	43	14.2	36	8.3	5	15.6	5	13.5
2–3	99	29.5	101	33.4	142	32.9	6	18.8	14	37.8
4–5	83	24.7	83	27.5	108	25.0	4	12.5	7	18.9
6–7	75	22.3	47	15.6	82	19.0	9	28.1	5	13.5
8–15	37	11.0	23	7.6	55	12.7	6	18.8	4	10.8
Daily	6	1.8	5	1.7	9	2.1	2	6.3	2	5.4
Total	336	100.0	302	100.0	432	100.0	32	100.0	37	100.0

Table 4–115

for city wives, 0.11 for village wives, and insignificant only for village husbands. As tables 4–119 to 4–122 show, the highest frequencies are found in those who were married for less than three years or between four and five years. The frequencies remained high up to six to fifteen years but declined thereafter.

OCCUPATION AND MONTHLY RATE OF SEXUAL INTERCOURSE (CITY WIVES)

	FACTORY		AGRICULTURE		SERVICE		COMMERCE	
	NO.	%	NO.	%	NO.	%	NO.	%
<=1	87	10.8	4	4.7	30	11.7	49	10.8
2–3	292	36.2	34	40.0	82	31.9	143	31.6
4–5	218	27.0	20	23.5	64	24.9	126	27.9
6–7	149	18.5	16	18.8	55	21.4	92	20.4
8–15	43	5.3	6	7.1	18	7.0	38	8.4
	17	2.1	5	5.9	8	3.1	4	0.9
Total	806	100.0	85	100.0	257	100.0	452	100.0

	OFFICIAL		S. OFFICIAL		PROFESSIONAL		SOLDIER		OTHERS	
	NO.	%	NO.	%	NO.	%	NO.	%	NO.	%
<=1	97	13.1	61	13.5	158	15.7	1	11.1	31	24.4
2–3	244	32.9	133	29.4	312	31.0	3	33.3	38	29.9
4–5	187	25.2	119	26.3	261	25.9	2	22.2	30	23.6
6–7	152	20.5	91	20.1	166	16.5	2	22.2	18	14.2
8–15	55	7.4	42	9.3	93	9.2	0	0	7	5.5
	6	0.8	6	1.3	18	1.8	1	11.1	3	2.4
Total	741	100.0	452	100.0	1008	100.0	9	100.0	127	100.0

Table 4–116

RELATIONSHIP BETWEEN PERCENTAGE OF CITY WIVES WITH DIFFERENT RATES OF SEXUAL INTERCOURSE

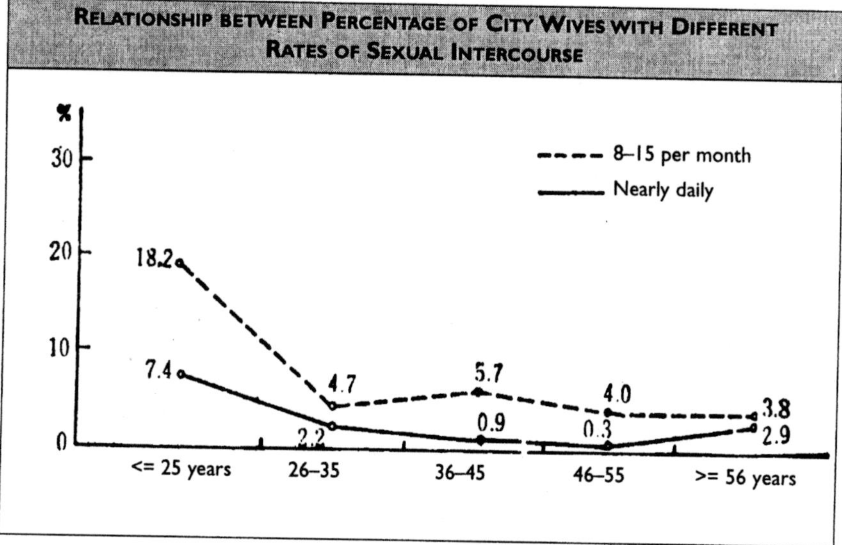

Figure 4–24

Occupation and Monthly Rate of Sexual Intercourse (Village Husbands)

	FACTORY		AGRICULTURE		SERVICE		COMMERCE	
	NO.	%	NO.	%	NO.	%	NO.	%
<=1	0	0	13	8.0	2	7.7	0	0
2–3	3	15.8	29	17.8	7	26.9	0	0
4–5	6	31.6	56	34.4	8	30.8	6	75.0
6–7	6	31.6	51	31.3	7	26.9	2	25.0
8–15	4	21.1	7	4.3	2	7.7	0	0
Daily	0	0	7	4.3	0	0	0	0
Total	19	100.0	163	100.0	26	100.0	8	100.0

	OFFICIAL		S. OFFICIAL		PROFESSIONAL		SOLDIER		OTHERS	
	NO.	%	NO.	%	NO.	%	NO.	%	NO.	%
<=1	1	6.7	2	7.7	0	0	0	0	0	0
2–3	1	6.7	5	19.2	2	15.4	1	33.3	2	12.5
4–5	5	33.3	6	23.1	5	38.5	1	33.3	6	37.5
6–7	5	33.3	8	30.8	3	23.1	1	33.3	4	25.0
8–15	3	20.0	4	15.4	2	15.4	0	0	3	18.8
Daily	0	0	1	3.8	1	7.7	0	0	1	6.3
Total	15	100.0	26	100.0	13	100.0	3	100.0	16	100.0

Table 4–117

Percentage of City and Village Subjects Who Had Sexual Intercourse Principally at Different Times

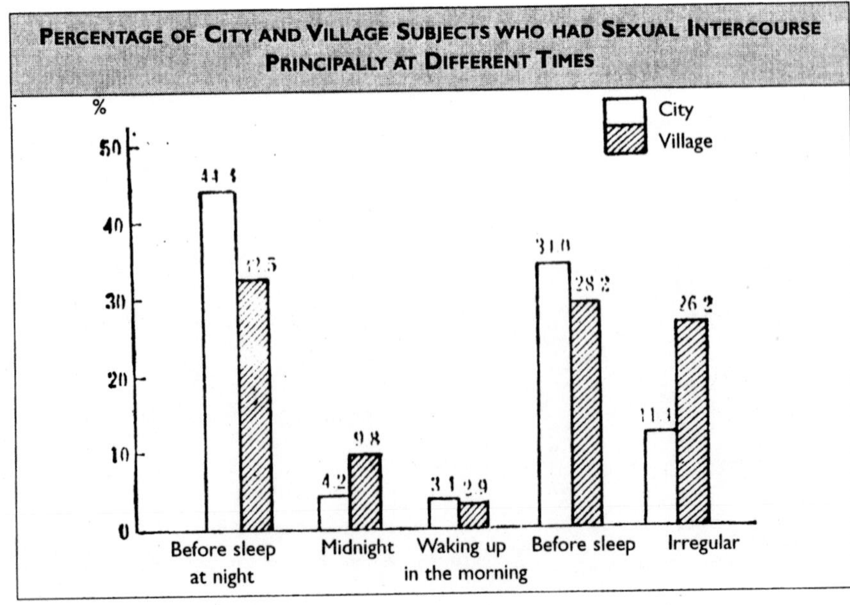

Figure 4–25

Occupation and Monthly Rate of Sexual Intercourse (Village Wives)

	FACTORY		AGRICULTURE		SERVICE		COMMERCE	
	NO.	%	NO.	%	NO.	%	NO.	%
<=1	14	6.4	52	9.1	8	9.1	0	0
2–3	50	22.9	129	22.5	18	20.5	5	20.0
4–5	77	35.3	162	28.3	19	21.6	9	36.0
6–7	58	26.6	139	24.3	23	26.1	11	44.0
8–15	17	7.8	78	13.6	15	17.0	0	0
Daily	2	0.9	13	2.3	5	5.7	0	0
Total	218	100.0	573	100.0	88	100.0	25	100.0

	OFFICIAL		S. OFFICIAL		PROFESSIONAL		SOLDIER		OTHERS	
	NO.	%	NO.	%	NO.	%	NO.	%	NO.	%
<=1	1	4.3	5	12.5	5	11.6	0	0	5	8.6
2–3	9	39.1	10	25.0	12	27.9	0	0	8	13.8
4–5	6	26.1	11	27.5	11	25.6	0	0	18	31.0
6–7	4	17.4	9	22.5	11	25.6	0	0	15	25.9
8–15	3	130	5	12.5	4	9.3	0	0	12	20.7
Daily	0	0	0	0	0	0	0	0	0	0
Total	23	100.0	40	100.0	43	100.0	0	0	58	100.0

Table 4–118

Duration of Marriage and Monthly Rate of Sexual Intercourse (City Husbands)

MONTHLY RATE	<=2		3–5		6–10		11–15		16–20		>=21	
	NO.	%	NO.	%	NO.	%	NO.	%	NO.	%	NO.	%
<=1	11	4.1	18	7.0	19	4.7	20	8.5	18	10.4	85	23.8
2–3	69	25.6	57	22.3	110	27.0	68	28.8	62	35.8	146	40.9
4–5	62	13.0	58	22.7	116	28.5	82	34.7	41	23.7	72	20.2
6–7	70	25.9	69	27.0	103	25.3	46	19.5	39	22.5	40	11.2
8–15	44	16.3	46	18.0	52	12.8	18	7.6	10	5.8	8	2.2
Daily	14	5.2	8	3.0	7	1.7	2	0.8	3	1.7	6	1.7
Total	270	100.0	256	100.0	407	100.0	236	100.0	173	100.0	357	100.0

Table 4–119

DURATION OF MARRIAGE AND MONTHLY RATE OF SEXUAL INTERCOURSE (CITY WIVES)												
MONTHLY RATE	<=2		3–5		6–10		11–15		16–20		>=21	
	NO.	%	NO.	%	NO.	%	NO.	%	NO.	%	NO.	%
<=1	34	6.8	44	8.1	88	8.3	89	14.4	62	12.6	205	27.2
2–3	135	26.9	155	28.7	336	31.6	216	35.1	180	26.7	263	34.9
4–5	112	22.4	140	25.9	325	30.5	153	24.8	141	28.7	162	21.5
6–7	128	25.5	133	24.6	208	19.5	110	17.9	83	16.9	89	11.8
8–15	69	13.8	55	10.2	92	8.6	39	6.3	20	4.1	31	4.1
Daily	23	4.6	14	2.6	15	1.4	9	1.5	5	1.0	4	0.5
Total	501	100.0	541	100.0	1064	100.0	646	100.0	491	100.0	254	100.0

Table 4–120

DURATION OF MARRIAGE AND MONTHLY RATE OF SEXUAL INTERCOURSE (VILLAGE HUSBANDS)												
MONTHLY RATE	<=2		3–5		6–10		11–15		16–20		>=21	
	NO.	%	NO.	%	NO.	%	NO.	%	NO.	%	NO.	%
<=1	1	2.9	3	7.1	2	4.1	3	8.6	4	6.5	5	6.9
2–3	6	17.6	7	16.7	11	22.4	7	20.0	13	21.0	7	9.7
4–5	8	23.5	18	42.9	13	26.5	13	37.1	20	32.3	28	38.9
6–7	14	41.2	12	28.6	18	36.7	8	22.9	18	29.0	20	27.8
8–15	2	5.9	2	4.8	4	8.2	4	11.4	5	8.1	8	11.1
Daily	3	8.8	0	0	1	2.0	0	0	2	3.2	4	5.6
Total	34	100.0	42	100.0	49	100.0	35	100.0	62	100.0	72	100.0

Table 4–121

The frequency of sexual intercourse had no significant relationship with the subjects' attitude to sexual intercourse. This shows that the professed sexual attitudes may not be genuine, or that they express ideals that most people simply cannot practice (tables 4–119 to 4–124).

In Kinsey's reports, the highest frequency of sexual intercourse for males was found between the ages of sixteen and twenty. The mean frequency was 3.9 per week. The rate deceased progressively to 0.9 per week at age sixty.[37] For the females, the rate was 2.8 per week below age twenty. It also decreased progressively to 0.6 per week at age sixty.[38] The rates were generally higher than our findings.

DURATION OF MARRIAGE AND MONTHLY RATE OF SEXUAL INTERCOURSE (VILLAGE WIVES)												
MONTHLY RATE	<=2		3–5		6–10		11–15		16–20		>=21	
	NO.	%	NO.	%	NO.	%	NO.	%	NO.	%	NO.	%
<=1	8	7.1	10	5.6	28	10.4	16	7.7	5	3.5	23	14.1
2–3	21	18.8	35	19.7	54	20.1	48	23.1	39	27.5	16	28.2
4–5	31	27.7	60	33.7	62	23.0	65	31.3	49	34.5	47	28.8
6–7	37	33.0	42	23.6	79	29.4	57	27.4	29	20.4	27	16.6
8–15	12	10.7	27	15.2	42	15.6	17	8.2	18	12.7	18	11.0
Daily	3	2.7	4	2.2	4	1.5	5	2.4	2	1.4	2	1.2
Total	112	100.0	178	100.0	269	100.0	208	100.0	142	100.0	163	100.0

Table 4–122

VIEW ON SEXUAL INTERCOURSE AND MONTHLY RATE OF SEXUAL INTERCOURSE (CITY)												
	WIFE'S DUTY		MUTUAL DUTY		MUTUAL PHYSICAL NEED		MUTUAL PSYCHO-PHYSICAL NEED		REPRO-DUCTION		ROUTINE	
	NO.	%	NO.	%	NO.	%	NO.	%	NO.	%	NO.	%
<=1	19	11.6	24	9.8	74	12.1	542	12.1	12	16.7	47	16.7
2–3	50	30.5	80	32.7	201	32.9	1425	31.8	22	30.6	87	31.0
4–5	40	24.4	53	21.6	154	25.2	1182	26.4	18	25.0	62	22.1
6–7	36	22.0	63	25.7	125	20.5	858	19.1	14	19.4	57	20.3
8–15	11	6.7	18	7.3	37	6.1	409	9.1	2	2.8	18	6.4
Daily	8	4.9	7	2.9	20	3.3	64	1.4	4	5.6	10	3.6
Total	164	100.0	245	100.0	611	100.0	4480	100.0	72	100.0	281	100.0

Table 4–123

4. Time of Sexual Intercourse

Most subjects had sexual intercourse at night before going to sleep, which occurred even more so for city subjects.

Age had little to do with the time of day subjects engaged in sexual intercourse. It appears that the older subjects tend to have intercourse at irregular hours (tables 4–126 to 4–129).

It could be argued that older people have more free time or that they need to adjust the timing of sexual intercourse according to their fluctuating physical states.

Educational level and occupation also have little to do with the time of day subjects engaged in sexual intercourse (tables 4–130 to 4–137).

View on Sexual Intercourse and Monthly Rate of Sexual Intercourse (Village)												
	Wife's Duty		Mutual Duty		Mutual Physical Need		Mutual Psycho-Physical Need		Repro-duction		Routine	
	NO.	%	NO.	%	NO.	%	NO.	%	NO.	%	NO.	%
<=1	2	10.5	2	4.9	24	10.6	60	7.2	4	6.1	17	9.6
2–3	2	10.5	10	24.4	45	19.9	185	22.2	12	18.2	37	20.9
4–5	5	26.3	16	39.0	67	29.6	247	29.7	20	30.3	57	32.2
6–7	6	31.6	9	22.0	55	24.3	224	26.9	23	34.8	44	24.9
8–15	4	21.1	4	9.8	28	12.4	97	11.6	5	7.6	21	11.9
Daily	0	0	0	0	7	3.1	20	2.4	2	3.0	1	0.6
Total	19	100.0	41	100.0	226	100.0	833	100.0	66	100.0	177	100.0

Table 4–124

Time for Sexual Intercourse													
	Total	Before Sleep		Midnight		Waking Up		Mostly Before Sleep		Irregular		Unknown	
		NO.	%	NO.	%	NO.	%	NO.	%	NO.	%	NO.	%
City	6210	2750	44.3	261	4.2	209	3.4	2112	34.0	710	11.4	168	2.7
Village	1392	403	32.5	137	9.8	41	2.9	393	28.2	365	26.2	3	0.2
Total	7602	3203	42.1	398	5.2	250	3.3	2505	33.0	1075	14.1	171	2.2

Table 4–125

Age and Time for Sexual Intercourse (City Husbands)										
	<=25		26–35		36–45		46–55		>=56	
	NO.	%	NO.	%	NO.	%	NO.	%	NO.	%
Before sleep	36	47.4	304	45.3	261	46.0	136	45.0	54	41.5
Midnight	2	2.6	21	3.1	29	5.1	19	6.3	11	8.5
Waking up	3	3.9	23	3.4	23	4.0	7	2.3	7	5.4
Mostly before sleep	22	28.9	256	38.2	191	33.6	102	33.8	46	35.4
Irregular	13	17.1	67	10.0	64	11.3	38	12.6	12	9.2
Total	76	100.0	671	100.0	568	100.0	302	100.0	130	100.0

P=0.20

Table 4–126

Age and Time for Sexual Intercourse (City Wives)										
	<=25		26–35		36–45		46–55		>=56	
	NO.	%	NO.	%	NO.	%	NO.	%	NO.	%
Before sleep	4	19.0	25	23.6	25	23.8	18	37.5	9	42.9
Midnight	3	14.3	18	17.0	17	16.2	5	10.4	2	9.5
Waking up	0	0	0	0	9	8.6	0	0	0	0
Mostly before sleep	7	33.3	31	29.2	28	26.7	11	22.9	7	33.3
Irregular	7	33.3	32	30.2	26	24.8	14	29.2	3	14.3
Total	21	100.0	106	100.0	105	100.0	48	100.0	21	100.0

P=0.05

Table 4–127

Age and Time for Sexual Intercourse (Village Husbands)										
	<=25		26–35		36–45		46–55		>=56	
	NO.	%	NO.	%	NO.	%	NO.	%	NO.	%
Before sleep	4	19.0	25	23.6	25	23.8	18	37.5	9	42.9
Midnight	3	14.3	18	17.0	17	16.2	5	10.4	2	9.5
Waking up	0	0	0	0	9	8.6	0	0	0	0
Mostly before sleep	7	33.3	31	29.2	28	26.7	11	22.9	7	33.3
Irregular	7	33.3	32	30.2	26	24.8	14	29.2	3	14.3
Total	21	100.0	106	100.0	105	100.0	48	100.0	21	100.0

P=0.05

Table 4–128

Age and Time for Sexual Intercourse (Village Wives)										
	<=25		26–35		36–45		46–55		>=56	
	NO.	%	NO.	%	NO.	%	NO.	%	NO.	%
Before sleep	40	36.7	163	29.9	133	39.5	30	37.5	5	35.7
Midnight	8	7.3	51	9.4	30	8.9	2	2.5	1	7.1
Waking up	4	3.7	15	2.8	10	3.0	3	3.8	0	0
Mostly before sleep	31	28.4	166	30.5	83	24.6	21	26.3	6	42.9
Irregular	26	23.9	150	27.5	81	24.0	2	30.0	2	14.3
Total	109	100.0	545	100.0	337	100.0	80	100.0	14	100.0

P=0.05

Table 4–129

The less educated appear to be more irregular in their timing probably due to their irregular life patterns.

EDUCATIONAL LEVEL AND TIME FOR SEXUAL INTERCOURSE (CITY HUSBANDS)										
	ILLITERATE		PRIMARY		J. HIGH		S. HIGH		C. & ABOVE	
	NO.	%	NO.	%	NO.	%	NO.	%	NO.	%
Before sleep	9	75.0	14	38.9	150	44.0	292	46.0	316	45.2
Midnight	1	8.3	5	13.9	25	7.3	24	3.8	24	3.4
Waking up	0	0	3	8.3	21	6.2	19	3.0	19	2.7
Mostly before sleep	1	8.3	9	25.0	99	29.0	228	35.9	277	3.6
Irregular	1	8.3	5	13.9	46	13.5	72	11.3	63	9.0
Total	12	100.0	36	100.0	341	100.0	635	100.0	699	100.0

Table 4–130

EDUCATIONAL LEVEL AND TIME FOR SEXUAL INTERCOURSE (CITY WIVES)										
	ILLITERATE		PRIMARY		J. HIGH		S. HIGH		C. & ABOVE	
	NO.	%	NO.	%	NO.	%	NO.	%	NO.	%
Before sleep	11	61.1	64	44.4	609	48.0	826	45.4	330	42.4
Midnight	0	0	7	4.9	62	4.9	73	4.0	29	3.7
Waking up	2	11.1	8	5.6	38	3.0	65	3.6	27	3.5
Mostly before sleep	2	11.1	43	29.9	395	31.2	651	35.8	312	40.1
Irregular	3	16.7	22	15.3	164	12.9	205	11.3	80	10.3
Total	18	100.0	144	100.0	1268	100.0	1820	100.0	778	100.0

Table 4–131

EDUCATIONAL LEVEL AND TIME FOR SEXUAL INTERCOURSE (VILLAGE HUSBANDS)										
	ILLITERATE		PRIMARY		J. HIGH		S. HIGH		C. & ABOVE	
	NO.	%	NO.	%	NO.	%	NO.	%	NO.	%
Before sleep	3	23.1	13	21.3	36	28.8	23	264	6	50.0
Midnight	1	7.7	10	16.4	17	13.6	15	17.2	0	0
Waking up	1	7.7	2	3.3	4	3.2	2	2.3	0	0
Mostly before sleep	3	23.1	20	32.8	36	28.8	22	25.3	2	11.7
Irregular	5	38.5	16	26.2	32	25.6	25	28.7	4	33.3
Total	13	100.0	61	100.0	125	100.0	87	100.0	12	100.0

Table 4–132

There is hardly any rule governing the time of day sexual intercourse is had. It seems to be more a matter of convenience. For the less potent people, sex therapists suggest intercourse in the morning as it is often the time when erection is most easily achieved.[39]

EDUCATIONAL LEVEL AND TIME FOR SEXUAL INTERCOURSE (VILLAGE WIVES)	ILLITERATE		PRIMARY		J. HIGH		S. HIGH		C. & ABOVE	
	NO.	%	NO.	%	NO.	%	NO.	%	NO.	%
Before sleep	12	34.3	75	30.7	176	35.2	107	36.4	1	8.3
Midnight	2	5.7	16	6.6	44	8.8	29	9.9	1	8.3
Waking up	1	2.9	12	4.9	12	2.4	7	2.4	0	0
Mostly before sleep	6	17.1	58	23.8	138	27.6	97	33.0	8	66.7
Irregular	14	40.0	83	34.0	130	26.0	54	18.4	2	16.7
Total	35	100.0	244	100.0	500	100.0	294	100.0	12	100.0

Table 4–133

OCCUPATION AND TIME FOR SEXUAL INTERCOURSE (CITY HUSBANDS)	FACTORY		AGRICULTURE		SERVICE		COMMERCE	
	NO.	%	NO.	%	NO.	%	NO.	%
Before sleep	135	45.2	10	34.5	30	48.4	74	45.4
Midnight	23	7.7	2	6.9	7	11.3	8	4.9
Waking up	18	6.0	1	3.4	2	3.2	7	4.3
Mostly before sleep	88	29.4	8	27.6	15	24.2	57	35.0
Irregular	35	11.7	8	27.6	8	12.9	17	10.4
Total	299	100.0	29	100.0	62	100.0	163	100.0

	OFFICIAL		S. OFFICIAL		PROFESSIONAL		SOLDIER		OTHERS	
	NO.	%	NO.	%	NO.	%	NO.	%	NO.	%
Before sleep	145	42.9	153	49.4	194	44.4	13	40.6	19	45.2
Midnight	11	3.3	11	3.5	16	3.7	1	3.1	2	4.8
Waking up	9	2.7	10	3.2	14	3.2	1	3.1	0	0
Mostly before sleep	133	39.3	110	35.5	169	38.7	14	43.8	14	33.3
Irregular	40	11.8	26	8.4	44	10.1	3	9.4	7	16.7
Total	338	100.0	310	100.0	437	100.0	32	100.0	42	100.0

Table 4–134

5. Form of Sexual Intercourse

The form of sexual intercourse mainly refers to sexual positions, something which is taboo in China. The same problem was mentioned by Kinsey, who reported that some American wives rejected all proposals by

OCCUPATION AND TIME FOR SEXUAL INTERCOURSE (CITY WIVES)	FACTORY		AGRICULTURE		SERVICE		COMMERCE	
	NO.	%	NO.	%	NO.	%	NO.	%
Before sleep	401	48.6	46	52.3	125	48.3	213	46.8
Midnight	32	3.9	1	1.1	21	8.1	21	4.6
Waking up	26	3.2	4	4.5	10	9.9	21	4.6
Mostly before sleep	262	31.8	25	28.4	82	31.7	144	31.6
Irregular	104	12.6	12	13.6	21	8.1	56	12.3
Total	825	100.0	88	100.0	259	100.0	455	100.0

	OFFICIAL		S. OFFICIAL		PROFESSIONAL		SOLDIER		OTHERS	
	NO.	%	NO.	%	NO.	%	NO.	%	NO.	%
Before sleep	325	44.7	210	45.4	438	42.8	5	55.6	54	40.3
Midnight	30	4.0	16	3.5	42	4.1	0	0	6	4.5
Waking up	18	2.4	23	5.0	35	3.4	0	0	3	2.2
Mostly before sleep	287	38.3	162	35.0	386	37.7	2	22.2	51	38.1
Irregular	80	10.7	52	11.2	122	11.9	2	22.2	20	14.9
Total	750	100.0	463	100.0	1023	100.0	9	100.0	134	100.0

Table 4–135

the husband to change intercourse positions. Indeed, some of them accused their husbands of being sex maniacs. This attitude is the cause of many divorces.[40]

Surveys in the United States showed that 70 percent of the couples never thought of trying other sexual positions, but a survey in more than two hundred societies showed that rear entry positions were rare in any case. Males and the better educated tend to change sexual positions more often.[41] Our survey, however (table 4–138 and figure 4–27), showed that 54.4 percent of the subjects (56.5 percent of city couples and 44.9 percent of village couples) surveyed change sexual positions at least occassionally.

This is an unexpected result, showing that Chinese couples are, in this respect, not very conservative after all. Kachadourian thought it ideal if couples were to choose their positions as a matter of course simply according to their own needs.[42]

The younger the couples are, the more of them tend to change sexual positions (G= 0.23 for city husbands, 0.16 for city wives, 0.10 for village wives and insignificant for viallage husbands). (tables 4–139 to 4–142 and figure 4–27).

Occupation and Time for Sexual Intercourse (Village Husbands)

	FACTORY		AGRICULTURE		SERVICE		COMMERCE	
	NO.	%	NO.	%	NO.	%	NO.	%
Before sleep	7	33.3	45	56.9	6	22.2	1	12.5
Midnight	1	4.8	24	14.4	6	22.2	1	12.5
Waking up	2	9.5	6	3.6	1	3.7	0	0
Mostly before sleep	8	38.1	45	26.9	9	33.3	1	12.5
Irregular	3	14.3	47	28.1	5	18.5	5	62.5
Total	21	100.0	167	100.0	27	100.0	8	100.0

	OFFICIAL		S. OFFICIAL		PROFESSIONAL		SOLDIER		OTHERS	
	NO.	%	NO.	%	NO.	%	NO.	%	NO.	%
Before sleep	4	26.7	7	26.9	4	30.8	1	33.3	5	31.3
Midnight	1	6.7	4	15.4	2	15.4	1	33.3	2	12.5
Waking up	0	0	0	0	0	0	0	0	0	0
Mostly before sleep	7	46.7	5	19.2	2	15.4	1	33.3	5	31.3
Irregular	3	20.0	10	38.5	5	38.5	0	0	4	25.0
Total	15	100.0	26	100.0	13	100.0	3	100.0	16	100.0

Table 4–136

Percentage of City and Village Subjects with Different Use of Sexual Positions

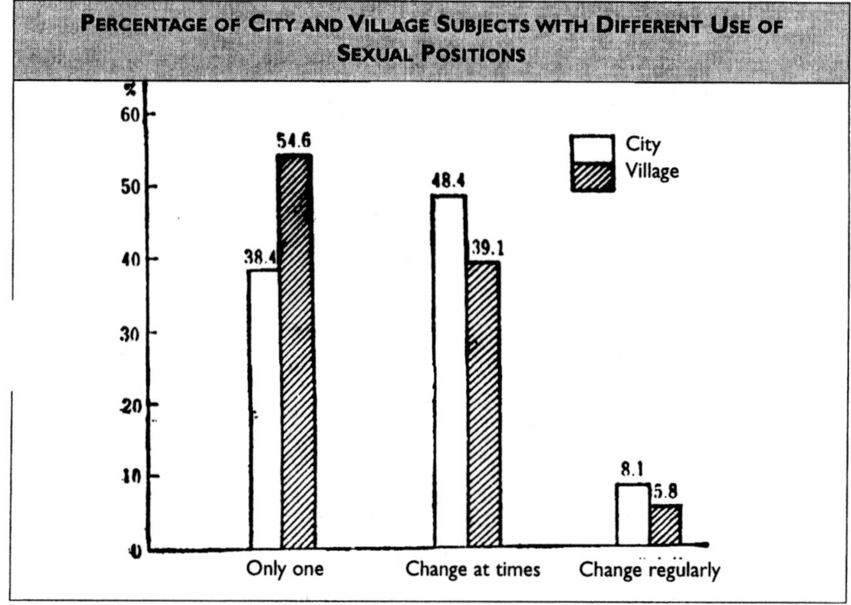

Figure 4–26

Occupation and Time for Sexual Intercourse (Village Wives)

	FACTORY		AGRICULTURE		SERVICE		COMMERCE	
	NO.	%	NO.	%	NO.	%	NO.	%
Before sleep	86	39.6	187	32.2	24	26.4	8	32.0
Midnight	11	5.1	55	9.5	8	8.8	1	4.0
Waking up	7	3.2	18	3.1	4	4.4	0	0
Mostly before sleep	52	24.0	171	29.5	29	31.9	6	24.0
Irregular	61	28.1	149	25.7	26	28.6	10	40.0
Total	217	100.0	580	100.0	91	100.0	25	100.0

	OFFICIAL		S. OFFICIAL		PROFESSIONAL		SOLDIER		OTHERS	
	NO.	%	NO.	%	NO.	%	NO.	%	NO.	%
Before sleep	10	41.7	18	43.9	19	43.2	0	0	17	28.8
Midnight	1	4.2	5	12.2	4	9.1	0	0	7	11.9
Waking up	0	0	1	2.4	2	4.5	0	0	0	0
Mostly before sleep	8	33.3	11	26.8	9	20.5	0	0	20	33.9
Irregular	5	20.8	6	16.6	10	22.7	0	0	15	25.4
Total	24	100.0	41	100.0	44	100.0	0	0	59	100.0

Table 4–137

Relationship Between Percentage of City Subjects who Regularly Change Sexual Positions and Their Age

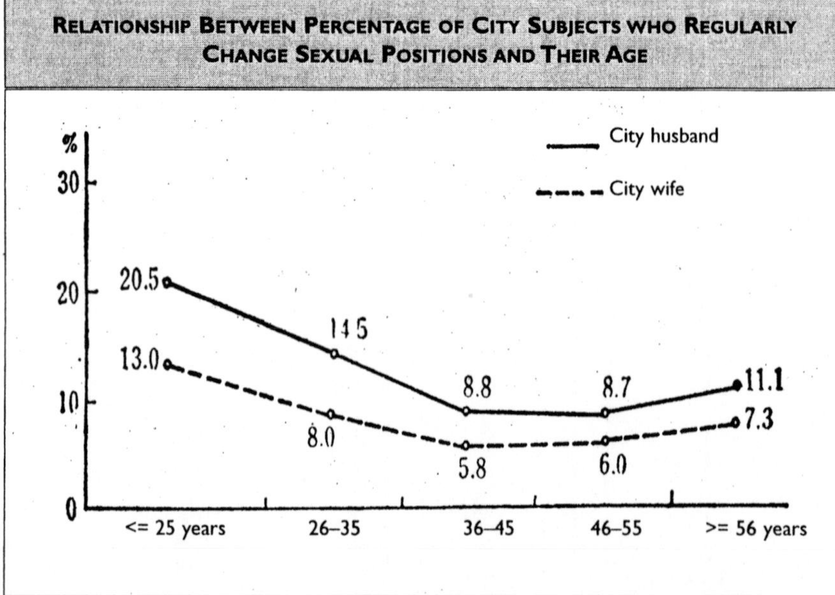

Figure 4–27

Sexual Positions Used									
	TOTAL	ONLY ONE		SOMETIMES CHANGE		OFTEN CHANGE		UNKNOWN	
		NO.	%	NO.	%	NO.	%	NO.	%
City	6210	2383	38.4	3006	48.4	502	8.1	319	5.1
Village	1392	760	54.6	543	39.1	81	5.8	8	0.6
Total	7602	3143	41.3	3549	46.7	583	7.7	327	4.3

Table 4–138

Age and Sexual Positions (City Husbands)										
	<=25		26–35		36–45		46–55		>=56	
	NO.	%	NO.	%	NO.	%	NO.	%	NO.	%
Only one	13	17.8	177	27.0	191	34.1	130	43.3	59	46.8
Sometimes change	45	61.6	384	58.5	320	57.1	144	48.0	53	42.1
Often change	15	20.5	95	14.5	49	8.8	26	8.7	14	11.1
Total	73	100.0	656	100.0	560	100.0	300	100.0	126	100.0

P=0.001

Table 4–139

Age and Sexual Positions (City Wives)										
	<=25		26–35		36–45		46–55		>=56	
	NO.	%	NO.	%	NO.	%	NO.	%	NO.	%
Only one	79	34.2	630	39.6	654	44.9	300	53.0	55	50.5
Sometimes change	122	52.8	835	52.4	719	49.3	232	41.0	46	42.2
Often change	30	13.0	127	8.0	85	5.8	34	6.0	8	7.3
Total	271	100.0	1592	100.0	1458	100.0	566	100.0	109	100.0

P=0.001

Table 4–140

Age and Sexual Positions (Village Husbands)										
	<=25		26–35		36–45		46–55		>=56	
	NO.	%	NO.	%	NO.	%	NO.	%	NO.	%
Only one	9	42.9	53	500	56	53.3	25	52.1	10	47.6
Sometimes change	11	52.4	44	41.5	41	39.0	17	35.4	10	47.6
Often change	1	4.8	9	8.5	8	7.6	6	12.5	1	4.8
Total	21	100.0	106	100.0	105	100.0	48	100.0	21	100.0

P=0.90

Table 4–141

AGE AND SEXUAL POSITIONS (VILLAGE WIVES)										
	<=25		26–35		36–45		46–55		>=56	
	NO.	%	NO.	%	NO.	%	NO.	%	NO.	%
Only one	56	51.4	295	54.5	198	58.8	48	60.8	8	57.1
Sometimes change	45	41.3	216	39.9	125	37.1	27	34.2	6	42.9
Often change	8	7.3	30	5.5	14	4.2	4	5.1	0	0
Total	109	100.0	541	100.0	337	100.0	79	100.0	14	100.0

P=0.50

Table 4–142

The educational level of our subjects did not have any significant relationship with sexual positions. (tables 4–143 to 4–146).

It is possible that in our society, with its low level of sexual sophistication, even the better educated are poorly educated when it comes to sex.

EDUCATIONAL LEVEL AND SEXUAL POSITIONS (CITY HUSBANDS)										
	ILLITERATE		PRIMARY		J. HIGH		S. HIGH		C. & ABOVE	
	NO.	%	NO.	%	NO.	%	NO.	%	NO.	%
Only one	5	45.5	8	22.9	132	39.3	214	34.6	205	29.8
Sometimes change	5	45.5	22	62.9	163	48.5	339	54.8	403	58.5
Often change	1	9.1	5	14.3	41	12.2	66	10.7	81	11.8
Total	11	100.0	35	100.0	336	100.0	619	100.0	689	100.0

Table 4–143

EDUCATIONAL LEVEL AND SEXUAL POSITIONS (CITY WIVES)										
	ILLITERATE		PRIMARY		J. HIGH		S. HIGH		C. & ABOVE	
	NO.	%	NO.	%	NO.	%	NO.	%	NO.	%
Only one	4	22.2	62	45.6	593	48.1	754	42.5	293	38.4
Sometimes change	11	61.1	57	41.9	568	46.1	898	50.6	406	53.2
Often change	3	16.7	17	12.5	72	5.8	121	6.8	64	8.4
Total	18	100.0	136	100.0	1233	100.0	1773	100.0	763	100.0

Table 4–144

Occupation had little to do with sexual positions as well (alpha all below 0.10 for different types of subjects, tables 4–147 to 4–150). The explanation given above might apply.

EDUCATIONAL LEVEL AND SEXUAL POSITIONS (VILLAGE HUSBANDS)										
	ILLITERATE		PRIMARY		J. HIGH		S. HIGH		C. & ABOVE	
	NO.	%	NO.	%	NO.	%	NO.	%	NO.	%
Only one	7	53.8	30	49.2	62	49.6	46	52.9	7	58.3
Sometimes change	3	23.1	27	44.3	53	42.4	35	40.2	3	25.0
Often change	3	23.1	4	6.6	10	8.0	6	6.9	2	16.7
Total	13	100.0	61	100.0	125	100.0	87	100.0	12	100.0

Table 4–145

EDUCATIONAL LEVEL AND SEXUAL POSITIONS (VILLAGE WIVES)										
	ILLITERATE		PRIMARY		J. HIGH		S. HIGH		C. & ABOVE	
	NO.	%	NO.	%	NO.	%	NO.	%	NO.	%
Only one	20	58.8	138	56.8	286	57.3	156	53.4	5	41.7
Sometimes change	12	35.3	92	37.9	183	36.7	126	43.2	6	50.0
Often change	2	5.9	13	5.3	30	6.0	10	3.4	1	8.3
Total	34	100.0	243	100.0	499	100.0	292	100.0	12	100.0

Table 4–146

OCCUPATION AND SEX POSITIONS: (CITY HUSBANDS)								
	FACTORY		AGRICULTURE		SERVICE		COMMERCE	
	NO.	%	NO.	%	NO.	%	NO.	%
One only	102	35.7	7	25.0	13	21.0	65	40.4
Sometimes change	149	52.1	18	64.3	41	66.1	79	49.1
Often change	35	12.2	3	10.7	8	12.9	17	10.6
Total	286	100.0	28	100.0	62	100.0	161	100.0

	OFFICAL		S. OFFICIAL		PROFESSIONAL		SOLDIER		OTHERS	
	NO.	%	NO.	%	NO.	%	NO.	%	NO.	%
One only	117	35.2	100	32.8	134	30.9	9	29.0	15	37.5
Sometimes change	181	54.5	168	55.1	252	58.2	15	48.4	21	52.5
Often change	34	10.2	37	12.1	47	10.9	7	22.6	4	10.0
Total	332	100.0	305	100.0	433	100.0	31	100.0	40	100.0

Table 4–147

OCCUPATION AND SEX POSITIONS (CITY WIVES)								
	FACTORY		AGRICULTURE		SERVICE		COMMERCE	
	NO.	%	NO.	%	NO.	%	NO.	%
One only	368	45.9	37	43.0	101	40.2	209	46.3
Sometimes change	379	47.3	41	47.7	131	52.2	219	48.6
Often change	54	6.7	8	9.3	19	7.6	23	5.1
Total	801	100.0	86	100.0	251	100.0	451	100.0

	OFFICIAL		S. OFFICIAL		PROFESSIONAL		SOLDIER		OTHERS	
	NO.	%	NO.	%	NO.	%	NO.	%	NO.	%
One only	300	41.1	192	43.0	430	13.1	2	22.2	54	41.9
Sometimes change	384	52.6	222	49.8	485	48.6	6	66.7	64	49.6
Often change	46	6.6	32	7.2	83	8.3	1	11.1	11	8.5
Total	730	100.0	446	100.0	998	100.0	9	100.0	129	100.0

Table 4–148

OCCUPATION AND SEX POSITIONS (VILLAGE HUSBANDS)								
	FACTORY		AGRICULTURE		SERVICE		COMMERCE	
	NO.	%	NO.	%	NO.	%	NO.	%
One only	9	42.9	81	48.5	16	59.3	5	62.5
Sometimes change	10	47.6	73	43.7	10	37.0	3	37.5
Often change	2	9.5	13	7.8	1	3.7	0	0
Total	21	100.0	167	100.0	27	100.0	8	100.0

	OFFICIAL		S. OFFICIAL		PROFESSIONAL		SOLDIER		OTHERS	
	NO.	%	NO.	%	NO.	%	NO.	%	NO.	%
One only	8	53.3	12	46.2	9	69.2	1	33.3	10	62.5
Sometimes change	4	26.7	11	42.3	4	30.8	2	66.7	4	25.0
Often change	3	20.0	3	11.5	0	0	0	0	2	12.5
Total	15	100.0	26	100.0	13	100.0	3	100.0	16	100.0

Table 4–149

OCCUPATION AND SEXUAL POSITIONS (VILLAGE HUSBANDS)								
	FACTORY		AGRICULTURE		SERVICE		COMMERCE	
	NO.	%	NO.	%	NO.	%	NO.	%
One only	145	67.4	297	51.5	49	54.4	14	56.0
Sometimes change	66	30.7	240	41.6	33	36.7	11	44.0
Often change	4	1.9	40	6.9	8	8.9	0	0
Total	215	100.0	577	100.0	90	100.0	25	100.0

	OFFICIAL		S. OFFICIAL		PROFESSIONAL		SOLDIER		OTHERS	
	NO.	%	NO.	%	NO.	%	NO.	%	NO.	%
One only	14	56.0	30	73.2	21	47.7	0	0	32	54.2
Sometimes change	11	44.0	8	19.5	23	52.3	0	0	26	44.1
Often change	0	0	3	7.3	0	0	0	0	1	1.7
Total	25	100.0	41	100.0	44	100.0	0	0	59	100.0

Table 4–150

6. Nudity in Sexual Intercourse

Nudity in sexual intercourse is an indication of sexual communication, but may also be related to cultural habits. For example, the Indians in southern Mexico are strict in clothing themselves during sex, despite a hot climate, whereas the Indians in northern Mexico go about their everyday lives more or less in the nude.[43] In the Victorian age, an Austrian woman boasted that although she had given birth to eight children, she had never allowed her husband to look at her breasts.[44] Kinsey came across some young men with a great deal of sexual experience who rejected their girl friends because they "had sunk so low" as to take all their clothes off during sexual intercourse.[45]

This type of physical distance between husband and wife seems hardly conducive to marital happiness. After all, as Ellis pointed out, if husband and wife cannot be comfortable with each other's bodies, how can they be frank with each other in other areas of marital life?[46]

However, things change over time. In Kinsey's survey, 90 percent of the couples of the higher social class were completely nude during sexual intercourse. During premarital sex, even if environment permitted it, only 55 percent of the couples were nude. Among the less educated, the respective figures were 43 percent and 32 percent.[47]

Total Nudity During Sexual Intercourse									
	TOTAL	OFTEN		SOMETIMES		NEVER		UNKNOWN	
		NO.	%	NO.	%	NO.	%	NO.	%
City	6210	794	12.8	3255	52.4	1866	30.0	295	4.8
Village	1392	186	13.4	609	43.8	592	42.5	5	0.4

Table 4–151

Regions and Total Nudity During Sexual Intercourse								
		TOTAL	OFTEN		SOMETIMES		NEVER	
			NO.	%	NO.	%	NO.	%
City	Shanghai	2475	196	7.9	1381	55.8	898	36.3
	Tienjin	993	215	21.3	527	52.2	251	24.9
	Chengdu	882	107	12.1	512	58.0	263	29.8
	Guangzhou	513	119	23.2	322	62.8	72	14.0
Village	Suzhou	494	28	5.7	209	42.3	257	52.0
	Yuci	893	158	17.6	400	44.7	335	37.5
	Shanghai	350	31	8.9	140	40.0	179	51.1

Table 4–152

Generally speaking, the Chinese, especially the Han, have been quite negative about nudity. There are records showing that a widow cut her arm after it was touched by another man, and of a women who refused to receive medical treatment for her diseased breast because she did not wish to expose her body to doctors.[48] In 1926, the famous artist Liu Hai-su was wanted by the police for using live nude models in his art school.[49] In the 1980s, a girl went insane, apparently because she was severely criticized for taking a job as a nude model.[50]

Yet there are signs that this type of conservatism is changing. Table 4–151 and figure 4–29 show that 63.7 percent of all the subjects surveyed were frequently nude during sexual intercourse, a fact especially true of city couples.

Table 4–152 shows that in cities of the southern (Guangdong) regions, those couples who were frequently nude were at 23.2 percent, occassionally nude were at 62.6 percent, higher than all other cities. This shows either that nudity during sexual intercoure is related to climate or that the people in southern regions are sexually less inhibited for other reasons.

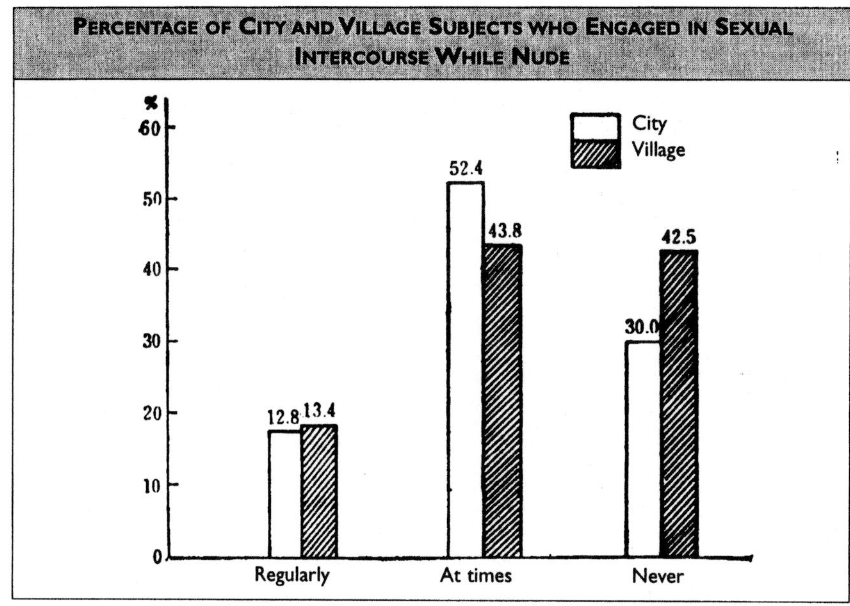

Figure 4–28

For the city couples, age and nudity during sex had a strong relationship (G=0.29 for husbands and 0.23 for wives). But for the villagers, the relationship was insignificant. The difference might be due to the location of most of the village subjects. They were mainly from Yuci and Qi Xian, where people habitually sleep in the nude. (tables 4-153 to 4-156).

There was some relationship between education and the city couples who were nude during sex (G=0.12 for husbands and 0.12 for wives). The higher the level of education, the more nudity. On the other hand,

AGE AND NUDITY DURING SEXUAL INTERCOURSE (CITY HUSBANDS)

	<=25		26–35		36–45		46–55		>=56	
	NO.	%	NO.	%	NO.	%	NO.	%	NO.	%
Often	26	35.1	138	20.9	80	14.3	37	12.3	17	13.4
Sometimes	39	52.7	407	61.8	343	61.4	167	55.5	71	55.9
Never	9	12.2	114	17.3	136	24.3	97	32.2	39	30.7
Total	74	100.0	659	100.0	559	100.0	301	100.0	127	100.0

P=0.001

Table 4–153

Age and Nudity during Sexual Intercourse (City Wives)										
	<=25		26–35		36–45		46–55		>=56	
	NO.	%	NO.	%	NO.	%	NO.	%	NO.	%
Often	62	26.7	232	14.6	126	8.5	48	8.4	7	6.5
Sometimes	122	52.6	915	57.7	781	52.9	243	42.3	37	34.3
Never	48	20.7	438	27.6	570	38.6	283	49.3	64	59.3
Total	232	100.0	1585	100.0	1477	100.0	574	100.0	108	100.0

P=0.001

Table 4–154

Age and Nudity during Sexual Intercourse (Village Husbands)										
	<=25		26–35		36–45		46–55		>=56	
	NO.	%	NO.	%	NO.	%	NO.	%	NO.	%
Often	4	19.0	15	14.2	13	12.4	11	23.4	2	9.5
Sometimes	12	57.1	47	44.3	49	46.7	23	48.9	11	52.4
Never	5	24.8	44	41.5	43	41.0	13	27.7	8	38.1
Total	21	100.0	106	100.0	105	100.0	47	100.0	21	100.0

P=0.50

Table 4–155

Age and Nudity during Sexual Intercourse (Village Wives)										
	<=25		26–35		36–45		46–55		>=56	
	NO.	%	NO.	%	NO.	%	NO.	%	NO.	%
Often	10	9.2	67	12.3	54	16.0	8	10.0	2	14.3
Sometimes	56	51.4	235	43.3	138	40.8	28	35.0	8	57.1
Never	53	39.4	241	44.4	146	43.2	44	55.0	4	28.6
Total	109	100.0	543	100.0	338	100.0	80	100.0	14	100.0

P=0.20

Table 4–156

Education and Nudity during Sexual Intercourse (City Husbands)										
	ILLITERATE		PRIMARY		J. HIGH		S. HIGH		C. & ABOVE	
	NO.	%	NO.	%	NO.	%	NO.	%	NO.	%
Often	2	20.0	4	11.1	58	17.1	90	14.4	139	20.3
Sometimes	5	50.0	23	63.9	184	54.3	391	62.6	412	60.1
Never	3	30.0	9	25.0	97	28.6	144	23.0	135	19.7
Total	10	100.0	36	100.0	339	100.0	625	100.0	686	100.0

Table 4–157

Education and Nudity During Sexual Intercourse (City Wives)										
	ILLITERATE		PRIMARY		J. HIGH		S. HIGH		C. & ABOVE	
	NO.	%	NO.	%	NO.	%	NO.	%	NO.	%
Often	3	17.6	20	14.0	116	9.4	223	12.5	112	14.7
Sometimes	10	58.8	56	39.2	635	51.3	957	53.7	421	55.1
Never	4	23.5	67	46.9	488	39.4	603	33.8	231	30.2
Total	17	100.0	143	100.0	1239	100.0	1783	100.0	764	100.0

Table 4–158

Education and Nudity During Sexual Intercourse (Village Husbands)										
	ILLITERATE		PRIMARY		J. HIGH		S. HIGH		C. & ABOVE	
	NO.	%	NO.	%	NO.	%	NO.	%	NO.	%
Often	2	5.4	13	21.3	7	13.7	12	13.8	0	0
Sometimes	6	46.2	29	47.5	62	50.0	37	42.5	7	58.3
Never	5	38.5	19	31.1	45	36.3	38	43.7	5	41.7
Total	13	100.0	61	100.0	124	100.0	87	100.0	12	100.0

Table 4–159

Education and Nudity During Sexual Intercourse (Village Wives)										
	ILLITERATE		PRIMARY		J. HIGH		S. HIGH		C. & ABOVE	
	NO.	%	NO.	%	NO.	%	NO.	%	NO.	%
Often	6	17.1	38	15.6	61	12.2	35	11.9	1	8.3
Sometimes	15	42.9	94	38.7	211	42.1	137	46.8	8	66.7
Never	14	40.0	111	45.7	229	45.7	121	41.3	3	25.0
Total	35	100.0	243	100.0	501	100.0	293	100.0	12	100.0

Table 4–160

for the village subjects, the husbands showed a G index of 0.14 in the relationship, but this was reversed, that is, the more educated, the less nudity. This may be because, in the villages, the better educated tend to give up the habit of sleeping in the nude (tables 4–157 to 4–160).

Occupation had an insignificant relationship with nudity during sex (alphas all below 0.10)(tables 4–161 to 4–164).

Along the same lines, we used another question to elicit the subjects views on nudity. We asked what the subjects thought about the job of being a nude model for artists. Tables 4–165 and 4–166 show that

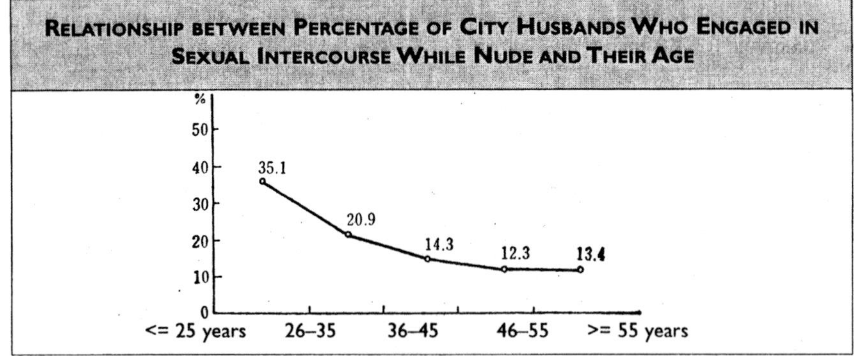

Figure 4–29

OCCUPATION AND NUDITY DURING SEXUAL INTERCOURSE (CITY HUSBANDS)

	FACTORY		AGRICULTURE		SERVICE		COMMERCE	
	NO.	%	NO.	%	NO.	%	NO.	%
Often	46	15.8	5	17.2	10	16.7	30	18.5
Sometimes	181	62.0	15	51.7	40	66.7	93	57.4
Never	65	22.3	9	31.0	10	16.7	39	24.1
Total	292	100.0	29	100.0	60	100.0	162	100.0

	OFFICIAL		S. OFFICIAL		PROFESSIONAL		SOLDIER		OTHERS	
	NO.	%	NO.	%	NO.	%	NO.	%	NO.	%
Often	59	17.9	42	13.8	87	20.0	11	34.4	5	12.8
Sometimes	195	59.1	185	60.7	257	58.9	16	50.0	23	59.0
Never	76	23.0	78	25.6	92	21.1	5	15.6	11	28.2
Total	330	100.0	305	100.0	436	100.0	32	100.0	39	100.0

Table 4–161

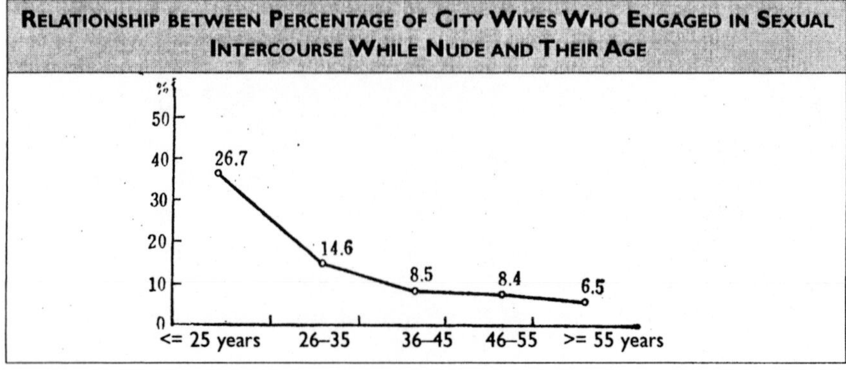

Figure 4–30

Occupation and Nudity During Sexual Intercourse (City Wives)								
	FACTORY		AGRICULTURE		SERVICE		COMMERCE	
	NO.	%	NO.	%	NO.	%	NO.	%
Often	110	13.7	7	8.0	31	12.1	51	11.3
Sometimes	399	49.6	45	51.7	128	49.8	258	57.3
Never	295	36.7	35	40.2	98	38.1	141	31.3
Total	804	100.0	87	100.0	257	100.0	450	100.0

	OFFICIAL		S. OFFICIAL		PROFESSIONAL		SOLDIER		OTHERS	
	NO.	%	NO.	%	NO.	%	NO.	%	NO.	%
Often	74	10.1	39	8.7	133	13.2	3	33.3	25	19.1
Sometimes	381	52.2	248	55.1	56	54.4	3	33.3	59	45.0
Never	275	37.7	163	36.2	325	32.4	3	33.3	47	35.9
Total	730	100.0	450	100.0	1004	100.0	9	100.0	131	100.0

Table 4–162

Occupation and Nudity During Sexual Intercourse (Village Husbands)								
	FACTORY		AGRICULTURE		SERVICE		COMMERCE	
	NO.	%	NO.	%	NO.	%	NO.	%
Often	3	14.3	25	15.1	8	29.6	0	0
Sometimes	8	38.1	84	50.6	8	29.6	6	75.0
Never	10	47.6	57	34.3	11	40.7	2	25.0
Total	21	100.0	166	100.0	27	100.0	8	100.0

	OFFICIAL		S. OFFICIAL		PROFESSIONAL		SOLDIER		OTHERS	
	NO.	%	NO.	%	NO.	%	NO.	%	NO.	%
Often	2	13.3	2	7.7	1	7.7	0	0	1	6.3
Sometimes	7	46.7	15	57.7	3	23.1	2	66.7	8	50.0
Never	6	40.0	9	34.6	9	69.2	1	33.3	7	43.8
Total	15	100.0	26	100.0	13	100.0	3	100.0	16	100.0

Table 4–163

fewer males and fewer city dwellers had a negative attitude in regard to this profession.

The educational level shows an insignificant relationship with the attitude toward nude models (G indices all insignificant except for village

OCCUPATION AND NUDITY DURING SEXUAL INTERCOURSE (VILLAGE WIVES)								
	FACTORY		AGRICULTURE		SERVICE		COMMERCE	
	NO.	%	NO.	%	NO.	%	NO.	%
Often	13	6.0	89	15.3	22	24.4	3	12.0
Sometimes	82	37.8	259	44.7	39	43.3	14	56.0
Never	122	56.2	232	40.0	29	32.2	8	32.0
Total	217	100.0	580	100.0	90	100.0	25	100.0

	OFFICIAL		S. OFFICIAL		PROFESSIONAL		SOLDIER		OTHERS	
	NO.	%	NO.	%	NO.	%	NO.	%	NO.	%
Often	1	4.2	2	4.9	4	9.1	0	0	6	10.2
Sometimes	15	62.5	15	36.6	20	45.5	0	0	21	35.6
Never	8	33.3	24	58.5	20	45.5	0	0	32	54.2
Total	24	100.0	41	100.0	44	100.0	0	0	59	100.0

Table 4–164

GENDER AND OPINION ON NUDE MODELS (CITY)							
GENDER	NORMAL		NOT IMPRESSED		LOW		TOTAL
	NO.	%	NO.	%	NO.	%	
Male	1222	68.5	510	28.6	53	3.0	1785
Female	2538	60.8	1471	35.3	162	3.9	4171

P=0.001

Table 4–165

GENEDER AND OPINION ON NUDE MODELS (VILLAGE)							
GENDER	NORMAL		NOT IMPRESSED		LOW		TOTAL
	NO.	%	NO.	%	NO.	%	
Male	154	51.7	95	31.9	49	16.4	298
Female	538	49.7	387	35.7	158	14.6	1083

P=0.10

Table 4–166

husbands which was 0.19). As the tables below show, however, the better educated tend to hold less negative attitudes, expecially those who are city dwellers.

EDUCATION AND VIEW ON NUDE MODELS (CITY HUSBANDS)										
	ILLITERATE		PRIMARY		J. HIGH		S. HIGH		C. & ABOVE	
	NO.	%	NO.	%	NO.	%	NO.	%	NO.	%
Low	3	23.1	4	11.1	19	5.5	19	3.0	6	0.9
Not a glory	3	23.1	12	33.3	95	27.5	209	32.9	171	24.5
Normal	7	53.8	20	55.6	231	67.0	407	64.1	520	74.6
Total	13	100.0	36	100.0	345	100.0	635	100.0	697	100.0

Table 4–167

EDUCATION AND VIEW ON NUDE MODELS (CITY WIVES)										
	ILLITERATE		PRIMARY		J. HIGH		S. HIGH		C. & ABOVE	
	NO.	%	NO.	%	NO.	%	NO.	%	NO.	%
Low	7	36.8	24	16.1	67	5.2	48	2.6	12	1.5
Not a glory	6	31.6	51	34.2	424	32.9	701	37.9	269	34.4
Normal	6	31.6	74	49.7	799	61.9	1102	59.5	501	64.1
Total	19	100.0	149	100.0	1290	100.0	1851	100.0	782	100.0

Table 4–168

EDUCATION AND VIEW ON NUDE MODELS (VILLAGE HUSBANDS)										
	ILLITERATE		PRIMARY		J. HIGH		S. HIGH		C. & ABOVE	
	NO.	%	NO.	%	NO.	%	NO.	%	NO.	%
Low	5	38.5	19	32.8	12	9.6	13	14.9	0	0
Not a glory	2	15.4	18	31.0	40	32.0	29	33.3	5	41.7
Normal	6	46.2	21	36.2	73	58.4	45	51.7	7	58.3
Total	13	100.0	58	100.0	125	100.0	87	100.0	12	100.0

Table 4–169

EDUCATION AND VIEW ON NUDE MODELS (VILLAGE WIVES)										
	ILLITERATE		PRIMARY		J. HIGH		S. HIGH		C. & ABOVE	
	NO.	%	NO.	%	NO.	%	NO.	%	NO.	%
Low	7	20.6	44	7.3	71	14.2	33	11.3	3	27.3
Not a glory	10	29.4	81	33.3	182	36.4	111	37.9	3	27.3
Normal	17	50.0	120	49.4	247	49.4	149	50.9	5	45.5
Total	34	100.0	245	100.0	500	100.0	293	100.0	11	100.0

Table 4–170

Occupation and View on Nude Models (City Husbands)

	FACTORY		AGRICULTURE		SERVICE		COMMERCE	
	NO.	%	NO.	%	NO.	%	NO.	%
Normal	202	67.6	16	53.3	38	61.3	108	65.9
Not a glory	85	28.4	11	36.7	19	30.6	50	30.5
Low	12	4.0	3	10.0	5	8.1	6	3.7
Total	299	100.0	30	100.0	62	100.0	164	100.0

	OFFICIAL		S. OFFICIAL		PROFESSIONAL		SOLDIER		OTHERS	
	NO.	%	NO.	%	NO.	%	NO.	%	NO.	%
Normal	229	67.8	212	67.7	320	73.4	24	75.0	30	71.4
Not a glory	100	29.6	89	28.4	112	25.7	8	25.0	11	26.2
Low	9	2.7	12	3.8	4	0.9	0	0	1	2.4
Total	338	100.0	313	100.0	436	100.0	32	100.0	42	100.0

Table 4–171

Occupation and View on Nude Models (City Wives)

	FACTORY		AGRICULTURE		SERVICE		COMMERCE	
	NO.	%	NO.	%	NO.	%	NO.	%
Normal	542	64.2	40	43.0	167	64.0	253	55.4
Not a glory	273	32.3	41	44.1	77	29.5	190	41.6
Low	29	3.4	12	12.9	17	6.5	14	3.1
Total	844	100.0	93	100.0	261	100.0	457	100.0

	OFFICIAL		S. OFFICIAL		PROFESSIONAL		SOLDIER		OTHERS	
	NO.	%	NO.	%	NO.	%	NO.	%	NO.	%
Normal	482	63.3	289	61.6	610	58.7	6	60.0	80	60.6
Not a glory	251	32.9	163	34.8	401	38.6	4	40.0	41	31.1
Low	29	3.8	17	3.6	28	2.7	0	0	11	8.3
Total	762	100.0	469	100.0	1039	100.0	10	100.0	132	100.0

Table 4–172

Occuaption is also not significantly associated with views toward nude models (alphas all below 0.10) (tables 4–171 to 4–174).

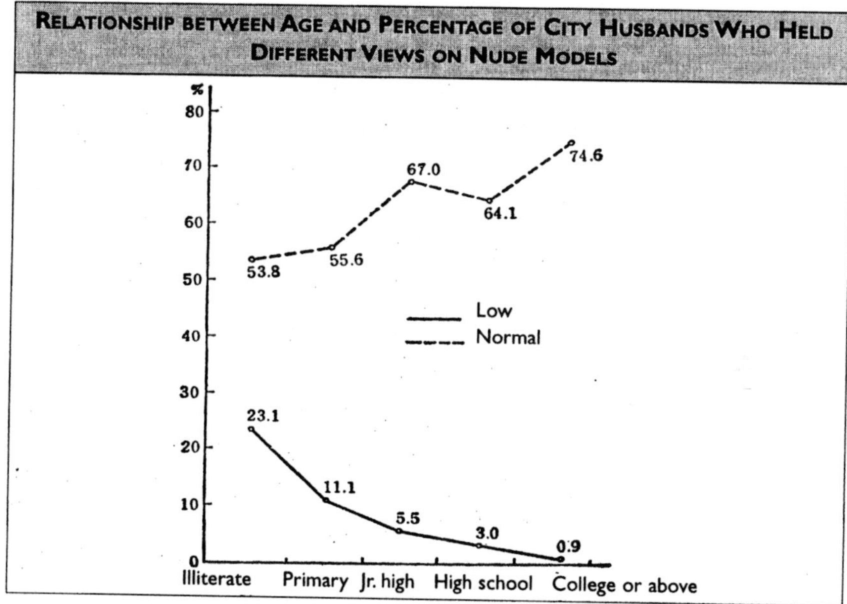

Figure 4–31

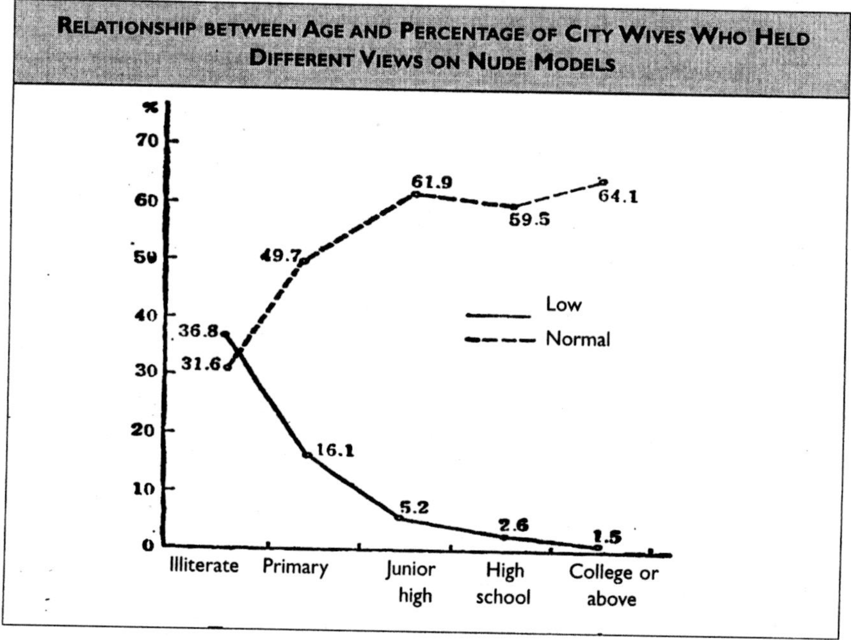

Figure 4–32

OCCUPATION AND VIEW ON NUDE MODELS (VILLAGE HUSBANDS)

	FACTORY		AGRICULTURE		SERVICE		COMMERCE	
	NO.	%	NO.	%	NO.	%	NO.	%
Normal	11	52.4	88	53.3	14	51.9	6	85.7
Not a glory	6	28.6	49	298.7	7	25.9	0	0
Low	4	19.0	28	17.0	6	22.2	1	14.3
Total	21	100.0	165	100.0	27	100.0	7	100.0

	OFFICIAL		S. OFFICIAL		PROFESSIONAL		SOLDIER		OTHERS	
	NO.	%	NO.	%	NO.	%	NO.	%	NO.	%
Normal	5	33.3	15	57.7	8	61.5	1	33.3	5	31.3
Not a glory	8	53.3	9	34.6	5	38.5	1	33.3	7	43.8
Low	2	13.3	2	7.7	0	0	1	33.3	4	25.0
Total	15	100.0	26	100.0	13	100.0	3	100.0	16	100.0

Table 4–173

OCCUPATION AND VIEW ON NUDE MODELS (VILLAGE WIVES)

	FACTORY		AGRICULTURE		SERVICE		COMMERCE	
	NO.	%	NO.	%	NO.	%	NO.	%
Normal	109	50.5	275	47.5	61	67.0	12	48.0
Not a glory	82	38.0	204	35.2	24	26.4	10	40.0
Low	25	11.6	100	17.3	6	6.6	3	12.0
Total	216	100.0	579	100.0	91	100.0	25	100.0

	OFFICIAL		S. OFFICIAL		PROFESSIONAL		SOLDIER		OTHERS	
	NO.	%	NO.	%	NO.	%	NO.	%	NO.	%
Normal	12	48.0	21	51.2	18	40.9	0	0	30	51.7
Not a glory	9	36.0	15	36.6	19	43.2	0	0	21	36.2
Low	4	16.0	5	12.2	7	15.9	0	0	7	12.1
Total	25	100.0	41	100.0	44	100.0	0	0	58	100.0

Table 4–174

7. Masturbation

Masturbation is practiced by adults as well as juveniles. As Ellis reported, after marriage, although 17 percent of males and 42 percent of females stopped masturbating, more females than males practiced

EXPERIENCE OF MASTURBATION BEFORE MARRIAGE							
	TOTAL	YES		NO		UNKNOWN	
		NO.	%	NO.	%	NO.	%
City	6210	1065	17.1	4679	75.3	466	7.5
Village	1392	141	10.1	1244	89.4	7	0.5
Total	7602	1206	15.9	5923	77.9	473	6.2

Table 4–175

FREQUENT MASTURBATION AFTER MARRIAGE					
	TOTAL	YES		NO	
		NO.	%	NO.	%
City	1061	93	8.7	972	91.3
Village	141	12	8.5	129	91.5
Total	1202	105	8.7	1101	91.3

Table 4–176

Note: This chart includes those who had masturbation experience only

frequent masturbation. This suggested that the married males probably masturbated more due to traveling alone or due to other environmental factors, and that the married females had masturbated because of an unsatisfactory sex life.[51]

Our subjects show a similar pattern. Table 4–175 and figure 4–33 show that 15.9 percent of the subjects masturbated before marriage, but table 4–176 shows that after marriage, 8.7 percent continued the practice frequently, and 91.3 percent did so occassionally.

REGIONS AND MASTURBATION EXPERIENCE								
	REGIONS	TOTAL	YES		NO		UNKNOWN	
			NO.	%	NO.	%		
City	Shanghai	2573	331	12.9	2123	82.5	119	4.6
	Tienjin	1010	142	14.1	824	81.6	44	4.4
	Chengdu	906	163	18.0	669	73.8	74	8.2
	Guangzhou	525	260	49.5	245	46.7	20	3.8
Village	Suzhou	494	35	7.1	458	92.7	1	0.2
	Yuci	898	106	11.8	786	87.5	6	0.7
	Shanghai	369	23	6.2	313	84.8	33	8.9

Table 4–177

Table 4–177 shows that the city and village subjects differed quite significantly in respect to masturbation before marriage. In the city subjects, 17.1 percent of them had masturbated. In the village subjects, the figure was 10.1 percent.

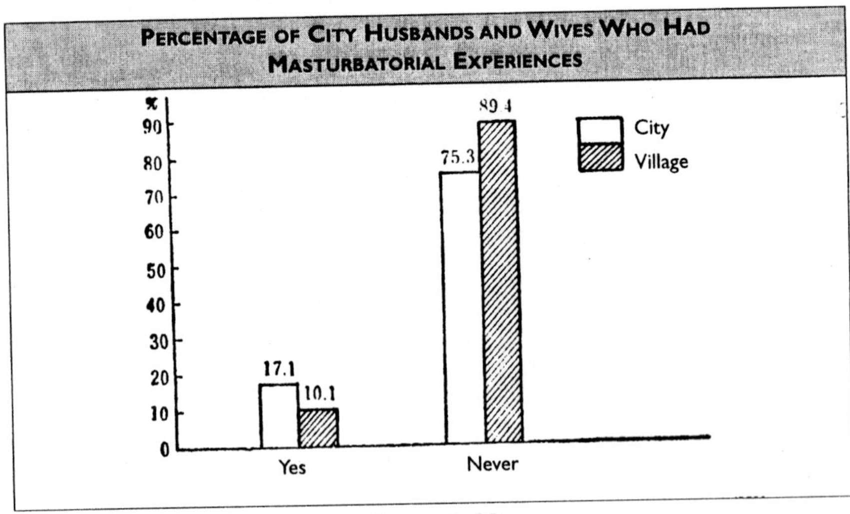

Figure 4–33

Table 4–177 shows that previous masturbation frequencies were lowest in the villages. For example, in Suzhou, the proportion was 7.1 percent, and in Yuci and Qixian 11.8 percent, all lower than in the cities. The proportion was much higher in Guangdong and along the costal areas, up to 49.5 percent. It could be that in the city and coastal regions, there is more sexual stimulation due to a more socially lax and open atmosphere.

Males and females differed in current masturbation rates. Table 4–178 shows that the males in the cities masturbated more, but in the villages, the females masturbated slightly more.

The previous masturbation rate of the married couples were much lower than that of today's young people. This demonstrates how much the general social atmosphere in China has changed.

SEX AND MASTURBATION EXPERIENCE

GENDER	CITY					VILLAGE				
	TOTAL					TOTAL				
		NO.	%	NO.	%		NO.	%	NO.	%
Male	1708	565	33.1	1143	66.9	299	27	9.0	272	91.0
Female	3900	477	12.2	3423	87.8	1085	114	10.5	971	89.5

Table 4–178

Of those surveyed, 13.1 percent of city subjects and 9.6 percent of village subjects did not hold any negative views toward masturbation. Of those who viewed masturbation as bad, 41.7 percent were city subjects and 73.4 percent were village subjects. This high proportion of subjects who held negative views about masturbation casts some doubt on their self-reports of masturbation. The rate may be higher than admitted. The fact that 30 percent of the city subjects did not answer the question on masturbation at all further supports this assumption.

VIEW ON MASTURBATION

	TOTAL	NATURAL		FORCED		BAD		LEISURE ACTIVITY		UNKNOWN	
		NO.	%	NO.	%	NO.	%	NO.	%	NO.	%
City	6210	813	13.1	356	5.7	2588	41.1	587	9.5	1866	30.0
Village	1392	133	9.6	85	6.1	1022	73.4	121	8.7	31	2.2

Table 4–179

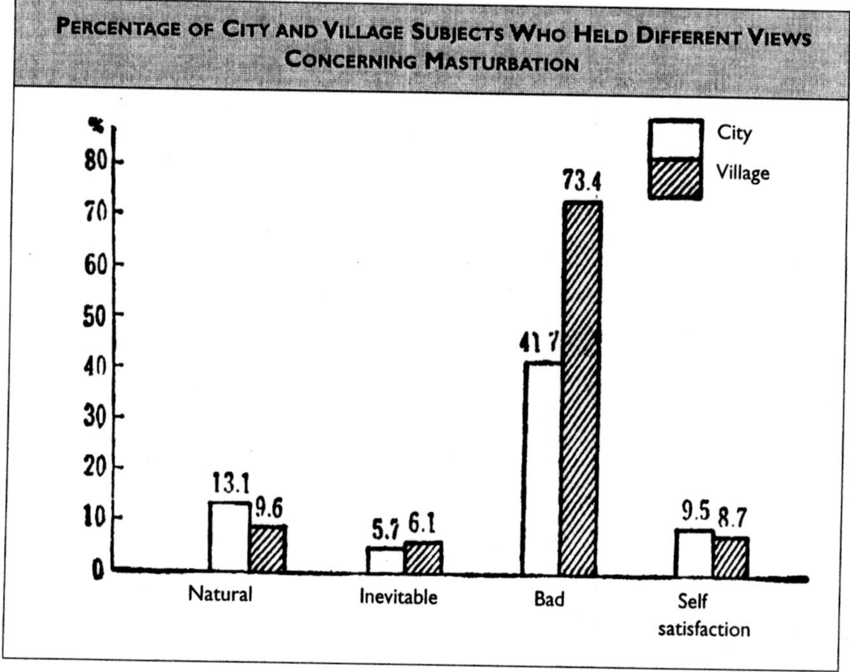

Figure 4–34

8. Homosexual Behavior

Because of the heavy pressure against homosexual behavior in China, in our survey we could ask about it only in a general way. The results show that city subjects knew more about it than the villagers, although the actual experience was very limited in both cases: 0.5 percent in the city and 2.3 percent in the village.

It has to be noted, however, that these experience figures do not represent the behavior of Chinese "homosexuals." Since we are talking about married subjects in this section, the figures are more a reflection of the rate of ambisexuality. In order to obtain more exact figures about homosexual behavior in China, a separate survey is necessary.

Understanding about Homosexuality

	TOTAL	HEARD OF		KNOW A LITTLE		EXPERIENCED IT		NEVER HEARD OF		UNKNOWN	
		NO.	%	NO.	%	NO.	%	NO.	%	NO.	%
City	6210	3533	56.4	1637	26.4	33	0.5	877	14.1	130	2.1
Village	1392	584	42.0	281	20.2	32	2.3	486	34.9	9	0.6

Table 4-180

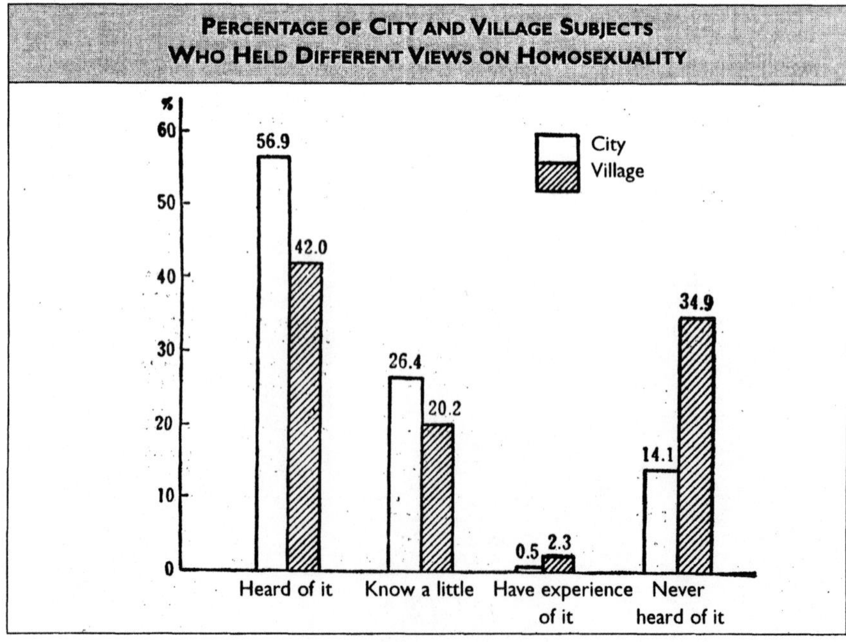

Figure 4–35

9. *Sex during Old Age*

A. Age at Which Subjects Stopped Having Sexual Intercourse

Before we asked this question, we asked the female subjects whether they had reached menopause. Table 4–181 shows their answers (as

Wives and Menopause									
	TOTAL	HAVE PASSED		NOT YET		CURRENT		UNKNOWN	
		NO.	%	NO.	%	NO.	%	NO.	%
City	6210	614	9.9	4266	68.7	186	3.0	1144	18.4
Village	1392	69	5.0	1222	87.8	29	2.1	72	5.1

Table 4–181

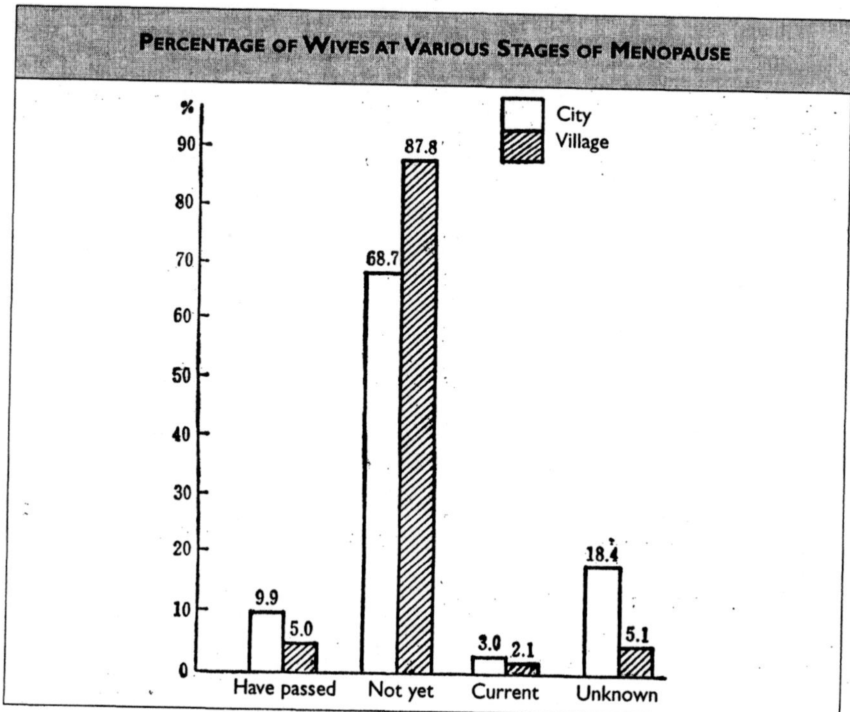

Figure 4–36

does figure 4–36). Then we asked the subjects their age at which they had ceased sexual intercourse (by cessation, we meant no sexual intercourse for over one year before the time of the survey). Results show that the wives mostly stopped after age forty-one and husband mostly

AGE OF STOPPING SEXUAL INTERCOURSE (WIVES)									
	TOTAL	<=30		31-40		41-50		>=51	
		NO.	%	NO.	%	NO.	%	NO.	%
City	238	37	15.5	34	14.3	83	34.9	84	35.3
Village	36	1	2.8	0	0	14	38.9	21	58.3

Table 4–182

AGE OF STOPPING SEXUAL INTERCOURSE (HUSBANDS)									
	TOTAL	<=30		31-40		41-50		>=51	
		NO.	%	NO.	%	NO.	%	NO.	%
City	222	19	8.6	33	14.9	44	19.8	126	56.8
Village	36	0	0	1	2.8	6	16.7	29	80.6

Table 4–183

at age fifty-one. The mean age of cessation for the wives was 46.19 (SD= 11.65), for the husbands 50.34 (SD= 10.62). The reasons for their giving up sexual intercourse, by decending order of frequency were: lack of desire (23.7 percent), fear of negative health effects (22.7 percent), unfavorable circumstances (13.5 percent), separated (12.7 percent), poor relationship (9.5 percent), and sexual dysfunctions (12.8 percent).

B. Views on Sex during Old Age

Table 4–184 shows that 6.9 percent of of city couples thought that they should not have sex after age sixty. The village couples were more conservative, with a corresponding figure of 17.7 percent.

VIEW ON A COUPLE HAVING SEX AFTER AGE FIFTY									
	TOTAL	YES IF POSSIBLE		BETTER LESS		SHOULD STOP		UNKNOWN	
		NO.	%	NO.	%	NO.	%	NO.	%
City	6210	2213	35.6	3254	52.4	430	6.9	313	5.0
Village	1392	352	25.3	785	56.4	246	17.7	9	0.6

Table 4–184

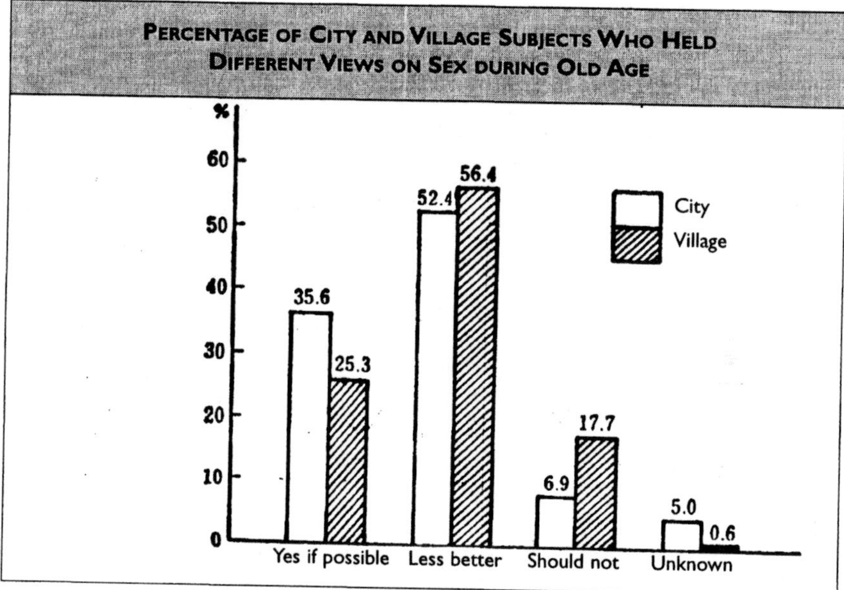

Figure 4–37

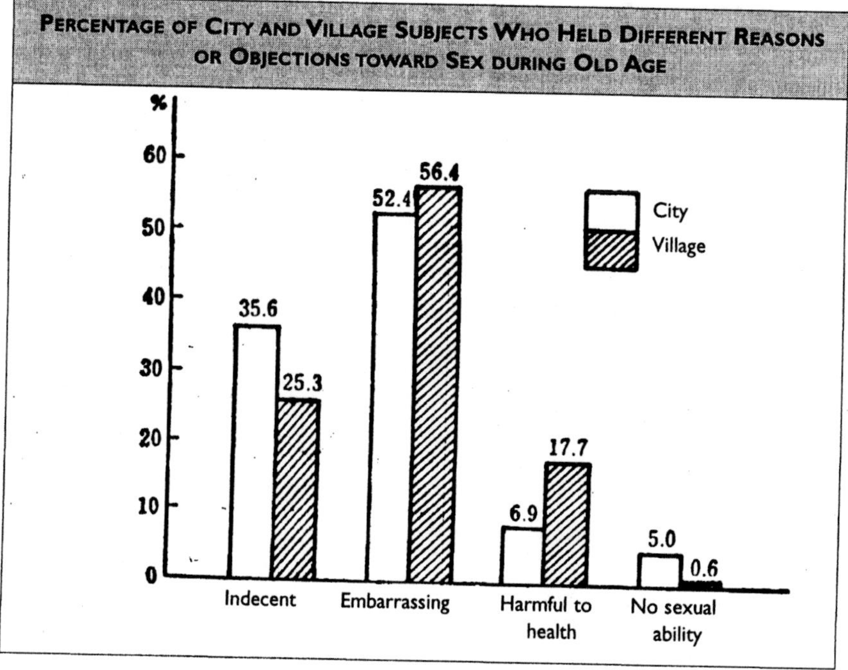

Figure 4–38

Reason for the Elderly Not to Have Sex											
	TOTAL	IMPROPER		EMBARRASSING		HARMFUL TO HEALTH		INFERTILE		UNKNOWN	
		NO.	%	NO.	%	NO.	%	NO.	%	NO.	%
City	485	15	3.1	46	9.5	279	57.5	145	29.9	0	0
Village	246	15	6.1	8	3.3	146	59.3	75	30.5	2	0.8

Table 4–185

Of the reasons provided against sex during old age, the one most frequently given was fear of harmful health effects (58.1 percent), followed by lack of sexual response.

Sex and View on the Elderly Having Sex							
	TOTAL	YES IF POSSIBLE		BETTER LESS		SHOULD STOP	
		NO.	%	NO.	%	NO.	%
Male	2008	791	39.4	1088	54.1	129	6.4
Female	5087	1714	33.7	2849	56.0	524	10.3

P=0.001

Table 4–186

Education and View on the Elderly Having Sex (City Husbands)										
	ILLITERATE		PRIMARY		J. HIGH		S. HIGH		C. & ABOVE	
	NO.	%	NO.	%	NO.	%	NO.	%	NO.	%
Yes if possible	4	30.8	9	26.5	121	36.4	250	40.7	318	46.9
Better less	7	53.8	21	61.8	182	54.8	341	55.4	344	50.7
Should stop	2	15.4	4	11.8	298	8.7	24	3.9	16	2.4
Total	13	100.0	34	100.0	332	100.0	615	100.0	678	100.0

Table 4–187

Education and View on the Elderly Having Sex (City Wives)										
	ILLITERATE		PRIMARY		J. HIGH		S. HIGH		C. & ABOVE	
	NO.	%	NO.	%	NO.	%	NO.	%	NO.	%
Yes if possible	8	44.4	42	30.2	411	33.0	636	35.6	321	42.1
Better less	6	33.3	73	52.5	693	55.7	1022	57.2	412	64.0
Should stop	4	22.2	24	17.3	140	11.3	128	7.2	30	3.9
Total	18	100.0	139	100.0	1244	100.0	1786	100.0	763	100.0

Table 4–188

Education and View on the Elderly Having Sex (Village Husbands)										
	ILLITERATE		PRIMARY		J. HIGH		S. HIGH		C. & ABOVE	
	NO.	%	NO.	%	NO.	%	NO.	%	NO.	%
Yes if possible	5	38.5	22	36.7	42	33.6	25	28.7	1	8.3
Better less	7	53.8	32	53.3	66	52.8	48	55.2	10	83.3
Should stop	1	7.7	6	10.0	17	13.6	14	16.1	1	8.3
Total	13	100.0	60	100.0	125	100.0	87	100.0	12	100.0

Table 4–189

Education and View on the Elderly Having Sex (Village Wives)										
	ILLITERATE		PRIMARY		J. HIGH		S. HIGH		C. & ABOVE	
	NO.	%	NO.	%	NO.	%	NO.	%	NO.	%
Yes if possible	9	25.7	64	26.2	125	25.1	56	19.3	1	8.3
Better less	18	51.4	127	52.0	284	56.9	180	62.1	11	91.7
Should stop	8	22.9	53	21.7	90	18.0	54	18.6	0	0
Total	35	100.0	244	100.0	499	100.0	290	100.0	12	100.0

Table 4–190

More females were opposed to sexual intecourse during old age (table 4–186).

In the cities, subjects who had sexual intercourse during old age increased with an increase in educational level (G+0.17 for husbands and 0.14 for wives). In the villages however, the reverse relationship is observed (G=0.13 for husbands and insignificant for wives). This shows that attitudes toward sex in old age is affected by the regional culture more than educational level. (Tables 4–187 to 4–190, figure 4–39).

C. Sexual Rights of the Elderly

Kinsey interviewed 14,080 males, of which eighty-seven were whites above age sixty years, and thirty-nine were blacks above the age of sixty. Of those, 20 percent at age sixty were impotent. The percentage was 25 percent at age sixty-five, 50 percent at seventy-five, and 75 percent at eighty.

Kinsey also interviewed fifty-six females at the age of sixty or above and found that their sexual interests had not diminished. Compared to the males, the only difference was that those without sexual partners reported higher levels of sexual activity. They also had a much higher rate of vaginal atresia.[52]

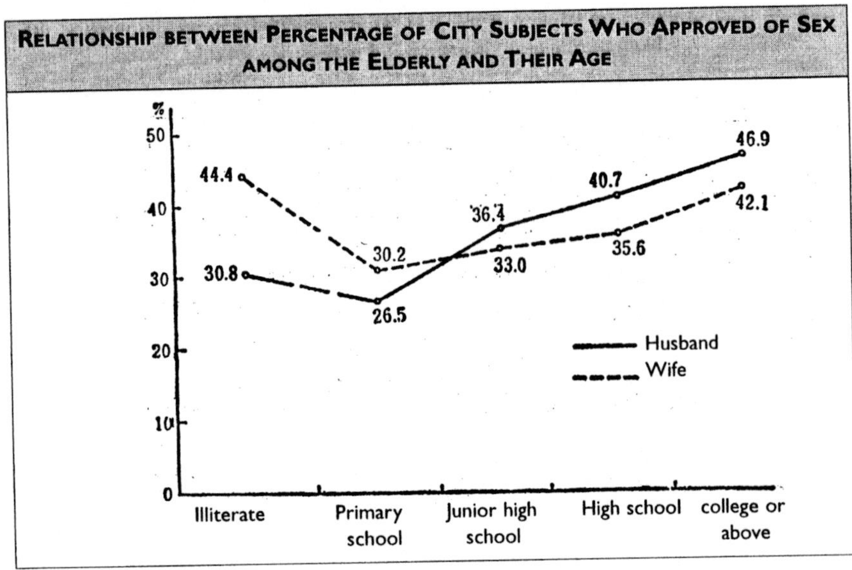

Figure 4–39

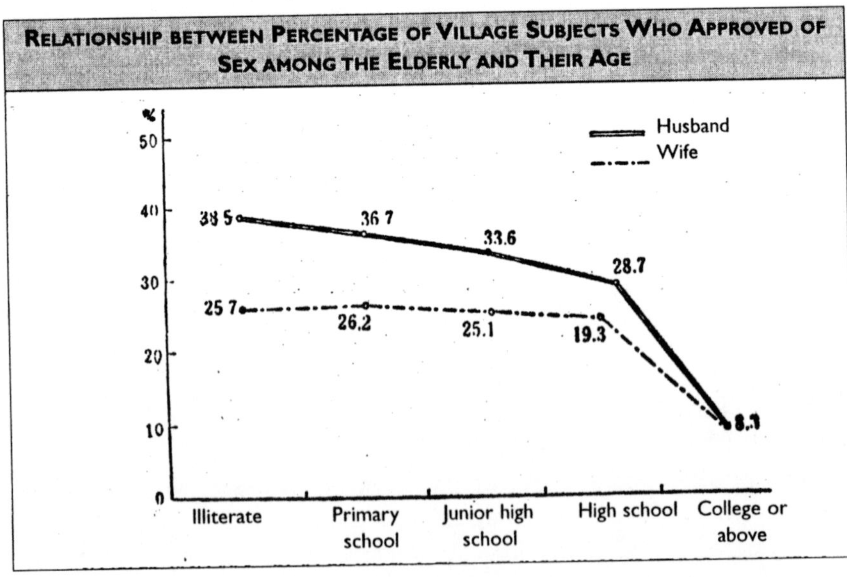

Figure 4–40

In 1979, Pfeiffer reported 70 percent of males at age sixty-eight and 25 percent at age seventy-eight still engaged in regular sexual activities. He concluded that except for illness, there is no obligatory reason for the elderly to abstain from sex.[53]

VIEW ON WIFE INITIATING SEX									
	TOTAL	SHOULD		SHOULD NOT		EMBARRASSING		UNKNOWN	
		NO.	%	NO.	%	NO.	%	NO.	%
City	6210	4173	67.2	670	10.8	1178	19.0	189	3.0
Village	1392	884	63.5	197	14.2	304	21.8	7	0.5

Table 4–191

Many old men are also capable of producing offspring. It was found that in age groups between sixty and seventy, 68.5 percent had sperm in their semen, at age seventy to eighty, the percentage was 59.5 percent and at age eighty to ninety, 48 percent.[54]

These and many other studies therefore show that although sexual desire, activities, and fertility of the elderly are lower, they are not completely absent.[55] Therefore, the sexual rights of older persons need to be protected. Society should accept sexual interests and activities in both the young and the old.

4. The Sexual Rights of Women

1. Initiative in Sexual Intercourse

In many cultures, females play a passive role in sexual activity. Traditional Chinese society even promotes the concept that it is a virtue for women to give up their right to sexual gratification.[56] In the West,

REGIONS AND VIEW ON WIFE INITIATING SEX								
	REGIONS	TOTAL	SHOULD		SHOULD NOT		EMBARRASSING	
			NO.	%	NO.	%		
City	Shanghai	2523	1735	68.9	324	12.8	461	18.3
	Tienjin	999	691	69.1	104	10.4	204	20.4
	Chengdu	875	603	68.9	87	9.9	185	21.1
	Guangzhou	511	402	78.6	16	3.1	93	18.2
Village	Suzhou	491	286	58.2	91	18.5	114	23.2
	Yuci	895	597	66.7	105	11.7	193	21.6
	Shanghai	349	232	66.5	59	16.9	58	16.6

Table 4–192

Freud[57] noted the tendency of a women to be highly dependant on the man with whom she has a sexual realtionship. But there is no biological or other compelling reason for this. An enlightened society should acknowledge women and their right to take a sexual initiative.

GENDER AND VIEW ON WIFE INITIATING SEX	MALE		FEMALE	
	NO.	%	NO.	%
Should	1515	74.4	3414	65.9
Should not	137	6.7	700	13.5
Embarrassing	382	18.8	1066	20.6
Total	2034	100.0	5180	100.0

Table 4–193

EDUCATION AND VIEW ON WIFE INITIATING SEX (CITY HUSBANDS)

	ILLITERATE		PRIMARY		J. HIGH		S. HIGH		C. OR ABOVE	
	NO.	%	NO.	%	NO.	%	NO.	%	NO.	%
Should	6	50.0	17	50.0	243	71.7	459	73.4	563	81.5
Should not	4	33.3	10	29.4	32	9.4	34	5.4	29	4.2
Embarrassing	2	16.7	7	20.6	64	18.9	132	21.1	99	14.3
Total	12	100.0	34	100.0	339	100.0	625	100.0	691	100.0

Table 4–194

PERCENTAGE OF CITY AND VILLAGE SUBJECTS WHO HELD DIFFERENT VIEWS TOWARD THEIR WIFE INITIATING SEX

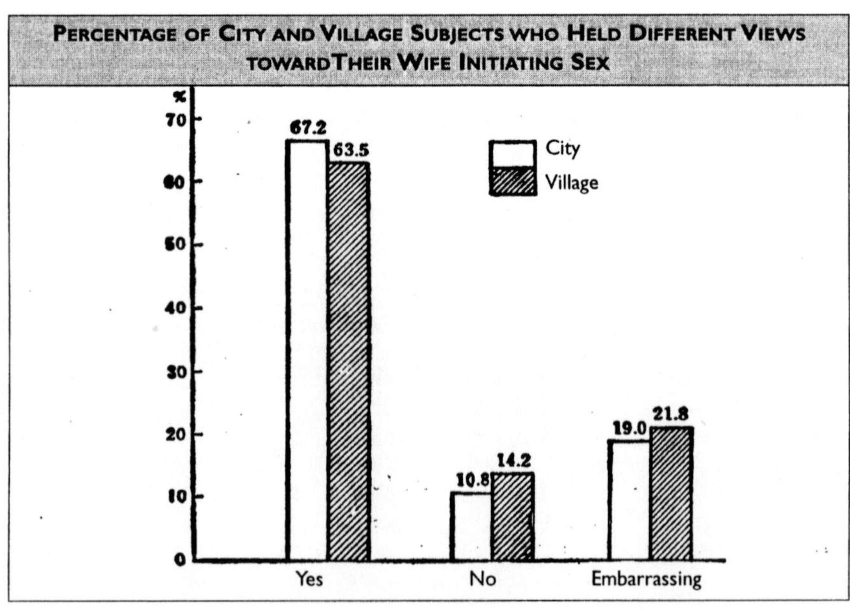

Figure 4–41

EDUCATION AND VIEW ON WIFE INITIATING SEX (CITY WIVES)										
	ILLITERATE		PRIMARY		J. HIGH		S. HIGH		C. & ABOVE	
	NO.	%	NO.	%	NO.	%	NO.	%	NO.	%
Should	8	44.4	72	49.3	772	60.5	1243	68.3	600	77.1
Should not	4	22.2	45	30.8	206	16.1	205	11.3	58	7.5
Embarrassing	6	33.3	29	19.9	299	23.4	371	20.4	120	15.4
Total	18	100.0	146	100.0	1277	100.0	1819	100.0	778	100.0

Table 4–195

EDUCATION AND VIEW ON WIFE INITIATING SEX (VILLAGE HUSBANDS)										
	ILLITERATE		PRIMARY		J. HIGH		S. HIGH		C. & ABOVE	
	NO.	%	NO.	%	NO.	%	NO.	%	NO.	%
Should	9	69.2	38	62.3	86	69.9	58	66.7	8	66.7
Should not	3	23.1	8	13.1	16	13.0	11	12.6	1	8.3
Embarrassing	1	7.7	15	24.6	21	17.1	18	20.7	3	25.0
Total	13	100.0	61	100.0	123	100.0	87	100.0	12	100.0

Table 4–196

EDUCATION AND VIEW ON WIFE INITIATING SEX (VILLAGE WIVES)										
	ILLITERATE		PRIMARY		J. HIGH		S. HIGH		C. & ABOVE	
	NO.	%	NO.	%	NO.	%	NO.	%	NO.	%
Should	18	51.4	153	62.7	306	61.2	196	67.1	8	66.7
Should not	7	20.0	38	15.6	80	16.0	30	10.3	2	16.7
Embarrassing	10	28.6	53	21.7	114	22.8	66	22.6	2	16.7
Total	35	100.0	244	100.0	500	100.0	292	100.0	12	100.0

Table 4–197

Table 4–191 shows that during sexual intercourse, slightly more city wives reported that they could take the initiative. More village wives reported that they felt too shy to take the initiative, although they wanted to do so.

Generally, there are no regional differences within these reports (table 4–192), if only in that a much higher proportion (78.6 percent) of the wives in Guangdong said they could take sexual initiative. The reason is probably that Guangdong is a city more open to the outside world.

More husbands than wives can accept female iniatives in sexual intercourse (table 4–193).

Initiator in Sex									
	TOTAL	HUSBAND		WIFE		BOTH		NOT CLEAR	
		NO.	%	NO.	%	NO.	%	NO.	%
Male	2052	1308	63.7	69	3.4	427	20.8	248	12.1
Female	5196	3739	71.9	67	1.3	802	15.4	588	11.3

P=0.001

Table 4–198

Regions and Initiator in Sex										
		TOTAL	HUSBAND		WIFE		BOTH		NOT CLEAR	
			NO.	%	NO.	%	NO.	%	NO.	%
City	Shanghai	2428	1817	74.8	24	1.0	332	13.7	255	10.5
	Tienjin	987	721	73.0	18	1.8	173	17.5	75	7.6
	Chengdu	872	644	73.9	16	1.8	126	14.4	86	9.9
	Guangzhou	499	357	71.5	9	1.8	100	20.0	33	6.6
Village	Suzhou	490	326	66.5	5	1.0	87	17.8	72	14.7
	Yuci	891	400	44.9	42	4.7	251	28.2	198	22.2

Table 4–199

Willingness to Cooperate in Sex							
GENDER	TOTAL	YES		NO		DEPENDS	
		NO.	%	NO.	%		
Male	2021	1522	75.3	51	2.5	448	22.2
Female	5114	2726	53.3	157	3.1	2231	43.6

P=0.001

Table 4–200

The acceptance of a woman's sexual initative shows a significant positive relationship with educational level (G=0.2). This relationship is less sigificant if the village couples are viewed separately (tables 4–194 to 4–197).

In reality, most husbands take the initiative in sex (table 4–198). The next common pattern found is a mutual, simultaneous initiative, and the least common is where wives take the initiative.

There is no regional difference in this regard (table 4–199).

Comparing the results of tables 4–191 and 4–198, it can be found that there was little if any validity behind the expectation that wives should take the sexual initiative. Table 4–200 shows that 75.3 percent of males and 53.3 percent of females were willing to cooperate with their partners in sex. More females depended on their mood to cooperate. There

REGION AND WILLINGNESS TO COOPERATE IN SEX								
		TOTAL	YES		NO		DEPENDS	
			NO.	%	NO.	%	NO.	%
City	Shanghai	2496	1425	57.1	67	2.7	1004	40.2
	Tienjin	989	620	26.7	26	2.6	343	34.7
	Chengdu	876	530	60.5	23	2.6	323	36.9
	Guangzhou	518	387	74.7	4	0.8	127	24.5
Village	Suzhou	494	230	46.6	14	2.8	250	50.6
	Yuci	888	561	63.2	37	4.2	290	32.7

Table 4–201

WILLINGNESS TO COOPERATE IN SEX AND VIEW ON SEXUAL INTERCOURSE														
WILLING-NESS	TOTAL	WIFE'S DUTY		MUTUAL DUTY		MUTUAL PHYSICAL NEED		MUTUAL PSYCHO-PHYSICAL NEED		REPRO-DUCTION		ROUTINE	
		NO.	%	NO.	%	NO.	%	NO.	%	NO.	%	NO.	%
Yes	4325	92	2.1	184	4.3	525	12.1	3204	74.1	86	2.0	234	5.4
No	209	15	7.2	10	4.8	35	16.7	116	55.5	10	4.8	23	11.0
Depends	2713	77	2.8	98	3.6	288	10.6	2006	73.9	42	1.5	202	7.4

P=0.001

Table 4–202

are no significant differences between the sexes in the will to be sexually cooperative (table 4–201).

The willingness to cooperate with the partner sexually shows a significant relationship with the views on marital sex. Those who think that sex is for satisfying emotional and physiological needs are more willing to cooperate (table 4–202).

Shortly before this survey, Xu An-qi surveyed five hundred married couples in Shanghai city. Of the subjects surveyed, 75.9 percent of the husbands said they took the initiative; 1.3 percent said the wives took the initiative; 22.8 percent said they share the initiatiative with their partners. For the wives, the corresponding figures were 86.3 percent, 1.3 percent, and 24 percent. The results were quite similar to ours in table 4–198. In the earlier survey, reasons for not taking the initiative were also explored. The reasons given by the husbands were situational difficulties (31.3 percent), fear of preganancy (26.1 percent), low sexual desire (29.2 percent), shyness (14.0 percent), physical problems or disease (8.6 percent), poor marital relationship (1.8 percent), and others

(5.5 percent). The corresponding figures from the wives were: 32.8 percent, 28.5 percent, 27.6 percent, 11.4 percent, 9.1 percent, 1.4 percent, and 5.7 percent.

In Xu's survey, another interesting finding was that taking the sexual initiative did not necessarily mean one had the right to suggest sexual intercourse. Of the husbands, 23.5 percent reported that they had the right to propose sexual intercourse, 39.8 percent said that their partners had, and 36.9 percent said that they had equal right with their partners. The corresponding figures for the wives were 16.7 percent, 52.9 percent, and 30.4 percent. The results demonstrate that many more wives had the right to propose sexual intercourse than those who actually took the initiative.[58]

2. Forced Sexual Intercourse

The above results suggest that the sexual attitudes of people in China are improving, but in certain areas, the picture is not as positive.

When the subjects were asked how they would deal with their spouses' sexual demands when they themselves were ill, 19.7 percent of the city subjects and 17.5 percent of the village subjects replied that they would reluctantly submit to the demands; 16.2 percent of the city subjects and 14.4

Response When Spouse Asks for Sex When One Is Uncomfortable

	TOTAL	SUBMIT RELUCTANTLY		PETTING BUT NO COITUS		EXPLAIN		REFUSE		UNKNOWN	
		NO.	%	NO.	%	NO.	%	NO.	%	NO.	%
City	6210	1223	19.7	1003	16.2	3283	52.9	439	7.1	262	4.2
Village	1392	244	17.5	200	14.4	809	58.1	134	9.6	5	0.4

Table 4–203

Response When Spouse Asks for Sex When One is Uncomfortable (City)

GENDER	TOTAL	SUBMIT RELUCTANTLY		PETTING BUT NO COITUS		EXPLAIN		REFUSE	
		NO.	%	NO.	%	NO.	%	NO.	%
Male	1723	380	22.0	399	23.1	858	79.8	86	5.0
Female	4067	806	19.8	577	14.2	2340	57.5	344	8.5

P=0.001

Table 4–204

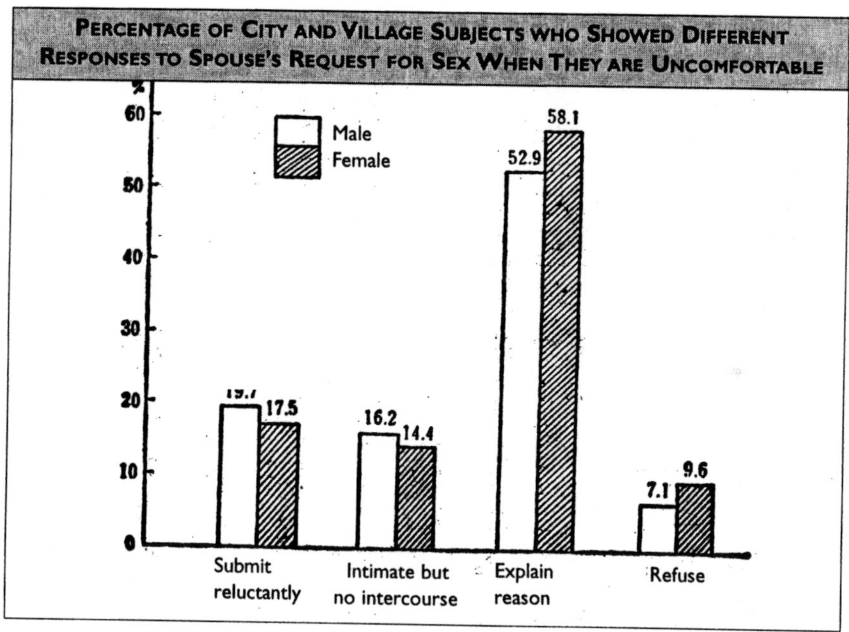

Figure 4–42

RESPONSE WHEN SPOUSE ASKS FOR SEX WHEN ONE IS UNCOMFORTABLE (VILLAGE)

GENDER	TOTAL	SUBMIT RELUCTANTLY		PETTING BUT NO COITUS		EXPLAIN		REFUSE	
		NO.	%	NO.	%	NO.	%	NO.	%
Male	301	52	17.3	54	17.9	163	54.2	32	10.6
Female	1083	191	17.6	146	13.5	645	59.6	101	9.3

P=0.20

Table 4–205

REACTION OF SPOUSE WHEN REQUEST FOR SEX IS REFUSED

	TOTAL	UNHAPPY		FORCE IT		ARGUMENT OR FIGHT		UNDERSTAND		UNKNOWN	
		NO.	%	NO.	%	NO.	%	NO.	%	NO.	%
City	6210	1688	27.2	162	2.6	72	1.2	3978	64.1	310	5.0
Village	1392	359	25.8	39	2.8	9	0.6	975	70.0	10	0.7

Table 4–206

REACTION OF SPOUSE WHEN REQUEST FOR SEX IS REFUSED (CITY)									
GENDER	TOTAL	UNHAPPY		FORCE IT		ARGUMENT OR FIGHT		UNDERSTAND	
		NO.	%	NO.	%	NO.	%	NO.	%
Male	1697	472	27.8	39	2.3	23	1.4	1163	68.5
Female	4049	1177	29.1	113	2.8	47	1.2	2712	67.0

P=0.50

Table 4–207

REACTION OF SPOUSE WHEN REQUEST FOR SEX IS REFUSED (VILLAGE)									
GENDER	TOTAL	UNHAPPY		FORCE IT		ARGUMENT OR FIGHT		UNDERSTAND	
		NO.	%	NO.	%	NO.	%	NO.	%
Male	300	83	27.7	9	3.0	2	0.7	206	68.7
Female	1079	276	25.6	30	2.8	7	0.6	766	70.9

P=0.90

Table 4–208

PERCENTAGE OF CITY AND VILLAGE SUBJECTS WHOSE SPOUSE SHOWED DIFFERENT RESPONSES WHEN REQUEST FOR SEXUAL INTERCOURSE WAS REJECTED

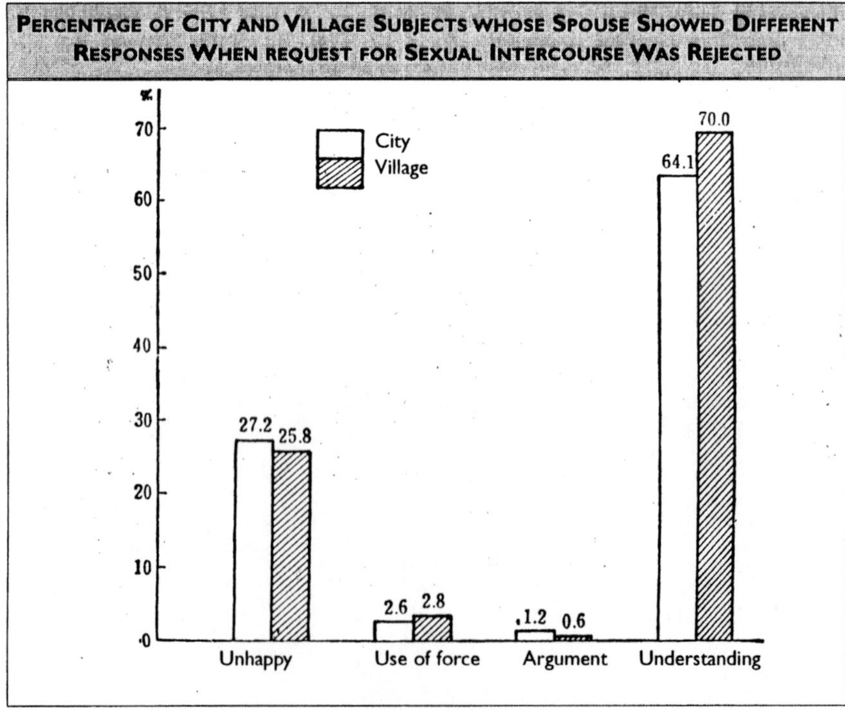

Figure 4–43

percent of the village subjects said they would allow a certain degree of physical intimacy; 52.9 percent and 58.1 percent would refuse with adequate explanations, while 7.1 percent and 9.6 percent would refuse bluntly.

The percentages did not differ significantly by sex of the subjects (tables 4–204 and 4–205).

After being rejected, 64.1 percent of the city subjects and 70.0 percent of the village subjects would accept the rejection well (4–206), but there was still a rather big proportion who would not accept any rejection; 2.6 percent of the city subjects and 2.8 percent of the village would even use sexual force on their spouses (table 4–206).

Integrating the results of tables 4–203 and 4–206, it can be seen that 23.6 percent of the city subjects and 24.0 percent of the village had their marital relationship adversely affected because of disagreement over sexual needs. From tables 4–207 and 4–208, there is no difference between the sexes.

Sexual disharmony as a cause for divorce has been increasing in recent years.[59] Pan Sui-Ming rightly pointed out that sexual harmony is

VIEW TOWARD RAPE VICTIMS

	TOTAL	REJECT		SYMPATHY		DISTANT		NOT TO BLAME		UNKNOWN	
		NO.	%	NO.	%	NO.	%	NO.	%	NO.	%
City	6210	171	2.8	3311	53.3	517	8.3	2007	32.3	204	3.3
Village	1392	61	4.4	743	53.4	102	7.3	477	34.3	9	0.6

Table 4–209

REGION AND VIEW TOWARD RAPE VICTIMS

		TOTAL	REJECT		SYMPATHY		DISTANT		NOT TO BLAME	
			NO.	%	NO.	%	NO.	%	NO.	%
City	Shanghai	2507	63	2.5	1396	55.7	203	8.1	845	33.7
	Tienjin	991	40	4.0	494	49.8	120	12.1	337	34.0
	Chengdu	878	21	2.4	519	59.1	58	6.6	280	31.9
	Guangzhou	516	8	1.5	264	51.2	36	7.0	208	40.3
Village	Suzhou	493	9	1.8	339	68.8	9	1.8	136	27.6
	Yuci	891	52	5.8	405	45.5	93.	10.4	341	38.3

Table 4–210

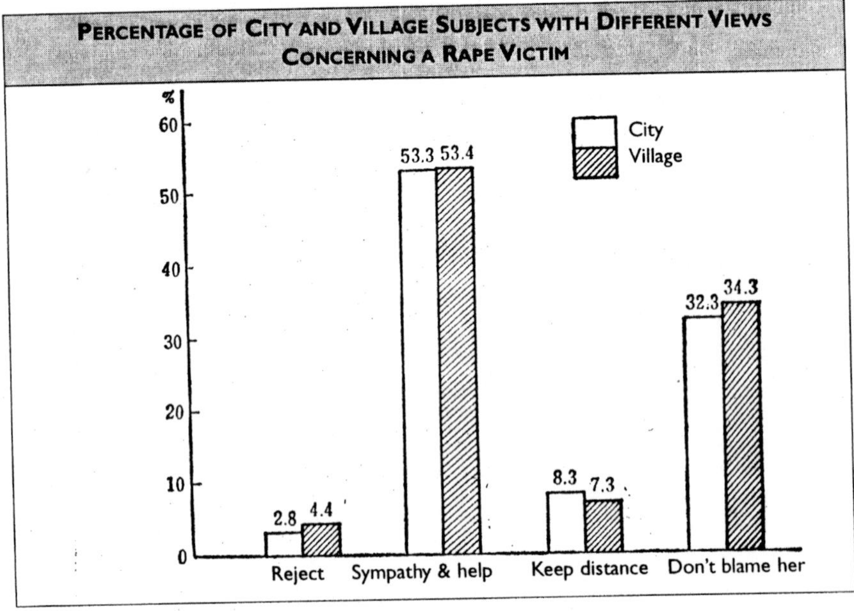

Figure 4–44

GENDER AND VIEW TOWARD RAPE VICTIMS

GENDER	TOTAL	REJECT		SYMPATHY		DISTANT		NOT TO BLAME	
		NO.	%	NO.	%	NO.	%	NO.	%
Male	2044	98	4.8	963	47.1	229	11.2	754	36.9
Female	5152	128	2.5	2988	58.0	377	7.3	1659	32.2

P=0.001

Table 4–211

EDUCATION AND VIEW TOWARD RAPE VICTIMS (CITY HUSBANDS)

	ILLITERATE		PRIMARY		J. HIGH		S. HIGH		C. & ABOVE	
	NO.	%	NO.	%	NO.	%	NO.	%	NO.	%
Reject	3	25.0	2	5.7	23	6.7	26	4.1	19	2.7
Sympathy	4	33.3	15	42.9	175	51.2	296	47.1	321	46.3
Distant	0	0	5	14.3	36	10.5	75	11.9	79	11.4
Not to blame	5	41.7	13	37.1	108	31.6	232	36.9	275	39.6
Total	12	100.0	35	100.0	342	100.0	629	100.0	694	100.0

Table 4–212

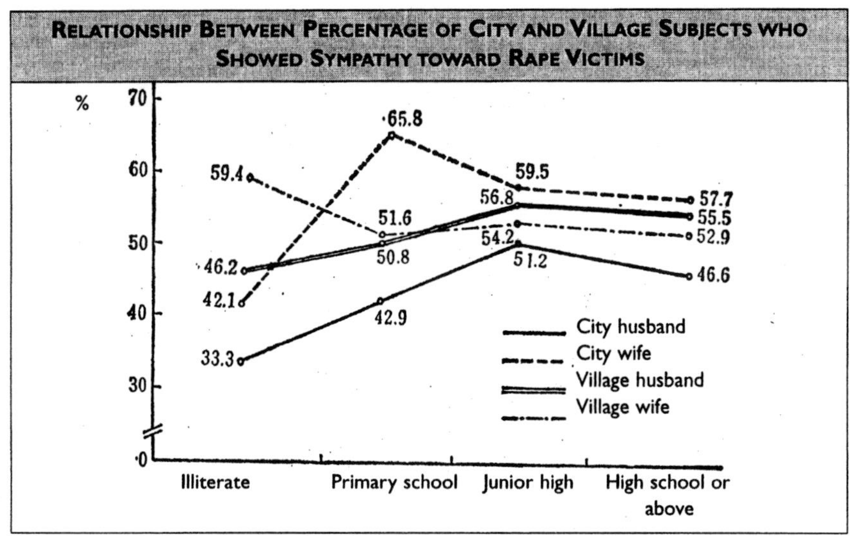

Figure 4–45

EDUCATION AND VIEW TOWARD RAPE VICTIMS (CITY WIVES)

	ILLITERATE		PRIMARY		J. HIGH		S. HIGH		C. & ABOVE	
	NO.	%	NO.	%	NO.	%	NO.	%	NO.	%
Reject	0	0	6	4.1	43	3.4	28	1.5	9	1.2
Sympathy	8	42.1	96	65.8	752	59.5	1070	59.1	419	54.4
Distant	5	26.3	18	12.3	100	7.9	128	7.1	50	6.5
Not to blame	6	31.6	26	17.8	369	29.2	585	32.3	292	37.9
Total	19	100.0	146	100.0	1264	100.0	1811	100.0	770	100.0

Table 4–213

EDUCATION AND VIEW TOWARD RAPE VICTIMS (VILLAGE HUSBANDS)

	ILLITERATE		PRIMARY		J. HIGH		S. HIGH		C. & ABOVE	
	NO.	%	NO.	%	NO.	%	NO.	%	NO.	%
Reject	2	15.4	3	5.1	8	6.4	2	2.3	0	0
Sympathy	6	46.2	30	50.8	71	56.8	51	58.6	4	33.3
Distant	1	7.7	8	13.6	4	3.2	3	3.4	0	0
Not to blame	4	30.8	18	30.5	42	33.6	31	35.6	8	66.7
Total	13	100.0	59	100.0	125	100.0	87	100.0	12	100.0

Table 4–214

Education and View toward Rape Victims (Village Wives)										
	ILLITERATE		PRIMARY		J. HIGH		S. HIGH		C. & ABOVE	
	NO.	%	NO.	%	NO.	%	NO.	%	NO.	%
Reject	1	3.1	17	7.0	19	3.8	8	2.7	0	0
Sympathy	19	59.4	126	51.6	271	54.2	156	53.2	6	50.0
Distant	0	0	27	11.1	39	7.8	17	5.8	3	25.0
Not to blame	12	37.5	74	30.3	171	34.2	112	38.2	3	25.0
Total	32	100.0	244	100.0	500	100.0	293	100.0	12	100.0

Table 4–215

a reflection of personal harmony between partners[60] and is more important to a couple than it appears.

3. Views on Virginity

The emphasis on premarital virginity has a long history in China.[61] This part of our survey explores how much this attitude is still prevalent.

With regard to a woman who has been raped, about 11 percent of all subjects would reject her, while 86 percent of them would be sympathetic and accepting. There was no significant difference in attitudes between the city and village subjects (table 4–209, figure 4–44).

There was no difference between subjects of different regions either, although a few more of the northern subjects were rejecting (table 4–210). In table 4–211 however, females appear to show more sympathy.

The educational level has a significant relationship with those having sympathetic attitudes (Figure 4–45).

Western scholars have, over time, held widely divergent views on the value of virginity.[62] In China it is, at present, difficult to change the traditional view. However, it may be possible to give the concept of virginity a new meaning and thus make it less harmful and degrading to females.[63]

5. Sexual Satisfaction

While the preceding section dealt with the objective data about sexual satisfaction, the following will deal with the subjective experience. The traditional Chinese culture gave priority to obligation and duty in marital relations. In contrast today, love and common interests are emphasized. Some contemporary Chinese scholars still emphasize love, spiritual values, and common interest, but there is also the view that sexual satisfaction is a bonding element in marriage. This largely agrees with modern Western views.[64]

1. Sexual Satisfaction:

Table 4–216 shows that 17.6 percent of the city couples felt very satisfied with their sexual lives, and 37.9 percent felt rather satisfied. The corresponding figures for village couples were 33.8 percent and 32.8 percent. On the whole, therefore, the village couples seemed more satisfied

SEXUAL SATISFACTION

	TOTAL	VERY GOOD		GOOD		FAIR		POOR		VERY POOR		CANNOT TELL		UNKNOWN	
		NO.	%	NO.	%	NO.	%	NO.	%	NO.	%	NO.	%	NO.	%
City	6210	1092	17.6	2351	37.9	1586	25.3	101	1.6	25	0.4	218	3.5	837	13.5
Village	1392	470	33.8	456	32.8	384	27.6	8	0.6	8	0.6	55	4.0	11	0.8

Table 4–216

PERCENTAGE OF CITY AND VILLAGE SUBJECTS WITH DIFFERENT LEVELS OF SEXUAL SATISFACTION

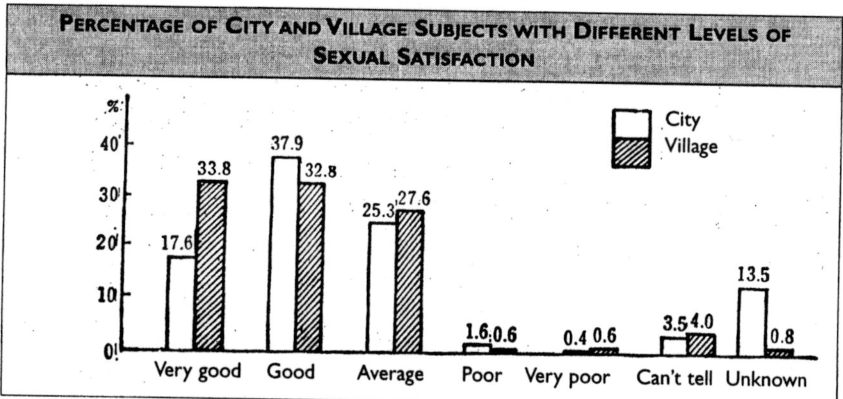

Figure 4–46

SEX AND SEXUAL SATISFACTION (CITY)

	TOTAL	VERY GOOD		GOOD		FAIR		POOR		VERY POOR		CANNOT TELL	
		NO.	%	NO.	%	NO.	%	NO.	%	NO.	%	NO.	%
Male	1503	431	28.7	732	48.7	288	19.2	20	1.3	8	0.5	24	1.6
Female	3870	661	17.1	1619	41.8	1298	33.5	81	2.1	17	0.4	194	5.0

Table 4–217

Gender and Sexual Satisfaction (Village)													
	TOTAL	VERY GOOD		GOOD		FAIR		POOR		VERY POOR		CANNOT TELL	
		NO.	%	NO.	%	NO.	%	NO.	%	NO.	%	NO.	%
Male	298	141	47.3	95	31.9	52	17.4	1	0.3	3	1.0	6	2.0
Female	1083	329	30.4	361	33.3	332	30.7	7	0.6	5	0.5	49	4.5

Table 4-218

Duration of Foreplay (in Minutes)															
	TOTAL	NONE		1		2-5		6-10		11-20		>20		UNKNOWN	
		NO.	%	NO.	%	NO.	%	NO.	%	NO.	%	NO.	%	NO.	%
City	6210	426	6.9	546	8.8	2194	35.3	1409	22.7	787	12.7	278	4.5	570	9.21
Village	1392	244	17.5	218	15.7	511	36.7	221	15.9	97	7.0	62	4.5	39	2.8

Table 4-219

Tables 4–217 and 4–218 show that more husbands than wives were equally satisfied, both in cities and villages.

Xu An-Qi in 1987 surveyed one thousand couples and found that 61.8 percent of the wives and 64.5 percent of the husbands were sexually satisfied. These figures are close to our own.

To verify what the subjects meant by being satisfied, we asked them about time taken during foreplay. In the city couples, 6.9 percent answered that they had none, and 8.8 percent took about one minute. The corresponding figures in the village subjects were 17.5 percent and

Duration of Foreplay (in Minutes) and Sexual Satisfaction (City Husbands)												
	NONE		1		2-5		6-10		11-20		>20	
	NO.	%	NO.	%	NO.	%	NO.	%	NO.	%	NO.	%
Very good	15	16.0	19	18.4	134	25.5	122	32.5	75	33.8	42	43.3
Good	25	26.6	44	42.7	287	54.6	198	52.8	110	49.5	36	37.1
Fair	42	44.7	37	35.9	95	18.1	45	12.0	31	14.0	13	13.4
Poor	4	4.3	3	2.9	6	1.1	4	1.1	1	0.5	1	1.0
Very poor	2	2.1	0	0	1	0.2	0	0	2	0.9	3	3.1
Cannot tell	6	6.4	0	0	3	0.6	6	1.6	3	1.4	2	2.1
Total	94	100.0	103	100.0	526	100.0	375	100.0	222	100.0	97	100.0

Table 4-220

Duration of Foreplay (in Minutes) and Sexual Satisfaction (City Wives)												
	NONE		1		2-5		6-10		11-20		>20	
	NO.	%	NO.	%	NO.	%	NO.	%	NO.	%	NO.	%
Very good	21	7.4	40	10.9	220	15.5	171	19.3	105	22.5	62	41.3
Good	49	17.3	105	28.6	634	44.8	444	50.2	244	52.2	47	31.3
Fair	139	49.1	172	46.9	489	34.5	233	26.4	102	21.8	32	21.3
Poor	20	7.1	11	3.0	21	1.5	15	1.7	3	0.6	3	2.0
Very poor	7	2.5	1	0.3	4	0.3	2	0.2	1	0.2	1	0.7
Cannot tell	47	16.6	38	10.4	48	3.4	19	2.1	12	2.6	5	3.3
Total	283	100.0	367	100.0	1416	100.0	884	100.0	467	100.0	150	100.0

P=0.001

Table 4-221

Duration of Foreplay (in Minutes) and Sexual Satisfaction (Village Husbands)												
	NONE		1		2-5		6-10		11-20		>20	
	NO.	%	NO.	%	NO.	%	NO.	%	NO.	%	NO.	%
Very good	17	27.9	27	56.3	46	45.5	23	62.2	10	47.6	11	57.9
Good	14	23.0	17	35.4	35	34.7	12	32.4	10	47.6	4	21.1
Fair	25	41.0	3	6.3	18	17.8	2	5.4	1	4.8	2	10.5
Poor	1	1.6	0	0	0	0	0	0	0	0	0	0
Very poor	0	0	1	2.1	1	1.0	0	0	0	0	1	5.3
Cannot tell	4	6.6	0	0	1	1.0	0	0	0	0	1	5.3
Total	61	100.0	48	100.0	101	100.0	37	100.0	21	100.0	19	100.0

P=0.001

Table 4-222

Duration of Foreplay (in Minutes) and Sexual Satisfaction (Village Wives)												
	NONE		1		2-5		6-10		11-20		>20	
	NO.	%	NO.	%	NO.	%	NO.	%	NO.	%	NO.	%
Very good	31	17.2	43	25.4	105	25.9	73	39.7	37	48.7	28	66.7
Good	31	17.2	61	36.1	152	37.5	72	39.1	27	35.5	5	11.9
Fair	97	53.9	52	30.8	132	32.6	32	17.4	11	14.5	7	16.7
Poor	2	1.1	0	0	4	1.0	1	0.5	0	0	0	0
Very poor	2	1.1	2	1.2	0	0	0	0	0	0	1	2.4
Cannot tell	17	9.4	11	6.5	12	3.0	6	3.3	1	1.3	1	2.4
Total	180	100.0	169	100.0	405	100.0	184	100.0	76	100.0	42	100.0

P=0.001

Table 4-223

15.7 percent. It is hardly plausible that such primitive ways of sexual intercourse should lead to the high percentages in sexual satisfaction.

Tables 4–220 to 4–223 show that the longer the foreplay reported, the higher the degree of sexual satisfaction of the couples. The correlation coefficient G for city husbands, city wives, village husbands, and village wives are 0.23, 0.32, 0.26, and 0.34 respectively. The correlation coefficient is highest for the wives, indicating a higher dependency on the duration of foreplay.

In order to find out more about possible sexual problems, we asked the subjects whether they felt pain at any time during sexual intercourse. Of the city subjects, 2.6 percent reported frequent pain, 39.2 percent occasional pain; the corresponding figures of village subjects were 2.2 percent and 34.4 percent.

This pain could be due to a lack of foreplay. Why? When we asked whether the couple had engaged in other types of physical intimacy (embraces, caresses, and so forth) in everyday life, 13.1 percent of the city couples and 16.5 percent of the village couples said that they never had. This indicates to us that the overall quality of their sex lives was rather poor.

The degree of physical intimacy seems to be different in different regions (table 4–226), but not necessarily higher in the more educated or modernized. For example, in Shanghai, the degree is one of the lowest,

Genital Pain during Sexual Intercourse

	TOTAL	OFTEN		SOMETIME		NEVER		UNKNOWN	
		NO.	%	NO.	%	NO.	%	NO.	%
City	6210	161	2.6	2435	39.2	3206	51.6	408	6.6
Village	1392	31	2.2	479	34.4	869	62.4	13	0.9

Table 4-224

Intimate Behavior Outside Intercourse

	TOTAL	OFTEN		SOMETIME		NEVER		UNKNOWN	
		NO.	%	NO.	%	NO.	%	NO.	%
City	6210	1123	18.1	3779	60.9	812	13.1	496	8.0
Village	1392	206	14.8	934	67.1	230	16.5	22	1.6

Table 4-225

REGION AND INTIMATE BEHAVIOR OUTSIDE INTERCOURSE								
		TOTAL	YES		NO		DEPENDS	
			NO.	%	NO.	%	NO.	%
City	Shanghai	2425	416	17.2	1615	66.5	394	16.2
	Tienjin	952	177	18.5	635	66.8	140	14.7
	Chengdu	842	193	22.9	568	67.5	81	9.6
	Guangzhou	479	135	28.2	289	60.3	55	11.5
Village	Suzhou	493	77	15.6	346	70.2	70	14.2
	Yuci	877	129	14.7	588	67.0	160	18.3

Table 4-226

probably because of the crowded living conditions and therefore the lack of privacy in the city.

Hence, it is plausible that the sexual life of Chinese couples is not as satisfactory as they claim. Perhaps some couples simply do not know what a satisfactory sex life is. There are reports that in certain places in China, some couples considered anal intercourse to be an alternative method for sexual intercourse. Therefore, despite the pain, these couples might still declare their sex lives satisfactory. In Shenyang, the court statistics from 1981 to 1982 showed that in one thousand divorce cases, 47 percent of males and 17 percent of females reported an unsatisfactory sexual life. In the Chang Ning region of Shanghai, of all the divorce cases in 1983, 23 percent gave sexual disharmony as their reason for divorce. During the last five years, the Shanghai Family Planning Bureau counseled about forty thousand subjects on methods of contraception or conception. Ten thousand infertility cases were found to be due to ignorance about the technique of vaginal sexual intercourse.

2. Factors Associated with Sexual Satisfaction

A. Sex

The wives were generally less satisfied than the husbands (tables 4–217 and 4–218)

B. Age

The correlation between age and sexual satisfaction is very low for both city and village couples (tables 4–227, 4–228, 4–229, and 4–230). As figure 4–48 shows, among the city wives, the younger ones reported more satisfaction while among the village wives, the older ones were more satisfied. It might be that age is related to some other factors in village and city life.

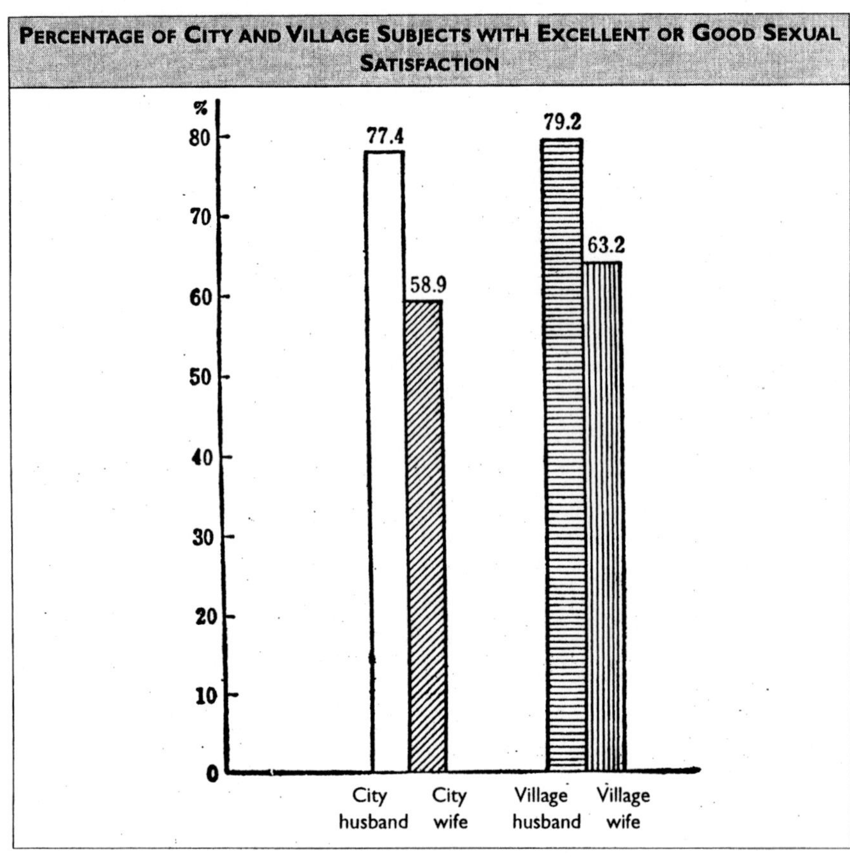

Figure 4–47

Age and Sexual Satisfaction (City Husbands)	<=25		26-35		36-45		46-55		>=56	
	NO.	%	NO.	%	NO.	%	NO.	%	NO.	%
Very good	21	34.4	182	32.1	122	25.7	71	27.1	28	25.5
Good	27	44.3	271	47.8	235	49.6	124	47.3	60	54.5
Fair	10	16.4	93	16.4	101	21.3	57	21.8	21	19.1
Poor	1	1.6	9	1.6	6	1.3	3	1.1	0	0
Very poor	0	0	5	0.9	1	0.2	2	0.8	0	0
Cannot tell	2	3.3	7	1.2	9	1.9	5	1.9	1	0.9
Total	61	100.0	567	100.0	474	100.0	262	100.0	110	100.0

P=0.70

Table 4–227

Age and Sexual Satisfaction (City Wives)	<=25		26-35		36-45		46-55		>=56	
	NO.	%	NO.	%	NO.	%	NO.	%	NO.	%
Very good	59	27.1	284	18.6	213	15.0	88	15.6	12	11.9
Good	91	41.7	669	43.8	610	43.0	197	34.9	39	38.6
Fair	55	25.2	473	31.0	485	34.2	231	40.9	38	37.6
Poor	4	1.8	30	2.0	35	2.5	8	1.4	2	2.0
Very poor	2	0.9	5	0.3	3	0.2	6	1.1	1	1.0
Cannot tell	7	3.2	65	4.3	74	5.2	35	6.2	9	8.9
Total	218	100.0	1526	100.0	1420	100.0	565	100.0	101	100.0

P=0.001

Table 4-228

Age and Sexual Satisfaction (Village Husbands)	<=25		26-35		36-45		46-55		>=56	
	NO.	%	NO.	%	NO.	%	NO.	%	NO.	%
Very good	10	47.6	52	49.5	41	39.8	28	58.3	10	47.6
Good	7	33.3	31	29.5	38	36.9	12	25.0	7	33.3
Fair	4	19.0	19	18.1	19	18.4	6	12.5	4	19.0
Poor	0	0	1	1.0	0	0	0	0	0	0
Very poor	0	0	0	0	2	1.9	1	2.1	0	0
Cannot tell	0	0	2	1.9	3	2.9	1	2.1	0	0
Total	21	100.0	105	100.0	103	100.0	48	100.0	21	100.0

P=0.95

Table 4-229

Age and Sexual Satisfaction (Village Wives)	<=25		26-35		36-45		46-55		>=56	
	NO.	%	NO.	%	NO.	%	NO.	%	NO.	%
Very good	32	29.4	181	29.7	106	31.4	26	32.9	4	28.6
Good	38	34.9	177	32.6	115	34.0	25	31.6	6	42.9
Fair	31	28.4	174	32.0	100	29.6	24	30.4	3	21.4
Poor	1	0.9	2	0.4	3	0.9	1	1.3	0	0
Very poor	0	0	2	0.4	3	0.9	0	0	0	0
Cannot tell	7	6.4	27	5.0	11	3.3	3	3.8	1	7.1
Total	109	100.0	543	100.0	338	100.0	79	100.0	14	100.0

P=0.99

Table 4-230

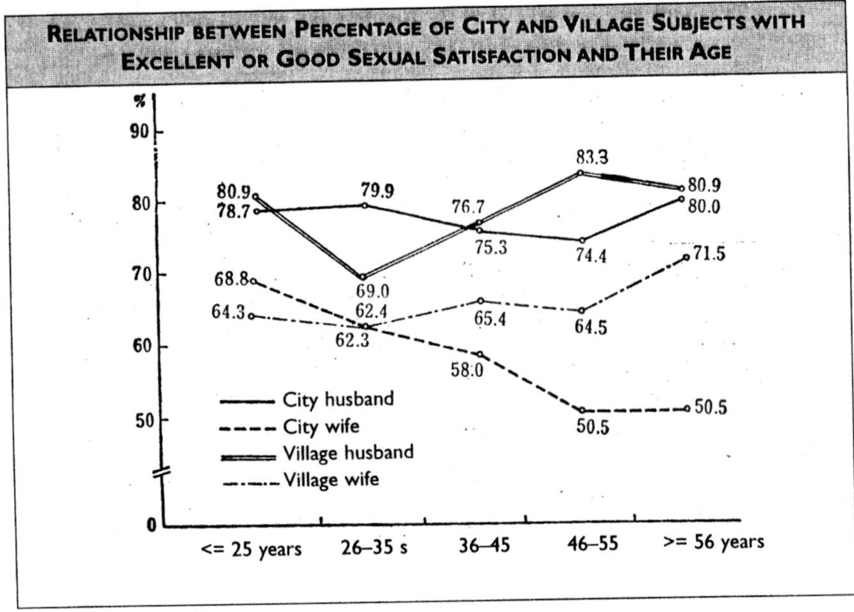

Figure 4–48

Perhaps sexual experience is decisive in the older village wives and sexual openness in the younger city wives.

BODILY HEALTH AND SEXUAL SATISFACTION (CITY HUSBANDS)						
SATISFACTION	HEALTHY		FAIR HEALTH		SICK	
	NO.	%	NO.	%	NO.	%
Very Good	316	36.2	87	17.0	12	19.4
Good	417	47.8	258	50.3	36	58.1
Fair	114	13.1	149	29.0	11	17.7
Poor	11	1.3	5	1.0	2	3.2
Very poor	5	0.6	2	0.4	0	0
Cannot tell	9	1.0	12	2.3	1	1.6
Total	872	100.0	513	100.0	62	100.0

Table 4-231

C. PHYSICAL HEALTH

The physical health of the subjects had a rather high correlation with the degree of sexual satisfaction (G=0.36 for city husbands, 0.33 for city wives, 0.50 for village husbands, and 0.40 for village wives). In tables 4–231 to 4–234, it can be seen that the health / sexual satisfaction correlation is higher in females.

D. YEARS OF MARRIAGE

The correlation of years of marriage with sexual satisfaction is low for both city and village couples. Figure 4–50 shows that the sexual satisfaction of city husbands had little variation with years of marriage. For city

BODILY HEALTH AND SEXUAL SATISFACTION (CITY WIVES)						
SATISFACTION	HEALTHY		FAIR HEALTH		SICK	
	NO.	%	NO.	%	NO.	%
Very Good	429	25.1	191	10.5	26	10.0
Good	763	44.6	727	40.1	95	36.5
Fair	434	25.4	734	40.4	106	40.8
Poor	22	1.3	47	2.6	8	3.1
Very poor	5	0.3	8	0.4	3	1.2
Cannot tell	59	3.4	108	6.0	22	8.5
Total	1712	100.0	1815	100.0	260	100.0

Table 4–232

BODILY HEALTH AND SEXUAL SATISFACTION (VILLAGE HUSBANDS)						
SATISFACTION	HEALTHY		FAIR HEALTH		SICK	
	NO.	%	NO.	%	NO.	%
Very Good	129	54.2	11	22.9	0	0
Good	67	28.2	19	39.6	6	75.0
Fair	35	14.7	15	31.3	2	25.0
Poor	1	0.4	0	0	0	0
Very poor	1	0.4	2	4.2	0	0
Cannot tell	5	2.1	1	2.1	0	0
Total	238	100.0	48	100.0	8	100.0

Table 4–233

BODILY HEALTH AND SEXUAL SATISFACTION (VILLAGE WIVES)						
SATISFACTION	HEALTHY		FAIR HEALTH		SICK	
	NO.	%	NO.	%	NO.	%
Very Good	271	37.7	48	14.5	9	32.1
Good	247	34.4	107	32.3	5	17.9
Fair	165	22.9	155	46.8	10	35.7
Poor	2	0.3	3	0.9	2	7.1
Very poor	5	0.7	0	0	0	0
Cannot tell	29	4.0	18	5.4	2	2.1
Total	719	100.0	331	100.0	28	100.0

Table 4-234

wives, the trend was greater satisfaction with longer marriage. For village husbands, the satisfaction was lowest in the middle–range duration while village wives showed no clear pattern.

E. EDUCATIONAL LEVEL

There was a low correlation between educational level and sexual satisfaction in both the city and village subjects, although in the city subjects, the correlation was higher. In general, there was a higher degree of satisfaction in those with a high school education. It may be that knowledge does contribute to sexual satisfaction, but the professionals or college graduates might be adversely affected by their quality of work or type of responsibility which they have to bear (tables 4–239 to 4–242).

DURATION OF MARRIAGE AND SEXUAL SATISFACTION (CITY HUSBANDS)												
SATISFACTION	<=2		3-5		6-10		11-15		16-20		>20	
	NO.	%	NO.	%	NO.	%	NO.	%	NO.	%	NO.	%
Very good	75	34.6	61	28.8	103	29.5	55	26.3	37	25.3	89	27.2
Good	95	43.8	103	48.6	166	47.6	106	50.7	79	54.1	162	49.5
Fair	39	18.0	36	17.0	69	19.8	42	20.1	26	17.8	66	20.2
Poor	3	1.4	4	1.9	7	2.0	1	0.5	3	2.1	1	0.3
Very poor	3	1.4	1	0.5	2	0.6	0	0	0	0	2	0.6
Cannot tell	2	0.9	7	3.3	2	0.6	5	2.4	1	0.7	7	2.1
Total	217	100.0	212	100.0	349	100.0	209	100.0	146	100.0	327	100.0

Table 4-235

DURATION OF MARRIAGE AND SEXUAL SATISFACTION (CITY WIVES)												
SATISFACTION	<=2		3-5		6-10		11-15		16-20		>20	
	NO.	%	NO.	%	NO.	%	NO.	%	NO.	%	NO.	%
Very good	115	24.2	93	18.0	173	16.9	95	16.2	74	15.7	104	14.1
Good	189	39.7	223	43.1	461	45.2	243	41.4	199	42.3	282	38.3
Fair	144	30.3	160	30.9	321	31.4	202	34.4	162	34.5	283	38.4
Poor	11	2.3	11	2.1	16	1.6	16	2.7	12	2.6	13	1.8
Very poor	1	0.2	3	0.6	4	0.4	1	0.2	0	0	8	1.1
Cannot tell	16	3.4	27	14.3	46	4.5	30	5.1	23	4.9	47	6.4
Total	476	100.0	517	100.0	1021	100.0	587	100.0	470	100.0	737	100.0

Table 4-236

DURATION OF MARRIAGE AND SEXUAL SATISFACTION (VILLAGE HUSBANDS)												
SATISFACTION	<=2		3-5		6-10		11-15		16-20		>20	
	NO.	%	NO.	%	NO.	%	NO.	%	NO.	%	NO.	%
Very good	17	50.0	18	41.9	26	54.2	14	37.8	29	46.8	37	50.0
Good	11	32.4	16	37.2	12	25.0	14	37.8	18	29.0	24	32.4
Fair	5	14.7	9	20.9	9	18.8	6	16.2	13	21.0	10	13.5
Poor	0	0	0	0	1	2.1	0	0	0	0	0	0
Very poor	0	0	0	0	0	0	1	2.7	1	1.6	1	1.4
Cannot tell	1	2.9	0	0	0	0	2	5.4	1	1.6	2	2.7
Total	34	100.0	43	100.0	48	100.0	37	100.0	62	100.0	74	100.0

Table 4-237

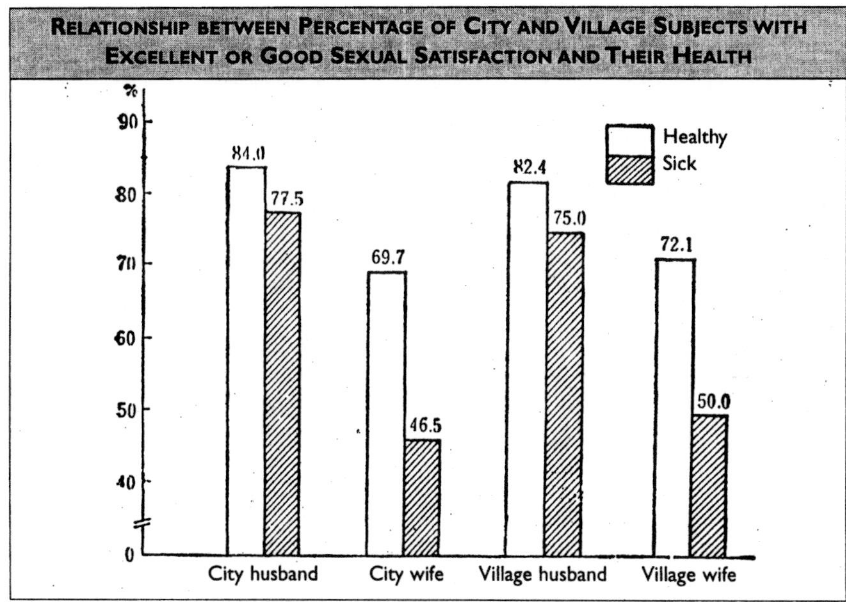

Figure 4–49

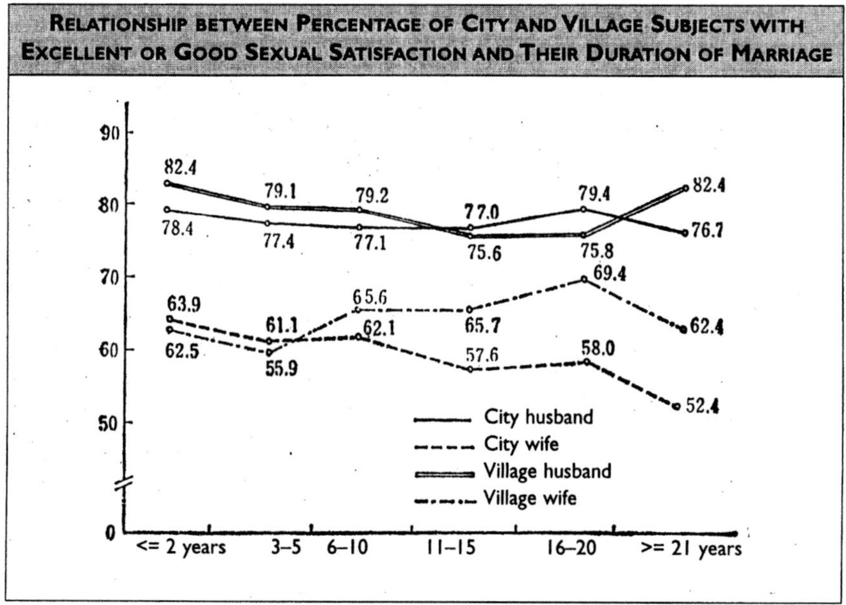

Figure 4–50

DURATION OF MARRIAGE AND SEXUAL SATISFACTION (VILLAGE WIVES)												
SATISFACTION	<=2		3-5		6-10		11-15		16-20		>20	
	NO.	%	NO.	%	NO.	%	NO.	%	NO.	%	NO.	%
Very good	31	27.7	48	26.8	84	30.8	66	31.4	52	36.1	48	29.1
Good	39	34.8	52	29.1	95	34.8	72	34.3	48	33.3	55	33.3
Fair	30	26.8	63	35.2	88	32.2	56	26.7	40	27.8	55	33.3
Poor	2	1.8	0	0	1	0.4	3	1.4	0	0	1	0.6
Very poor	0	0	1	0.6	1	0.4	2	1.0	1	0.7	0	0
Cannot tell	10	8.9	15	8.4	4	1.5	11	5.2	3	2.1	6	3.6
Total	112	100.0	179	100.0	273	100.0	210	100.0	144	100.0	165	100.0

Table 4-238

EDUCATION AND SEXUAL SATISFACTION (CITY HUSBANDS)										
	ILLITERATE		PRIMARY		J. HIGH		S. HIGH		C. & ABOVE	
	NO.	%	NO.	%	NO.	%	NO.	%	NO.	%
Very good	1	9.1	7	21.9	92	32.3	156	29.3	165	27.4
Good	4	36.4	13	40.6	117	41.1	270	50.8	310	51.4
Fair	4	36.4	12	37.5	62	21.8	86	16.2	114	18.9
Poor	2	18.2	0	0	3	1.1	10	1.9	3	0.5
Very poor	0	0	0	0	1	0.4	4	0.8	3	0.5
Cannot tell	0	0	0	0	10	3.5	6	1.1	8	1.3
Total	11	100.0	32	100.0	285	100.0	532	100.0	603	100.0

Table 4-239

EDUCATION AND SEXUAL SATISFACTION (CITY WIVES)										
	ILLITERATE		PRIMARY		J. HIGH		S. HIGH		C. & ABOVE	
	NO.	%	NO.	%	NO.	%	NO.	%	NO.	%
Very good	4	23.5	25	18.1	205	17.3	282	16.4	132	17.8
Good	4	23.5	47	34.1	481	40.6	733	42.6	328	44.1
Fair	7	41.2	54	39.1	421	35.5	574	33.4	222	29.9
Poor	0	0	1	0.7	28	2.4	34	2.0	16	2.2
Very poor	0	0	1	0.7	3	0.3	10	0.6	3	0.4
Cannot tell	2	11.8	10	7.2	48	4.0	88	5.1	42	5.7
Total	17	100.0	138	100.0	1186	100.0	1721	100.0	743	100.0

Table 4-240

EDUCATION AND SEXUAL SATISFACTION (VILLAGE HUSBANDS)										
	ILLITERATE		PRIMARY		J. HIGH		S. HIGH		C. & ABOVE	
	NO.	%	NO.	%	NO.	%	NO.	%	NO.	%
Very good	6	40.2	32	52.5	58	47.2	36	41.9	7	58.3
Good	4	30.8	16	26.2	45	36.6	27	31.4	2	16.7
Fair	1	7.7	12	19.7	15	12.2	21	24.4	3	25.0
Poor	0	0	0	0	1	0.8	0	0	0	0
Very poor	0	0	1	1.6	1	0.8	1	1.2	0	0
Cannot tell	2	15.4	0	0	3	2.4	1	1.2	0	0
Total	13	100.0	61	100.0	123	100.0	86	100.0	12	100.0

Table 4-241

EDUCATION AND SEXUAL SATISFACTION (VILLAGE WIVES)										
	ILLITERATE		PRIMARY		J. HIGH		S. HIGH		C. & ABOVE	
	NO.	%	NO.	%	NO.	%	NO.	%	NO.	%
Very good	11	31.4	81	33.3	145	29.0	91	31.1	1	8.3
Good	11	31.4	71	29.2	163	32.6	112	38.2	4	33.3
Fair	11	31.4	81	33.3	164	32.8	72	24.6	4	33.3
Poor	1	2.9	0	0	3	0.6	1	0.3	2	16.7
Very poor	0	0	1	0.4	3	0.6	1	0.3	0	0
Cannot tell	1	2.9	9	3.7	22	4.4	16	5.5	1	8.3
Total	35	100.0	243	100.0	500	100.0	293	100.0	12	100.0

Table 4-242

F. Coital Frequency

There was a significant correlation between coital frequency and sexual satisfaction (g=0.22 for city husbands, 0.26 for city wives, 0.25 for village husbands, and 0.21 for village wives) (tables 4–243 to 4–246).

The correlation is easy to understand. The more satisfied two people are with their sexual intercourse, the more likely they are to repeat it. This is simply a matter of positive reinforcement. There seems to be a limit to the reinforcement effect, however, since satisfaction shows a less steep rise in those who engaged in coitus nearly every day (figures 4–51, 4–52).

G. Initiation of Coitus

Sexual satisfaction is higher in those whose coital activity is initiated either mutually or by the wife (tables 4–247, 4–248, 4–249 and 4–250). Figure 4–53 shows that this is the rule except for city husbands. It is easy

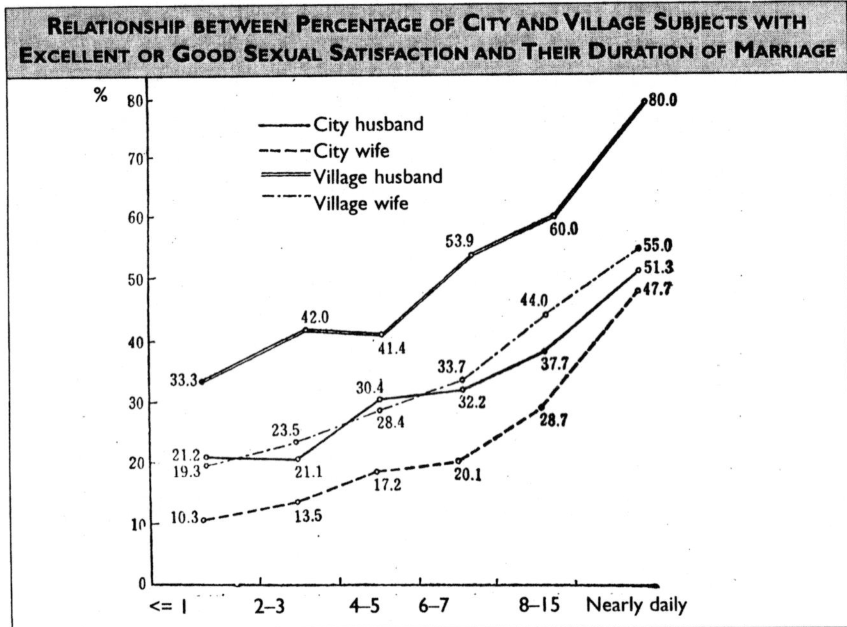

Figure 4–51

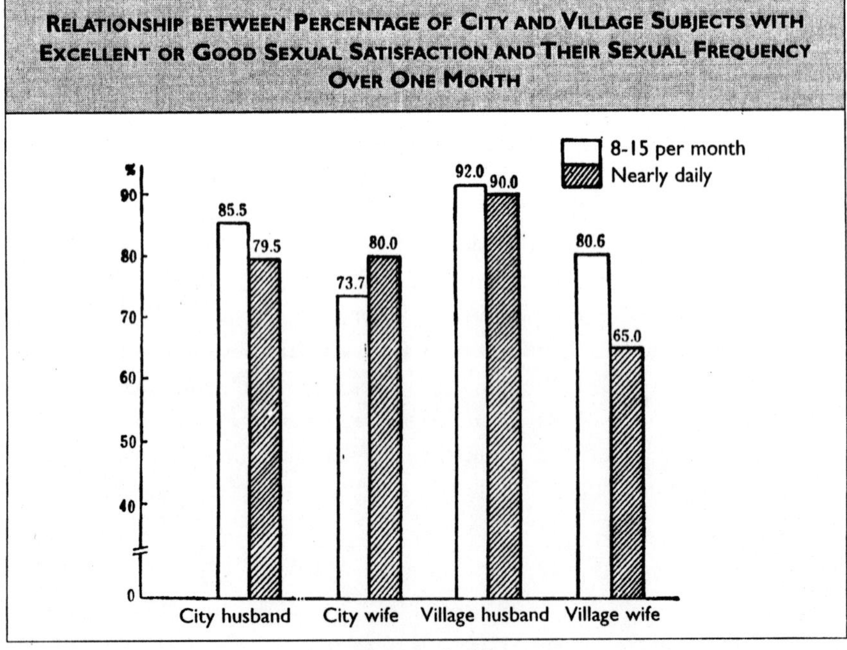

Figure 4–52

MONTHLY RATE OF SEXUAL INTERCOURSE AND SEXUAL SATISFACTION (CITY HUSBANDS)												
SATISFACTION	<=1		2-3		4-5		6-7		8-15		DAILY	
	NO.	%	NO.	%	NO.	%	NO.	%	NO.	%	NO.	%
Very good	31	21.2	89	21.1	112	30.4	106	32.2	60	37.7	20	51.3
Good	62	42.5	211	50.1	189	51.4	167	50.8	76	47.8	11	28.2
Fair	43	29.5	101	24.0	61	16.6	52	15.8	19	11.9	3	7.7
Poor	4	2.7	11	2.6	0	0	1	0.3	2	1.3	0	0
Very poor	0	0	3	0.7	3	0.8	0	0	0	0	2	5.1
Cannot tell	6	4.1	6	1.4	3	0.8	3	0.9	2	1.3	3	7.7
Total	146	100.0	421	100.0	368	100.0	329	100.0	159	100.0	39	100.0

Table 4-243

MONTHLY RATE OF SEXUAL INTERCOURSE AND SEXUAL SATISFACTION (CITY WIVES)												
SATISFACTION	<=1		2-3		4-5		6-7		8-15		DAILY	
	NO.	%	NO.	%	NO.	%	NO.	%	NO.	%	NO.	%
Very good	49	10.3	166	13.5	167	17.2	144	20.1	83	28.7	31	47.7
Good	129	27.0	493.	40.2	462	47.6	351	49.0	130	45.0	21	32.3
Fair	224	16.9	491	40.0	286	29.5	184	25.7	59	20.4	7	10.8
Poor	19	4.0	24	2.0	18	1.9	9	1.3	3	1.0	5	7.7
Very poor	7	1.5	0	0	2	0.2	3	0.4	1	0.3	0	0
Cannot tell	50	10.5	52	4.2	35	3.6	26	3.6	13	4.5	1	1.5
Total	478	100.0	1226	100.0	970	100.0	717	100.0	289	100.0	65	100.0

Table 4-244

MONTHLY RATE OF SEXUAL INTERCOURSE AND SEXUAL SATISFACTION (VILLAGE HUSBANDS)												
SATISFACTION	<=1		2-3		4-5		6-7		8-15		DAILY	
	NO.	%	NO.	%	NO.	%	NO.	%	NO.	%	NO.	%
Very good	6	33.3	21	42.0	41	41.4	48	53.9	15	60.0	8	80.0
Good	6	33.3	14	28.0	36	36.4	27	30.3	8	32.0	1	10.0
Fair	4	22.2	13	26.0	18	18.2	13	14.6	2	8.0	0	0
Poor	0	0	1	2.0	0	0	0	0	0	0	0	0
Very poor	0	0	0	0	2	2.0	0	0	0	0	1	10.0
Cannot tell	2	11.1	1	2.0	2	2.0	1	1.1	0	0	0	0
Total	18	100.0	50	100.0	99	100.0	89	100.0	25	100.0	10	100.0

Table 4-245

MONTHLY RATE OF SEXUAL INTERCOURSE AND SEXUAL SATISFACTION (VILLAGE WIVES)												
SATISFACTION	<=1		2-3		4-5		6-7		8-15		DAILY	
	NO.	%	NO.	%	NO.	%	NO.	%	NO.	%	NO.	%
Very good	17	19.3	57	23.5	89	28.4	91	33.7	59	44.0	11	55.0
Good	17	19.3	66	27.2	103	32.9	119	44.1	49	36.6	2	10.0
Fair	40	45.5	106	43.6	111	35.5	44	16.3	21	15.7	5	25.0
Poor	3	3.4	0	0	0	0	3	1.1	0	0	1	5.0
Very poor	1	1.1	1	0.4	0	0	1	0.4	1	0.7	1	5.0
Cannot tell	10	11.4	13	5.3	10	3.2	12	5.4	4	3.0	0	0
Total	88	100.0	243	100.0	313	100.0	270	100.0	134	100.0	20	100.0

Table 4-246

INITIATOR IN SEX AND SEXUAL SATISFACTION (CITY HUSBANDS)								
SATISFACTION	HUSBAND		WIFE		BOTH		NOT CLEAR	
	NO.	%	NO.	%	NO.	%	NO.	%
Very good	260	26.7	6	16.7	124	39.1	36	22.8
Good	492	50.5	17	47.2	142	44.8	72	45.6
Fair	188	19.3	10	27.8	48	15.1	39	24.7
Poor	17	1.7	1	2.8	0	0	2	1.3
Very poor	6	0.6	1	2.8	1	0.3	0	0
Cannot tell	12	1.2	1	2.8	2	0.6	9	5.7
Total	975	100.0	36	100.0	317	100.0	158	100.0

P=0.001

Table 4-247

INITIATOR IN SEX AND SEXUAL SATISFACTION (CITY WIVES)								
SATISFACTION	HUSBAND		WIFE		BOTH		NOT CLEAR	
	NO.	%	NO.	%	NO.	%	NO.	%
Very good	431	14.6	14	36.8	157	32.4	49	14.5
Good	1226	41.5	13	34.2	229	47.2	130	38.3
Fair	1062	35.9	10	26.3	87	17.9	127	37.5
Poor	73	2.5	0	0	4	0.8	3	0.9
Very poor	16	0.5	0	0	0	0	1	0.3
Cannot tell	149	5.0	1	2.6	8	1.6	29	8.6
Total	2957	100.0	38	100.0	485	100.0	339	100.0

P=0.001

Table 4-248

INITIATOR IN SEX AND SEXUAL SATISFACTION (VILLAGE HUSBANDS)								
SATISFACTION	HUSBAND		WIFE		BOTH		NOT CLEAR	
	NO.	%	NO.	%	NO.	%	NO.	%
Very good	61	48.4	8	53.3	49	52.7	23	36.5
Good	43	34.1	4	26.7	28	30.1	20	31.7
Fair	18	14.3	2	13.3	13	14.0	18	28.6
Poor	1	0.8	0	0	0	0	0	0
Very poor	1	0.8	0	0	2	2.2	0	0
Cannot tell	2	1.6	1	6.7	1	1.1	2	3.2
Total	126	100.0	15	100.0	93	100.0	63	100.0

P=0.50

Table 4-249

INITIATOR IN SEX AND SEXUAL SATISFACTION (VILLAGE WIVES)								
SATISFACTION	HUSBAND		WIFE		BOTH		NOT CLEAR	
	NO.	%	NO.	%	NO.	%	NO.	%
Very good	153	25.6	14	43.8	108	44.4	53	25.7
Good	225	37.6	11	34.4	76	31.3	48	23.3
Fair	185	30.9	5	15.6	53	21.8	87	42.2
Poor	4	0.7	0	0	0	0	3	1.5
Very poor	1	0.2	2	6.3	1	0.4	1	0.5
Cannot tell	30	5.0	0	0	5	2.1	14	6.8
Total	598	100.0	32	100.0	243	100.0	206	100.0

P=0.001

Table 4-250

VIEW ON WIFE INITIATING SEX AND SEXUAL SATISFACTION (CITY HUSBANDS)						
SATISFACTION	SHOULD		SHOULD NOT		EMBARRASSED	
	NO.	%	NO.	%	NO.	%
Very good	315	29.1	31	30.4	72	26.1
Good	528	48.7	37	36.3	149	54.0
Fair	207	19.1	29	28.4	45	16.3
Poor	13	1.2	2	2.0	4	1.4
Very poor	7	0.6	0	0	1	0.4
Cannot tell	14	1.3	3	2.9	5	1.8
Total	1084	100.0	102	100.0	276	100.0

Table 4-251

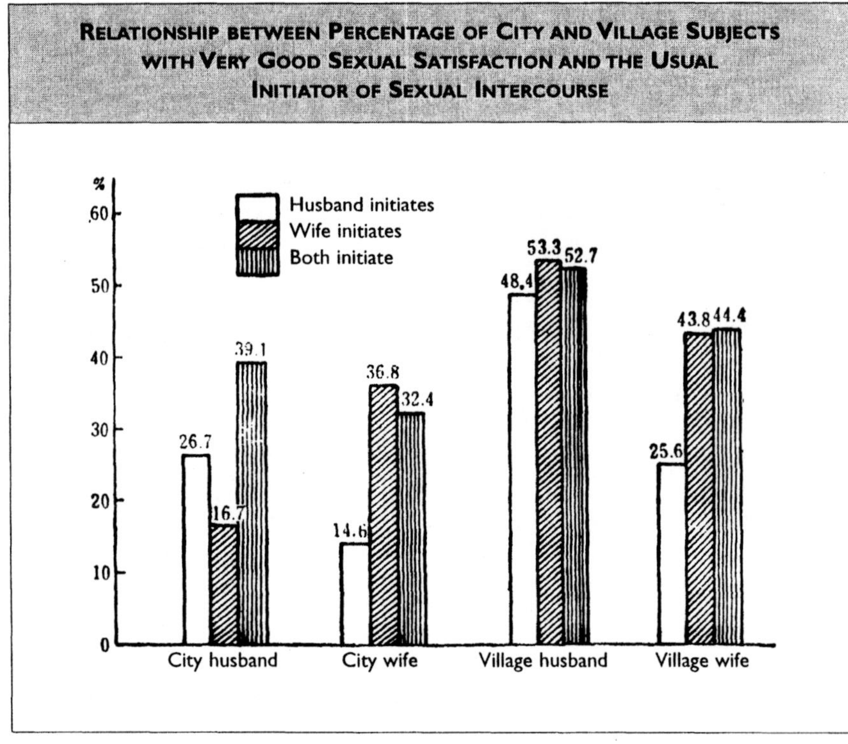

Figure 4–53

to understand why sex is more satisfying if it is by mutual desire. As for its being more satisfactory if initiated by the wife, it is probably because under such circumstances, the husbands are rarely totally passive, meaning that the coitus is in fact initiated mutually.

Tables 4– 251 to 4–254 show that except for the village husbands, if the wife proposes sexual intercourse, sexual satisfaction is higher for both the husband and the wife, especially for the wife.

H. Mutual Cooperation

Tables 4–255 to 4–258 show that sexual satisfaction is higher for those husbands and wives who cooperate with their partners in sex. The correlation is quite high, G being 0.32 for city husbands, 0.51 for city wives, 0.43 for village husbands, and 0.47 for village wives.

I. Coital Positions

Tables 4–259 to 4–262 and figure 4–54 show obvious positive relationships between sexual satisfaction and frequency of changing coital positions.

VIEW ON WIFE INITIATING SEX AND SEXUAL SATISFACTION (CITY WIVES)						
SATISFACTION	SHOULD		SHOULD NOT		EMBARRASSED	
	NO.	%	NO.	%	NO.	%
Very good	483	19.1	53	11.0	109	14.1
Good	1130	44.8	153	31.7	301	38.8
Fair	762	30.2	216	44.8	288	37.2
Poor	36	1.4	23	4.8	21	2.7
Very poor	7	0.3	3	0.6	7	0.9
Cannot tell	106	4.2	34	71	49	6.3
Total	2524	100.0	482	100.0	775	100.0

Table 4-252

VIEW ON WIFE INITIATING SEX AND SEXUAL SATISFACTION (VILLAGE HUSBANDS)						
SATISFACTION	SHOULD		SHOULD NOT		EMBARRASSED	
	NO.	%	NO.	%	NO.	%
Very good	92	46.5	27	69.2	21	35.6
Good	66	33.3	5	12.8	23	39.0
Fair	36	18.2	5	12.8	11	18.6
Poor	0	0	1	2.6	0	0
Very poor	0	0	0	0	3	5.1
Cannot tell	4	2.0	1	2.6	1	1.7
Total	198	100.0	39	100.0	59	100.0

Table 4-253

VIEW ON WIFE INITIATING SEX AND SEXUAL SATISFACTION (VILLAGE WIVES)						
SATISFACTION	SHOULD		SHOULD NOT		EMBARRASSED	
	NO.	%	NO.	%	NO.	%
Very good	195	28.8	49	31.2	84	34.3
Good	242	35.8	43	27.4	73	29.8
Fair	203	30.0	53	33.8	75	30.6
Poor	4	0.6	1	0.6	2	0.8
Very poor	2	0.3	2	1.3	1	0.4
Cannot tell	30	4.4	9	5.7	10	4.1
Total	676	100.0	157	100.0	245	100.0

Table 4-254

WILLINGNESS TO COOPERATE IN SEX AND SEXUAL SATISFACTION (CITY HUSBANDS)						
SATISFACTION	WILLING		NOT WILLING		DEPENDS	
	NO.	%	NO.	%	NO.	%
Very good	361	30.9	2	69.7	58	21.3
Good	593	50.8	9	30.0	119	43.8
Fair	189	16.2	13	43.3	76	27.9
Poor	9	0.8	2	6.7	8	2.9
Very poor	5	0.4	2	6.7	1	0.4
Cannot tell	10	0.9	2	6.7	10	3.7
Total	1167	100.0	30	100.0	272	100.0

Table 4-255

WILLINGNESS TO COOPERATE IN SEX AND SEXUAL SATISFACTION (CITY WIVES)						
SATISFACTION	WILLING		NOT WILLING		DEPENDS	
	NO.	%	NO.	%	NO.	%
Very good	506	25.9	10	8.9	129	7.6
Good	966	49.4	11	9.8	608	35.6
Fair	430	22.0	41	36.6	793	46.5
Poor	16	0.8	23	20.5	42	2.5
Very poor	1	0.1	6	5.4	10	0.6
Cannot tell	37	1.9	21	18.8	125	7.3
Total	1956	100.0	112	100.0	1707	100.0

Table 4-256

WILLINGNESS TO COOPERATE IN SEX AND SEXUAL SATISFACTION (VILLAGE HUSBANDS)						
SATISFACTION	WILLING		NOT WILLING		DEPENDS	
	NO.	%	NO.	%	NO.	%
Very good	104	57.5	4	36.4	33	31.4
Good	54	29.8	3	27.3	37	35.2
Fair	20	11.0	3	27.3	29	27.6
Poor	0	0	0	0	1	1.0
Very poor	0	0	0	0	3	2.9
Cannot tell	3	1.7	1	9.1	2	1.9
Total	181	100.0	11	100.0	105	100.0

Table 4-257

Willingness to Cooperate in Sex and Sexual Satisfaction (Village Wives)						
SATISFACTION	WILLING		NOT WILLING		DEPENDS	
	NO.	%	NO.	%	NO.	%
Very good	251	41.4	4	10.3	69	19.0
Good	217	35.8	5	12.8	137	31.9
Fair	120	19.8	21	33.8	190	44.2
Poor	1	0.2	3	7.7	3	0.7
Very poor	2	0.3	1	2.6	2	0.5
Cannot tell	15	2.5	5	12.8	29	6.7
Total	606	100.0	39	100.0	430	100.0

Table 4-258

Varied Sex Positions and Sexual Satisfaction (City Husbands)						
SATISFACTION	ONE POSITION ONLY		CHANGE SOMETIMES		CHANGE	
	NO.	%	NO.	%	NO.	%
Very good	113	24.8	215	25.7	95	53.7
Good	185	40.7	476	56.9	56	31.6
Fair	133	29.2	128	15.3	19	10.7
Poor	12	2.6	5	0.6	2	1.1
Very poor	2	0.4	3	0.4	3	1.7
Cannot tell	10	2.2	10	1.2	2	1.1
Total	455	100.0	837	100.0	177	100.0

P=0.001

Table 4-259

Varied Sex Positions and Sexual Satisfaction (City Wives)						
SATISFACTION	ONE POSITION ONLY		CHANGE SOMETIMES		CHANGE	
	NO.	%	NO.	%	NO.	%
Very good	198	12.2	347	18.8	104	39.7
Good	575	35.4	887	48.0	118	45.0
Fair	674	41.5	527	28.5	34	12.0
Poor	55	3.4	23	1.2	1	0.4
Very poor	11	0.7	4	0.2	0	0
Cannot tell	113	6.9	59	3.2	5	1.9
Total	1626	100.0	1847	100.0	262	100.0

P=0.001

Table 4-260

Varied Sex Positions and Sexual Satisfaction (Village Husbands)

SATISFACTION	ONE POSITION ONLY		CHANGE SOMETIMES		CHANGE	
	NO.	%	NO.	%	NO.	%
Very good	66	44.0	59	48.0	16	64.0
Good	43	28.7	48	39.0	4	16.0
Fair	35	23.3	14	11.4	3	12.0
Poor	1	0.7	0	0	0	0
Very poor	2	1.3	0	0	1	4.0
Cannot tell	3	2.0	2	1.6	1	4.0
Total	150	100.0	123	100.0	25	100.0

P=0.10

Table 4-261

Relationship between Percentage of City and Village Subjects with Excellent or Good Sexual Satisfaction and Their Use of Varied Sexual Positions

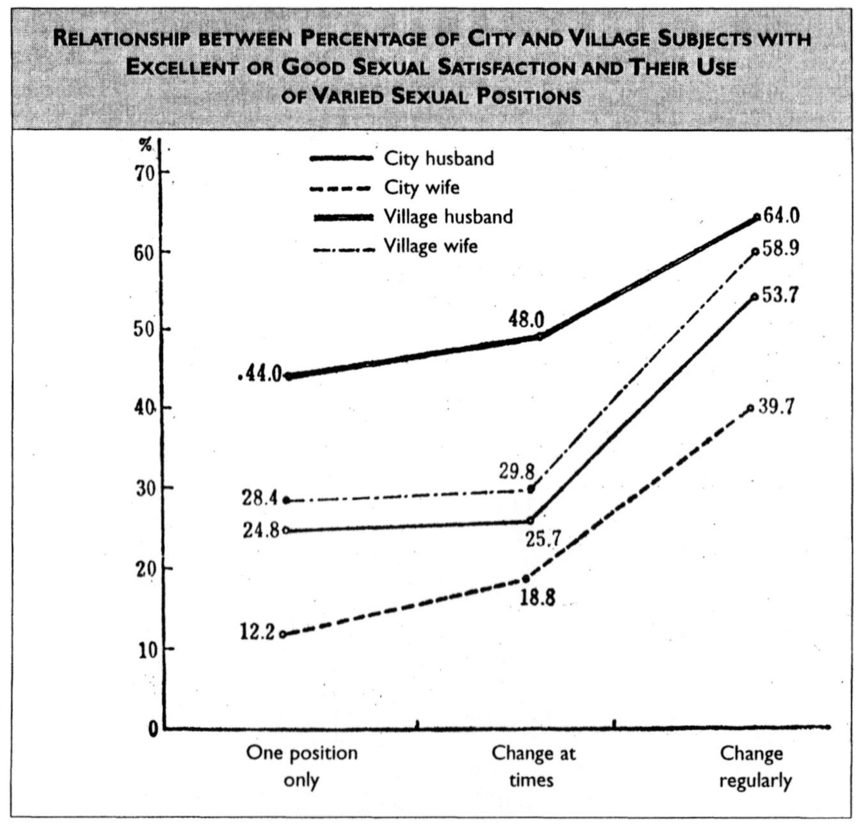

Figure 4–54

SEX POSITIONS AND SEXUAL SATISFACTION (VILLAGE WIVES)						
SATISFACTION	ONE POSITION ONLY		CHANGE SOMETIMES		CHANGE	
	NO.	%	NO.	%	NO.	%
Very good	171	28.4	125	29.8	33	58.9
Good	165	27.4	184	43.9	10	17.9
Fair	225	37.4	92	22.0	11	19.6
Poor	4	0.7	3	0.7	0	0
Very poor	3	0.5	1	0.2	1	1.8
Cannot tell	34	5.6	14	3.3	1	1.8
Total	602	100.0	419	100.0	56	100.0

P=0.001

Table 4-262

J. NUDITY

Sexual satisfaction is positively related to nudity during coitus too. G is 0.29 for city husbands, 0.37 for city wives, 0.24 for village husbands, and 0.36 for village wives (tables 4–263 to 4–266 and figure 4–55).

RELATIONSHIP BETWEEN PERCENTAGE OF CITY AND VILLAGE SUBJECTS WITH EXCELLENT OR GOOD SEXUAL SATISFACTION AND FREQUENCY OF NUDITY DURING SEXUAL INTERCOURSE

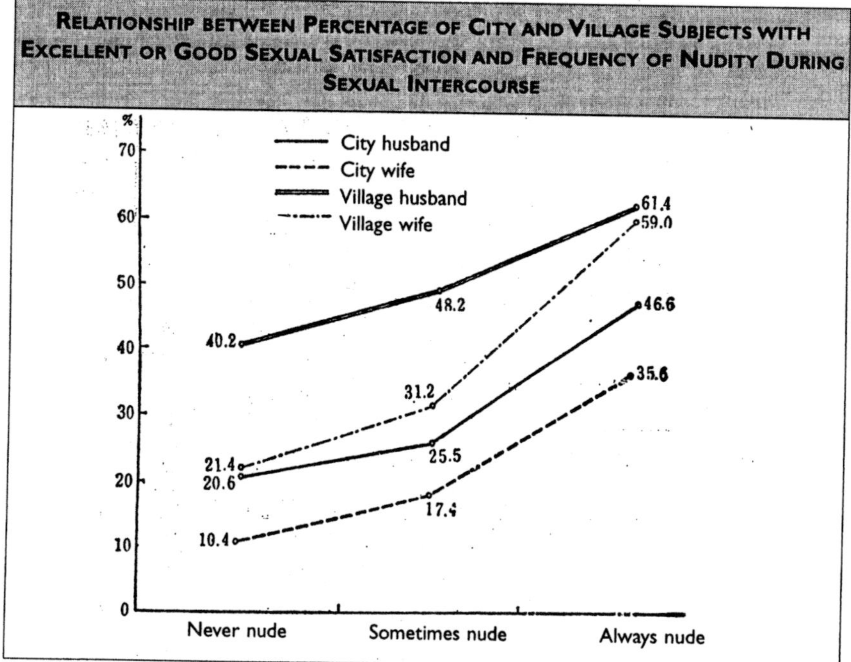

Figure 4–55

NUDITY IN SEXUAL INTERCOURSE AND SEXUAL SATISFACTION (CITY HUSBANDS)						
SATISFACTION	OFTEN NUDE		SOMETIMES		NEVER	
	NO.	%	NO.	%	NO.	%
Very good	129	46.6	226	25.5	64	20.6
Good	108	39.0	471	53.2	142	45.8
Fair	31	11.2	168	19.0	85	27.4
Poor	2	0.7	8	0.9	9	2.9
Very poor	4	1.4	2	0.2	2	0.6
Cannot tell	3	1.1	11	1.2	8	2.6
Total	277	100.0	886	100.0	310	100.0

P=0.001

Table 4-263

NUDITY IN SEXUAL INTERCOURSE AND SEXUAL SATISFACTION (CITY WIVES)						
SATISFACTION	OFTEN NUDE		SOMETIMES		NEVER	
	NO.	%	NO.	%	NO.	%
Very good	161	35.6	341	17.4	140	10.4
Good	204	45.1	919	46.8	455	33.9
Fair	70	15.5	582	29.6	609	45.3
Poor	8	1.8	34	1.7	39	2.9
Very poor	3	0.7	5	0.3	7	0.5
Cannot tell	6	0.3	82	4.2	94	7.0
Total	452	100.0	1963	100.0	1344	100.0

P=0.001

Table 4-264

NAKEDNESS IN SEXUAL INTERCOURSE AND SEXUAL SATISFACTION (VILLAGE HUSBANDS)						
SATISFACTION	OFTEN NUDE		SOMETIMES		NEVER	
	NO.	%	NO.	%	NO.	%
Very good	27	61.4	68	48.2	45	40.2
Good	9	20.5	53	37.6	33	29.5
Fair	7	15.9	19	13.5	26	23.2
Poor	0	0	0	0	1	0.9
Very poor	1	2.3	1	0.7	1	0.9
Cannot tell	0	0	0	0	6	5.4
Total	44	100.0	141	100.0	112	100.0

P=0.02

Table 4-265

NUDITY IN SEXUAL INTERCOURSE AND SEXUAL SATISFACTION (VILLAGE WIVES)						
SATISFACTION	OFTEN NUDITY		SOMETIMES		NEVER	
	NO.	%	NO.	%	NO.	%
Very good	82	59.0	145	31.2	102	21.4
Good	33	24.7	184	39.6	144	30.3
Fair	19	13.7	111	23.9	199	41.8
Poor	0	0	3	0.6	4	0.8
Very poor	1	0.7	2	0.4	2	0.4
Cannot tell	4	2.9	20	4.3	25	5.3
Total	139	100.0	465	100.0	476	100.0

P=0.001

Table 4-266

K. SEXUAL ATTITUDES

For the city couples, sexual satisfaction is higher for those who consider sex an emotional and physiological need, and lowest for those who see it as a routine matter or as a means of reproduction. In the village couples, low satisfaction is reported by those who see sex as a duty or routine, but the correlations are not as high as those in the city couples. (tables 4–267 to 4–270)

L. SEXUAL PLEASURE

There is a significant correlation between sexual satisfaction and sexual pleasure, with the G index at 0.53 for city husbands, 0.75 for city wives,

VIEW ON SEXUAL INTERCOURSE AND SEXUAL SATISFACTION (CITY HUSBANDS)												
SATISFACTION	WIFE'S DUTY		MUTUAL DUTY		MUTUAL PHYSICAL NEED		MUTUAL PSYCHO-PHYSICAL NEED		REPRO-DUCTION		ROUTINE	
	NO.	%	NO.	%	NO.	%	NO.	%	NO.	%	NO.	%
Very good	7	23.3	24	32.4	49	27.8	316	28.4	8	40.0	21	31.3
Good	14	46.7	33	44.6	75	42.6	573	51.6	6	30.0	22	32.8
Fair	6	20.0	15	20.3	46	26.1	189	17.0	3	15.0	20	29.9
Poor	1	3.3	0	0	5	2.8	13	1.2	0	0	1	1.5
Very poor	1	3.3	0	0	1	0.6	5	0.5	1	5.0	0	0
Cannot tell	1	3.3	2	2.7	0	0	15	1.4	2	10.0	3	4.5
Total	30	100.0	74	100.0	176	100.0	1111	100.0	20	100.0	67	100.0

Table 4-267

VIEW ON SEXUAL INTERCOURSE AND SEXUAL SATISFACTION (CITY WIVES)												
SATISFACTION	WIFE'S DUTY		MUTUAL DUTY		MUTUAL PHYSICAL NEED		MUTUAL PSYCHO-PHYSICAL NEED		REPRO-DUCTION		ROUTINE	
	NO.	%	NO.	%	NO.	%	NO.	%	NO.	%	NO.	%
Very good	14	11.7	32	21.1	71	18.9	504	17.2	5	11.1	27	13.9
Good	48	10.0	60	39.5	141	37.5	1280	43.6	14	31.1	61	31.4
Fair	43	35.8	56	36.8	142	37.8	928	31.6	19	42.2	90	46.4
Poor	3	2.5	1	0.7	5	1.3	64	2.2	3	6.7	3	1.5
Very poor	2	1.7	0	0	1	0.3	12	0.4	0	0	2	1.0
Cannot tell	10	8.3	3	2.0	16	4.3	147	5.0	4	8.9	11	5.7
Total	120	100.0	152	100.0	376	100.0	2935	100.0	45	100.0	194	100.0

Table 4–268

VIEW ON SEXUAL INTERCOURSE AND SEXUAL SATISFACTION (VILLAGE HUSBANDS)												
SATISFACTION	WIFE'S DUTY		MUTUAL DUTY		MUTUAL PHYSICAL NEED		MUTUAL PSYCHO-PHYSICAL NEED		REPRO-DUCTION		ROUTINE	
	NO.	%	NO.	%	NO.	%	NO.	%	NO.	%	NO.	%
Very good	5	83.3	4	66.7	23	43.4	93	47.0	3	33.3	13	50.0
Good	1	16.7	1	16.7	17	32.1	65	32.8	4	44.4	7	26.9
Fair	0	0	1	16.7	12	22.6	33	16.7	0	0	6	23.1
Poor	0	0	0	0	1	1.9	0	0	0	0	0	0
Very poor	0	0	0	0	0	0	2	1.0	1	11.1	0	0
Cannot tell	0	0	0	0	0	0	5	2.5	1	11.1	0	0
Total	6	100.0	6	100.0	53	100.0	198	100.0	3	100.0	26	100.0

Table 4–269

0.53 for village husbands, and 0.53 for village wives. Tables 4–271 to 4–274 show that the more couples enjoyed sex, the more sexually satisfied they were.

Tables 4–271 to 4–274 show however, that without sexual pleasure, some couples can still be satisfied. This suggests that some people can obtain satisfaction by means other than sexual pleasure. This type of satisfaction could also be due to ignorance or to low expectations, since tables 4–272 and 4–274 show that many more village wives than city wives are satisfied without sexual pleasure.

View on Sexual Intercourse and Sexual Satisfaction (Village Wives)												
SATISFACTION	WIFE'S DUTY		MUTUAL DUTY		MUTUAL PHYSICAL NEED		MUTUAL PSYCHO-PHYSICAL NEED		REPRO-DUCTION		ROUTINE	
	NO.	%	NO.	%	NO.	%	NO.	%	NO.	%	NO.	%
Very good	5	38.5	9	25.7	53	29.8	204	31.7	14	24.1	44	29.5
Good	4	30.8	9	25.7	58	32.8	219	34.0	21	36.2	47	31.5
Fair	2	15.4	14	40.0	58	32.8	184	28.6	19	32.8	52	34.9
Poor	0	0	0	0	3	1.7	3	0.5	1	1.7	0	0
Very poor	1	7.7	0	0	1	0.6	3	0.5	0	0	0	0
Cannot tell	1	7.7	3	8.6	4	2.3	31	4.8	3	5.2	6	4.0
Total	13	100.0	35	100.0	177	100.0	644	100.0	58	100.0	149	100.0

Table 4–270

Sexual Pleasure and Sexual Satisfaction (City Husbands)						
SATISFACTION	OFTEN		SOMETIMES		NEVER	
	NO.	%	NO.	%	NO.	%
Very good	329	37.3	86	15.7	7	17.1
Good	453	51.4	261	47.6	7	17.1
Fair	87	9.9	176	32.1	17	41.5
Poor	4	0.5	12	2.2	3	7.3
Very poor	5	0.6	1	0.2	2	4.9
Cannot tell	4	0.5	12	2.2	5	12.2
Total	882	100.0	548	100.0	41	100.0

P=0.001

Table 4–271

Sexual Pleasure and Sexual Satisfaction (City Wives)						
SATISFACTION	OFTEN		SOMETIMES		NEVER	
	NO.	%	NO.	%	NO.	%
Very good	409	39.1	231	9.2	9	3.8
Good	552	52.8	1016	40.5	19	8.1
Fair	76	7.3	1081	43.1	114	48.7
Poor	3	0.3	41	1.6	37	15.8
Very poor	0	0	6	0.2	10	4.3
Cannot tell	5	0.5	132	5.3	45	19.2
Total	1045	100.0	2507	100.0	234	100.0

P=0.001

Table 4–272

SEXUAL PLEASURE AND SEXUAL SATISFACTION (VILLAGE HUSBANDS)						
SATISFACTION	OFTEN		SOMETIMES		NEVER	
	NO.	%	NO.	%	NO.	%
Very good	57	68.7	81	42.2	2	10.0
Good	21	25.3	66	34.4	7	35.0
Fair	4	4.8	39	20.3	9	45.0
Poor	0	0	1	0.5	0	0
Very poor	1	1.2	2	1.0	0	0
Cannot tell	0	0	3	1.6	2	10.0
Total	83	100.0	192	100.0	20	100.0

P=0.001

Table 4–273

SEXUAL PLEASURE AND SEXUAL SATISFACTION (VILLAGE WIVES)						
SATISFACTION	OFTEN		SOMETIMES		NEVER	
	NO.	%	NO.	%	NO.	%
Very good	130	50.6	179	24.3	16	19.3
Good	103	40.1	250	33.9	8	9.6
Fair	17	6.6	268	36.3	46	55.4
Poor	1	0.4	3	0.4	3	3.6
Very poor	3	1.2	0	0	2	2.4
Cannot tell	3	1.2	38	5.1	8	9.6
Total	257	100.0	738	100.0	83	100.0

P=0.001

Table 4–274

M. MENSTRUAL PERIOD

Menstruation is known to have some influence on sexual desire. In our survey, about 40 percent of the wives reported increased sexual desires in the first week after menstruation, 20 percent reported no increase, and 40 percent could not give a definite answer.

DESIRE FOR SEX ONE WEEK AFTER MENSTRUATION									
	TOTAL	YES		NO		NOT SURE		UNKNOWN	
		NO.	%	NO.	%	NO.	%	NO.	%
City	6210	2445	39.4	1191	19.2	2194	35.3	380	6.1
Village	1392	500	35.9	262	18.8	616	44.3	14	1.0

Table 4–275

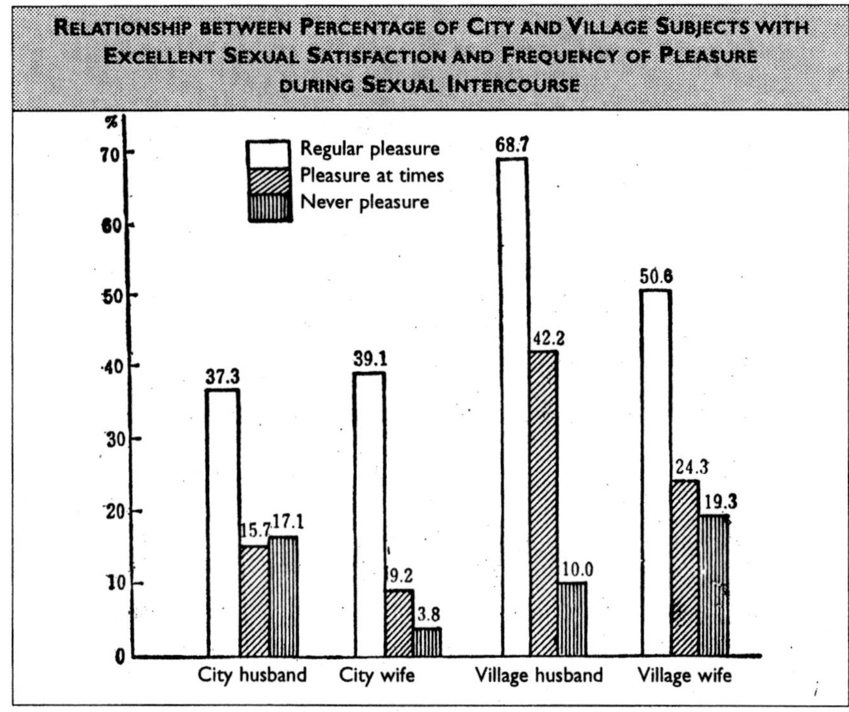

Figure 4–56

Of those surveyed,42.7 percent of the city couples and 42.2 percent of the village couples thought that sex was most pleasurable immediately after the end of menstruation; 35.4 percent of the city couples and 43.4 percent of the village couples thought the time was best in the middle of menstruation periods (Table 4–276). The least percentage of couples thought sex was pleasurable before menstruation. These findings are comparable with those found in other countries.[65]

N. LIVING CONDITIONS

Privacy is usually required for sexual satisfaction. Living conditions are therefore an important factor. Table 4–277 shows that for most of the subjects, their living environments were hardly soundproof. Of those asked, 50 percent even had to live with children in the same room. So it would seem that living conditions in China, therefore, are rather unfavorable for an unhurried and fulfilling sex life.

Living conditions and sexual satisfaction appeared to have no relationship. Table 4–278 to 4–281 show that with no other people living in

SUBJECTIVELY THE BEST TIME FOR SEX IN A MONTH									
	TOTAL	AFTER MENSTRUATION		BEFORE MENSTRUATION		BETWEEN MENSTRUATIONS		UNKNOWN	
		NO.	%	NO.	%	NO.	%	NO.	%
City	6210	2650	42.7	559	9.0	1760	28.3	1241	20.0
Village	1392	588	42.2	182	13.1	584	42.5	38	2.7

Table 4–276

LIVING CONDITION																
	WITH CHILDREN/OTHERS IN SAME ROOM							SOUND INSULATION								
	YES		NO		UNKNOWN		TOTAL	GOOD		FAIR		POOR		UNKNOWN		TOTAL
	NO.	%	NO.	%	NO.	%		NO.	%	NO.	%	NO.	%	NO.	%	
City	2713	43.7	3039	48.9	458	7.4	6210	1720	27.7	3306	53.2	825	13.3	359	5.8	6210
Village	801	57.5	572	41.1	19	1.4	1392	382	27.4	814	58.5	181	13.0	15	1.1	1392

Table 4–277

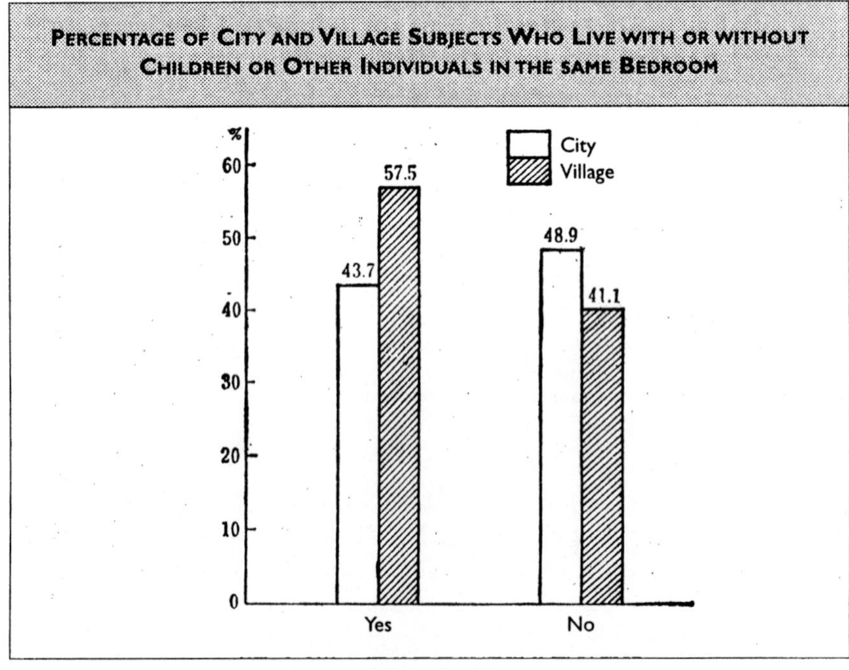

Figure 4–57

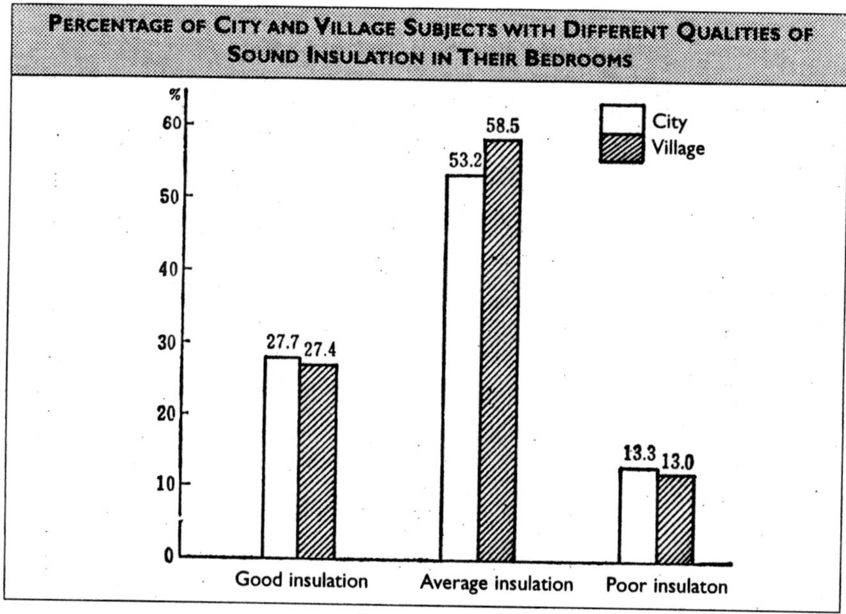

Figure 4–58

the same room, 80.3 percent of the city husbands were rather satisfied sexually, but when there were other people in the same room, 74.8 percent of the husbands still felt sexually satisfied. For the wives, the respective percentages are similar at 59.1 percent and 59.2 percent respectively. For the village husbands, the respective percentages are 73.8 percent and 82.3 percent, and for the village wives, 61.5 percent and 75.3 percent. In present China it is still quite common for relatives to live together in one room, especially in the villages. By tradition, many couples are quite used to the situation, so much so that they are hardly affected sexually. In some villages in northern China, it is not uncommon for a few couples to sleep in a large,

SEXUAL SATISFACTION AND LIVING WITH CHILDREN OR OTHERS IN THE SAME ROOM (CITY HUSBANDS)

SATISFACTION	YES		NO	
	NO.	%	NO.	%
Very good	184	28.4	224	28.5
Good	301	46.4	407	51.8
Fair	133	20.5	137	17.5
Poor	11	1.7	6	0.8
Very poor	5	0.8	3	0.4
Cannot tell	15	2.3	8	1.0
Total	649	100.0	785	100.0

Table 4–278

common bed (tables 4–278 to 4–281)

Yet, tables 4–282 to 4–286 show that sound insulation did have some association with sexual satisfaction, with the G index being 0.18, 0.11, 0.23, and 0.12 for city husbands, city wives, village husbands, and village wives respectively. Sound insulation may be an important factor because it determines not only whether noises within the a room could be heard outside, but also whether outside noises could interfere with a couple's sexual activity. The association is obvious in figure 4–59.

3. Sexual Pleasure

Sexual pleasure has long been associated strongly with sexual satisfaction. Sexual pleasure can be obtained in many ways, such as petting, embracing, and kissing, and the peak of sexual pleasure is usually orgasm.[66] In the second Kinsey report, 36 percent to 44 percent of American women could not achieve orgasm from every sexual intercourse. Only one third of them could achieve orgasm in

Sexual Satisfaction and Living with Children or Others in the Same Room (City Wives)

SATISFACTION	YES		NO	
	NO.	%	NO.	%
Very good	274	15.8	345	18.3
Good	754	43.4	772	40.8
Fair	584	33.6	627	33.2
Poor	40	2.3	38	2.0
Very poor	6	0.3	8	0.4
Cannot tell	79	4.5	100	5.3
Total	1737	100.0	1890	100.0

Table 4–279

Sexual Satisfaction and Living with Children or Others in the Same Room (Village Husbands)

SATISFACTION	YES		NO	
	NO.	%	NO.	%
Very good	96	50.0	44	42.7
Good	62	32.3	32	31.1
Fair	30	15.6	21	20.4
Poor	0	0	1	1.0
Very poor	2	1.0	1	1.0
Cannot tell	2	1.0	4	3.9
Total	192	100.0	103	100.0

Table 4–280

Sexual Satisfaction and Living with Children or Others in the Same Room (Village Wives)

SATISFACTION	YES		NO	
	NO.	%	NO.	%
Very good	184	30.6	139	29.9
Good	209	34.7	147	31.6
Fair	165	27.4	163	35.1
Poor	6	1.0	1	0.2
Very poor	4	0.7	1	0.2
Cannot tell	34	5.6	14	3.0
Total	602	100.0	465	100.0

Table 4–281

SOUND INSULATION IN ROOM AND SEXUAL SATISFACTION (CITY HUSBANDS)						
SATISFACTION	GOOD INSULATION		FAIR INSULATION		POOR INSULATION	
	NO.	%	NO.	%	NO.	%
Very good	144	38.6	221	25.4	46	21.5
Good	157	42.1	454	52.2	106	49.5
Fair	61	16.4	166	19.1	50	23.4
Poor	5	1.3	11	1.3	3	1.4
Very poor	3	0.8	4	0.5	1	0.5
Cannot tell	3	0.8	13	1.5	8	3.7
Total	373	100.0	869	100.0	214	100.0

P=0.001

Table 4–282

SOUND INSULATION IN ROOM AND SEXUAL SATISFACTION (CITY WIVES)						
SATISFACTION	GOOD INSULATION		FAIR INSULATION		POOR INSULATION	
	NO.	%	NO.	%	NO.	%
Very good	238	21.3	316	15.5	81	15.4
Good	439	39.2	935	45.7	172	32.7
Fair	378	33.8	651	31.8	210	39.9
Poor	15	1.3	38	1.9	23	4.4
Very poor	3	0.3	7	0.3	4	0.8
Cannot tell	46	4.1	98	4.8	36	6.8
Total	1119	100.0	2045	100.0	526	100.0

P=0.001

Table 4–283

more than 50 percent of the time during intercourse (but never 100 percent), one third in about 50 percent of the time, and another one third in less than 50 percent.[67]

In our survey, we only surveyed sexual pleasure, not orgasm, because we found in our pilot studies that many women were unable to understand what was meant. Many women already felt that sex was satisfactory if they experienced at least some sexual pleasure.

Our findings show that most of the couples derived regular sexual pleasure from sexual intercourse. Only 5.7 percent of the couples had never experienced it. Generally, fewer female subjects had experienced sexual pleasure, probably because of the still pervasive sexual repression of females (Tables 4–287 and 4–288).

SOUND INSULATION IN ROOM AND SEXUAL SATISFACTION (VILLAGE HUSBANDS)						
SATISFACTION	GOOD INSULATION		FAIR INSULATION		POOR INSULATION	
	NO.	%	NO.	%	NO.	%
Very good	50	61.0	78	42.6	12	38.7
Good	20	24.4	63	34.4	11	35.5
Fair	7	8.5	37	20.2	8	25.8
Poor	1	1.2	0	0	0	0
Very poor	0	0	3	1.6	0	0
Cannot tell	4	4.9	2	1.1	0	0
Total	82	100.0	183	100.0	31	100.0

P=0.001

Table 4–284

SOUND INSULATION IN ROOM AND SEXUAL SATISFACTION (VILLAGE WIVES)						
SATISFACTION	GOOD INSULATION		FAIR INSULATION		POOR INSULATION	
	NO.	%	NO.	%	NO.	%
Very good	10	36.9	184	29.3	32	21.9
Good	89	29.9	217	34.6	51	34.9
Fair	77	25.8	198	31.6	52	35.6
Poor	3	1.0	2	0.3	2	1.4
Very poor	1	0.3	1	0.2	3	2.1
Cannot tell	18	6.0	25	4.0	6	4.1
Total	298	100.0	627	100.0	146	100.0

P=0.001

Table 4–285

This difference in sexual pleasure between women and men is compatible with the findings of other countries. Although males in general reach puberty a year later than the females, they can reach orgasm when they are still in their teens, while many females have their first orgasm after age twenty.[68]

Tables 4–287 and 4–288 show that there are some regional differences in sexual pleasure. For both males and females, sexual pleasure is lower in the village subjects (figures 4–60 and 4–61), and among the cities, Guangzhou has the highest percentage of subjects reporting sexual pleasure.

We also analyzed the various factors which could relate to sexual pleasure in the categories on the following pages:

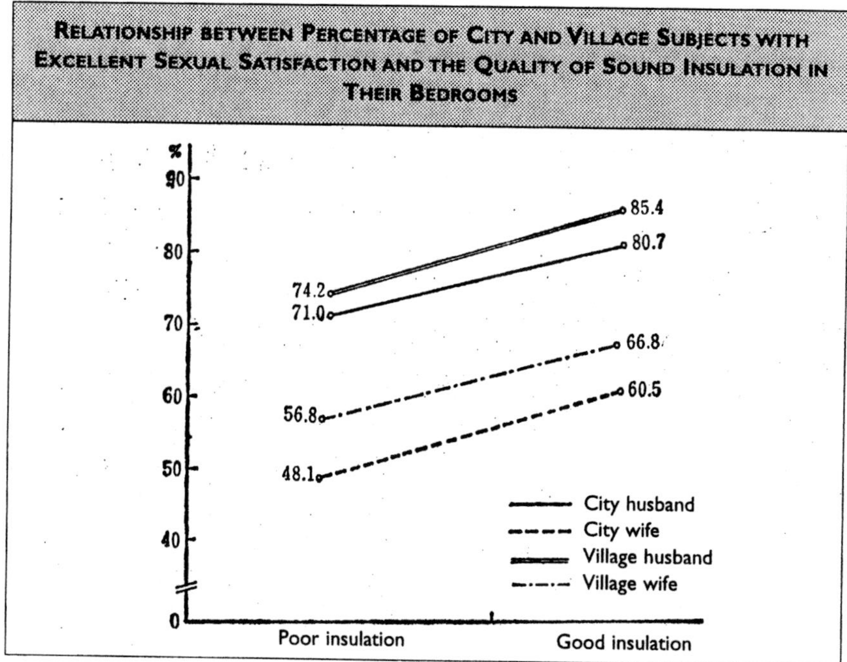

Figure 4–59

A. YEARS OF MARRIAGE

Except for city wives with a G index of 0.12, other subjects did not show any significant relationship between years of marriage and percentage of subjects experiencing sexual pleasure. For the city husbands, the rise of sexual pleasure with years of marriage is the most steady, with the peak at eleven to fifteen years, slightly higher at eleven. For city wives, the trend is towards a lowering of sexual pleasure over the years of

FREQUENCY OF PLEASURE IN SEXUAL INTERCOURSE

GENDER	TOTAL	OFTEN		SOMETIMES		NEVER	
		NO.	%	NO.	%	NO.	%
Male	2026	1062	52.4	885	43.7	79	3.9
Female	5116	1385	27.1	3403	66.5	328	6.4

P=0.001

Table 4–286

SEX AND FREQUENCY OF PLEASURE (CITY)

GENDER	TOTAL	OFTEN		SOMETIMES		NEVER	
		NO.	%	NO.	%	NO.	%
Male	1750	949	54.2	742	42.4	59	3.4
Female	4050	1170	28.9	2633	65.0	274	6.1

P=0.001

Table 4–287

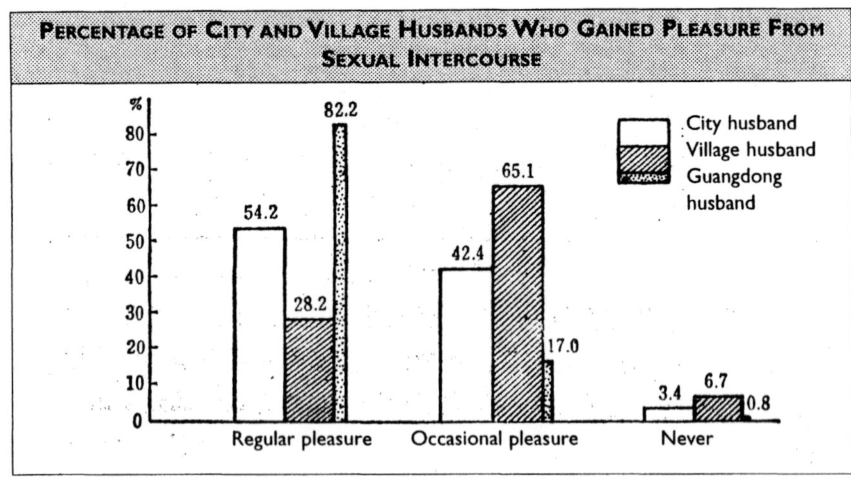

Figure 4–60

marriage. The peak is second year of marriage. For village husbands, the peaks of sexual pleasure are found more at the two extremes of marriage years, with the peak at more than twenty-one years for 34.2 percent. For village wives, the curve fluctuates, with peaks at around six to ten years (tables 4–289 to 4–292 and figure 4–62).

Gender and Frequency of Pleasure (Village)

GENDER	TOTAL	OFTEN		SOMETIMES		NEVER	
		NO.	%	NO.	%	NO.	%
Male	298	84	28.2	194	65.1	20	6.7
Female	1082	258	23.8	741	68.5	83	7.7

P=0.05

Table 4–288

Such results are slightly different from foreign studies which found generally that sexual pleasure increases with years of marriage.

Duration of Marriage (in Years) and Frequency of Pleasure (City Husbands)

	<=2		3-5		6-10		11-15		16-20		>20	
	NO.	%	NO.	%	NO.	%	NO.	%	NO.	%	NO.	%
Often	149	54.8	132	52.0	216	53.2	131	56.0	95	54.3	200	55.6
Sometimes	116	42.6	114	44.9	172	42.4	98	41.9	74	42.3	147	40.8
Never	7	2.6	8	3.1	18	4.4	5	2.1	6	3.4	13	3.6
Total	272	100.0	254	100.0	406	100.0	234	100.0	175	100.0	360	100.0

Table 4–289

Duration of Marriage (in Years) and Frequency of Pleasure (City Wives)												
	<=2		3-5		6-10		11-15		16-20		>20	
	NO.	%	NO.	%	NO.	%	NO.	%	NO.	%	NO.	%
Often	192	37.6	179	32.6	325	30.3	146	24.0	129	36.3	182	24.0
Sometimes	288	56.5	338	61.6	683	63.6	422	69.3	331	67.6	529	69.9
Never	30	5.9	32	5.8	66	6.1	41	6.7	30	6.1	46	6.1
Total	510	100.0	549	100.0	1074	100.0	609	100.0	490	100.0	757	100.0

Table 4–290

Duration of Marriage (in Years) and Frequency of Pleasure (Village Husbands)												
	<=2		3-5		6-10		11-15		16-20		>20	
	NO.	%	NO.	%	NO.	%	NO.	%	NO.	%	NO.	%
Often	10	30.3	12	27.9	13	27.1	8	21.6	16	25.0	25	34.2
Sometimes	19	57.6	29	67.4	32	66.7	28	75.7	42	65.6	44	60.3
Never	4	12.1	2	4.7	3	6.3	1	2.7	6	9.4	4	5.5
Total	33	100.0	43	100.0	48	100.0	37	100.0	64	100.0	73	100.0

Table 4–291

Duration of Marriage (in Years) and Frequency of Pleasure (Village Wives)												
	<=2		3-5		6-10		11-15		16-20		>20	
	NO.	%	NO.	%	NO.	%	NO.	%	NO.	%	NO.	%
Often	25	22.3	44	24.3	75	27.6	46	21.9	36	25.4	32	19.4
Sometimes	79	70.5	122	67.4	179	65.8	148	70.5	94	66.2	119	72.1
Never	8	7.1	15	8.3	18	6.6	16	7.6	12	8.5	14	8.5
Total	112	100.0	181	100.0	272	100.0	210	100.0	142	100.0	165	100.0

Table 4–292

Schnabel[69] of Germany reported that of females, 19 percent experienced sexual pleasure in the first year, another 15 percent in the next year, 11 percent in the third year, 14 percent in the fourth and fifth year, 11 percent from six to nine years, and 9 percent after ten years. There were only 11 percent who had never had sexual orgasm at the time of the survey. In Kinsey's report,[70] similar figures were quoted—63 percent of the women could reach orgasm in the first year, cumulating to 71 percent in the fifth year, 77 percent in the tenth, 81 percent in the fifteenth, and 85

PERCENTAGE OF CITY AND VILLAGE WIVES WHO HAD PLEASURE FROM SEXUAL INTERCOURSE
%
70
60
50
40
30
20
10
0
City wives
Village wives
Guangdong wives
28.9
23.6
37.4
65.0
68.5
60.0
6.1
7.7
2.6
Regular pleasure
Occasional pleasure
Never

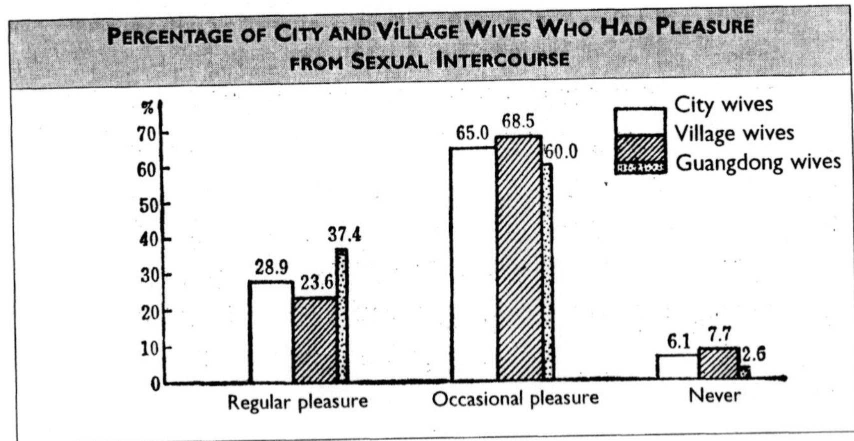

Figure 4–61

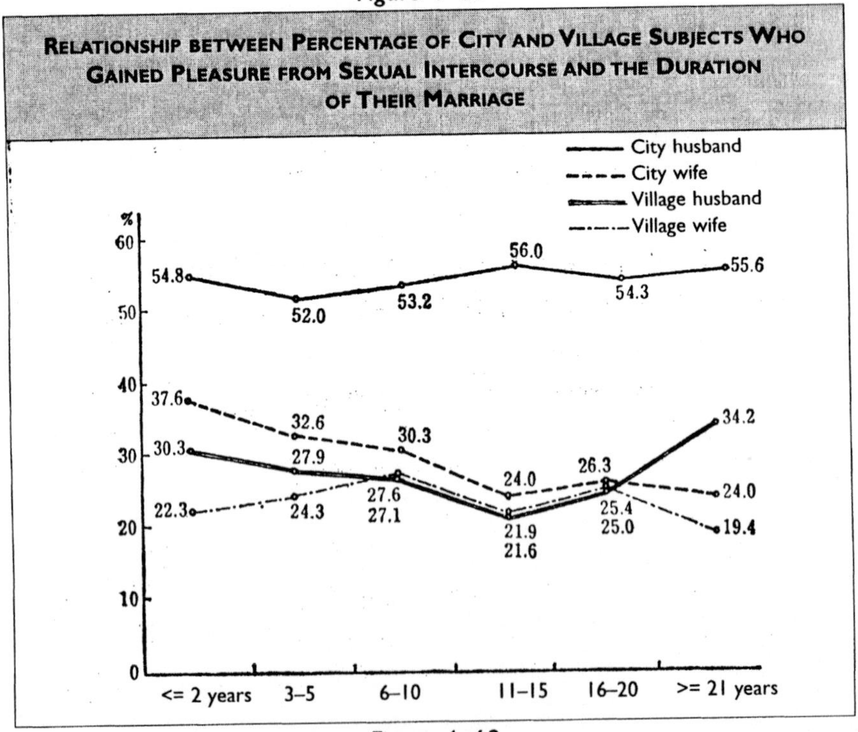

RELATIONSHIP BETWEEN PERCENTAGE OF CITY AND VILLAGE SUBJECTS WHO GAINED PLEASURE FROM SEXUAL INTERCOURSE AND THE DURATION OF THEIR MARRIAGE
City husband
City wife
Village husband
Village wife
%
60
50
40
30
20
10
0
54.8
52.0
53.2
56.0
54.3
55.6
37.6
32.6
30.3
24.0
26.3
24.0
30.3
27.9
27.6
27.1
21.9
21.6
25.4
25.0
34.2
19.4
22.3
24.3
<= 2 years
3–5
6–10
11–15
16–20
>= 21 years

Figure 4–62

percent at the twentieth year. The difference of the Chinese subjects might be due to their heavy workload in their middle years or their misunderstanding of the nature of sexual pleasure.

Age and Pleasure in Sexual Intercourse (City Husbands)										
	<=25		26-35		36-45		46-55		>=56	
	NO.	%	NO.	%	NO.	%	NO.	%	NO.	%
Often	46	36.0	369	55.7	287	51.4	159	43.5	69	53.1
Sometimes	26	35.6	274	41.4	248	44.4	125	42.1	59	45.4
Never	1	1.4	19	2.9	23	4.1	13	4.4	2	1.5
Total	73	100.0	662	100.0	558	100.0	297	100.0	130	100.0

P=0.30

Table 4–293

Age and Pleasure in Sexual Intercourse (City Wives)										
	<=25		26-35		36-45		46-55		>=56	
	NO.	%	NO.	%	NO.	%	NO.	%	NO.	%
Often	96	40.7	521	32.5	373	25.1	140	24.3	28	25.2
Sometimes	126	53.8	993	61.9	1014	68.3	398	69.2	76	68.5
Never	14	5.9	90	5.6	98	6.6	37	6.4	7	6.3
Total	236	100.0	1604	100.0	1485	100.0	575	100.0	111	100.0

P=0.001

Table 4–294

Age and Pleasure in Sexual Intercourse (Village Husbands)										
	<=25		26-35		36-45		46-55		>=56	
	NO.	%	NO.	%	NO.	%	NO.	%	NO.	%
Often	8	38.1	26	25.0	27	25.7	16	33.3	7	35.0
Sometimes	10	47.6	72	69.2	70	66.7	30	62.5	12	60.0
Never	3	14.3	6	5.8	8	7.6	2	4.2	1	5.0
Total	21	100.0	104	100.0	105	100.0	48	100.0	20	100.0

P=0.05

Table 4–295

Age and Pleasure in Sexual Intercourse (Village Wives)										
	<=25		26-35		36-45		46-55		>=56	
	NO.	%	NO.	%	NO.	%	NO.	%	NO.	%
Often	27	24.8	129	23.7	86	25.6	14	17.7	2	14.3
Sometimes	74	67.9	374	68.8	226	67.3	56	70.9	11	78.6
Never	8	7.3	41	7.5	24	7.1	9	11.4	1	7.1
Total	109	100.0	544	100.0	336	100.0	79	100.0	14	100.0

P=0.90

Table 4–296

Education and Pleasure in Sexual Intercourse (City Husbands)										
	ILLITERATE		PRIMARY		J. HIGH		S. HIGH		C. & ABOVE	
	NO.	%	NO.	%	NO.	%	NO.	%	NO.	%
Often	6	54.5	13	36.1	151	44.8	314	50.3	435	63.2
Sometimes	4	36.4	22	1.1	170	50.4	282	45.2	242	35.2
Never	1	9.1	1	2.8	16	4.7	28	4.5	11	1.6
Total	11	100.0	36	100.0	337	100.0	624	100.0	688	100.0

Table 4–297

B. Age

Subjects' age was closely related to years of marriage. The findings about age and sexual pleasure were therefore similar to years of marriage (Tables 4–293 to 4–296).

C. Educational Level

Table 4–297 to 4–300 show the exception of village husbands, whose sexual pleasure increased with the increase of educational level, with the

Education and Pleasure in Sexual Intercourse (City Wives)										
	ILLITERATE		PRIMARY		J. HIGH		S. HIGH		C. & ABOVE	
	NO.	%	NO.	%	NO.	%	NO.	%	NO.	%
Often	4	23.5	35	24.6	339	27.2	513	28.4	256	33.4
Sometimes	12	70.6	97	68.3	830	66.6	1175	65.1	472	61.5
Never	1	5.9	10	7.0	77	6.2	116	6.4	39	5.1
Total	17	100.0	142	100.0	1246	100.0	1804	100.0	767	100.0

Table 4–298

Education and Pleasure in Sexual Intercourse (Village Husbands)										
	ILLITERATE		PRIMARY		J. HIGH		S. HIGH		C. & ABOVE	
	NO.	%	NO.	%	NO.	%	NO.	%	NO.	%
Often	4	36.4	17	27.9	38	30.6	21	24.1	3	25.0
Sometimes	7	63.6	42	68.9	76	61.3	58	66.7	9	75.0
Never	0	0	2	3.3	10	8.1	8	9.2	0	0
Total	11	100.0	61	100.0	124	100.0	87	100.0	12	100.0

Table 4–299

EDUCATION AND PLEASURE IN SEXUAL INTERCOURSE (VILLAGE WIVES)										
	ILLITERATE		PRIMARY		J. HIGH		S. HIGH		C.& ABOVE	
	NO.	%	NO.	%	NO.	%	NO.	%	NO.	%
Often	5	14.3	54	22.2	118	23.7	77	26.2	4	33.3
Sometimes	26	74.3	170	70.0	338	67.9	202	68.7	5	41.7
Never	4	11.4	19	7.8	42	8.4	15	5.1	3	25.0
Total	35	100.0	243	100.0	498	100.0	294	100.0	12	100.0

Table 4–300

G index at 0.25 for city husbands, 0.07 for city wives, 0.08 for village husbands, and 0.09 for village wives.

Similar findings are reported in foreign studies. Kinsey found, for example, that in the first year of marriage, 34 percent of subjects of a junior high school educational level could not reach orgasm, but only 28 percent of senior high school students could not, compared to 24 percent for college level, and 22 percent for postgraduate level. These differences became smaller as the years of marriage reached fifteen years. If women who could reach orgasm in every sexual intercourse were selected, the factor of educational level was even more prominent. For these women during their first year of marriage, 31 percent had a junior high school education, 35 percent senior high school, 39 percent college, and 43 percent postgraduate. This difference persisted even after fifteen years of marriage, with 43 percent at senior high level education and 53 percent at college education.[71] Kinsey's explanation of this correlation was that the more educated women married at a later stage and hence the correlation was primarily with age. However, for our Chinese subjects, age of marriage is similar for different educational levels, and because of a general repression of sexual knowledge, educational level does not correlate with sexual knowledge. This explains why in our data, the relationship of sexual pleasure and educational level is neither clear nor consistent.

D. Sexual Attitudes

Of the city subjects, those who reported frequent sexual pleasure were those who considered sex mostly as the duty of a married couple, or as a psychological or physical need; those who experienced pleasure occasionally saw sex mostly as a routine activity, a duty of the wife, or a necessity for reproduction. Of the village subjects, those who reported frequent sexual pleasure considered sex mostly the duty of the wife, the duty of the married couple, or the physical need of both partners; those who reported occasional sexual pleasure saw sex as a reproductive need, for the mutual psychological or physical satisfaction or for the mutual physical need; those who never had any sexual pleasure were those who took sex mostly as the wife's duty, a routine matter, or a reproductive necessity (tables 4–301 and 4–302).

The findings show that sexual pleasure has a strong relationship with a subject's sexual attitude. For example, those who believed that sex is a psychological or physical need experienced more sexual pleasure, and those who viewed sex as a couple's routine duty or a reproductive necessity had less. Differences in sexual attitudes may be the underlying factor as well for the lower level of sexual pleasure in the village subjects.

View on Sexual Intercourse and Pleasure in Sexual Intercourse (City)

	WIFE'S DUTY		MUTUAL DUTY		MUTUAL PHYSICAL NEED		MUTUAL PSYCHO-PHYSICAL NEED		REPRO-DUCTION		ROUTINE	
	NO.	%	NO.	%	NO.	%	NO.	%	NO.	%	NO.	%
Often	47	28.8	98	38.6	211	34.6	1694	37.6	16	22.9	78	27.7
Sometimes	101	62.0	138	54.3	373	61.1	2590	57.6	43	61.4	180	63.8
Never	15	9.2	18	7.1	26	4.3	215	4.8	11	15.7	24	8.5
Total	163	100.0	254	100.0	610	100.0	4499	100.0	70	100.0	282	100.0

Table 4–301

View on Sexual Intercourse and Pleasure in Sexual Intercourse (Village)

	WIFE'S DUTY		MUTUAL DUTY		MUTUAL PHYSICAL NEED		MUTUAL PSYCHO-PHYSICAL NEED		REPRO-DUCTION		ROUTINE	
	NO.	%	NO.	%	NO.	%	NO.	%	NO.	%	NO.	%
Often	9	47.4	11	26.8	59	25.8	209	24.8	12	17.9	41	23.2
Sometimes	8	42.1	29	70.7	153	66.8	576	68.3	49	73.1	118	66.7
Never	2	10.5	1	2.4	17	7.4	58	6.9	6	9.0	18	10.2
Total	19	100.0	41	100.0	229	100.0	843	100.0	67	100.0	177	100.0

Table 4–302

INITIATOR IN SEX AND SEXUAL PLEASURE (CITY)								
	HUSBAND		WIFE		MUTUAL		CANNOT TELL	
	NO.	%	NO.	%	NO.	%	NO.	%
Often	1433	32.9	39	42.9	508	56.5	169	30.7
Sometimes	2687	61.7	48	52.7	367	40.8	339	61.6
Never	237	5.4	4	4.4	24	2.7	42	7.6
Total	4357	100.0	91	100.0	899	100.0	550	100.0

Table 4–303

INITIATOR IN SEX AND SEXUAL PLEASURE (VILLAGE)								
	HUSBAND		WIFE		MUTUAL		CANNOT TELL	
	NO.	%	NO.	%	NO.	%	NO.	%
Often	179	24.7	20	42.6	92	27.3	50	18.7
Sometimes	495	68.3	25	53.2	230	68.2	183	68.3
Never	51	7.0	2	4.3	15	4.5	35	13.1
Total	725	100.0	47	100.0	337	100.0	268	100.0

Table 4–304

E. Initiative in Sexual Intercourse

Tables 4–303 and 4–304 shows that sexual pleasure is experienced mostly by couples whose sexual intercourse is initiated either mutually or by the wife. This finding is in agreement with the previous finding about sexual satisfaction and initiative in sexual intercourse.

F. Nudity

Sexual pleasure has a strong correlation with nudity during sexual intercourse (G=0.51). Table 4–305 shows that 62.9 percent of couples who

NUDITY IN SEXUAL INTERCOURSE AND PLEASURE							
	TOTAL	OFTEN NUDE		SOMETIMES		NEVER	
		NO.	%	NO.	%	NO.	%
Often	973	612	62.9	336	34.5	25	2.6
Sometimes	3836	1436	27.4	2259	58.9	141	3.7
Never	2407	430	17.9	1736	72.1	241	10.0

Table 4–305

have sexual intercourse in the nude report three times as much sexual pleasure as those who never went completely nude (17.9 percent).

G. First Sexual Partner
Tables 4–306 and 4–307 show that the kind of first sexual partner had a high correlation with sexual pleasure (G=0.25 for city subjects and 0.48 for village subjects). Those whose first sexual intercourse occurred before marriage experienced more sexual pleasure than those who began within marriage. Perhaps the excitement with premarital partners had a positive effect on the ability to experience sexual pleasure in marriage.

Type of First Sexual Partner and Sexual Pleasure (City)

	NON-SPOUSE		SPOUSE	
	NO.	%	NO.	%
Often	101	52.6	1816	36.4
Sometimes	77	40.1	2917	58.5
Never	14	7.3	250	5.0
Total	192	100.0	4983	100.0

Table 4–306

Type of First Sexual Partner and Sexual Pleasure (Village)

	NON-SPOUSE		SPOUSE	
	NO.	%	NO.	%
Often	23	51.1	307	23.9
Sometimes	20	44.4	881	68.7
Never	2	4.4	94	7.4
Total	45	100.0	1282	100.0

Table 4–307

Sexual Positions and Sexual Pleasure

	TOTAL	NEVER		SOMETIMES		OFTEN	
		NO.	%	NO.	%	NO.	%
One only	3088	285	9.2	2165	70.1	638	20.7
Sometimes change	3525	90	2.5	1983	56.3	1452	41.2
Often change	577	15	2.6	173	30.0	389	67.4

P=0.001

Table 4–308

H. Variation in Sexual Intercourse Techniques
Sexual satisfaction is associated positively with variations in sexual techniques (G=0.50). Table 4–308 and figure 4–63 shows that 67.4 percent of couples who changed their sexual intercourse techniques frequently experienced regular sexual satisfaction, while only 20.7 percent of those who used only one technique were satisfied with the results.

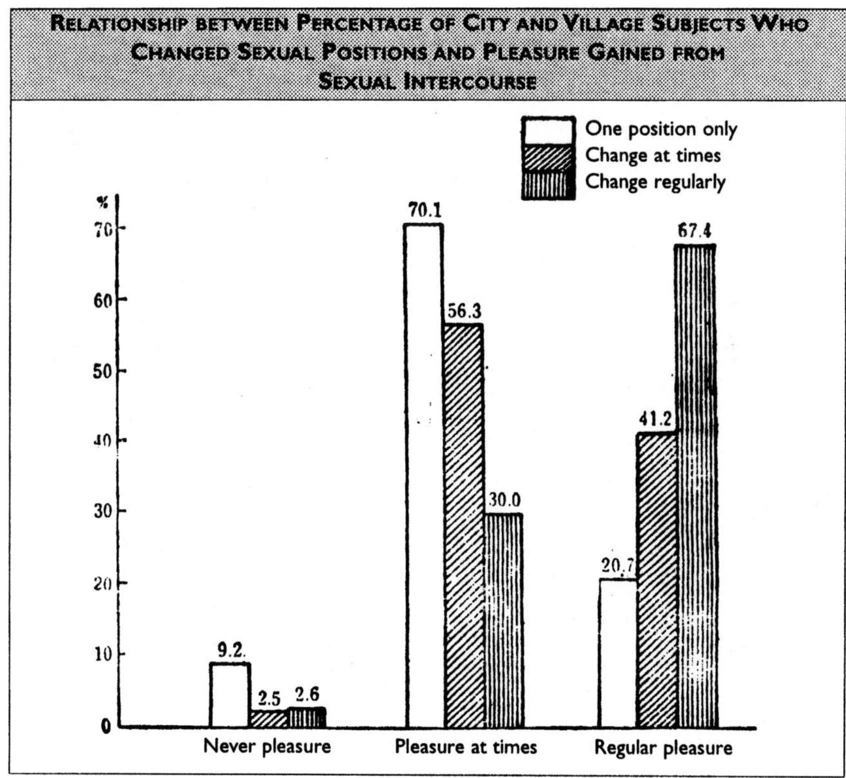

Figure 4–63

6. Marital Changes

We studied some of the common factors which tend to cause marital changes, with the hope that they could be better understood or perhaps even prevented.

1. Extramarital Sex

Extramarital sex or love has been praised or scorned at different times in both the Western or Eastern civilizations.[72] In any case,the Western churches and the Chinese neo-Confucians severely condemned such behavior. In contemporary China, extramarital affairs appear to be on the rise.

In our survey, we asked "How many sexual partners do you have?"[73] If the answer is one, it could be presumed that this is the subject's marital partner; if the answer is more than one, then it could be assumed that the subject has extramarital affairs. Table 4–309 and figure 4–64 show

Number of Sexual Partners Including Spouse

	TOTAL	1		2		3		4		5		UNKNOWN	
		NO.	%	NO.	%	NO.	%	NO.	%	NO.	%	NO.	%
City	6210	5471	88.1	275	4.4	52	0.8	18	0.3	26	0.4	368	5.9
Village	1892	1304	93.7	63	4.5	16	1.1	4	0.3	4	0.3	1	0.1

Table 4–309

Percentage of City and Village Subjects with Different Numbers of Sex Partners

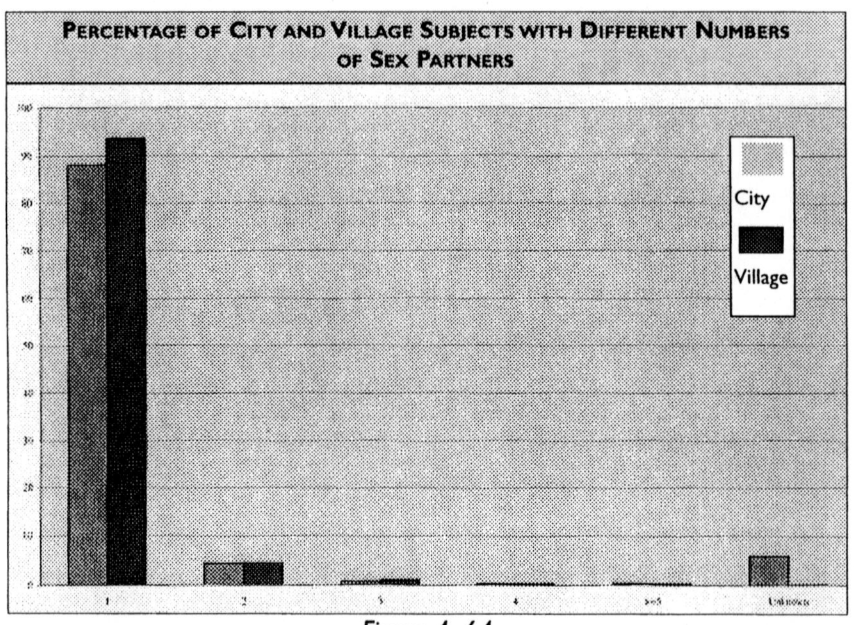

Figure 4–64

Gender and Number of Sex Partners (City)

	TOTAL	1		2		3		4		>=5	
		NO.	%	NO.	%	NO.	%	NO.	%	NO.	%
Male	1732	1556	89.8	121	7.0	32	1.8	10	0.6	13	0.8
Female	3968	3781	95.3	147	3.7	20	0.5	8	0.2	12	0.3

P=0.001

Table 4–310

that the city and village subjects did not differ significantly in the rates of having extramarital sexual partners. If those who did not give any definite answers were excluded, the rates were both around 6.0 percent.

GENDER AND NUMBER OF SEX PARTNERS (VILLAGE)											
	TOTAL	1		2		3		4		>=5	
		NO.	%	NO.	%	NO.	%	NO.	%	NO.	%
Male	301	273	90.7	17	5.6	7	2.3	2	0.7	2	0.7
Female	1087	1028	94.6	46	4.2	9	0.8	2	0.2	2	0.2

P=0.05

Table 4–311

PERCENTAGE OF CITY AND VILLAGE SUBJECTS WITH EXTRAMARITAL SEX PARTNERS

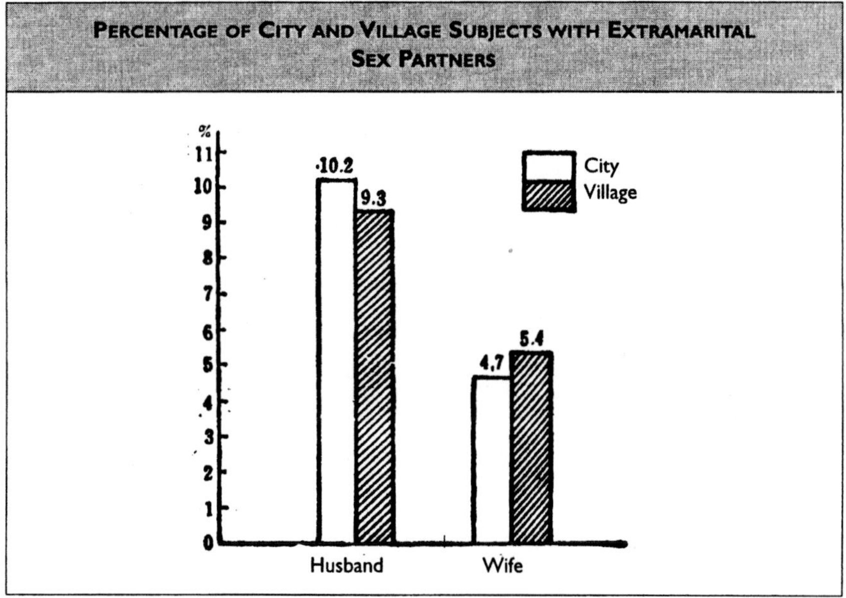

Figure 4–65

Both in the village and city subjects, more males than females had extramarital sex (Tables 4–310 and 4–311)

We also analyzed the factors which could be associated with extramarital sex:

A. EDUCATIONAL LEVEL

Tables 4–312 to 4–315 show that a low level of education is only weakly associated with extramarital sex (G=0.13 for city wives, 0.17 for village husbands and 0.17 for village wives). On the other hand, some well-educated people in China feel a need for what they call "a spiritual partner." These relationships are in fact often sexual.

EDUCATION AND NUMBER OF SEX PARTNERS (CITY HUSBANDS)										
NO. OF PARTNERS	ILLITERATE		PRIMARY		J. HIGH		S. HIGH		C. & ABOVE	
	NO.	%	NO.	%	NO.	%	NO.	%	NO.	%
1	7	70.0	30	83.3	305	89.2	556	91.0	614	90.4
2	2	20.0	5	13.9	24	7.0	39	6.4	43	6.3
3	0	0	1	2.8	10	2.9	8	1.3	11	1.6
4	0	0	0	0	1	0.3	6	1.0	3	0.4
>=5	1	10.0	0	0	2	0.6	2	0.3	8	1.2
Total	10	100.0	36	100.0	342	100.0	611	100.0	679	100.0

Table 4–312

EDUCATION AND NUMBER OF SEX PARTNERS (CITY WIVES)										
NO. OF PARTNERS	ILLITERATE		PRIMARY		J. HIGH		S. HIGH		C. & ABOVE	
	NO.	%	NO.	%	NO.	%	NO.	%	NO.	%
1	16	94.1	121	90.3	1152	94.7	1698	95.8	729	95.9
2	1	5.9	12	9.0	56	4.6	57	3.2	19	2.5
3	0	0	0	0	5	0.4	9	0.5	6	0.8
4	0	0	0	0	1	0.1	2	0.1	4	0.5
>=5	0	0	1	0.7	2	0.2	6	0.3	2	0.3
Total	17	100.0	134	100.0	1216	100.0	1772	100.0	760	100.0

Table 4–313

EDUCATION AND NUMBER OF SEX PARTNERS (VILLAGE HUSBANDS)										
NO. OF PARTNERS	ILLITERATE		PRIMARY		J. HIGH		S. HIGH		C. & ABOVE	
	NO.	%	NO.	%	NO.	%	NO.	%	NO.	%
1	12	92.3	53	86.9	114	91.2	81	93.1	11	91.7
2	1	7.7	4	6.6	6	4.8	4	4.6	1	8.3
3	0	0	2	3.3	3	2.4	2	2.3	0	0
4	0	0	0	0	2	1.6	0	0	0	0
>=5	0	0	2	3.3	0	0	0	0	0	0
Total	13	100.0	61	100.0	125	100.0	87	100.0	12	100.0

Table 4–314

EDUCATION AND NUMBER OF SEX PARTNERS (VILLAGE WIVES)										
NO. OF PARTNERS	ILLITERATE		PRIMARY		J. HIGH		S. HIGH		C. & ABOVE	
	NO.	%	NO.	%	NO.	%	NO.	%	NO.	%
1	34	97.1	224	91.8	477	95.0	282	95.9	11	91.7
2	0	0	13	5.3	21	4.2	11	3.7	1	8.3
3	1	2.9	5	2.0	2	0.4	1	0.3	0	0
4	0	0	1	0.4	1	0.2	0	0	0	0
>=5	0	0	1	0.4	1	0.2	0	0	0	0
Total	35	100.0	244	100.0	502	100.0	294	100.0	12	100.0

Table 4–315

B. OCCUPATION

As for the city husbands, more extramarital sex was found among factory workers, farmers, fishermen, and skilled technicians; as for the city wives, they are service workers, farmers, fisherwomen, and administrators. Of the village husbands those with higher rates of extramarital sex are factory workers, farmers, fishermen, and businessmen; for the village

OCCUPATION AND NUMBER OF SEX PARTNERS (CITY HUSBANDS)								
	FACTORY		AGRICULTURE		SERVICE		COMMERCE	
	NO.	%	NO.	%	NO.	%	NO.	%
1	264	89.5	25	93.3	59	96.7	146	90.1
2	21	7.1	3	10.0	2	3.3	12	7.4
3	7	2.4	1	3.3	0	0	2	1.2
4	2	0.7	1	3.3	0	0	0	0
>=5	1	0.3	0	0	0	0	2	1.2
Total	295	100.0	30	100.0	61	100.0	162	100.0

	OFFICIALS		S. OFFICIAL		PROFESSIONAL		SOLDIERS		OTHERS	
	NO.	%	NO.	%	NO.	%	NO.	%	NO.	%
1	298	92.3	263	90.7	378	87.3	30	100.0	36	87.8
2	19	5.9	20	6.9	35	8.1	0	0	4	9.8
3	4	1.2	4	1.4	11	2.5	0	0	0	0
4	2	0.6	1	0.3	4	0.9	0	0	0	0
>=5	0	0	2	0.7	5	1.2	0	0	1	2.4
Total	323	100.0	290	100.0	433	100.0	30	100.0	41	100.0

Table 4–316

Occupation and Number of Sex Partners (City Wives)

	FACTORY		AGRICULTURE		SERVICE		COMMERCE	
	NO.	%	NO.	%	NO.	%	NO.	%
1	760	94.9	82	94.3	236	93.7	421	94.6
2	33	4.1	5	5.7	13	5.2	19	4.3
3	5	0.6	0	0	1	0.4	4	0.9
4	0	0	0	0	0	0	1	0.2
>=5	3	0.4	0	0	2	0.8	0	0
Total	801	100.0	87	100.0	252	100.0	445	100.0

	OFFICIALS		S. OFFICIAL		PROFESSIONAL		SOLDIERS		OTHERS	
	NO.	%	NO.	%	NO.	%	NO.	%	NO.	%
1	688	95.8	416	94.5	967	96.5	8	100.0	117	93.6
2	25	3.5	18	4.1	24	2.4	0	0	8	6.4
3	2	0.3	3	0.7	5	0.5	0	0	0	0
4	2	0.3	1	0.2	3	0.3	0	0	0	0
>=5	1	0.1	2	0.5	3	0.3	0	0	0	0
Total	718	100.0	440	100.0	1002	100.0	8	100.0	125	100.0

Table 4–317

Occupation and Number of Sex Partners (Village Husbands)

	FACTORY		AGRICULTURE		SERVICE		COMMERCE	
	NO.	%	NO.	%	NO.	%	NO.	%
1	18	85.7	149	89.2	26	96.3	7	87.5
2	2	9.5	12	7.2	0	0	0	0
3	1	4.8	3	1.8	0	0	1	12.5
4	0	0	1	0.6	1	3.7	0	0
>=5	0	0	2	1.2	0	0	0	0
Total	21	100.0	167	100.0	27	100.0	8	100.0

	OFFICIALS		S. OFFICIAL		PROFESSIONAL		SOLDIERS		OTHERS	
	NO.	%	NO.	%	NO.	%	NO.	%	NO.	%
1	14	93.3	24	92.3	12	92.3	3	100.0	16	100.0
2	0	0	1	3.8	1	7.7	0	0	0	0
3	1	6.7	1	3.8	0	0	0	0	0	0
4	0	0	0	0	0	0	0	0	0	0
>=5	0	0	0	0	0	0	0	0	0	0
Total	15	100.0	26	100.0	13	100.0	3	100.0	16	100.0

Table 4–318

OCCUPATION AND NUMBER OF SEX PARTNERS (VILLAGE WIVES)								
	FACTORY		AGRICULTURE		SERVICE		COMMERCE	
	NO.	%	NO.	%	NO.	%	NO.	%
1	208	96.3	543	93.5	84	93.3	23	92.0
2	8	3.7	26	4.5	6	6.7	2	8.0
3	0	0	8	1.4	0	0	0	0
4	0	0	2	0.3	0	0	0	0
>=5	0	0	2	0.3	0	0	0	0
Total	216	100.0	581	100.0	90	100.0	25	100.0

	OFFICIALS		S. OFFICIAL		PROFESSIONAL		SOLDIERS		OTHERS	
	NO.	%	NO.	%	NO.	%	NO.	%	NO.	%
1	24	96.0	41	100.0	42	95.5	0	0	58	98.3
2	1	4.0	0	0	2	4.5	0	0	1	1.7
3	0	0	0	0	0	0	0	0	0	0
4	0	0	0	0	0	0	0	0	0	0
>=5	0	0	0	0	0	0	0	0	0	0
Total	25	100.0	41	100.0	44	100.0	0	0	59	100.0

Table 4–319

wives, they are farmers, fisherwomen, service workers, and businesswomen (Tables 4–316 to 4–319).

C. Age

There is insignificant association between age and the number of extramarital sexual partners (Table 4–320 to 4–323). There is a higher rate of extramarital sexual partners in subjects age below twenty-five or above fifty-six.

AGE AND NUMBER OF SEX PARTNERS (CITY HUSBANDS)										
	<=25		26-35		36-45		46-55		>=56	
	NO.	%	NO.	%	NO.	%	NO.	%	NO.	%
1	63	87.5	597	90.3	495	89.8	268	90.2	106	85.5
2	5	6.9	42	6.4	40	7.3	19	6.4	15	12.1
3	0	0	15	2.3	13	2.4	3	1.0	1	0.8
4	0	0	1	0.2	3	0.5	6	2.0	0	0
>=5	4	5.6	6	0.9	0	0	1	0.3	2	1.6
Total	72	100.0	661	100.0	551	100.0	297	100.0	124	100.0

Table 4–320

AGE AND NUMBER OF SEX PARTNERS (CITY WIVES)										
	<=25		26-35		36-45		46-55		>=56	
	NO.	%	NO.	%	NO.	%	NO.	%	NO.	%
1	211	92.5	1505	95.7	1397	95.9	534	94.2	94	91.3
2	17	7.5	49	3.1	45	3.1	27	4.8	9	8.7
3	0	0	12	0.8	5	0.3	3	0.5	0	0
4	0	0	1	0.1	5	0.3	1	0.2	0	0
>=5	0	0	5	0.3	5	0.3	2	0.4	0	0
Total	228	100.0	1572	100.0	1457	100.0	567	100.0	103	100.0

Table 4–321

AGE AND NUMBER OF SEX PARTNERS (VILLAGE HUSBANDS)										
	<=25		26-35		36-45		46-55		>=56	
	NO.	%	NO.	%	NO.	%	NO.	%	NO.	%
1	18	85.7	95	89.6	97	92.4	44	91.7	19	90.5
2	2	9.5	6	5.7	6	5.7	2	4.2	1	4.8
3	1	4.8	4	3.8	2	1.9	0	0	0	0
4	0	0	1	0.9	0	0	1	2.1	0	0
>=5	0	0	0	0	0	0	1	2.1	1	4.8
Total	21	100.0	106	100.0	105	100.0	48	100.0	21	100.0

Table 4–322

AGE AND NUMBER OF SEX PARTNERS (VILLAGE WIVES)										
	<=25		26-35		36-45		46-55		>=56	
	NO.	%	NO.	%	NO.	%	NO.	%	NO.	%
1	106	96.4	513	94.0	320	95.0	75	93.8	14	100.0
2	4	3.6	26	4.8	13	3.9	3	3.8	0	0
3	0	0	6	1.1	2	0.6	1	1.3	0	0
4	0	0	1	0.2	1	0.3	0	0	0	0
>=5	0	0	0	0	1	0.3	1	1.3	0	0
Total	110	100.0	546	100.0	337	100.0	80	100.0	14	100.0

Table 4–323

For those who have three or more extramarital partners, the female subjects are concentrated mostly in the middle years, while the males spread rather evenly over all age ranges.

VIEW ON SEX FOR LOVE (WITHOUT MARRIAGE) AND NUMBER OF SEX PARTNERS (CITY)						
	AGREE		NOT AGREE		NOT MIND	
	NO.	%	NO.	%	NO.	%
1	493	81.9	4303	95.5	616	92.1
2	64	10.6	171	3.8	37	5.5
3	25	4.2	14	0.3	12	1.8
4	7	1.2	9	0.2	2	0.3
>=5	13	2.2	11	0.2	2	0.3
Total	602	100.0	4508	100.0	669	100.0

Table 4–324

VIEW ON SEX FOR LOVE (WITHOUT MARRIAGE) AND NUMBER OF SEX PARTNERS (VILLAGE)						
	AGREE		NOT AGREE		NOT MIND	
	NO.	%	NO.	%	NO.	%
1	109	92.4	1074	94.0	115	93.5
2	6	5.1	50	4.4	6	4.9
3	0	0	14	1.2	2	1.6
4	2	1.7	2	0.2	0	0
>=5	1	0.8	3	0.3	0	0
Total	118	100.0	1143	100.0	123	100.0

Table 4–325

D. SEXUAL ATTITUDES

There is a strong relationship between sexual attitude and extramarital sex. Tables 4–324 to 4–326 show that those subjects who felt "sex is all right as long as people are in love" or that "sex is unimportant" had more sexual partners than those who did not subscribe to these concepts. The association between extramarital sex is stronger for the city subjects than the village subjects.

E. SEXUAL PLEASURE

The G index between number of extramarital sexual partners and sexual pleasure is 0.31 for city subjects and 0.26 for village. Tables 4–326 and 4–327 also show that the more extramarital sexual partners, the more experience of sexual pleasure. Perhaps those with more partners had a stronger sexual desire and hence more easily experienced sexual pleasure. On the other hand, it could also be that the excitement and novelty of different partners is more conducive to sexual pleasure.

Our findings in this section could be matched with the divorce data in different parts of China in the last few years. In 1985, in Shanghai, Tienjin, Guangzhou, Zhengzhou, and Nanjing, 24 –40 percent of divorce cases involved extramarital affairs. If we assume that about two third of these affairs involved sex, then about 16 to 27 percent of divorce cases dealt with extramarital sex.[74] In 1987, in a town in Yiwu Xian of Zhejiang, 69.2 percent of divorce cases involved etramarital affairs.[75] In Bao'an Xian of Zhenzhun of Guangdong province, the rate in the same year went even up to 91.8 percent.[76]

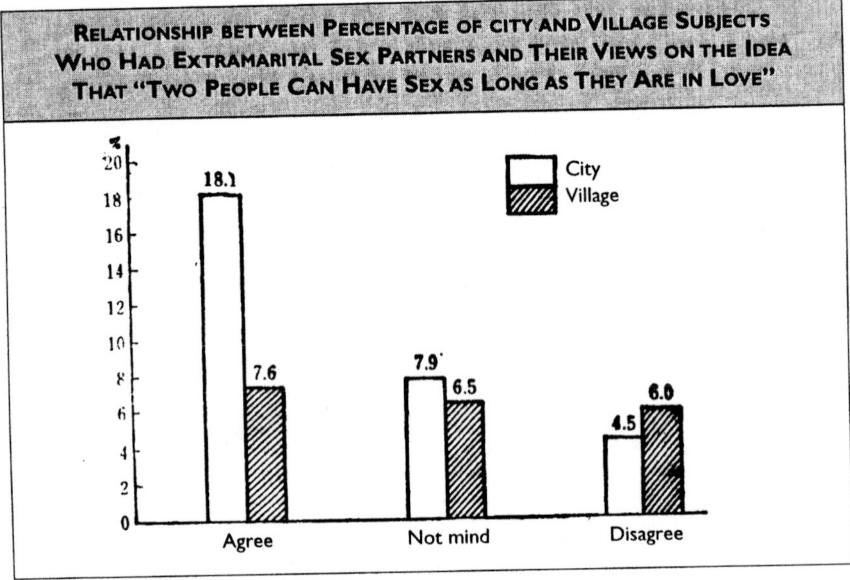

Figure 4–66

Number of Sex Partners and Pleasure in Sex (City)

	1		2		3		4		>=5	
	NO.	%	NO.	%	NO.	%	NO.	%	NO.	%
Often	1915	35.9	119	44.2	31	63.3	12	66.7	19	73.1
Sometimes	3144	58.9	139	51.7	16	32.7	4	22.2	5	19.2
Never	280	5.2	11	4.1	2	4.1	2	11.1	2	7.7
Total	5339	100.0	269	100.0	49	100.0	18	100.0	26	100.0

P=0.001

Table 4–326

Number of Sex Partners and Pleasure in Sex (Village)

	1		2		3		4		>=5	
	NO.	%	NO.	%	NO.	%	NO.	%	NO.	%
Often	309	23.9	17	27.0	10	62.5	3	75.0	3	75.0
Sometimes	888	68.6	42	66.7	6	37.5	1	25.0	1	25.0
Never	98	7.6	4	6.3	0	0	0	0	0	0
Total	1295	100.0	63	100.0	16	100.0	4	100.0	4	100.0

P=0.01

Table 4–327

Similar findings were obtained in other countries. For example, in Russia, an extramarital affair is the third most common cause of divorce, following emotional disharmony, and personality incompatibility. In Bulgaria, it is the first cause, and in Czechoslovakia, it is the second.[77]

In the first Kinsey Report, 75 percent of American males below the age of fifty had sex outside of marriage and at least half had sex with prostitutes on more than one occasion.[78] For extramarital sex, the rate of husbands between ages sixteen to twenty was 37 percent and that of husbands at age fifty was 30 percent.[79] Kinsey estimated that in general 5–10 percent of American husbands used extramarital sex for sexual release and their frequencies were 1.3 times per week for husbands below age 25 and 0.7 times per week from age 36 to 60.[80]

Our findings are similar to Kinsey's, including the higher rates of extramarital sex in the city subjects. Kinsey's explanation was that the less-educated social classes took time to learn the value of remaining faithful to their partners.[81]

In the 1980s, attitudes toward extramarital sex have undergone great changes which may be reflected in the high incidence reported here. In the past, extramarital sex was hardly approved, but table 4–328 shows that of the contemporary city dwellers 53.0 percent think that in the case of a poor relationship with one's partner, extramarital sex is understandable and should not be interfered with. For village subjects, the rate is still as high as 43.9 percent. Table 4–329 shows that females are less tolerant of extramarital sex.

Tables 4–330 to 4–333 show that for the city subjects, the better educated are more tolerant. This phenomenon is less obvious in the village subjects and even less so for the males.

The above tolerance regarding extramarital sex rested on the assumption that one had a poor relationship with one's partner to start with. From the answer to another question which removed this assumption, we

VIEW ON EXTRAMARITAL SEX DUE TO MARITAL DISHARMONY

	TOTAL	UNDER-STANDABLE		NO NEED TO INTERFERE		NOT GLORIOUS		SINFUL		UNKOWN	
		NO.	%	NO.	%	NO.	%	NO.	%	NO.	%
City	6210	1677	27.0	1614	26.0	1958	31.5	843	13.6	118	1.9
Village	1392	371	26.7	240	17.2	501	36.0	274	19.7	6	0.4

Table 4–328

GENDER AND VIEW ON EXTRAMARITAL SEX DUE TO MARITAL DISHARMNONY										
GENDER	TOTAL	UNDER-STANDABLE		NO NEED TO INTERFERE		NOT GLORIOUS		SINFUL	
		NO.	%	NO.	%	NO.	%	NO.	%
Male	2058	654	31.8	541	26.3	606	29.4	257	12.5
Female	5221	1349	25.8	1260	24.1	1788	34.2	824	15.8

P=0.001

Table 4–329

EDUCATION AND VIEW ON EXTRAMARITAL SEX DUE TO MARITAL DISHARMONY (CITY HUSBANDS)										
	ILLITERATE		PRIMARY		J. HIGH		S. HIGH		C. & ABOVE	
	NO.	%	NO.	%	NO.	%	NO.	%	NO.	%
Understandable	1	8.3	11	31.4	122	35.7	188	29.6	246	35.3
No need to interfere	6	50.0	8	22.9	71	20.8	190	29.9	208	29.8
Not glorious	2	16.7	8	22.9	102	29.8	182	28.6	177	25.4
Sinful	3	25.0	8	22.9	47	13.7	76	11.9	66	9.5
Total	12	100.0	35	100.0	342	100.0	636	100.0	697	100.0

Table 4–330

EDUCATION AND VIEW ON EXTRAMARITAL SEX DUE TO MARITAL DISHARMONY (CITY WIVES)										
	ILLITERATE		PRIMARY		J. HIGH		S. HIGH		C.OR ABOVE	
	NO.	%	NO.	%	NO.	%	NO.	%	NO.	%
Understandable	4	21.1	36	24.2	291	22.7	479	26.0	230	29.5
No need to interfere	3	15.8	14	9.4	314	24.5	510	27.7	214	27.5
Not glorious	9	47.4	67	45.0	461	35.9	613	33.3	236	30.3
Sin	3	15.8	32	21.5	218	17.0	241	13.1	99	12.7
Total	19	100.0	149	100.0	1284	100.0	1843	100.0	779	100.0

Table 4–331

learn that an average of 50 percent of the respondents believe that the adulterous person should be dissuaded from continuing the infidelity in order to save the marriage, but the city subjects feel less strongly about saving marriages and favor divorce (Table 4–334). Males are also less tolerant than females. More males (34.1 percent) than females (28.6 percent) opted for a divorce. This is probably because China is still a male-centered society.

EDUCATION AND VIEW ON EXTRAMARITAL SEX DUE TO MARITAL DISHARMONY (VILLAGE WIVES)										
	ILLITERATE		PRIMARY		J. HIGH		S. HIGH		C. & ABOVE	
	NO.	%	NO.	%	NO.	%	NO.	%	NO.	%
Understandable	6	46.2	18	30.0	34	27.9	26	29.9	4	33.3
No need to interfere	2	15.4	9	15.0	21	17.2	13	14.9	2	16.7
Not glorious	4	30.8	24	40.0	41	33.6	26	29.9	3	25.0
Sinful	1	7.7	9	15.0	26	21.3	22	25.3	3	25.0
Total	13	100.0	60	100.0	122	100.0	87	100.0	12	100.0

Table 4–332

EDUCATION AND VIEW ON EXTRAMARITAL SEX DUE TO MARITAL DISHARMONY (VILLAGE HUSBANDS)										
	ILLITERATE		PRIMARY		J. HIGH		S. HIGH		C. & ABOVE	
	NO.	%	NO.	%	NO.	%	NO.	%	NO.	%
Understandable	9	25.7	66	27.0	126	25.1	78	26.5	2	16.7
No need to interfere	10	28.6	32	13.1	93	18.6	56	19.0	1	8.3
Not glorious	12	34.3	99	40.6	195	338.9	90	30.6	6	50.0
Sinful	4	11.4	47	19.3	87	17.4	70	23.8	3	25.0
Total	35	100.0	244	100.0	501	100.0	294	100.0	12	100.0

Table 4–333

ATTITUDE TOWARD SPOUSE WHO COMMITTED ADULTERY															
	TOTAL	DISSUADE		KEEP QUIET		MAKE A FUSS		GO TO COURT		DIVORCE		REVENGE		UNKNOWN	
		NO.	%	NO.	%	NO.	%	NO.	%	NO.	%	NO.	%	NO.	%
City	6210	3250	52.3	184	3.0	62	1.0	390	6.3	2089	33.6	139	2.3	96	1.5
Village	1392	927	66.6	123	88	61	4.4	64	4.6	178	12.8	35	2.5	4	0.3

Table 4–334

Tables 4–336 to 4–339 and figures 4–69 and 4–70 show how that educational level had a rather complicated association with sexual attitudes. Generally, we have found that the more educated an individual is, the more liberal her/his sexual attitudes are. But for the married, the educational level did not appear to have any association with the views of adultery. More city wives chose divorce in case their partners committed adultery, showing that they are the more independent and conscious of their rights.

Gender and Attitude toward Spouse Who Committed Adultery													
	TOTAL	DISSUADE		KEEP QUIET		MAKE A FUSS		GO TO COURT		DIVORCE		REVENGE	
		NO.	%	NO.	%	NO.	%	NO.	%	NO.	%	NO.	%
Male	2054	1021	49.7	92	4.5	33	1.6	146	7.1	700	34.1	62	3.0
Female	5244	3049	58.1	207	3.9	87	1.7	297	5.7	1500	28.6	104	2.0

Table 4–335

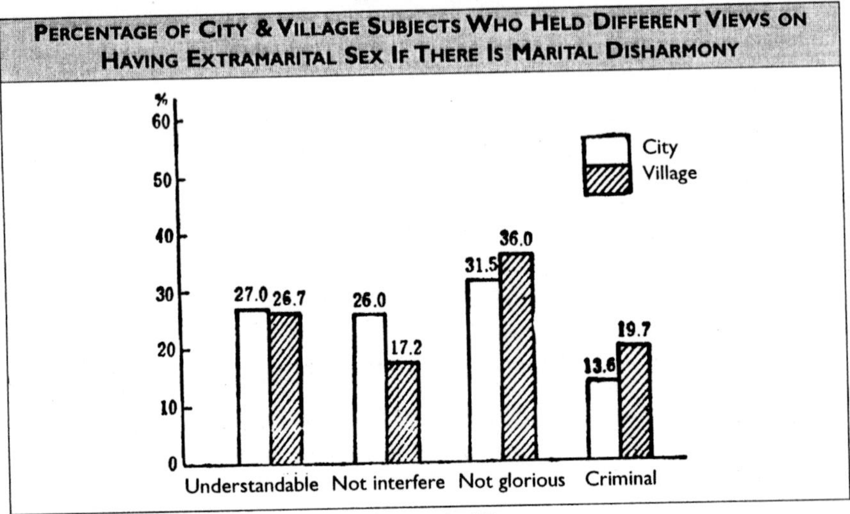

Figure 4–67

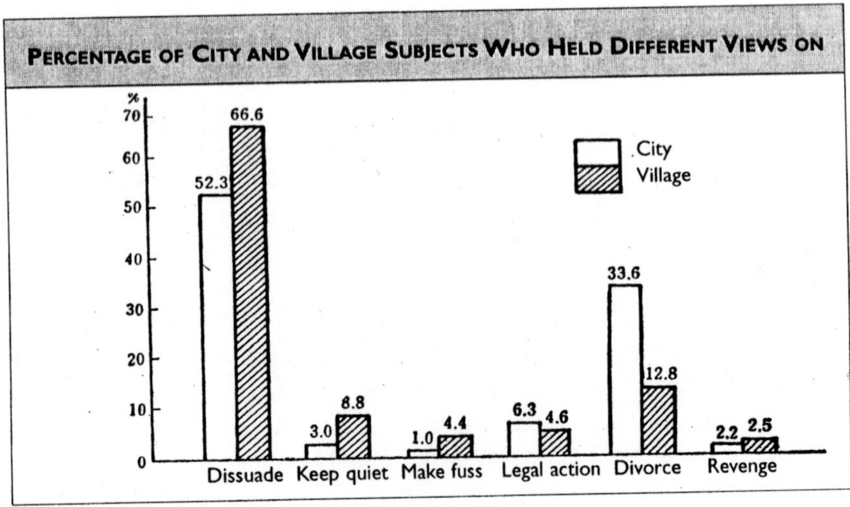

Figure 4–68

EDUCATION AND ATTITUDE TOWARD SPOUSE WHO COMMITTED ADULTERY (CITY HUSBANDS)	ILLITERATE		PRIMARY		J. HIGH		S. HIGH		C. & ABOVE	
	NO.	%	NO.	%	NO.	%	NO.	%	NO.	%
Dissuade	4	33.3	16	45.7	157	45.6	291	45.7	351	50.8
Keep quiet	2	16.7	2	5.7	12	3.5	23	3.6	17	2.5
Make a fuss	0	0	1	2.9	7	2.0	3	0.5	4	0.6
Go to court	0	0	1	2.9	30	8.7	58	9.1	48	6.9
Divorce	4	33.3	14	40.0	126	36.6	236	37.0	260	37.6
Revenge	2	16.7	1	2.9	12	3.5	26	4.1	11	1.6
Total	12	100.0	35	100.0	344	100.0	637	100.0	691	100.0

Table 4–336

EDUCATION AND ATTITUDE TOWARD SPOUSE WHO COMMITTED ADULTERY (CITY WIVES)	ILLITERATE		PRIMARY		J. HIGH		S. HIGH		C. & ABOVE	
	NO.	%	NO.	%	NO.	%	NO.	%	NO.	%
Dissuade	10	52.6	88	58.3	777	60.0	974	52.7	414	52.9
Keep quiet	3	15.8	15	9.9	45	3.5	39	2.1	13	1.7
Make a fuss	1	5.3	3	2.0	18	1.4	17	0.9	6	0.8
Go to court	2	10.5	15	9.9	72	5.6	114	6.2	39	5.0
Divorce	1	5.3	28	18.5	355	27.4	671	36.3	295	37.7
Revenge	2	10.5	2	1.3	28	2.2	33	1.8	15	1.9
Total	19	100.0	151	100.0	1295	100.0	1848	100.0	782	100.0

Table 4–337

EDUCATION AND ATTITUDE TOWARD SPOUSE WHO COMMITTED ADULTERY (VILLAGE HUSBANDS)	ILLITERATE		PRIMARY		J. HIGH		S. HIGH		C. & ABOVE	
	NO.	%	NO.	%	NO.	%	NO.	%	NO.	%
Dissuade	8	61.5	39	66.1	89	71.2	60	69.0	9	75.0
Keep quiet	4	30.8	8	13.6	9	7.2	5	5.7	0	0
Make a fuss	0	0	2	3.4	4	3.2	2	2.3	0	0
Go to court	0	0	5	6.5	6	4.8	3	3.4	0	0
Divorce	1	7.7	4	6.8	13	10.4	16	18.4	2	16.7
Revenge	0	0	1	1.7	4	3.2	1	1.1	1	8.3
Total	13	100.0	59	100.0	125	100.0	87	100.0	12	100.0

Table 4–338

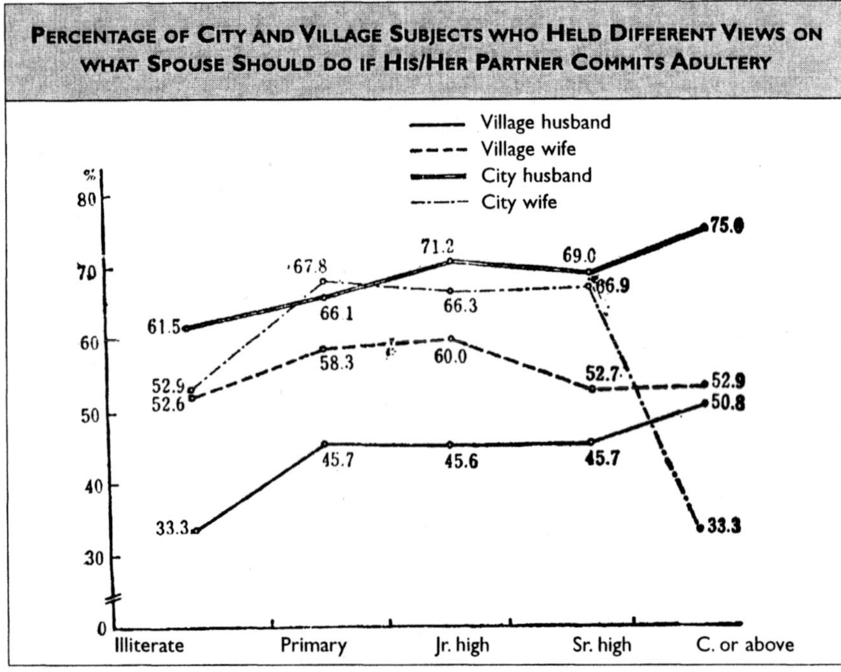

Figure 4–69

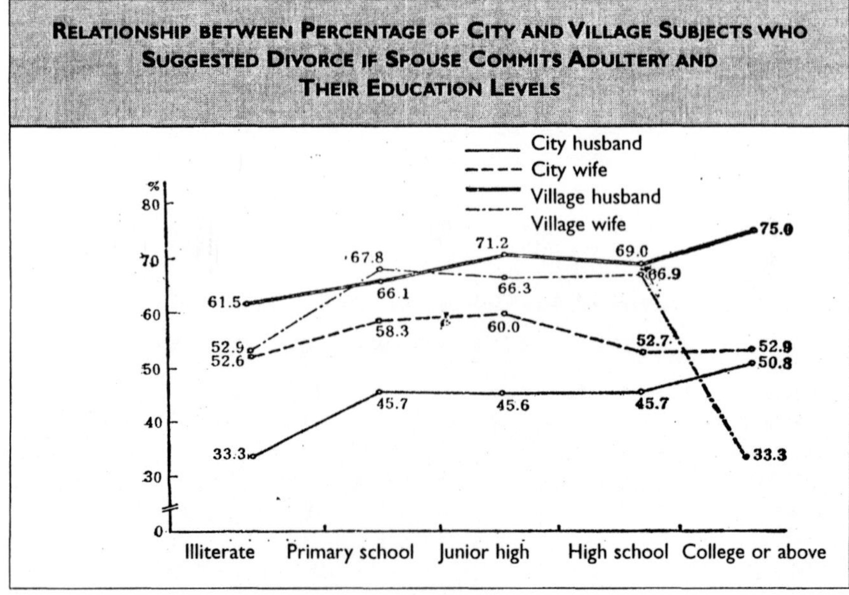

Figure 4–70

Education and Attitude toward Spouse Who Committed Adultery (Village Wives)										
	ILLITERATE		PRIMARY		J. HIGH		S. HIGH		C. & ABOVE	
	NO.	%	NO.	%	NO.	%	NO.	%	NO.	%
Dissuade	18	52.9	166	67.8	333	66.3	196	66.9	4	33.3
Keep quiet	3	8.8	28	11.4	37	7.4	24	8.2	5	41.7
Make a fuss	3	8.8	12	4.9	24	4.8	11	3.8	2	16.7
Go to court	2	5.9	9	3.7	23	4.6	16	5.5	0	0
Divorce	8	23.5	28	11.4	72	14.3	33	11.3	1	8.3
Revenge	0	0	2	0.8	13	2.6	13	4.4	0	0
Total	34	100.0	245	100.0	502	100.0	293	100.0	12	100.0

Table 4–339

Attitude toward the "Third Party"									
GENDER	TOTAL	LEGAL ACTION		SIGN OF PROGRESS		LET IT BE		EDUCATION OR COUNSELING	
		NO.	%	NO.	%	NO.	%	NO.	%
Male	2048	361	17.6	76	3.7	170	8.3	1441	70.3
Female	5228	837	16.0	85	1.6	270	5.2	4036	77.2

P=0.001

Table 4–340

Education and Attitude toward the "Third Party" (City Husbands)										
	ILLITERATE		PRIMARY		J. HIGH		S. HIGH		C. & ABOVE	
	NO.	%	NO.	%	NO.	%	NO.	%	NO.	%
Legal action	4	30.8	15	41.7	76	22.3	120	18.9	84	12.5
Sign of progress	1	7.7	2	5.6	17	5.0	19	3.0	25	3.7
Let it be	0	0	4	11.1	20	5.9	50	7.9	68	10.1
Educate or counsel	8	61.5	15	41.7	228	66.9	447	70.3	514	76.6
Total	13	100.0	36	100.0	341	100.0	636	100.0	671	100.0

Table 4–341

As for the views toward the third party in extramarital affairs (the "home wrecker"), table 4–340 shows that about 70 percent of subjects, with females being in a slight majority, voted for educating and counseling the third party.

In the city subjects, the more educated voted for counseling the third party, but in the village subjects, there was no obvious relationship

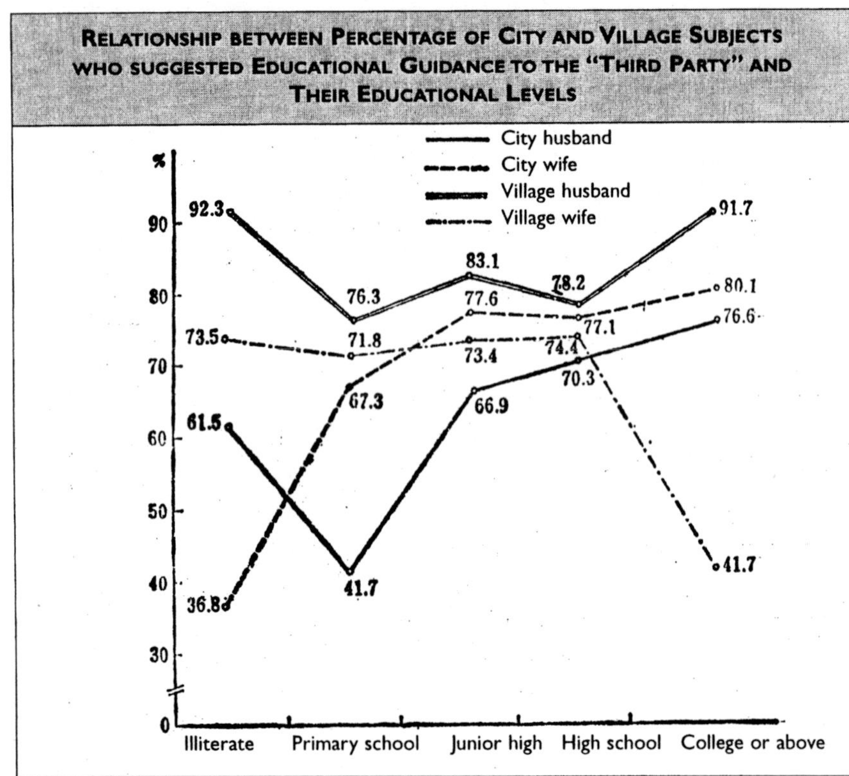

Figure 4–71

EDUCATION AND ATTITUDE TOWARD THE "THIRD PARTY" (CITY WIVES)

	ILLITERATE		PRIMARY		J. HIGH		S. HIGH		C. & ABOVE	
	NO.	%	NO.	%	NO.	%	NO.	%	NO.	%
Legal action	11	57.9	34	22.7	198	15.3	305	16.5	101	13.0
Sign of progress	0	0	4	2.7	28	2.2	25	1.4	7	0.9
Let it be	1	5.3	11	7.3	62	4.8	91	4.9	47	6.0
Educate or counsel	7	36.8	101	67.3	1002	77.6	1421	77.1	624	80.1
Total	19	100.0	150	100.0	1290	100.0	1842	100.0	779	100.0

Table 4–342

between this view and educational level (tables 4–341 to 4–344 and figure 4–71).

Our results show that in China people have gradually become more tolerant and have developed a more understanding attitude toward extramarital sex. However, there is still quite a sizeable part of the

Education and Attitude toward the "Third Party" (Village Husbands)										
	ILLITERATE		PRIMARY		J. HIGH		S. HIGH		C. & ABOVE	
	NO.	%	NO.	%	NO.	%	NO.	%	NO.	%
Legal action	0	0	7	11.9	12	9.7	15	17.2	1	8.3
Sign of progress	0	0	2	3.4	2	1.6	1	1.1	0	0
Let it be	1	7.7	5	8.5	7	5.6	3	3.4	0	0
Educate or counsel	12	92.3	45	76.3	103	83.1	68	78.2	11	91.7
Total	13	100.0	59	100.0	124	100.0	87	100.0	12	100.0

Table 4–343

Education and Attitude toward the "Third Party" (Village Wives)										
	ILLITERATE		PRIMARY		J. HIGH		S. HIGH		C. & ABOVE	
	NO.	%	NO.	%	NO.	%	NO.	%	NO.	%
Legal action	3	8.8	54	22.0	86	17.2	52	17.7	6	50.0
Sign of progress	2	5.9	3	1.2	10	2.0	8	2.7	0	0
Let it be	4	11.8	12	4.9	37	7.4	15	5.1	1	8.3
Educate or counsel	25	73.5	176	71.8	367	73.4	218	74.4	5	41.7
Total	34	100.0	245	100.0	500	100.0	293	100.0	12	100.0

Table 4–344

Attitude toward the Spouse Getting Close to the Other Sex													
	TOTAL	NOT WORRY		MAKE A FUSS		KEEP QUIET		REMIND SPOUSE		FIND THE CAUSE FIRST		UNKNOWN	
		NO.	%	NO.	%	NO.	%	NO.	%	NO.	%	NO.	%
City	6210	2166	34.9	58	0.9	163	2.6	1761	28.4	1977	32.8	85	1.4
Village	1392	419	30.1	71	5.1	74	5.3	331	23.8	491	35.3	6	0.4
Total	7602	2585	34.0	129	1.7	237	3.1	2092	27.5	2468	32.5	91	1.2

Table 4–345

population who cannot accept it. For example, table 4–328 shows that 45.1 percent of the city subjects and 55.7 percent of the village subjects still hold that it is shameful or worse.

In modern China, where the law recognizes only monogamous marriage, society is bound to interfere with extramarital relationships. However, it is the method of interference that is important.

Attitude toward the Spouse Getting Close to the Opposite Sex											
	TOTAL	NOT WORRY		MAKE A FUSS		KEEP QUIET		REMIND SPOUSE		FIND THE CAUSE FIRST	
		NO.	%	NO.	%	NO.	%	NO.	%	NO.	%
Male	2061	827	40.1	39	1.9	57	2.8	530	25.7	608	29.5
Female	5246	1684	32.1	89	1.7	174	3.3	1505	28.7	1794	34.2

Table 4–346

Education and Attitude toward the Spouse Getting Close to the Opposite Sex (City Husbands)										
	ILLITERATE		PRIMARY		J. HIGH		S. HIGH		C. & ABOVE	
	NO.	%	NO.	%	NO.	%	NO.	%	NO.	%
Not worrry	6	46.2	12	34.3	169	49.0	251	39.4	261	37.4
Make a fuss	1	7.7	1	2.9	6	1.7	7	1.1	0	0
Keep quiet	1	7.7	0	0	14	4.1	8	1.3	13	1.9
Remind spouse	1	7.7	8	22.9	68	19.7	182	28.6	213	30.6
Find the cause first	4	30.8	14	40.0	88	25.5	189	29.7	210	30.1
Total	13	100.0	35	100.0	345	100.0	637	100.0	697	100.0

Table 4–347

Education and Attitude toward the Spouse Getting Close to the Opposite Sex (City Wives)										
	ILLITERATE		PRIMARY		J. HIGH		S. HIGH		C.OR ABOVE	
	NO.	%	NO.	%	NO.	%	NO.	%	NO.	%
Not worrry	3	15.8	38	25.2	441	34.0	605	32.7	275	35.0
Make a fuss	2	10.5	5	3.3	16	1.2	14	0.8	3	0.4
Keep quiet	3	15.8	18	11.9	48	3.7	39	2.1	8	1.0
Remind spouse	5	26.3	36	23.8	351	27.1	585	31.6	231	29.4
Find the cause first	6	31.6	54	35.8	440	34.0	608	32.8	268	34.1
Total	19	100.0	151	100.0	1296	100.0	1851	100.0	785	100.0

Table 4–348

Due to the general increase in social contacts and the broadening of social circles, there is now also another type of mixed-gender relationship: Males and females become very close friends with no sex involved. Table 4–346 shows that most city subjects and males do not worry about this. But even the village wives who worry a great deal are few, and their

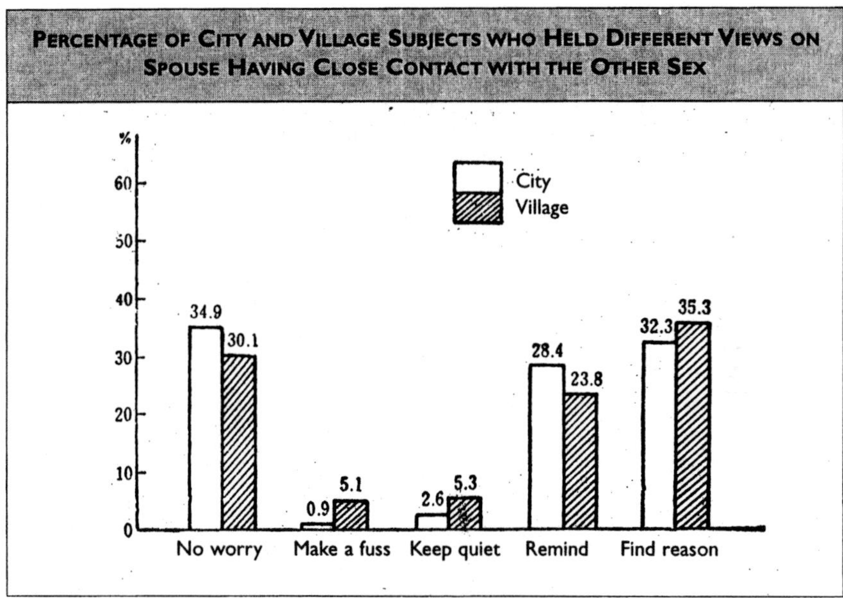

Figure 4–72

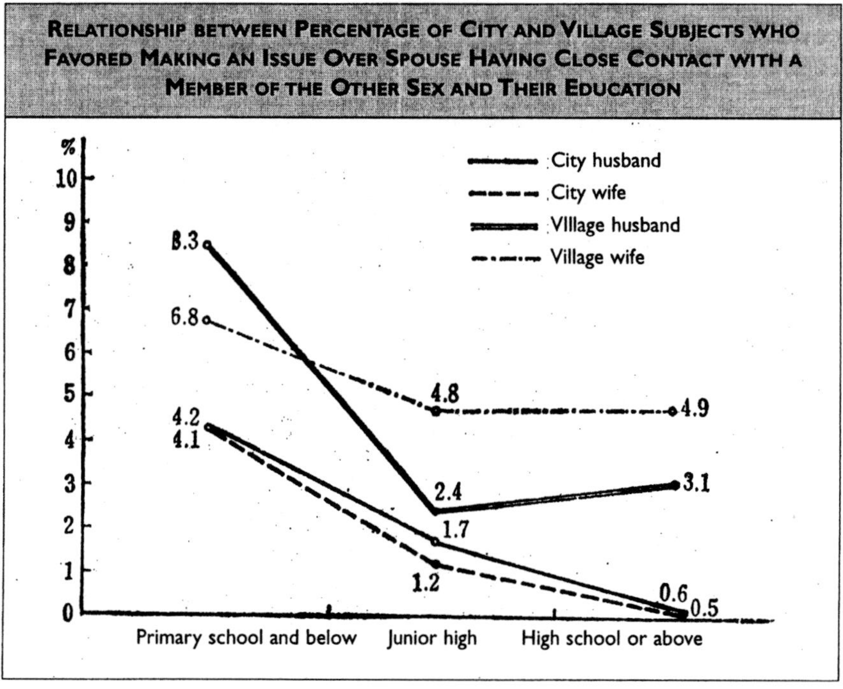

Figure 4–73

EDUCATION AND ATTITUDE TOWARD THE SPOUSE GETTING CLOSE TO THE OTHER SEX (VILLAGE HUSBANDS)										
	ILLITERATE		PRIMARY		J. HIGH		S. HIGH		C. & ABOVE	
	NO.	%	NO.	%	NO.	%	NO.	%	NO.	%
Not worrry	3	32.1	20	33.9	52	41.6	29	33.7	3	25.0
Make a fuss	2	15.4	4	6.8	3	2.4	3	3.5	0	0
Keep quiet	0	0	0	0	3	2.4	2	2.3	0	0
Remind spouse	3	23.1	13	22.0	27	21.6	20	23.3	6	50.0
Find the cause first	5	38.5	22	37.3	40	32.0	32	37.2	3	25.0
Total	13	100.0	59	100.0	125	100.0	86	100.0	12	100.0

Table 4–349

EDUCATION AND ATTITUDE TOWARD THE SPOUSE GETTING CLOSE TO THE OTHER SEX (VILLAGE WIVES)										
	ILLITERATE		PRIMARY		J. HIGH		S. HIGH		C. & ABOVE	
	NO.	%	NO.	%	NO.	%	NO.	%	NO.	%
Not worrry	11	32.4	66	26.9	153	30.5	77	26.3	2	16.7
Make a fuss	1	2.9	18	7.3	24	4.8	13	4.4	2	16.7
Keep quiet	2	5.9	15	6.4	34	6.8	15	5.1	3	25.0
Remind spouse	9	26.5	52	21.2	113	22.6	86	29.4	1	8.3
Find the cause first	11	32.4	94	38.4	177	35.3	102	34.8	4	33.3
Total	34	100.0	245	100.0	501	100.0	293	100.0	12	100.0

Table 4–350

worries are unrelated to their educational level (figure 4–73). It could be that village wives are now more educated and their position in marriage is becoming more elevated.

2. Broken Marriage

According to the teachings of the Neo-Confucians about one thousand years ago, divorce is something to be avoided at all costs, but the modern Chinese are beginning to change their attitude.

1. Increase in Divorce Rates

There is generally an increase in the divorce rate all over the world. It is estimated that in the United States about 40 percent of all marriages will end in divorce.[82] Beginning in the 1980s, it has been said that there is one case of divorce every twenty-seven seconds in America.

The same trend could also be observed in the former USSR. The divorce rate was 3.5 percent 1950, 10 percent in 1960, 18 percent in 1965, 31 percent in 1966, 26 percent in 1971, and rose to 34 percent in 1980.[83] In France, the rate was 23.8 percent in 1981, but 27 percent in 1983.[84] In Germany, the number of divorce cases was 492,128 in 1965, 3,121,370 in 1983, that is a rise from 11.9 percent to 32.8 percent in a matter of 18 years.[85] The divorce rate in East Germany was one in five, in Britain one in seven, in Czechoslovakia one and four[86] and in other European countries it was about the same.

In the past, the Chinese believed that the high divorce rate was due to the problems of Western civilization, because before 1983 or thereabouts, for more than thirty years, the divorce rate in China had remained rather stable at about four hundred thousand cases per year. After 1983 however, there has been a rapid rise by forty thousand per year. By 1986, the rate went beyond five hundred thousand, became 580,000 in 1987, and thus, the divorce rate was one in one thousand.[87] For example, in the province of Kiangsi, if the number of divorce cases was taken to be one hundred in 1981, then the number was 113.01 in 1985, 143.35 in 1985, and 185.47 in 1989.[88]

There are two other special features of interest in our Chinese divorce statistics. First, most divorce cases were initiated by women. For example, in Liaoning, of one thousand cases of divorce in 1981 to 1982, 89..1 percent were filed by women. In the 1980s in Beijing, Tienjin, Shanghai, and Guangdong, about 60 percent of all divorce cases were filed by women. In small cities like Jiaocheng Xian, the rate was 73.4 percent in 1983.[89] The second feature is that there is a rise in negotiated divorces (divorce by mutual consent). In 1981, the national figure for negotiated divorce was 187,000. In 1989, it was 280,000, an increase of 49.7 percent.[90] These features also reflect a change of attitude toward marriage and divorce in China.

B. Social Attitude toward Divorce

Table 4–351 and figure 4–74 show that 87.1 percent of the city subjects and 86.7 percent of the village subjects considered divorce to be shameful or possibly shameful. The percentages were quite close. There were also no significant differences between the male and female subjects (table 4–352). However, more females than males took extreme views on divorce. That is, more of them either accepted or rejected the idea that divorce was shameful, showing that females were generally more sensitive to the idea of divorce.

REGION AND ATTITUDE TOWARD A DIVORCED WOMAN										
	TOTAL	NOT GLORIOUS		NOT A SHAME		NOT MIND		UNKNOWN		
		NO.	%	NO.	%	NO.	%	NO.	%
City	6210	690	11.1	4504	72.5	904	14.6	112	1.8
Village	1392	179	12.9	907	65.2	299	21.5	7	0.5
	7602	869	11.4	5411	71.2	1203	15.8	119	1.6

Table 4–351

PERCENTAGE OF CITY AND VILLAGE SUBJECTS WHO DID OR DID NOT CONSIDER DIVORCE A DISGRACE TO WOMEN

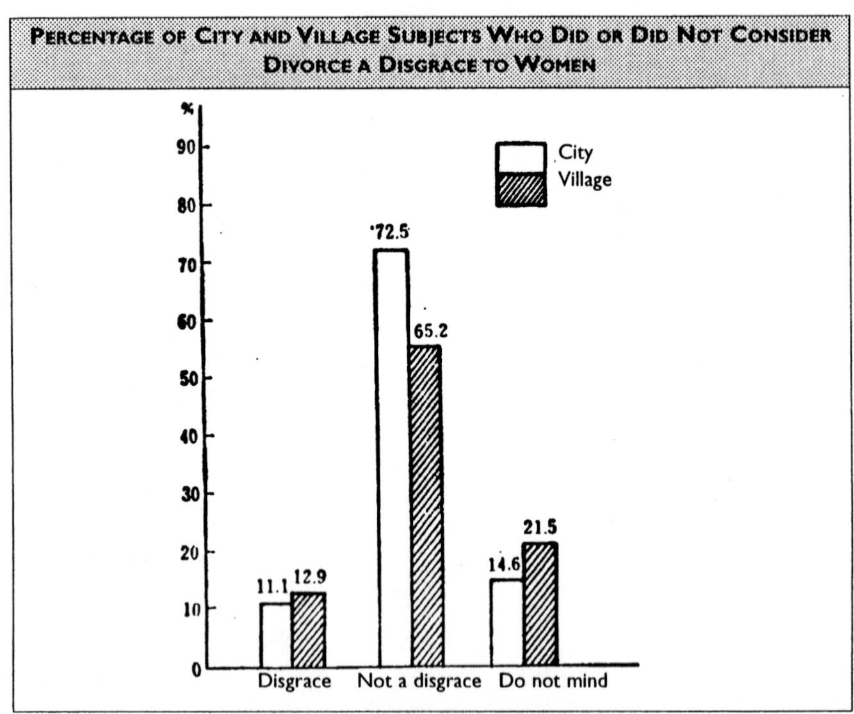

Figure 4–74

Attitudes toward divorce show a significant corrrelation with educational level. Tables 4–353 to 4–356 show that the more educated people are, the more open-minded they are about divorce.

Chinese sociologist Pei Xiao Tong, for example[91] agreed that a rise in divorce rates has nothing to do with moral decadence. Engels[92] even thought that it was moral for a couple to divorce if they were no longer

GENDER AND ATTITUDE TOWARD A DIVORCED WOMAN							
GENDER	TOTAL	NOT GLORIOUS		NOT A SHAME		NOT MIND	
		NO.	%	NO.	%	NO.	%
Male	2048	180	8.8	1419	69.3	449	21.9
Female	5223	651	12.4	3857	73.7	725	13.9

P=0.001

Table 4–352

EDUCATION AND ATTITUDE TOWARD A DIVORCED WOMAN (CITY HUSBANDS)										
	ILLITERATE		PRIMARY		J. HIGH		S. HIGH		C. & ABOVE	
	NO.	%	NO.	%	NO.	%	NO.	%	NO.	%
Not glorious	3	27.3	7	20.6	35	10.2	52	8.2	42	6.1
Not a shame	6	54.5	16	47.1	231	67.5	456	71.6	504	72.8
Not mind	2	18.2	11	32.4	76	22.2	129	20.3	146	21.1
Total	11	100.0	34	100.0	342	100.0	637	100.0	692	100.0

Table 4–353

EDUCATION AND ATTITUDE TOWARD A DIVORCED WOMAN (CITY WIVES)										
	ILLITERATE		PRIMARY		J. HIGH		S. HIGH		C. & ABOVE	
	NO.	%	NO.	%	NO.	%	NO.	%	NO.	%
Not glorious	5	26.3	34	22.7	226	17.5	188	10.2	54	6.9
Not a shame	5	26.3	90	60.0	884	68.8	1475	79.9	629	80.4
Not mind	9	47.4	26	17.3	180	14.0	184	10.0	99	12.7
Total	19	100.0	150	100.0	1290	100.0	1847	100.0	782	100.0

Table 4–354

EDUCATION AND ATTITUDE TOWARD A DIVORCED WOMAN (VILLAGE HUSBANDS)										
	ILLITERATE		PRIMARY		J. HIGH		S. HIGH		C. & ABOVE	
	NO.	%	NO.	%	NO.	%	NO.	%	NO.	%
Not glorious	2	15.4	14	24.1	21	16.8	8	9.2	0	0
Not a shame	8	61.5	30	51.7	76	60.8	64	73.6	8	66.7
Not mind	3	23.1	14	24.1	28	22.4	15	17.2	4	33.3
Total	13	100.0	58	100.0	125	100.0	87	100.0	12	100.0

Table 4–355

EDUCATION AND ATTITUDE TOWARD A DIVORCED WOMAN (VILLAGE WIVES)										
	ILLITERATE		PRIMARY		J. HIGH		S. HIGH		C. & ABOVE	
	NO.	%	NO.	%	NO.	%	NO.	%	NO.	%
Not glorious	1	2.9	39	16.0	65	13.0	28	9.6	1	8.3
Not a shame	19	55.9	159	65.2	343	68.5	185	63.1	10	83.3
Not mind	14	41.2	46	18.9	93	18.6	80	27.3	1	8.3
Total	34	100.0	244	100.0	501	100.0	293	100.0	12	100.0

Table 4–356

RELATIONSHIP BETWEEN PERCENTAGE OF CITY AND VILLAGE SUBJECTS WHO FELT THAT DIVORCE WAS NOT A DISGRACE TO WOMEN AND THEIR EDUCATIONAL LEVEL

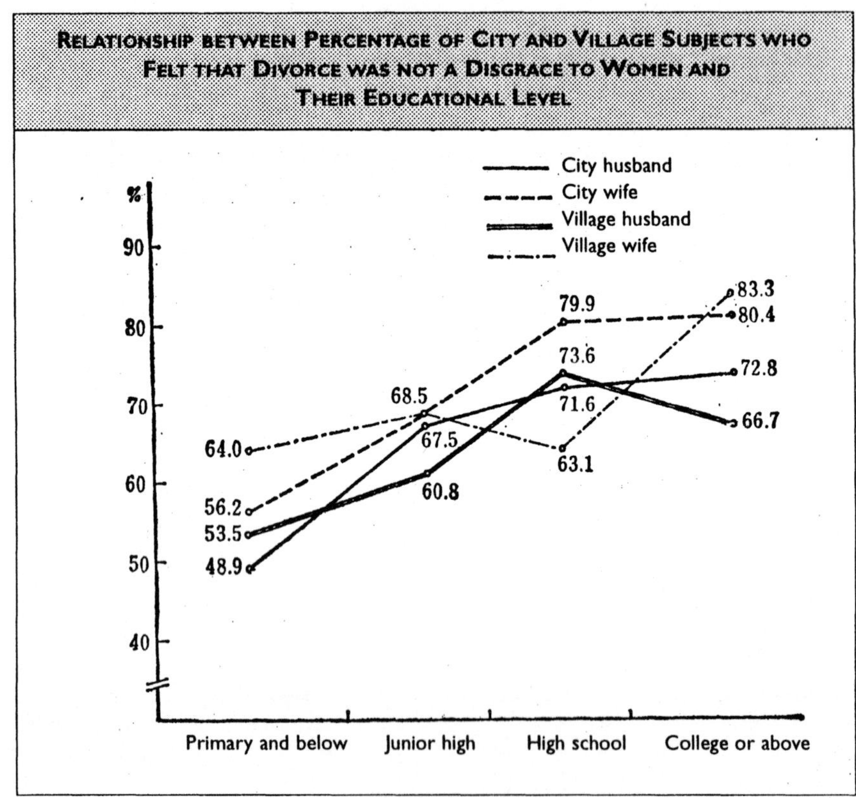

Figure 4–75

in love. Russell had similar ideas, taking into account the welfare of the children.[93] It appears that the modern Chinese are becoming aware of this type of thinking and no longer consider all divorce shameful and immoral.

7. Other Aspects of Married Sexual Life

1. Birth Control

Today the threat of overpopulation in China is serious. Fertility control is a basic policy of the Chinese government, and its success depends very much on the people's attitude toward fertility.

AIM OF REPRODUCTION

	TOTAL	FOR OLD AGE		HEIR		ADD MANPOWER		A BLESSING	
		NO.	%	NO.	%	NO.	%	NO.	%
City	6210	850	13.7	301	4.8	53	0.9	26	0.4
Village	1392	425	30.5	232	16.7	34	2.4	25	1.8

	ADD FUN		SOCIAL DUTY		NOT THOUGHT OF IT		OTHERS		UNKNOWN	
	NO.	%	NO.	%	NO.	%	NO.	%	NO.	%
City	2160	34.8	2312	37.2	378	6.1	37	0.6	93	1.5
Village	94	6.8	462	33.2	114	8.2	5	0.4	1	0.1

Table 4–357

A. Aim of Reproduction

Table 4–357 shows that of the city subjects, 34.8 percent took reproduction as a means of adding interest to life, and 37.2 percent took it as a social duty. For village subjects, the two most important aims were to find care during old age (30.5 percent) and to continue the family name (16.7 percent). It shows that although in many aspects of sexual behavior, village subjects resemble city subjects, on the issue of reproduction, the hold very different views. The reason could be financial, since the villagers lack retirement pensions or other forms of financial support in old age.

B. Number and Gender of Children Hoped For

Table 4–358 shows that about 80 percent of both city and village subjects hoped for one son and one daughter. As for the "one child policy," 66.2 percent of the city subjects and 48.5 percent of the village subjects considered it acceptable and strongly supported it. This shows that the government has been quite successful in the promotion of the one-child con-

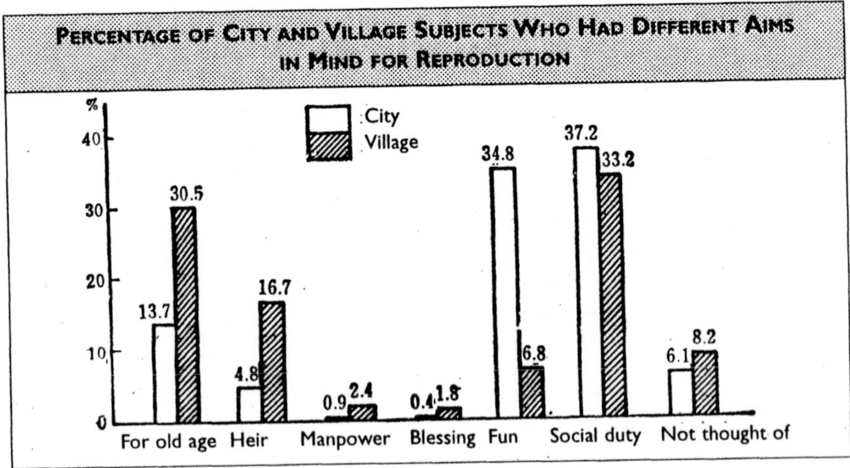

Figure 4–76

IDEAL NUMBER AND GENDER OF CHILDREN

	TOTAL	NONE		ONE SON		ONE DAUGHTER		ONE SON & ONE DAUGHTER	
		NO.	%	NO.	%	NO.	%	NO.	%
City	6210	109	1.8	437	7.0	535	8.6	4695	75.6
Village	1392	3	0.2	36	2.6	60	4.3	1123	80.7

	TWO SONS		TWO DAUGHTERS		MANY		LEAVE TO NATURE		UNKNOWN	
	NO.	%	NO.	%	NO.	%	NO.	%	NO.	%
City	42	0.7	49	0.8	27	0.4	255	4.1	61	1.0
Village	32	2.3	18	1.3	29	2.1	90	6.5	1	0.1

Table 4–358

ATTITUDE TOWARD ONE CHILD POLICY

	TOTAL	CORRECT & SUPPORT		ACCEPT RELUCTANTLY		NOT CORRECT		UNKNOWN	
		NO.	%	NO.	%	NO.	%	NO.	%
City	6210	4112	66.2	1770	28.5	186	3.0	142	2.3
Village	1392	675	48.5	644	46.3	69	5.0	4	0.3

Table 4–359

ATTITUDE IF ONLY CHILD IS A DAUGHTER										
	TOTAL	ONE IS ENOUGH		ONE MORE IF POLICY ALLOWS		ONE MORE EVEN IF PENALTY		UNKNOWN		
		NO.	%	NO.	%	NO.	%	NO.	%
City	6210	3674	59.2	2205	35.5	50	0.8	281	4.5
Village	1392	467	33.5	839	60.3	83	6.0	3	0.2

Table 4–360

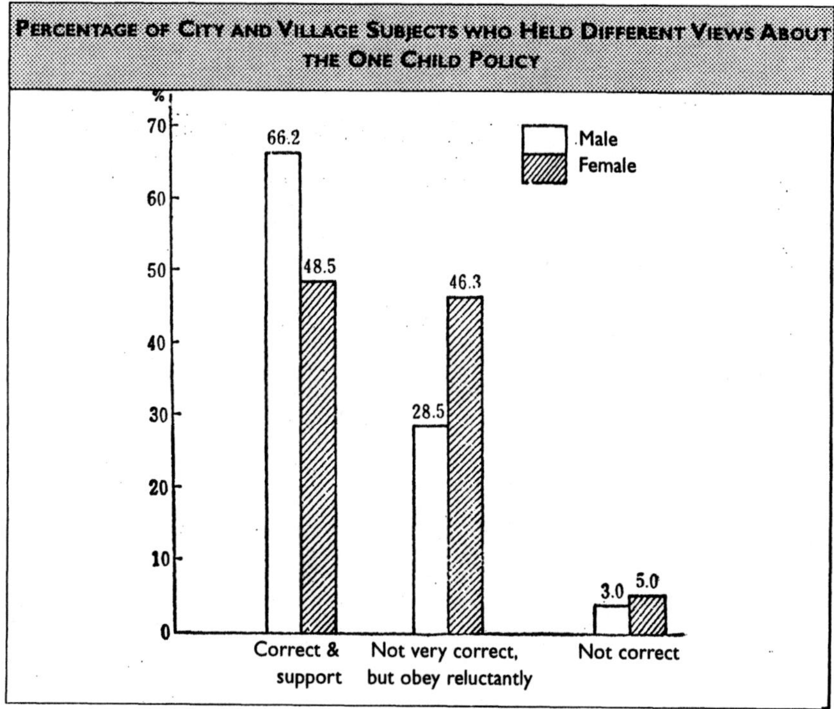

Figure 4–77

cept. The reported personal wishes do not necessarily contradict this, but rather express some abstract ideal.

Yet, table 4–360 shows that if the subjects had a daughter as their first child, 35.5 percent of the city subjects and 60.3 percent of the village subjects said that if the policy allowed, they would try to have a second child. Furthermore, 0.8 percent of the city dwellers and 6.0 percent of the villagers went further and said they would try to have a second child even in the face of punishment. This is a matter for serious concern.[94]

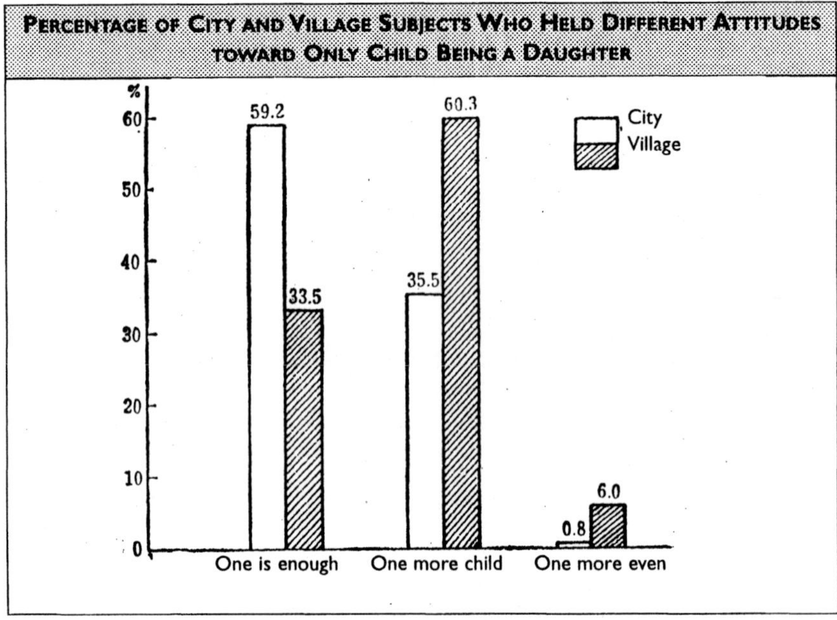

Figure 4–78

Our findings are in agreement with similar studies. In 1987, the Chinese Academy of Social Science and Social Science Research Center conducted a family survey in villages of fourteen provinces. Of 6733 subjects, 388 replied that they hoped to have one child, 3131 (46.5 percent)

CONTRACEPTIVE METHODS

	TOTAL	TUBAL LIGATION		VASECTOMY		IUD		PILLS		EXTERNAL APPLICATION	
		NO.	%	NO.	%	NO.	%	NO.	%	NO.	%
City	6210	585	9.4	144	2.3	2657	42.8	365	5.9	1135	18.3
Village	1392	303	21.8	17	1.2	707	50.8	105	7.5	71	5.4

	SAFE PERIOD		COITUS INTERUPTUS		NONE		OTHERS		UNKNOWN	
	NO.	%	NO.	%	NO.	%	NO.	%	NO.	%
City	563	9.1	106	1.7	358	5.8	119	1.9	178	2.9
Village	56	4.0	10	0.7	89	6.4	25	1.8	9	0.6

Table 4–361

hoped for two children, 1319 (20.7 percent) for three, 1085 (16.1 percent) for four, 282(4.2 percent) for five, 136 (2 percent) for six.[95]

A similar study conducted in Beijing city and other small Szechuan towns also showed similar results.[96]

C. Contraception

Both in the city and the village, the most commonly used contraceptive method is the diaphragm (table 4–361). This could be due to patriarchal ideas still persisting in China. There were still 5.8 percent of the city subjects and 6.4 percent of the village subjects who did not use any contraceptive methods, showing that contraceptive education is still in need of reinforcement.

2. Domestic Work

Table 4–362 shows that most couples shared domestic work, i.e., 53.6 percent of the city subjects and 65.8 percent of the village subjects. In the villages, many couples do their production works also at home. This may explain the slightly higher percentage for the village couples who share work at home. Another obvious finding, however, is that for a much higher percentage of couples, wives did more work than the husbands. Also, for a much higher percentage of couples, wives did all the housework. This shows that the traditional Chinese concept "The man works outside of the home and the woman works inside" is still alive for some people.

Share of Housework														
	TOTAL	WIFE MORE		HUSBAND MORE		EQUAL SHARE		ALL WIFE		ALL HUSBAND		UNKNOWN	
		NO.	%	NO.	%	NO.	%	NO.	%	NO.	%	NO.	%
City	6210	2021	32.5	587	9.5	3330	53.6	207	3.3	28	0.5	37	0.6
Village	1392	347	24.9	77	5.5	916	65.8	43	3.1	4	0.3	5	0.4

Table 4–362

We also explored the relationship of some other factors to the type of sharing in domestic work by the couples.

A. Affection Between the Couples

Table 4–363 shows that the better the couple's affection was within their relationship, the higher the percentage of housework sharing occurred housework (Figure 4–80).

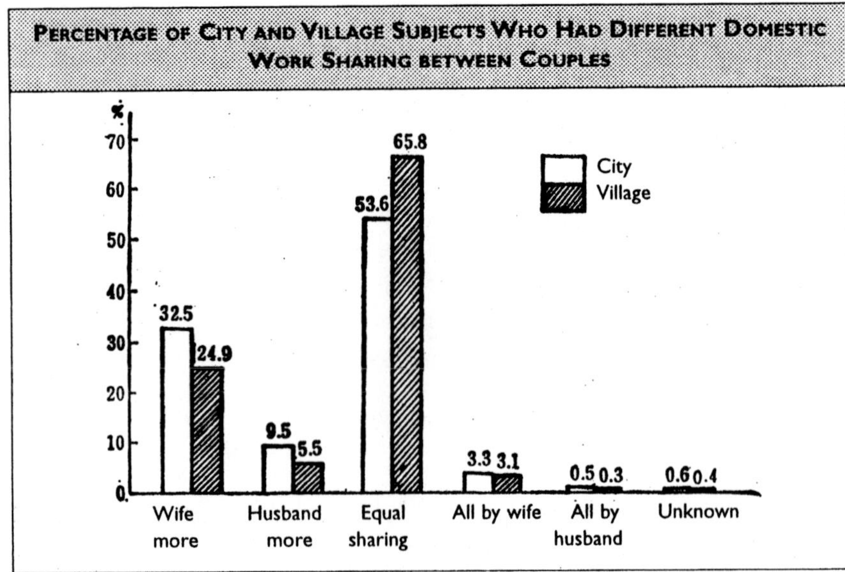

Figure 4–79

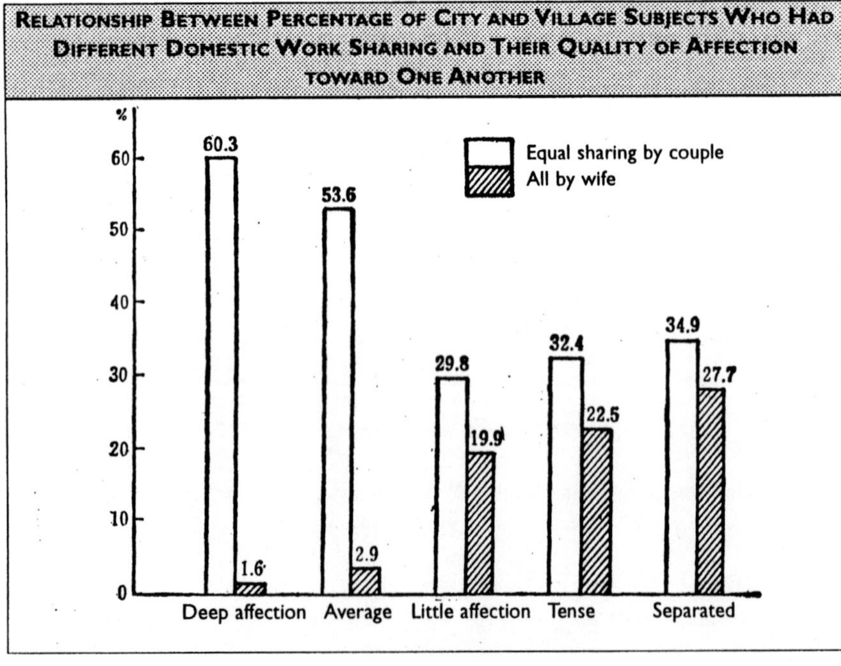

Figure 4–80

COUPLE'S RELATIONSHIP AND SHARE OF HOUSEWORK											
RELATION	TOTAL	WIFE MORE		HUSBAND MORE		EQUAL SHARE		ALL WIFE		ALL HUSBAND	
		NO.	%	NO.	%	NO.	%	NO.	%	NO.	%
Good	4309	1250	29.0	382	8.9	2600	60.3	67	1.6	10	0.2
Fair	2642	908	34.4	232	8.8	1416	53.6	77	2.9	9	0.3
Poor	151	61	40.4	15	9.9	45	29.8	30	19.9	0	0
Tense	71	27	38.0	3	4.2	16	22.5	23	22.4	2	2.8
Separated	83	23	27.7	6	7.2	23	27.7	29	34.9	2	2.4
Cannot tell	247	80	32.4	19	7.7	120	48.6	19	7.7	9	3.6

Table 4–363

MARITAL SATISFACTION AND SHARE OF HOUSEWORK											
MARITAL SATISFACTION	TOTAL	WIFE MORE		HUSBAND MORE		EQUAL SHARE		ALL WIFE		ALL HUSBAND	
		NO.	%	NO.	%	NO.	%	NO.	%	NO.	%
Good	4555	1318	28.9	379	8.3	2782	61.1	68	1.5	8	0.2
Fair	2353	824	35.0	221	9.4	1221	51.8	79	3.4	8	0.3
Poor	890	106	36.6	32	11.0	77	26.6	67	23.1	8	2.7
Cannot tell	342	113	33.0	31	9.1	156	45.6	35	10.2	7	2.0

Table 4–364

AGE AND SHARE OF HOUSEWORK (CITY HUSBANDS)										
SHARE OF WORK	<=25		26-35		36-45		46-55		>=56	
	NO.	%	NO.	%	NO.	%	NO.	%	NO.	%
Wife more	15	20.0	233	34.5	215	37.5	126	41.0	63	48.8
Husband more	6	8.0	69	10.2	55	9.6	22	7.2	4	3.1
Equal	52	69.3	350	51.8	291	50.7	149	48.5	56	43.4
All by wife	2	2.7	16	2.4	11	1.9	8	2.6	6	4.7
All by husband	0	0	8	1.2	2	0.3	2	0.7	0	0
Total	75	100.0	676	100.0	574	100.0	307	100.0	129	100.0

P=0.001

Table 4–365

Table 4–364 shows that the higher the degree of marital satisfaction, the higher the percentage of couples who shared housework.

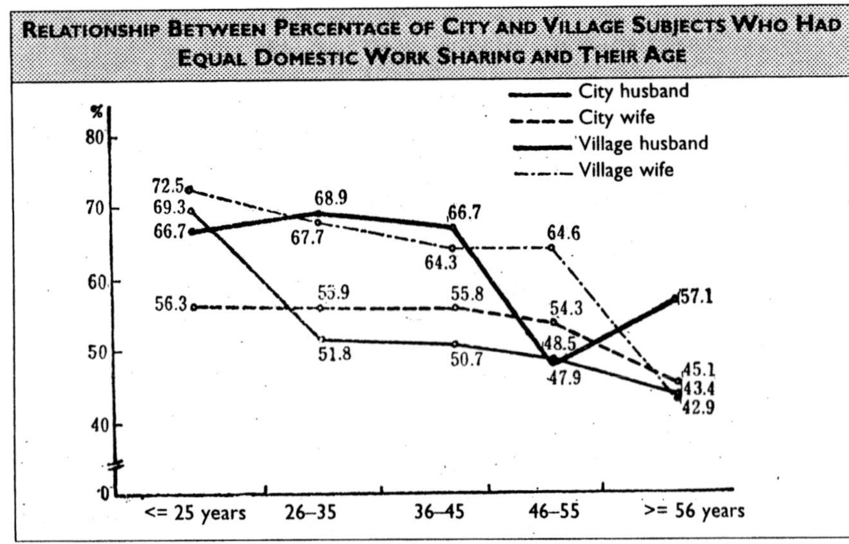

Figure 4–81

AGE AND SHARE OF HOUSEWORK (CITY WIVES)										
SHARE OF WORK	<=25		26-35		36-45		46-55		>=56	
	NO.	%	NO.	%	NO.	%	NO.	%	NO.	%
Wife more	68	28.3	490	29.9	494	32.0	197	31.9	43	35.2
Husband more	27	11.3	175	10.7	137	8.9	49	7.9	13	10.7
Equal	135	56.3	918	55.9	860	55.8	335	54.3	55	45.1
All by wife	10	4.2	51	3.1	49	3.2	33	5.3	8	6.6
All by husband	0	0	7	0.4	2	0.1	3	0.5	3	2.5
Total	240	100.0	1641	100.0	1542	100.0	617	100.0	122	100.0

P=0.001

Table 4–366

AGE AND SHARE OF HOUSEWORK (VILLAGE HUSBANDS)										
SHARE OF WORK	<=25		26-35		36-45		46-55		>=56	
	NO.	%	NO.	%	NO.	%	NO.	%	NO.	%
Wife more	3	14.3	25	23.6	24	22.9	17	35.4	5	23.8
Husband more	3	14.3	6	5.7	9	8.6	2	4.2	3	14.3
Equal	14	66.7	73	68.9	70	66.7	23	47.9	12	57.1
All by wife	1	4.8	2	1.9	2	1.9	6	12.5	1	4.8
All by husband	0	0	0	0	0	0	0	0	0	0
Total	21	100.0	106	100.0	105	100.0	48	100.0	21	100.0

P=0.10

Table 4–367

AGE AND SHARE OF HOUSEWORK (VILLAGE WIVES)										
SHARE OF WORK	<=25		26-35		36-45		46-55		>=56	
	NO.	%	NO.	%	NO.	%	NO.	%	NO.	%
Wife more	21	19.3	132	24.2	91	27.1	24	30.4	5	35.7
Husband more	8	7.3	28	5.1	17	5.1	0	0	1	7.1
Equal	79	72.5	369	67.7	216	64.3	51	64.6	6	42.9
All by wife	1	0.9	14	2.6	11	3.3	4	5.1	1	7.1
All by husband	0	0	2	00.4	1	0.3	0	0	1	7.1
Total	109	100.0	545	100.0	336	100.0	79	100.0	14	100.0

P=0.01

Table 4–368

EDUCATION AND SHARE OF HOUSEWORK (CITY HUSBANDS)										
SHARE OF WORK	ILLITERATE		PRIMARY		J. HIGH		S. HIGH		C. & ABOVE	
	NO.	%	NO.	%	NO.	%	NO.	%	NO.	%
Wife more	5	38.5	14	38.9	134	38.5	248	38.1	251	35.9
Husband more	1	7.7	2	5.6	37	10.6	60	9.4	54	7.7
Equal	5	38.5	15	41.7	161	46.3	317	49.7	382	54.6
All by wife	2	15.4	4	11.1	12	3.4	15	2.4	9	1.3
All by husband	0	0	1	2.8	4	1.1	3	0.5	4	0.6
Total	13	100.0	36	100.0	348	100.0	638	100.0	700	100.0

Table 4–369

EDUCATION AND SHARE OF HOUSEWORK (CITY WIVES)										
SHARE OF WORK	ILLITERATE		PRIMARY		J. HIGH		S. HIGH		C. & ABOVE	
	NO.	%	NO.	%	NO.	%	NO.	%	NO.	%
Wife more	10	52.6	61	39.6	440	33.5	551	29.6	226	28.8
Husband more	0	0	9	5.8	131	10.0	185	9.9	73	9.3
Equal	4	21.1	67	43.5	680	51.8	1070	57.5	461	58.7
All by wife	4	21.1	15	9.7	55	4.2	50	2.7	24	3.1
All by husband	1	5.3	2	1.3	6	0.5	4	0.2	2	0.3
Total	19	100.0	154	100.0	1312	100.0	1860	100.0	786	100.0

Table 4–370

B. AGE

Tables 4–365 to 4–368 show that the younger the couple, the higher the percentage of shared housework. For the older age groups, there

EDUCATION AND SHARE OF HOUSEWORK (VILLAGE HUSBANDS)										
SHARE OF WORK	ILLITERATE		PRIMARY		J. HIGH		S. HIGH		C. & ABOVE	
	NO.	%	NO.	%	NO.	%	NO.	%	NO.	%
Wife more	6	46.2	15	24.6	26	20.8	20	23.0	6	50.0
Husband more	3	23.1	10	16.4	7	5.6	2	2.3	1	8.3
Equal	4	30.8	31	50.8	89	71.2	63	72.4	3	25.0
All by wife	0	0	5	8.2	3	2.4	2	2.3	2	16.7
All by husband	0	0	0	0	0	0	0	0	0	0
Total	13	100.0	6	100.0	125	100.0	87	100.0	12	100.0

Table 4–371

EDUCATION AND SHARE OF HOUSEWORK (VILLAGE WIVES)										
SHARE OF WORK	ILLITERATE		PRIMARY		J. HIGH		S. HIGH		C. & ABOVE	
	NO.	%	NO.	%	NO.	%	NO.	%	NO.	%
Wife more	8	22.9	58	24.0	126	25.1	73	24.9	8	66.7
Husband more	1	2.9	14	5.8	27	5.4	10	3.4	2	16.7
Equal	23	65.7	162	66.9	330	35.9	204	69.6	2	16.7
All by wife	2	5.7	7	2.9	16	3.2	6	2.0	0	0
All by husband	1	2.9	1	0.4	2	0.4	0	0	0	0
Total	35	100.0	242	100.0	501	100.0	293	100.0	12	100.0

Table 4–372

were higher percentages of couples with wives doing most or all of the daily housework.

C. EDUCATIONAL LEVEL

For the city couples, the highly educated couples shared housework more (table 4–369) and had less percentage of wives doing most or all of the housework. For the village couples, the more educated wives did more housework. This is difficult to explain, but could be due simply to the small sample of educated wives in the villages (table 4–372).

In table 3–369, there is another significant finding. The more educated the city husbands were, the more the couples shared housework. For the village couples, the higher educated couples shared housework more except that for couples where the husbands were college graduates, the more their wives had to do housework.

In general, it has to be realized that housework is quite burdensome for most couples in China because of a lack of modern household tools or even a lack of electrical power. A survey in the early eighties showed that in households with modern equipment a couple had to spend on the average three hours and thirty-five minutes per day on housework. In those with less adequate facilities, the average time was four hours and forty-four minutes.[97]

In Shanghai, a survey of 146 married female workers found that 57.5 percent of them had no older relatives to help them or they had to take care of their older relatives. They had to do a mean of three to four hours of housework after their day time work, with a maximum of eight hours per day for some. Another finding showed that 46.6 percent had a low attendance rate at their day time workplace and 75.4 percent had to give up recreation time or their social life.[98]

In Tienjin, of one thousand female workers surveyed, 841 had their work performance adversely affected by their housework, and all of them had been warned and investigated.[99]

In Henan, of 1,316 female workers surveyed, 43.9 percent spent three to four hours per day for housework, 41.8 percent spent more than four hours.

Where heavy housework is required, the wives usually do more of it than the husbands. According to a survey in Helungjiang, on an average working day, the husbands did 3.3 to 3.5 hours per day of housework while the wives spent 3.9 to 4.7 hours. On holidays, the hours were 6.5 to 7.3 for the husbands and 8.7 to 9.1 for the wives.[100] In Tienjin in 1985, the relative work hours between wives and husbands were 265:195 for shopping, 414:67 for laundry, 366:91 for cooking, 163:36

Chief Cause of Marital Conflicts

	TOTAL	CHILDREN		HOUSEWORK		DAILY MATTERS		FINANCE		TEMPER	
		NO.	%	NO.	%	NO.	%	NO.	%	NO.	%
City	6210	1474	23.7	461	7.4	1562	25.1	220	3.5	583	9.4
Village	1392	223	16.0	164	11.8	463	33.3	83	6.0	116	8.3

	RELATIVES		HABITS		SOCIAL		SEX		OTHERS		UNKNOWN	
	NO.	%	NO.	%	NO.	%	NO.	%	NO.	%	NO.	%
City	452	7.3	369	5.9	212	3.4	106	1.7	214	3.4	557	9.0
Village	108	7.8	131	9.4	44	3.2	15	1.1	21	1.5	24	1.7

Table 4–73

GENDER AND CAUSE OF MARITAL CONFLICTS (CITY)											
	TOTAL	CHILDREN		HOUSEWORK		DAILY MATTERS		FINANCE		TEMPER	
		NO.	%	NO.	%	NO.	%	NO.	%	NO.	%
Male	1670	360	21.6	119	7.1	498	29.8	86	5.1	192	11.5
Female	3834	1069	27.9	329	8.6	1028	26.8	124	3.2	376	9.8

	RELATIVES		HABITS		SOCIAL		SEX		OTHERS	
	NO.	%	NO.	%	NO.	%	NO.	%	NO.	%
Male	139	8.3	124	7.4	72	4.3	35	2.1	45	2.7
Female	304	7.9	238	6.2	132	3.4	68	1.8	166	4.3

P=0.001

Table 4–374

GENDER AND CAUSE OF MARITAL CONFLICTS (VILLAGE)											
	TOTAL	CHILDREN		HOUSEWORK		DAILY MATTERS		FINANCE		TEMPER	
		NO.	%	NO.	%	NO.	%	NO.	%	NO.	%
Male	297	45	15.2	37	12.5	99	33.3	24	8.1	35	11.8
Female	1068	178	16.7	127	11.9	764	34.1	58	5.4	80	7.5

	RELATIVES		HABITS		SOCIAL		SEX		OTHERS	
	NO.	%	NO.	%	NO.	%	NO.	%	NO.	%
Male	18	6.1	23	7.7	10	3.4	3	1.0	3	1.0
Female	89	8.3	108	10.1	34	3.2	12	1.1	18	1.7

P=0.30

Table 4–375

for baby-sitting, 87:122 for helping with children's studies, 96:65 for caring for sick members in the family, 554:16 for dress making, and 20:80 for other kinds of housework.[101]

3. Other Marital Conflicts

There are conflicts between married couples which do not threaten the marriage. Table 4–373 shows that problems with the children were the most common cause, 23.7 percent for the city subjects, 16.0 percent for the village. Conflicts due to sexual problems were quite few, being 1.9 percent of all the conflicts for the city subjects and 1.1 for the

MARITAL SATISFACTION AND CAUSE OF MARITAL CONFLICTS (CITY)										
	CHILDREN		HOUSEWORK		DAILY MATTERS		FINANCE		TEMPER	
	NO.	%	NO.	%	NO.	%	NO.	%	NO.	%
Good	1012	68.8	255	56.0	1036	66.4	93	42.3	134	23.0
Fair	416	28.3	172	37.8	469	30.1	92	41.8	299	51.4
Poor	17	1.2	9	2.0	17	1.1	15	6.8	96	16.5
Cannot tell	27	1.8	19	4.2	38	2.4	20	9.1	53	9.1
Total	1472	100.0	455	100.0	1560	100.0	220	100.0	582	100.0
	RELATIVES		HABITS		SOCIAL		SEX		OTHERS	
	NO.	%	NO.	%	NO.	%	NO.	%	NO.	%
Good	247	54.9	190	51.9	109	51.4	32	30.2	117	54.7
Fair	168	37.3	138	37.7	79	37.3	37	34.9	39	18.2
Poor	9	2.0	20	5.5	10	4.7	20	18.9	38	17.8
Cannot tell	26	5.8	18	4.9	14	6.6	17	16.0	20	9.3
Total	450	100.0	366	100.0	212	100.0	106	100.0	214	100.0

Table 4–376

MARITAL SATISFACTION AND CAUSE OF MARITAL CONFLICTS (VILLAGE)										
	CHILDREN		HOUSEWORK		DAILY MATTERS		FINANCE		TEMPER	
	NO.	%	NO.	%	NO.	%	NO.	%	NO.	%
Good	161	72.2	103	62.8	331	71.5	49	59.0	29	25.0
Fair	48	21.5	51	31.1	108	23.3	22	26.5	62	53.4
Poor	1	0.4	3	1.8	4	0.9	5	6.0	16	13.8
Cannot tell	13	5.8	7	4.3	20	4.3	7	8.4	9	7.8
Total	223	100.0	164	100.0	463	100.0	83	100.0	116	100.0
	RELATIVES		HABITS		SOCIAL		SEX		OTHERS	
	NO.	%	NO.	%	NO.	%	NO.	%	NO.	%
Good	69	63.9	91	69.5	21	47.7	8	53.3	20	95.2
Fair	33	30.6	25	19.1	14	31.8	4	26.7	0	0
Poor	2	1.9	4	3.1	2	4.5	2	13.3	1	4.8
Cannot tell	4	3.7	11	8.4	7	15.9	1	6.7	0	0
Total	108	100.0	131	100.0	44	100.0	15	100.0	21	100.0

Table 4–377

village. This does not mean that sexual problems were rare for them, but rather that the subjects had a high tolerance with regard to sexual problems. Tables 4–374 and 4–375 show that males and females did not differ significantly in the rate of causes of these conflicts.

More city subjects, however, mentioned problems with children as a cause of conflict. It could be because they had higher expectation than the village subjects of their children. In the city, more wives had conflicts because of their children, indicating that they had even higher expectations than their husbands of their children.

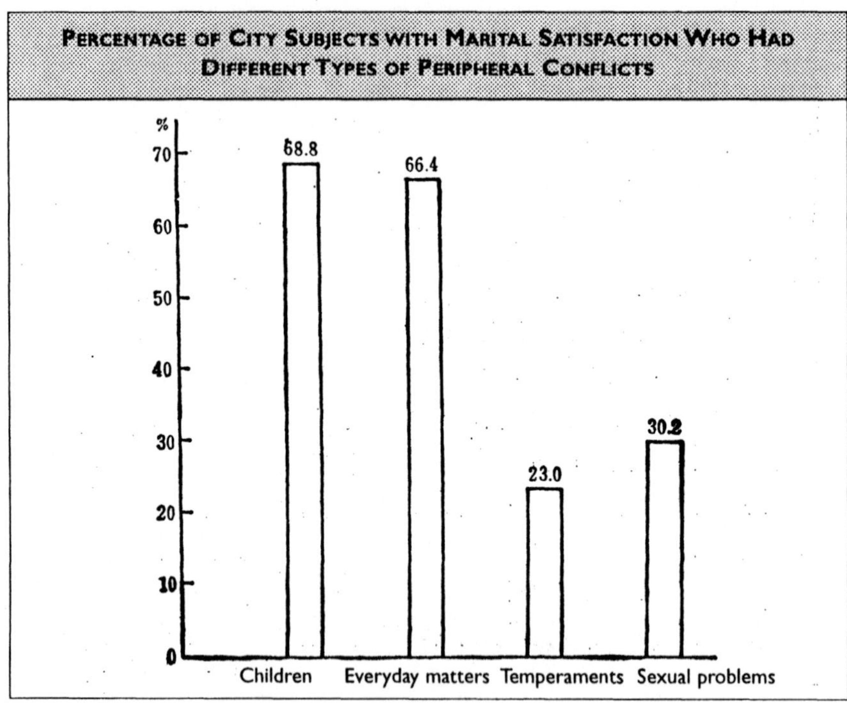

Figure 4–82

We also explored the association of following factors on the occurrence of marital conflicts:

A. Marital Satisfaction

Some marital conflicts had significant relationship with marital satisfaction, some others had not. Tables 4–376 and 4–377 shows that for both the city and village subjects, children problems and domestic trivialities were associated with high marital satisfaction, and incompatible personality and sexual problems were associated with poor satisfaction.

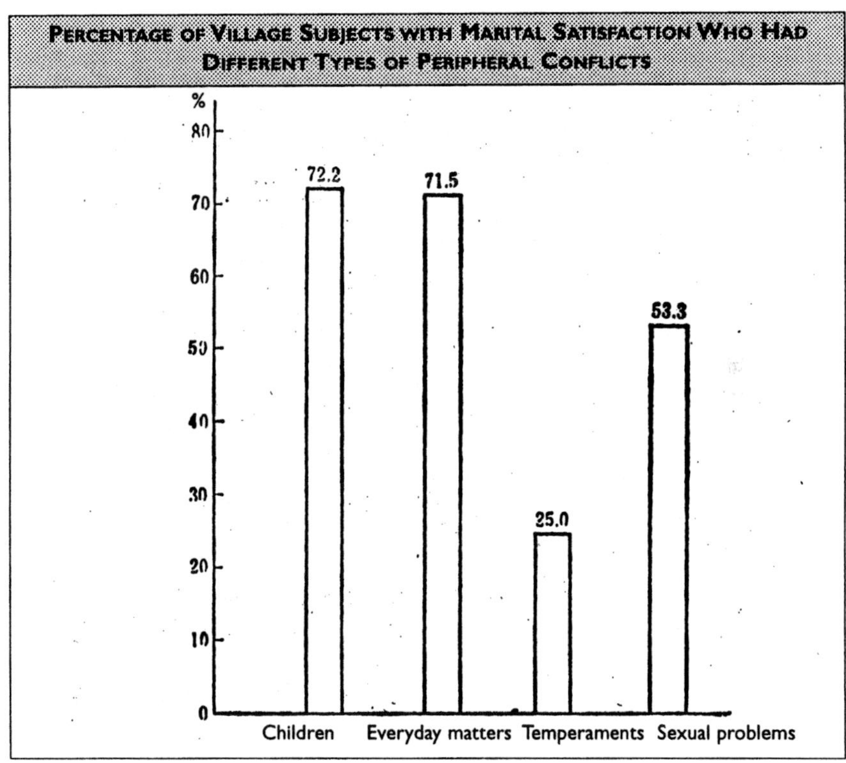

Figure 4–83

EDUCATION AND CAUSE FOR PERIPHERAL MARITAL CONFLICTS (CITY HUSBANDS)	ILLITERATE		PRIMARY		J. HIGH		S. HIGH		C. & ABOVE	
	NO.	%	NO.	%	NO.	%	NO.	%	NO.	%
Children	1	9.1	12	37.5	69	22.0	131	22.1	133	20.0
Housework	1	9.1	1	3.1	33	10.5	45	7.6	34	5.1
Daily matters	1	9.1	9	28.1	90	28.8	166	27.9	215	32.3
Finance	4	36.4	4	12.5	19	6.1	33	5.6	25	3.8
Temper	2	18.2	2	6.3	33	10.5	67	11.3	81	12.2
Relative	0	0	1	3.1	23	7.3	47	7.9	63	9.5
Habits	1	9.1	1	3.1	20	6.4	45	7.6	56	8.4
Social	1	9.1	2	6.3	11	3.5	26	4.4	30	4.5
Sex	0	0	0	0	8	2.6	13	2.2	13	2.0
Others	0	0	0	0	7	2.2	21	3.5	16	2.4
Total	11	100.0	32	100.0	313	100.0	594	100.0	666	100.0

Table 4–378

EDUCATION AND CAUSE OF MARITAL CONFLICTS (CITY WIVES)										
	ILLITERATE		PRIMARY		J. HIGH		S. HIGH		C. & ABOVE	
	NO.	%	NO.	%	NO.	%	NO.	%	NO.	%
Children	5	26.3	26	19.0	349	29.4	468	27.5	196	27.1
Housework	2	10.5	13	9.5	100	8.4	148	8.7	61	8.4
Daily matters	4	21.1	31	22.6	332	28.0	457	26.9	183	25.3
Finance	1	5.3	11	8.0	47	4.0	50	2.9	14	1.9
Temper	2	10.5	18	13.1	109	9.2	173	10.2	70	9.7
Relative	2	10.5	12	8.8	93	7.8	133	7.8	59	8.2
Habits	0	0	8	5.8	48	4.0	112	6.6	67	9.3
Social	0	0	6	4.4	31	2.6	63	3.7	29	4.0
Sex	2	10.5	4	2.9	20	1.7	27	1.6	14	1.9
Others	1	5.3	8	5.8	57	4.8	70	4.1	29	4.0
Total	19	100.0	137	100.0	1186	100.0	1701	100.0	722	100.0

Table 4–379

EDUCATION AND CAUSE OF MARITAL CONFLICTS (VILLAGE HUSBANDS)										
	ILLITERATE		PRIMARY		J. HIGH		S. HIGH		C. & ABOVE	
	NO.	%	NO.	%	NO.	%	NO.	%	NO.	%
Children	3	23.1	12	20.0	17	13.8	10	11.6	3	25.0
Housework	0	0	4	6.7	16	13.0	15	17.4	1	8.3
Daily matters	6	46.2	15	25.0	46	37.4	28	32.6	3	25.0
Finance	0	0	5	8.3	11	8.9	5	5.8	2	16.7
Temper	3	23.1	8	13.3	17	13.8	6	7.0	1	8.3
Relative	1	7.7	3	5.0	3	2.4	11	12.8	0	0
Habits	0	0	5	8.3	8	6.5	8	9.3	2	16.7
Social	0	0	4	6.7	4	3.3	2	2.3	0	0
Sex	0	0	3	5.0	0	0	0	0	0	0
Others	0	0	1	1.7	1	0.8	1	1.2	0	0
Total	13	100.0	60	100.0	123	100.0	86	100.0	12	100.0

Table 4–380

B. Educational Level

There was a low correlation between educational level and rate of marital conflict in both the city and village subjects. If considered together with marital satisfaction, it can be seen that in those with a low educational level (below junior high school), there were more marital conflicts which were associated with low marital satisfaction. For the higher educated, the common conflicts were not those which could lower marital satisfaction (table 4–378 to 4–381).

EDUCATION AND CAUSE OF MARITAL CONFLICTS (VILLAGE WIVES)										
	ILLITERATE		PRIMARY		J. HIGH		S. HIGH		C. & ABOVE	
	NO.	%	NO.	%	NO.	%	NO.	%	NO.	%
Children	5	14.7	40	16.7	81	16.5	50	17.1	2	16.7
Housework	2	5.9	33	13.8	59	12.0	33	11.3	0	0
Daily matters	11	32.4	80	33.3	164	33.5	102	34.9	7	58.3
Finance	3	8.8	14	5.8	28	5.7	13	4.5	0	0
Temper	4	11.8	17	7.1	36	7.3	22	7.5	1	8.3
Relative	3	8.8	14	5.8	43	8.8	27	9.2	2	16.7
Habits	5	14.7	22	9.2	50	10.2	31	10.6	0	0
Social	1	2.9	10	4.2	13	2.7	10	3.4	0	0
Sex	0	0	5	2.1	6	1.2	1	0.3	0	0
Others	0	0	5	2.1	10	2.0	3	1.0	0	0
Total	34	100.0	240	100.0	490	100.0	292	100.0	12	100.0

Table 4–381

AGE AND CAUSE OF MARITAL CONFLICTS (CITY HUSBANDS)										
	<=25		26-35		36-45		46-55		>=56	
	NO.	%	NO.	%	NO.	%	NO.	%	NO.	%
Children	5	7.7	111	17.4	144	26.7	74	26.7	20	16.7
Housework	8	12.3	47	7.4	38	7.0	14	5.1	8	6.7
Daily matters	13	20.0	183	28.6	161	29.8	85	30.7	53	44.2
Finance	6	9.2	30	4.7	19	3.5	20	7.2	7	5.8
Temper	9	13.8	70	11.0	62	11.5	33	11.9	12	10.0
Relative	8	12.3	65	10.2	41	7.6	17	6.1	6	5.0
Habits	6	9.2	59	9.2	35	6.5	15	5.4	7	5.8
Social	6	9.2	36	5.6	21	3.9	8	2.9	1	0.8
Sex	2	3.1	16	2.5	10	1.9	4	1.4	3	2.5
Others	2	3.1	22	3.4	9	1.7	7	2.5	3	2.5
Total	65	100.0	639	100.0	540	100.0	277	100.0	120	100.0

Table 4–382

C. AGE

Age had insignificant association with marital conflicts also. But some common characteristics can be found in the city and village subjects. Problems with children arose most commonly in the middle years, but came a little later for the village subjects. Personality incompatibility occurred commonly in late middle or early old age. Sexual problems arose at age ranges between forty-six and fifty-five for the wives and

AGE AND CAUSE OF MARITAL CONFLICTS (CITY WIVES)

	<=25		26-35		36-45		46-55		>=56	
	NO.	%	NO.	%	NO.	%	NO.	%	NO.	%
Children	23	10.2	413	27.1	434	30.8	167	31.3	18	18.2
Housework	11	4.9	132	8.7	128	9.1	42	7.9	13	13.1
Daily matters	62	27.6	403	26.4	376	26.7	151	28.3	27	27.3
Finance	15	6.7	43	2.8	42	3.0	16	3.0	7	7.1
Temper	25	11.1	132	8.7	138	9.8	67	12.5	11	11.1
Relative	35	15.6	149	9.8	94	6.7	19	3.6	5	5.1
Habits	20	8.9	97	6.4	73	5.2	33	6.2	9	9.1
Social	25	11.1	55	3.6	42	3.0	7	1.3	2	2.0
Sex	2	0.9	26	1.7	25	1.8	13	2.4	2	2.0
Others	7	3.1	76	5.0	58	4.1	19	3.6	5	5.1
Total	225	100.0	1526	100.0	1410	100.0	534	100.0	99	100.0

Table 4–383

AGE AND CAUSE OF MARITAL CONFLICTS (VILLAGE HUSBANDS)

	<=25		26-35		36-45		46-55		>=56	
	NO.	%	NO.	%	NO.	%	NO.	%	NO.	%
Children	4	19.0	11	10.6	16	15.4	11	23.4	3	14.3
Housework	0	0	21	20.2	12	11.5	3	6.4	1	4.8
Daily matters	9	42.9	27	26.0	38	36.5	16	34.0	9	24.9
Finance	4	19.0	8	7.7	7	6.7	4	8.5	1	4.8
Temper	1	4.8	12	11.5	11	10.6	6	12.8	5	23.8
Relative	1	4.8	9	8.7	7	6.7	0	0	1	4.8
Habits	2	9.5	11	10.6	5	4.8	4	8.5	1	4.8
Social	0	0	4	3.8	4	3.8	2	4.3	0	0
Sex	0	0	0	0	2	1.9	1	2.1	0	0
Others	0	0	1	1.0	2	1.9	0	0	0	0
Total	21	100.0	104	100.0	104	100.0	47	100.0	21	100.0

Table 4–384

between twenty-six and thirty-five for the husbands. Financial problems were commonly found among the younger ages for the husbands and in late middle ages for the wives.

Marital conflicts have been studied in China frequently in the 1980s. In 1985, a survey of one thousand subjects in Beijing showed that those couples with less frequent fights were more satisfied with their marriages. Furthermore, 27.1 percent of the marital conflicts were caused by

Age and Cause of Marital Conflicts (Village Wives)										
	<=25		26-35		36-45		46-55		>=56	
	NO.	%	NO.	%	NO.	%	NO.	%	NO.	%
Children	16	14.7	93	17.3	52	15.7	15	19.5	2	14.3
Housework	14	12.8	60	11.2	46	13.9	7	9.1	0	0
Daily matters	43	39.4	178	33.1	119	36.0	20	26.0	4	28.6
Finance	7	6.4	24	4.5	17	5.1	9	11.7	1	7.1
Temper	9	8.3	37	6.9	22	6.6	9	11.7	3	21.4
Relative	3	2.8	54	10.1	23	6.9	7	9.1	2	14.3
Habits	11	10.1	55	10.2	36	10.9	5	6.5	1	7.1
Social	3	2.8	18	3.4	9	2.7	3	3.9	1	7.1
Sex	1	0.9	9	1.7	2	0.6	0	0	0	0
Others	2	1.8	9	1.7	5	1.5	2	2.6	0	0
Total	109	100.0	537	100.0	331	100.0	77	100.0	14	100.0

Table 4–385

children problems, 21.9 percent by domestic trivialities, 15.2 percent by domestic chores, 13.4 percent by financial problems, 9 percent by personality incompatibility, 6.1 percent by family relationship problems, 4.6 percent by life habits, 2.3 percent by social problems, 1.8 percent by sexual problems, and 2.2 percent by other reasons.[102] These findings are similar to ours except for the frequency due to domestic chores. It is probably because in the recent years, much domestic work has been made easier by electric tools.

In theory, these nonfundamental conflicts should be preventable. A survey of eighty cases of marital disputes found that 75 percent were due to harsh accusations of one party, and subsequent counter accusations of the other party over matters which were not insoluble or even important.[103]

4. Source of Sexual Knowledge

Sexual knowledge is difficult to obtain, even for adults. Early in this century, China's first sexologist, Chang Jing Sheng, was harrassed and pressured to the extent that he attempted suicide.[104] Even in the United States and Europe, harsh laws against unrestricted sex education still existed in the 1920s and 1930s.[105] This situation was, of course, quite ridiculous. As Bertand Russell has rightly pointed out, if a system can be sustained only by ignorance, it is not going to last.[106]

During the 1980s in China, there was a great change in attitudes. How knowledgeable about sex were the adults at the time of our survey?

A. Knowledge of Sex Books

In the late 1980s, a few books have been published in China for the purpose of public sex education. They are *The Knowledge of Sex*, *The Essentials for the Newlywed*, *Handbook of Sex Knowledge*, and *Sexual Medicine*. Table 4–386 shows that these books had been widely read by the subjects. It shows that sexual ignorance and fear of sexual knowledge are gradually disappearing in China.[107]

Yet a figure of 37.6 percent of city subjects and 22.9 percent of village subjects who have not read any of these books is high. That more village subjects than city dwellers have read sex education books is a slight surprise. It could be due to the energetic attempts of family planning educators in recent years, or it may be because most of the village subjects had at least a primary school education (tables 4–2 and 4–3).

For the less formal type of sex education materials such as recreational sex books or movies, the rate of contact was quite low (table 4–387). The reason is that these types of material are still rare in China and are also denigrated, making many people reluctant to come in contact with them. Yet, the percentage of people who really did not want to read them was low. This shows that people are in fact still quite interested in them.

Books Read Before Marriage											
	TOTAL	KNOWLEDGE OF SEX		ESSENTIALS FOR THE NEWLYWED		HANDBOOK OF SEXUAL KNOWLEDGE		SEXUAL MEDICINE		NONE	
		NO.	%	NO.	%	NO.	%	NO.	%	NO.	%
City	6210	1495	24.1	1436	23.1	354	5.7	588	9.5	2337	37.6
Village	1392	361	25.9	441	31.7	123	8.8	148	10.6	319	22.9
Total	7602	1856	24.4	1877	24.7	477	6.3	736	9.7	2656	34.9

Table 4–386

Experience Watching Books or Videos or Movies Which Depict Mainly Sex											
	TOTAL	YES		NO CHANCE		WISH TO		NOT WISH		UNKNOWN	
		NO.	%	NO.	%	NO.	%	NO.	%	NO.	%
City	6210	1125	18.1	3038	48.9	209	3.4	1618	26.1	220	3.5
Village	1392	171	12.3	687	49.4	88	6.3	439	31.5	7	0.5
Total	7602	1296	17.0	3725	49.0	297	3.9	2057	27.1	227	3.0

Table 4–387

PERCENTAGE OF CITY AND VILLAGE SUBJECTS WHO HAD READ DIFFERENT SEX EDUCATION BOOKS

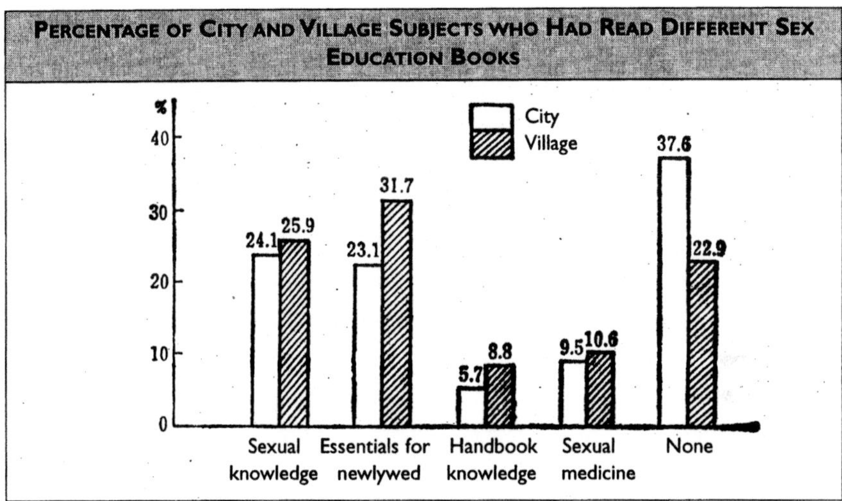

Figure 4–84

PERCENTAGE OF CITY AND VILLAGE SUBJECTS WHO HAD READ BOOKS OR SEEN MOVIES OR VIDEOS IN WHICH SEX WAS PRINCIPALLY DEPICTED

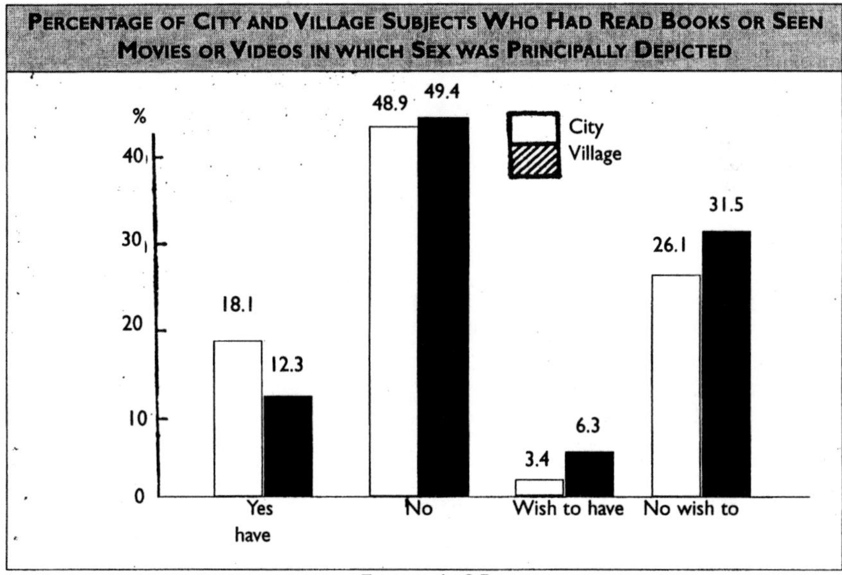

Figure 4–85

2. Other Sources of Sexual Knowledge

Table 4–388 shows that informal sex books or movies did not form the principal source of the subjects' sexual knowledge. For the city subjects, the top five sources, by order of frequency, were books, personal experience, female peers, teachers, and other printed materials; for

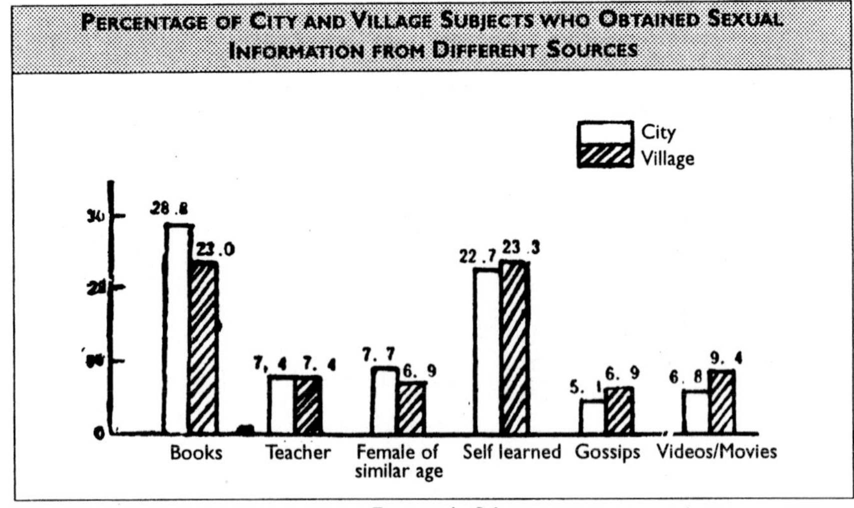

Figure 4–86

SOURCE OF SEXUAL KNOWLEDGE

	TOTAL	MOTHER		FATHER		SENIORS		FEMALE OF SIMILAR AGE		MALE OF OF SIMILAR AGE		BOOKS	
		NO.	%	NO.	%	NO.	%	NO.	%	NO.	%	NO.	%
City	14574	515	3.5	155	1.1	355	2.4	1115	7.7	492	3.4	4198	28.8
Village	1099	139	3.4	44	1.1	63	1.5	282	6.9	135	3.3	942	23.0

	DOCTOR		TEACHER		FAMILY PLANNING OFFICER		SELF-TAUGHT		FROM GOSSIPS		VIDEOS, RADIO, MOVIES		OTHERS	
	NO.	%	NO.	%	NO.	%	NO.	%	NO.	%	NO.	%	NO.	%
City	611	4.2	1079	7.4	546	3.7	3315	22.7	744	5.1	993	6.8	456	3.1
Village	155	3.8	302	7.4	262	6.4	956	23.3	283	6.9	385	9.4	151	3.7

Table 4–388

villagers, they were experience, books, other printed materials, teachers, female peers, and gossip. It is interesting to find that sexual knowledge comes more from female peers both for the city and village subjects.Perhaps sex is more often talked about by females, in some structured or formal fashion.

It must be noted that a large percentage of subjects obtained their sexual knowledge from informal sources. This is in agreement with

PRINCIPLE KNOWLEDGE DEFICIENCY IN MARITAL LIFE											
	TOTAL	PHYSIOLOGY & HYGIENE		SEXUAL TECHNIQUES		INTERPERSONAL SKILLS		CHILDREN EDUCATION		UNKNOWN	
		NO.	%	NO.	%	NO.	%	NO.	%	NO.	%
City	6210	471	7.6	967	15.6	1784	28.7	2418	38.9	570	9.2
Village	1392	250	18.0	139	10.0	294	21.1	693	49.8	16	1.1
Total	7602	721	9.5	1106	14.5	2078	27.3	3111	40.9	586	7.7

Table 4–389

results from other surveys in China, such as the one performed in Helungjiang in 1986.[108] This shows that in the absence of sexual knowledge, people have their own ways of obtaining information. It is known that in the villages, old women like to sit in groups at street corners talking excitedly about sexual matters. Young boys and girls, though not participating, are free to listen from a distance.The chat could center on some funny incident befalling newlyweds, there could be jokes about the courtship between some relatives or other anecdotes. The cramped living conditions of married couples, with their children and the

PERCENTAGE OF CITY AND VILLAGE SUBJECTS WHO FELT DIFFERENT TYPES OF DEFICIENCIES CONCERNING SEXUAL KNOWLEDGE

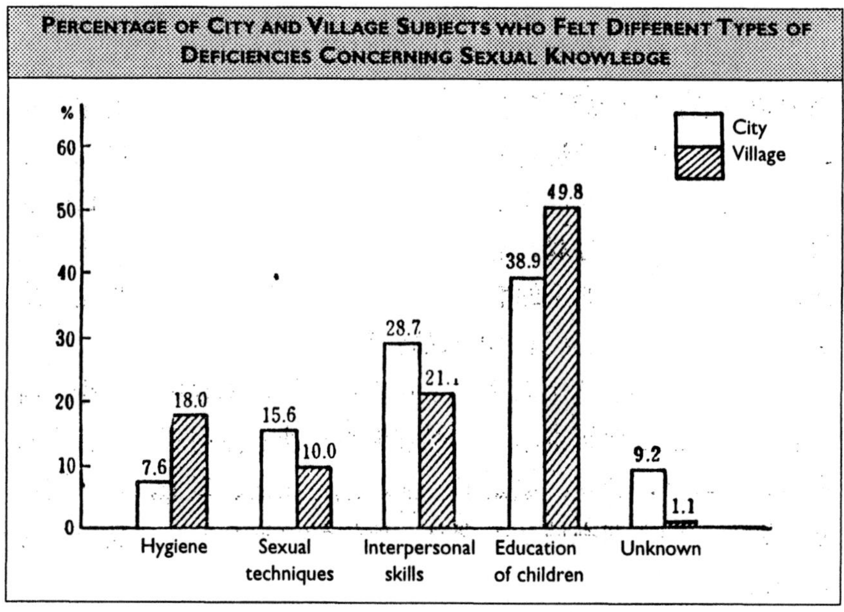

Figure 4–87

"carelessness" in sexual intercourse could also be a source of sexual information for the children.

Table 4–389 shows that most subjects believed that they lacked most of the knowledge to handle interpersonal relationships successfully and to teach their children. Sex knowledge only came next. They still do not think it is the most important. It could be that the Chinese tend to focus more on the benefit of the society rather than oneself. This may be a good point, but also a reason why they cannot fully express their own needs.

Response If Child Asks "Where Do I Come From?"

	TOTAL	TELL THE TRUTH		IGNORE		DECEIVE		SCOLD		DISTRACT		UNKNOWN	
		NO.	%	NO.	%	NO.	%	NO.	%	NO.	%	NO.	%
City	6210	3837	61.8	207	3.3	447	7.2	38	0.6	1578	25.4	103	1.7
Village	1392	665	47.8	127	9.1	86	6.2	35	2.5	471	33.8	8	0.6
Total	7602	4502	59.2	334	4.4	533	7.1	73	1.0	2049	27.0	111	1.5

Table 4–390

Sex and Response If Child Asks "Where Do I Come From?" (City)

	TOTAL	TELL THE TRUTH		IGNORE		DECEIVE		SCOLD		DISTRACT	
		NO.	%	NO.	%	NO.	%	NO.	%	NO.	%
Male	1778	1157	65.1	62	3.5	74	4.2	19	1.1	466	26.2
Female	4170	2595	62.2	140	3.4	356	8.5	17	0.4	1062	25.5

P=0.001

Table 4–391

Sex and Response If Child Asks "Where Do I Come From?" (Village)

	TOTAL	TELL THE TRUTH		IGNORE		DECEIVE		SCOLD		DISTRACT	
		NO.	%	NO.	%	NO.	%	NO.	%	NO.	%
Male	300	151	50.3	14	4.7	20	6.7	5	1.7	110	36.7
Female	1081	513	47.5	113	10.5	66	6.1	28	2.6	361	33.4

P=0.001

Table 4–392

PERCENTAGE OF CITY AND VILLAGE SUBJECTS WITH DIFFERENT RESPONSES TO CHILDREN ASKING ABOUT SEX

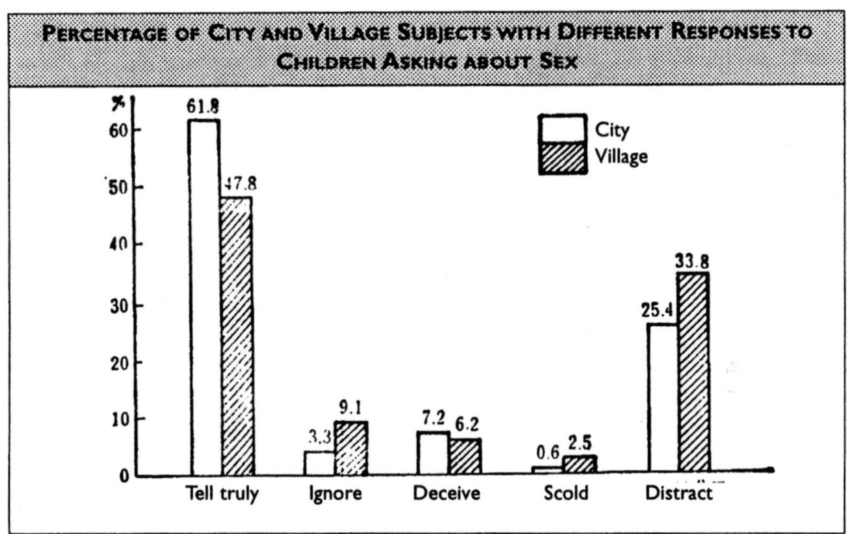

Figure 4–88

EDUCATION AND RESPONSE IF CHILD ASKS "WHERE DO I COME FROM?" (CITY HUSBANDS)

	ILLITERATE		PRIMARY		J. HIGH		S. HIGH		C. & ABOVE	
	NO.	%	NO.	%	NO.	%	NO.	%	NO.	%
Tell truth	7	53.8	16	45.7	218	63.7	398	62.7	488	70.2
Ignore	1	7.7	2	5.7	24	7.0	20	3.1	13	1.9
Deceive	0	0	5	14.3	18	5.3	22	3.5	26	3.7
Scold	2	15.4	1	2.9	5	1.5	8	1.3	2	0.3
Distract	3	23.1	11	31.4	77	22.5	187	29.4	166	23.9
Total	13	100.0	35	100.0	342	100.0	635	100.0	695	100.0

Table 4–393

EDUCATION AND RESPONSE IF CHILD ASKS "WHERE DO I COME FROM?" (CITY WIVES)

	ILLITERATE		PRIMARY		J. HIGH		S. HIGH		C. & ABOVE	
	NO.	%	NO.	%	NO.	%	NO.	%	NO.	%
Tell truth	9	52.9	77	51.3	763	59.0	1145	62.0	549	70.2
Ignore	2	11.8	11	7.3	61	4.7	49	2.7	15	1.9
Deceive	3	17.6	24	16.0	141	10.9	148	8.0	33	4.2
Scold	1	5.9	3	2.0	4	0.3	6	0.3	2	0.3
Distract	2	11.8	35	23.3	325	25.1	500	27.1	183	23.4
Total	17	100.0	150	100.0	1294	100.0	1848	100.0	782	100.0

Table 4–394

EDUCATION AND RESPONSE IF CHILD ASKS "WHERE DO I COME FROM?" (VILLAGE HUSBANDS)										
	ILLITERATE		PRIMARY		J. HIGH		S. HIGH		C. & ABOVE	
	NO.	%	NO.	%	NO.	%	NO.	%	NO.	%
Tell truth	4	30.8	19	31.1	76	61.3	48	55.2	3	25.0
Ignore	0	0	7	11.5	4	3.2	3	3.4	0	0
Deceive	3	23.1	6	9.8	7	5.6	2	2.3	1	8.3
Scold	0	0	2	3.3	2	1.6	1	1.1	0	0
Distract	6	46.2	27	44.3	35	28.2	33	37.9	8	66.7
Total	13	100.0	61	100.0	124	100.0	87	100.0	12	100.0

Table 4–395

EDUCATION AND RESPONSE IF CHILD ASKS "WHERE DO I COME FROM?" (VILLAGE WIVES)										
	ILLITERATE		PRIMARY		J. HIGH		S. HIGH		C. & ABOVE	
	NO.	%	NO.	%	NO.	%	NO.	%	NO.	%
Tell truth	17	48.6	114	46.9	234	47.0	144	49.1	4	33.3
Ignore	2	5.7	34	14.0	45	9.0	30	10.2	2	16.7
Deceive	1	2.9	21	8.6	26	5.2	16	5.5	2	16.7
Scold	4	11.4	6	2.5	11	2.2	7	2.4	0	0
Distract	11	31.4	68	28.0	182	36.5	96	32.8	4	33.3
Total	35	100.0	243	100.0	498	100.0	293	100.0	12	100.0

Table 4–396

5. Sex Education for Children

Table 4–390, figure 4–88, table 4–391, and 4–392 show that of those who were asked the question "Where do I come from?" by their children, a large percentage of the subjects, city more than the village, answered truthfully. Wives and husbands did not differ significantly though slightly fewer wives answered truthfully.

Tables 4–393 to 4–396 show that the likelihood of answering truthfully is related to the educational level. G indices were 0.15, 0.14, and 0.20 for city husbands, city wives, and village husband respectively.

Obviously, the well educated have the same idea as Bertrand Russell, who maintained that lying to children will only make them stupid, hypocritical, and cowardly.[109]

Conclusions

1. Contemporary Chinese society is undergoing rapid change. Many obsolete ideas have been rejected, but not all. Our survey shows many of these contradictions:
   - (A) Many women and men want to marry for love, but often have only the vaguest concept of love , i.e., they do not know what exactly love is and is not.
   - (B) Many claim satisfaction with their marital sex lives, but are not satisfied with many of its details.
   - (C) Many are interested in knowing more about sex and are open-minded about it, but take no initiative to look for information.
   - (D) The status of women has improved, but few are concerned with the quality of their sex lives, including the women themselves.
   - (E) Many have some sexual knowledge, but it is often fragmentary and not comprehensive enough.
   - (F) Many try various ways of enhancing sexual pleasure (e.g., different sexual techniques and positions), but they only do so secretly, and there is no open agreement that it is all right.
   - (G) Many understand the importance of family planning for the nation, but many still practice contraception reluctantly, or deliberately avoiding it.
   - (H) There is a general open-mindedness about divorce and extramarital sex, but not necessarily when it comes down to one's personal life.
   - (I) There is an increase in premarital and extramarital sex, but there is a great deal of controversy concerning its meaning.
   - (J) The problem of sex in the aged has been identified but not yet given its due attention.

   These and many similar matters have to be dealt with in the future sex civilization of China. In order to find solutions, one will have to improve the people's quality of life, and this is inseparable from an improvement in economic circumstances.

2. The usual idea about Chinese families is that they are very stable and this is believed to be an asset in Chinese society Our survey, however, raises the point that it is not always enough to be satisfied with

outward stability. We must look at the basic reason for the stability. It is obvious that marriage and family as examined and described by us are of high stability but low quality. For example, outward satisfaction often hides underlying frustration. Therefore, one may ask whether outward stability is, in fact, hiding inward instability? It is important to identify these problems and to solve them.

3. To improve the quality of marital sex, it is important to help people to have a proper attitude toward sex. Previously, sex was considered "dirty" by many people, but now we encounter many different attitudes. It may be appropriate today to emphasize the pleasure function of sex and to put it in a social perspective.

4. To enhance the quality of sex for married couples, it may be necessary to emphasize the role of affection and love in marriage. Our survey shows that there are still many married couples who consider sex as nothing more than a duty or a means of producing offspring. This is likely to make sex monotonous, lowering the quality of the marriage.

5. There are still moral controversies about some sexual issues, such as masturbation, premarital and extramarital sex, divorce, and chastity. It is quite impossible to find one universal morality governing such matters. Sex education should probably teach the moral principle that any behavior is permissible as long as it is harmless to others and takes place by mutual consent.

6. There is a need for adult sex education. It should emphasize the importance of and difference between affection and moral duties, rights, and responsibilities. To maintain a happy and enduring marital relationship, it is not effective to depend only on the force of morality and the law, because they can, at best, maintain only a superficial stability. Teachings about mutual respect and love, on the other hand, will strengthen the foundations of a stable and happy marriage.

7. A greater emphasis should be placed on the sexual needs of women and the aged. Our survey shows that women remain largely under the influence of traditional concepts and are therefore more removed from factual sexual knowledge and flexible sexual attitudes. The sex life of the elderly is also largely neglected by most people.

8. Our survey shows that sexual behavior is determined very much by sexual knowledge and sexual attitudes. If we want to minimize con-

flict in this area, we must popularize sex education and see it as part of our society's civilizing process. In view of the now occurring social changes, we must work for a more open and tolerant atmosphere. Only this way can we hope to adapt well to the rapidly modernizing world.

NOTES

1. Pan Yun-Kang, *Thoughts in an Asian Society* (Beijing: China Women Publications, 1989), 34.
2. Chang Yi-Bing, *Division and Change* (Harbin, Helungjiang: People's Publications, 1989), 27–28.
3. Dalin Liu, *Marital Sociology* (Tianjin: Tianjin People's Publications, 1987), 39.
4. Chang Yi-Bing, *Division and Change*, 28.
5. Dalin Liu, *Marital Sociology*, 39.
6. Chang Yi-Bing, *Division and Change*, 25.
7. Ye Ling, "Diversions in Marital Behavior," *Marriage and Family*. 2 (1988): 6.
8. Chang Yi-Bing, *Division and Change*, 34.
9. Herbert Spencer, *The Principles of Psychology* (London: Williams and Norgate, 1899).
10. Havelock Ellis, *Psychology of Sex* (Chinese Edition) (Beijing: Joint Publications, 1987), 453.
11. Ibid., 429.
12. K. Bachniev, *Treatise on Love* (Chinese Edition) (Beijing: Joint Publications, 1984), 158–59.
13. Chang Yi-Bing, *Division and Change*, 90.
14. Guo Da Li, trans., *Selections from Marx and Engels* (Beijing: Beijing People's Publications, 1911), vol. 4, p. 78.
15. Fu Lei, *Letters of Fu Lei's Family* (Beijing: Joint Publications, 1981), 224–25.
16. Bertrand Russell, *Marital Revolution* (Chinese Edition) (Shanghai: Eastern Publications, 1988), 96.
17. Pei Yi-De, *Ideal Marriage* (Beijing: Ethnic Publications, 1989), 3.
18. Chang Yi-Bing, *Division and Change*, 87; Liu Da-Lin, *Marital Sociology*, 90; Havelock Ellis, *Psychology of Sex*, 453.
19. Zha Cai-Bin, *A Treatise on Marital Life*, 36.

20. Ellis, *Psychology of Sex*, 348–51.
21. Dalin Liu, *Sex Sociology* (Jinan: Shandong People's Publications, 1986), 7.
22. Pan Sui Ming, *Kinsey Report—Sexual Behavior in the Human Male* (Chinese Edition) (Beijing: Guong Ming Daily Publications, 1988), 46.
23. Bertrand Russell, *Why I Am Not a Christian* (Chinese edition) (Shanghai: Commercial Press, 1982), 128.
24. Ellis, *Psychology of Sex*, 334.
25. Chang Yi-Bing, *Division and Change*, 21–22.
26. Ellis, *Psychology of Sex*, 371.
27. Pan Sui Ming, *Kinsey Report—Sexual Behavior in the Human Male*, 75–75, 102–103.
28. Hua Wen-Ying, "Why Is Premarital Sex So Prevalent?" *Marriage and Family* (special issue on sexual problems and marriage), (1989) 28.
29. Dalin Liu, *Marital Sociology*, 50.
30. Dalin Liu, "Current Trends in Sexual Problems," *Marriage and Family*, 12 (1989): 12-13.
31. Pan Sui Ming, *Kinsey Report—Sexual Behavior in the Human Male*, 167.
32. Zha Cai-Bin, *A Treatise on Marital Life*, 129.
33. Pan Sui Ming, *Kinsey Report—Sexual Behavior in the Human Male*, 168–69.
34. Chang Yi-Bing, *Division and Change*, 123–24.
35. Cai Heng-Zi (Qing Dynasty), *Chong Ming Talks*, vol. 2, p. 22.
36. Ellis, *Psychology of Sex*, 70
37. Pan Sui Ming, *Kinsey Report—Sexual Behavior in the Human Male*, 69.
38. Pan Sui-Ming, *Kinsey Report—Sexual Behavior in the Human Female* (Chinese Edition) (Beijing: Solidarity Publications, 1990), 143.
39. Ellis, *Psychology of Sex*, 384.
40. Pan Sui Ming, *Kinsey Report—Sexual Behavior in the Human Male*, 162.
41. Desmond Morris, *The Naked Ape* (Chinese Edition) (Shanghai: Xue Lin Publications, 1987), 44.
42. H. A. Kachadourian and T. L. Donald, *Fundamentals of Human Sexuality*. (New York: Holt, Rinehart and Winston, 1972). Chinese Edition by Li Hong-Kuan (Beijing: Village Publications, 1989), 264–66, 83.
43. R. H. Lowie, *Human Culture in Perspective* (Chinese edition) (Beijing: Joint Publications, 1984), 80–81.
43. Ibid.
45. Pan Sui Ming, *Kinsey Report—Sexual Behavior in the Human Male*, 93–95.
46. Ellis, *Psychology of Sex*, 346.

47. Pan Sui Ming, *Kinsey Report—Sexual Behavior in the Human Male*, 167.
48. Dalin Liu, *Sex Sociology*, 154.
49. Ningxia People Publications, *Events of the Nude Models* (Yinchuan: Ningxia Publications, 1989), 131.
50. Zhu Zhao-Rui, "The Incident of Selecting Female Nude Models," *Family* 10 (1988): 35.
51. Ellis, *Psychology of Sex*, 449–50.
52. Pan Sui Ming, *Kinsey Report—Sexual Behavior in the Human Male*, 63–76.
53. R. Michener, *Sex—a Practical Manual* (New York: 1982), 247.
54. Pan Sui Ming, *Kinsey Report—Sexual Behavior in the Human Male*, 157.
55. Gangsu Publications, *Dictionary of Geriatrics*, (Lanzhou: Gangsu Publications, 1988), 107.
56. "Civilized Mind or Feudal Ignorance?," *Renmin Daily*, Nov. 22, 1986, 4. The paper reported on the following women:

    - Tin was married to a husband who was sexually impotent right from the first day of marriage. She stayed in the marriage for eight years.
    - Li gave up her career and spent seventeen years taking care of her sick husband and his father.
    - Wong took care of her parents-in-law for twenty-three years after the death of her husband.
    - Liu took care of her paralyzed father-in-law and mentally ill mother-in-law while she still had to farm.
    - Jiu who was forced to marry a husband for exchange but did not ask for divorce.
    - Gao stayed for fifteen years with a husband who was waiting to be sentenced for a criminal offence.

    It was controversial whether these were respectable women or simply victims of the traditional oppression of women.
57. Sigmund Freud, *Sex, Love and Civilization* (Chinese Edition) (Hefei: Anhui Literary Publications, 1987), 237.
58. Xu An-Qi, "On Female Sexual Rights," *Sociological Research* 3 (1990): 103–104.
59. The following are extracts from records of divorce cases handled in a court in China in recent years:

    a. "Yuen had excessive sexual desire. He needed sex every night and every time he took more than an hour to finish. For my bodily health, I had to leave him for a few days every month. I cannot tolerate this torture any more."

b. "During all the seven years of marriage, he rarely smiled at me or gave me a greeting. He never took care of me but forced me to have sex with him repeatedly. When I could not satisfy his strong desire, his mother taught him to burn my genital."

c. "We lived in a poor flat of thirteen square meters together with our parents or children, but he never cared about this. He asked for sex as soon as he came to the bed. Thinking that all the others might not be asleep, I could not get myself excited. Then, he would force me. I could not struggle. I could only sob. He did it although I was sobbing."

d. "He forced me to have sex even when I was menstruating. He stripped me naked, tore my underwear, and pressed me to have sex, ignoring my plea that it was painful. He took out scissors to cut my genital. I sobbed, but he threatened that if I made any noise, he would whip me."

e. "Every time, less than two weeks after I had taken an induced abortion, he forced me to have sex, not caring even when I was bleeding. If I refused, he used his fingers to probe my vagina at will. Now, I keep bleeding from my vagina. He never cared whether I had the baby or not, and he never gave any financial or emotional support for my abortion."

60. Pan Sui-Ming, "On Sexual Dissatisfaction," *Chinese Sexology* (Guangzhou: Guangdong People's Publications, 1990), 1:521.
61. Yosano Akiko, "A Treatise on Chastity," quoted in *New Youths*. 4:5, 12.
62. Ellis, *Psychology of Sex*, 392.
63. Russell, *Marital Revolution*, 2.
64. Ellis, *Psychology of Sex*, 392
65. Ibid.
66. Kachadourian and Donald, *Fundamentals of Human Sexuality*, 83.
67. Pan Sui-Ming, *Kinsey Report—Sexual Behavior in the Human Female*, 168–69; Pan Sui Ming, *Kinsey Report—Sexual Behavior in the Human Male*, 181.
68. Morris, *The Naked Ape*, 35.
69. Dalin Liu, *Sex Sociology*, 127.
70. Pan Sui-Ming, *Kinsey Report—Sexual Behavior in the Human Female*, 167–68.
71. Ibid., 171.
72. Guo Da Li, trans., *Selections from Marx and Engels*, vol. 4, p. 66; Li Yu (Late Tang Dynasty) Pu Sha Man.
73. Sex partner in this survey means "partner with whom one has sexual intercourse." This was explained to all subjects surveyed.
74. Dalin Liu, *Sex Sociology*, 170.

75. Dalin Liu "Current Trends in Sexual Problems," 12–13.
76. He Ming, "A Different View on 'the Third Party,'" *Marriage and Family* 10 (1988): 34-35.
77. Zha Cai-Bin, *A Treatise on Marital Life*, 149.
78. Pan Sui Ming, *Kinsey Report—Sexual Behavior in the Human Male*, 66.
79. Ibid., 83.
80. Ibid., 68.
81. Ibid., 186.
82. W. Good, *Family* (Chinese Edition) (Shanghai: Social Archives Publications, 1986), 100.
83. Zha Cai-Bin, *A Treatise on Marital Life*, 121.
84. Anon., "Divorce Rates around the World," *New Observer* 1 (1986): 4.
85. Anon., "Divorce Rates in Germany," *Sociological Reference International* 6 (1986): 48.
86. Xu An-Qi, *Psychology of Divorce* (Beijing: China Women Publications, 1988), 121.
87. Chinese Government (1987) Population Census by one-percent sampling.
88. Unpublished data.
89. Dalin Liu, *Marital Sociology*, 224.
90. Anon., "Divorce Patterns in China," *Marriage and Family* 6 (1990): 5.
91. Pan Yun-Kang, *Thoughts in an Asian Society*, 165–66.
92. Guo Da Li, trans., *Selections from Marx and Engels*, vol. 4, pp. 78–79.
93. Russell, *Marital Revolution*, 154.
94. Chang Yi-Bing, *Division and Change*, 173–74.
95. Pan Yun-Kang, "Reproductive Desire of Current Chinese Women," *Marriage and Family* 5 (1989): 6.
96. Pan Yun-Kang, *Thoughts in an Asian Society*, 101–102.
97. Dalin Liu, *Modern Art of Family Management* (Jinan: Shandong Scientific and Technological Publications, 1987), 91.
98. Dalin Liu, *Management for Family Life* (Shenyang: Liaoning Scientific Publications), 85.
99. Ibid.
100. Zhang Yi-Bing , "Female Conflicts between Social and Family Duties — an Analysis," *Chinese Social Science* 1 (1982): 177-190.
101. Pan Yun-Kang, *Thoughts in an Asian Society*, 145.
102. Dalin Liu, *Sociology of Marriage* (Tienjin: Tienjin People's Publications, 1987), 130.

103. Xu An-Qi, *Psychology of Divorce*, 88.

104. Dalin Liu, *Sex Sociology*, 42–47.

105. Russell, *Marital Revolution*, 65, 69.

106. Ibid., 69–71.

107. Gao Cai-Qin, "Sexual Life and Attitudes of Helungjiang Villagers," *Marriage and Family* (special issue) 5 (1989): 11

108. Ibid.

109. Russell, *Marital Revolution*, 64.

5
Sex Offenders

1. Overview

This part of the survey was conducted in Suzhou, Shanghai, Chengdu, Mishan, Beijing, Qingdao, Nanjing, Xiamen, and Shenzhen, with 2,136 effective responses. The distribution of the cases in the different regions are in table 5–1.

The regions were selected for reasons of convenience and feasibility Most of the subjects came from the prisons in these regions, some others from the Correctional Institutions or Youth Correctional Homes. The cases were selected at random or by intention as conditions allowed in these institutions. Self-completed questionnaires were used for data collection. If the selected subjects were illiterate, a trained interviewer helped them to fill in the questionnaires.

Sample Distribution of Sex Offenders		
REGIONS	NO.	%
Suzhou	234	11.0
Shanghai	1047	49.0
Chengdu	486	22.8
Mishan	88	4.1
Beijing	82	3.8
Qingdao	45	2.1
Nanjing	98	4.6
Xiamen	47	2.2
Shenzhen	9	0.4
Total	2136	100.0

Table 5-1

Since all the subjects under survey were serving their sentences, it was not difficult to contact them and get their cooperation. With the help of the prison or correctional officers, the offenders were gathered, given explanations on the purpose of the survey, and assured of confidentiality. They were reminded repeatedly that the questionnaires were to be completed and returned anonymously and that nobody had any wish to know who filled in which questionnaire, so that how they filled in the information would not affect their sentences or how they would be treated in the future.

Of all the subjects surveyed, 1,441 (67.5 percent) were males, 630 (29.5 percent) were females, and 65 (3.0 percent) did not reveal their gender.

The mean age of the subjects was 27.39 (SD=9.69); 50.8 percent were below age twenty-six, 70.6 percent below thirty-one. This shows that in China, the age of sex offenders tends to be young. For females, the age was even lower: 74.1 percent of the female offenders were below age twenty-five while male offenders of the same age group were only 43.2 percent (table 5–2).

GENDER AND AGE DISTRIBUTION OF THE SEX OFFENDERS

		<=20		21–25		26–30		31–35		>=36	
		NO.	%	NO.	%	NO.	%	NO.	%	NO.	%
Male	1404	259	18.4	348	24.8	312	22.2	178	12.7	307	21.9
Female	609	250	41.1	201	33.0	97	15.9	38	6.2	23	3.8

Table 5–2

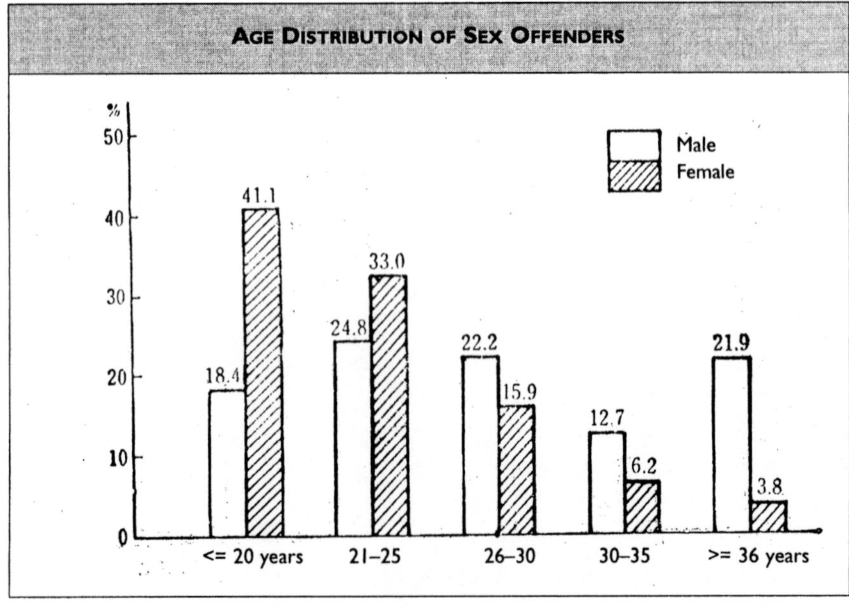

Figure 5–1

EDUCATIONAL LEVEL OF THE SEX OFFENDERS										
GENDER	TOTAL	ILLITERATE		PRIMARY		J. HIGH		ABOVE J. HIGH		
		NO.	%	NO.	%	NO.	%	NO.	%	
Male	1425	128	9.0	289	20.3	724	50.8	284	19.9	
Female	618	12	1.9	137	22.2	407	65.9	62	10.0	

P=0.001

Table 5–3

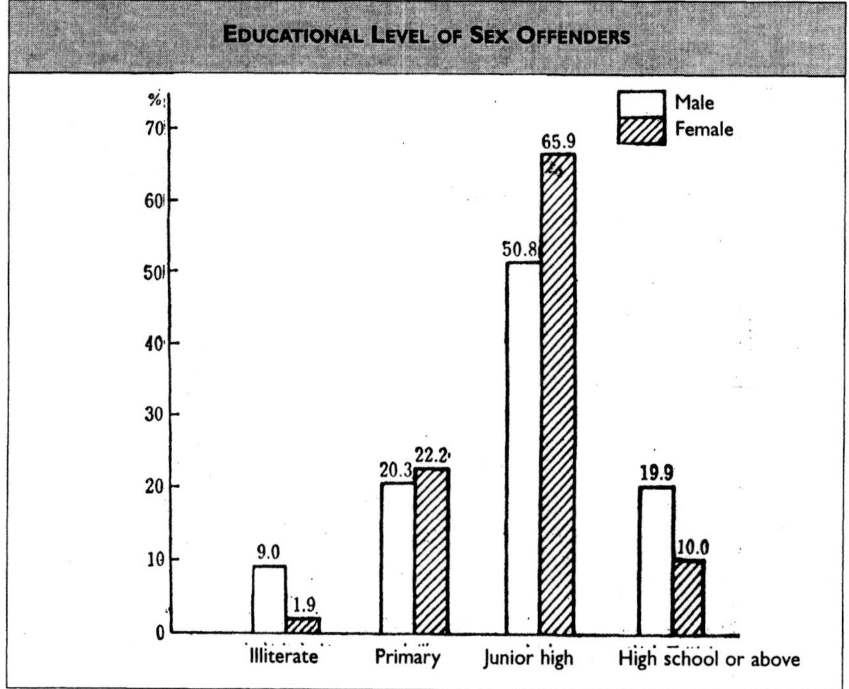

Figure 5–2

The educational level of the subjects was low. In the females it was generally lower than in the males (table 5–3).

Table 5–4 shows that of the youngest age groups, the sex offenders were of the middle educational rage. Of the older sex offenders, they were either of very low or very high educational level.

The subjects were mostly workers, farmers, or professionals, constituting a total of 71.4 percent. The professionals were primarily teachers or officials. The rest of the subjects were students (table 5–5).

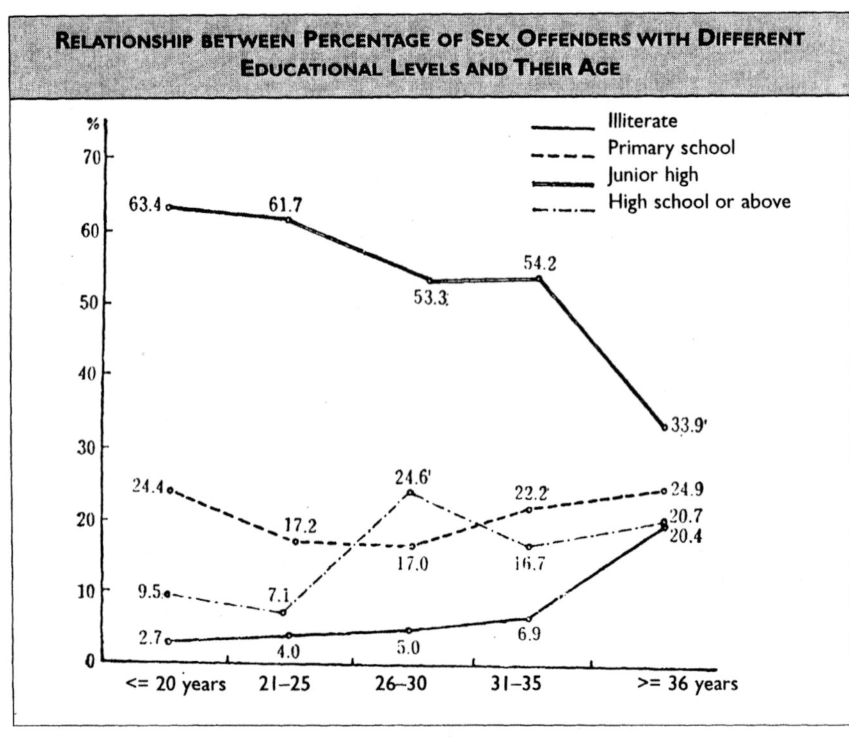

Figure 5–3

AGE AND EDUCATION LEVEL OF THE SEX OFFENDERS										
AGE	TOTAL	ILLITERATE		PRIMARY		J. HIGH		ABOVE J. HIGH		
		NO.	%	NO.	%	NO.	%	NO.	%
<=20	517	14	2.7	126	24.4	328	63.4	49	9.5
21–25	553	22	4.0	95	17.2	341	61.7	95	7.1
26–30	418	21	5.0	71	17.0	223	53.3	103	24.6
31–35	216	15	6.9	48	22.2	117	54.2	36	16.7
>=36	333	68	20.4	83	24.9	113	33.9	69	20.7

Table 5–4

Table 5–5 shows that the unemployed ranked third in those with the highest sex crime rates. The crime problems of this group are becoming increasingly prominent in recent China.

Among the workers, generally the rate of sex crimes increased with age. Among the farmers, there is no such obvious relationship. Among

Occupations of the Sex Offenders

FACTORY		AGRICULTURE		SERVICE		COMMERCE		TEACHER	
NO.	%	NO.	%	NO.	%	NO.	%	NO.	%
736	34.5	455	21.3	86	4.0	77	3.6	36	1.7

MEDICAL		ARTS		OFFICIAL		TECHNICIAN		FINANCE	
NO.	%	NO.	%	NO.	%	NO.	%	NO.	%
19	0.9	6	0.3	36	1.7	11	0.5	7	0.3

SOLDIER		STUDENTS		SELF BUSINESS		NONE		OTHERS		UNKNOWN	
NO.	%	NO.	%	NO.	%	NO.	%	NO.	%		
12	0.6	130	6.1	114	5.3	328	15.4	42	2.0	41	1.9

Table 5–5

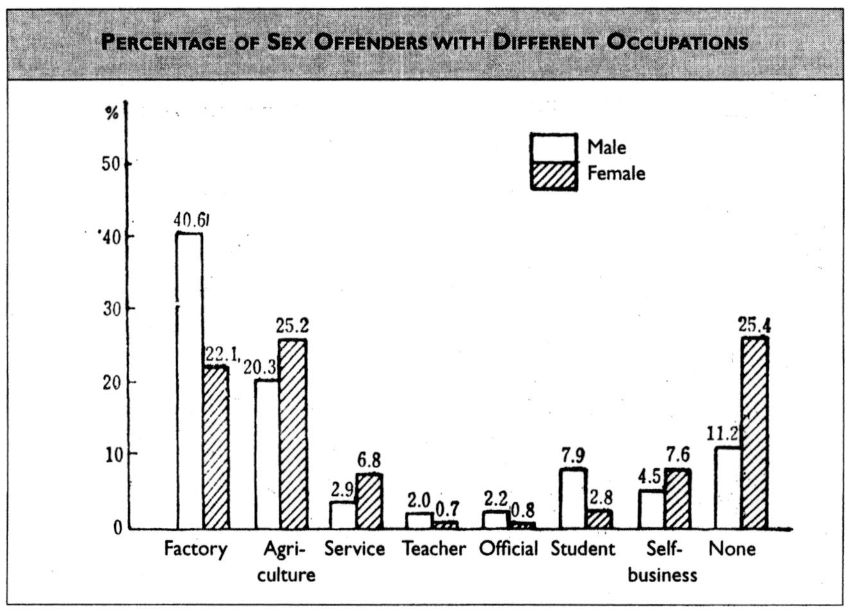

Figure 5–4

teachers and officials, the sex crime rate increased sharply after age thirty-six. Among the unemployed and the students, there was a trend for crime rate to drop with increasing age.

GENDER AND OCCUPATION OF THE SEX OFFENDERS

	TOTAL	FACTORY		AGRICULTURE		SERVICE		COMMERCE		TEACHER	
		NO.	%	NO.	%	NO.	%	NO.	%	NO.	%
Male	1423	578	40.6	289	20.3	42	2.9	56	3.9	29	2.0
Female	614	136	22.1	155	25.2	42	6.8	19	3.1	4	0.7

	MEDICAL		ARTS		OFFICIAL		TECHNICIAN		FINANCE	
	NO.	%	NO.	%	NO.	%	NO.	%	NO.	%
Male	14	1.0	2	0.1	31	2.2	11	0.8	3	0.2
Female	5	0.8	3	0.5	5	0.8	0	0	4	0.7

	SOLDIER		STUDENTS		SELF BUSINESS		NONE		OTHERS	
	NO.	%	NO.	%	NO.	%	NO.	%	NO.	%
Male	10	0.7	112	7.9	64	4.5	159	11.2	23	1.6
Female	2	0.3	17	2.8	47	7.6	156	25.4	19	3.1

Table 5–6

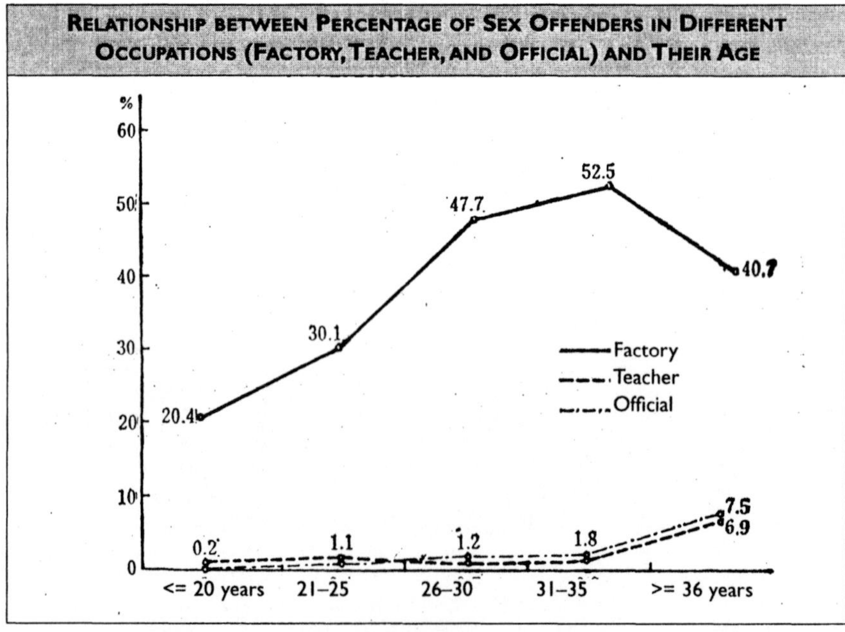

RELATIONSHIP BETWEEN PERCENTAGE OF SEX OFFENDERS IN DIFFERENT OCCUPATIONS (FACTORY, TEACHER, AND OFFICIAL) AND THEIR AGE

Figure 5–5

AGE AND OCCUPATION OF THE SEX OFFENDERS

AGE	TOTAL	FACTORY		AGRICULTURE		SERVICE		COMMERCE		TEACHER	
		NO.	%	NO.	%	NO.	%	NO.	%	NO.	%
<=20	509	104	20.4	95	18.7	21	4.1	12	2.4	1	0.2
21–25	554	167	30.1	130	23.5	20	3.6	18	3.2	6	1.1
26–30	415	198	47.7	77	18.6	23	5.5	19	4.6	3	0.7
31–35	217	114	52.5	46	21.2	9	4.1	15	6.9	2	0.9
>=36	334	136	40.7	86	25.7	9	2.7	11	3.3	23	6.9

AGE	MEDICAL		ARTS		OFFICIAL		TECHNICIAN		FINANCE	
	NO.	%	NO.	%	NO.	%	NO.	%	NO.	%
<=20	2	0.4	1	0.2	0	0	0	0	0	0
21–25	4	0.7	2	0.4	2	0.4	5	0.9	1	0.2
26–30	3	0.7	0	0	5	1.2	2	0.5	2	0.5
31–35	3	1.4	0	0	4	1.8	1	0.5	1	0.5
>=36	7	2.1	3	0.9	25	7.5	3	0.9	3	0.9

AGE	SOLDIER		STUDENTS		SELF BUSINESS		NONE		OTHERS	
	NO.	%	NO.	%	NO.	%	NO.	%	NO.	%
<=20	0	0	79	15.5	27	5.3	153	30.0	14	2.7
21–25	6	1.1	41	7.4	35	6.3	106	19.1	11	2.0
26–30	3	0.7	8	1.9	28	6.7	37	8.9	7	1.7
31–35	0	0	0	0	6	2.8	14	6.5	2	0.9
>=36	1	0.3	0	0	13	3.9	7	2.1	7	2.1

Table 5–7

Among the subjects, 1,363 (63.8 percent) were unmarried, 480 (22.5 percent) were married, and 29 (1.4 percent) were remarried; 15 (0.7 percent) were widowed at the time of conviction, 2 (0.1 percent) were widowed after conviction; 47 (2.2 percent) were divorced before conviction, 82 (3.8 percent) were divorced after conviction, and 118 (5.5 percent) did not give clear indication of their marital status.

If those unmarried and those who were widowed or divorced before conviction were categorized as "without partners," and the rest as "with partners," the former group show had a greater sex crime rate, with the females slightly higher than the males (73.1 percent against 69.2 percent). For those with partners, males were slightly higher (30.8 percent against 26.9 percent) (table 5–8).

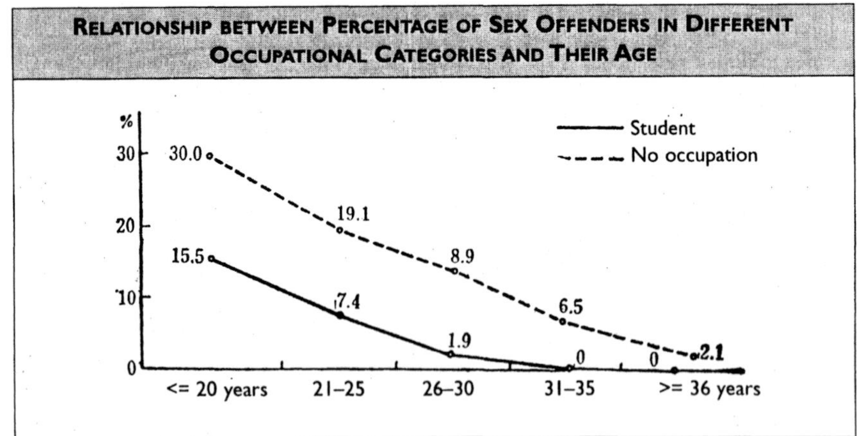

Figure 5–6

Marital Status															
	TOTAL	SINGLE		MARRIED		RE-MARRIED		WIDOWED BEFORE ARREST		WIDOWED AFTER ARREST		DIVORCE BEFORE ARREST		DIVORCED AFTER ARREST	
		NO.	%	NO.	%	NO.	%	NO.	%	NO.	%	NO.	%	NO.	%
Male	1373	918	66.9	338	24.6	12	0.9	10	0.7	2	0.1	22	1.6	71	5.2
Female	590	406	68.8	134	22.7	16	2.7	5	0.8	0	0	20	3.4	9	1.5

P=0.001

Table 5–8

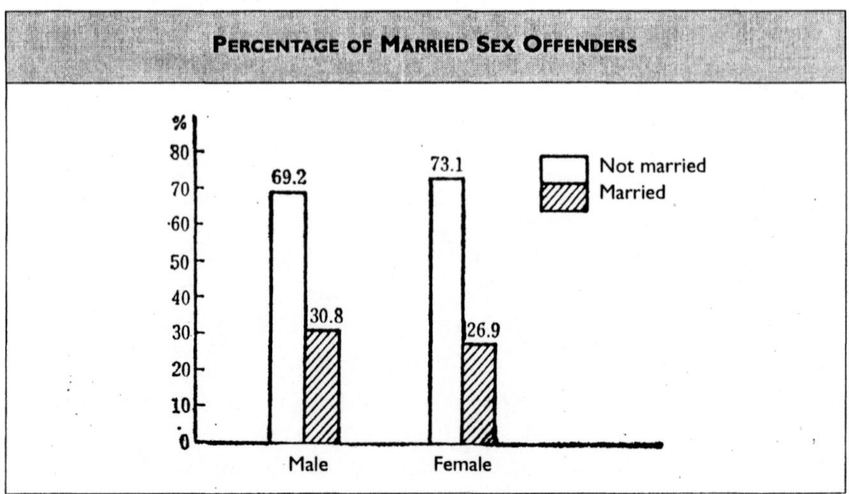

Figure 5–7

2. Definition of Sex Crime

According to the law in China, sex crimes include rape, gang rape, statutory rape (victim age below fourteen), forcing women into prostitution, seducing and accommodating prostitutes, hooliganism (insulting females and sexual promiscuity), bigamy, and the breaking of the marriage of a military man. In daily life, some other behaviors are considered sexual misconduct. They include extramarital affairs, as well as minor hooliganism offenses. If this misconduct cannot be corrected by education or persuasion, the Regulations for Social Security Management and the Regulations for Correctional Work stipulate clear guidelines for handling such behavior.

In 1988, the total yearly crime rate in China rose by 45.1 percent as compared with 1987; 4.1 percent of these crimes were rape, gang rape, and statutory rape; 10.7 percent were prostitution peddling, insulting females, promiscuity, and hooliganism. The yearly crime rates increased further by 138 percent in 1989.

1. Types of Sex Crimes

The highest types were rape and hooliganism, adding up to 53.2 percent of the total sex crimes (table 5–9).

TYPE OF SEX OFFENSES AS RECORDED										
TOTAL	RAPE		GANG RAPE		CHILD ASSAULT		PROMISCUITY		PROSTITUTION	
	NO.	%	NO.	%	NO.	%	NO.	%	NO.	%
2136	565	26.5	65	3.0	300	14.0	51	2.4	385	18.0

HOOLIGANISM		KEEP PROSTITUTES		BIGAMY		SEDUCE TO PROSTITUTION		FORCE TO PROSTITUTION		UNKNOWN	
NO.	%	NO.	%	NO.	%	NO.	%	NO.	%		
570	26.7	17	0.8	7	0.3	22	1.0	10	0.5	144	6.7

Table 5–9

The sex distribution of the criminals in the various types of sex crimes can be found in table 5–10 and figure 5–8.

Rape, gang rape, and statutory rape were clearly the predominant male crimes. Females were usually convicted for these crimes for their

GENDER AND TYPE OF SEX OFFENSES AS RECORDED [1]

GENDER	TOTAL	RAPE		GANG RAPE		CHILD ASSAULT		PROMISCUITY		PROSTITUTION	
		NO.	%	NO.	%	NO.	%	NO.	%	NO.	%
Male	1337	538	40.2	60	4.5	287	21.5	25	1.9	5	0.4
Female	601	12	2.0	3	0.5	6	1.0	25	4.2	365	60.7

GENDER	HOOLIGANISM		KEEP PROSTITUTES		BIGAMY		SEDUCE TO PROSTITUTION		FORCE TO PROSTITUTION	
	NO.	%	NO.	%	NO.	%	NO.	%	NO.	%
Male	407	30.4	8	0.6	1	0.1	5	0.4	1	0.1
Female	151	25.1	8	1.3	6	1.0	17	2.8	8	1.3

P=0.001

Table 5–10

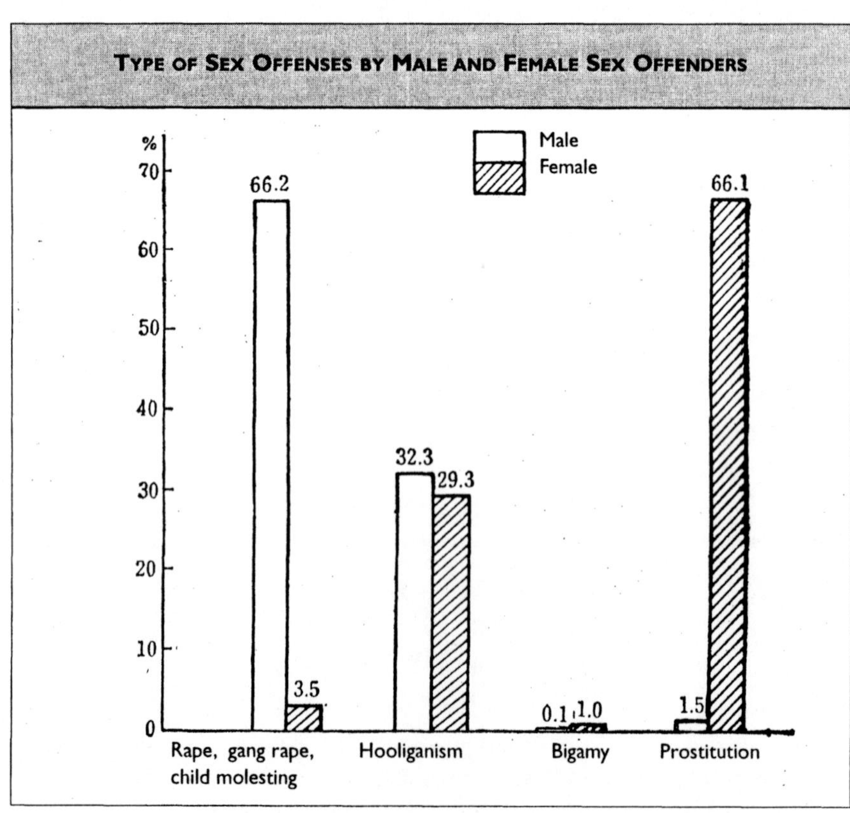

Figure 5–8

PERIOD OF WORK CORRECTIONAL SENTENCE						
TOTAL	<2 YEARS		2 TO <3 YRS.		3 YEARS	
	NO.	%	NO.	%	NO.	%
673	193	28.7	197	29.3	283	42.0

Table 5–11

PERIOD OF IMPRISONMENT (IN YEARS)																
TOTAL	<3		3 TO <5		5 TO <7		7 TO<10		10 TO<15		>=15		LIFE		DEATH	
	NO.	%	NO.	%	NO.	%	NO.	%	NO.	%	NO.	%	NO.	%	NO.	%
1435	139	9.7	257	17.9	308	21.5	311	21.7	264	18.4	78	5.4	42	2.9	36	2.5

Table 5–12

being an accomplice. Prostitution was practically an all-female sex crime. It involves 57.9 percent of the total females surveyed. For promiscuity, female rates were much higher than male. It is understood, however, that in China prostitutes are both offenders and victims. Therefore, in general, if their behavior has not caused any serious consequences, they are not punished, only criticized, educated, given administrative penalties, or at most sentenced to correctional work. Only prostitution peddlers are given criminal sentences.

Tables 5–11 and 5–12 show the type of sentences for the subjects.

2. Crime Methods

Of the sex crimes committed, 11.3 percent were through violence or force, and 47.7 percent by seduction or deceit (table 5–13).

Table 5–14 and figure 5–9 show that more males used the method of violence and force, and were still higher in the use of deceit or administrative superiority. Females were the predominant individuals committing prostitution.

There is a tendency for sex offenders to use psychological methods more in the recent years. In 1986, in Beijing, a male had illicit sex with fifty women. He was not attractive by appearance, but because of his special social position, he manipulated the minds of the females and succeeded in the crime.[2] Other types of methods include the technological method, with the use of drugs and technological instruments. This was not found yet in this survey.

MEANS OF COMMITTING THE OFFENSE								
TOTAL	PROSTITUTION		VIOLENCE		THREAT		SEDUCTION	
	NO.	%	NO.	%	NO.	%	NO.	%
2136	217	10.2	150	7.0	92	4.3	316	14.8

DATING		INTRODUCED BY OTHERS		GROUP SEX		OFFICIAL POWER	
NO.	%	NO.	%	NO.	%	NO.	%
688	32.2	163	7.6	58	2.7	40	1.9

RECOMMEND JOB		OFFER HOUSING		OTHERS		UNKNOWN	
NO.	%	NO.	%	NO.	%	NO.	%
14	0.7	26	1.2	83	3.9	289	13.5

Table 5–13

GENDER AND MEANS OF CRIME											
GENDER	TOTAL	PROSTITUTION		VIOLENCE		THREAT		SEDUCTION		DATING	
		NO.	%	NO.	%	NO.	%	NO.	%	NO.	%
Male	1229	20	1.6	134	10.9	84	6.8	257	20.9	484	39.4
Female	565	193	34.2	7	1.2	7	1.2	50	8.8	185	32.7

	INTRODUCED BY OTHERS		GROUP SEX		OFFICIAL POWER		RECOMMEND JOB		OFFER HOUSING		OTHERS	
	NO.	%	NO.	%	NO.	%	NO.	%	NO.	%		
Male	73	5.9	48	3.9	37	3.0	5	0.4	18	1.5	69	5.6
Female	84	14.9	10	1.8	1	0.2	9	1.6	7	1.2	12	2.1

P=0.001

Table 5–14

3. Sex Crime Victims

By the reports of 1,534 offenders, 70 percent of their victims were ordinary members of the other sex, i.e., those between the age of eighteen and sixty, of normal physical and psychological health, and not closely related to the offenders. Outside these normal subjects, young girls below the age of fourteen were the most frequent victims (table 5–15). It shows that they need more social attention for sex education and protection.

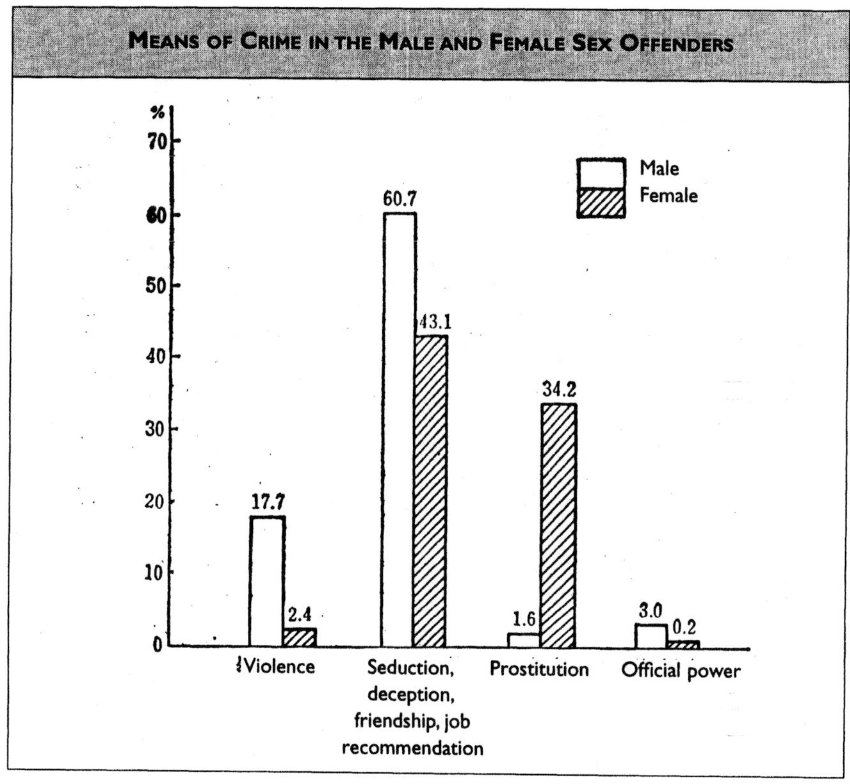

Figure 5–9

TYPE OF SEX CRIME VICTIMS

TOTAL	USUALLY OTHER SEX		YOUNG GIRLS		OLD PEOPLE		CLOSE RELATIVE		MENTALLY DISABLED	
	NO.	%	NO.	%	NO.	%	NO.	%	NO.	%
1534	1104	71.9	335	21.8	26	1.7	25	1.6	44	2.9

Table 5–15

Of those surveyed, 690 subjects (45.0 percent) reported to have one to two victims, 334 (21.8 percent) reported three to four, 192 (12.5 percent) five to six, 113 (7.4 percent) seven to eight, 89 (5.8 percent) nine to ten, and 116 (7.4 percent) over ten. The mean number of victims per offender was 4.5 (SD=5.13). Table 5–16 shows that the female criminals had the greatest number of sexual victims, an obvious result of prostitution.

NUMBER OF VICTIMS (PER OFFENDER) BELONGING TO THE OTHER SEX

	TOTAL	1–2		3–4		5–6		7–8		9–10		>=11	
		NO.	%	NO.	%	NO.	%	NO.	%	NO.	%	NO.	%
Male	1036	591	57.0	212	20.5	106	10.2	68	6.6	31	3.0	28	2.7
Female	470	89	18.9	115	24.5	83	17.7	41	8.7	56	11.9	86	18.3

P=0.001

Table 5–16

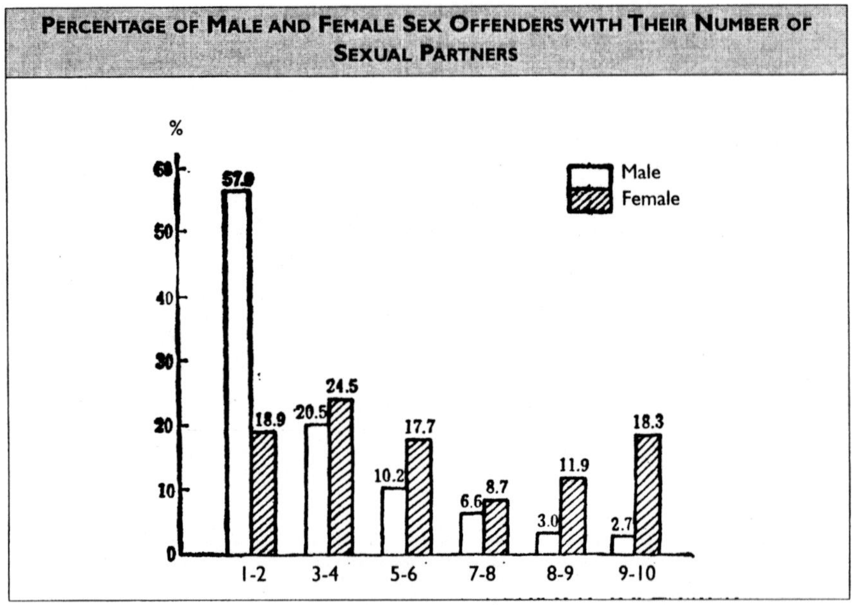

PERCENTAGE OF MALE AND FEMALE SEX OFFENDERS WITH THEIR NUMBER OF SEXUAL PARTNERS

Figure 5–10

NUMBER OF VICTIMS (PER OFFENDER) BELONGING TO THE SPECIAL GROUPS

	TOTAL	1		2–3		4–5		6–7	
		NO.	%	NO.	%	NO.	%		
Young girl	335	261	77.9	64	19.1	8	2.4	2	0.6
Elderly	26	17	65.4	9	34.6	0	0	0	0
Close relative	25	16	64.0	6	24.0	3	12.0	0	0
Ment. / Phys. disabled	44	37	84.1	6	13.6	1	2.3	0	0

Table 5–17

NUMBER OF CLOSE RELATIVE VICTIMS PER OFFENDER									
GENDER OF OFFENDER	TOTAL	1		2		3		4	
		NO.	%	NO.	%	NO.	%	NO.	%
Male	15	9	60.0	4	26.7	2	13.3	0	0
Female	10	7	70.0	0	0	0	0	3	30.0

Table 5–18

Tables 5–17 to 5–20 show the type and rate of "unusual" victims the sex criminals had sexual relations with. Those who had sex with young girls were all males. Those who had sex with psychiatric patients and the mentally impaired were predominantly males. Males were also more for having sex with close relatives and the elderly.

NUMBER OF ELDERLY VICTIMS PER OFFENDER							
SEX OF OFFENDER	TOTAL	1		2		3	
		NO.	%	NO.	%	NO.	%
Male	14	8	57.1	4	28.6	2	14.3
Female	11	8	72.7	2	18.2	1	9.1

Table 5–19

NUMBER OF MENTALLY OR PHYSICALLY DISABLED VICTIMS PER OFFENDER									
GENDER OF OFFENDER	TOTAL	1		2		3		4–5	
		NO.	%	NO.	%	NO.	%	NO.	%
Male	43	36	83.7	2	4.7	4	9.3	1	2.3
Female	1	1	100.0	0	0	0	0	0	0

Table 5–20

4. Age at First Offense

There is a general tendency, overall, for sex criminals to be quite young.[3] From the self-reports of 1990 criminals, 85.7 percent had their first offense below age twenty-nine, 50.7 percent below nineteen. For those who committed offenses before marriage, the mean age of first offense was 18.35 (SD=6.43). For the married criminal, the mean age of first offense was 30.75 (SD=8.32); for the divorced and widowed, mean age was 35.37 (11.55). The overall mean age was 20.91 (SD=8.71) (table 5–21).

Age of First Offense													
	TOTAL	<=14		15–19		20–29		30–39		40–49		>=50	
		NO.	%	NO.	%	NO.	%	NO.	%	NO.	%	NO.	%
Before marriage	1597	105	6.6	904	56.6	505	31.6	65	4.1	13	0.8	5	0.3
When married	342	0	0	2	0.6	170	49.7	123	35.9	31	9.1	16	4.7
Divorced/ widowed	51	0	0	0	0	20	39.2	15	29.4	5	9.8	11	21.6

Table 5–21

Age of First Offense of the Unmarried Offenders													
	TOTAL	<=14		15–19		20–29		30–39		40–49		>=50	
		NO.	%	NO.	%	NO.	%	NO.	%	NO.	%	NO.	%
Male	1080	63	5.8	541	50.1	399	36.9	59	5.5	13	1.2	5	0.5
Female	473	39	8.2	340	71.9	91	19.2	3	0.6	0	0	0	0

Table 5–22

Table 5–21 also shows that the large majority (80.3 percent) of the sex crimes were committed before marriage and most of them (88.2 percent) were between age fifteen to twenty-nine.

There is some difference between unmarried males and females in their age of first sex offense. For the females, many more were age nineteen or below, and nearly none were thirty or above (table 5–22). This shows the dangers faced by young women today.

The peak age of first offense for married male sex criminals was thirty to thirty-nine, for married females twenty to twenty-nine, much lower than the males.

Age of First Offense of the Married Offenders											
GENDER	TOTAL	15–19		20–29		30–39		40–49		>=50	
		NO.	%	NO.	%	NO.	%	NO.	%	NO.	%
Male	233	0	0	81	34.8	107	45.9	29	12.4	16	6.9
Female	102	2	2.0	86	84.3	14	13.7	0	0	0	0

P=0.001

Table 5–23

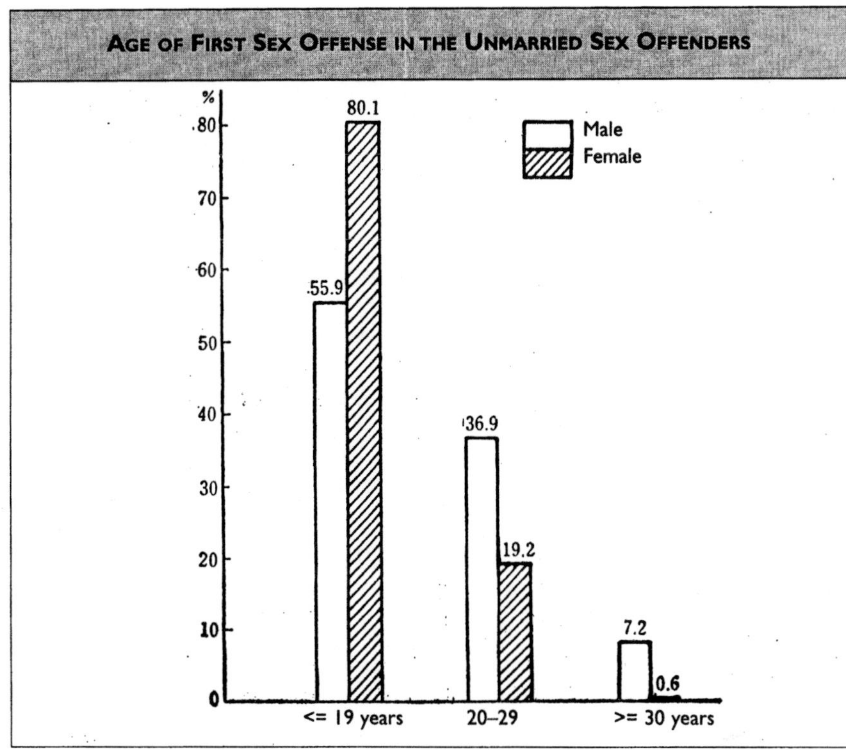

Figure 5–11

5. Motive of the Crime

Of those surveyed, 339 (15.9 percent) reported money as the principle motive for their crime, 781 (36.6 percent) committed the crime for pleasure, 579 (27.1 percent) for curiosity, 166 (7.8 percent) for revenge, 107 (5.0 percent) for other motives, and 164 (7.7 percent) were unclear.

Table 5–24 shows that the sexes differ a lot in their motives. Males concentrated on pleasure (49.7 percent) and curiosity (35.8 percent). Females concentrated on money (44.1 percent) and revenge (19.5 percent).

Table 5–25 shows that age has a definite relationship with sex crimes. The younger subjects had more curiosity and money motives. The older subjects had pleasure as their primary motive. The younger subjects had revenge as a primary motive as well. This motive decreased sharply above age thirty-six.

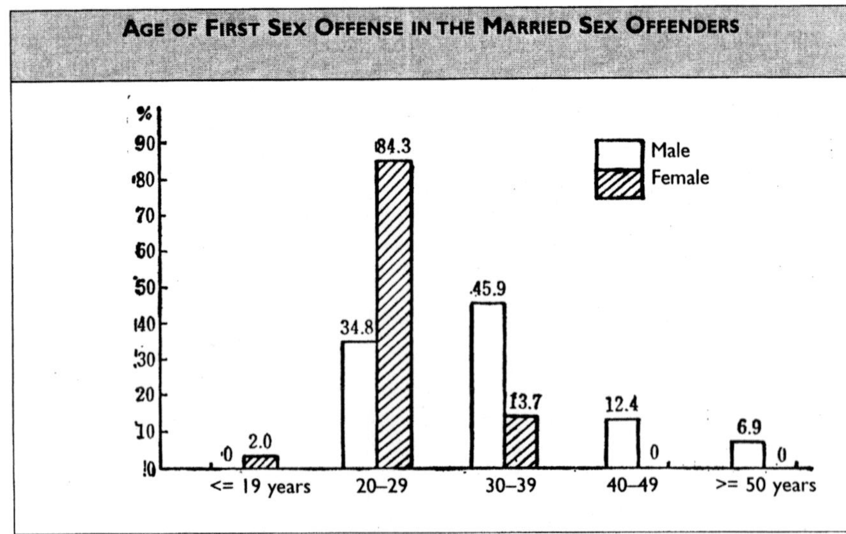

Figure 5–12

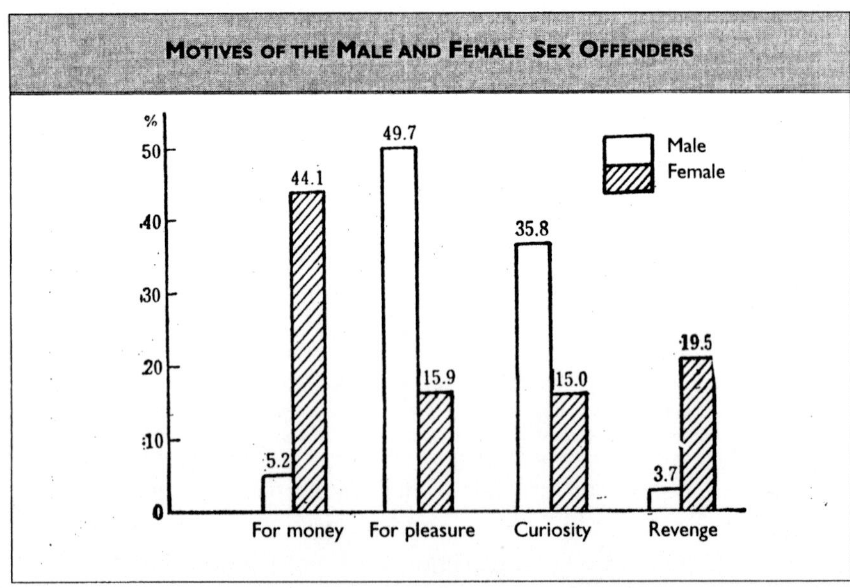

Figure 5–13

It has to be noted that the revenge motive occured much more in the females. It may show the level of unfair treatment females are receiving in our society. The finding is also in agreement with Feng's survey

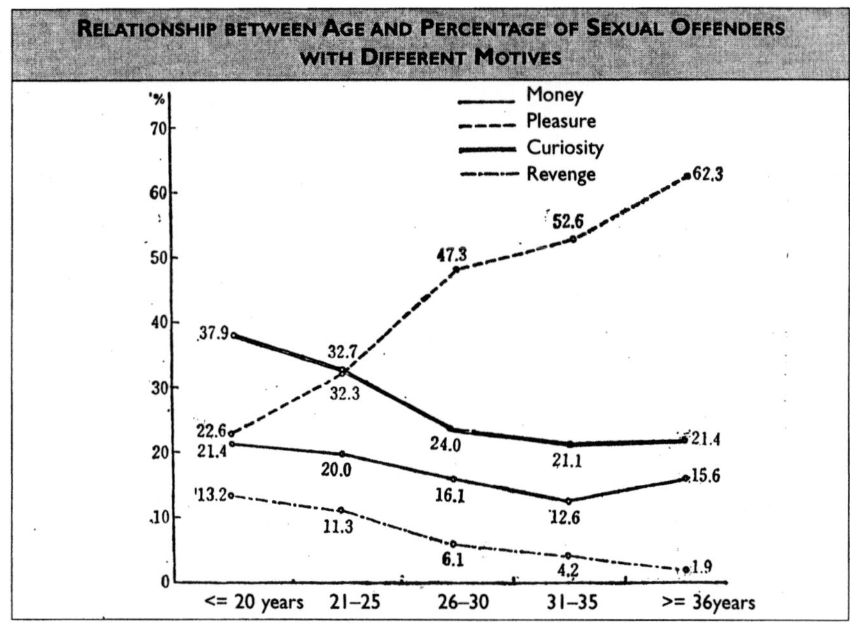

Figure 5–14

MOTIVE OF OFFENSE

GENDER	TOTAL	MONEY		PLEASURE		CURIOSITY		REVENGE		OTHERS	
		NO.	%	NO.	%	NO.	%	NO.	%	NO.	%
Male	1342	70	5.2	667	49.7	481	35.8	50	3.7	74	5.5
Female	580	256	44.1	92	15.9	57	15.0	113	19.5	32	5.5

P=0.001

Table 5–24

MOTIVE AND AGE

GENDER	TOTAL	MONEY		PLEASURE		CURIOSITY		REVENGE		OTHERS	
		NO.	%	NO.	%	NO.	%	NO.	%	NO.	%
<=20	499	107	21.4	113	22.6	189	37.9	66	13.2	24	4.8
21–25	520	104	20.0	168	32.3	170	32.7	59	11.3	19	3.7
26–30	391	63	16.1	185	47.3	94	24.0	24	6.1	25	6.4
31–35	190	24	12.6	100	52.6	40	21.1	8	4.2	18	9.5
>=36	308	24	7.8	192	62.3	66	21.4	6	1.9	20	6.5

Table 5–25

Age of First Ejaculation												
TOTAL	<=10		11–12		13–14		15–16		17–18		>=19	
	NO.	%	NO.	%	NO.	%	NO.	%	NO.	%	NO.	%
1305		7	0.5	24	1.8	250	19.2	514	39.4	326	25.0	184

Table 5–26

Age of First Menstruation												
TOTAL	<=10		11–12		13–14		15–16		17–18		>=19	
	NO.	%	NO.	%	NO.	%	NO.	%	NO.	%	NO.	%
602	19	3.2	112	18.6	245	40.7	185	30.7	36	6.0	5	0.8

Table 5–27

Age and Interval of Nocturnal Emissions													
	TOTAL	<=1 WEEK		2 WEEKS		1 MONTH		2 MONTHS		3 MONTHS		IRREGULAR	
		NO.	%	NO.	%	NO.	%	NO.	%	NO.	%	NO.	%
<=20	258	25	9.7	68	26.4	68	26.4	15	5.8	7	2.7	75	29.1
21–25	340	35	10.3	92	27.1	95	27.9	14	4.1	6	1.8	98	28.8
26–30	300	27	9.0	70	23.3	82	27.3	15	5.0	7	2.3	99	33.0
31–35	166	17	10.2	35	21.1	50	30.1	8	4.8	6	3.6	50	30.1
>=36	259	21	8.1	32	12.4	66	25.4	25	9.7	23	8.9	92	35.6

Table 5–28

performed in Shanghai in 1988 on 205 female criminals.[4] There, he found 24 percent of them were between age thirteen and seventeen, and 36 percent between eighteen and twenty. In the age range between thirteen and twenty, 23.9 percent reported being sexually abused in their early childhood; 13.7 percent of the abused said they committed crimes as revenge for their abuse experience.

Males may have a revenge motive too, e.g., because their relatives or wives had been sexually abused, or because they had the experience of being despised or mistreated by members of the opposite sex.[5]

3. Sexual Development and Experience

1. Sexual Development

The mean age of male sex criminals for first ejaculation was 16.34 (SD=2.61), of the females for menarche was 13.7 (SD=2.69). Of the

1,360 male criminals, 129 (9.5 percent) reported that they had nocturnal emission once a week or more, 307 (22.6 percent) once every two weeks, 372 (27.4 percent) once a month, 77 (5.7 percent) once every two months, 49 (3.6 percent) once every three months, and 426 (31.3 percent) irregularly.

Age has some relationship with the frequency of nocturnal emission, with the younger subjects having more frequent nocturnal emissions (table 5–28).

2. *Having Watched Sexual Intercourse*

There are theories which say that the experience of having watched sexual intercourse causes youngsters to commit sexual crimes because of

Age and Circumstances of Watching Sexual Intercourse

AGE	TOTAL	PARENTS AT HOME		SIBLINGS AT HOME		FRIEND'S HOUSE		VIDEO MOVIES		PUBLIC PLACE	
		NO.	%	NO.	%	NO.	%	NO.	%	NO.	%
<=15	374	54	14.4	16	4.3	76	20.3	174	46.5	54	14.4
16–20	628	12	1.9	15	2.4	130	20.7	361	57.5	110	17.5
>20	112	7	6.3	2	1.8	14	12.5	64	57.1	25	22.3

Table 5–29

Relationship between the Percentage of Sex Offenders Witnessing Sexual Intercourse in Different Situations and Their Age

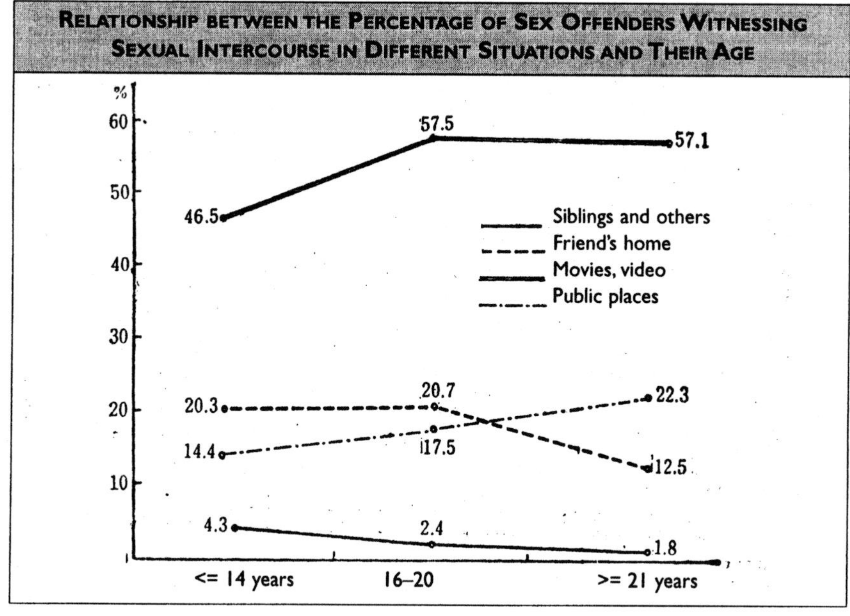

Figure 5–15

the impulse, curiosity, and emotion it arouses. In Shanghai, a fifteen-year-old boy was reported having experimented sexually with his sister because he had inadvertently watched his parents having sex.[6]

Of the 1,355 criminals, 80 (5.9 percent) reported that their first exposure to sexual intercourse was watching their parents, 36 (2.7 percent) watching their siblings, 262 (19.3 percent) watching friends, 753 (55.6 percent) watching videos, 221 (16.3 percent) watching strangers in public, and 3 (0.2 percent) unclear.

Response and Age of First Watching Sexual Depictions from Videos, Movies, or Books

AGE OF WATCHING	TOTAL	CALM		EXCITED		WISH TO TRY	
		NO.	%	NO.	%	NO.	%
<=15	371	155	41.8	142	38.3	74	19.9
16–20	625	294	46.9	242	38.6	91	14.5
>20	114	69	60.5	34	29.8	11	9.6

Table 5–30

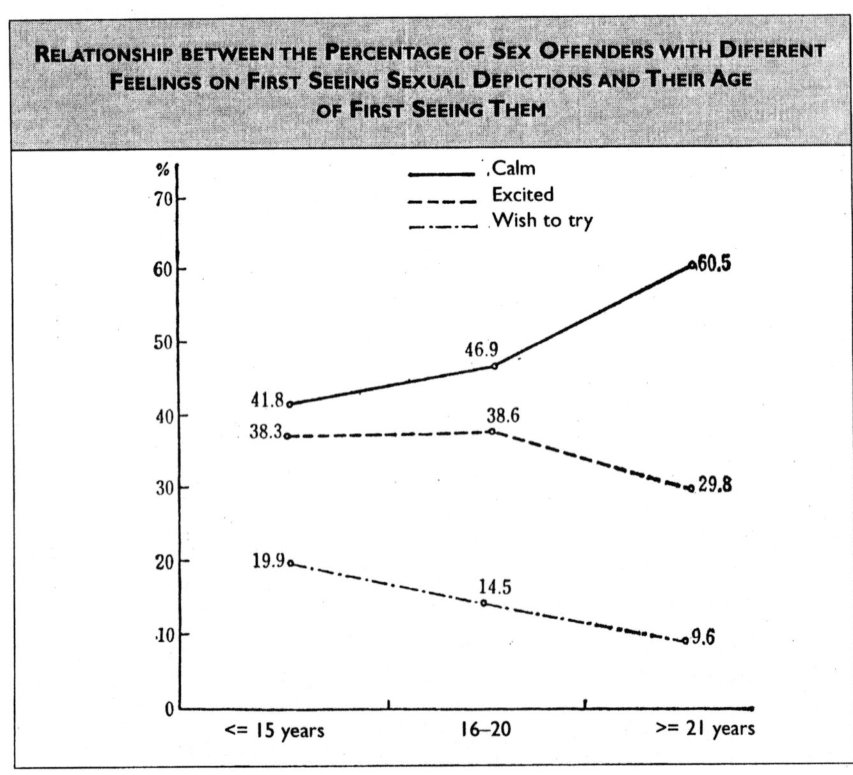

Relationship between the Percentage of Sex Offenders with Different Feelings on First Seeing Sexual Depictions and Their Age of First Seeing Them

Figure 5–16

AGE OF FIRST WATCHING SEXUAL INTERCOURSE AND SUBJECTIVE STRENGTH OF SEX DRIVE										
AGE OF WATCHING	TOTAL	HIGH		USUAL		LOW		UNCONTROLLABLE	
		NO.	%	NO.	%	NO.	%	NO.	%
<=15	362	73	20.2	239	66.0	27	7.5	23	6.3
16–20	628	99	15.8	446	71.0	51	8.1	32	5.1
>20	117	19	16.2	82	70.1	13	11.1	3	2.6

Table 5–31

Of those surveyed, 1,163 subjects reported the age at which they first watched sexual intercourse. Of these subjects, 38 (3.3 percent) were below age eleven, 344 (29.6 percent) between eleven and fifteen, 654 (56.2 percent) between sixteen and twenty, 91 (7.8 percent) between twenty-one and twenty-five, and 36 (3.1 percent) above twenty-five. The mean age was 17.1, SD=4.81.

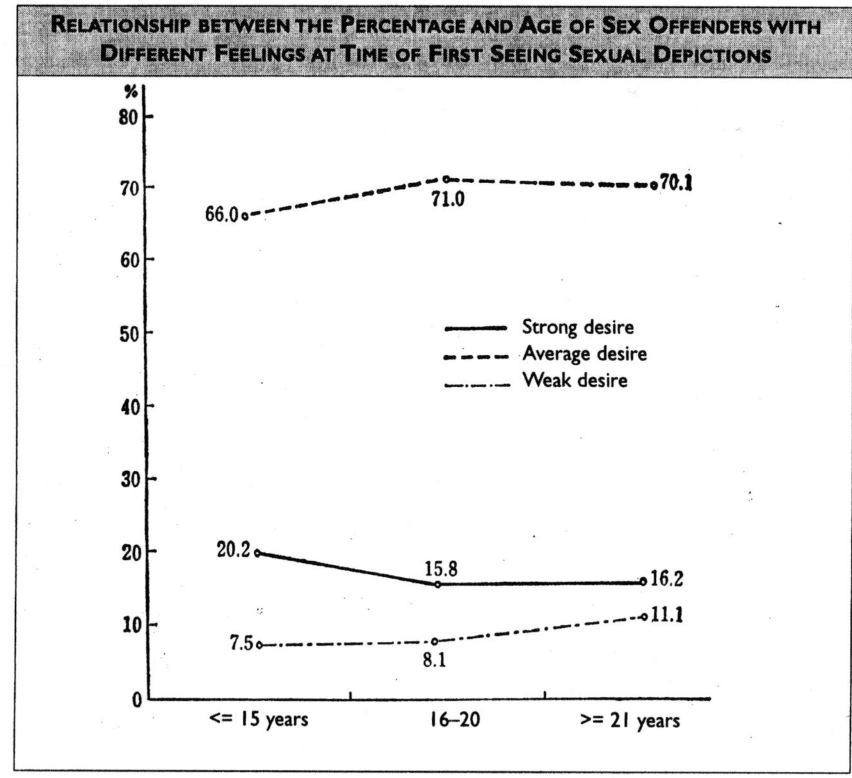

Figure 5–17

AGE OF FIRST WATCHING SEXUAL INTERCOURSE AND AGE OF FIRST SEX OFFENSE									
AGE OF WATCHING	TOTAL	<=14		15–19		20–29		>=30	
		NO.	%	NO.	%	NO.	%	NO.	%
<=15	324	47	14.5	223	68.8	44	13.6	10	3.1
16–20	512	13	2.5	305	59.6	184	35.9	10	2.0
>20	72	1	1.4	5	6.9	54	75.0	12	16.7

Table 5–32

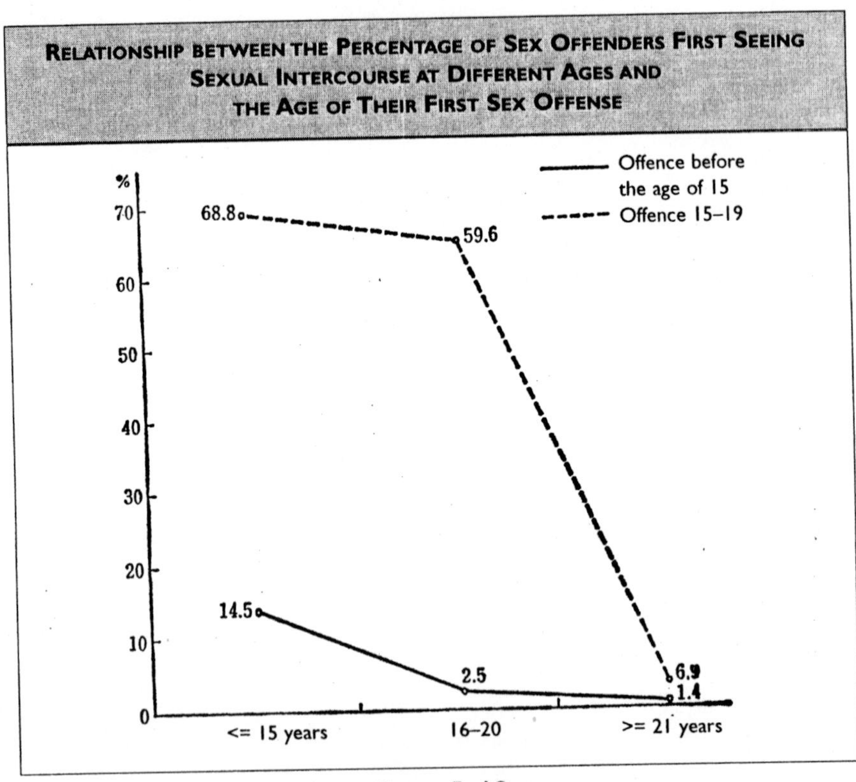

Figure 5–18

Table 5–29 and figure 5–15 shows the age and environment of the subjects' first watching sexual intercourse.

Table 5–29 shows that most of those who watched before age fifteen watched their parents or siblings. Friends were the most common for those who first watched between sixteen and twenty. As age increases, the rate of first seeing sexual intercourse from videos or friends increased as well (G=0.24).

Those individuals who witnessed sexual intercourse at an early age also reported the desire to try the act at that age (G=0.16, table 5–30).

Table 5–31 also shows that the earlier the subject had witnessed the act of sexual intercourse, the more of them felt their sexual desires were strong or up to an uncontrollable level.

Table 5–32 shows that the earlier the subjects had watched sexual intercourse, the earlier their age of first sex offense occurred (G=0.63).

Our figures have demonstrated some association between watching sexual intercourse and sex crime, but we cannot conclude any direct causal relationship, since there could be many other related factors. Our survey did not have any control to really look into the matter. Our figures, however, may be used in future studies on this issue, when normal control and other comparative data are available.

3. Masturbation

Experience of Masturbation

GENDER	TOTAL	YES		NO		UNKNOWN	
		NO.	%	NO.	%	NO.	%
Male	1441	275	19.1	1017	70.6	149	10.3
Female	630	55	8.7	408	64.8	167	26.5

P=0.001

If masturbation rate is a measure of the strength of sexual desire, the rate of the sex criminals did not show they had

Experience of Masturbation and Educational Level

MASTURBATION	TOTAL	ILLITERATE		PRIMARY		J. HIGH		S. HIGH AND ABOVE	
		NO.	%	NO.	%	NO.	%	NO.	%
Yes	283	12	11.2	63	18.6	151	15.8	57	17.6
No	1443	95	88.8	276	81.4	806	84.2	266	82.4

Table 5–34

greater sexual desire than other groups we surveyed. Only 337 subjects (15.8 percent) in this part of the survey admitted masturbation habits, with males being much higher than females (table 5–33), and no relationship with educational level (table 5–34).

The frequency of masturbation in the subjects was also low compared with our other groups in the survey; 148 (43.9 percent) reported less than once a week, 95 (28.2 percent) once a week, 46 (13.6 percent) twice a week, 19 (5.6 percent) three times a week, 8 (2.4 percent) four

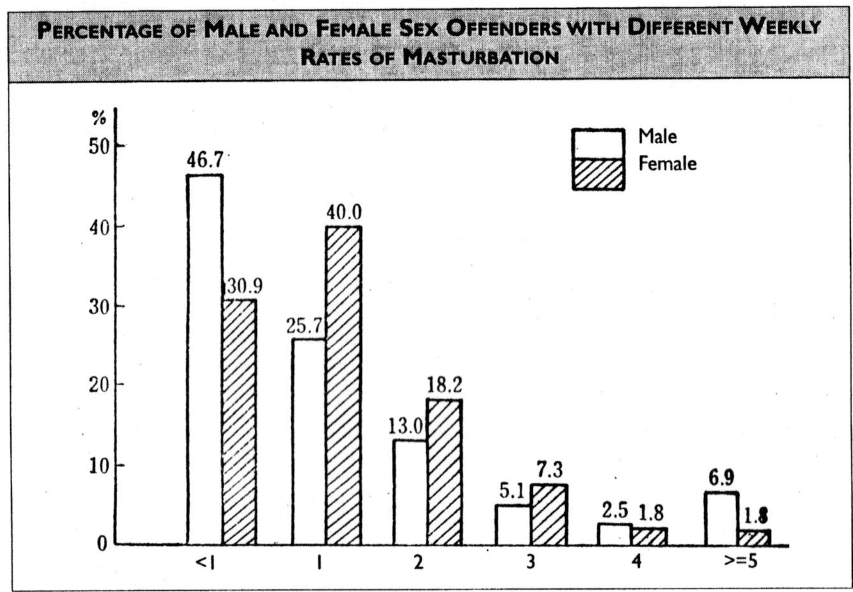

PERCENTAGE OF MALE AND FEMALE SEX OFFENDERS WITH DIFFERENT WEEKLY RATES OF MASTURBATION

Figure 5–19

CURRENT NUMBER OF TIMES MASTURBATING PER WEEK

	TOTAL	<1		1		2		3		4		>=5	
		NO.	%	NO.	%	NO.	%	NO.	%	NO.	%	NO.	%
Male	276	129	46.7	71	25.7	36	13.0	14	5.1	7	2.5	19	6.9
Female	55	17	30.9	22	40.0	10	18.2	4	7.3	1	1.8	1	1.8

P=0.001

Table 5–35

EDUCATIONAL LEVEL AND CURRENT MASTURBATION PER WEEK

	TOTAL	<1		1		2		3		4		>=5	
		NO.	%	NO.	%	NO.	%	NO.	%	NO.	%	NO.	%
Illiterate	16	3	18.8	6	37.5	0	0	2	12.5	2	12.5	3	18.8
Primary	87	31	35.6	32	36.8	12	13.8	4	4.6	2	2.3	6	6.9
J. high	175	80	45.7	46	26.3	27	15.4	10	5.7	4	2.3	8	4.6
S. high & above	52	32	61.5	10	19.2	6	11.5	2	3.9	0	0	2	3.9

Table 5–36

AGE AND CURRENT MASTURBATION PER WEEK													
AGE	TOTAL	<1		1		2		3		4		>=5	
		NO.	%	NO.	%	NO.	%	NO.	%	NO.	%	NO.	%
<=20	93	36	38.7	32	34.4	12	12.9	5	5.4	4	4.3	4	4.3
21–25	86	43	50.0	16	18.6	20	23.3	4	4.7	0	0	3	3.5
26–30	65	27	41.5	23	35.4	5	7.7	6	9.2	2	3.1	2	3.1
31–35	36	14	38.9	14	38.9	4	11.1	1	2.8	0	0	3	8.3
>=36	50	24	48.0	8	16.0	5	10.0	3	6.0	2	4.0	8	16.0

Table 5–37

times a week, and 21 (6.2 percent) five or more times a week. The mean frequency for males was 1.4 times per week, for females 1.3 times.

It is difficult to explain this lower frequency. It could be due to difference in age distribution of the surveyed groups, or that it was not so convenient to masturbate in prison or correctional centers, which may run the subject a risk of further ridicule or punishment.

Table 5–36 show that the more highly educated masturbated less than the less educated.

SUBJECTIVE SEX DRIVE STRENGTH									
GENDER	TOTAL	STRONG		AVERAGE		WEAK		UNCONTROLLABLE	
		NO.	%	NO.	%	NO.	%	NO.	%
Male	1333	274	20.6	886	66.5	95	7.1	78	5.8
Female	584	46	7.9	454	77.7	75	12.8	9	1.5

P=0.001

Table 5–38

AGE AND SUBJECTIVE SEX DRIVE STRENGTH									
AGE	TOTAL	STRONG		AVERAGE		WEAK		UNCONTROLLABLE	
		NO.	%	NO.	%	NO.	%	NO.	%
<=20	452	71	15.7	311	68.8	46	10.2	24	5.3
21–25	536	75	14.0	389	72.6	40	7.5	32	6.0
26–30	400	73	18.3	289	72.3	21	5.2	17	4.2
31–35	206	35	17.0	148	71.8	18	8.7	5	2.4
>=36	317	65	20.5	195	61.5	49	15.5	8	2.5

Table 5–39

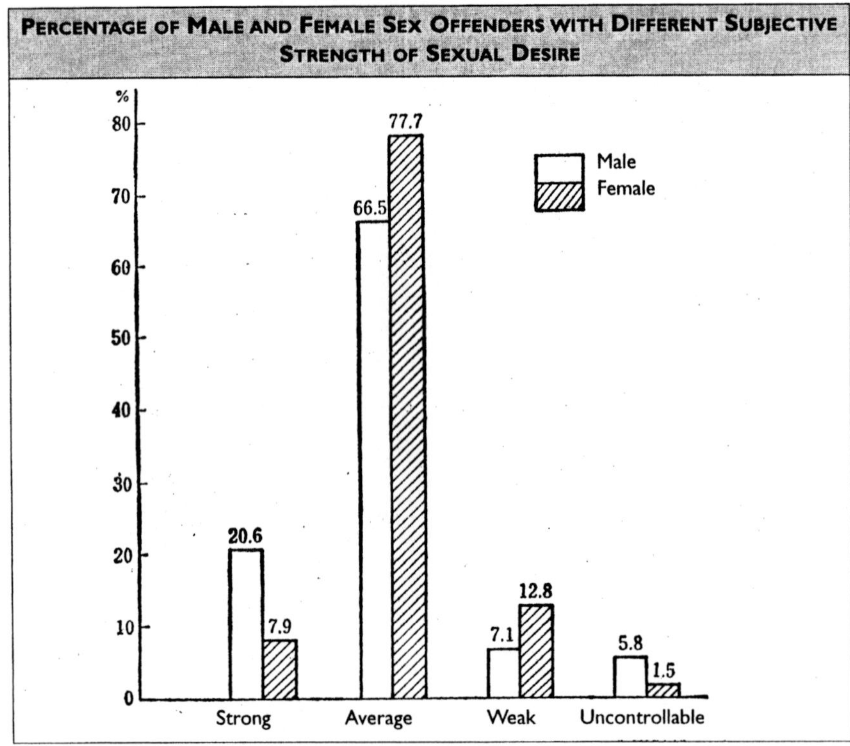

Figure 5–20

Age of the masturbators had no significant relationship with the frequency of masturbation (table 5–37).

4. Sexual Desire

Of those surveyed, 325 (15.2 percent) of the sex criminals reported high sexual desire, 1,370 (64.1 percent) reported ordinary desire, 180 (8.4 percent) reported low desire, 88 (4.1 percent) reported exceptionally high desire to uncontrollable outbursts at any time, and 173 (8.1 percent) did not give any clear answer.

Males with high subjective sexual desires were 3.72 times more than those with low desires. For females the high-low ratio was only 3:4. The female subjects were of lower desires probably because of cultural reasons only. But if their cultural controls are broken by early sexual experiences, it may be their desire to seek self-destruction, causing them to commit sex crimes, especially prostitution.[7]

Table 5–39 shows that subjects above age thirty-five had the highest

EDUCATION OF PARENTS													
	TOTAL	ILLITERATE		PRIMARY		J. HIGH		S. HIGH		C. OR ABOVE		UNKNOWN	
		NO.	%	NO.	%	NO.	%	NO.	%	NO.	%	NO.	%
Father	2136	549	25.7	512	24.0	535	25.0	276	12.9	139	6.5	125	5.9
Mother	2136	919	43.0	478	22.4	369	17.3	146	6.8	58	2.7	166	7.8

Table 5–40

OCCUPATION OF PARENTS											
	TOTAL	FACTORY		AGRICULTURE		SERVICE		COMMERCE		OFFICIAL	
		NO.	%	NO.	%	NO.	%	NO.	%	NO.	%
Father	2136	919	43.0	484	22.7	31	1.5	79	3.7	276	12.9
Mother	2136	776	36.3	669	31.3	54	2.5	62	2.9	80	3.7

	PROFESSIONAL		ARTS		SOLDIER		SELF BUSINESS		NO JOB		OTHERS		UNKNOWN	
	NO.	%	NO.	%	NO.	%	NO.	%	NO.	%	NO.	%	NO.	%
Father	47	2.2	73	3.4	13	0.6	67	3.1	21	1.0	28	1.3	98	4.6
Mother	30	1.4	80	3.7	3	0.1	57	2.7	143	6.7	33	1.5	149	7.0

Table 5–41

FAMILY FINANCIAL SITUATION BEFORE CONVICTION											
GENDER	TOTAL	VERY GOOD		GOOD		AVERAGE		POOR		VERY POOR	
		NO.	%	NO.	%	NO.	%	NO.	%	NO.	%
Male	1410	75	5.3	319	22.6	835	59.2	131	9.3	50	3.5
Female	606	36	5.9	138	22.8	329	54.3	82	13.5	21	3.5

P=0.10

Table 5–42

percentage of high desire and low desire subjects. The individuals with uncontrollable desires decreased as age advanced.

4. Marriage

1. Parental Status

The educational level of the parents were lower than general, with 50.7 percent of them at primary level, and 65.4 percent in the illiterate to semi-illiterate range.

By occupation, most of the parents (65.7 percent of fathers, 67.6 percent of mothers) were workers or farmers, agreeing to the general occupation distribution in China. It has to be noted that the third most common occupation of the parents was government officials.

Family economic conditions showed nothing particular. Most of them (83.5 percent) were from average to above-average range. There was also no significant difference between male and female criminals (table 5–42).

Ability of Financial Situation to Satisfy One's Needs Before Conviction

GENDER	TOTAL	YES		NO	
		NO.	%	NO.	%
Male	1417	915	64.6	502	35.4
Female	608	303	49.8	305	50.2

P=0.001

Table 5–43

Percentage of Male and Female Offenders Who Are Financially Unsatisfied and Have Financial Difficulties

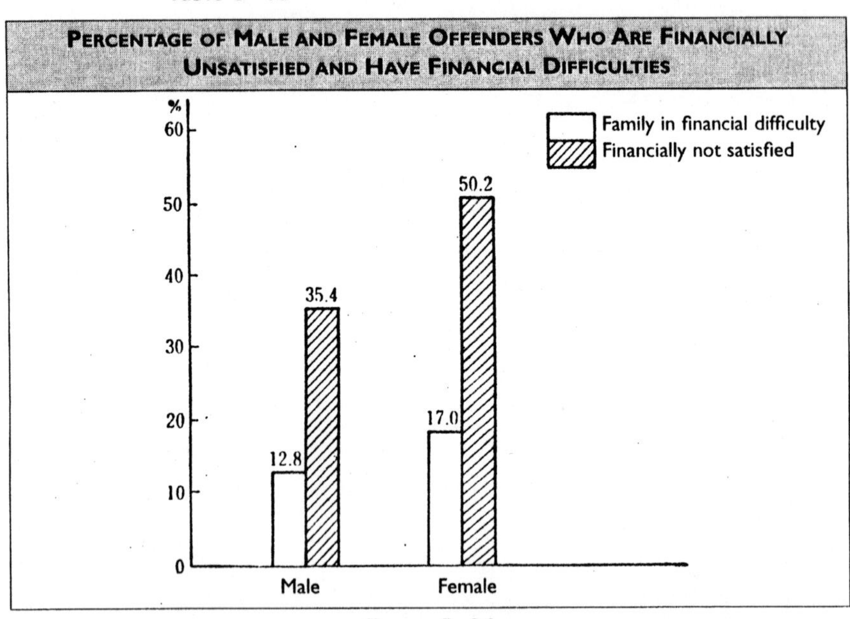

Figure 5–21

However, quite a sizable proportion of criminals were dissatisfied with their families financial situation; 1,251 (58.6 percent) felt the family could satisfy their needs, but 830 (38.9 percent) said they thought not. Taking out those whose families were really financially inadequate, there were 25.2 percent who were not satisfied with an average or above average family. Males with such dissatisfactions were 35.4 percent and females 50.2 percent (table 5–42 and 5–43).

Parental criminal records could be a factor for sex crimes among their children. In Shanghai, it was reported that when a father was imprisoned due to a sex crime, the mother had promiscuous sex at home. Her three daughters learned this and all sexually misbehaved at age twelve or thirteen.[8] Of the subjects surveyed, 59 (2.8 percent) reported sex criminals among their family members, 110 (5.1 percent) reported promiscuous sex in the members. More females gave such reports.

History of Sex Offense in Family Members					
GENDER	TOTAL	YES		NO	
		NO.	%	NO.	%
Male	1375	36	2.6	1339	97.4
Female	594	23	3.9	571	96.1

Table 5–44

History of Promiscuity in Family Members					
GENDER	TOTAL	YES		NO	
		NO.	%	NO.	%
Male	1381	68	4.9	1313	95.1
Female	595	40	6.7	555	93.3

Table 5–45

2. Relationship with Parents

Of those surveyed, 1175 (55.0 percent) reported a good relationship, 746 (34.9 percent) ordinary, 105 (4.9 percent) bad, and 110 (5.1 percent) unclear. More females had bad relationship with their parents (table 5–46).

Relation with Parents Before Arrest							
GENDER	TOTAL	GOOD		AVERAGE		POOR	
		NO.	%	NO.	%	NO.	%
Male	1370	840	61.3	471	34.4	59	4.3
Female	604	299	49.5	264	43.7	41	6.8

P=0.001

Table 5–46

Although the overall parental relationships were not worse than that of the general population, communication with the parents appeared bad. Out of all the subjects, 1,137 (53.2 percent) reported rare communication or chatting with the parents, 127 (5.9 percent) never, 769 (36.0 percent) regularly, and 103 (4.8 percent) unknown (table 5–47).

Verbal Communication with Parents Before Arrest							
GENDER	TOTAL	OFTEN		RARE		NEVER	
		NO.	%	NO.	%	NO.	%
Male	1369	532	38.9	750	54.8	87	6.4
Female	611	218	35.7	359	58.8	34	5.6

Table 5–47

FEELINGS TOWARD FAMILY LIFE									
GENDER	TOTAL	MATERIAL & MENTAL SATISFACTION		MATERIAL SATISFACTION ONLY		NO WARMTH		MONOTONOUS	
		NO.	%	NO.	%	NO.	%	NO.	%
Male	1371	421	30.7	319	23.3	241	17.6	390	28.4
Female	602	95	15.8	158	26.2	149	24.8	200	33.2

P=0.001

Table 5–48

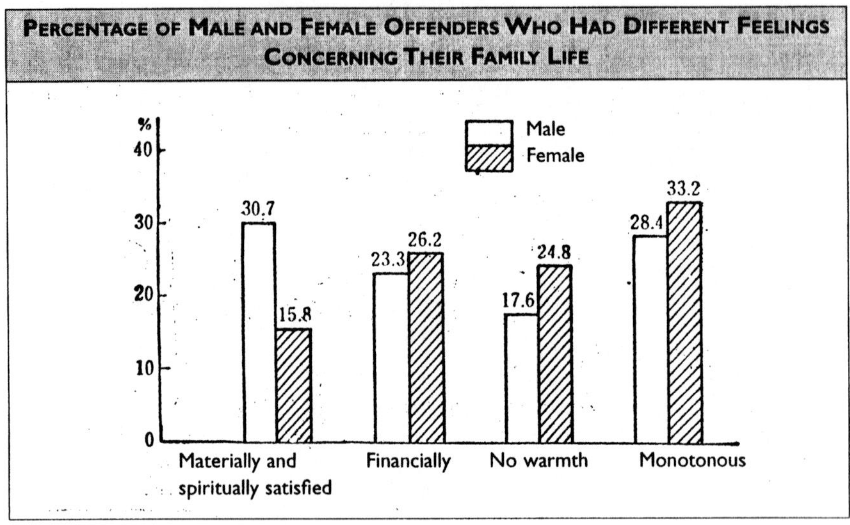

Figure 5–22

Table 5–48 shows the subjects' general feeling concerning the family; 527 (24.7 percent) said they were both materially and emotionally satisfied, 497 (23.3 percent) said only materially satisfied, 401 (18.8 percent) said lack of family warmth or concern, 601 (28.1 percent) felt boredom in family, and 110 (5.1 percent) unclear. It confirms that many sex criminals lack strong family ties.[9]

Table 5–48 and figure 5–22 show that family dissatisfaction is found more often in female offenders.

About one third of the subjects' parents did not give them any formal sex education. When the subjects came to the age of socializing with the opposite sex, 598 (27.9 percent) of the parents demanded that they

PARENTAL ATTITUDE TOWARD DATING FRIENDS OF THE OTHER SEX											
GENDER	TOTAL	TOTAL SUPPORT		CONDITIONAL SUPPORT		NO CONCERN		OPPOSE BAD COMPANY		ABSOLUTELY OPPOSE	
		NO.	%	NO.	%	NO.	%	NO.	%	NO.	%
Male	1285	65	5.1	396	30.8	255	19.8	350	27.2	219	17.0
Female	594	5	0.8	183	30.8	84	14.1	176	29.6	146	24.6

Table 5–49

not do it casually; 537 (25.1 percent) demanded them to make friends with righteous people only; only 74 (3.5 percent) supported their children unconditionally. Furthermore, 377 (17.6 percent) opposed any heterosexual contacts under any circumstances; 346 (16.2 percent) did not pay any attention; 206 (9.6 percent) were unclear in their attitudes. Table 5–49 shows that the parental attitudes did not differ between the son and daughters, although there was a slight suggestion that the parents controlled their daughters more.

Some parents continued with their prohibitive attitude after their children had sexually misbehaved. In a survey done in Sichuan, it was found that in a group of female sex offenders, 2 percent of the parents were ambivalent in their attitude, 20.2 percent remained as before, 49.5 percent scolded or beat them up, 14.1 percent threw them out of the home, and 5.1 percent treated them better than before. Only 9.1 percent tried to better educate their daughters.[10]

3. Marital Relationship

Of the 2,136 surveyed, 27.8 percent were married. Of the married offenders, 47.4 percent subjectively felt affection with their partners, 29.5 percent did not feel bad, and 22.6 percent felt that theirs was a poor relationship.

CURRENT RELATIONSHIP WITH SPOUSE											
GENDER	TOTAL	GOOD		FAIR		POOR		MUTUAL NEGLECT		SEPARATED	
		NO.	%	NO.	%	NO.	%	NO.	%	NO.	%
Male	465	266	57.2	127	27.3	46	9.9	8	1.7	18	3.9
Female	196	53	27.0	70	35.7	47	24.0	9	4.6	17	8.7

P=0.001

Table 5–50

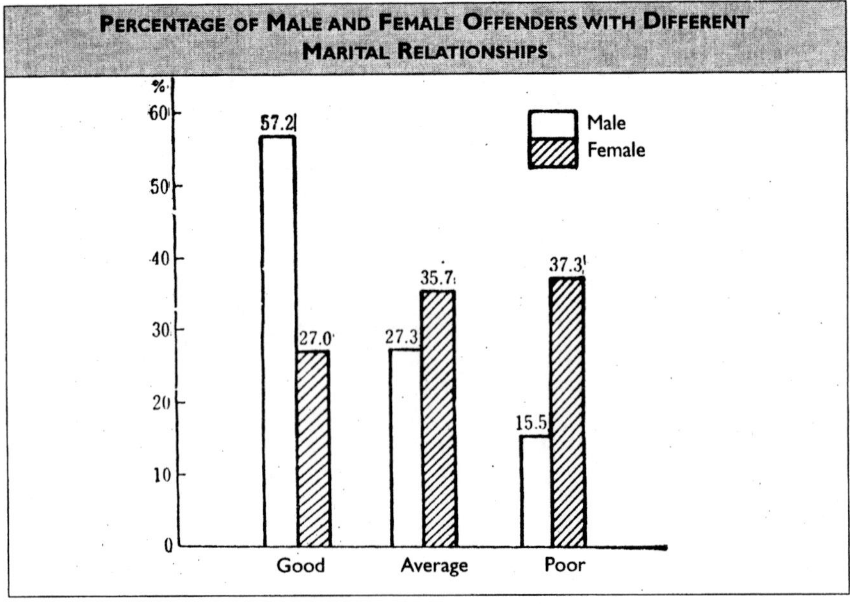

Figure 5–23

VERBAL COMMUNICATION WITH SPOUSE BEFORE CONVICTION

GENDER	TOTAL	OFTEN		RARE		NEVER	
		NO.	%	NO.	%	NO.	%
Male	486	283	58.2	183	37.7	20	4.1
Female	196	89	45.4	89	45.4	18	9.2

Table 5–51

The overall marital relationship was worse than the city and village couples surveyed in the last chapter.

In table 5–50, we can see that less than half as many female as male offenders felt

SEXUAL SATISFACTION BEFORE CONVICTION

GENDER	TOTAL	VERY GOOD		GOOD		NOT KNOW		POOR		VERY POOR	
		NO.	%	NO.	%	NO.	%	NO.	%	NO.	%
Male	449	64	14.2	239	53.2	58	12.9	72	16.0	16	3.6
Female	166	18	10.8	70	42.2	37	22.3	28	16.9	13	7.8

P=0.001

Table 5–52

that they had a good relationship with their spouse, suggesting that marital dissatisfaction could be a principal cause for female sex offenses.

The married offenders did not communicate well with their spouses in general. Out of those who responded, 46.4 percent of them talked little with their spouses, 53.6 percent did so regularly. Since 76.9 percent felt satisfied with their marriages, the high percentage of poor communication suggest that the marriages were in fact of poor quality. The female offenders communicated even less with their spouses which may also contribute to their sex offenses (table 5–51).

For sexual satisfaction, 63.2 percent of the married offenders reported very high or high satisfaction within their marriage before convic-

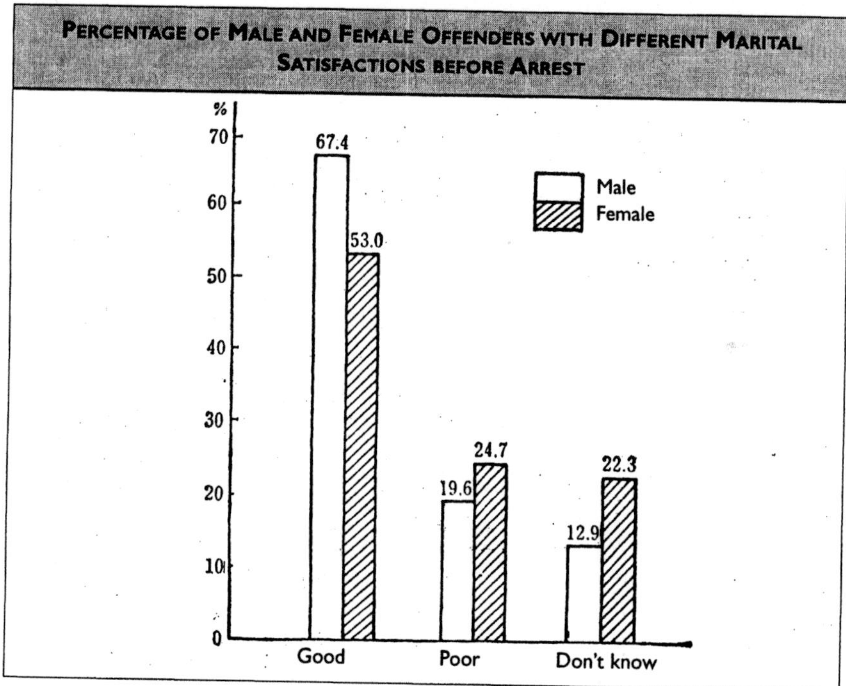

Figure 5–24

tion, 21.1 percent reported not satisfied, and 15.4 percent did not know. The percentage of sexual dissatisfaction was similar to the percentage on marital dissatisfaction.

Table 5–52 and figure 5–24 show that the more females were dissatisfied with sex than were males, similar to the findings on city and village couples in the previous chapter.

AGE AND SEXUAL SATISFACTION BEFORE CONVICTION											
AGE	TOTAL	VERY GOOD		GOOD		NOT KNOW		POOR		VERY POOR	
		NO.	%	NO.	%	NO.	%	NO.	%	NO.	%
<=25	98	12	12.2	39	39.8	28	28.6	15	15.3	4	4.1
26-30	131	17	13.0	67	51.1	23	17.6	18	13.7	6	4.6
31-35	121	19	15.7	71	58.7	16	13.2	9	7.4	6	5.0
36-45	167	22	13.2	81	48.5	16	9.6	37	22.2	11	6.6
46-55	58	6	10.3	30	51.7	9	15.5	11	19.0	2	3.5
>=56	33	5	15.2	18	54.5	3	9.1	7	21.2	0	0

Table 5–53

The age of the offenders had no significant relationship with sexual satisfaction before conviction.

Of the married offenders, 72.4 percent reported that their spouses could satisfy their sexual needs; 27.6 percent said they could not, and 1.1 percent did not give a clear answer. More males then females felt that

PERCENTAGE OF MALE AND FEMALE OFFENDERS WITH DIFFERENT WEEKLY RATES OF SEXUAL INTERCOURSE BEFORE ARREST

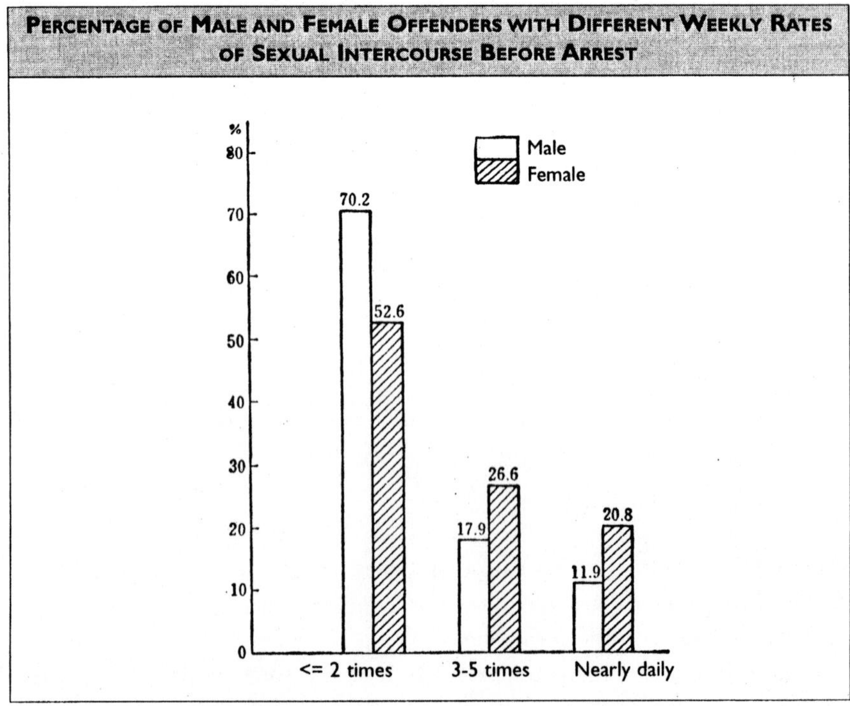

Figure 5–25

their spouses could not satisfy them (table 5–54).

WHETHER OR NOT SPOUSE WAS SEXUALLY SATISFYING BEFORE CONVICTION					
GENDER	TOTAL	YES		NO	
		NO.	%	NO.	%
Male	425	302	71.1	123	28.9
Female	163	124	74.1	39	23.9

Table 5–54

The frequency of sexual intercourse for the sex offenders before conviction was generally more than that of the general population. The mean rate was ten times per month, about double of the city and village couples surveyed in the last chapter. More males had sex twice per month. More females had it for three times per month, showing discrepancies in frequencies between the sexes (table 5–55 and figure 5–25).

FREQUENCY OF SEXUAL INTERCOURSE PER WEEK WITH SPOUSE BEFORE CONVICTION									
GENDER	TOTAL	<=1		2		3		DAILY	
		NO.	%	NO.	%	NO.	%	NO.	%
Male	436	128	29.4	178	40.8	78	17.9	52	11.9
Female	154	39	25.3	42	27.3	41	26.6	32	20.8

P=0.001

Table 5–55

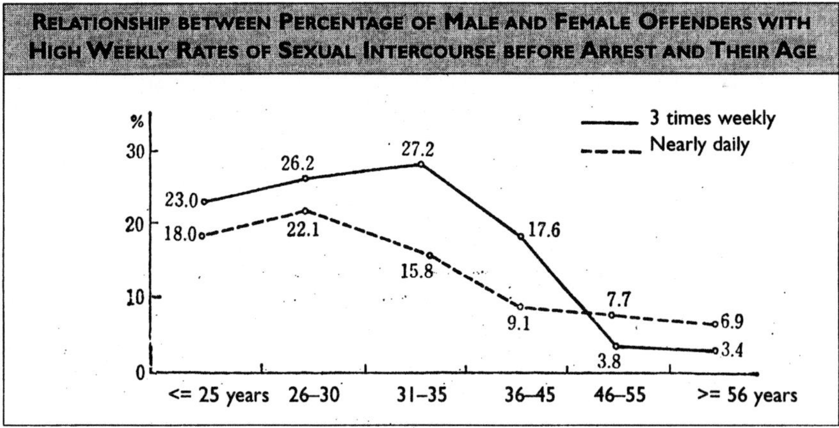

Figure 5–26

The frequency of sexual intercourse had some association with age. The younger the subject the more frequently they had sex (G=0.25). Figure 5–26 shows that the peak frequency occurred in age range of twenty-six to thirty.

AGE AND FREQUENCY OF SEXUAL INTERCOURSE PER WEEK WITH SPOUSE BEFORE CONVICTION									
AGE	TOTAL	<=1		2		3		DAILY	
		NO.	%	NO.	%	NO.	%	NO.	%
<=25	100	28	28.0	31	31.0	23	23.0	18	18.0
26–30	122	22	18.0	41	33.6	32	26.2	27	22.1
31–35	114	20	17.5	45	39.5	31	27.2	18	15.8
36–45	165	47	28.5	74	44.8	29	17.6	15	9.1
46–55	52	24	46.2	22	42.3	2	3.8	4	7.7
56	29	20	69.0	6	20.7	1	3.4	2	6.9

Table 5–56

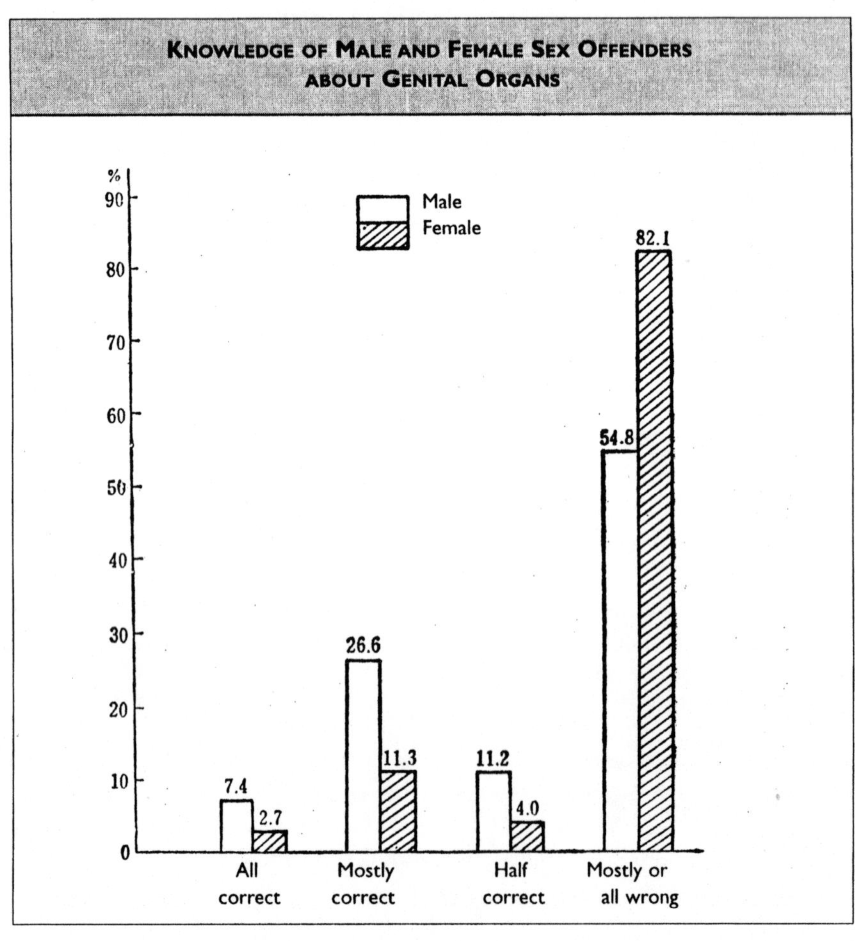

Figure 5–27

KNOWLEDGE ABOUT GENITAL ORGANS									
GENDER	TOTAL	ALL CORRECT		MAJORITY CORRECT		HALF CORRECT		MOSTLY WRONG	
		NO.	%	NO.	%	NO.	%	NO.	%
Male	1441	106	7.4	383	26.6	162	11.2	790	54.8
Female	630	17	2.7	71	11.3	25	4.0	517	82.1

P=0.001

Table 5–57

5. Sexual Knowledge and Attitude

1. SOURCE OF SEXUAL KNOWLEDGE

On a short test on sexual knowledge consisting of various questions, 126 subjects (5.9 percent) answered all questions correctly, 462 (21.6 percent) did fairly well, 191 (8.9 percent) answered half of the questions correctly, and 1,357 (63.5 percent) failed badly or did not answer. The percentage of correct answers was 27.8 percent. The females did not do

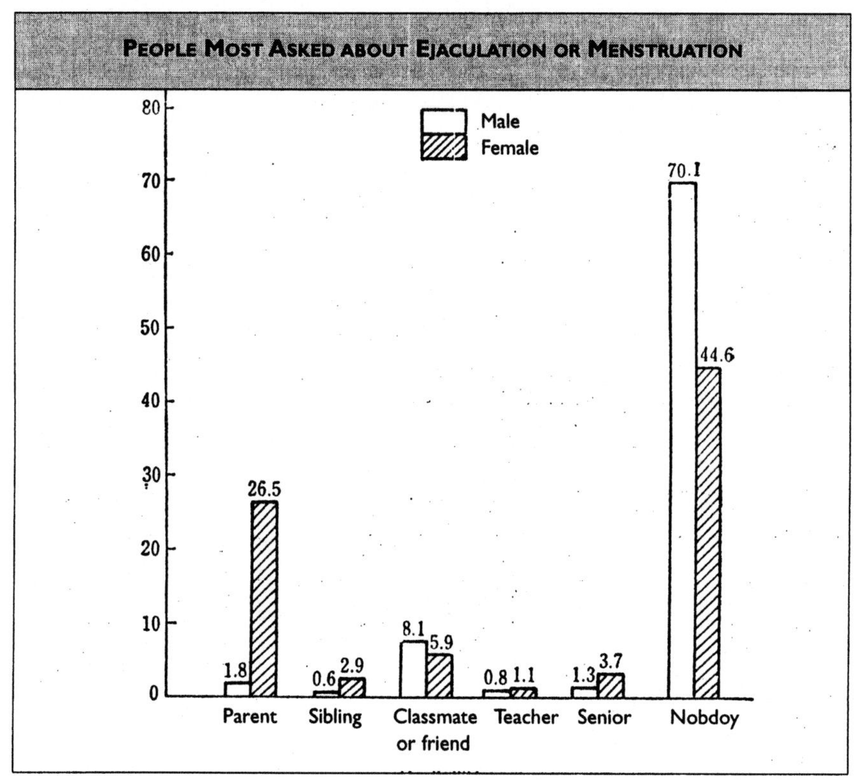

Figure 5–28

Knowledge about Ejaculation								
TOTAL	HARMFUL TO HEALTH		NORMAL		CANNOT TELL		UNKNOWN	
	NO.	%	NO.	%	NO.	%	NO.	%
1441	137	9.5	920	63.8	344	23.9	40	2.8

Table 5–58

as well as the males (table 5–57).

On the topic of ejaculation, only 63.8 percent of the male subjects thought it was a natural phenomenon (table 5–58).

Person Consulted on First Ejaculation or Menstruation																		
	TOTAL	PARENT		SIBLING		FRIEND		TEACHER		SENIOR OF SAME SEX		NOBODY		OTHERS		UNKOWN		
		NO.	%	NO.	%	NO.	%	NO.	%	NO.	%	NO.	%	NO.	%	NO.	%
Male	1441	26	1.8	8	0.6	117	8.1	12	0.8	19	1.3	1010	70.1	51	3.5	198	13.7
Female	630	167	26.5	18	2.9	37	5.9	7	1.1	23	3.7	281	44.6	6	1.0	91	14.4

P=0.001

Table 5–59

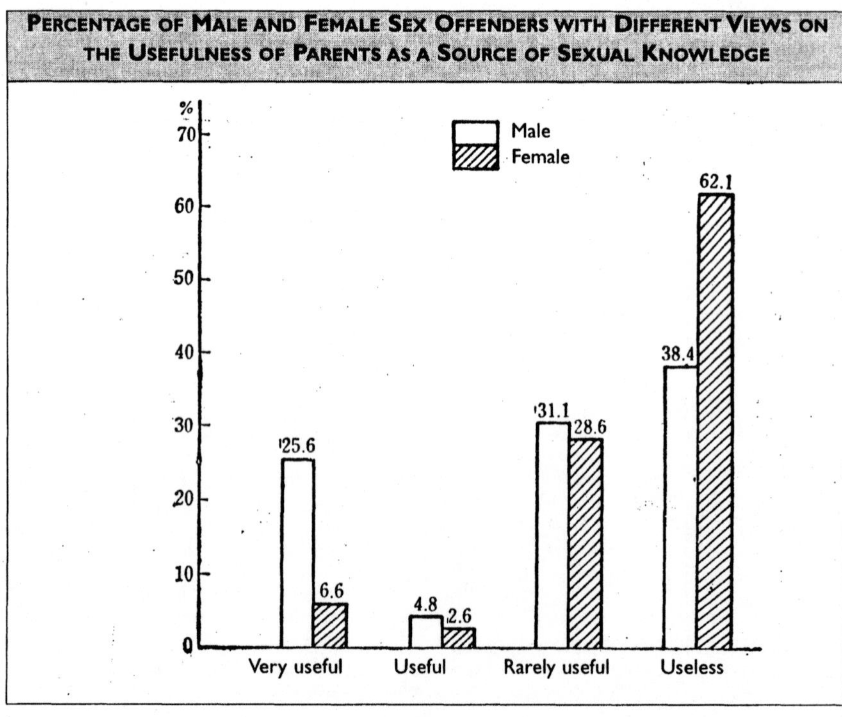

Percentage of Male and Female Sex Offenders with Different Views on the Usefulness of Parents as a Source of Sexual Knowledge

Figure 5–29

GENDER AND VIEW ON SEXUAL INFORMATION FROM PARENTS										
GENDER	TOTAL	VERY USEFUL		USEFUL		RARELY USEFUL		USELESS		
		NO.	%	NO.	%	NO.	%	NO.	%
Male	289	74	25.6	14	4.8	90	31.1	111	38.4
Female	227	15	6.6	6	2.6	65	28.6	141	62.1

Table 5–60

AGE AND VIEW ON SEXUAL INFORMATION FROM PARENTS									
AGE	TOTAL	VERY USEFUL		USEFUL		RARELY USEFUL		USELESS	
		NO.	%	NO.	%	NO.	%	NO.	%
<=20	139	8	5.8	5	3.6	57	41.0	69	49.6
21–25	150	20	13.3	3	2.0	47	31.3	80	53.3
26–30	94	19	20.2	3	3.2	12	12.8	60	63.8
31–35	52	13	25.0	3	5.8	17	32.7	19	36.5
>=36	79	26	32.9	5	6.3	24	30.4	24	30.4

Table 5–61

RELATIONSHIP BETWEEN PERCENTAGE OF MALE AND FEMALE SEX OFFENDERS WITH DIFFERENT VIEWS ON THE USEFULNESS OF PARENTS AS A SOURCE OF SEXUAL KNOWLEDGE AND THEIR AGE

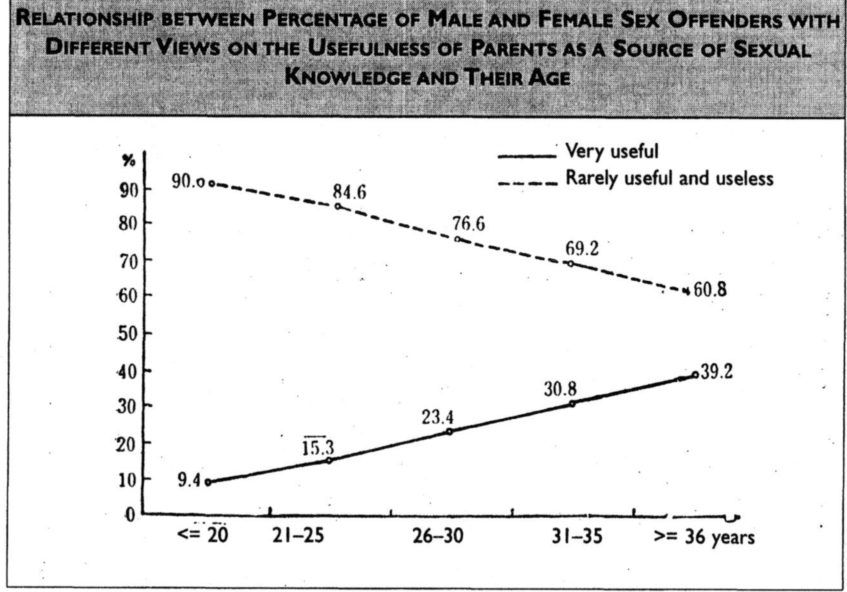

Figure 5–30

GENDER AND VIEW ON SEXUAL INFORMATION FROM SIBLINGS									
GENDER	TOTAL	VERY USEFUL		USEFUL		RARELY USEFUL		USELESS	
		NO.	%	NO.	%	NO.	%	NO.	%
Male	183	17	9.3	18	9.8	60	32.8	88	48.1
Female	113	3	2.7	12	10.6	30	26.5	68	60.2

Table 5–62

AGE AND VIEW ON SEXUAL INFORMATION FROM SIBLINGS									
AGE	TOTAL	VERY USEFUL		USEFUL		RARELY USEFUL		USELESS	
		NO.	%	NO.	%	NO.	%	NO.	%
<=20	90	1	1.1	15	16.7	34	37.8	40	44.4
21–25	93	8	8.6	7	7.5	21	22.6	57	61.3
26–30	49	6	12.2	4	8.2	10	20.4	29	59.2
31–35	28	1	3.6	1	3.6	10	35.7	16	57.1
>=36	37	6	16.2	3	8.1	15	40.5	13	35.1

Table 5–63

GENDER AND VIEW ON GENDERUAL INFORMATION FROM TEACHERS									
GENDER	TOTAL	VERY USEFUL		USEFUL		RARELY USEFUL		USELESS	
		NO.	%	NO.	%	NO.	%	NO.	%
Male	268	70	26.1	51	19.0	53	19.8	94	35.1
Female	126	21	26.7	12	9.5	26	20.6	67	53.2

Table 5–64

For the early source of knowledge, we asked the males and females from whom they sought advice when they had their first ejaculation or menstruation. Most of the males did not ask anybody. Most females asked their parents (table 5–59, figure 5–28).

On the usefulness of the parents as a source of sexual knowledge, most subjects answered negatively. The total percentage of negative answers was much higher than the high school students, but much more males (30.4 percent) than females (9.2 percent) thought that the parents were a useful source of information (table 5–60, Figure 5–29).

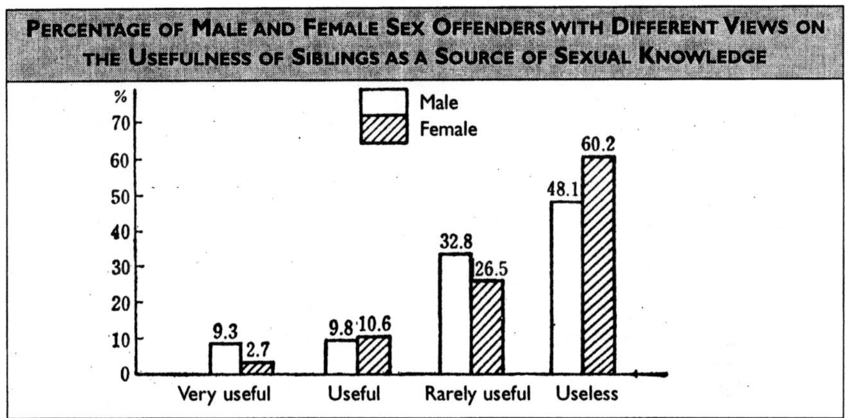

Figure 5–31

Age and View on Sexual Information from Teachers

AGE	TOTAL	VERY USEFUL		USEFUL		RARELY USEFUL		USELESS	
		NO.	%	NO.	%	NO.	%	NO.	%
>=20	113	15	13.3	23	20.4	28	24.8	47	41.6
21=25	126	26	20.6	16	12.7	23	18.3	61	48.4
26–30	68	24	25.3	8	11.8	7	10.3	29	42.6
31–35	36	7	19.4	10	27.8	7	19.4	12	33.3
>=36	50	18	36.0	5	10.0	16	32.0	11	22.0

Table 5–65

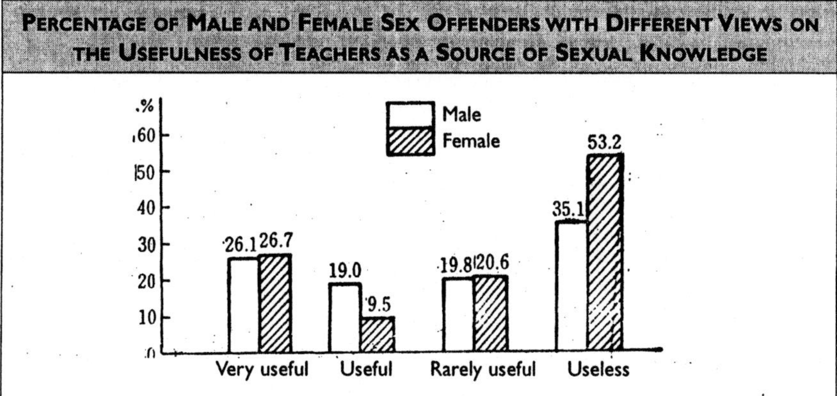

Figure 5–32

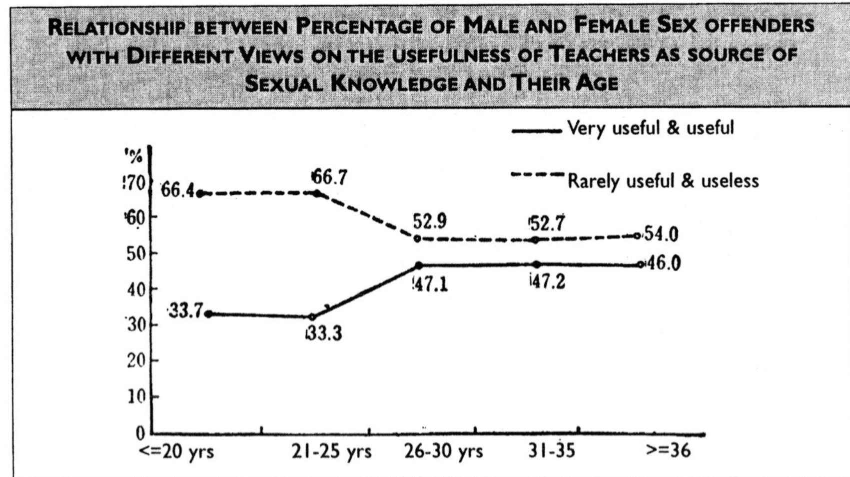

RELATIONSHIP BETWEEN PERCENTAGE OF MALE AND FEMALE SEX OFFENDERS WITH DIFFERENT VIEWS ON THE USEFULNESS OF TEACHERS AS SOURCE OF SEXUAL KNOWLEDGE AND THEIR AGE

Figure 5–33

SEX AND VIEW ON SEXUAL INFORMATION FROM CLASSMATES AND FRIENDS

GENDER	TOTAL	VERY USEFUL		USEFUL		RARELY USEFUL		USELESS	
		NO.	%	NO.	%	NO.	%	NO.	%
Male	696	287	41.2	201	28.9	154	22.1	54	7.8
Female	273	88	32.2	36	13.2	78	28.6	71	26.0

Table 5–66

The older the subjects, the more useful they found their parents as a source of sexual knowledge (G=0.17) (table 5–61, figure 5–30).

AGE AND VIEW ON SEXUAL INFORMATION FROM CLASSMATES AND FRIENDS

AGE	TOTAL	VERY USEFUL		USEFUL		RARELY USEFUL		USELESS	
		NO.	%	NO.	%	NO.	%	NO.	%
<=20	293	112	38.2	61	20.8	83	28.3	37	12.6
21–25	289	115	39.8	70	24.2	62	21.5	42	14.5
26–30	184	73	39.7	46	25.0	39	21.2	26	14.1
31–35	86	37	43.0	18	20.9	24	27.9	7	8.1
>=36	116	38	32.7	43	37.1	24	20.7	11	9.5

Table 5–67

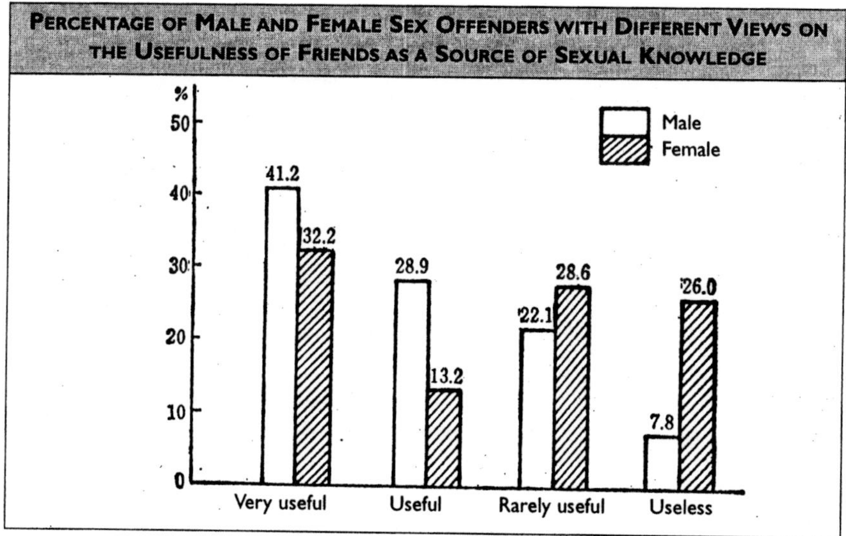

Figure 5–34

On the usefulness of siblings as a source of sexual knowledge, a large majority gave a negative answer, similar to the high school students. The males however, again found the source more useful.

Age does not appear to correlate with the feeling of the usefulness of the siblings as a source of sexual knowledge (table 5–63).

On teachers as a source of sexual knowledge, still a little bit more than half of the subjects gave negative answers (61.5 percent), which was much higher than the high school students (table 5–64, figure 5–32). The males felt more negatively about this than the females.

ATTITUDE TOWARD LOVE

GENDER	TOTAL	FOR AFFECTION		FOR COITUS		NO TRUE LOVE BETWEEN MALE & FEMALE		A DECEPTION		CAN HAVE MULTIPLE LOVERS	
		NO.	%	NO.	%	NO.	%	NO.	%	NO.	%
Male	1380	896	64.9	201	14.6	93	6.7	111	8.0	79	5.7
Female	600	300	50.0	35	5.8	87	14.5	150	25.0	28	4.7

Table 5–68

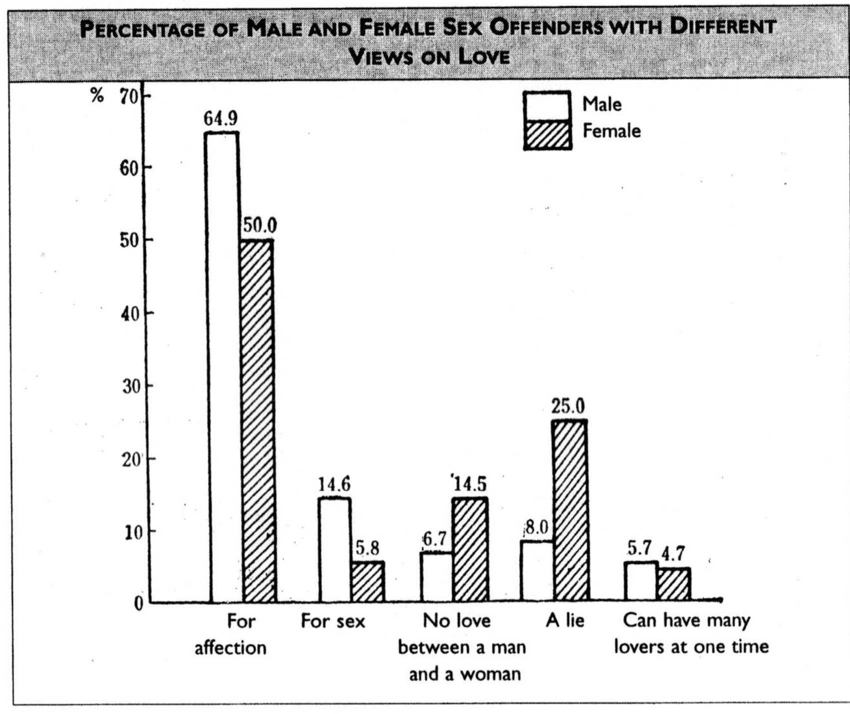

Figure 5–35

Age related positively with the feeling of teachers as a useful source (G=0.16) (table 5–56, figure 5–33).

On the usefulness of friends or classmates, only 36.7 percent of the subjects who responded answered negatively, much lower than the high school students. The males thought more highly of their peers than the females (table 5–66, figure 5–34).

Age did not show any significant relationship with the feeling on friends or classmates as a useful source (table 3–67).

The change of feelings concerning the usefulness of the source of sexual knowledge could be due to the gradual accumulation of insight and experience. Certain sources which were thought at one time to be useless may in retrospect be correct and useful as one learns more and has more life experience.

2. Views on Love

On the subject of love, 37.8 percent did not take affection to be love itself. The female offenders thought more so than the males. It could be

AGE AND ATTITUDE TOWARD LOVE											
AGE	TOTAL	FOR AFFECTION		FOR COITUS		NO TRUE LOVE BETWEEN MALE & FEMALE		A DECEPTION		CAN HAVE MULTIPLE LOVERS	
		NO.	%	NO.	%	NO.	%	NO.	%	NO.	%
<=20	503	271	53.9	55	10.9	63	12.5	84	16.7	30	6.0
21–25	539	296	54.9	61	11.3	51	9.5	96	17.8	35	6.5
26–30	396	250	63.1	58	14.6	30	7.6	38	9.6	20	5.1
31–35	208	137	65.9	19	9.1	19	9.1	21	10.1	12	5.8
>=36	317	227	71.6	41	12.9	18	5.7	20	6.3	11	3.5

Table 5–69

that the females were psychologically traumatized and that is why many of them committed sex offenses as a means of revenge (table 5–24).

Age relates significantly with attitudes toward love, with the older subjects viewing affection more as an objective itself (G=0.18) (table 5–69).

Educational level also has a significant relation in the same direction (Table 5-70).

However, from table 5–69 and 5–70, it can be seen that the age and educational level do not seem to be associated with the view that one could have many lovers and still be in love.

When asked what was most important concerning their ideal lover, 67.3 percent took affection, education, personality, and temperament as most important. The others took materialistic objectives (table 5–71), thus negating the importance of love.

EDUCATION AND ATTITUDE TOWARD LOVE											
	TOTAL	FOR AFFECTION		FOR COITUS		NO TRUE LOVE BETWEEN MALE & FEMALE		A DECEPTION		CAN HAVE MULTIPLE LOVERS	
		NO.	%	NO.	%	NO.	%	NO.	%	NO.	%
Illiterate	125	61	48.8	26	20.8	10	8.0	20	16.0	8	6.4
Primary	407	221	54.3	71	17.4	45	11.1	52	12.8	18	4.4
J. High	1120	669	59.7	118	10.5	99	8.8	166	14.8	68	6.1
S. High & above	348	254	73.0	21	6.0	33	9.5	24	6.9	16	4.6

Table 5–70

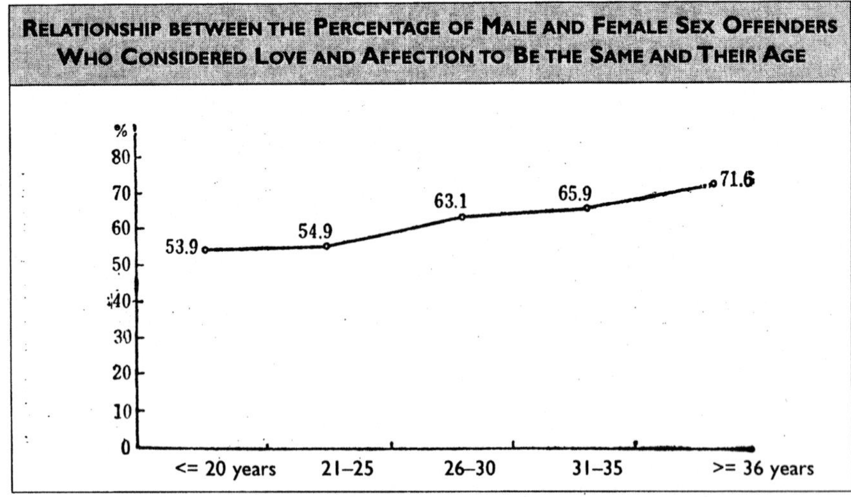

Figure 5–36

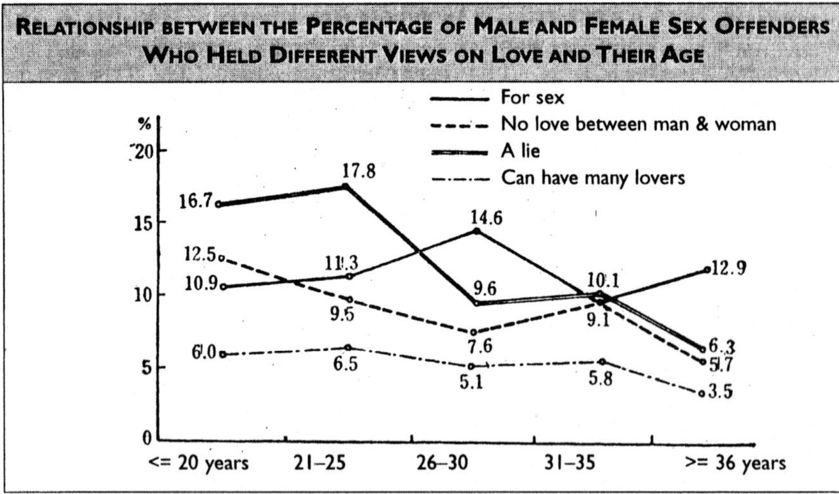

Figure 5–37

The females centered more on monetary importance in their criteria, while the males focused more on outward attractiveness, personality, and affection (table 5–72, figure 5–39).

Table 5–73 shows that as age advances, less importance is placed on money or physical attraction. More emphasis is placed on personality and temperament.

Educational level shows a positive association with the emphasis on physical attraction, education, and affection. There is no significant relationship between educational level and the emphasis on money.

CONDITIONS AFFECTING CHOICE OF SPOUSE										
TOTAL	WEALTH		APPEARANCE		LEARNEDNESS		SOCIAL STATUS		PERSONALITY	
	NO.	%	NO.	%	NO.	%	NO.	%	NO.	%
2136	223	10.4	320	15.0	86	4.0	32	1.5	493	23.1

AFFECTION		HOUSE		RELATION ABROAD		SEXUALLY SATISFYING		UNKNOWN	
NO.	%	NO.	%	NO.	%	NO.	%	NO.	%
858	40.2	29	1.4	10	0.5	30	1.4	55	2.6

Table 5–71

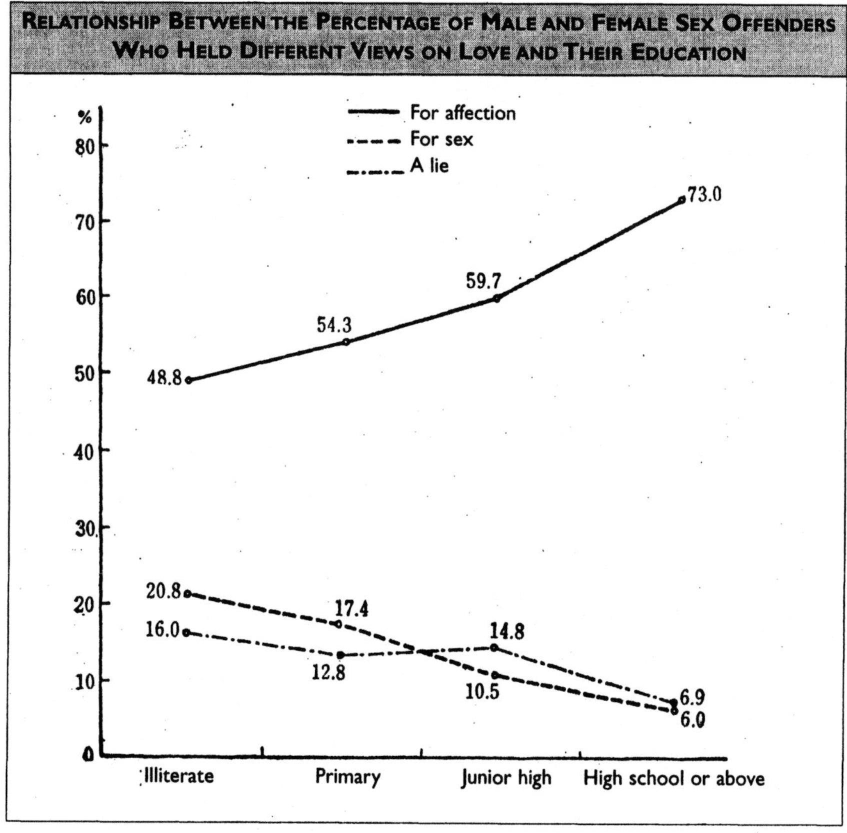

Figure 5–38

GENDER AND CONDITIONS AFFECTING CHOICE OF SPOUSE										
GENDER	TOTAL	WEALTH		APPEARANCE		LEARNEDNESS		SOCIAL STATUS	
		NO.	%	NO.	%	NO.	%	NO.	%
Male	1406	92	6.5	256	18.2	53	3.8	18	1.3
Female	617	123	19.9	53	8.6	31	5.0	14	2.3

GENDER	PERSONALITY		AFFECTION		HOUSE		RELATION ABROAD		SEXUALLY SATISFYING	
	NO.	%	NO.	%	NO.	%	NO.	%	NO.	%
Male	356	25.3	586	41.7	16	1.1	2	0.1	27	1.9
Female	127	20.6	247	40.0	12	1.9	7	1.1	3	0.5

P=0.001

Table 5–72

AGE AND CONDITIONS AFFECTING CHOICE OF SPOUSE										
AGE	TOTAL	WEALTH		APPEARANCE		LEARNEDNESS		SOCIAL STATUS	
		NO.	%	NO.	%	NO.	%	NO.	%
<=20	514	79	15.4	83	16.1	19	3.7	10	1.9
21–25	542	69	12.7	87	16.1	20	3.7	8	1.5
26–30	411	28	6.8	70	17.0	18	4.4	6	1.5
31–35	214	10	4.7	41	19.2	8	3.7	0	0
>=36	332	27	8.1	25	7.5	17	5.1	6	1.8

AGE	PERSONALITY		AFFECTION		HOUSE		RELATION ABROAD		SEXUALLY SATISFYING	
	NO.	%	NO.	%	NO.	%	NO.	%	NO.	%
<=20	102	19.8	205	39.9	3	0.6	2	0.4	11	2.1
21–25	123	22.7	226	41.7	3	0.6	3	0.6	3	0.6
26–30	102	24.8	170	41.4	9	2.2	2	0.5	6	1.5
31–35	52	24.3	95	44.4	6	2.8	1	0.5	1	0.5
>=36	100	30.1	138	41.6	8	2.4	2	0.6	9	2.7

Table 5–73

On early love, 53.6 percent of the subjects took a positive view, more than the high school students. This could be related to the principle of

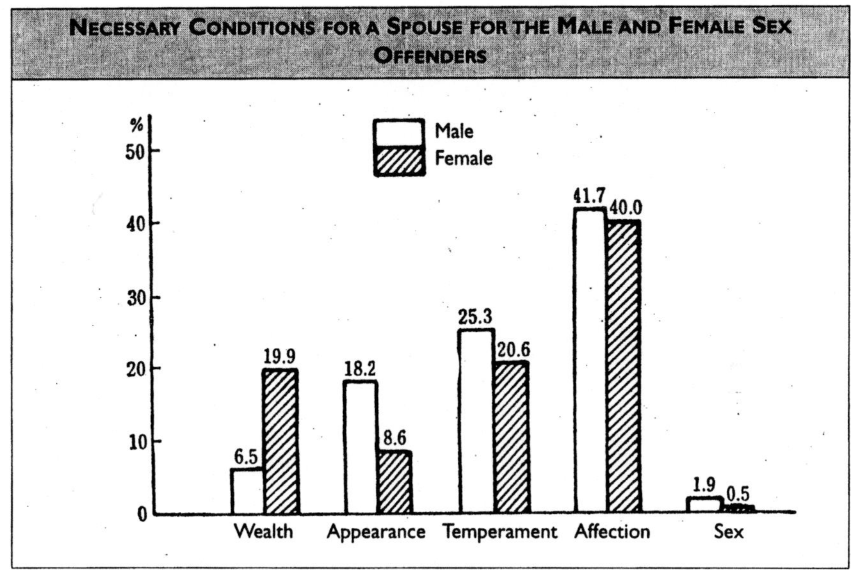

Figure 5–39

Education and Conditions Affecting Choice of Spouse

	TOTAL	WEALTH		APPEARANCE		LEARNEDNESS		SOCIAL STATUS	
		NO.	%	NO.	%	NO.	%	NO.	%
Illiterate	136	22	16.2	15	11.0	4	2.9	3	2.2
Primary	427	42	9.8	56	13.1	16	3.7	7	1.6
J. High	1134	129	11.4	183	16.1	41	3.6	15	1.3
S. High & above	351	23	6.6	59	16.8	25	7.1	6	1.7

	PERSONALITY		AFFECTION		HOUSE		RELATION ABROAD		SEXUALLY SATISFYING	
	NO.	%	NO.	%	NO.	%	NO.	%	NO.	%
Illiterate	40	29.4	37	27.2	5	3.7	0	0	10	7.4
Primary	110	25.8	172	40.3	13	3.0	3	0.7	8	1.9
J. High	265	23.4	476	42.0	10	0.9	5	0.4	10	0.9
S. High & above	73	20.8	160	45.6	1	0.3	2	0.6	2	0.6

Table 5–74

View on Early Love													
	TOTAL	NATURAL		WAY TO MATURITY		USEFUL FOR CHOOSING SPOUSE		USEFUL FOR WORK & STUDY		EASILY RUIN A PERSON		BAD FOR WORK OR STUDY	
		NO.	%	NO.	%	NO.	%	NO.	%	NO.	%	NO.	%
Male	1393	376	27.0	242	17.4	153	11.0	52	3.7	252	18.1	318	22.8
Female	568	109	19.2	93	16.4	78	13.7	11	1.9	188	33.1	89	15.7

P=0.01

Table 5–75

enjoyment , a lack of higher ideals, or lack of social responsibility among the offenders.

Table 5–75 shows that more females took a negative view on early love. It may be because many of the female offenders had bad experiences from their own early sexual love affairs.

Older subjects viewed early love more negatively (G=0.16, table 5–76), but educational level did not show any clear relation to different views on early love, reflecting probably that in our society, different and reasonable views do exist on this issue (table 5–76).

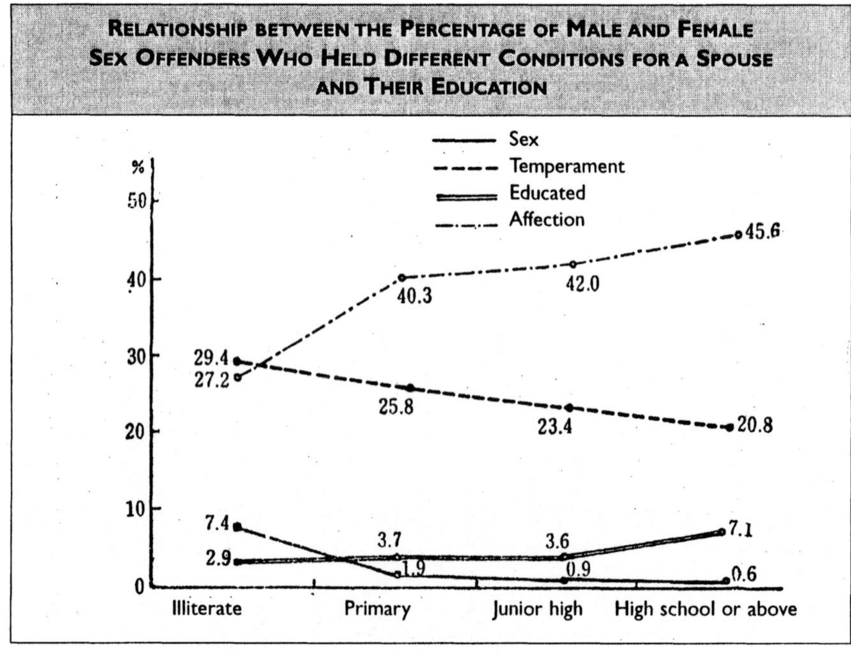

Figure 5–40

AGE AND VIEW ON EARLY LOVE													
AGE	TOTAL	NATURAL		WAY TO MATURITY		USEFUL FOR CHOOSING SPOUSE		USEFUL FOR WORK & STUDY		EASILY RUIN A PERSON		BAD FOR WORK OR STUDY	
		NO.	%	NO.	%	NO.	%	NO.	%	NO.	%	NO.	%
<=20	502	142	28.3	93	18.5	56	11.2	12	2.4	128	25.5	71	14.1
21–25	530	140	26.4	105	19.8	58	10.9	11	2.1	135	25.5	81	15.3
26–30	390	114	29.2	76	19.5	52	13.3	18	4.6	65	16.7	65	16.7
31–35	206	37	18.0	31	15.0	38	18.4	11	5.3	38	18.4	51	24.8
>=36	322	54	16.8	33	10.2	25	7.8	12	3.7	58	18.0	140	43.5

P=0.01

Table 5–76

EDUCATION AND VIEW ON EARLY LOVE													
	TOTAL	NATURAL		WAY TO MATURITY		USEFUL FOR CHOOSING SPOUSE		USEFUL FOR WORK & STUDY		EASILY RUIN A PERSON		BAD FOR WORK OR STUDY	
		NO.	%	NO.	%	NO.	%	NO.	%	NO.	%	NO.	%
Illiterate	128	33	25.8	18	14.1	16	12.5	4	3.1	20	15.6	37	28.9
Primary	393	83	21.1	71	18.1	54	13.7	18	4.6	88	22.4	79	20.1
J. High	1112	276	24.8	203	18.3	137	12.3	29	2.6	262	23.6	205	18.4
S. High & above	353	102	28.9	50	14.2	26	7.4	14	4.0	68	19.3	96	26.3

Table 5–77

VIEW ON SEXUAL FREEDOM											
GENDER	TOTAL	SHOULD PROMOTE		BENEFIT, NO HARM		NEUTRAL		CONDITIONAL SUPPORT		OBJECT	
		NO.	%	NO.	%	NO.	%	NO.	%	NO.	%
Male	1404	166	11.8	103	7.3	681	48.5	227	16.2	227	16.2
Female	580	20	3.4	21	3.6	350	60.3	63	10.9	126	21.7

P=0.001

Table 5–78

3. Views on Sexual Freedom

Table 5–78 shows that 29.1 percent of the subjects gave total support for sexual freedom, the males more than the females. There seems to be a trend for total support or total rejection of sexual freedom to decrease with

Education and View on Sexual Freedom											
	TOTAL	SHOULD PROMOTE		BENEFIT, NO HARM		NEUTRAL		CONDITIONAL SUPPORT		OBJECT	
		NO.	%	NO.	%	NO.	%	NO.	%	NO.	%
Illiterate	130	23	17.7	11	8.5	55	42.3	14	10.8	27	20.8
Primary	395	44	11.1	41	10.4	176	44.6	47	11.9	87	22.0
J. High	1128	95	8.4	58	5.1	620	55.0	172	15.2	1831	16.2
S. High & above	354	29	8.2	18	5.1	184	52.0	64	18.1	59	16.7

Table 5–79

Age and View on Sexual Freedom											
AGE	TOTAL	SHOULD PROMOTE		BENEFIT, NO HARM		NEUTRAL		CONDITIONAL SUPPORT		OBJECT	
		NO.	%	NO.	%	NO.	%	NO.	%	NO.	%
>=20	497	46	9.3	22	4.4	270	54.3	89	17.9	70	14.1
21–25	535	50	9.3	27	5.0	282	52.7	88	16.4	88	16.4
26–30	400	36	9.0	35	8.8	212	53.0	56	14.0	61	15.3
31–35	212	21	9.9	15	7.1	105	49.5	28	13.2	43	20.3
>=36	331	37	11.2	26	7.9	144	43.5	31	9.4	93	28.1

Table 5–80

Gender and View of Chastity											
GENDER	TOTAL	IMPORTANT		FEUDALISM		FOR WOMAN ONLY		NO PROBLEM IF LOVE		SEXUAL NEED OVERRIDES	
		NO.	%	NO.	%	NO.	%	NO.	%	NO.	%
Male	1263	284	22.5	166	13.1	227	18.0	523	41.4	63	5.0
Female	588	223	37.9	50	8.5	61	10.4	232	39.5	22	3.7

P=0.001

Table 5–81

educational level. Instead, conditional support or neutral views increased (table 5–79). The percentage of total rejection increased with age.

On chastity, 40.3 percent of the subjects did not think this was of any importance, as long as there was affection or sexual needs being satisfied. Another 10.3 percent rejected the idea as being a feudal idea.

More female subjects considered chastity to be important to them, showing the effects of Chinese traditional concepts on females.

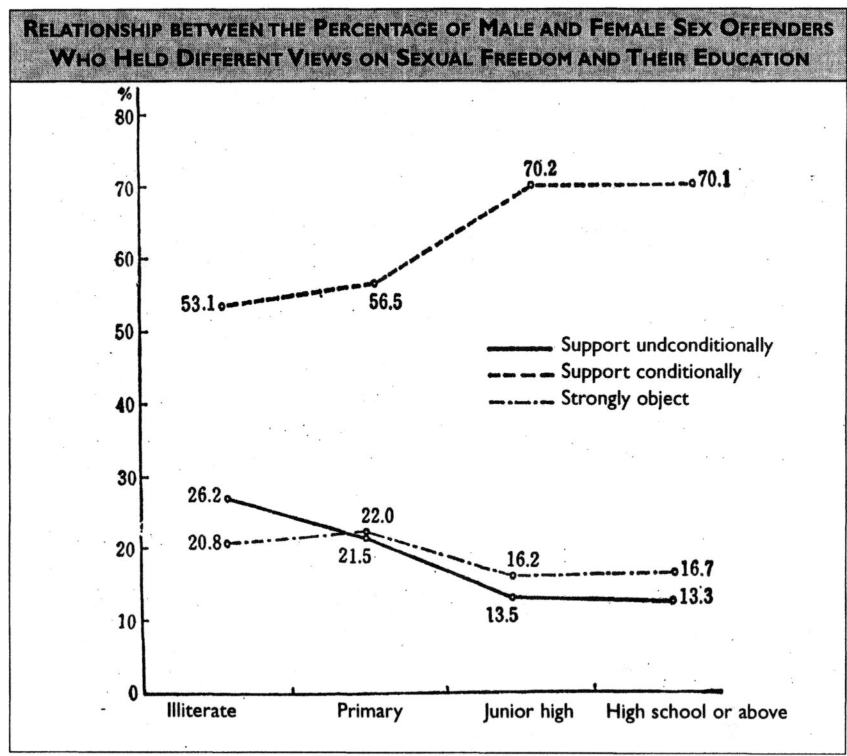

Figure 5–41

AGE AND VIEW OF CHASTITY											
AGE	TOTAL	IMPORTANT		FEUDALISM		FOR WOMAN ONLY		NO PROBLEM IF LOVE		SEXUAL NEED OVERRIDES	
		NO.	%	NO.	%	NO.	%	NO.	%	NO.	%
<=20	475	115	24.2	46	9.7	70	14.7	221	46.5	23	4.8
21–25	506	128	25.3	64	12.6	80	15.8	217	42.9	17	3.4
26–30	378	106	28.0	39	10.3	61	16.1	153	40.5	19	5.0
31–35	190	53	27.9	21	11.1	34	17.9	72	37.9	10	5.3
>=36	294	89	30.3	49	16.7	45	15.3	95	32.3	16	5.4

Table 5–82

Age did not show any significant relationship with views concerning chastity (table 5–82).

Concerning the life pursuits of women, 23.1 percent of the female respondents looked for career success, 53.4 percent strove to be a good wife and mother, and 23.4 percent sought reckless enjoyment. Table

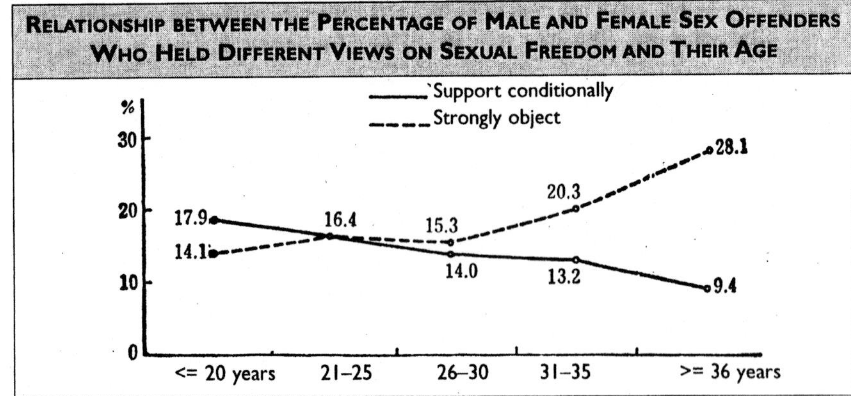

Figure 5–42

LIFE AIM OF A WOMAN OF THE FEMALE OFFENDERS								
TOTAL	PLEASURE		BE A GOOD MOTHER & WIFE		DEPEND ON A MAN		CAREER	
	NO.	%	NO.	%	NO.	%	NO.	%
592	168	28.4	256	43.2	11	1.9	157	26.5

Table 5–83

5–84 shows that older women looked less toward reckless enjoyment as their life pursuit. More were inclined to become a wife and mother.

The highly educated women looked for career success more than the other females (table 5–85 and figure 5–46).

4. Attitude toward Premarital and Extramarital Sex

A total of 71.4 percent of respondents showed positive attitudes toward premarital sex, which wasn't much different from the 74.9 percent support given by the college students (table 5–86, figure 5–47).

Females showed less support than males toward premarital sex by mutual consent, but more support was given if the couple eventually got married (table 5–86).

The older the respondents, the more negative their attitudes were toward premarital sex, agreeing to their attitudes to sexual freedom (G=0.1) (table 5–87) The highly educated took a more positive view toward premarital sex (table 5–88, figure 5–48).

On the way to handle premarital sex, 59.4 percent showed accepting opinions, similar to those (55.5 percent) of the college students.

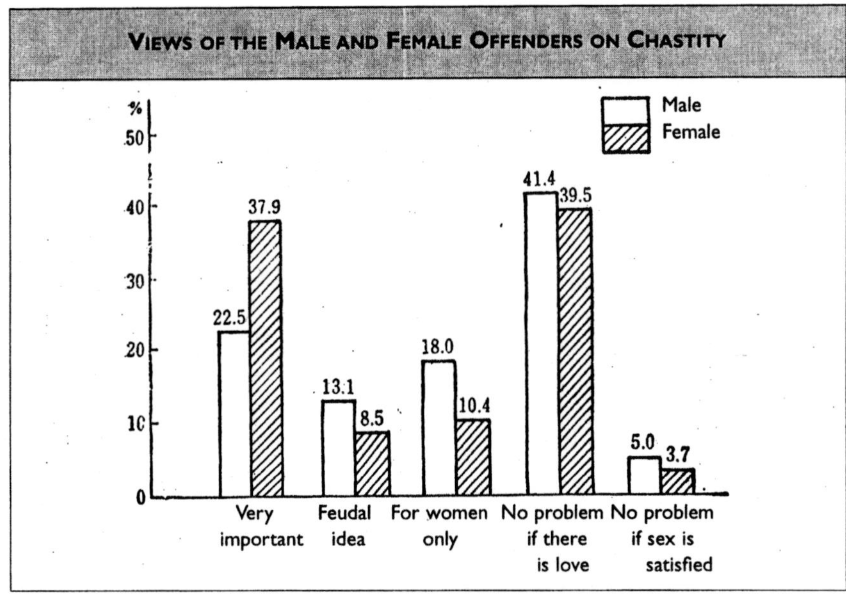

Figure 5–43

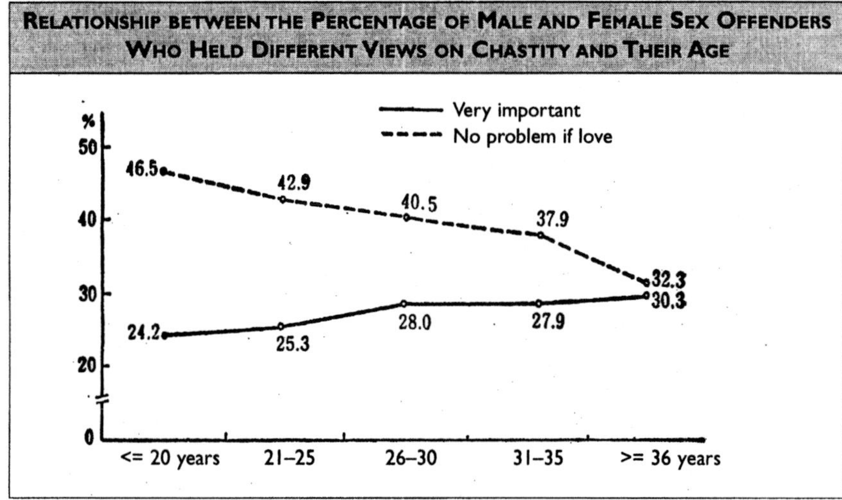

Figure 5–44

Table 5–89 and 5–86 showed that about double the percentage of subjects disapproved of extramarital sex than premarital sex. Females could accept extramarital sex more if it was based on affection; 14.8 percent of the males, in contrast with 7.5 percent of the females, felt that

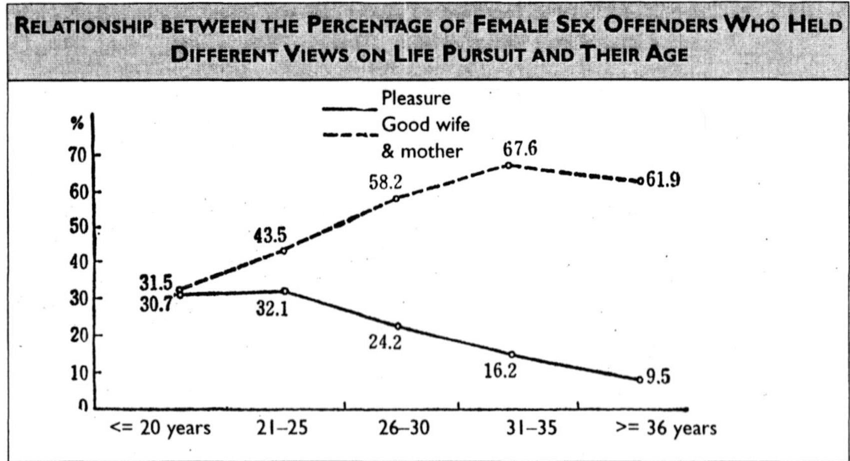

Figure 5–45

Age and Life Aim as a Woman of the Female Offenders

AGE	TOTAL	PLEASURE		BE A GOOD MOTHER & WIFE		DEPEND ON A MAN		CAREER	
		NO.	%	NO.	%	NO.	%	NO.	%
<=20	238	75	31.5	73	30.7	5	2.1	85	35.7
21–25	184	59	32.1	80	43.5	2	1.1	43	23.4
26–30	91	22	24.2	53	58.2	1	1.1	15	16.5
31–35	37	6	16.2	25	67.6	3	8.1	3	8.1
>=36	21	2	9.5	13	61.9	0	0	6	28.6

Table 5–84

Education and Life Aim as a Woman of the Female Offenders

	TOTAL	PLEASURE		BE A GOOD MOTHER & WIFE		DEPEND ON A MAN		CAREER	
		NO.	%	NO.	%	NO.	%	NO.	%
Illiterate	10	2	20.0	8	80.0	0	0	0	0
Primary	123	27	22.0	69	56.1	4	3.2	23	18.7
J. High	392	132	33.7	145	37.0	6	1.5	109	27.8
S. High & above	57	6	10.5	25	43.9	1	1.7	25	43.9

Table 5–85

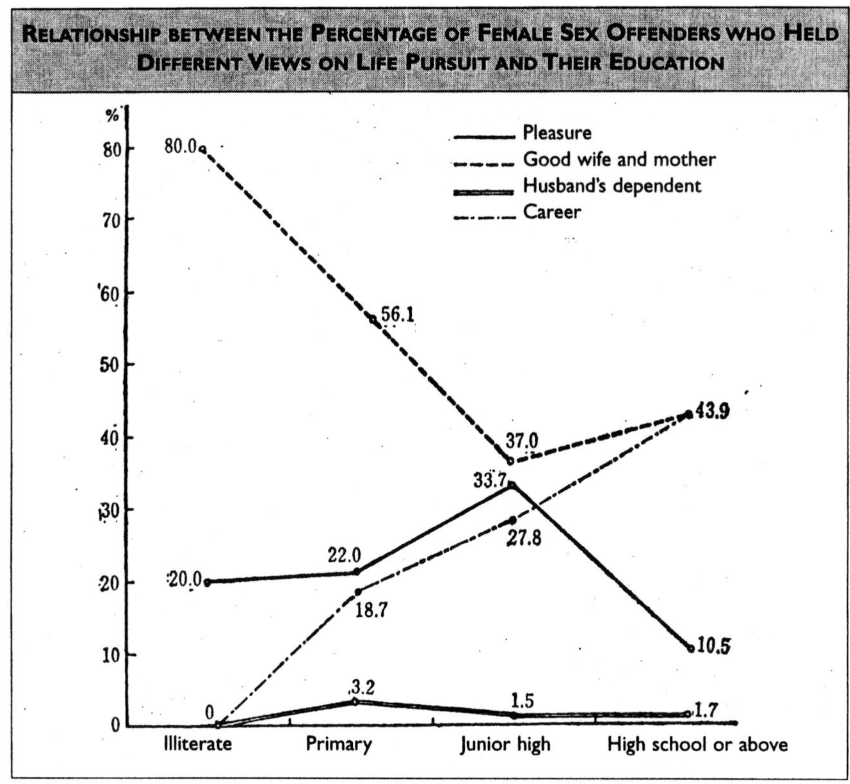

Figure 5–46

extramarital sex was acceptable if it were with the spouse's consent, showing a greater desire by males to have extramarital affairs.

Age did not show any significant relationship with views on extramarital sex. Generally, there is a trend for the older age groups to reject it, but to conditionally accept it if the spouse did not object or there was sexual disharmony. More highly educated subjects vote for permitting extramarital sex for reasons of affection but less for extramarital sex if consent were given by the spouse.

How sexual attitudes relate to sexual offenses still requires clarification from other surveys. In 1984, Sichuan Social Science Institute surveyed 850 young criminals; most of them insisted that money and personal enjoyment were their biggest aims in life; 74 percent of them felt that they must enjoy life while they were young, and among those subjects the greatest proportion were the rapists. They viewed heterosexual relationships as a mutual loss.[11]

View on Premarital Sex											
GENDER	TOTAL	OK IF MUTUAL CONSENT		OK IF MARRIED AFTERWARD		NO PROBLEM		HARM SELF BUT NOT SOCIETY		HARM SOCIETY, OBJECT	
		NO.	%	NO.	%	NO.	%	NO.	%	NO.	%
Male	1368	758	55.4	252	18.4	146	10.7	42	3.1	170	12.4
Female	565	205	36.3	163	28.8	77	13.6	23	4.1	97	17.3

Table 5–86

Age and View on Premarital Sex											
AGE	TOTAL	OK IF MUTUAL CONSENT		OK IF MARRIED AFTERWARD		NO PROBLEM		HARM SELF BUT NOT SOCIETY		HARM SOCIETY, OBJECT	
		NO.	%	NO.	%	NO.	%	NO.	%	NO.	%
<=20	479	244	50.9	100	20.9	65	13.6	15	3.1	55	11.5
21–25	525	286	54.5	105	20.0	62	11.8	18	3.4	54	10.3
26–30	389	198	50.9	92	23.7	47	12.1	9	2.3	43	11.1
31–35	206	96	46.6	53	25.7	17	8.3	9	4.4	31	15.0
>=36	322	136	42.2	60	18.6	26	8.1	12	3.7	88	27.3

Table 5–87

Education and View on Premarital Sex											
	TOTAL	OK IF MUTUAL CONSENT		OK IF MARRIED AFTERWARD		NO PROBLEM		HARM SELF BUT NOT SOCIETY		HARM SOCIETY, OBJECT	
		NO.	%	NO.	%	NO.	%	NO.	%	NO.	%
Illiterate	133	61	45.9	15	11.3	19	14.3	5	3.8	33	24.8
Primary	390	180	46.2	71	18.2	49	12.6	18	4.6	72	18.5
J. High	1086	546	50.3	251	23.1	131	12.1	27	2.5	131	12.1
S. High & above	348	188	54.0	83	23.9	25	7.2	13	3.7	39	11.2

Table 5–88

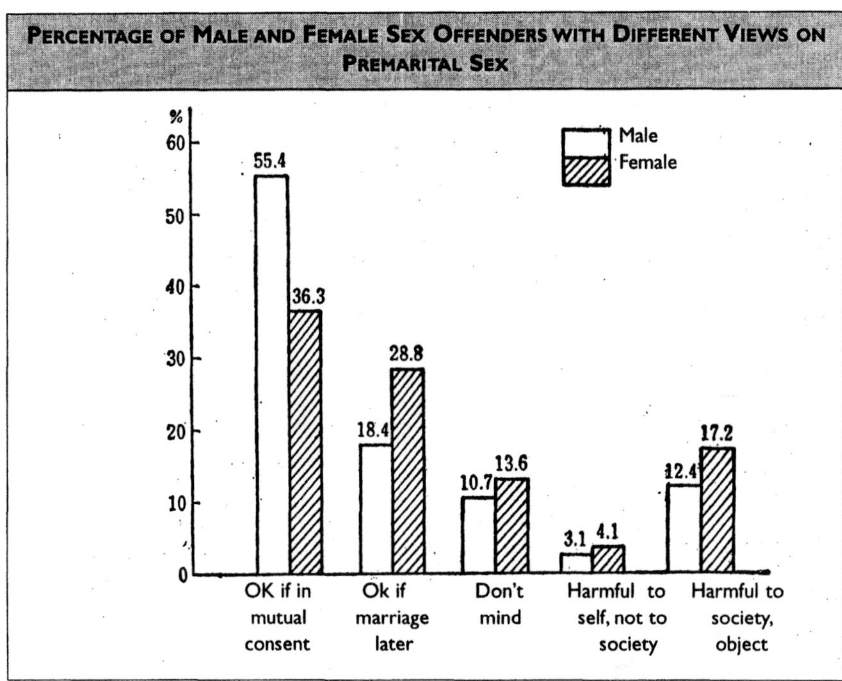

Figure 5–47

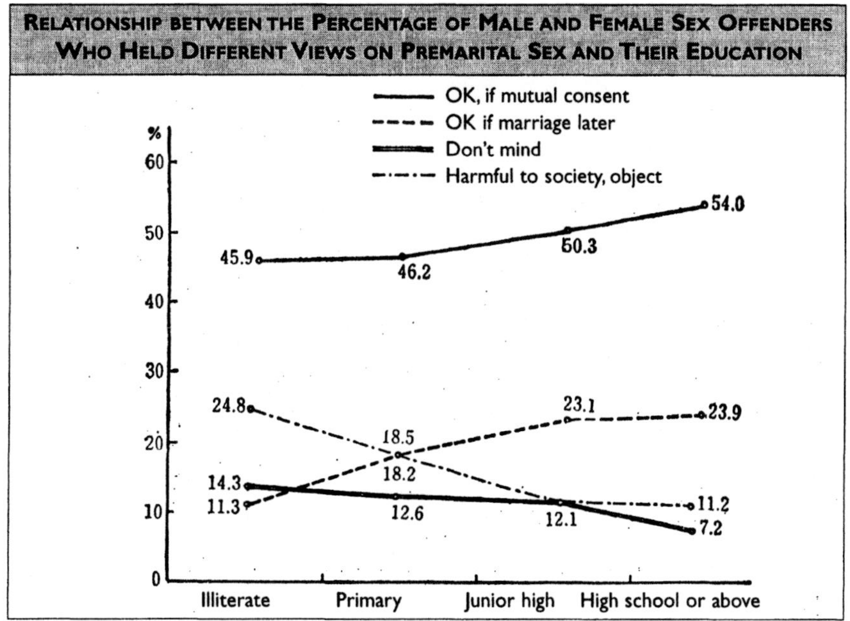

Figure 5–48

View on Extramarital Sex														
	TOTAL	OK IF IN LOVE		OK IF SPOUSE AGREE		ACCEPTABLE IF POOR MARITAL SEX		NO HARM, NO BENEFIT		HARMFUL TO FAMILY, OBJECT		UNKNOWN	
		NO.	%	NO.	%	NO.	%	NO.	%	NO.	%	NO.	%
Male	1441	494	34.2	213	14.8	81	5.6	89	6.2	429	29.8	135	9.4
Female	630	239	37.9	47	7.5	33	5.2	38	6.0	176	27.9	97	15.4

P=0.001

Table 5–89

Percentage of Male and Female Sex Offenders with Different Views on Extramarital Sex

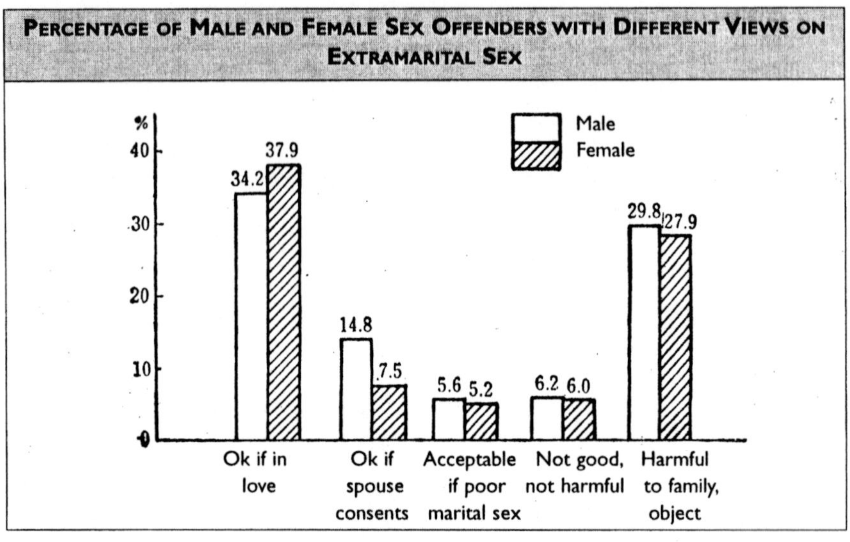

Figure 5–49

6. Recreational Life

1. Types of Recreation

Table 5–92 shows that the sex offenders had a large variety of recreations. The top five were movies, clothing, music, and making friends with the opposite sex, chatting, and eating.

2. Factors Relating to Type of Recreation:

A. Gender

Females liked dancing and clothing most. Males liked eating, gambling, making heterosexual friends, reading, and watching videos.

AGE AND VIEW ON EXTRAMARITAL SEX											
AGE	TOTAL	OK IF IN LOVE		OK IF SPOUSE AGREE		ACCEPTABLE IF POOR MARITAL SEX		NO HARM, NO BENEFIT		HARMFUL TO FAMILY, OBJECT	
		NO.	%	NO.	%	NO.	%	NO.	%	NO.	%
<=20	436	206	47.2	53	12.1	24	5.5	17	3.9	136	31.2
21–25	481	208	43.2	60	12.5	27	5.6	47	9.8	139	28.9
26–30	384	149	38.8	59	15.4	27	7.0	32	8.3	117	30.5
31–35	202	73	36.1	40	19.8	12	5.9	10	5.0	67	33.2
>=36	323	98	30.3	39	12.1	28	8.7	20	6.2	138	42.7

Table 5–90

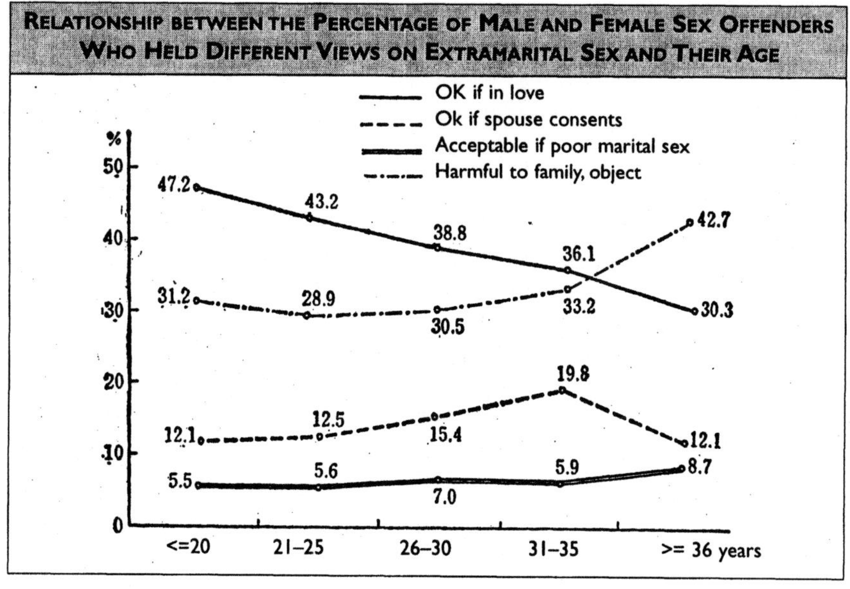

Figure 5–50

B. AGE

Table 5–94 shows that the young subjects liked videos, going to bars and cafes, dancing, and clothing. The older subjects liked movies, eating, and reading. Making heterosexual friends as a recreation did not differ with age.

C. EDUCATIONAL LEVEL

There are more obvious associations of recreation with educational level. The educated subjects liked more cultural activities such as

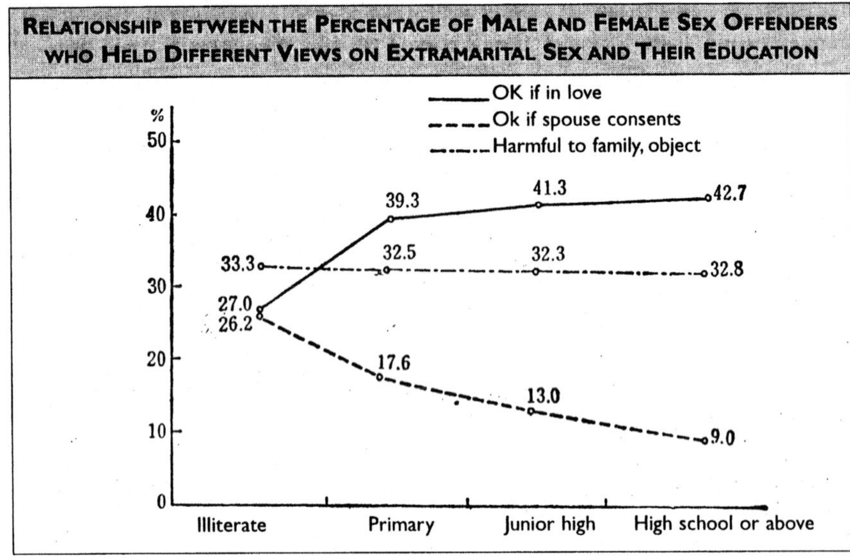

Figure 5–51

EDUCATION AND VIEW ON EXTRAMARITAL SEX											
	TOTAL	OK IF MUTUAL CONSENT		OK IF MARRIED AFTERWARD		NO PROBLEM		HARM SELF BUT NOT SOCIETY		HARM SOCIETY, OBJECT	
		NO.	%	NO.	%	NO.	%	NO.	%	NO.	%
Illiterate	126	34	27.0	33	26.2	8	6.3	9	7.1	42	33.5
Primary	369	145	39.3	65	17.6	16	4.3	23	6.2	120	32.5
J. High	1031	426	41.3	134	13.0	69	6.7	69	6.7	333	32.3
S. High & above	335	143	42.7	30	9.0	24	7.2	28	8.4	110	32.8

Table 5–91

reading, music, and travel. Making heterosexual friends and chatting did not differ much with education (table 5–94, 5–95).

The conversational subjects among female subjects focused mostly on eating and make-up (table 5–96).

The predominantly favorite content of videos (table 5–97) for the males were those with sexual or violent contents, the others were detective or family stories. For the females, the favorites were love stories with soft-core erotic scenes. These subjects were recieved well by those

LEISURE ACTIVITIES OF OFFENDERS BEFORE CONVICTION

TOTAL	MOVIES		VIDEOS		BAR		DANCING		CARDS		MUSIC		CLOTHES	
	NO.	%	NO.	%	NO.	%	NO.	%	NO.	%	NO.	%	NO.	%
5158	806	15.6	317	6.1	265	5.1	322	6.2	294	5.7	445	8.6	460	8.9

FOOD		POPULAR READING		SERIOUS READING		TRAVELING		FRIENDS WITH OTHER SEX		CHATTING		OTHERS	
NO.	%	NO.	%	NO.	%	NO.	%	NO.	%	NO.	%	NO.	%
379	7.3	368	7.1	297	5.8	268	5.2	446	8.6	384	7.4	107	2.1

Table 5–92

LEISURE ACTIVITIES OF MALE AND FEMALE SEX OFFENDERS

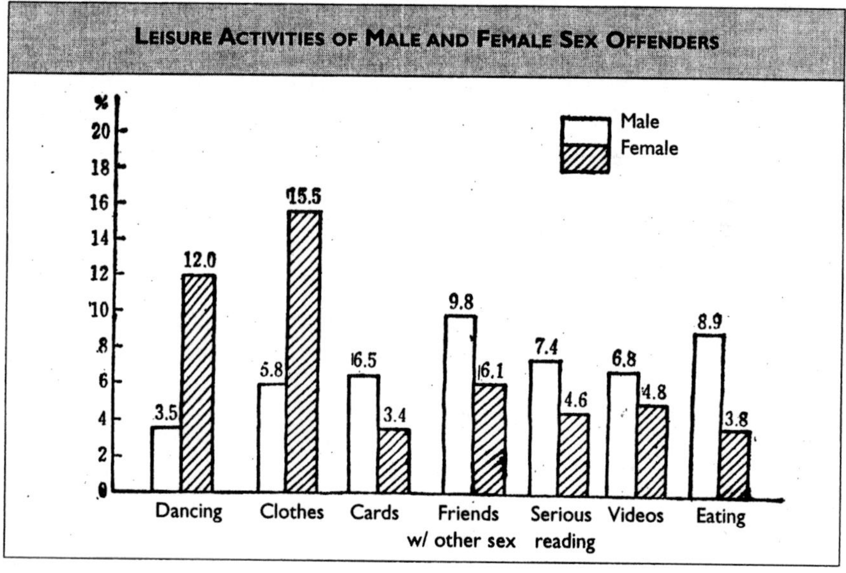

Figure 5–52

falling in the age range between twenty-six and forty-five. As they grow older, they liked more detective and family stories (table 5–98, G=0.11).

Educational level had a definite association with the type of videos the subjects liked (table 5–99). The higher educated liked more of the detective and family type videos. Love and erotic contents were liked by subjects of all educational levels (G=0.1).

GENDER AND LEISURE ACTIVITIES OF OFFENDERS BEFORE CONVICTION

	TOTAL	MOVIES		VIDEOS		BAR		DANCING		CARDS		MUSIC		CLOTHES	
		NO.	%	NO.	%	NO.	%	NO.	%	NO.	%	NO.	%	NO.	%
Male	3511	535	15.2	238	6.8	166	4.7	122	3.5	229	65	305	8.7	205	5.8
Female	1538	246	16.0	74	4.8	90	5.9	185	12.0	53	3.4	120	7.8	239	15.5

TOTAL	FOOD		POPULAR READING		SERIOUS READING		TRAVELING		FRIENDS WITH OTHER SEX		CHATTING		OTHERS	
	NO.	%	NO.	%	NO.	%	NO.	%	NO.	%	NO.	%	NO.	%
Male	312	8.9	249	7.1	259	7.4	186	5.3	345	9.8	268	7.6	92	2.6
Female	54	3.5	113	7.3	70	4.6	79	5.1	93	6.1	109	7.1	13	0.8

P=0.001

Table 5–93

AGE AND LEISURE ACTIVITIES OF OFFENDERS BEFORE CONVICTION

AGE	TOTAL	MOVIES		VIDEOS		BAR		DANCING		CARDS		MUSIC		CLOTHES	
		NO.	%	NO.	%	NO.	%	NO.	%	NO.	%	NO.	%	NO.	%
<=20	1359	167	12.3	108	7.9	92	6.8	128	9.4	66	4.9	121	8.9	156	11.5
21–25	1383	200	14.5	83	6.0	73	5.3	112	8.1	85	6.1	113	8.2	141	10.2
26–30	984	162	16.5	52	5.3	52	5.3	46	4.7	62	6.3	93	9.5	74	7.5
30–35	523	103	19.7	31	5.9	18	3.4	11	2.1	32	6.1	50	9.6	45	8.6
>=36	718	151	21.0	28	3.9	19	2.6	13	1.8	40	2.6	52	7.2	26	3.6

AGE	FOOD		POPULAR READING		SERIOUS READING		TRAVELING		FRIENDS WITH OTHER SEX		CHATTING		OTHERS	
	NO.	%	NO.	%	NO.	%	NO.	%	NO.	%	NO.	%	NO.	%
<=20	63	4.6	109	8.0	53	4.0	64	4.7	123	9.1	90	6.6	19	1.4
21–25	77	5.6	100	7.2	72	5.2	69	5.0	134	9.7	108	7.8	16	1.2
26–30	89	9.0	51	5.2	52	5.3	59	6.0	92	9.3	81	8.2	19	1.9
30–35	45	8.6	36	6.9	20	3.8	37	7.1	35	6.7	44	8.4	16	3.1
>=36	93	12.9	62	8.6	66	9.2	29	4.0	51	7.1	55	7.7	33	4.6

Table 5–94

As for offenders reactions to videos with sex or love contents, more males reported an increase in sexual impulse and a wish to engage in

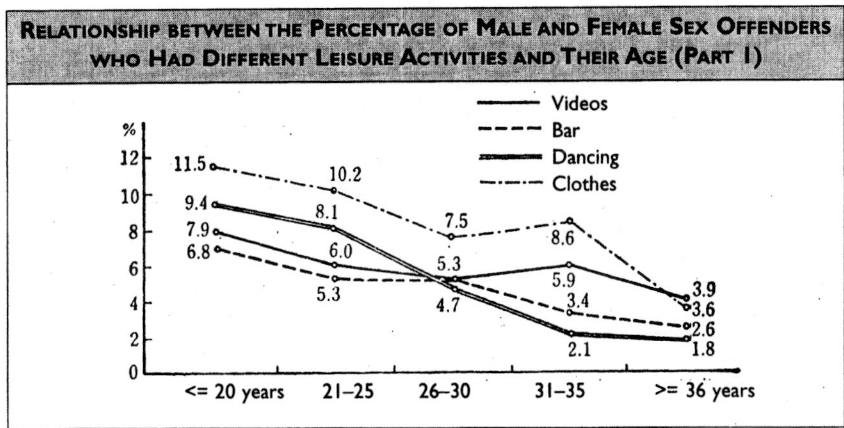

Figure 5–53

these activities (table 5–100, figure 5–58). More subjects in the older age group felt calm when seeing sex or love videos, as well as a slight feeling of impulsiveness (G=0.1) (table 5–101).

Educational level did not appear to associate significantly with the

EDUCATION AND LEISURE ACTIVITIES OF OFFENDERS BEFORE CONVICTION

	TOTAL	MOVIES		VIDEOS		BAR		DANCING		CARDS		MUSIC		DRESSING	
		NO.	%	NO.	%	NO.	%	NO.	%	NO.	%	NO.	%	NO.	%
Illiterate	388	90	23.2	34	8.8	20	5.2	15	3.9	31	8.0	12	3.1	20	5.2
Primary	1069	214	20.0	88	8.2	40	3.7	41	3.8	58	5.4	97	9.1	101	9.4
J. High	2741	386	14.1	162	5.9	153	5.6	215	7.8	156	5.7	238	8.7	269	9.8
S. High & above	725	84	11.6	15	2.1	41	5.7	37	5.1	39	5.4	74	10.2	48	6.6

	FOOD		POPULAR READING		SERIOUS READING		TRAVELING		FRIENDS WITH OTHER SEX		CHATTING		OTHERS	
	NO.	%	NO.	%	NO.	%	NO.	%	NO.	%	NO.	%	NO.	%
Illiterate	62	16.0	16	4.1	12	3.1	7	1.8	25	6.4	29	7.5	15	3.9
Primary	99	9.3	60	5.6	33	3.1	37	3.5	83	7.8	96	9.0	22	2.1
J. High	164	6.0	217	7.9	125	4.6	152	5.5	262	9.6	193	7.0	49	1.8
S. High & above	42	5.8	64	8.8	87	12.0	59	8.1	61	8.4	55	7.6	19	2.6

Table 5–95

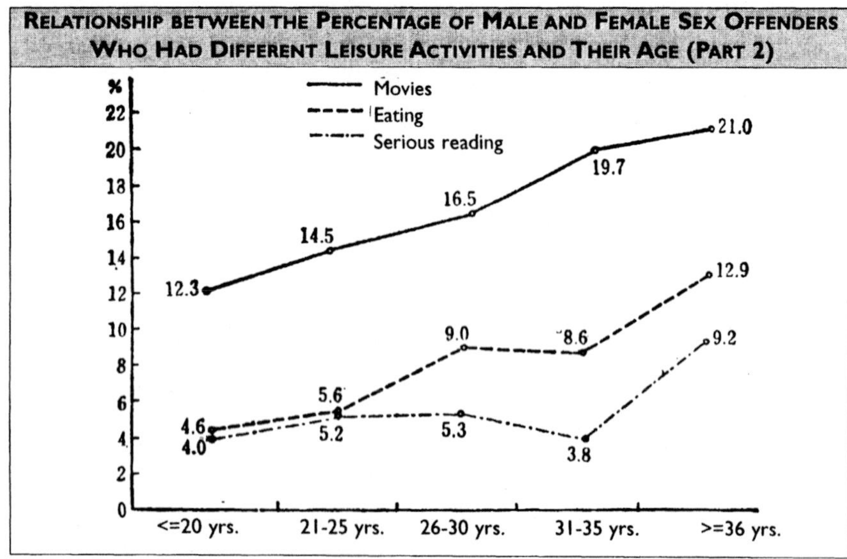

Figure 5–54

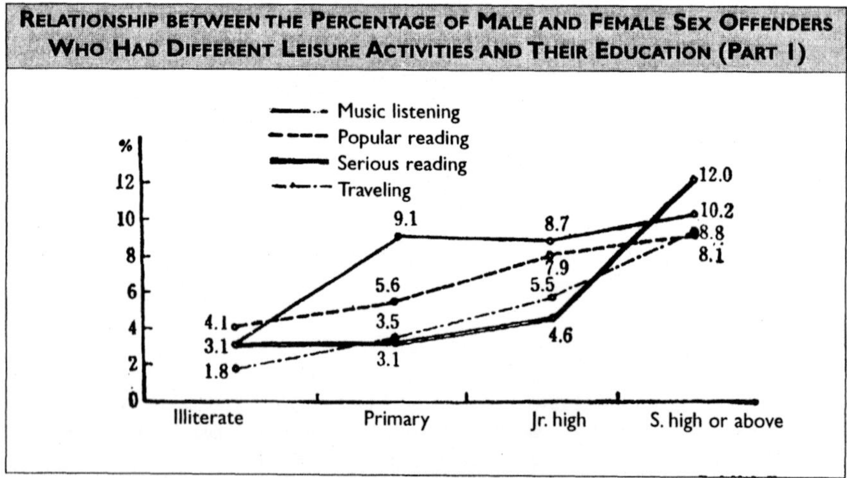

Figure 5–55

type of reaction upon seeing the sexual videos (table 5–102, figure 5–60).

Table 5–103 shows that as reported by the subjects, up to 52.3 percent of the sexual videos or books were from the open market and 42.5 percent from friends or classmates. Females usually came across the materials in friends' houses, while the males bought or borrowed the material from friends.

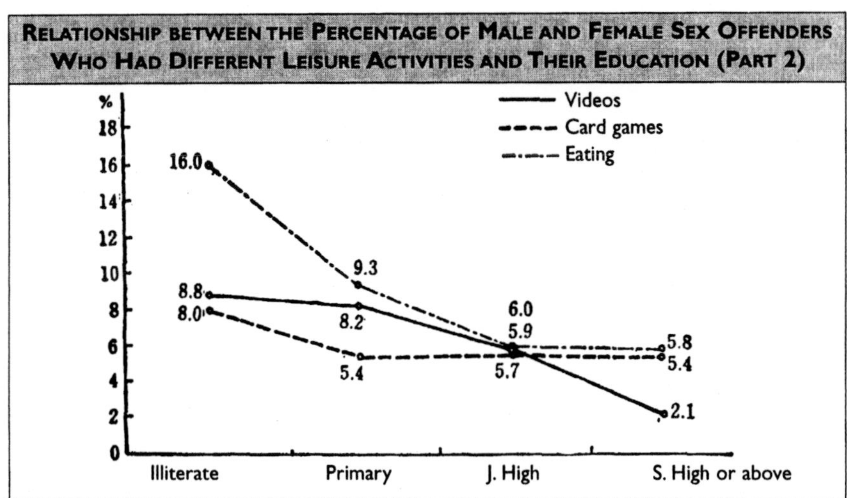

Figure 5–56

TOPICS OF CONVERSATION WITH FRIENDS

	TOTAL	POLITICS		BUSINESS		SEX		SEDUCE OTHER SEX		FOOD & DRESSING		MOVIES, VIDEOS, MAGAZINES	
		NO.	%	NO.	%	NO.	%	NO.	%	NO.	%	NO.	%
Male	1336	203	15.2	398	29.8	249	18.6	84	6.3	209	15.6	193	14.4
Female	550	48	8.7	145	26.4	60	10.9	13	2.4	202	36.7	82	14.9

P=0.001

Table 5–96

FAVORITE TYPE OF MOVIES, VIDEOS, OR MAGAZINES

	TOTAL	LOVE STORY		SEXUAL		VERY SEXUAL		VIOLENCE		DETECTIVE		FAMILY	
		NO.	%	NO.	%	NO.	%	NO.	%	NO.	%	NO.	%
Male	1360	267	19.6	156	11.5	97	7.1	528	38.8	174	12.8	138	10.1
Female	548	190	34.7	74	13.9	27	4.9	161	29.4	58	10.6	36	6.6

P=0.001

Table 5–97

The older age groups bought the materials or watched them in movie theatres, probably due to their financial situation (table 5–104).

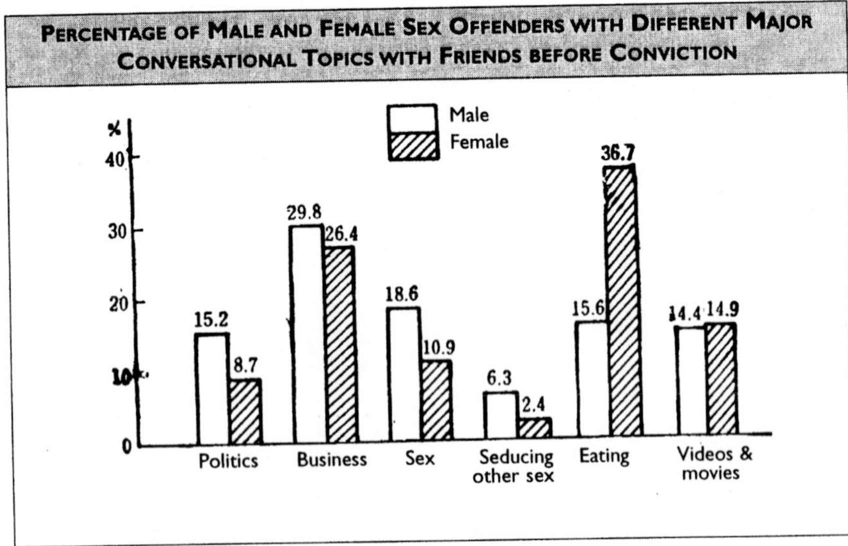

Figure 5–57

AGE AND FAVORITE TYPE OF MOVIES, VIDEOS, OR MAGAZINES

AGE	TOTAL	LOVE STORY		SEXUAL		VERY SEXUAL		VIOLENCE		DETECTIVE		FAMILY	
		NO.	%	NO.	%	NO.	%	NO.	%	NO.	%	NO.	%
<=20	494	150	30.4	59	11.9	27	5.5	185	37.4	40	8.1	33	6.7
21–25	528	127	24.1	54	10.2	29	5.5	222	42.0	56	10.6	40	7.6
26–30	374	89	23.8	52	13.9	27	7.2	115	30.7	52	13.9	39	10.4
31–35	199	37	18.6	28	14.1	20	10.1	60	30.2	30	15.1	24	12.1
>=36	303	55	18.2	40	13.2	21	6.9	101	33.3	46	15.2	40	13.2

Table 5–98

EDUCATION AND FAVORITE TYPE OF MOVIES, VIDEOS, OR MAGAZINES

	TOTAL	LOVE STORY		SEXUAL		VERY SEXUAL		VIOLENCE		DETECTIVE		FAMILY	
		NO.	%	NO.	%	NO.	%	NO.	%	NO.	%	NO.	%
Illiterate	160	31	19.4	11	6.9	13	8.1	77	48.1	18	11.3	10	6.3
Primary	414	108	26.1	53	12.8	28	6.7	176	42.5	36	8.7	13	3.1
J. High	1033	250	24.2	144	13.9	64	6.2	351	34.0	140	13.6	84	8.1
S. High	278	89	21.2	28	10.1	19	6.8	67	24.1	38	13.7	67	24.1

Table 5–99

REACTION UPON WATCHING SEXUAL DEPICTIONS							
	TOTAL	CALM		EXCITED		WISH TO TRY	
		NO.	%	NO.	%	NO.	%
Male	1347	549	40.8	557	41.4	241	17.9
Female	572	415	72.6	107	18.7	50	8.7

P=0.001

Table 5–100

AGE AND FEELING UPON WATCHING SEXUAL DEPICTIONS							
AGE	TOTAL	CALM		EXCITED		WISH TO TRY	
		NO.	%	NO.	%	NO.	%
<=20	487	222	45.6	151	31.0	114	23.4
21–25	528	264	50.0	185	35.0	79	15.0
26–30	385	206	53.5	137	35.6	42	10.9
31–35	201	101	50.2	79	39.3	21	10.4
>=36	306	167	54.6	108	35.3	31	10.1

Table 5–101

The educated bought the materials themselves or had them supplied by friends (table 5–105).

The findings confirm the idea that young people are highly affected by their peer groups or subculture. A study shows that every young criminal had about two to five friends of questionable conduct, or who were criminals as well, some up to ten.[12]

EDUCATION AND REACTION UPON WATCHING SEXUAL DEPICTIONS							
	TOTAL	CALM		EXCITED		WISH TO TRY IT	
		NO.	%	NO.	%	NO.	%
Illiterate	158	75	47.5	54	34.2	29	18.4
Primary	425	215	50.6	138	32.5	72	16.9
J. High	1037	527	50.8	356	34.3	154	14.9
S. High & above	276	131	47.5	111	40.2	34	12.3

Table 5–102

CIRCUMSTANCE OF WATCHING THE MOST IMPRESSIVE SEXUAL DEPICTION													
	TOTAL	BOUGHT OWN		FRIENDS' SUPPLY		AT FRIENDS' PLACE		IN SECRET VIDEO PLACES		PUBLIC SHOW PLACES		OTHERS	
		NO.	%	NO.	%	NO.	%	NO.	%	NO.	%	NO.	%
Male	1666	217	13.0	429	25.7	241	14.5	108	6.5	552	33.1	119	7.1
Female	720	73	10.1	145	20.1	177	24.6	46	6.4	251	34.9	28	3.9

P=0.001

Table 5–103

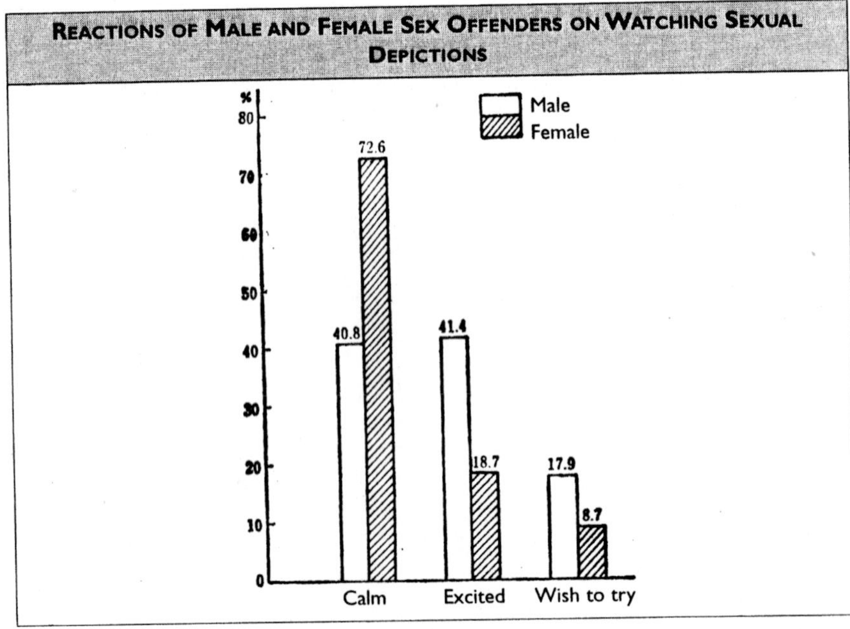

Figure 5–58

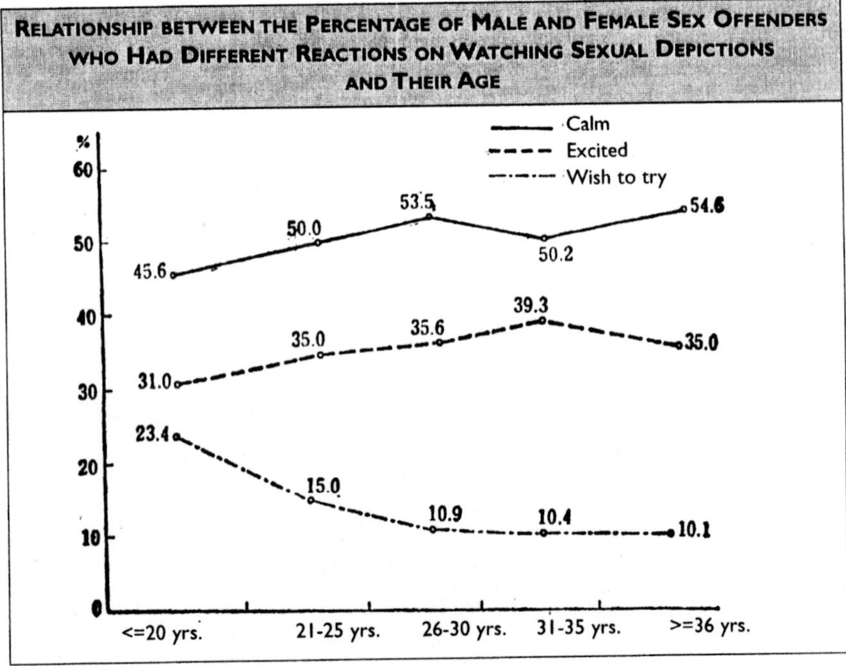

Figure 5–59

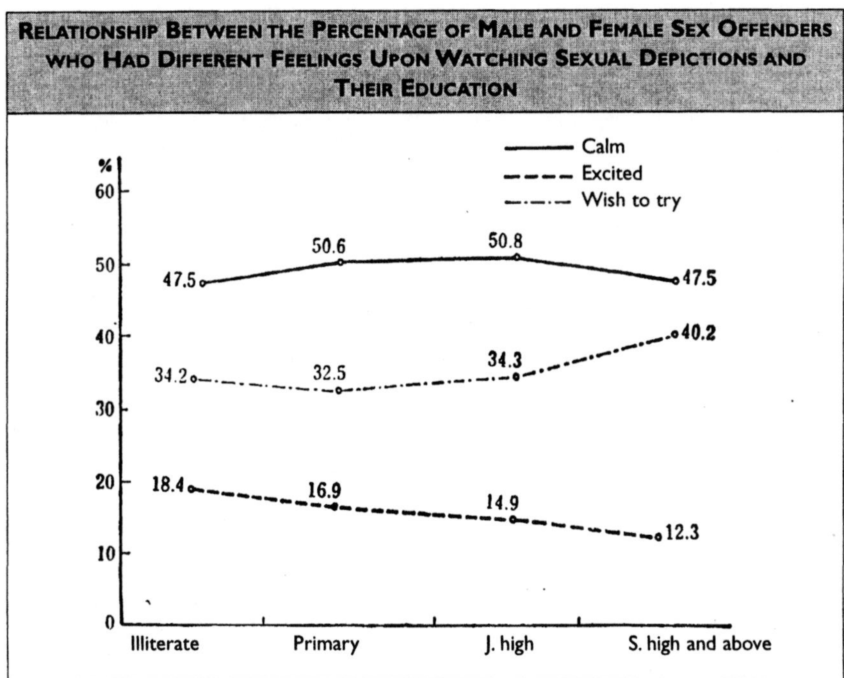

Figure 5–60

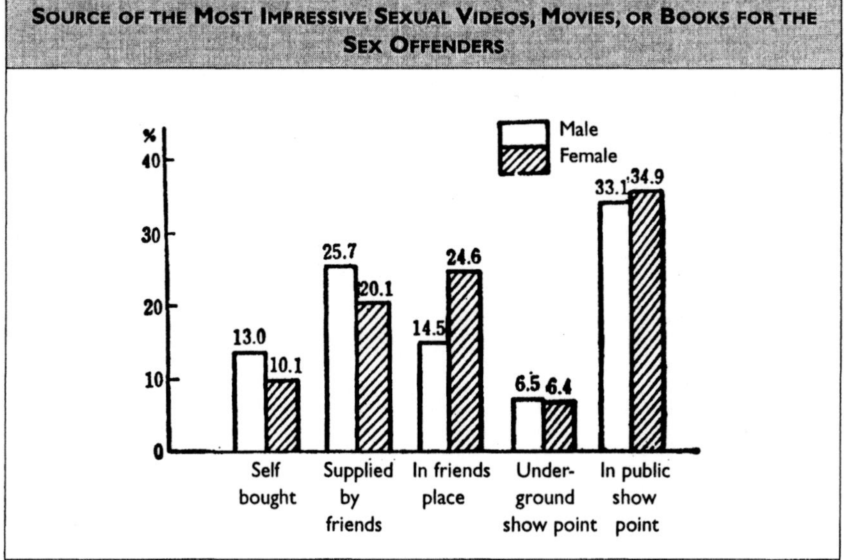

Figure 5–61

Age and Circumstance of Watching the Most Impressive Sexual Depiction													
	TOTAL	BOUGHT OWN		FRIENDS' SUPPLY		AT FRIENDS' PLACE		IN SECRET VIDEO PLACES		PUBLIC SHOW PLACES		OTHERS	
		NO.	%	NO.	%	NO.	%	NO.	%	NO.	%	NO.	%
<=20	673	83	12.3	177	26.3	151	22.4	59	8.8	175	26.0	28	4.2
21–25	681	70	10.3	180	26.4	124	18.2	47	6.9	228	33.5	32	4.7
26–30	468	62	13.2	108	23.1	68	14.5	26	5.6	178	38.0	26	5.6
30–35	244	33	13.5	54	22.1	35	14.3	9	3.7	94	38.5	19	7.8
>=36	304	44	14.5	50	16.4	30	9.9	16	5.3	122	40.1	42	13.8

Table 5–104

Education and Circumstance of Watching the Most Impressive Sexual Depiction													
	TOTAL	BOUGHT OWN		FRIENDS' SUPPLY		AT FRIENDS' PLACE		IN SECRET VIDEO PLACES		PUBLIC SHOW PLACES		OTHERS	
		NO.	%	NO.	%	NO.	%	NO.	%	NO.	%	NO.	%
Illiterate	175	21	12.0	28	16.0	20	11.4	16	9.1	71	40.6	19	10.9
Primary	505	59	11.7	85	16.8	90	17.8	34	6.7	206	40.8	31	6.1
J. High	1318	155	11.8	357	27.1	236	17.9	87	6.6	410	31.1	73	5.5
S. High & above	355	48	13.5	91	25.6	67	18.9	15	4.2	108	30.4	26	7.3

Table 5–105

7. Prostitution

In the early years of modern China, the hard work of the Chinese government had eradicated prostitution for some time, but beginning in the late 1970s, prostitution reappeared in the coastal regions and then

Age of Prostitution Offenders												
TOTAL	<=20		21–25		26–30		31–35		>=36		UNKNOWN	
	NO.	%	NO.	%	NO.	%	NO.	%	NO.	%	NO.	%
385	147	38.2	143	37.1	52	18.8	17	4.4	9	2.3	17	4.4

Table 5–106

Education of Prostitution Offenders												
TOTAL	ILLITERATE		PRIMARY		J. HIGH		S. HIGH		C. OR ABOVE		UNKNOWN	
	NO.	%	NO.	%	NO.	%	NO.	%	NO.	%	NO.	%
385	6	1.6	87	22.6	235	61.0	23	6.0	1	0.3	33	8.6

Table 5–107

Occupation of Prostitution Offenders										
TOTAL	FACTORY		AGRICULTURE		SERVICE		COMMERCE		TEACHER	
	NO.	%	NO.	%	NO.	%	NO.	%	NO.	%
385	56	14.5	112	29.1	28	7.3	11	2.9	3	0.9

MEDICAL		ARTS		OFFICIAL		FINANCE		SOLDIER	
NO.	%	NO.	%	NO.	%	NO.	%	NO.	%
3	0.8	2	0.5	1	0.3	3	0.8	1	0.3

STUDENT		SELF-EMPLOYED		NONE		OTHERS		UNKNOWN	
NO.	%	NO.	%	NO.	%	NO.	%	NO.	%
4	1.0	35	9.1	102	26.5	15	3.9	9	2.3

Table 5–108

spread to the big cities. Eventually the villages saw an increase in such activities. In 1985 in Guangzhou, only forty-nine people were arrested for prostitution and associated crimes; in 1985 the number rose to two thousand. In mid 1987, it was twelve thousand. In Shanghai, it was reported that the number of inmates charged for prostitution and associated crimes, as well as those admitted to correctional homes for youths had increased by five times within three years.[13]

1. Basic Data

Of the 2136 subjects in this part of the survey, 385 women were charged for prostitution, constituting up to 61.1 percent of all female offenders. Their age tended to be low; 75.3 percent were below age 25, 89.1 percent below thirty.

Compared with table 5–3, the educational level of these offenders was on the average lower than the sex offenders in general; 6.3 percent

FAMILY FINANCES BEFORE ARREST												
TOTAL	VERY GOOD		GOOD		AVERAGE		POOR		VERY POOR		UNKNOWN	
	NO.	%	NO.	%	NO.	%	NO.	%	NO.	%	NO.	%
385	16	4.2	85	22.1	197	51.2	63	16.4	11	2.9	13	3.4

Table 5–109

ABILITY OF FAMILY FINANCE TO SATISFY PERSONAL NEED						
TOTAL	YES		NO		UNKNOWN	
	NO.	%	NO.	%	NO.	%
385	166	43.1	200	51.9	19	4.9

Table 5–110

AGE OF FIRST SEXUAL OFFENSE (DIVORCED OR WIDOWED)				
TOTAL	20–29		>=30	
	NO	%	NO.	%
12	9	75.0	3	25.0

Table 5–114

MOTIVE FOR BECOMING A PROSTITUTE												
TOTAL	MONEY		PLEASURE		CURIOSITY		REVENGE		OTHERS		UNKNOWN	
	NO.	%	NO.	%	NO.	%	NO.	%	NO.	%	NO.	%
385	193	50.1	46	11.9	44	11.4	63	16.4	15	3.9	24	6.2

Table 5–111

AGE OF FIRST SEXUAL OFFENSE (BEFORE MARRIAGE)						
TOTAL	<=14		15–19		>=20	
	NO.	%	NO.	%	NO.	%
282	20	7.1	211	74.8	51	18.1

Table 5–112

AGE OF FIRST SEXUAL OFFENSE (MARRIED)				
TOTAL	20– 29		>=30	
	NO.	%	NO.	%
69	64	92.8	5	7.2

Table 5–113

were of high school level (table 5–107) compared with 10.0 percent of the general sex offenders.

Table 5–108 shows that the female prostitution offenders came from a large variety of occupations. There were more offenders from the villages, due to the fact that some villagers believed prostitution was a fast way to get rich, so much so that some husbands took their wives, some fathers took their daughters, and some sisters went together to the cities to become prostitutes.

Table 5–109 shows that 77.5 percent of the offenders had satisfactory or above satisfactory financial situations at home, but 51.9 percent found their family finances could not meet their personal needs (table 5–110).

The major purpose for prostitution was therefore money (50.1 percent), much higher than the 15.9 percent of the general sex offenders. Of the subjects, 16.4 percent also took revenge as the purpose for prostitution, also a higher rate than the general sex offenders (table 5–111).

Among these offenders, the age of committing the first offense was also earlier than the general sex offenders. Table 5–112 and 5–113 reveal that in those who had their offense committed at the age range between fifteen and nineteen, the prostitution offenders were of higher proportion (64.8 percent) than the general sex offenders (56.6 percent). Of the married subjects (table 5–113), 92.8 percent of them had their first offence committed between age twenty and twenty-nine.

2. Marital Relationship

Of the prostitute offenders, 31.4 percent were married or divorced. Compared with the marital relationship of the general female sex offenders, the prostitute offenders did not differ much (38.3 percent

Marital Status of Prostitution Offenders

TOTAL	SINGLE		MARRIED		REMARRIED		WIDOWED BEFORE ARREST		WIDOWED AFTER ARREST		DIVORCED BEFORE ARREST		DIVORCED AFTER ARREST	
	NO.	%	NO.	%	NO.	%	NO.	%	NO.	%	NO.	%	NO.	%
385	243	63.1	89	23.1	11	2.9	3	0.8	15	3.9	3	0.8	21	5.5

Table 5–115

Marital Relationship of Prostitution Offenders

TOTAL	GOOD		AVERAGE		OFTEN FIGHTS		MUTUAL NEGLECT		SEPARATED	
	NO.	%	NO.	%	NO.	%	NO.	%	NO.	%
128	30	23.4	49	38.3	32	25.0	7	5.5	10	7.8

Table 5–116

SEXUAL SATISFACTION WITH SPOUSE										
TOTAL	VERY GOOD		GOOD		NOT CLEAR		POOR		VERY POOR	
	NO.	%	NO.	%	NO.	%	NO.	%	NO.	%
105	7	6.7	44	41.9	25	23.8	20	19.0	9	8.6

Table 5–117

COMPARISON OF MARRIED FEMALE SEX OFFENDERS ON MARITAL SATISFACTION											
	TOTAL	GOOD		AVERAGE		OFTEN FIGHTS		MUTUAL NEGLECT		SEPARATED	
		NO.	%	NO.	%	NO.	%	NO.	%	NO.	%
Prostitute	128	30	23.4	49	38.3	32	25.0	7	5.5	10	7.8
Non-prostitute	68	23	33.8	21	30.9	15	22.1	2	2.9	7	10.3

Table 5–118

COMPARISON OF MARRIED FEMALE SEX OFFENDERS ON SEXUAL SATISFACTION											
	TOTAL	VERY GOOD		GOOD		NOT CLEAR		POOR		VERY POOR	
		NO.	%	NO.	%	NO.	%	NO.	%	NO.	%
Prostitute	105	7	6.7	44	41.9	25	23.8	20	19.0	9	8.6
Non-prostitute	61	11	18.0	26	42.6	12	19.7	8	13.1	4	6.6

Table 5–119

ABILITY OF HUSBAND TO SATISFY SEXUAL NEED					
	TOTAL	YES		NO	
		NO.	%	NO.	%
Prostitute	103	81	78.6	22	21.4
Non-prostitute	60	43	71.7	17	28.3

Table 5–120

not satisfactory compared with 35.3 percent), but the percentage of sexual dissatisfaction was much higher, 27.0 percent compared with 19.7 percent. Harmonious relationships among the prostitute offenders was 23.4 percent, in the general sex offenders 33.8 percent. Table 5–119 also shows that only 6.7 percent of the prostitution

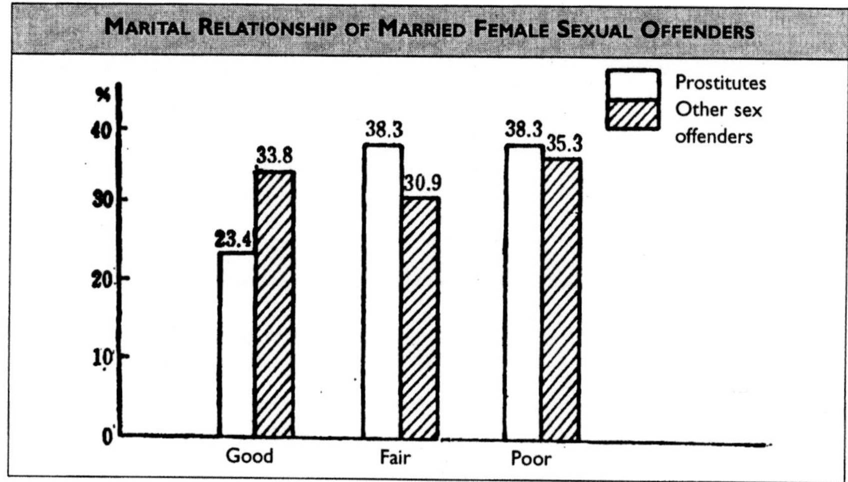

Figure 5–62

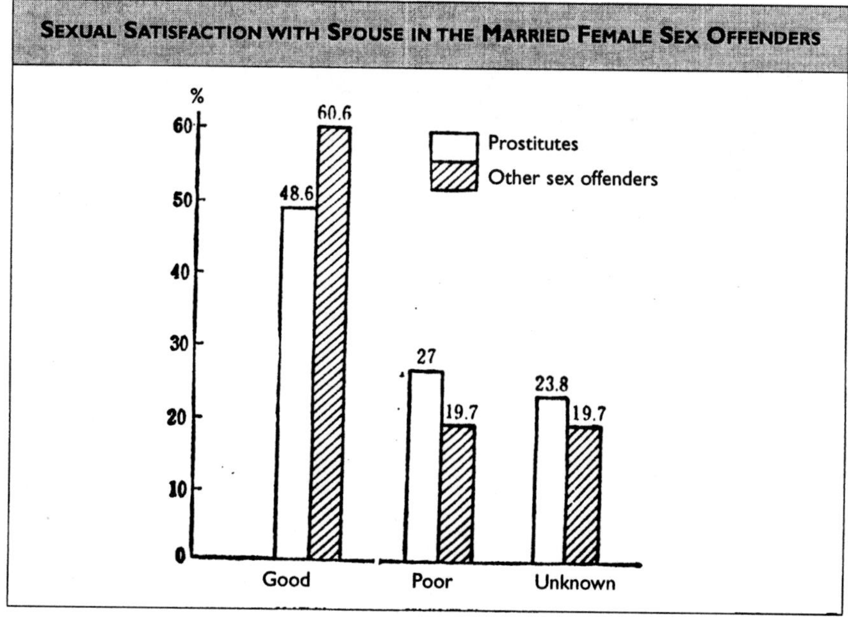

Figure 5–63

offenders were highly satisfied with their sex life, compared with 18.0 percent in the general sex offenders.

Table 5–120, however, shows that less prostitute offenders felt their husband could not meet their sexual needs. It shows that the main problem

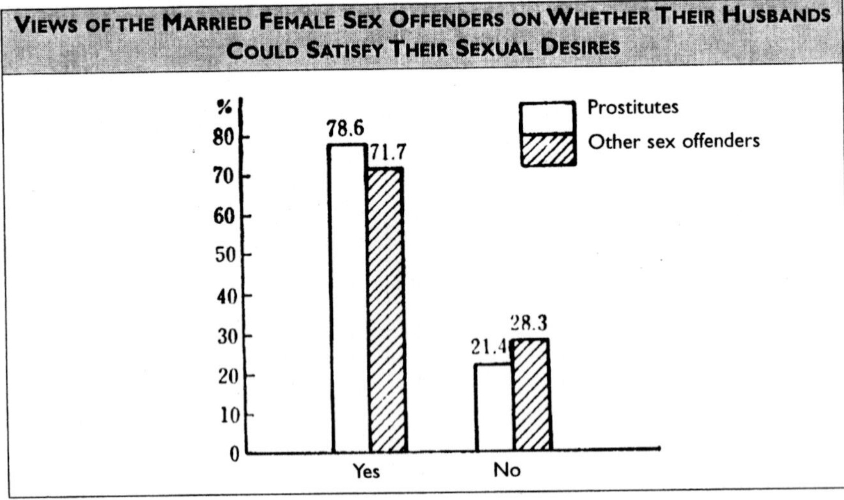

Figure 5–64

ATTITUDE TOWARD LOVE

	TOTAL	FOR AFFECTION		FOR SEX		NOT BETWEEN MALE & FEMALE		A DECEPTION		CAN HAVE MULTIPLE LOVERS	
		NO.	%	NO.	%	NO.	%	NO.	%	NO.	%
Prostitute	362	175	48.3	22	6.1	52	14.4	97	26.8	16	4.4
Non-prostitute	238	125	52.5	13	5.5	35	14.7	53	22.3	12	5.0

Table 5–121

VIEW ON SEXUAL FREEDOM

	TOTAL	SHOULD PROMOTE		BENEFIT, NO HARM		NEUTRAL		CONDITIONAL SUPPORT		OBJECT	
		NO.	%	NO.	%	NO.	%	NO.	%	NO.	%
Prostitute	349	11	3.2	18	5.2	202	57.9	32	9.2	86	24.6
Non–prostitute	231	9	3.9	3	1.3	148	64.1	31	13.4	40	17.3

Table 5–122

Requirements in Choosing a Spouse										
	TOTAL	WEALTH		APPEARANCE		LEARNED		STATUS		
		NO.	%	NO.	%	NO.	%	NO.	%	
Prostitute	375	84	22.4	25	6.7	14	3.7	5	1.3	
Non-prostitute	242	39	16.1	28	11.6	17	7.0	9	3.7	

	TEMPER		AFFECTION		HOUSING		FOREIGN CONTACTS		SEXUAL SATISFACTION	
	NO.	%	NO.	%	NO.	%	NO.	%	NO.	%
Prostitute	81	21.6	156	41.6	6	1.6	2	0.5	2	0.5
Non-prostitute	46	19.0	91	37.6	6	2.5	5	2.1	1	0.4

Table 5–122

Comparison between the Prostitution Female Offenders and the Other Female Offenders on Their Requirements for the Ideal Spouse

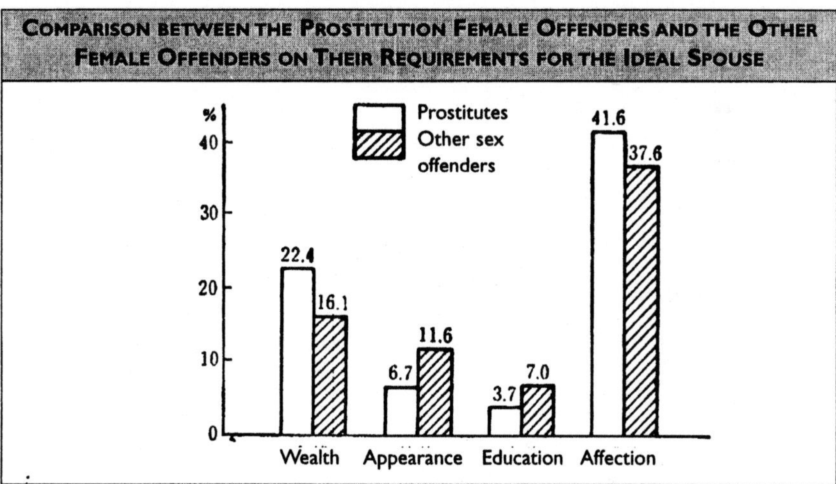

Figure 5–65

in the prostitute offenders was not sexual dissatisfaction, but the lack of affection in their relationships.

3. Sexual Attitudes:

On the purpose of love in a relationship, 48.3 percent of the prostitute offenders stated it was for affection. Their views were not significantly different from the general sex offenders (table 5–121, table 5–68).

View on Chastity											
	TOTAL	IMPORTANT		FEUDALISM		ONLY FOR WOMAN		NO PROBLEM IF IN LOVE		SEXUAL NEED OVERIDES	
		NO.	%	NO.	%	NO.	%	NO.	%	NO.	%
Prostitute	353	138	38.5	34	9.5	47	13.1	129	36.0	10	2.8
Non-prostitute	230	85	37.0	16	7.0	14	6.1	103	44.8	12	5.2

Table 5–124

View on Aim in Life for a Woman									
	TOTAL	PLEASURE		GOOD WIFE AND MOTHER		DEPENDENT ON MAN		CAREER	
		NO.	%	NO.	%	NO.	%	NO.	%
Prostitute	365	105	28.8	159	43.6	6	1.6	95	26.0
Non-prostitute	227	63	27.8	97	42.7	5	2.2	62	27.3

Table 5–125

On criteria for their ideal spouse, compared with the general sex offenders, the prostitute offenders took money and affection to be important factors.

On sexual freedom, there were no obvious differences among the general offenders except a suggestion of a high rate of rejection. The prostitutes more then likely worked more for money than sexual freedom.

About 50 percent of the prostitute offenders did not think chastity was important, differing little from the general sex offenders.

On life pursuits, the prostitute offenders differed little from the general population of subjects surveyed, (table 5–125) but they showed less regret (table 5–126).

4. Characteristics Currently Found Among Prostitutes in China

In our survey, we found the following characteristics among the prostitute offenders:

[a] Currently prostitution in China is all underground.

[b] They are mostly part-time. As shown in table 5–108, 71.2 percent of them had other occupations. This is in agreement with previous findings.[14]

[c] They are young prostitutes, some below age fourteen, but mostly below nineteen.

[d] Their family financial situation, more often than not, was relatively good. They worked as prostitutes simply for enjoyment and money.

[e] They have a particular view of life which centers on self-enjoyment, with a low sense of social responsibility.

The problem of prostitution in China could be caused by many factors, lack of education, modernization, the open-door policy, or the weakening of political education. A female Chinese writer once said, "Our society has neglected sex education. Time has therefore taken revenge on us."[15]

8. The Road to a New Life

1. Attitude toward Confession

Of all offenders, 54.7 percent confessed being guilty of the crime and

Reaction to Conviction

TOTAL	REGRET		BLAME SELF		BLAME VICTIM		BLAME OTHERS		WISH TO CHANGE		NO FEELING		NOT REGRET	
	NO.	%	NO.	%	NO.	%	NO.	%	NO.	%	NO.	%	NO.	%
375	105	28.0	51	13.6	23	6.1	39	10.4	112	29.9	42	11.2	3	0.8
238	88	37.0	41	17.2	15	6.3	21	8.8	54	22.7	13	5.5	6	2.5

Table 5–126

Attitude toward Penalty Received

	TOTAL	GUILTY		GUILTY BUT NOT ACCEPT PENALTY		NOT VERY GUILTY		NO CRIME	
		NO.	%	NO.	%	NO.	%	NO.	%
Male	1387	789	56.9	399	27.9	160	11.5	50	3.6
Female	598	346	57.9	206	34.4	34	5.7	12	2.0

P=0.001

Table 5–127

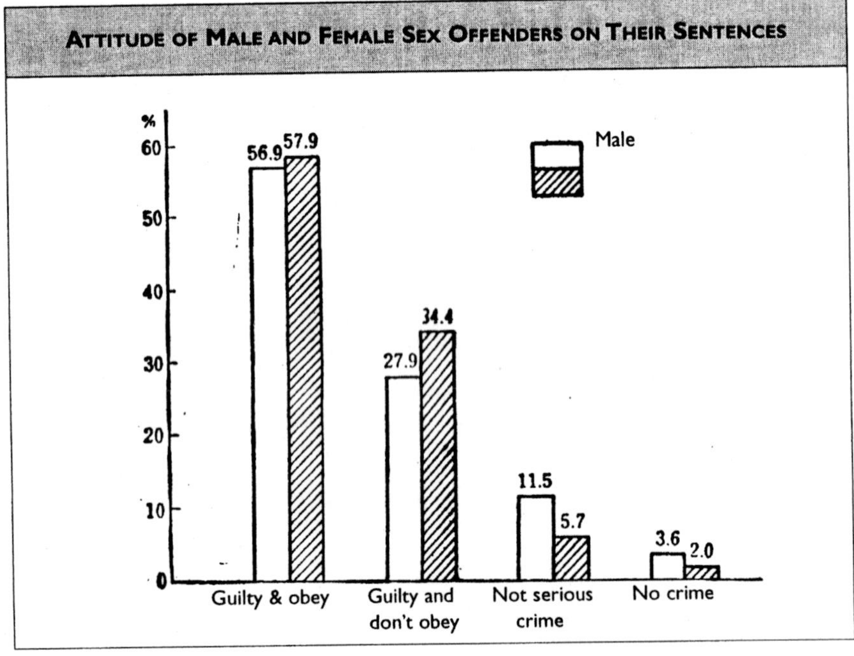

Figure 5–66

REACTION TO CONVICTION

TOTAL	REGRET		BLAME SELF		BLAME VICTIM		BLAME OTHERS		WISH TO CHANGE		NO FEELING		NOT REGRET		UNKOWN	
	NO.	%	NO.	%	NO.	%	NO.	%	NO.	%	NO.	%	NO.	%	NO.	%
2136	749	35.1	404	18.9	124	5.8	140	6.6	500	23.4	93	4.4	49	2.3	77	3.6

Table 5–128

GENDER AND REACTION TO CONVICTION

	TOTAL	REGRET		BLAME SELF		BLAME VICTIM		BLAME OTHERS		WISH TO CHANGE		NO FEELING		NOT REGRET	
		NO.	%	NO.	%	NO.	%	NO.	%	NO.	%	NO.	%	NO.	%
Male	1387	538	38.8	302	21.8	80	5.8	77	5.6	316	22.8	37	2.7	37	2.7
Female	613	193	31.5	92	15.0	38	6.2	60	9.8	166	27.1	55	9.0	9	1.5

Table 5–129

GREATEST LOSS AFTER BEING CONVICTED													
	TOTAL	NAME		CHASTITY		FUTURE		CAREER OR STUDY		MONEY		FAMILY	
		NO.	%	NO.	%	NO.	%	NO.	%	NO.	%	NO	%
Male	1404	342	24.4	14	1.0	547	39.0	133	9.5	224	16.0	144	10.3
Female	608	187	30.8	37	6.1	141	23.2	67	11.0	98	16.1	78	12.8

P=0.001

Table 5–130

were willing to accept the penalty, but the others who did not confess were a problem for the correctional service.

Females were less apt to confess and accept their penalty than the males, probably because they had more complicated causes for their offenses. They tend to see themselves as victims, forced into crime by the community or others (table 5-127, figure 5-66).

Of the offenders 77.4 percent felt regret, self-blame, or a wish to change their ways (table 5–128), but the number of females with these feelings were less. They blamed others more then themselves. Three times more females than males felt nothing about their penalty (table 5–129). More females felt that their conviction cost them their name and chastity. More males thought it ruined their career (table 5–130, figure 5–68).

Table 5–131 shows that twice as many females as males felt that their conviction was worthy of what they had gained, reflecting upon the psychology of the female offenders.

GENDER AND VIEW ON BEING CONVICTED							
GENDER	TOTAL	GOOD BARGAIN		NOT GOOD BARGAIN		UNKNOWN	
		NO.	%	NO.	%	NO.	%
Male	1355	31	2.3	1034	76.3	290	21.4
Female	594	35	5.9	354	59.6	205	34.5

P=0.001

Table 5–131

AGE AND VIEW ON BEING CONVICTED							
AGE	TOTAL	GOOD BARGAIN		NOT GOOD BARGAIN		UNKNOWN	
		NO.	%	NO.	%	NO.	%
<=20	500	24	4.8	294	58.8	182	36.4
21–25	525	16	3.0	370	70.5	139	26.5
26–30	399	11	2.8	297	74.4	91	22.8
31–35	204	6	2.9	157	77.0	41	20.1
>=36	313	8	2.6	269	85.9	36	11.5

Table 5–132

Reactions of the Male and Female Sex Offenders on Being Sentenced

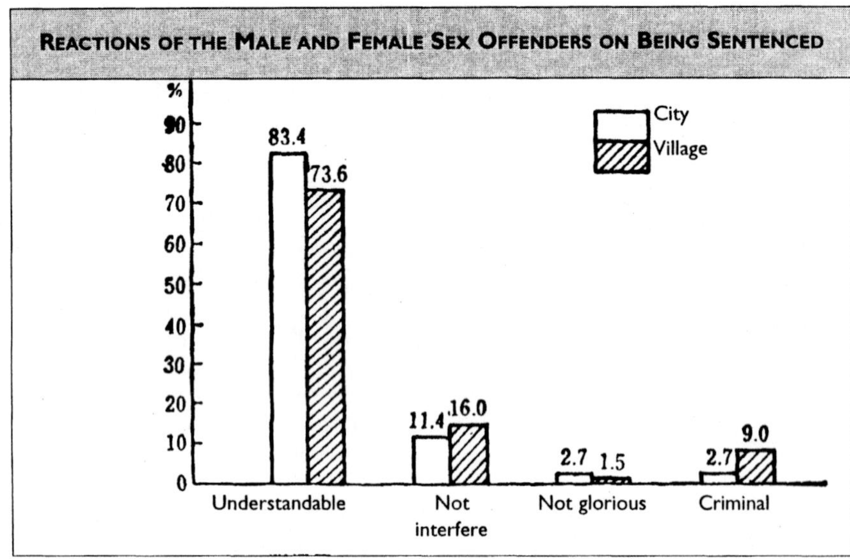

Figure 5–67

Subjective Greatest Loss as Perceived by the Male and Female Sex Offenders on Being Sentenced

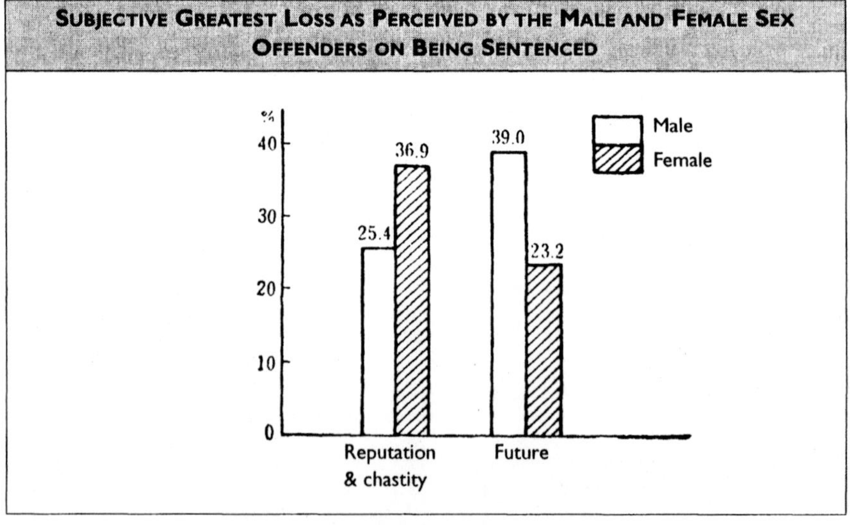

Figure 5–68

The older offenders felt less about their conviction being worthy of their gain and many more felt it was not worthy (G=-0.24).

Of the offenders, 692 (32.4 percent) had appealed against their conviction; 55.8 percent of the appeals were unsuccessful, 12.4 percent were

VIEW OF THE MALE AND FEMALE SEX OFFENDERS ON THE SENTENCE THEY RECEIVED

%
80
70
60
50
40
30
20
10
0
Male
Female
76.3
59.6
34.5
21.4
2.3
5.9
Gained from the crime
No gain
Not know

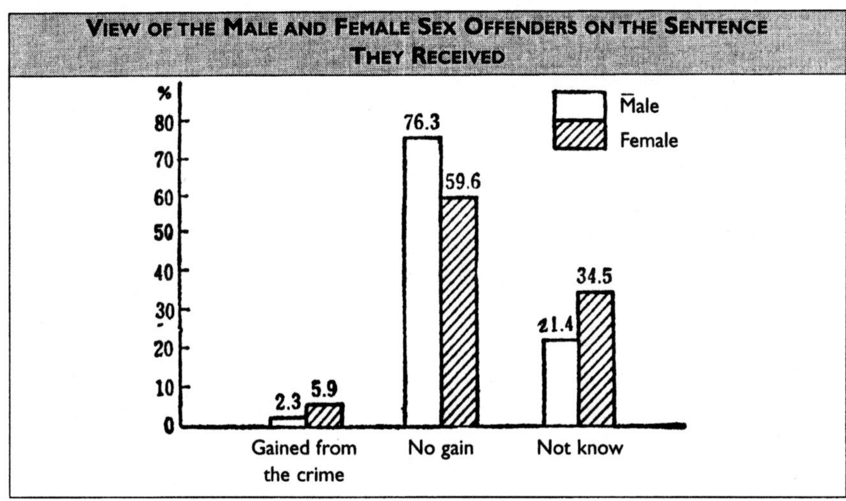

Figure 5–69

RELATIONSHIP BETWEEN THE PERCENTAGE OF MALE AND FEMALE SEX OFFENDERS WHO HAD DIFFERENT VIEWS ON THE SENTENCES THEY RECEIVED AND THEIR AGE

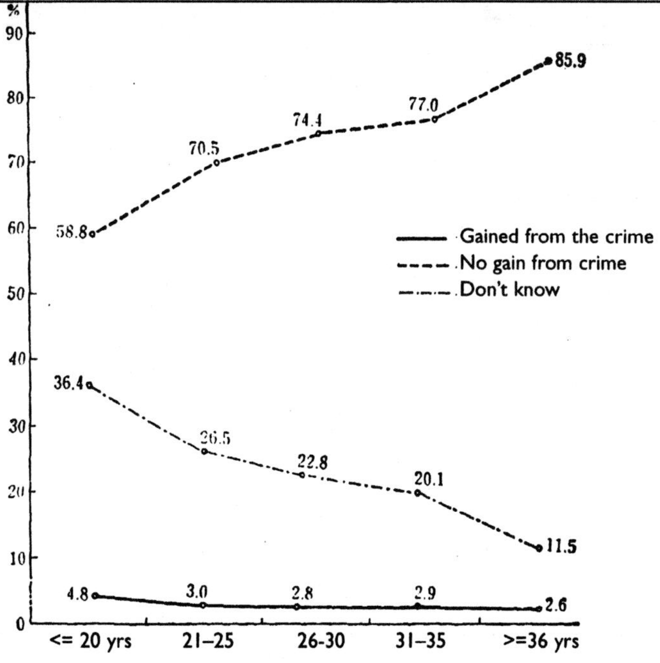

%
90
80
70
60
50
40
30
20
10
0
85.9
77.0
74.4
70.5
58.8
Gained from the crime
No gain from crime
Don't know
36.4
26.5
22.8
20.1
11.5
4.8
3.0
2.8
2.9
2.6
<= 20 yrs
21–25
26-30
31–35
>=36 yrs

Figure 5–70

RELATIONSHIP BETWEEN THE PERCENTAGE OF MALE AND FEMALE SEX OFFENDERS WHO HAD DIFFERENT VIEWS ON THE SENTENCES THEY RECEIVED AND THEIR AGE

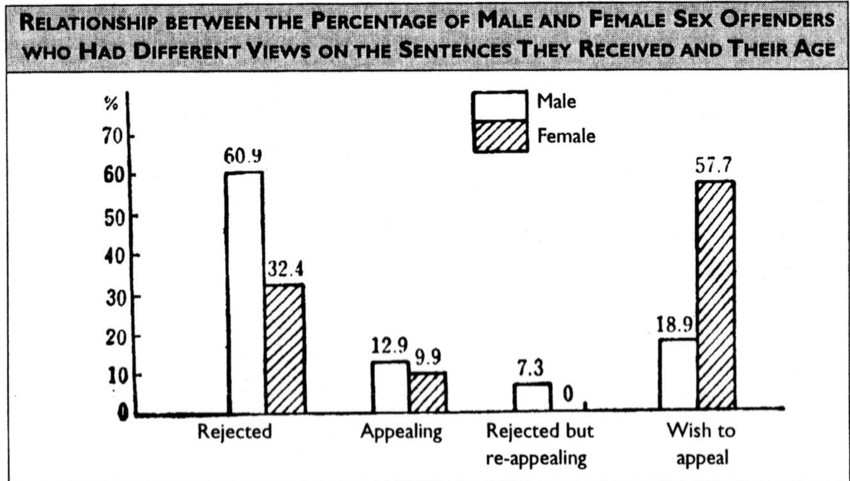

Figure 5–71

APPEALS									
	TOTAL	REJECTED		PENDING		REJECTED BUT REAPPEALING		WISH TO APPEAL	
		NO.	%	NO.	%	NO.	%	NO.	%
Male	565	344	60.9	73	12.9	41	7.3	107	18.9
Female	111	36	32.4	11	9.9	0	0	64	57.7

P=0.001

Table 5–133

being heard, 6.2 percent had been rejected but were being appealed, 25.6 percent pending (table 5–133, figure 5–71). Females who wished to appeal were obviously more, but fewer of them really put it into action.

2. Sexual Needs While Serving Sentence

Table 5–134 shows the various methods the offenders used to channel their sexual needs during their sentence period. In the "other" channel, there is one common method called "spiritual meeting." In this meeting a number of the inmates gather, talking about their past sexual enjoyments and glories and disclose their own sexual fantasies as a way of sexual gratification.

Table 5–135 shows that female offenders tended to suppress their desires less, but rather wrote love and sexual poems or sang love songs. Males suppressed or masturbated more. The prison usually did not interfere with suppression or writing poetry, but masturbation or mutual masturbation would be severely punished. Another way is to channel their needs through recreation, sports, or cultural activities, or have medication administered by doctors.

Older offenders suppressed their desires more than other methods. The younger offenders resorted more to singing and writing poetries. Bodily contacts including hugging, kissing, or masturbation were evenly distributed.

Way of Suppressing Sexual Desire During Sentence Period

TOTAL	SUPPRESS ONLY		COPY LOVE POEMS		DRAW SEXY PAINTINGS		SING LOVE SONGS	
	NO.	%	NO.	%	NO.	%	NO.	%
2136	1097	51.4	70	3.3	17	0.8	190	8.9

CARESS INMATES		MASTURBATION		OTHERS		UNKNOWN	
NO.	%	NO.	%	NO.	%	NO.	%
15	0.7	96	4.5	110	5.1	541	25.3

Table 5–134

Gender and Way of Suppressing Sexual Desires

	TOTAL	SUPPRESS ONLY		COPY LOVE POEMS		DRAW SEXY PAINTINGS		SING LOVE SONGS	
		NO.	%	NO.	%	NO.	%	NO.	%
Male	1441	931	64.6	39	2.7	14	1.0	97	6.7
Female	630	144	22.9	28	4.4	3	0.5	91	14.4

	CARESS INMATES		MASTURBATION		OTHERS		UNKNOWN	
	NO.	%	NO.	%	NO.	%	NO.	%
Male	10	0.7	91	6.3	71	4.9	188	13.0
Female	5	0.8	5	1.0	35	5.6	319	50.6

P=0.001

Table 5–135

The subjects who had watched sexual intercourse below the age of fifteen tended to masturbate more. It is in agreement with the previous finding that these subjects claimed to have strong sexual desires (table 5–137).

The problems of sexual release for the prisoners are still unsolved. A more humane approach seems to be needed.

AGE AND WAY OF SUPPRESSING SEXUAL DESIRE										
AGE	TOTAL	SUPPRESS ONLY		COPY LOVE POEMS		DRAWINGS, PAINTINGS		SING LOVE SONGS		
		NO.	%	NO.	%	NO.	%	NO.	%	
<=20	380	241	63.4	27	7.1	3	0.8	61	14.6	
21–25	417	283	67.9	17	4.1	4	1.0	54	12.9	
26–30	321	225	70.1	18	5.6	4	1.2	39	12.1	
31–35	165	121	73.3	5	3.0	3	1.8	15	9.1	
>=36	267	196	73.4	2	0.7	3	1.1	14	5.2	

AGE	CARESS INMATES		MASTURBATION		OTHERS	
	NO.	%	NO.	%	NO.	%
<=20	3	0.8	22	5.8	23	6.1
21–25	4	1.0	30	7.2	25	6.0
26–30	4	1.2	12	3.7	19	5.9
31–35	3	1.8	9	5.5	9	5.5
>=36	0	0	22	8.2	30	11.2

Table 5–136

AGE OF FIRST WATCHING SEXUAL INTERCOURSE AND WAYS OF SUPPRESSING SEXUAL DESIRE									
AGE	TOTAL	SUPPRESS ONLY		COPY LOVE POEMS		DRAWINGS, PAINTINGS		SING LOVE SONGS	
		NO.	%	NO.	%	NO.	%	NO.	%
<=15	320	207	64.7	13	4.1	4	1.3	36	12.3
16–20	534	365	68.4	27	5.1	8	1.5	77	14.4
>=21	94	68	72.3	4	4.3	0	0	11	11.7

AGE	CARESS INMATES		MASTURBATION		OTHERS	
	NO.	%	NO.	%	NO.	%
<=15	3	0.9	37	11.6	20	6.3
16–20	4	0.7	23	4.3	30	5.6
>=21	2	2.1	4	4.3	5	5.3

Table 5–137

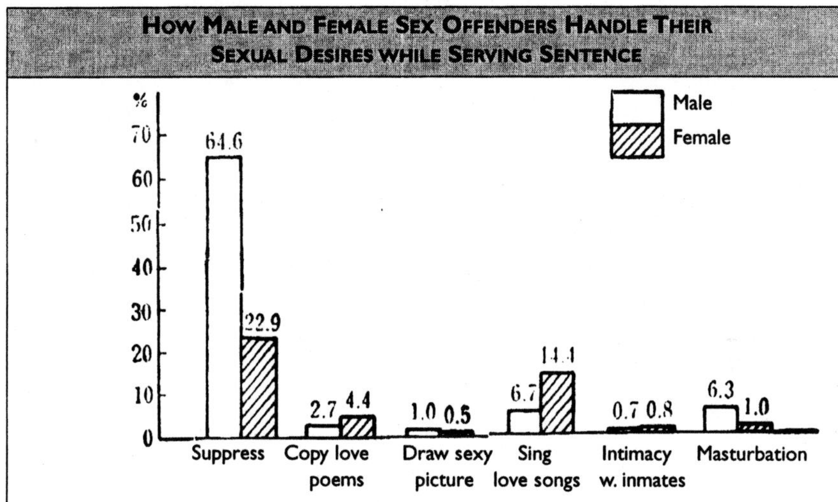

Figure 5–72

3. Effect of Re-education

A Shanghai correctional center estimated that about 80 percent of the female convicts had a genuine willingness to change, but in 1985, a study showed that the recidivism rate of female offenders was between 25 percent to 30 percent. Some studies concluded that the factors for recidivism were egocentrism, uncontrolled desire to possess, antisocial attitude, resistance to normal education, acceptance of antisocial messages, lack of moral and duty sense, lack of self control, risk-taking tendency, abnormal physical or psychological make-up, rigid stereotyping, susceptibility to temptations.[16]

In 1972, youth correctional centers followed up twenty-six hundred discharged youths in the past ten years and found that of those without job placement, 36.57 percent of them had committed minor offenses, 23.61 percent regular offenses; for those with placement, the percentages were 13.73 percent and 6.57 percent, showing the importance of proper placement.

Conclusion

There seems to be a tendency for the age of sex offenders to lower as time goes on. The female offenders are very different from the males with respect to their background, aim, and causes for crimes.

The educational level of the offenders' parents was low. The lack of family cohesiveness could be a cause for the sex crime. The lack of proper sex education and the low educational standard of the offenders could also contribute to the problem. At a time when China is opening up and modernizing, an improvement of education and living standards should go along with the social changes that must be made to minimize the social factors which could induce sex crimes.

Notes

1. Females are convicted for rape, gang rape, and child sexual assault as accomplices.
2. Cao Lu, "Be Aware of Psychological Crimes" in *Society* 7 (1988): 17
3. Crimes committed by adolescents have increased rapidly in recent years in various Western countries. In the United States, FBI statistics show that in the past three decades, adolescent crimes have increased tremendously. Half of the serious crimes were committed by people of age ten to seventeen, some as young as six to seven. In San Francisco, 75 percent of those arrested for serious physical assaults were below age nineteen. In Chicago, in 1978, one third of murder crimes were by youngsters below twenty. [L.D. Schwartz, *Studies on Sex Crimes* (Wuhan: Wuhan Publications, 1988), Chinese version, 1st ed., 78.]

   According to the 1981 *Japan White Paper on Crimes*, based on population, the rate of adolescent crime rate was 5.3 percent in the United States, 4.8 percent in Germany, and 4.4 percent in Japan. In Japan, in one thousand adolescents, 9.2 were arrested for crimes in 1955, 12.3 in 1975, 14.1 in 1978, and 22.4 in 1981,while the adult rate was only 8.1 in one thousand in the same year. [Hung Je-He, *Education on Sex* (Shanghai: Shanghai People's Publications, 1989), 1st ed., 276.]

   In China, the age of sex criminals is also decreasing. In Shanghai for example, one hundred adolescents were arrested for rape or gang rape in 1980. The number was 150 in 1981, 192 in 1982, and 311 in 1983. The rate in 1985 was 42.5 percent higher than that of 1984, and 11.7 percent of the total sex crimes were committed by adolescents. [Gu Ying-Chun, *A Comprehensive Study on the Treatment of Adolescent Crimes* (Shanghai: Public Publications, 1986), 1st ed.,272.]

   The statistics in Beijing of 1980 showed that most of the first sex crimes were committed by persons between the ages of thirteen and sixteen, with females earlier than the males. [Xu Yin-Long, *Psychological and Biological Characteristics of Adolescents and Their Methods of Education* (Shanghai: Shanghai People's Publications, 1982), 1st ed., p. 61.]

   In the province of Zhejiang, a random sample of twenty-three prostitutes found that their mean age was 17.2; seventeen of them (74 percent) were between the ages of fourteen and eighteen. [Gu Ying-Chun, *Archive of Studies on Adolescent Crimes* (Hangzhou: Zhejiang Social Science Research Institute, 1983), 93.]

In Shanghai, the youngest rapist arrested so far was age twelve. He raped a girl of three in his neighborhood. In Liaoning, a rapist of age fifteen raped an old lady of age seventy-five. [*People's Law Report* (1990), Issue No. 6.]

4. Fung Tian-Yun, "Women's Sexual Revenge on Men," *Society* 7 (1990): 15.
5. Schwartz, *Studies on Sex Crimes*, 36.
6. Dalin Liu, *Sexual Sociology* (Jinan: Shandong People's Publications, 1986), 1st ed., 201.
7. Schwartz, *Studies on Sex Crimes*, 82.
8. Dalin Liu, *Sexual Sociology*.
9. Schwartz, *Studies on Sex Crimes*, 88–89.
10. Gu Ying-Chun, *Archive of Studies on Adolescent Crimes*, 92.
11. Sichuan Social Science Institute and Adolescent Research Centre, *Sichuan Adolescent Criminals—Case Report Studies* (Chengdu: The Institute, 1985), 10.
12. Chen Shu-Hen, *How to Predict and Prevent Adolescent Crimes.* (Shanghai: Shanghai Social Science Publications, 1989), 1st ed., 102.
13. Huang Jia-Xin, "New Trends of Sex Crimes," *Society* 6 (1989): 24.
14. Ibid.
15. Yi Ni, *Contemplations Under the Sun* (Beijing: China Joint Literature Publications, 1988), 116–17.
16. Gu Ying-Chun, *Archive of Studies on Adolescent Crimes*, 203.

6
Comparative Studies

In our survey, we studied four groups of subjects, each apparenetly different from the others, but they are in fact very much interrelated because one group may develop or change to the other group. For example, the students will likely become married adults and some of the non-criminals could become criminals. We hope to be able to find some patterns in this change or development, so that we can predict or help to prevent some of the unfavorable outcomes possible. This could be accomplished by making comparisons: comparisons between the four groups as well as with similar groups in other countries. We have done a bit of the latter in the previous chapters, but more detailed comparisons among the groups will be made in this chapter.

1. Psychophysiological Development

A. Sexual Physiology

For the high school students, the mean age of first ejaculation was 14.4 and menarche was 13.4; for the college students, it was a bit older, at 14.59 and 13.43 respectively. This is not difficult to understand, since it is well known that our youngsters are maturing faster progressively and that there is a mean age gap of about five years between the high school and college students.

For the sex offenders, the respective ages were 16.34 and 13.70. Since the mean age of the offenders was 27.39, it is also understandable that they mature even more slowly. There is no evidence that the sex offenders mature sexually earlier than the general population, something which some researchers suspect is a factor associated with sexual offenses.

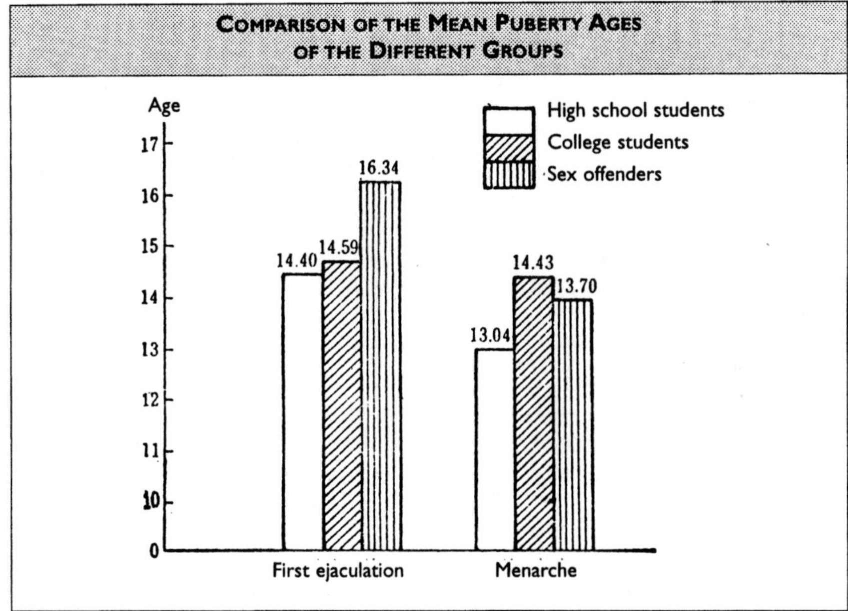

Figure 6–1

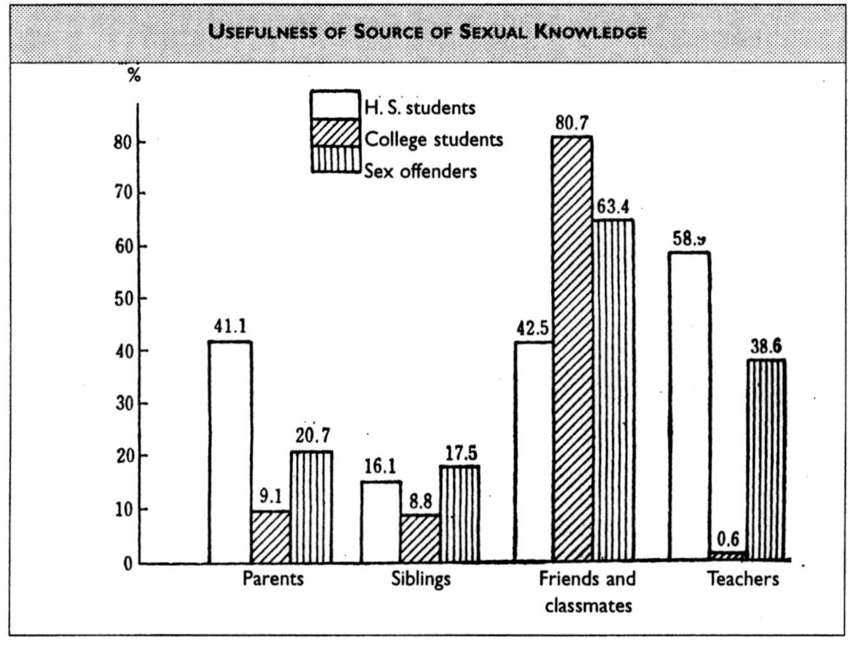

Figure 6–2

B. Sexual Knowledge and Attitude

Figure 6–2 shows that more high school students considered their parents and teachers as useful sources of sexual information, while the college students had the lowest proportion. This shows that probably the high school students trusted their parents and teachers more. On the other hand, the college students may be getting independent and untrusting, or the parents and teachers are really not up-to-date in their sexual knowledge. Both the college students and the sex offenders resorted most to their friends or classmates for sexual information, probably as a result of their larger social environment than the high school students.

C. Experience with Erotica

Figure 6–3 shows that more college than high school students felt excited upon experiencing erotica. This probably only shows a natural increase in interest and feeling as one matures psychosexually. Comparison with sexual offenders cannot be made since different questions were asked about their feelings concerning sexual matters.

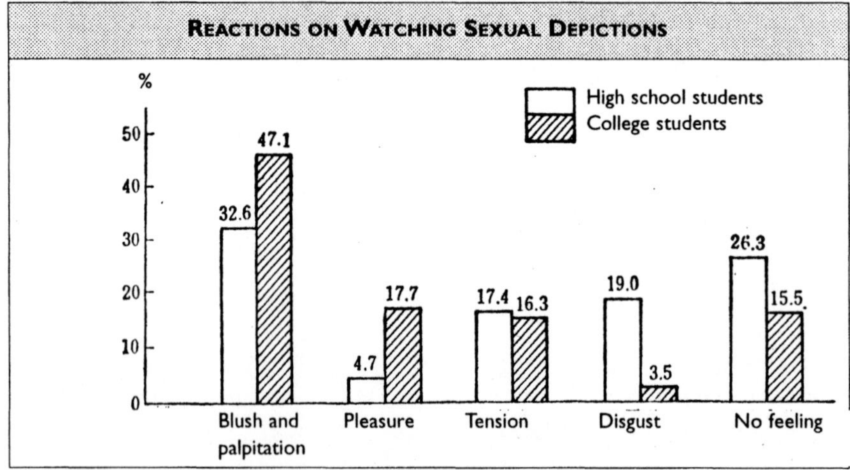

Figure 6–3

2. Sexual Behavior

A. Courtship

Figure 6–4 shows the rate of high school and college students who had entered into courtship. The latter were much more than the former, and females somewhat higher than the males.

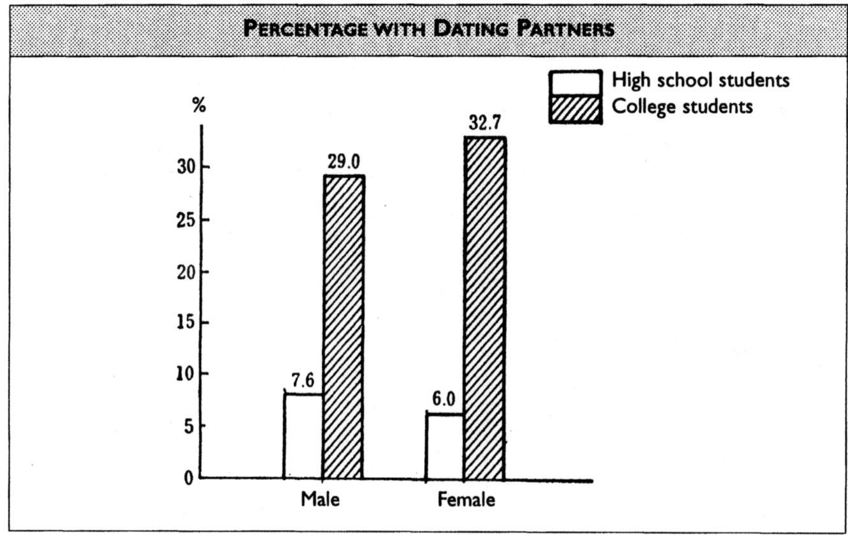

Figure 6–4

The high school and college students had different attitudes toward courtship as well; 95.2% of the college students considered courtship as proper for students, more than three times that of the high school students. This reflects two different stages in attitude towards courtship (figure 6–5).

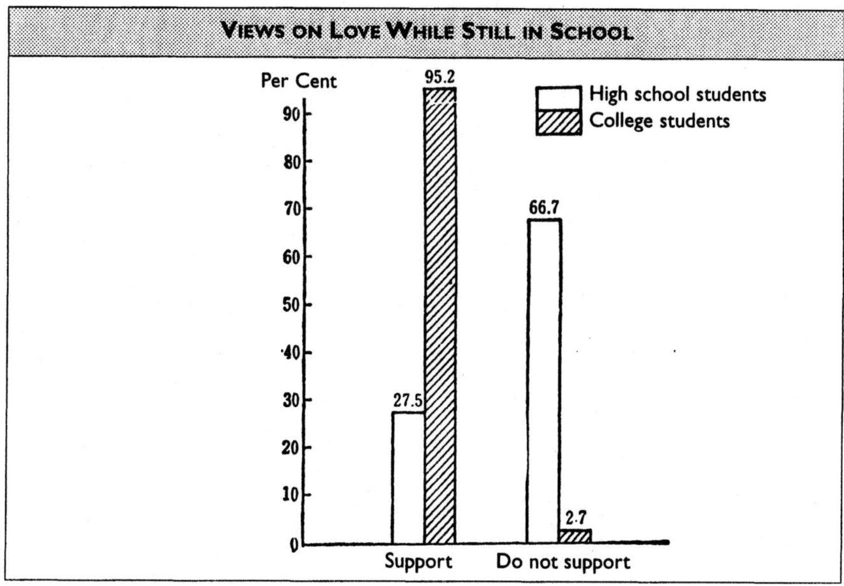

Figure 6–5

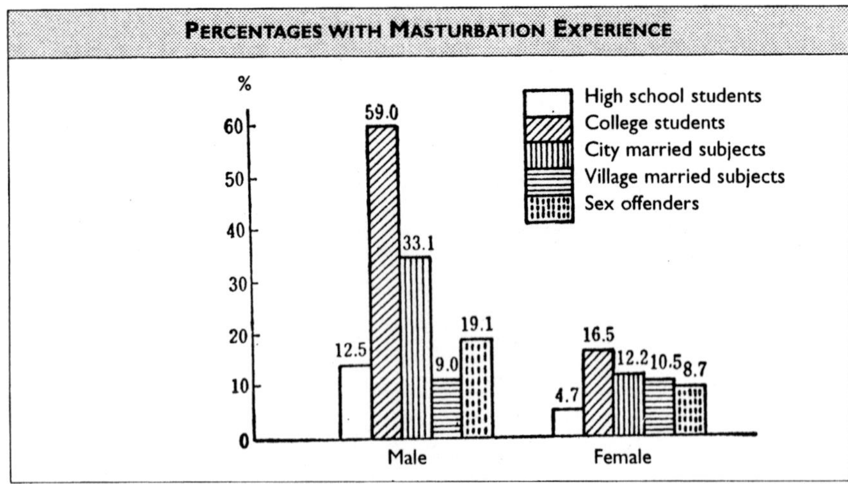

Figure 6–6

B. Masturbation

Figure 6–6 shows that of all the subject groups surveyed, college students were highest in their masturbation rates. The female college students also had the highest rate among all female subjects. This could be that for the college students, they had reached the peak time for their sexual desire or activities, and yet, because of the restrictions imposed by their studies, they could not get release from sexual intercourse. Hence, they had to resort to masturbation.

Comparatively, the sex offenders did not show high masturbation rates. It could be that they had already found their channels of sexual release, although some of these channels may be improper or even criminal.

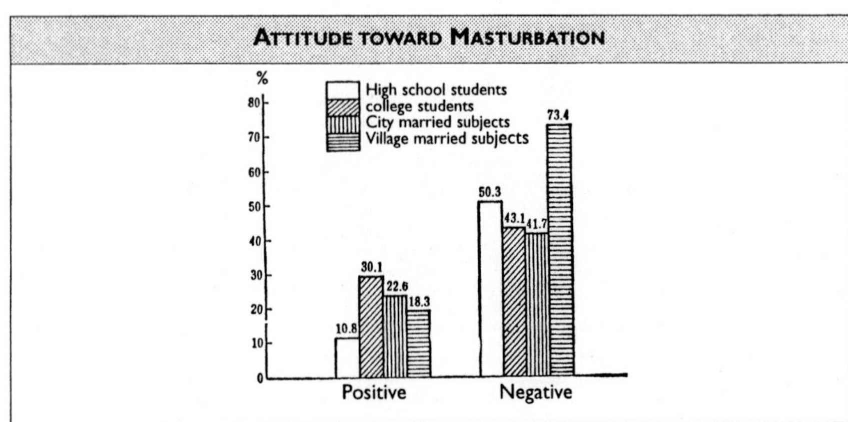

Figure 6–7

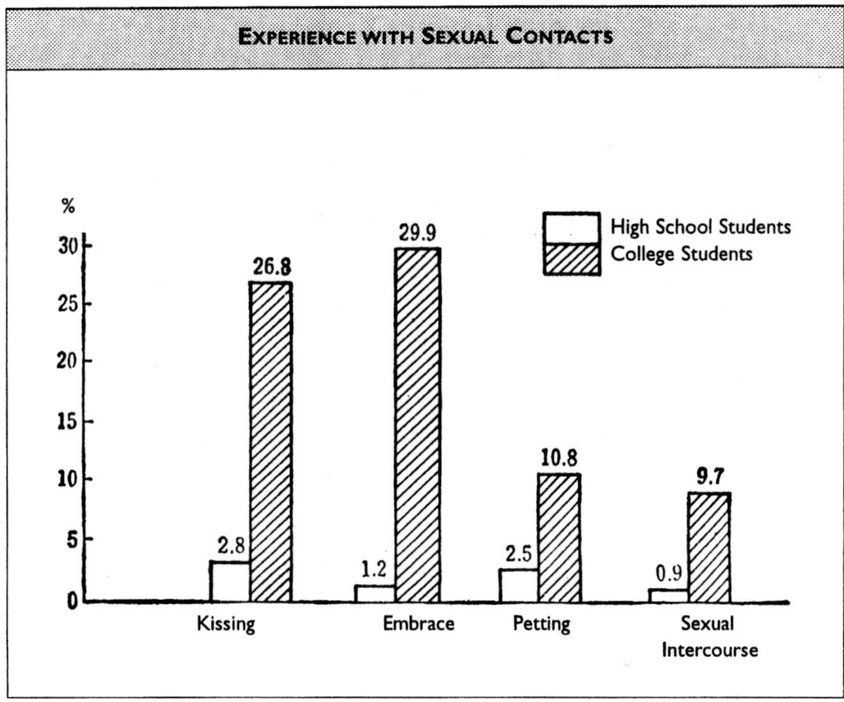

Figure 6–8

The college students also showed the highest rate of positive attitude toward masturbation.

C. Sexual Contact

Figure 6–8 shows that much more college than high school students had a variety of sexual activities and contacts; 9.7% of the college students had sexual intercourse compared with 0.9% of the high school students.

D. Premarital Sex

The rate of premarital sex in the college students was not higher than the married adults. Table 6–9 shows that in fact, more (one to two times) married couples had premarital sex than the college students. This could be because of the yet shorter exposure period the college students had compared with the married adults, or that the college students were really more self-disciplined or involved with their studies.

Figure 6–10 shows that college students and sexual offenders had the highest proportion of those who took a positive attitude toward premarital sex. The high school students were the most ambiguous.

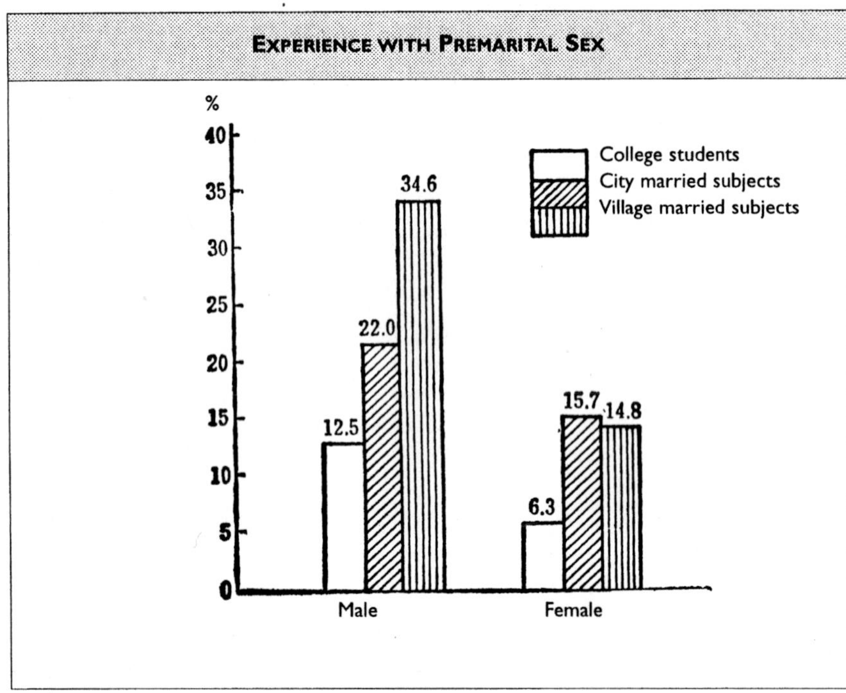

Figure 6–9

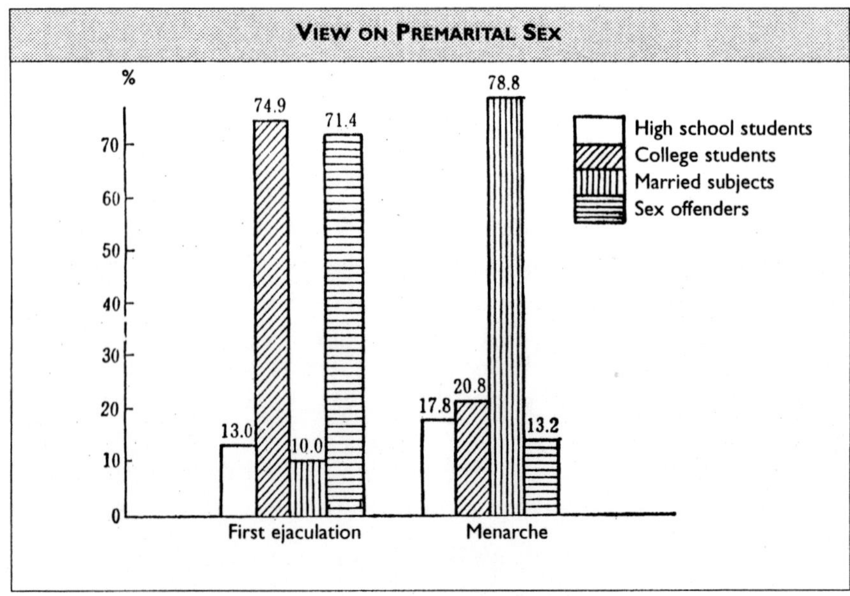

Figure 6–10

They had the proportion both in the positive and negative attitudes, showing their perplexity over this issue.

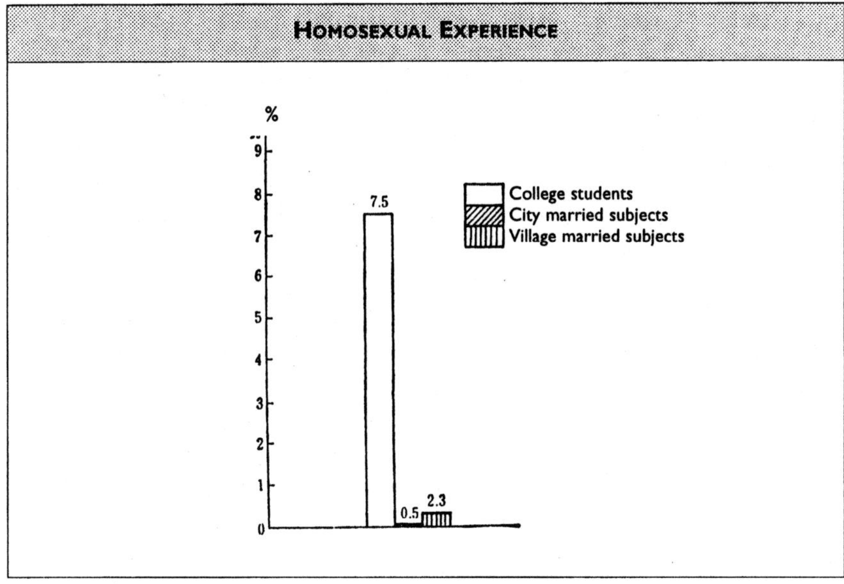

Figure 6–11

E. Homosexual Behavior

Figure 6–11 shows that among all the groups, college students had the highest proportion of those who had homosexual behavior.

3. Marriage and Family:

A. Educational Level of the Parents

Table 6–1 shows that the educational level of the city couples were obviously higher than the village couples.

The parents of the college subjects were not much more highly educated than the rest. Compared with the city subjects, most of them had a college education, but some of them had education only at the primary level or below. This means that most college students were from ordinary families.

For the sex offenders, the difference in parental educational level is more obvious. A low percentage of their parents were of college education, about the same as that of the village couples. As for the percentage with primary education or below, it was about double that of the village couples. This suggests that poorly educated parents may be a cause for sex crimes because they could not educate their children properly or form a good cohesive family.

Table 6–1 also shows that the sex offenders themselves were poorly educated, about the same as that of the village wives, suggesting further the important effect of education on sex crimes.

COMPARISON OF EDUCATIONAL LEVEL IN DIFFERENT GROUPS OF SUBJECTS			
	ILLITERATE OR PRIMARY	HIGH SCHOOL	COLLEGE OR ABOVE
City husband	2.7%	54.9%	39.1%
City wife	4.1%	75.3%	18.7%
Village husband	24.6%	70.4%	4.0%
Village wife	25.7%	73.1%	1.1%
Father of college student	18.8%	34.3%	41.7%
Mother of college student	30.7%	36.7%	28.4%
Father of sex offender	49.7%	37.9%	6.5%

Table 6–1

B. Marital Satisfaction

A much higher proportion of sex offenders than married couples were dissatisfied with their marriage. This could be a cause of sex crimes or poor quality of the sex offenders personalities.

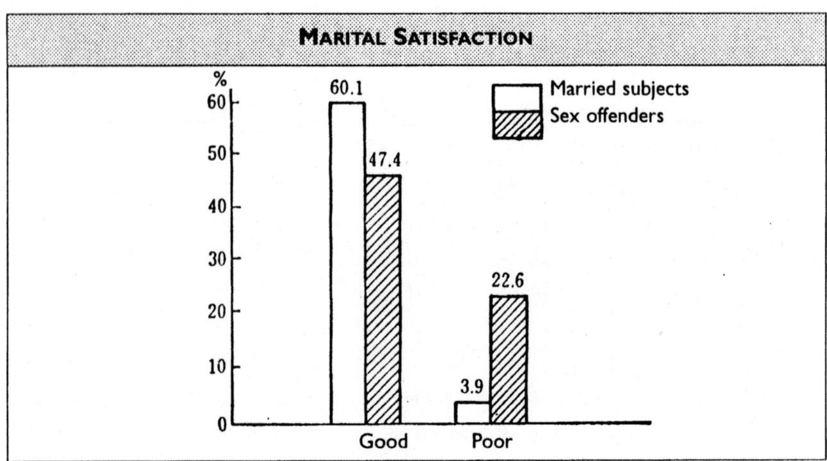

Figure 6–12

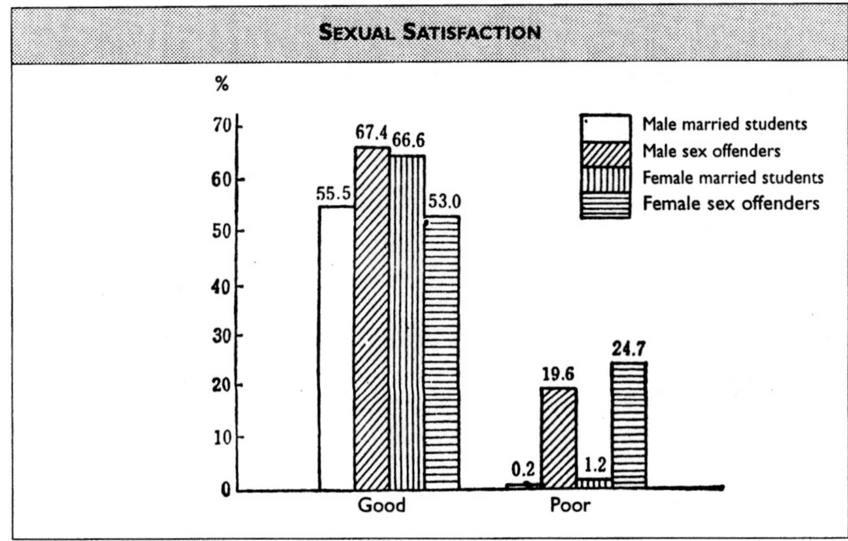

Figure 6–13

C. Sexual Satisfaction

Figure 6–13 shows that the sexual satisfaction of the sex offenders and the married couples did not differ much, but more sex offenders (especially the females) had sexual dissatisfaction. This dissatisfaction could be the cause or the result of their sex crimes.

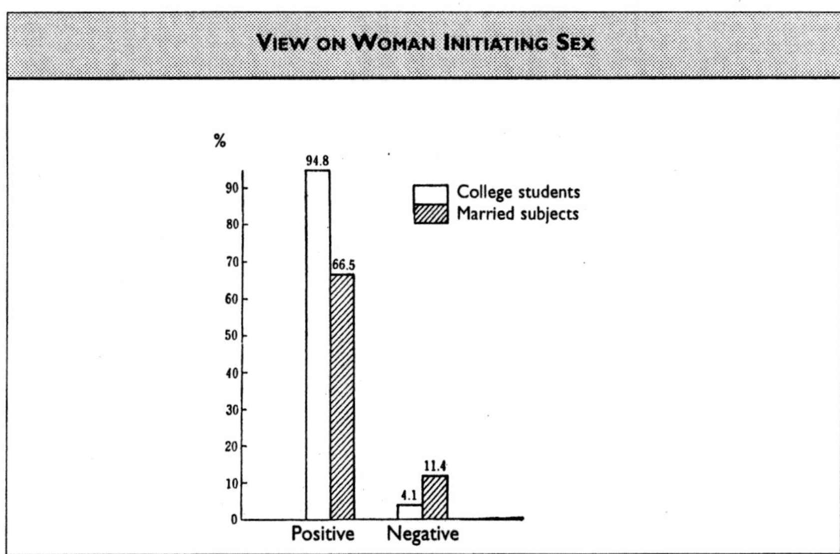

Figure 6–14

4. Sexual Attitudes

A. Whether Women Should Take the Initiative In Sex

Answers to this question reflects the attitude toward sex and sexual equality. The college students had the highest percentage (94.8 percent) of affirmation to this question. 66.5 percent of the maried couples also affirmed. This is not a low percentage. It shows that people are getting more enlightened in this respect as society advances.

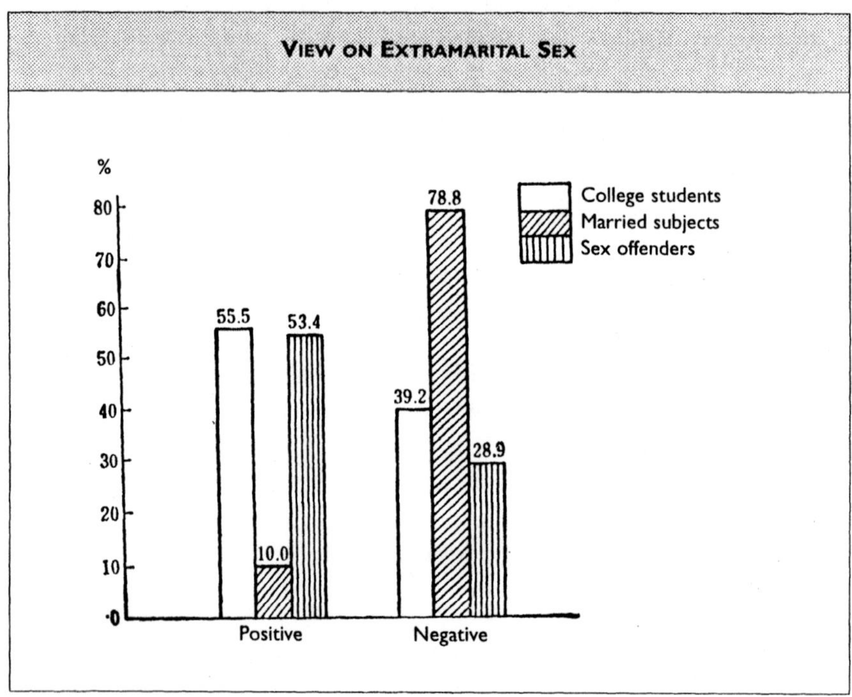

Figure 6–15

B. Attitude toward Extramarital Sex

Figure 6–15 shows that a very low proportion of married couples approved extramarital sex, but the percentages of the college students and the sex offenders were quite similarily high, both more than 50 percent. It is difficult to see that attitudes toward extramarital sex have anything to do with sex crimes. The differences might be due to the difference in mean age of the different groups of subjects only, again reflecting different sexual attitudes amongst different generations.

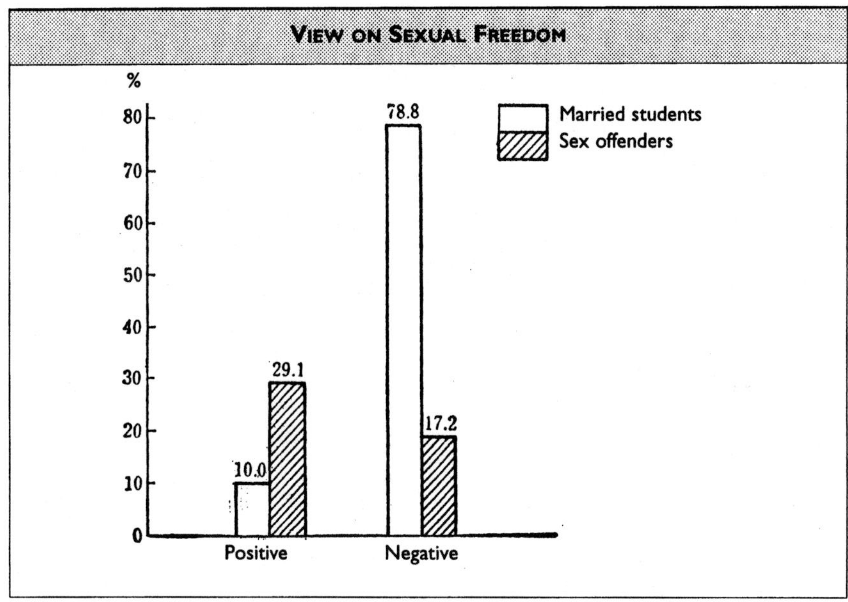

Figure 6–16

5. Conclusion

We had chosen a few items of interest to us for comparison. We could not obtain any new findings, but some of the comparisons do confirm some of our previous conclusions, making them more clear and obvious.

Appendix I
Questionnaires

Instructions

(Applicable to all questionnaires of this survey)

Sex is an important activity in our life. It is closely related to the healthy development of young people, to the happiness and harmony between the spouses, and to social stability and cohesiveness. Because of the long-lasting sexual inhibitions in our society along with other reasons, we are still having many sexual problems. The aim of this survey is to look at these problems, to understand them, and to find ways to solve them, if possible. Therefore, this survey is very important for our society and its future. Please give us your support and cooperation.

You are kindly requested to note that:

1. The questionnaires are anonymous. All information you put in will be treated as strictly confidential.
2. Please put in all the information honestly and truthfully.
3. Except where indicated otherwise, choose only one answer for each question.
4. Except where indicated otherwise, make your choice by putting a check in one of the empty boxes.
5. Fill in the blanks indicated by the lines.
6. Fill in the questionnaire on your own. Do not ask others for answers.

Thank you for your cooperation.

NATIONAL "SEX CIVILIZATION" SURVEY TASK FORCE
MAY, 1989

High School Student Questionnare

Your current address:

Province: ______________________________

City: ______________________________

Town: ______________________________

1. Gender:

Male	[ ]	Female	[ ]

2. Age: __________

3. Class:

Junior 1	[ ]	Junior 2	[ ]
Junior 3	[ ]	Senior 1	[ ]
Senior 2	[ ]	Senior 3	[ ]

4. Parental Occupation:

	Father	Mother
Worker	[ ]	[ ]
Farmer	[ ]	[ ]
Business	[ ]	[ ]
Service	[ ]	[ ]
Junior Official	[ ]	[ ]
Senior Official	[ ]	[ ]
Professional	[ ]	[ ]
Other	[ ]	[ ]

5. Parental education:

	Father	Mother
Illiterate	[ ]	[ ]
Primary	[ ]	[ ]
Junior high	[ ]	[ ]
Senior high	[ ]	[ ]
College	[ ]	[ ]
Post-graduate	[ ]	[ ]

6. Affectionate relationship between the parents:

Very good	[ ]	Good	[ ]
Fair	[ ]	Argue a lot	[ ]
Frequent fights	[ ]	Separated	[ ]
Divorced	[ ]	Unknown	[ ]

7. Do you have any siblings?
   No [ ] Yes [ ]
   Number of elder brothers _______
   Number of elder sisters _______
   Number of younger brothers _______
   Number of younger sisters _______

8. Your school performance:
   Excellent [ ] Good [ ]
   Fair [ ] Poor [ ]
   Very poor [ ]

9. Have you already experienced ejaculation? (Males only)
   No [ ] Yes [ ]
   a. Age of first ejaculation:_______
   b. Circumstances of first ejaculation:
      Asleep [ ] Awake [ ]
      Masturbation [ ] Other _______
   c. Your current frequency of ejaculation is once:
      A week [ ] 2 weeks [ ]
      3 weeks [ ] A month [ ]
      2 months [ ] 3 months [ ]
      Irregular [ ]
   d. Your reaction to your first ejaculation:
      Psychologically prepared, not worried [ ]
      Psychologically prepared, but worried [ ]
      Psychologically unprepared, not worried [ ]
      Psychologically prepared, but worried [ ]
      Other:_______
   e. Did you know about ejaculation before you had the first one?
      No [ ] Yes [ ]
   f. From where did you get this information?
      Class [ ] Reading [ ]
      Parents [ ] Siblings [ ]
      Classmate [ ] Others: _______

10. Your view on ejaculation: (Males only)
    Nocturnal emission is harmful to the body [ ]
    Normal physiology [ ] Cannot say clearly [ ]
    Obscene, shameful [ ] Other: _______

11. How do you take care of your penis? (Male only)
    - Aviod cleaning it [ ]
    - Phimosis is natural, need no treatment [ ]
    - Clean the member regularly [ ]
    - Do not know [ ]

12. Your development of sexual charateristics (male only):

	Not yet	Developing	Developed
Adam's apple	[ ]	[ ]	[ ]
Beard	[ ]	[ ]	[ ]
Axillary hair	[ ]	[ ]	[ ]
Pubic hair	[ ]	[ ]	[ ]
Acne	[ ]	[ ]	[ ]

13. Have you started menstruation? (Female only)
    No [ ] Yes [ ]
    a. Age of first menstruation ________
    b. Month of first menstruation ________
    c. Your reaction to first menstruation:
       - Psychologically prepared, not worried [ ]
       - Psychologically prepared, but worried [ ]
       - Psychologically unprepared, not worried [ ]
       - Psychologically prepared, but worried [ ]
       - Other:________________________________
    d. Did you know about menstruation before your menarche?
       No [ ] Yes [ ]
       From where did you get this knowledge?
       - Class [ ] Reading [ ]
       - Parents [ ] Siblings [ ]
       - Classmate [ ]
       - Others:________________________
    e. Your bodily symptoms during menstruation:
       - No symptoms [ ] Abdominal pain [ ]
       - Nausea/vomiting [ ] Low back pain [ ]
       - Loss of appetite [ ] Several of above [ ]
    f. Your mood during menstruation:
       - Not special [ ] Good mood [ ]
       - Restless [ ] Depressed [ ]

14. How do you handle your menstruation? (Female only)
    - Wash and hang dry my menstruation napkins under the sun. [ ]

Wash and hang dry my menstruation napkins
in cool dark places [ ]
Use disposable napkins [ ] Don't know [ ]

15. Your development of secondary sexual charateristics (female only):

	Not yet	Developing	Developed
Breasts	[ ]	[ ]	[ ]
Axillary hair	[ ]	[ ]	[ ]
Pubic hair	[ ]	[ ]	[ ]
Acne	[ ]	[ ]	[ ]

16. Do you look forward to heterosexual contacts?
Yes [ ] No [ ]

17. At what age did you start relating to the other sex? ______________
What made you do so? He/she was:
Attractive by appearance [ ]
Kind and tender [ ]
Strong in character [ ]
Optimistic, made me happy [ ]
Helpful to me [ ]
Gain sense of security [ ]
Necessary for me socially [ ]
Others:____

18. If you had not already made any heterosexual contacts, why?
Do not like it [ ]
Not have the courage [ ]
No need [ ]
Fear of gossip [ ]
Busy studying [ ]
Others:____

19. Do you have intimate friends of the other sex?
No [ ]Yes [ ]
Since what age?____________

20. Do you have the following with your intimate friend of the other sex? (Multiple answers allowed)
Kissing [ ] Hugging [ ]
Petting [ ] Sexual intercourse [ ]

21. Do you wish to touch the body of the other sex?
No [ ] Yes [ ]
Since what age?____________

22. Have you felt sexual desire?
    No [ ] Yes [ ]
    Since what age?____________

23. If you have had sexual desire, what do you think triggers it? (Choose any three)
    Seeing the nude body of the other sex [ ]
    Accidental contact with body of the other sex [ ]
    Dating with the other sex [ ]
    When talking about sex [ ]
    Reading books about sex [ ]
    Watching videos about sex [ ]
    At leisure [ ]
    Dancing with the opposite sex [ ]
    Others:______________________________

24. Do you masturbate?
    Don't know [ ] No [ ] Yes [ ]
    Since what age?____________
    Current frequency :
    Less than once per week [ ]
    Once per week [ ] Twice per week [ ]
    More than twice per week [ ] Not fixed [ ]

25. What do you think of masturbation?
    Normal [ ] Not good [ ]
    A neccessity [ ] Don't know [ ]
    Other ______________________________

26. Have you ever talked about sexual matters with people of the same sex?
    No [ ] Yes [ ]
    Who are the people you've talked to about sex?
    Father [ ] Mother [ ]
    Teacher [ ] Brothers [ ]
    Sisters [ ] Others [ ]

27. Have you ever talked about sexual matters with people of the other sex?
    No [ ] Yes [ ]
    Who are they?
    Father [ ] Mother [ ]
    Teacher [ ] Brothers [ ]
    Sisters [ ] Others [ ]

28. Have you had formal sex education?

No [ ] Yes [ ]

What were the contents received?

Sexual Physiology [ ]
Pregnancy and birth [ ]
Adolescent psychology [ ]
Heterosexual social manners [ ]
Heterosexual friendship and courtship [ ]
Population and birth control [ ]
STD and its prevention and treatment [ ]
Sex morals [ ]
Others________________________

29. Your principal source of sexual knowledge? (Check one only)

Newspapers and magazines [ ]
Chinese videos [ ]
Foreign videos [ ]
Chinese literature [ ]
Foreign literature [ ]
Medical books [ ]
Social chats [ ]
Erotica [ ]
Schools [ ]
Others________________________

30. How useful have the following people been as a source of sexual knowledge? (Check one only for the most useful)

	Parents	Siblings	Friend/classmates	Teachers
Most useful	[ ]	[ ]	[ ]	[ ]
Useful	[ ]	[ ]	[ ]	[ ]
Not very useful	[ ]	[ ]	[ ]	[ ]
Useless	[ ]	[ ]	[ ]	[ ]

31. What is the most important sexual topic you want to know about right now?

Sexual physiology [ ]
What is love [ ]
Adolescent psychology [ ]
Heterosexual social manners [ ]
How to handle sexual impulses [ ]
Sexual intercourse [ ]

Population and birth control [ ]
STD's and their prevention and treatment [ ]
Homosexuality and sexual variations [ ]
Others________________________

32. Where does the fetus grow?

Vas deference	[ ]	Sperm cell	[ ]
Urethra	[ ]	Uterus	[ ]
Penis	[ ]	Abdomen	[ ]
Ovarian duct	[ ]	Ovary	[ ]
Vagina	[ ]		

33. From where is baby born?

Vas deference	[ ]	Sperm cell	[ ]
Urethra	[ ]	Belly button	[ ]
Penis	[ ]	Testis	[ ]
Ovarian duct	[ ]	Ovary	[ ]
Vagina	[ ]		

34. The cause of sexually transmitted disease is:
Promiscuity [ ]
Autoimmune disorder [ ]
Bodily contact with the opposite sex [ ]
Don't know [ ]

35. Which of the following diseases are related to sex? (may choose more than one)

Tuberculosis	[ ]	Gonnorrhea	[ ]
Leukemia	[ ]	AIDS	[ ]
Syphilis	[ ]		

36. Do you have a dating partner already?
No [ ] Yes [ ]
Since what age?__________

37. What do you think "early love" is?
Has a lover before age fifteen [ ]
Has a lover while in high school [ ]
Has a lover before legal age for marriage [ ]
Can't say clearly [ ]

38. What is your attitude toward early love?
Normal [ ]
Not advisable [ ]
Can help studying [ ]

Can harm studying [ ]
Cannot avoid the possibility of having lover once you leave school [ ]
Others____________________

39. If one of your female classmate became pregnant, what would your attitude be:

Laugh at and reject her [ ]
Advise her to have an abortion [ ]
Ask the school to punish her [ ]
Normal, no cause for concern [ ]
Others____________________

40. Have you ever read the following books?

Dream of the Red Chamber [ ]
Jin-Ping-Mei [ ]
Red and Black [ ]
Nana [ ]
Life [ ]
If Tomorrow Comes [ ]
The Life of the Hollywood Stars [ ]
Lady Chatterley's Lover [ ]
Rosy Dream [ ]
The Heart of a Young Girl [ ]
Sexual Medicine [ ]
Handbook of Sex Knowledge [ ]
Sexual Psychology [ ]
Book with Nude Paintings [ ]
Book with Nude Photography [ ]

41. Your feeling toward erotic depictions are:

Flushing, palpitation, and panting [ ]
Joyful [ ]
Tense [ ]
Feel offended [ ]
No feeling [ ]

42. Do you think high schol students should be allowed to read or watch erotic books, videos, or movies?

Yes [ ]
Yes, under adult guidance [ ]
No [ ]

College Student Questionnaire

1. Age of first ejaculation or menstruation:________________
2. Age of first beard or breast growth________________________
3. Age of first pubic hair growth____________________________
4. Check below the following terms which you understand:

Impregnation	[ ]	Pregnancy	[ ]
Menstruation	[ ]	Love	[ ]
Kissing	[ ]	Parturition	[ ]
Nocturnal emission	[ ]	Masturbation	[ ]
Penis	[ ]	Vagina	[ ]
Uterus	[ ]	Ovulation	[ ]
Orgasm	[ ]	Contraception	[ ]
Testosterone	[ ]	Ejaculation	[ ]
Sexual intercourse	[ ]	Homosexuality	[ ]
Prostitution	[ ]	Rape	[ ]
STD	[ ]	Testes	[ ]
Ovary	[ ]		

5. During menstruation, you frequently feel: (female only)

Breast enlargement	[ ]	Abdominal pain	[ ]
Mild discomfort	[ ]	Tiredness	[ ]
As usual	[ ]		

6. Your earliest source of sexual knowledge is from:

Father	[ ]	Mother	[ ]
Siblings	[ ]	Teacher	[ ]
Classmates	[ ]	Friends	[ ]
Books	[ ]	Other adults	[ ]

7. Do you feel the following sources of sex knowledge useful?

	Very useful	Useful	A little useful	No
Father	[ ]	[ ]	[ ]	[ ]
Mother	[ ]	[ ]	[ ]	[ ]
Siblings	[ ]	[ ]	[ ]	[ ]
Friends	[ ]	[ ]	[ ]	[ ]
Teachers	[ ]	[ ]	[ ]	[ ]

8. Your principal source of sexual knowledge is (check one only):

Newspaper/Magazine	[ ]	Chinese videos/movies	[ ]
Foreign videos/movies	[ ]	Literature	[ ]

Medical books [ ] Pornography [ ]
Others______________________________

9. Do you like your gender?
Yes [ ] No [ ] Don't mind [ ]

10. If you could choose, what gender would you pick?
Male [ ] Female [ ] Don't mind [ ]

11. Please rank six people with whom you feel most intimate, by putting number one to six in the boxes with one meaning most intimate, six least

Father	[ ]	Mother	[ ]
Brothers	[ ]	Sisters	[ ]
Grandpa	[ ]	Grandma	[ ]
Same sex friends	[ ]	Opposite sex friends	[ ]
Teacher	[ ]	Doctor	[ ]
Colleagues	[ ]	Neighbors	[ ]

12. Do you have people to whom you can talk about personal matters?
No [ ]
Yes [ ]
Who are they (choose only one principal type):

Parents	[ ]	Brothers	[ ]
Sisters	[ ]	Same sex friends	[ ]
Opposite sex friends	[ ]	Teacher	[ ]

Others______________

13. When did you first wear bras? (Female only)
When breasts first developed [ ]
When breasts have fully developed [ ]
Never [ ]

14. Why do you wear bra?
For the healthy growth of the breast [ ]
For feminine beauty [ ]
To restrict breast growth [ ]

15. Do you have the desire to relate with members of the other sex?
Yes [ ] No [ ]

16. Take two of the following movies stars you like best:

Yang Jai-Bu	[ ]	Liu Siu-sin	[ ]
Pan Han	[ ]	Jiang Min	[ ]
Kung Sue	[ ]	Chen Chung	[ ]
Alan Delon	[ ]		

17. The following has been troubling you most: (Check one only)

Short statue	[ ]	Pimples and acne	[ ]
Thick beard	[ ]	No beard	[ ]
Obesity	[ ]	Baldness	[ ]
Grey hair	[ ]	Hair on the legs	[ ]

18. The following has been causing you anxiety most: (check one only)

Thin pubic hair	[ ]	Penis too big	[ ]
Penis too small	[ ]	Breasts too big	[ ]
Breasts too small	[ ]	Others________________	

19. For first ejculation (or menstruation), you asked whom for advice?

Father	[ ]	Mother	[ ]
Friend/classmate	[ ]	Teacher	[ ]
Other same sex adults	[ ]	Nobody	[ ]

20. On first ejculation (or menstruation), your reaction was:

Psychologically prepared, not worried [ ]
Psychologically prepared, but worried [ ]
Psychologically unprepared, not worried [ ]
Psychologically prepared, but worried [ ]

21. Before your first ejaculation or menstruation, did you know that it was a natural part of adolescent growth?

No [ ]
Yes [ ]

You knew it from:

Hygiene lessons	[ ]	Outside reading	[ ]
Parents	[ ]	Siblings	[ ]
Elder classmates	[ ]	Others________________	

22. Your circumstances on first ejaculation:

Asleep [ ]
Self masturbation [ ]
Mutual masturbation with same sex [ ]
Mutual masturbation with the opposite sex [ ]
Coitus [ ]

23. Do you have day dreams about sexual intercourse?

Frequently [ ] Occassionally [ ] Never [ ]

24. Have you ever worried about having a sexual dysfunction?

Yes [ ] Never [ ]
Have not thought of that [ ]

25. Have you ever had sexual dreams?
    Never [ ] Rarely [ ] Frequently [ ]
    What are the dream contents? (Multiple checks allowed)
    Kissing [ ] Petting [ ]
    Coitus [ ] Others ______________

26. Have you ever seen a nude body of the opposite sex?
    Never [ ] Yes [ ]
    From where? (Pick one principle source only)
    Newspaper and magazine [ ]
    Popular movies/videos [ ]
    Pornographic videos [ ]
    Pornographic photos [ ]
    Live subjects [ ]

27. Have you masturbated?
    Never [ ] Yes [ ]
    Age of first masturbation______________.
    Mean frequuncy during adolescence was ___ per week.
    Top frequency was ______ per day/week/month.
    Current frequency_______ per day/week/month.
    Age of stopping masturbation (if stopped)________.

28. You think masturbation is:
    Normal [ ]
    Immoral [ ]
    Criminal [ ]

29. You think the effect of masturbation on the body is:
    Beneficial if properly performed [ ]
    Neither harmful nor beneficial [ ]
    A little bit harmful [ ]
    Very harmful [ ]

30. Have you even masturbated mutually with the same sex?
    Yes [ ] Never [ ]

31. You think your penile foreskin is:
    Normal [ ] Too long [ ]
    Too tight [ ] Has been circumcised [ ]

32. You think courtship among college students should be:
    Forbidden [ ] Restricted [ ]
    Given proper guidence [ ] Free [ ]

33. What is your view toward the following?

	Normal	Inconceivable	Unhygienic	Unethical
Sex among the elderly	[ ]	[ ]	[ ]	[ ]
Sex among the handicapped	[ ]	[ ]	[ ]	[ ]
Female taking initiative in sex	[ ]	[ ]	[ ]	[ ]
Sex during menstruation	[ ]	[ ]	[ ]	[ ]

34. From the twenty qualities below, choose six that you like best for each sex and fill in their respective letters in the boxes below.

a. Confident
b. Tender
c. Independent
d. Asertive
e. Loyal
f. Resilient
g. Kind
h. Sedentary
i. Active
j. Competitive
k. Forgiving
l. Courageous
m. Warm
n. Persistent
o. Intelligent
p. Considerate
q. Truthful
r. Aggresive
s. Sensitive

	1	2	3	4	5	6
Male	[ ]	[ ]	[ ]	[ ]	[ ]	[ ]
Female	[ ]	[ ]	[ ]	[ ]	[ ]	[ ]

35. Rank what you feel should be the aims of sexual intercourse and put their respective letters in the empty boxes.

a. Physical pleasure
b. To develope love relations
c. To form a family
d. For reproduction
e. To have a companion
f. To satisfy the partner

Ranks	1	2	3	4	5	6
Aims	[ ]	[ ]	[ ]	[ ]	[ ]	[ ]

36. Do you drink alcohol?

Never [ ]   Occasionally [ ]
Frequently [ ]   Drunk all the time [ ]

37. Do you smoke?

Never [ ]   Occasionally [ ]   Frequently [ ]

38. Have you ever tried aphrodisiacs?

Yes	[ ]	Never	[ ]

39. What do you think of the saying that "one drop of semen is as precious as ten drops of blood?"

Correct	[ ]	May be correct	[ ]	Unfounded	[ ]

40. Your age of first sexual intercourse:

Below 13	[ ]	13	[ ]	14	[ ]
15	[ ]	16	[ ]	17	[ ]
18	[ ]	19	[ ]	20	[ ]
21	[ ]	22	[ ]	23	[ ]
24	[ ]	Not yet	[ ]		

41. Your number of sexual partners:

0	[ ]	1	[ ]	2-5	[ ]
6-10	[ ]	More than 10	[ ]		

42. Your principal contraceptive method used (check one only):

Oral pills	[ ]	Spermicides	[ ]
Condom	[ ]	Diaphragm	[ ]
Safe period	[ ]	Coitus Interruptus	[ ]

Others____

43. Have you engaged in the following behavior with the other sex? If you have, since what age? What is your attitude, feeling, and frequency?

	Hugging	Kissing	Genital play	Coitus	Genital anal	Genital oral
FREQUENCY						
Regularly	[ ]	[ ]	[ ]	[ ]	[ ]	[ ]
At times	[ ]	[ ]	[ ]	[ ]	[ ]	[ ]
Never	[ ]	[ ]	[ ]	[ ]	[ ]	[ ]
INITIATION						
Active	[ ]	[ ]	[ ]	[ ]	[ ]	[ ]
Passive	[ ]	[ ]	[ ]	[ ]	[ ]	[ ]
Forced	[ ]	[ ]	[ ]	[ ]	[ ]	[ ]
FEELING						
Enjoy	[ ]	[ ]	[ ]	[ ]	[ ]	[ ]
Offended	[ ]	[ ]	[ ]	[ ]	[ ]	[ ]
Not mind	[ ]	[ ]	[ ]	[ ]	[ ]	[ ]
AGE STARTED	____	____	____	____	____	____

44. Have you engaged in the following behavior with the same sex? If you have, at what age did you start? What is your attitude about this, how do you feel about it, and how often did you do it?

	Hugging	Kissing	Genital play	Simulated Coitus	Genital anal	Genital oral
FREQUENCY						
Regularly	[ ]	[ ]	[ ]	[ ]	[ ]	[ ]
At times	[ ]	[ ]	[ ]	[ ]	[ ]	[ ]
Never	[ ]	[ ]	[ ]	[ ]	[ ]	[ ]
INITIATION						
Active	[ ]	[ ]	[ ]	[ ]	[ ]	[ ]
Passive	[ ]	[ ]	[ ]	[ ]	[ ]	[ ]
Forced	[ ]	[ ]	[ ]	[ ]	[ ]	[ ]
FEELING						
Enjoy	[ ]	[ ]	[ ]	[ ]	[ ]	[ ]
Offended	[ ]	[ ]	[ ]	[ ]	[ ]	[ ]
Not mind	[ ]	[ ]	[ ]	[ ]	[ ]	[ ]
AGE STARTED	____	____	____	____	____	____

45. Your view on premarital sex is:

- Alright if based on love [ ]
- Alright if by mutual consent [ ]
- Should be condemned morally [ ]
- Should be punished administratively [ ]
- Should be punished by law [ ]

46. If your engaged marital partner tells you that he/she had sex with someone before, you will:

- Terminate relationship with him/her immediately [ ]
- Marry him/her anyway, but feel hurt [ ]
- Not let past behavior affect your relationship [ ]

47. If extramarital affair is by the consent of the marital partner, you think:

- It should be punished by law [ ]
- Should be condemned morally [ ]
- Should be punished administratively [ ]
- It is alright if based on love [ ]
- Others should not interfere [ ]

48. If you saw the nude body of the other sex in some proper public places, e.g., in a public bath, would you:

Like it [ ] Feel offened [ ]
Not notice it [ ]

49. If a friend tells you that he/she has homosexual tendencies, would you:

Feel offended. Stop relating with him/her [ ]
Show sympathy but keep a distance from him/her [ ]
Give consolation and advise psychiatric help [ ]
Show sympathy and have homosexual activity with him/her [ ]

50. If a relative had engaged in homosexual activity, you would feel:

Ashamed [ ]
Feel like someone in your house is seriously sick [ ]
Feel nothing special [ ]

51. If you are told that someone you admire is a homosexual, his/her image in your mind will be:

Not a bit affected [ ] Less perfect [ ]
Changed to low and disgusting [ ]

52. If Tchaikovsky had been executed for being a homosexual, you think:

He deserved it [ ]
The punishment was too severe [ ]
The punishment was totally wrong [ ]

53. You think sexual activties between homosexuals are:

Normal behavior of a minority [ ]
Deviant [ ] Unethical [ ]
Criminal [ ]

54. Have you ever felt sexually excited in the following situations:

Bodily contact with the other sex in crowded places [ ]
Watching a nude human statue [ ]
Wearing clothing of the other sex [ ]
Bodily contact with children [ ]
Experience physical torture [ ]
Torturing others physically [ ]
Exposing your genitals to other sex [ ]
Contact with animals [ ]
Forcing others to have sex with you [ ]
Watching the body of the other sex, live or in photos [ ]

55. Your gender Male [ ] Female [ ]
Your age:______________________________

56. Your grade:

First year	[ ]	Second year	[ ]	Third year	[ ]
Fourth year	[ ]	Fifth year	[ ]	Post-grad	[ ]

57. Your professional subject is:

Arts	[ ]	Science	[ ]
Engineering	[ ]	Agriculture	[ ]
Medicine	[ ]		

58. Educational level of parents:

	Father	Mother
Illiterate	[ ]	[ ]
Primary	[ ]	[ ]
Junior high	[ ]	[ ]
Senior high	[ ]	[ ]
College	[ ]	[ ]
Post-graduate	[ ]	[ ]

59. Parental occupation:

	Father	Mother
Worker	[ ]	[ ]
Farmer	[ ]	[ ]
Business	[ ]	[ ]
Service	[ ]	[ ]
Junior Official	[ ]	[ ]
Senior Official	[ ]	[ ]
Professional	[ ]	[ ]
Others	[ ]	[ ]

60. Have you ever read the following books?

Dream of the Red Chamber	[ ]
Jin-Ping-Mei (Golden Lotus)	[ ]
Red and Black	[ ]
Nana	[ ]
Life	[ ]
Love Gambler	[ ]
The Life of the Hollywood Stars	[ ]
Lady Chatterley's Lover	[ ]
Rosy Dream	[ ]

The Missing Woman [ ]
Sadistic Violence [ ]
Nude Paintings [ ]
Nude Photography [ ]

61. Your feeling toward sexual depictions are:
Flushing, palpitation, and panting [ ]
Joyful [ ] Tense [ ]
Feel offended [ ] No feeling [ ]

62. You think literature with sexual depictions are for students something that:
Can be read [ ]
Should be read [ ]
Should be selectively read [ ]
Should be forbidden [ ]

63. You think sex education in our country is at present:
Very appropriate [ ]
Too conservative [ ]
Too open [ ]

Married Couples Questionnaire

1. Age of husband ________________
Age of wife ________________
Sex of respondent: Male [ ] Female [ ]

2. Educational level

	Wife	Husband
Illiterate	[ ]	[ ]
Primary	[ ]	[ ]
Junior high	[ ]	[ ]
Senior high	[ ]	[ ]
College	[ ]	[ ]
Post-graduate	[ ]	[ ]

3. Current occupation:

	Wife	Husband
Worker	[ ]	[ ]
Farmer	[ ]	[ ]
Business	[ ]	[ ]

	Wife	Husband
Service	[ ]	[ ]
Junior Official	[ ]	[ ]
Senior Official	[ ]	[ ]
Professional	[ ]	[ ]
Soldier	[ ]	[ ]
Others	[ ]	[ ]

4. How were you first married?
   Parental arrangement [ ]   Introduced by relatives [ ]
   Introduced by friends [ ]   By self choice [ ]

5. Age at first marriage:
   Wife________   Husband__________

6. Do you miss your spouse if you are separated for more than a week?
   Yes [ ]   No [ ]
   Not sure/do not know [ ]

7. Do you feel more free if your spouse is not at home?
   Yes [ ]   No [ ]
   Not sure/do not know [ ]

8. Do you have this feeling frequently, leading you to think that you might be happier married to someone else?
   Frequently [ ]   Sometimes [ ]   Never [ ]

9. Do you have this feeling, leading you to think that if not for the children, you would have asked for a divorce?
   Yes [ ]   No [ ]   Not thought of it [ ]

10. Do you still remember your wedding anniversary?
   Yes [ ]   No [ ]

11. Are you satisfied with your marriage?
   Yes [ ]   No [ ]   Partly [ ]   Not clear [ ]

12. Your affection for your spouse is:
   Deep [ ]   Ordinary [ ]
   Shallow [ ]   Tense [ ]
   Living or sleeping separately [ ]   Not clear [ ]

13. On household work, the sharing between you two is:
   Wife doing more [ ]   Husband doing more [ ]
   Equal sharing [ ]   Totally by the wife [ ]
   Totally by the husband [ ]

14. The chief source of conflict between you two is:

Children	[ ]	Housework	[ ]
Trivial family problems	[ ]	Financial	[ ]
Personality clash	[ ]	Life habits	[ ]
Kinship problems	[ ]	Social habits	[ ]
Sexual	[ ]	Others____________	

15. Do you think marriage must be for love?
    Yes [ ] No [ ] May be [ ]

16. Your attitude toward love scenes in movies is:
    Like it a lot [ ] Feel offended [ ] Not mind [ ]

17. If a married person has an extramarital affair because of an unhappy marriage, would you think it:
    Understandable [ ]
    A personal matter that should not be interfered with by anybody [ ]
    Shameful [ ]
    Sinful [ ]

18. If a women has been raped, you will:
    Reject her [ ]
    Show sympathy and help her [ ]
    Keep her at a distance [ ]
    Not blame her. It's not her fault [ ]

19. If a married person is close to someone of the other sex, do you think the spouse should:
    Not worry, since it is usual social activity [ ]
    Make a fuss [ ]
    Keep quiet though feeling hurt [ ]
    Send out a warning [ ]
    Clarify what is going on first [ ]

20. If a married person had extramarital sex, you would think the spouse should:
    Dissuade him/her patiently [ ]
    Keep quiet to save face [ ]
    Make a fuss [ ]
    Tell someone superior [ ]
    Insist divorce [ ]
    Take revenge [ ]

21. Do you agree that as long as two people are in love, they could have sex without marriage?

Yes [No [ ] Neutral [ ]

22. To the "third party" in a marriage, you will

Report him/her to the police [ ]
Respect him/her for being so able [ ]
Leave it as it is [ ]
Educate him/her, to solve the problem [ ]

23. Is divorce shameful to a woman?

Yes [ ] No [ ] Neutral [ ]

24. To a woman who takes up nude modelling, your view is:

A normal job [ ]
Not glorious though acceptable [ ]
Not acceptable [ ]

25. If your child asks "Where do I come from?", you will :

Tell the truth tactfully [ ]
Ignore them [ ]
Lie to them [ ]
Scold them [ ]
Distract them [ ]

26. Regarding a couple above fifty still having sex, your view is:

Acceptable so long as they need it [ ]
Acceptable, but not too often [ ]
Should stop it [ ]

27. If you think old people should not have sex, your reason is:

It is not respectable [ ]
It is embarrassing [ ]
It is harmful to the body [ ]
Old people have no sexual ability [ ]

28. You think for a couple to have sex,

It is the duty of the wife to satisfy the husband [ ]
It is a mutual duty [ ]
It is a mutual physical need [ ]
It is a mutual emotional and physical need [ ]
It is for reproduction [ ]
It is a routine for all couples [ ]

29. Do you think that the wife should initiate sex with the husband?

Yes [ ] No [ ] Should, but rather embarrassing [ ]

30. Do you think sex for a couple is an embarrassing matter?
    Yes [ ]   No [ ]   No comment [ ]

31. Do you understand what homosexuality is?
    Heard about it [ ]
    Know a little [ ]
    Have personal experience [ ]
    Never heard of it [ ]

32. Have you ever read publications or videos which principally depict sex?
    Yes [ ]   Never had a chance [ ]
    Wish to have read [ ]
    Will not read even if I have the chance [ ]

33. Your obstetric history:
    Total deliveries________________
    Males________   Females______________
    Deaths before adulthood____________
    Number given to others_____________

34. Your ideal number of children is:
    None [ ]   One son [ ]
    One daughter [ ]
    One son, one daughter [ ]
    Two sons [ ]
    Two daughters [ ]
    Many sons and daughters [ ]
    Leave it to nature [ ]

35. If your first child is a daughter, your view is:
    One is enough, to respond to the call of the nation [ ]
    Have another one as policy allows [ ]
    Try to get a son even if punished [ ]
    Hide somewhere and give birth to a second child [ ]

36. You think the aim of having children is :
    To prepare for old age [ ]
    To extend the family tree [ ]
    Increase the labor force [ ]
    More children, more blessings [ ]
    Add fun to life [ ]
    Social duty [ ]
    Never thought of it [ ]
    Others______________________________

37. Check if you agree with the following statements (multiple checks allowed):

Greatest sin against filial piety is having no children [ ]
Having no children is hurtful to one's ancestors [ ]
Daughters are spilled water [ ]
Sons earn money, daughters spend money [ ]

38. What do you think of the government's call for one child per family?

Correct, all should follow [ ]
Not very reasonable, but we have to obey since we would otherwise be punished [ ]
Not correct at all [ ]

39. What contraceptive method do you use principally?

Tubal ligation [ ] Vasectomy [ ] IUD [ ]
Oral pills [ ] Douching [ ]
Safe period [ ] Coitus interruptus [ ]
None [ ]]Others________________

40. Have you masturbated>

No [ ] Yes frequently [ ]
Yes occasionally [ ]

What do you think of masturbation?

Natural behavior [ ]
Acceptable only if forced by circumstances [ ]
Bad behavior [ ]
Not a problem [ ]

41. Your frequency of sexual intercourse in the last year is:

Once per month or less [ ]
2-3 times per month [ ]
4-5 times per month [ ]
6-7 times per month [ ]
8 to 15 times per month [ ]
Nearly once a day or more [ ]

42. Who usually takes the initiative in sexual intercourse?

Husband [ ] Wife [ ]
Both [ ] Cannot say clearly [ ]

43. Has the wife heightened her sexual desire after menstruation?

Yes [ ] No [ ]
Not clear [ ]

44. From your experience, which period of your life is sexually most satisfying?

Before 30	[ ]	Between 30 and 40	[ ]
Between 40 and 50	[ ]	After 50	[ ]
Not clear	[ ]		

45. From your experience, which period of the month is sexually most satisfying?

Immediately after wife's menstruation [ ]
Before wife's menstruation [ ]
Between wives two menstruation periods [ ]

46. How much time do you usually spend in foreplay before sexual intercourse?

None	[ ]	Less than 1 minute	[ ]
2-5 minutes	[ ]	6-10 minutes	[ ]
10- 20 minutes	[ ]	More than 20 min.	[ ]

47. Are you willing to cooperate with your partner during sexual intercourse?

Yes [ ] No [ ]
Depend on mood [ ]

48. How many sexual positions do you use in sexual intercourse?

Only one [ ]
A few different positions [ ]
Frequently change positions [ ]

49. At what hour do you usually have sexual intercourse?

Before sleep	[ ]	Middle of the night/sleep	[ ]
On waking up	[ ]	No fixed pattern	[ ]

Usually before sleep but also at some other times [ ]

50. Do you feel pleasure from sexual intercourse?

Frequently [ ] At times [ ]
Never [ ]

51. Do you feel pain during sexual intercourse?

Frequently [ ] At times [ ]
Never [ ]

52. Do you both go naked during sexual intercourse?

Always [ ] At times [ ]
Never [ ]

53. Generally speaking, your feeling toward sexual intercourse with your marital partner is:

	Wife	Husband
Very satisfied	[ ]	[ ]
Satisfied	[ ]	[ ]
Acceptable	[ ]	[ ]
Not satisfied	[ ]	[ ]
Very unsatisfied	[ ]	[ ]
Cannot say clearly	[ ]	[ ]

54. If you feel ill and yet your partner asks for sex, your usual response is:

Submit to it reluctantly [ ]
Show love and caring but not have sex [ ]
Express your difficulty honestly [ ]
Refuse firmly [ ]

55. If you refuse the request for sex, what is your partner's reactions:

Unhappy [ ] Forces it upon you [ ]
Argument or fight [ ] Understanding [ ]

56. Other than sexual intercourse, do you also perform loving behavior with your partner?

Regularly [ ] At times [ ] Never [ ]

57. Your age of first sexual intercourse:________________

58. If you have stopped having sexual intercourse already, what was the age of stopping for the wife__________, for the husband__________.

59. What is your reason for stopping sexual intercourse:

Old age, no more desire [ ]
One of us has infectious disease [ ]
No affection [ ]
Afraid of harm to the body [ ]
Sexual difficulties [ ]
Separated [ ]
Old age, embarrassing [ ]
Circumstances do not allow [ ]
Wife frigid [ ]
Husband impotent [ ]

60. Do you have children or other relatives sleeping in the same room with you?

Yes [ ] No [ ]

61. How is the sound insulation in your bedroom?

Very good	[ ]	Partial insulation only	[ ]
None at all	[ ]		

62. How is your physical health?

	Wife	Husband
Very Healthy	[ ]	[ ]
Fair	[ ]	[ ]
Have disease	[ ]	[ ]

63. If you have a disease, what type?

	Wife	Husband
Cardiovascular	[ ]	[ ]
Digestive	[ ]	[ ]
Renal	[ ]	[ ]
Endocrine	[ ]	[ ]
Neurological	[ ]	[ ]
Reproductive	[ ]	[ ]
Respiratory	[ ]	[ ]
Physically impaired	[ ]	[ ]

64. Has wife had menopaus?

Yes	[ ]	No	[ ]
In the process of it			[ ]

65. Your principle sources of sexual knowledge (check any three):

Father	[ ]	Mother	[ ]
Elderly	[ ]	Teacher	[ ]
Books or magazines	[ ]	Doctors	[ ]
Females of about the same age			[ ]
Males of about the same age			[ ]
Family Planning officials			[ ]
My own experience			[ ]
Gossip			[ ]
Videos, movies, or broadcast			[ ]
Others			[ ]

66. Your first sexual intercourse was:

Before marriage	[ ]	At wedding night	[ ]
After marriage	[ ]		

67. Your first sexual partner was:

Your spouse	[ ]
Someone not your spouse	[ ]

68. How many sexual partners have you, including your spouse?

One	[ ]	Two	[ ]
Three	[ ]	Four	[ ]
Five or more	[ ]		

69. Have you read the following books?
   - *Sexual Knowledge* [ ]
   - *Essentials for the Newlywed* [ ]
   - *Handbook of Sexual Knowledge* [ ]
   - *Sexual Medicine* [ ]

70. For your marriage, you feel most deficient in knowledge on what subjects:
   - Human physiology and hygiene [ ]
   - Sexual techniques [ ]
   - Interpersonal skills [ ]
   - Child education [ ]

71. If you have marital sexual problems, you will:
   - Consult a doctor [ ]
   - Talk with an intimate friend [ ]
   - Talk frankly with your spouse [ ]
   - Let it be [ ]

SEX OFFENDER QUESTIONNAIRE

1. Your age____________________

   Your sex: Male [ ] Female [ ]

2. Your educational level:

	Before conviction	Now
Illiterate	[ ]	[ ]
Primary	[ ]	[ ]
Junior high	[ ]	[ ]
Senior high	[ ]	[ ]
College	[ ]	[ ]
Postgraduate	[ ]	[ ]

3. Your occupation before conviction:

Worker	[ ]	Farmer	[ ]
Business	[ ]	Service	[ ]

Junior Official	[ ]	Senior Official	[ ]
Teacher	[ ]	Medical	[ ]
Artist	[ ]	Technician	[ ]
Finance	[ ]	Soldier	[ ]
Student	[ ]	Self-owned business	[ ]
None	[ ]	Others	[ ]

4. Your political identity before conviction:

Member of the Communist Party [ ]
Member of the Democratic Party [ ]
Member of the Young Communist Party [ ]
No political membership [ ]

5. Marital status:

Single [ ]
Married [ ]
Remarried [ ]
Widowed before conviction [ ]
Widowed after conviction [ ]
Divorced before conviction [ ]
Divorced after conviction [ ]

6. Your relationship with your last spouse

Good and affectionate [ ]
Fair [ ]
Frequent arguments [ ]
Separated [ ]

7. Did you need to leave your spouse at home to work often?

Frequently [ ] Rarely [ ]
Never [ ]

8. Do you think your last spouse could satisfy you sexually?

[ ] Yes [ ] No [ ]

9. With your last spouse, your feeling toward your sex life was:

Very satisfactory	[ ]	Satisfactory	[ ]
Do not know	[ ]	Unsatisfactory	[ ]
Very unsatisfactory	[ ]		

10. With your last spouse, the mean frequency of sexual intercourse in the last one year was:

Less than once a week	[ ]	Twice a week	[ ]
Three times a week	[ ]	Nearly daily	[ ]

11. Your financial condition before conviction was:

Very good	[ ]	Good	[ ]
Ordinary	[ ]	Difficult	[ ]
Very difficult	[ ]		

12. Your relationship with parents before conviction was:

Very good	[ ]	Fair	[ ]
Bad	[ ]	No parents	[ ]

13. Your relationship with siblings before conviction was:

Very good	[ ]	Fair	[ ]
Bad	[ ]	No siblings	[ ]

14. Did you talk with your parents before conviction?

Often	[ ]	Rarely	[ ]
Never	[ ]	No parents	[ ]

15. Did you talk with spouse before conviction?

Often	[ ]	Rarely	[ ]
Never	[ ]	No spouse	[ ]

16. Did you talk or meet with your siblings before conviction?

Often	[ ]	Rarely	[ ]
Never	[ ]	No siblings	[ ]

17. Before conviction, your feeling for your original family was:

Spiritually and materially satisfying	[ ]
Loved by parents, financially adequate	[ ]
No parental concern, lack of warmth	[ ]
Monotonous life, boring	[ ]

18. Before conviction, was your family or your own financial condition able to satisfy your daily needs?

Yes	[ ]	No	[ ]

19. Are your family members (parents, siblings etc.) casual with sexual relationships?

Yes	[ ]	No	[ ]

20. Have your family members (parents, siblings etc.) committed any sexual offenses?

Yes	[ ]	No	[ ]

21. Your biological parents are:

Both alive and living together			[ ]
Dead (at least one of them	[ ]	Divorced	[ ]
Working away from home (at least one of them)			[ ]

22. Parental educational level:

	Father	Mother
Illiterate	[ ]	[ ]
Primary	[ ]	[ ]
Junior high	[ ]	[ ]
Senior high	[ ]	[ ]
College	[ ]	[ ]
Postgraduate	[ ]	[ ]

23. Parental occupation:

	Father	Mother
Worker	[ ]	[ ]
Farmer	[ ]	[ ]
Business	[ ]	[ ]
Service	[ ]	[ ]
Junior official	[ ]	[ ]
Senior official	[ ]	[ ]
Teacher	[ ]	[ ]
Medical	[ ]	[ ]
Artist	[ ]	[ ]
Technician	[ ]	[ ]
Finance	[ ]	[ ]
Soldier	[ ]	[ ]
Student	[ ]	[ ]
Self-owned business	[ ]	[ ]
None	[ ]	[ ]
Others	[ ]	[ ]

24. Your view toward sexual liberation or freedom is:

Should be promoted [ ]
Beneficial, not harmful [ ]
Not support, but not interfere either [ ]
Can be promoted if STD can be prevented [ ]
Strongly against [ ]

25. Your view toward premarital sex is:

Should not interfere if by mutual consent [ ]
All right if the two will finally get married [ ]
Not a problem in any way [ ]
Harmful to the person, but not to society [ ]
Harmful to society, should be opposed [ ]

26. Your view toward extramarital sex is:
    - Should not interfere if based on affection [ ]
    - Alright if the spouse is not against it [ ]
    - Not harmful or beneficial [ ]
    - Acceptable if spouse cannot provide satisfactory sex [ ]
    - Harmful to family, should be opposed [ ]

27. Your view toward early love is:
    - Should not interfere, normal youth behavior [ ]
    - Can improve maturation of youths [ ]
    - Beneficial to work or studies [ ]
    - Can ruin one's life [ ]
    - Harmful to work or studies [ ]

28. Your view toward love is:
    - For building up of affection [ ]
    - Should be accompanied by sex to confirm love [ ]
    - No real love between the sexes [ ]
    - The more love partners, the better [ ]

29. Your most important condition for a spouse is:

Money	[ ]	Appearance	[ ]
Learned	[ ]	Social position	[ ]
Personality	[ ]	Affection	[ ]
Has a apt. or home	[ ]	Has relatives abroad	[ ]
Sexually satisfying	[ ]		

30. You think a woman should (for female responders only):
    - Satisfy one's need for pleasure liberally [ ]
    - Enjoy life while she is young [ ]
    - Make life happy for the husband and children [ ]
    - Should depend on man, get the husband's affection [ ]

31. Your view toward chastity is:
    - absolutely important [ ]
    - is a feudal concept [ ]
    - applied to women only, not to men [ ]
    - is not a problem if there is affection [ ]
    - not a concern if only sexual need can be satisfied [ ]

32. Before conviction, what were your three most favorite pastimes?

movies	[ ]	videos	[ ]

going to bars [ ] dancing [ ]
music [ ] clothes, makeup [ ]
reading serious books [ ] travelling [ ]
majong or card games [ ]
socializing with the opposite sex [ ]
chatting with friends [ ]
other ___________________________

33. What is your most favorite type of book, video, or movie?
about love and physical intimacy [ ]
partially erotic [ ]
mainly erotic [ ]
heros and violence [ ]
detective [ ]
family and social [ ]

Please give one book, video, or movie which you think has affected you most:___________________________

34. While you are watching erotic materials, your feeling is:
calm and peaceful [ ] excited [ ]
wish to have a try [ ]

35. From which two sources you get the most impressive experience on erotic materials?
your own or your friend's purchase [ ]
supplied by friends or classmates [ ]
watched in the friend's or classmate's home [ ]
watched in secret video establishments [ ]
watched in public theatres, entertainment centers [ ]
Others___________________________

36. From where did you get your first sight of heterosexual intercourse:
parents at home [ ]
siblings at home [ ]
in friend's house [ ]
movies and videos [ ]
in public places [ ]
at that time, your age was __________.

37. When chatting with your friend, you most frequent topic is:
administrative or political matters [ ]
business [ ]
sexual matters [ ]

how to flirt with the other sex [ ]
eating and dressing [ ]
movies, TV, and books [ ]

38. Before conviction, your parents' attitude toward your making friends with the other sex was:

supportive [ ]
supportive if not promiscuous [ ]
not to concern [ ]
oppose if the other one was not to their liking [ ]
absolutely oppose [ ]

39. You were convicted in the year __________.

40. Your crime as decided by the court is:

rape [ ] gang rape [ ]
child sexual assault [ ] promiscuous sex [ ]
prostitution [ ] hooliganism [ ]
accommodating prostitutes [ ]
bigamy [ ]
soliciting women to be prostitutes [ ]
forcing women to be prostitutes [ ]
other crimes:______________________________

41. Your period of sentence (for correctional sentence only):

less than 2 years [ ] 2-3 years [ ]
3 years [ ]

42. Your period of sentence (for imprisonment sentence only):

less than 3 years [ ] 3-5 years [ ]
5-7 years [ ] 7-10 years [ ]
10-15 years [ ] more than 15 years [ ]
indefinite [ ] death [ ]

43. Do you have a previous criminal record?

No [ ] Yes [ ]
Imprisonment______times
Correctional______times
Work/study duty___times
Young correctional______times
Security management_____times
Total: ________________times

44. What type of sentence in your previous criminal record was due to sex crimes?____________________________.

45. Your means of sex crime was principally:

prostitution	[ ]	violence	[ ]
threat	[ ]	seduction	[ ]
love/friendship	[ ]	Group sex	[ ]
through introduction by a third party			[ ]
by means of official position			[ ]
pretend to be a job agent			[ ]
provide housing			[ ]
other________________________			

46. With how many people of the other sex have you had sex with, including your crime victims?

Young children ______________

Elderly people (over 65)________

Mentally ill or impaired________

Close relatives:

Parent_______ Children__________

Siblings_____ Grandchildren_____

Nephews or nieces______ Half-siblings _________

Others (please specify type and number)_________

Total:____________________________

47. Age at which you committed your first crime:

	Before marriage	During marriage	After divorce or widowed
Below 14	[ ]	[ ]	[ ]
15-19	[ ]	[ ]	[ ]
20-29	[ ]	[ ]	[ ]
30-39	[ ]	[ ]	[ ]
40-49	[ ]	[ ]	[ ]
Above 50	[ ]	[ ]	[ ]

48. Your main motive for the crime was:

money	[ ]	pleasure	[ ]
curiosity	[ ]	revenge	[ ]
other___________________			

49. Your view about your current sentence is:

Guilty and obey sentence [ ]

Guilty but not accept the sentence [ ]

Why don't you accept it?________________________________

Not guilty [ ] No crime at all [ ]

Why not?____

50. Have you appealed?
    yes, but turned down [ ]
    pending [ ]
    yes, turned down, but re-appealing [ ]
    planning to appeal [ ]

51. How do you feel after being sentenced?
    regret [ ] blame self [ ]
    blame others [ ] blame the victim [ ]
    wish to change [ ] not mind [ ]
    no regret [ ]

52. What do you think is your greatest loss after being convicted:
    reputation ruined [ ] chastity lost [ ]
    future ruined [ ] broken family [ ]
    lost opportunity to work or study [ ]
    lost opportunity to earn money [ ]

53. Your view on the sentence received is:
    worthy of the gain received [ ]
    not worthy of the gain received [ ]
    do not know [ ]

54. Your age of first ejaculation (Male only) is _______.

55. Your current frequency of ejaculation is once per (male only):
    week or less [ ] 2 weeks [ ]
    month [ ] 2 months [ ]
    3 months [ ] irregular [ ]

56. Your age of first menstruation (female only) is _______.

57. Do you masturbate?
    No [ ] Yes [ ]
    Frequency of masturbation per week:
        less than once [ ] once [ ]
        twice [ ] 3 times [ ]
        4 times [ ] 5 times and above [ ]

58. You think your sexual desire is:
    high [ ] ordinary [ ] weak [ ]
    unpredictable and uncontrollable [ ]

59. While serving your sentence, how do you handle your sexual desire?
    Suppress [ ] copy love poems [ ]

sexual drawings [ ] sing love songs [ ]
hug and pet inmates [ ] masturbation [ ]
other___________________

60. From the supplied diagrams, pick the appropriate numbers and fill them into the respective boxes:

male genitalia [ ] female genitalia [ ]
vagina [ ] uterus [ ]
Fallopian tube [ ] ovary [ ]
testes [ ] vas deference [ ]
sperm [ ] penis [ ]
ureter [ ]

61. Your view on nocturnal emission is (male only):

harmful to health [ ]
normal physiological phenomenon [ ]
do not know [ ]

62. On your first ejaculation or menstruation, from whom did you seek advice?

Parents [ ] Siblings [ ]
Teacher [ ] Classmates and friends [ ]
Seniors of the same sex [ ] Nobody [ ]
Others___________________________

63. Which source of sexual knowledge do you think has been most useful:

	Very useful	Useful	A little	No
Parents	[ ]	[ ]	[ ]	[ ]
Siblings	[ ]	[ ]	[ ]	[ ]
Friends	[ ]	[ ]	[ ]	[ ]
Teachers	[ ]	[ ]	[ ]	[ ]

Appendix 2

Development of Adolescent Sex Education in China

1. Before the Liberation

Since the "New Culture (May Fourth) Movement" of 1919, there has been efforts to promote sex education. Chang Jing-sheng (1889 - 1970) is the pioneer of Chinese sex education. In 1920, he proposed contraception and population control and put sex education as part of aesthetics and life education, trying to combine it with social structure and law. Zhou Zou-ren (1885-1967) introduced the work of Havelock Ellis in 1933. When he was Dean of the Arts Faculty of Beijing University, he encouraged students to study sex education, to do research, and write on this topic. Pan Guang-dan (1899-1976) translated Ellis' Psychology of Sex in 1939 and continued to translate sexological works until the late 1940s. Lu Xun (1881-1936) in 1909 taught students about sex himself. He wrote, "For a good society, human nature must be released, sex education popularized, and this is the work for all educators."

2. After the Liberation

Since the establishment of modern China, the development of sex education can be divided into four stages:

1. Introductory Stage (1949–1978)

In the early 1950s, China published a number of sex education books, including Russell's *Sexual Psychology*. Premier Zhou was very supportive of this type of work. In 1954, he gave a speech in Beijing

University, calling for a breaking of taboos and the introduction of sex education for the students. In 1963, at a National Health Technology Congress, he gave instruction to offer sex education courses.

Ye Gong-shao, in one of his articles, remembers how, in 1963, Premier Zhou instructed the medical profession to provide adolescent sex education in order to promote their health and proper growth. Zhou related how when he was still a student, he was greatly benefited by the sex education course held at his school. He said sex education should be given before the children reach puberty. He understood that some may worry over the bad effects of early sex education upon the children, but he said this should be rare, and that we should trust that most of our children are good children.

Following Premier Zhou's instruction, many medical professionals began writing sex education articles in newspapers and magazines. The response was overwhelming. Many youths wrote to the authors asking about sexual information or facts concerning personal sexual problems.

Despite these efforts, conservative attitudes were still strong. In 1972, in the preparation for the textbook on *Physiology and Hygiene for High School*, half of the editors opposed the inclusion of a chapter on genital organs, causing a lot of arguments. The chapter was finally approved after Ye Gong-shao mentioned Premier Zhou's instructions, but the genital diagrams were censored before they could be distributed.

In 1973, Premier Zhou insisted on the further progress of sex education and pointed out again its importance. He suggested that the textbook above should be strengthened on sexual physiology and hygiene, but also large, colored hanging diagrams should be made to facilitate class instructions. In 1975, when Premier Zhou was terminally ill, he still reminded those around him of the need to make adolescent sex education a top priority.

In 1974, the Education Bureau and Health Bureau jointly issued a memo on "Suggestions on Further Strengthening Hygiene Education". It suggested putting the emphasis on "adolescent physiology and hygiene, including the changes and growth of adolescent sex organs." To put this in action, in 1976, Shanghai junior high schools added in their biology class a section on human anatomy and made pilot trials of adolescent sex education.

In 1978, the draft on "Full Time Ten Year System of High School Physiology and Hygiene Curriculum" emphasized the need for education on adolescent physiology and hygiene, including late marriages and planned parenthood. The arrangement was to teach about adolescent physiology and hygiene in junior high and the rest in senior high.

In this period, the high school biology syllabi all required the teaching of sex physiology topics (Table 7-1)

REQUIREMENT FOR SEXUAL PHYSIOLOGY CONTENTS IN HIGH SCHOOL BIOLOGY CURRICULUM IN CHINA

1952 Syllabus: "Draft of Biology Curriculum"

Year taught: Senior High School, first year
Teaching hours: four hours, including one practical.
Contents: Chapter 11— physiological characteristics of growth, reproductive cells, fertilization, intrauterine growth, fetus and its relationship with the mother, similarity between animal fetal growth and human fetal growth, fetal nutrition and growth, characteristics of baby and adolescent growth. Health care of woman and baby in China.

1956 Syllabus: "Draft of Biology Curriculum"

Year taught: Senior High School, first year
Teaching hours: three hours.
Contents: same as above

1963 Syllabus: Fulltime High School Biology Curriculum (Draft)

Year taught: Junior second year, physiology and hygiene
Teaching hours: two hours
Contents: Chapter 10 (reproduction and growth). Structure of male and female sex organs, reproductive cells, the formation and structure of sperm and egg, menstruation and ovulation, fertilization, embryonic growth, characteristics of human growth in various stages, hygiene and health in each stage of growth, late marriage and planned parenthood.

1978 Syllabus: Fulltime Ten-year System High School Physiology and Hygiene Curriculum (Draft)

Year taught: Junior second and third years, physiology and hygiene
Teaching hours: Junior second — one hour, Junior third, two hours.
Contents: Chapter 10 (reproductive system), the function and structure of male and female external and internal sex organs, formation and morphology of sperm, ovum. Embryonic growth and nutrition. Chapter 11 (adolescent physiology and hygiene): The concept of adolescence, adolescent growth and characteristics, growth changes and the health of internal organs. Growth and maturation of sex organs. Adolescent hygiene, menstruation, and ejaculation. Adolescent health problems and their prevention (amenorrhea, dysmenorrhea, functional uterine bleeding, vaginal discharge, balanitis, and so forth).

Table 7-1

Despite the draft syllabus however, there were difficulties in putting it into real practice. It could be said, therefore, in this period real sex education for adolescents was practically nonexistent.

2. The Rising Stage (1979–1983)

Because of the open door policy, foreign information about sex gradually entered China in this period. Ethical education in schools could not catch up with the changes. Sexual misconduct in the young increased, with students participating in more dating and sexual activities. Many people began to realize the pressing need for adolescent sex education. In 1979, the Education Bureau and Health Bureau jointly published a "Interim Regulation on Hygiene Work in Primary and High School." It required the strengthening of adolescent hygiene education. From 1980 on, senior high school education courses were provided for the population.

Also in 1980, in Shanghai, led by the municipal council and the municipal committee, Shanghai's education department formally set up pilot high schools for adolescent sex education, to explore the adolescent growth pattern and need for this type of education.

In 1981, the principle of Qizhong High School in Beijing, Liu Feng-Wu started an Adolescent Budding Period Education study group, also exploring ways to provide sex education for the students in the school.

In 1982, Wu Jia-ping translated, edited, and published *Sexual Medicine* so that contemporary American sexological knowledge and findings were introduced into China. In the foreword of the book, he gave in-depth and enlightening comments on youth sex problems and a way to give them sex education.

At the same time, many educators and medical professionals wrote sex education articles from the point of view of sexual medicine, sexual misconduct, and other subjects. Some schools in Shanghai and Beijing produced sex education teaching materials of their own to teach sexual knowledge and sexual ethics, obtaining some first hand results and experience.

3. Development Stage (1984–1987)

In this stage, scientific sexual studies began in the fields of sexual medicine, sexual psychology, sexual ethics, and sexual sociology. Some regional academic groups were established to promote adolescent sex education.

In 1984, in the Shanghai meeting on high school political work, party members on municipal education and hygiene affirmed the importance of adolescent sex education for the building up of the socialist mental culture. They wished to put adolescent sex education on track, and required pilot testing in order to provide such education. After that meeting,

Shanghai's education department selected ninety-eight high schools as the first expanded group for the pilot study. From 1985 onward, with the help of the Shanghai Social Science Institute, sex education was offered in these schools. In 1986, in the Shanghai Educational Workers meeting, the need for providing education on sexual physiology, sexual psychology, and sexual ethics was further emphasized.

In September 1984, Beijing's education department and the Municipal Health Quarantine Unit established a group on the "Teaching and Study of Adolescent Hygiene Education." It directed twelve high schools in the city and surrounding towns to try a two year plan of sex education, beginning from the first year of junior high. The principal content was adolescent physiology and hygiene. From 1987, Beijing's education department set up a leader group on adolescent education in the political teaching unit to be responsible for promoting, organizing, and ensuring adolescent sex education in the Beijing schools.

In this period, medical and educational professionals wrote many articles exploring the ways, suitable times, principles, and contents of adolescent sex education. Some made small surveys on adolescent growth patterns and sexual psychology. Some made suggestions on the organization of teaching teams and training of suitable teachers. Yao Pei-kuan wrote *Adolescent Education for High Schools* in which she comprehensively introduced the contents of adolescent sex education, providing the first reference book for teachers and parents on this topic. In March 1987, Yao and others wrote *A Primer for Adolescent Knowledge*, in which the contents of adolescent sex education were introduced to students in simple language. These two books ended the problem of a lack of reference books and teaching materials in China for adolescent sex education.

In May 1986, in the book *The Work of High School Masters*, edited by Li De-xia, sex education was formally presented for the first time as part of the content for the training of school teachers. In July of the same year, the book *A Curriculum on Education* edited by Shao Zong-je also for the first time put adolescent education as one of the important topics in his book.

In June 1985, Shanghai organized an Adolescent Education Teaching Material Seminar, where the methods and means of teaching were discussed. In 1986, Beijing's western district organized a seminar on adolescent education where the experience of teaching these topics were summarized and exchanged, and thus requiring all high schools to include this part of the teaching in their curriculum.

Some other regions also began this process. For example, in Sichuan, Chongqing, in the district of Sha-ping-bei, the Teachers Training College began, in 1985, to put adolescent education as part of their biological education studies. In Shenyang, the Education Scientific Research Institute, in the first half of 1987, began experimenting with adolescent education in high schools. In Nanjing, the education department in August 1987 published an *Outline of Adolescent Education*. The publication came from the experience and results of a pilot trial of the *Nanjing High School Behaviour and Conduct Outline*. The Department required that adolescent education should be combined with the teaching of physiology and hygiene, and put into the teaching plans, with topical seminars be ing run in high schools.

On October 1, 1987, the Shanghai Municipal Regulation on the Protection of Youths required that adolescent education be given to students entering their adolescent period. It was the beginning of adolescent sex education's integration into our national laws. Hence, adolescent sex education began to be established in China.

4. The Promotion Period (1988–Present)

On August 24, 1988, the National Education Committee and National Family Planning Committee circulated an "Announcement on Developing Adolescent Education," representing the nation's formal affirmation of adolescent sex education throughout the country.

In 1988, the National Work Meeting on Primary and High School Ethical Teaching required that all education units place importance on adolescent education in high schools. In June 1988, the National Education Committee and National Family Planning Committee called a meeting in Shanghai to discuss the principles and methods of putting the requirement into action. In view of the lack of formal documents to unify efforts, the "Announcement on Developing Adolescent Education" by the two committees was a timely document, setting out the three important tasks for implementing adolescent sex education: teachers training, curriculum development, production of teaching material, and research.

At around the same time, adolescent sex education in various places continued to develop. In Shanghai, the education department did a lot of work. (1) It put adolescent education into the "Outline of Shanghai Primary and High School Ethical Teaching." (2) It conducted surveys on the physiological and psychological characteristics of high school students, and based on the results, organized the production of teaching materials. (3) It set up an elective course on general knowledge of adolescence in junior high schools. In two hundred and fifty high schools in twenty-two regions, it tried to set out five to six teaching hours in every year of high school in the politics and thought classes to do this elective course. Of the high schools, 36 percent accomplished this, amounting to about one fourth of the total students in Shanghai obtaining the education. (4) It set up a three-tier network of instruction. The municipal education department organized an instruction group to run regular topical seminars on teaching methods. The district department made regular course and teaching reviews. The schools organized teaching groups composed of political workers, counsellors, biology teachers, politics teachers, class teachers, and grade leaders to decide on teaching plans and collect feedback. In 1987 Beijing's education department collected the experience of its twelve pilot schools and produced a book called *Adolescent Health Education* as teaching material for the whole city.

The development of adolescent sex education in this period can be described in the following areas:

I. CLEARER EDUCATIONAL OBJECTIVES

This was accomplished through the "Announcement on Developing Adolescent Education."

II. TEACHING METHODS AND HOURS WERE SPECIALLY SET

On teaching methods, a survey found that 53.5 percent of schools made use of physiology and hygiene courses, 30 percent made use of political and educational courses, 2 percent used extracurricular counseling, 10 percent through the teacher's work, 1.4 percent through school administration, and 0.5 percent did the teaching jointly with parents.

In October 1988, Shanghai's education department required all schools to provide ten to twelve teaching hours to junior first year students for adolescent sex education.

III. CONSOLIDATION OF TEACHING MATERIALS

In September 1989, the Committee on Shanghai High School Political Teaching Resources, the Shanghai Social Science Youth Study Institute, and the Shanghai Education Science Research Institute jointly wrote the *Reader on Adolescent General Knowledge.*

In October 1988 Zhu Wai-bin edited *One Hundred Adolescent Problems of High School Students.* In November 1988, the Secretary for National Education and the Editorial Board of People's Education produced the *One Hundred Questions and Answers on Adolescent Sex Education in High Schools.* In 1988 in Tienjin, *The Knowledge on High School Adolescent Hygiene* was produced in two volumes. In December 1989, Yao Pei-kuan and others published *Adolescent Education.*

IV. CONSOLIDATION OF TEACHING CONTENTS
Table 7-2 shows the contents taught in four standard books *Reader on Adolescent General Knowledge* (Shanghai), *Outline of Adolescent Education* (Nanjing), *The Knowledge on High School Adolescent Hygiene* (Tienjin), and *Adolescent Health Education* (Beijing). A gradual consolidation of the teaching contents could be seen. Contents on masturbation, sexual intercourse, contraception, STD's, and sexual ethics and aesthetics are gradually introduced.

V. TEACHERS' TRAINING
In October 1988, the National Education Committee took up the duty of training adolescent-education teachers. In May 1989, it organized the first national Adolescent Education Resources and Teaching Method course. The course was rerun in October. Each course trained up to about one hundred teachers.

For broader training, in 1989 the National Education Committee sponsored Shanghai Wen Wei Po (newspaper) and Shanghai Sex Education Association, for a Correspondence Course on Adolescent Sex Education. Some regional education institutes also tried to give teachers' training. For example, in Hunan Teachers' Training College, adolescent education was included in the teachers' training curriculum.

VI. SCIENTIFIC RESEARCH AND EXCHANGE:
In July 1989, the National Education Committee and Shanghai Social Science Institute organized a national workshop on the Theory and Practice of National Adolescent Education in Wuxi.

In October 1990, they organized in Sichuan a second national meeting on adolescent sexual psychology. The family Planning units also contributed much in this area. In October 1986, the National Family Planning Association organized a national seminar on sexual knowledge and education. In January 1992, a second similar workshop was run in Shanghai.

In the late 1980s, many academic organizations had also run many workshops and seminars on this topic. From 1987 to 1991, the organization committee of the China Sexology Association had run five national sexology meetings in various cities in China. Each of these meeting were attended by three hundred to five hundred participants.

Sex Education Contents in Four Standard Textbooks on Adolescent Sex Education

"Reader on Adolescent General Knowledge" (Shanghai)

Sexual physiology: Birth of a new life, fertilization, pregnancy, gender determination. Adolescent development, external and internal changes, male/female differences. Adolescent hygiene, menstruation, breast care, nocturnal emission, prepuce, undescended testes.
Sexual psychology: Adolescent psychology, sexual psychology, psychological characteristics in adolescence. Psychological health, mood, gender acceptance, self control training.
Sexual ethics: The social meaning of adolescence, ethical norms. Equality of the sexes, mutual respect. Self respect and decency. Development of sexual morals, knowledge, and habits.
Sexual esthetics: Nothing.

"Outline of Adolescent Education" (Nanjing),

Sexual physiology: Adolescent physiological characteristics: neurological, motor, respiratory, digestive, urinary, reproductive, visual, and auditory systems. Care of adolescent growth: nutrition, food, hygiene, sports, school life, common diseases, and prevention.
Sexual Psychology: Psychological characteristics, health education, mood, and self regulation of mood.
Sexual ethics: Honesty, humility, hard work, friendship, obedience, and self-realization.
Sexual aesthetics: What is beauty, beauty in human relationships. Physical beauty: dresses, manners, hairstyle, and so forth.

"Knowledge on High School Adolescent Hygiene (Tienjin)

Sexual physiology: Characteristics of adolescent development, external appearance, internal organs, reproductive organs, and intelligence. Adolescent hygiene, work and rest, sleep, training, nutrition. Common diseases and prevention. Development of the genital organs, male and female, structure and function. Nocturnal emission and menstruation. Smoking, drinking, tight underwear, masturbation, prepuce, phimosis, balanitis, undescended testes, dysmenorrhoea, amennorrhoea, menorrhagia, vaginal discharge, vaginitis.
Sexual psychology: Search for sexual knowledge. Sexual identity, gender, friendship, no love in schools.
Sexual ethics: Nothing.
Sexual esthetics: Nothing

"Adolescent Health education" (Beijing).

Sexual physiology: Adolescent growth changes: external appearance, internal organs, sex organs, nocturnal emission, and menstruation.
Hygiene, nutrition, pimples, breasts, smoking, drinking.
Sexual psychology: Developmental characteristics, mood, intelligence, and sexual awareness.
Sexual ethics: Establishment of moral standards, sexual ethics, self-respect, mutual respect, manners, career importance, and friendship.

PRINCIPLES OF ADOLESCENT SEX EDUCATION

These principles pay attention to adolescent growth patterns, scientific sex education characteristics, and the general social expectations. They developed in a long process of experience, revision, and research.

1. Combination of Sexual Knowledge and Moral Education

Together with the knowledge, adolescents should also acquire the ability to regulate and control their desires, to integrate them into their personality, to build up a concept of responsibility, to realize how one's behavior affects others and society.

2. Positive Channeling and Enrichment of Activities

Sexual knowledge should be imparted positively, honestly, naturally, seriously and scientifically, in an active manner.

It is not desirable to try to stop sexual desire in adolescents, but offering of useful activities may help channelling the energy into constructive areas, such as sports, arts, dancing, music, etc. Sexual stimulation should be avoided.

3. Appropriate Time, Place, and Extent

Materials taught should be appropriate to the stage of development of the youth, neither too early nor too late. To get the most appropriate results, the teacher must have a good understanding of the adolescent psychology and bodily changes, sexological knowledge, and the social expectations to which young people must respond.

Appropriate methods should include a consideration of the students' mood and personality. There should be a belief that every youth has his/her own personal worth. Respect confidentiality and personal dignity. Use a truthful, trusting, and non-condescending attitude.

4. Combination of Sex Education with Sexual Enrichment

Sexual enrichment means an internalization of the sexual knowledge provided to enable self-control, thus enabling individuals to handle selectively external sexual stimulations, help them adapt to different circumstances, and avoid or resist psychosexual traumas.

5. Pay Attention to Commonalities and Differences

Every adolescent is unique and may show great difference from other individuals of the same sex or age, physically or psychologically. Other than teaching the whole class following the general guidelines, there must be flexibility, such as small group or individual teaching or counseling in accordance with needs.

6. Concerted Efforts with School, Family, and Society

Sex education is part of personality education. Personality is influenced also by family and society. Close contact with society and family in conducting sex education is important for its effectiveness. Teachers must be sensitive to the social events and family environments of the students, so that they may adjust their education material and tactics accordingly.

METHODS OF ADOLESCENT SEX EDUCATION

1. Classroom Teaching

This is most suitable for the systematic teaching of sexual physiology, psychology and ethics.

2. Topical Studies

Based on the students' age, psychological characteristics, and educational level, while noting those problems which most students tend to have at certain times, lead us to look for information on particular topics. This could be done through essay competition, speech competition, poster exhibition, movie review, book review, and other activities students are interested in. If the students can bring out their personal experiences for discussion, the effects are usually better than the teacher's lessons.

3. Individual Conversation

To provide individual information or advice based on personal need.

4. Educational Counseling

Offer sexual advice in individual educational counselling sessions, to be done by teachers, biology teachers, or school physicians, in order to meet personal needs.

5. Multimedia Teaching Methods

The use of videos and movies is an attractive learning method for students. They can learn more easily, with impressive results. Many of these educational videos and movies have now been produced.

6. Exhibitions

To educate through accessible means, such as specimens, diagrams, models, videos, and movies. This can be run by social service organizations. Teachers would simply bring the students to watch. Small exhibitions could also be organized within schools or as joint school functions.

7. Visits

To visit part-time schools, correctional facilities (especially on sex offenders), to learn the importance of sexual ethics, its problems and how to handle them properly.

8. Channeling

Positive channelling of sexual desire or preoccupation using other activities.

9. Opportune Education

Sexual matters and events come up from time to time in our society, in news, movies, and literature. When these arise, they are good opportunities for sex education, which prove to be more impressive and useful than regular teaching.

10. Three-Dimensional Teaching

Join forces with school, family, and society to form an educational network. Make the educational efforts well coordinated in objective and direction. Teachers need to educate parents and social leaders regularly on updated sexual information in order to get the proper support form them.

(This chapter is an edited summary of two articles, one by Yao Pei-kuan on "The Study and Practice of Adolescent Sex Education in China", the other by Liu Wen-li on "The History and Development of Sex Education in High Schools in China.")

Postscript

This survey took one year and three months to complete (February 1989 to May 1990). The analysis and the composition took one year and three months as well (May 1990 to August 1991).

The writing was done as follows: The overview and chapter six were by Dalin Liu. Chapter two was by Yao Peikuan, Sun Zhongxiong. Fan Minsheng wrote the first draft of Chapter four, and Dalin Liu wrote the final version; Liu also wrote chapter four, amended by Li Ping Zhou. Chapter five was analyzed by Chen Shuheng and written by Liu.

Man Lun Ng and Li Ping Zhou reviewed the whole text. Xu Anqi, Yeng Hong Tai, Lu Han Long, and Yao Peikuan reviewed part of the text also.

Thanks are due to the manager of Shanghai Joint Publication Company, Lin Yao Shen. In the spring of 1990, I mentioned this survey in a seminar organized by *Family Doctor* magazine. Lin came to me during the break to ask about the manuscript. Since then, he had taken pains to ensure the scholastic quality of the production, reviewed the manuscript personally, and helped in the organization of the publication, showing his great ability as a publisher.

We had some financial problems with copying the manuscripts during the preparation period. *Family Doctor* magazine helped greatly at this juncture. The chief editor, Li Jin and the assistant editor Liu Ming helped us to apply for a fund from its Publication Grant. The Fund management committee, in which Bing Sin was a member, finally approved a sum sufficient to enable us to carry on with our work. This support was definitely more than just financial.

We did feel pressure from many areas as we proceeded with our work. We had constant worries on how people in and outside China would evaluate it, and whether it would meet international standards. Man Lun Ng of the Hong Kong Sex Education Association (who was later also the Foundation President of the Asian Federation for Sexology) made a highly critical review of the manuscript. He wrote down many remarks, questions, and amendments on nearly every page, but as a respect to the manuscript, he photocopied it and only marked on the copies. I am very grateful for his deep concern. His wife Sui May told me that she had never seen him taking a work so seriously before. Sometimes, I had mixed feelings about Ng's criticism, and had expressed a few times to him frankly that he was overcritical. He replied that this criticism would also come from international readers, and by then it would be too late to do anything about it. So, we did our best to improve based on his criticism, but I dare not say we have met Ng's requirements, because many of them, under the limitation of our country and ability, are simply impossible to satisfy. We could only say, we are humble and alert to our inadequacies. At the same time, Erwin J. Haeberle also gave us much valuable advice and suggestions on the survey, but because of cultural differences, he could only advise us mainly on matters of principle and not on the details. Obviously, we could not translate every bit of our work at every stage for him to give advice.

Statistical matters rested on our statistician, Li Ping Zhou. He worked hard, staying up late at night for many months, and yet did not make any complaint or ask for any extra reward. Without him, our report would have had a much lower quality.

I would like also to thank Professor Pan Sui Ming of the China People's University. He is one of the few sex sociologists in our country. He had overcome a lot of difficulties to complete translating the two Kinsey reports and mailed them to me so that I could use them for more detailed reference. He had encouraged and helped me to take up this piece of work, aimed at international use.

I am happy for having completed this work and yet I am not without some apprehension. Ng warned me that this report would certainly receive many serious criticisms. As a researcher, especially in sexology, I think we should be brave to receive criticism. Sexologists like Hirschfeld and Kinsey were severely criticized when their work came out. Of course, our work could not be compared with Hirschfeld's or Kinsey's, but we are just as open and ready to receive them as a stimulation for better work in the future.

One common question expected—and in fact raised already even during the preparation of this book—is whether our survey is "scientific" i.e. "representative of the Chinese" or not. Our view is that there are many grades of scientific work, depending on resources and conditions. This report represents the best a group of sexologists could do in China in the late eighties. They had as far as possible followed the requirements of science. It is their first step towards a scientific enquiry. It may be childish or even laughable, but a first step is essential so that there can be second, third, and better steps. Like many sociological surveys, this survey cannot represent the whole population of China (if one knows the heterogenous nature of the Chinese people and culture). Although, it can give a rough idea of the population close to the survey samples, which is already important and interesting information.

Some foreign scholars have commented on some of the figures as unexpectedly low or high. It might be noted that on some of the same figures, local scholars gave exactly opposite comments. It simply shows how unreliable estimations based on common sense can be, but our findings may be a stimulation for further research.

Others commented on the social effect of our report. "The report tells us how abundant sex crimes are in China. Is that telling people that these things are natural and reasonable?" "Masturbation and homosexual behavior are so frequent in our youths. Where is the forty years of educational effort by our communist party?" It is always controversial to link scientific work to politics. If they must be linked, then I would say that, without the improved and open leadership of our communist party there would not be such a survey. Without the party's realistic approach, all scientific advances in recent years would not have appeared. Things that exist are not necessarily correct, but they must be admitted, for only then we can look for their causes, change them or perfect them in order to facilitate social development.

This book may be preserved as a scientific document of some use, or at least, as a record of scientific failure. If the latter, it still serves some scientific purpose.

After the completion of this report, there are still three things ahead:

1. The analysis so far is rather incomplete and superficial. There is still a lot in our data waiting to be analyzed and dug out. This part of the endeavor will take many more years of work with more people to help.

2. The findings and analysis results will need to be distributed to various policy making organizations such as the education department and health organizations for reference, information that can be put to practical use.

3. This survey only looks at the ordinary people. For some special populations with specific problems, more in-depth and specialized

studies are required. In 1991, I started a homosexuality survey. I may also plan a study on sexuality among the elderly. Sexuality surveys could later be extended to the physically disabled, soldiers, and minority groups.

Finally, I thank our society and everyone else who contributed and showed concern for this survey.

DALIN LIU
SHANGHAI UNIVERSITY, FACULTY OF ARTS

Bibliography

Du Jian-hai. 1988. *The Study and Practice of Adolescent Sex Education in Current China.* Shanghai Education Study. 1:22

Office of the National Primary and High School Teaching Resource Committee. 1986. *A Collection of Biology Teaching Outlines in Primary and High Schools in Modern China, 1949 to 1985.* Beijing: The Office.

Secretary for the National Education Committee on Sports and Hygiene. 1988. *One Hundred Questions and Answers on Adolescent Sex Education in High Schools.* Beijing: Beijing University Publications.

Wu Je-ping. 1984. *Sexual Medicine.* Beijing: Science and Technology Publication Company.

Yao Pei-kuan. 1988. *A Reader of General Knowledge on Adolescence.* Shanghai: Shanghai People's Publication.

——— 1989. *Adolescent Education.* Guangsi: Guangsi Science and Technology Publications.

——— 1990. *A Report on Adolescent Education Survey.* Shanghai: Xue Lin Publications.

Ye Gong-shao. 1985. "Premier Zhou Is Concerned about Sex Education." *Essential for Parents* 4:15

Zhu Wai-bin. 1988. *One Hundred Adolescent Problems of High School Students.* Shanghai: Shanghai Medical University Publications.

ALSO PUBLISHED BY CONTINUUM

Rob Baker
THE ART OF AIDS: FROM STIGMA TO CONSCIENCE

"Rob Baker was one of the first — and one of the very best — to write seriously about pop culture in the Sixties. Now he gives us an essential, remarkably concise, analytic yet personal, and constantly readable overview of plague art." — LINDA WINER in *New York Newsday*

Harriet Evans
WOMEN AND SEXUALITY IN CHINA: FEMALE SEXUALITY AND GENDER SINCE 1949

"This is a subtle and nuanced work that greatly enhances our understanding of the connections between sex, gender, and changing visions of modernity in China."
— GAIL HERSHATTER, University of California, Santa Cruz

Marie M. Fortune
LOVE DOES NO HARM: SEXUAL ETHICS FOR THE REST OF US

"This is a feminist ethical contribution with substance."
— MARY E. HUNT

Robert T. Francoeur, Editor-in-Chief
Martha Cornog, Timothy Perper, and Norman A. Scherzer, Coeditors
THE COMPLETE DICTIONARY OF SEXOLOGY: NEW EXPANDED EDITION

In paperback. "Well executed . . . a remarkable job."
— *Booklist*

Robert T. Francoeur, Editor
THE INTERNATIONAL ENCYCLOPEDIA OF SEXUALITY

An indispensable three-volume set: 30 countries, 130 contributors.

Sigmund Freud
PSYCHOLOGICAL WRITINGS AND LETTERS
Edited by Sander L. Gilman

Many of the classic works on sexuality, infant sexuality, dreams, psychological procedure, telepathy, jokes, and the uncanny — also featuring a selection of Freud's correspondence. Available in hardcover and paperback.

Erwin J. Haeberle and Rolf Gindorf, Editors
BISEXUALITIES: THE IDEOLOGY AND PRACTICE OF SEXUAL CONTACT WITH BOTH MEN AND WOMEN

A scholarly analysis of the whys and wherefores of people who love people of both sexes.

James Vaughn Kohl and Robert T. Francoeur
THE SCENT OF EROS: MYSTERIES OF ODOR IN HUMAN SEXUALITY
Foreword by William E. Hartman and Marilyn A. Fithian

"This is science at its best, with adventures, ideas, and lots of facts. . . .You will never look at your lover or your family the same way again." — HELEN FISHER, New York University Human Sexuality Program

John Money
GENDERMAPS: SOCIAL CONSTRUCTIONISM, FEMINISM, AND SEXOSOPHICAL HISTORY

"Dr. John Money was one of my principal influences when I was writing *Sexual Personae.* He is the leading sexologist in the world today." — CAMILLE PAGLIA

John Money
PRINCIPLES OF DEVELOPMENTAL SEXOLOGY

A seminal work. "Perhaps no one since Freud has provided us with such a blend of biological and psychological facts, theory, and clinical material intensively integrated into an increasingly coherent picture of the origins of human experience." — DR. JUNE REINISCH, former director of the Kinsey Institute

John Money
REINTERPRETING THE UNSPEAKABLE: HUMAN SEXUALITY 2000

"Dr. John Money has exercised a major influence on the development of sexology over the last half of the twentieth century." — DR. VERN BULLOUGH

Charles Moser, M.D., and JJ Madeson
BOUND TO BE FREE: THE SM EXPERIENCE

"The first intelligent, fully informed, fact-based discussion of what SM is. . . .The authors provide a perspective that is uniquely accurate, sensitive, and fair in its depiction and interpretation of erotic sadomasochism." — *Library Journal*

William E. Prendergast
SEXUAL ABUSE OF CHILDREN AND ADOLESCENTS

A thoughtful and compassionate guide for those who are touched by sexual abuse themselves or care for others who are.

Dr. Ruth K. Westheimer
DR. RUTH'S ENCYCLOPEDIA OF SEX

"Entries address all aspects of sexuality — from mechanics and biology to cultural, legal, and religious concerns. The range of material covered in this volume is impressive." — *Publishers Weekly*